W9-BIX-133

Following the Fairways

Editor Nick Edmund

KENSINGTON WEST PRODUCTIONS LTD

HEXHAM ENGLAND

KENNETH REED

Artist: **Kenneth Reed** **TRADITION** *Courtesy of:* **Old Troon Sporting Antiques**

Acknowledgements

There have been all manner of hands that have guided the production of this, our updated, revised and expanded eighth edition of Following the Fairways.

The company acknowledges the kind and generous advice of many golf professionals, secretaries and enthusiasts from all parts of Great Britain and Ireland. It is only by constant updating that a guide of this type maintains its value. This is particularly so given that we have updated every single detail in the Complete Golf Section – quite tough I assure you.

In our endeavour to illustrate the book, we have been kindly assisted by the Burlington Gallery, Rosenstiel's and other passionate colectors of golfing memorabilia. A particular big thank you to Bob Pringle of Old Troon Antiques (0292) 311822. A number of new illustrations have been provided from this gallery and in future editions we hope also to add numerous examples of golfing memorabilia, a specialist subject of this gallery. The colour work is all credited and we are most grateful to all our featured artists for kindly allowing us permission to use their works.

We greatly appreciate the assistance of the many people who helped us in selecting hotels, restaurants and pubs around the country. We are confident that you will relish savouring some of our suggestions, but do please let us know if you come across one that you can recommend. We are also grateful to the hoteliers who have helped us produce feature pages for the book which I hope you feel adds to both the look and usefulness of Following the Fairways. As publisher, I would also like to thank the staff at Kensington West Productions for their hard work, dedication and enormous enthusiasm for the task which enabled us to meet our tight schedules. The company is greatly indebted to a legion of typists who put together all the facts, figures and fairways collated in this book.

I would like to thank Ian Botham for penning our foreword. His prowess as a sportsman is renowned and respected throughout the world. It is a great bonus to have such a passionate enthusiast for the game of golf add his sentiments to this work which has been lovingly compiled, written and of course researched!

Finally, I would like to thank Nick Edmund, author of the golf editorial, for his tremendous efforts in providing such distinguished copy and I thank all those companies who have helped with the production for their accomplished work.

Julian West

Kensington West Productions Ltd
5 Cattle Market, Hexham,
Northumberland NE46 1NJ
Tel: (0434) 609933 Fax: (0434) 600066

Editor
Nick Edmund

Consultant Editors
Simon Tilley, Jane Chambers, Karen Ryan
Sarah Hedley Kathrine Harrison
Sarah Mann Janet Blair

Design
Kensington West Productions Ltd

Cartography
Camilla Charnock, Craig Semple

Typesetting
Gask and Howley Limited

Origination
Pre-Press Limited Hong Kong

Printing
Rotolito Lombarda Italy

*Front cover Artist: Linda Hartough,
Royal Dornoch,
Courtesy of Old Troon Sporting Antiques
Title page Artist: Linda Hartough,
Royal St George's
Courtesy of Old Troon Sporting Antiques
Back cover Artist: Kenneth Reed,
The Postage Stamp,
Artist: Terence Gilbert, St Andrews,
Artist: Linda Hartough , Turnberry
Courtesy of Old Troons Sporting Antiques*

All rights reserved. No part of this publication may be reproduced, stored in a retrieval system, or transmitted in any form or by any means, electronic, mechanical, photocopying, recording or otherwise, without the prior permission of Kensington West Productions Ltd. While every effort has been made to ensure the accuracy of the facts and data contained in this publication, no responsibility can be accepted by the editor, or Kensington West Productions Ltd, for errors or omissions or their consequences.

© Copyright 1994 Kensington West Productions Ltd

Artist: **Linda Hartough** ROYAL TROON *Courtesy of* **Old Troon Sporting Antiques**

Introduction

Two Americans are on a golfing vacation in Scotland. They are playing one of the famous old links courses – let's say Carnoustie – and it is blowing a gale. They are struggling with the elements but trying desperately to keep their heads down. One of them slashes at his tee shot and, suspecting the worst, cries out, 'where on earth did that go, did you see it?' His caddie interjects, 'I'm afraid you've hit a Clark Gable.' The two Americans look at each other incredulously, 'what in heavens name does that mean? And the caddie replies, 'Gone with the wind, sir' ...

Welcome to the fully revised and updated 8th edition of Following the Fairways. First published in October 1986, Following the Fairways seeks to lead the golfer (and perhaps his or her non-golfing partner) on a leisurely journey around the golf courses of Great Britain and Ireland, suggesting some of the best 18 holes–links, parkland, cliff-top and heathland and recommending superior 19th holes–places to eat, drink and sleep along the way.

To adopt golfers' vernacular, Following the Fairways is a 'where to play–where to stay' guide. Over the years our simple objective has been to try to establish it as the most informative, entertaining and authoritative book of its type. Certainly the book's content has altered considerably these past eight years–with so much happening on and off the fairways it has needed to. Moreover, the first edition was a purely British affair whereas now something like a quarter of the book is devoted to a celebration of golf in the Emerald Isle.

Perhaps the most striking difference between Following the Fairways and other golf course guides is that we have chosen to illustrate the main body of the golf text with fine art (from classics to contemporary) rather than photographs. This is partly to be different and partly because we discovered some wonderful pictures many of which had not been seen in print before.

Apart from extending the book's scope to include golf in Ireland, the biggest single impact on its content has been the 'golf course boom' of the 1980s and early 1990s. Several of the 'Championship Courses' featured (see below) were not in existence or not fully operational in 1986; indeed our current 'Golf Club of the Year', Portal is a prime example.

It is precisely because it explores the best of these new developments that Following The Fairways can claim to be the most up to date golf course guide.

So how does the book work? How does it help the reader to follow the fairways? Beyond the introductory pages, which in addition to the annual **'Golf Club of the Year'** award include our unique **Golf Course Rankings**, the journey begins in Cornwall and eventually ends in the West of Ireland. For easy reference the book is divided into 30 chapters or 'golfing areas', each with its own attractive, hand drawn map. Each golf course within the area is included within a detailed directory section which we term **'Complete Golf'**. For each club we list the telephone number, address, course yardages, together with approximate green fees and visitor policy. Some 2,000 golf clubs are listed. Over 700 of the golf courses, as well as perhaps three times as many nearby hotels, inns and restaurants are recommended in the golf area text or **'Choice Golf'** section.

Many of the leading golf courses of Great Britain and Ireland are given special attention, each having an entire page of editorial with an accompanying course plan. These featured courses comprise the aforementioned **'Championship Golf'** section and over 100 such courses are now included. Among their number are all the famous courses of Great Britain and Ireland, i.e. every one of the Open Championship venues, plus the likes of Gleneagles, Sunningdale, Royal Dornoch and Ballybunion. All details relating to these entries are carefully revised each year. In addition to the greats, many lesser known but beautifully situated courses are also featured–places which we believe no holidaying golfer would wish to miss; for instance: Machrihanish on the Mull of Kintyre, Connemara in Co Galway, Nefyn in North Wales, Castletown on the Isle of Man and delightful St Enodoc in Cornwall. The 'new' courses are also well represented by the likes of Chart Hills, Hanbury Manor, Mount Juliet, Letham Grange and Collingtree Park. Overall we think it is a well balanced collection of the old, the new, inland and seaside courses.

Before inviting you to read on, as editor, I would quickly like to thank everyone in Britain and Ireland who has helped me compile the golf text; special thanks are owing to Sean McCann of Golf and Travel in Dublin for his help over a number of years and, of course, to my wife Teresa for continuing to put up with my golfing wanderlust. Finally, I must say I am delighted that Ian Botham has provided the foreword to this edition–a true cricketing legend who genuinely loves his golf. I wish him, and all of you, an enjoyable 1995–both on and off the fairways.

Nick Edmund,
Editor
August, 1994

J Burrow **THE BERKSHIRE** *Burlington Gallery*

Foreword

The announcement of my retirement in 1993 from 21 years of professional cricket was not as hard to make as everyone expected. In fact, it came as rather a relief. Over those years the first item into the car boot for the away game was not the cricket coffin but the golf bag! Travelling up and down the motorway system of the UK I would many a time pray for rain at some stage of the game to allow me to get away onto the golf course where I could relax from the world of cricket and take out my frustrations on the little white ball.

Now in my 'retirement' (only from cricket I hasten to add) I am able to enjoy my golf even more, in fact, my wife, having spent years as a cricket widow is now the golf widow. Every spare minute away from business is spent either on the river bank or on the golf course and I have been extremely privileged over the years to have played on most of the major courses in the British Isles and beyond.

'Following The Fairways' is my constant companion in the car alongside my clubs and what an excellent companion it makes. As much as time allows, my business appointments are made in order to allow 18 holes. Out comes the book, a phone call is made and I am on my way to renew an old acquaintance or explore a new course.

On thumbing through last year's edition of Following The Fairways I am delighted to see two of my favourite nine hole courses mentioned, Alderney in the Channel Islands and St. Fillans in Tayside. I hope to be able to make many more discoveries over the next twelve months during my travels, thanks to my invaluable companion.

Ian Botham OBE

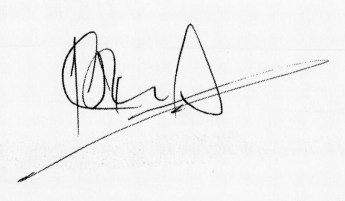

Choice Golf

The Opening Strokes

Choice Golf (30 Golfing Areas)

England

Wales

Scotland

Ireland

Artist: **Kenneth Reed** *THE OLD COURSE ST ANDREWS*

Courtesy of Old Troon Sporting Antiques

Complete Golf

(The Course Directory)

England

Wales

Scotland

Ireland

Championship Golf

King's Course, Gleneagles – Robert Turnbull.

Championship Golf

When reviewing this country's top new golf facilities the national press, especially the golf magazines, are guilty of concentrating almost exclusively on the big budget developments situated in southern England. Granted, there has been a far greater amount of activity south of Birmingham and a number of very fine courses have been built but things haven't exactly been standing still in the north these past five or six years. One of the most outstanding creations in Great Britain, not just in the north, is the Portal Golf and Country Golf Club at Tarporley in Cheshire.

Portal exudes quality: a strikingly modern, yet very elegant clubhouse (even Prince Charles would approve of its design) and a truly first rate golf course fashioned by Donald Steel, one of Britain's foremost golf architects. Steel has worked on many projects, both in this country and overseas but he regards the layout at Portal as perhaps his most accomplished work. Finest or not, it is difficult to imagine that he can have designed a more beautiful course.

The word 'beautiful' is sometimes derided when applied to new golf projects: 'challenge is far more important than aesthetics' has become the slogan. But if golf is to be an enjoyable recreation surely they are both important.

It is not the site or its location that is especially impressive at Portal, although it probably scores eight out of ten in this department but the way the course has been landscaped and is presented ie. the care that went into its design and construction and the aftercare that maintains it in superb condition and has seen the planting of numerous flower beds, banks of heather and rockeries around the trees and greens. At Portal the lakes and ponds aren't merely water hazards - they are works of art. Some critics might say that cascading water and the 'Kew Gardens nursery effect' have no place in golf, but would Augusta be quite as great if you removed all the dogwoods and azalea? At Britain's leading heathland courses purple heather isn't cultivated purely to frustrate the wayward golfer; it pleases the eye and there is no reason why a good parkland golf course shouldn't possess some of the delights of a beautiful park.

In order to make a point, the aesthetic attributes of Portal have been emphasised but there is also plenty of challenge in the 18 holes (Portal is one of our featured Championship Courses, see ahead) moreover it hasn't gained our 'Golf Club of the Year' award purely for its on-course treats - the off-course ambience is equally special. Portal is very much a Golf Club (or Golf and Country Club to be precise) and is run as such. Youthful it may be, but there is a genuine 'Club atmosphere' at the nineteenth hole whereas, again, at some of the prestigious new developments in the south the club-house seems to operate in a manner more akin to a hotel than a golf club. Visitors are made to feel welcome at Portal; the facilities are excellent and the building has great character. In fact, Portal exudes more than quality and character...it has style.

Artist: Nick Jones Winter Portal

Golf Course of the year

Artist: Nick Jones Summer Portal

MORWENSTOW
Bude & North Cornwall GC
BUDE
CRACKINGTON HAVEN

Launceston GC
LAUNCESTON

PORT ISAAC
St.Enodoc GC
Trevose G & CC   ROCK   ST.KEW
ST. MERRYN   PADSTOW
WADEBRIDGE
ST.MAWGAN   BODMIN   St. Mellion
Newquay GC   G & CC
NEWQUAY   LISKEARD   ST MELLION   SALTASH
Loswithiel GC   Looe GC   TIDEFORD
Perranporth GC   CARLYON   TALLAND   Whitsand Bay
BAY   GOLANT   BYLOOE   EAST LOOE   Hotel & G.C.
MOUNT HAWKE   Truro   FOWEY   POLPERRO
Tehidy Park GC   GC   Carlyon Bay Hotel & GC
ST.IVES   TRURO   St.Austell GC
GARBIS BAY   West Cornwall   TREGONWY
PENZANCE   G.C.   PHILLEIGH
MYLOR BRIDGE
Budock Vean   ST. MAWES
Hotel & G.C.   FALMOUTH
Falmouth GC
HELFORD
LANDS END   MANACCAN
Mullion GC   MULLION
LIZARD POINT

Artist: **G. Wallace LINKS GOLF** *Courtesy of:* **Burlington Gallery**

14

Brandy for the Parson, Baccy for the Clerk'—Cornwall is the land of the smuggler's cove. It is also the land of King Arthur and the Knights of the Round Table—a land of legends. To cross the Tamar is to enter foreign soil: for centuries the Cornish Celts had more in common with the Welsh and the French Bretons than the ever-invading Anglo Saxons. Well, the Anglo-Saxons still invade but nowadays in a more peaceful manner. 'Grockles' they are called in Cornwall and they come in search of sun, sand and sea (not to mention a holiday home!) But there is also a fairly recent addition, a subspecies commonly known as the 'golfing-grockle' who comes to Cornwall to seek out some of the finest golfing country in the Kingdom.

The South Coast

If one commences an imaginary tour by crossing the Tamar at Plymouth, **St Mellion** Golf and Country Club (0579) 50101 has surely to be the first port of call. It is one of the few places in Britain where one might bump into Jack Nicklaus. St Mellion has an onsite hotel and two fine courses, one of which was designed by the great man and is featured later in this chapter. Also convenient for St Mellion are the hotels in Plymouth, the pick of which is the Moat House (0752) 662866. Not far away in Saltash, a new course has recently opened called **China Fleet**, apparently the Navy (British—not Oriental) is the guiding force behind it.

Heading westwards **Looe** Golf Club (formerly, Looe Bin Down) is situated on high ground to the north of Looe, near Widegates. An 18 hole moorland course, it lies somewhat at the mercy of the elements and can get exceptionally windy. Not too far away at Portwinkle the **Whitsand Bay Hotel** (0503) 30276 is an ideal place to break a journey with its own gentle 18 hole golf course stretching out along the cliffs and looking down over Whitsand Bay.

The area around Looe abounds with good hotels and restaurants with seafood not surprisingly a speciality. In Fowey, two restaurants to consider are the Food For Thought (0726) 832221 and Cordon Bleu. Another hotel where the visitor can enjoy a little extra walking—on the cliffs as well as on the fairways is at Talland-on-Looe, the Talland Bay Hotel (0503) 72667. The Kitchen (0503) 72780 is an excellent restaurant in Polperro and in Golant, the Cormorant Hotel (0726) 833426 enjoys a glorious setting. Further inland the Old Rectory (0579) 342617 at St Keyne offers excellent value.

We'll now, if you'll pardon the expression, leave the Looe area and, still heading in a clockwise direction set sail for St Austell where we find a twin attraction for golfers: the redoubtable **Carlyon Bay** and the **St Austell** Golf Club. The St Austell course is situated on the western edge of the town off the A390. Rather shorter than Carlyon Bay but with an ample spread of gorse and numerous bunkers, it possesses plenty of challenges and attractions of its own.

Carlyon Bay is surely one of Britain's best loved hotel courses. Not a Turnberry or a Gleneagles perhaps, but very pleasing with several challenging holes and views over a number of beaches—one of which is frequented by naturists!

St Austell is a pleasant place to spend a day or two and golfers of course may decide to stay at Carlyon Bay Hotel itself (0726) 812304: obviously very convenient but four-star comfort as well. As a first rate alternative though, Boscundle Manor (0726) 813557 at Tregrehan is also highly recommended—the food alone is worth a trip. Heading northwards will bring one to the recently

opened **Lostwithiel** Golf and Country Club (0208) 873550, where fine golf and agreeable accommodation are the order of the day. Note also the 13th century Globe Inn (0208) 872501 while in Lostwithiel.

Falmouth—a glorious harbour and seagulls aplenty. More good golf awaits. Like St Austell, there are two sets of fairways on which to exercise the swing (and maybe burn off all these extra calories we've accumulated!) They are to be found at the **Falmouth** Golf Club, south west of the town (fine clifftop views over Falmouth Bay) and at the **Budock Vean Hotel**. This latter course has only nine holes but plenty of variety and is exceptionally well kept.

For hotels, Budock Vean (0326) 250288 takes pride of place but others to note include the Crill Manor Hotel (0326) 211880 and the Hotel St Michael's (0326) 312707. The opening words of The Wind in the Willows were written at the Greenbank (0326) 312440, clearly an inspiring place, while the Penmere Manor (0326) 211411 also has much to commend it. Three final thoughts for places to stay in this area are the Idle Rocks (0326) 270771 at St Mawes on the Roseland peninsula and the Meudon Hotel (0326) 250541 back in Falmouth.

Still heading along the south coast, the course at **Mullion** is one of the short but sweet brigade. Situated seven miles south of Helston, it can lay claim to being the most southerly on the British mainland. Nestling around the cliff edges overlooking some particularly inviting sands and with distant views towards St Michael's Mount, Mullion typifies the charm of Cornish holiday golf. With the spectacular scenery of the Lizard area, it's another good spot to spend a few days. In Mullion, or perhaps more precisely, Mullion Cove, Henscath House (0326) 240537 is perfect for the golf course and a strong mention also for the Riverside (0326) 231443 at Helford where there is some good accommodation and first rate cuisine. Penzance is another place where people may wish to base themselves—golfers especially now that the 18 hole **Cape Cornwall** Golf and Country Club has been opened at nearby St Just.

North Cornwall

The **West Cornwall** Golf Club lies just beyond St Ives at Lelant. A beautiful and very natural old-fashioned type of links, it was laid out a hundred years ago by the then vicar of Lelant. Like St Enodoc, it is a genuine links course—sand dunes and plenty of sea breezes!—and quite short. Jim Barnes, who won both the Open and US Open was born in Lelant village.

In St Ives, two hotels to note are the Tregenna Castle (0736) 795254 and the Garrack (0736) 796199—ideal for the nearby cliffs and beaches as well as the new 18 hole par 59 **Treganna Castle** golf course. Slightly further afield at Carbis Bay, the Boskerris Hotel (0736) 795295 is particularly friendly.

Passing numerous derelict tin and copper mines the inland course at **Tehidy Park** is soon reached. Located midway between Camborne and Portreath it presents a considerable contrast to the golf at Lelant: here we are amidst the pine trees, rhododendrons and bluebells—hopefully not right amidst them! Getting back to the northern coast, **Perranporth** and **Newquay** look closer on the map than they are by road. Both are links type courses with outstanding sea views. Not far away at St Mawgan a 9 hole course, **Treloy,** has recently opened.

In Newquay, where the crash of the Atlantic waves offers a surfers' paradise there are several welcoming establishments. The Atlantic Hotel (0637) 872244 is an ideal holiday base, as is the Hotel Bristol (0637) 875181. A less expensive but still superb option is the Priory Lodge

Hotel (0637) 874111. Connoisseurs of the public house might care to visit the Falcon at St Mawgan. Golfers at Tehidy may note the Tregarthan Country Cottage at Mount Hawke—quite small but friendly and good value, the Beach Dunes Hotel at Perranporth is clearly very convenient for the Perranporth links while a recommended guest house in this area is Aviary Court (0209) 842256 at Mary's Well, Redruth.

Further along the coast lie two marvellous golfing challenges—**St Enodoc** at Rock and **Trevose** at Constantine Bay. Trevose is the longer course but much more open and it doesn't possess the massive sandhills that are the feature of St Enodoc's links.

The most convenient places for the golfing gourmet to stay are, at Trevose, the splendid Treglos Hotel (0841) 520727 and for St Enodoc, the St Enodoc Hotel (0208) 863394 in Rock and the St Morritz Hotel (0208) 862242 near Wadebridge. An early start can also be made from Padstow, where the Seafood Restaurant has a great reputation – and a few fine rooms for those who may have over-indulged the night before; from Crackington Manor (0840) 230397 at Crackington Haven and from the Castle Rock Hotel at Port Isaac (0208) 880300. This delightful fishing village also houses the 17th century Port Gaverne Inn (0208) 880244—tremendous food and a charming atmosphere await.

Our coastal tour ends appropriately at Bude—a pleasant and unassuming seaside resort with a very good golf links, **Bude and North Cornwall,** situated almost in the town centre and renowned for its rolling fairways and excellent greens. The town has an impressive array of hotels: the Burn Court Hotel (0288) 352872 is as comfortable as any and has the advantage of overlooking the golf course. One other popular spot for golfers in town is the Camelot (0288) 352361. In Morwenstow, a fine old pub the Bush is well worth visiting if only for the breathtaking clifftop views.

The golf course at Tehidy was mentioned on our coastal tour, but three other inland courses definitely merit attention: the first is **Truro,** a shortish parkland course, close to the lovely cathedral, the second is at **Launceston,** one of the best parkland courses in the county, and the third, the outstanding new course near Camelford, called **Bowood,** which we explore in some detail ahead.

For stylish accommodation Truro golfers might wish to base themselves at the picturesque Trevispian-Vean Farm House (0872) 79514, and visitors to Bowood (which isn't all that far from Trevose) may opt for the comforts of the aforementioned Treglos, or the even closer Lanteglos Hotel (0840) 213551. The White Hart coaching inn is an admirable base to explore the countryside around Launceston. However, the golf course itself is where some of the best views can be enjoyed. Located on high ground, to the west stretches Bodmin Moor—bogs and mystery—and to the east, Dartmoor.

Artist: **Cecil Aldin** ***CHIPPING TO THE FLAG*** *Courtesy of:* **Burlington Gallery**

To some, mention of the north coast of Cornwall will invoke thoughts of golden sandy beaches and cool, inviting seas. For others, it may conjure up images of romantic coves, wild, spectacular cliffs and incessant crashing waves. Either way, the place has a certain magic; after all it was here that King Arthur is said to have met Merlin. Such is the setting of the Trevose Golf and Country Club.

Located near the quaint little fishing port of Padstow, Trevose is an ideal spot for a golfing holiday - or any kind of holiday come to that, but those who haven't made space in the boot for the golf clubs are missing out on something rather special. The Club has long boasted a splendid 18 hole Championship course plus an adjacent nine hole short course; now Trevose can entice the visiting golfer with a new 'full length' par 35 nine hole course - thus making 36 holes in total.

All administrative matters at Trevose are in the capable hands of Messrs **Peter Gammon** and **Lionel Grindley**. Both can be contacted by telephone on **(0841) 520208** and by fax on (0841) 521057. The Club's **professional Gary Alliss**, can be reached on **(0841) 520261**. Not surprisingly the course (or courses) are at their busiest during the summer months, but whatever the time of year visitors looking for a game would be wise to make a quick telephone call before setting off - they should find the Club very accommodating. Societies are also welcomed at Trevose. Those organising, should address written applications to the Secretary at **Trevose Golf and Country Club, Constantine Bay, Padstow, Cornwall PL28 8JB**. Proof of handicap is required to play on the Championship course.

The 1994 green fee varies according to the time of year with major reductions available to those wishing to obtain temporary membership of the Club. From November to mid-March a day's golf on the 18 hole course can be purchased for £20. From mid-March to the end of May, plus the month of October, the green fee is £25 per day, whilst between June and September (inclusive) the same is priced at £28. The green fee for a day's golf on either of the 9 hole courses again varies with the season: the corresponding green fee rates for these courses are, 'Short Course' - £8, £9 and £10; and 'New Course' - £14, £16, and £18. Junior golfers can usually obtain fifty per cent reductions on all the above rates. Finally, as an example of temporary membership, a fortnight's golf on the Championship course during the peak summer peri-

od can be obtained for £145.

Whereas the image of north Cornwall maybe a romantic one, the same could hardly be said of the journey to get there! Travelling to this part of the West Country however, is not the painful slog it once was. The roads have been improved and there are regular flights from Heathrow to nearby Newquay Airport (six miles from the Golf Club). Motorists will normally head for Bodmin (via the A30 from Exeter or the A38 from Plymouth). From Bodmin the A30 should be taken towards Padstow. The Club is about four miles west of Padstow off the B3276.

From the Championship tees the 18 hole course measures 6608 yards (par 71, SSS 72). The forward tees reduce the length by about 150 yards, while the ladies play over 5713 yards, par 73. The course can properly be described as a golf links though the visitor need not distress himself with fears of having to carry Himalayan-like sandhills, and as a rule the rough is kept fairly short. The latter should ensure that the golfer spends more time admiring the scenery than searching for his golf ball - and a word about the views - they are indeed tremendous, particularly those across Booby's Bay which provide such a dramatic backdrop to the 4th green.

The wind at Trevose can often play a decisive role and prevent low scoring (no one, at least at the time of writing, has bettered 66). There are a great number of well-positioned bunkers and a stream meanders through much of the course. Trevose certainly provides a good test for any standard of golfer.

The Clubhouse with its prime situation overlooking the course offers a whole range of first class facilities. There is a large comfortable Bar and a Dining Room which can cater for over a hundred people. Breakfast, lunches and dinners are served daily in the Dining Room and in addition light snacks can be obtained at all times. For children, a separate games room is provided. Swimming, snooker and tennis are also all very much a part of the Country Club scene - what's more, there's even a trendy boutique!

There is an unmistakably relaxed, holiday flavour about Trevose. The atmosphere is perhaps best epitomised by the story of four lady Members involved in a foursomes game: apparently, when playing the short 16th they arrived at the green only to discover that they had been so busy chattering not one of them had remembered to tee off.... so much for women drivers!

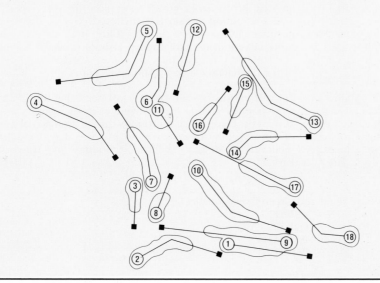

Hole	Yards	Par	Hole	Yards	Par
1	443	4	10	467	4
2	386	4	11	199	3
3	166	3	12	448	4
4	500	5	13	507	5
5	461	4	14	317	4
6	323	4	15	327	4
7	428	4	16	225	3
8	156	3	17	388	4
9	451	5	18	416	4
Out	**3,314**	**36**	**In**	**3,294**	**35**
			Out	3,314	36
			Totals	6,608	71

Port Gaverne Hotel and Green Door Cottages

This delightful hotel is situated in a spectacular small cove only ½ a mile away from the 1,000 year old fishing village of Port Isaac on the North Cornish Heritage Coast. Rich in history, much of the surrounding area consists of cliffs, headlands, beaches and old buildings which are preserved by the National Trust.

The hotel is an early seventeenth century Cornish Coastal Inn that has been carefully restored by resident proprietor Midge Ross whilst still retaining its original character, ambience and charm.

The nineteen bedrooms are all en suite with colour television, radio and direct dial telephone. The hotel is extremely comfortable with a relaxed and friendly atmosphere.

Dining at the Port Gaverne is a memorable experience with good food prepared from the best ingredients available. Chef Ian Brodey and his staff use fresh garden produce, local lamb and beef, locally landed fish, lobster and crab when in season, to create an excellent a la carte menu.

Only a few steps away from this internationally known hotel are the Green Door Cottages. These are seven splendidly restored eighteenth century self contained Cornish fishermen's cottages built around an enclosed and sheltered courtyard. All are attractively and comfortably furnished with their own central heating, colour television and direct dial telephone. Each cottage has its own fully equipped kitchen.

Whether staying at the Hotel or Cottages this is a truly an ideal centre from which to explore this very special area. Swimming within the sheltered cove is always a popular choice as are diving, sailing and surfing. The more adventurous may choose inshore or shark fishing and the less energetic may choose to wander along one of the particularly spectacular coastal paths.

For golf enthusiasts Cornwall is fast becoming one of the most popular golfing holiday venues in the country and at the Port Gaverne Hotel rounds can be arranged at any of the twenty-six courses within the Royal Duchy including St Mellion, St Enodoc, Bodmin and Bowood Park.

Port Gaverne Hotel and Green Door Cottages
Nr Port Isaac
North Cornwall PL29 3SQ
Tel: (0208) 880244
Fax: (0208) 880151

'It lay content
Two paces from the pin;
A steady putt and then it went
Oh, most securely in.
The very turf rejoiced to see
That quite unprecedented three.'

I suppose only Cornwall, and probably only St Enodoc come to that, could have inspired someone to write a poem about a birdie. Actually, it wasn't just 'someone' it was the Poet Laureate Sir John Betjeman who loved, and in later years lived, beside the glorious west country links.

Everyone who visits St Enodoc, it seems, falls under a spell of some sorts. So why is it such a favourite and what are these charms?

Imagine a really classic links course: huge sandhills; meandering, tumbling fairways; plenty of humps and hillocks; the odd awkward stance and blind shot perhaps but firm, fast greens and plenty of invigorating sea air. This is St Enodoc to a tee. Exhilarating, dramatic scenery? St Enodoc most definitely, being situated on the northern coast of Cornwall and not too far from Padstow and Trevose the views could hardly be mundane. The chance of a good score? Again yes—providing you stay on the fairways! St Enodoc, unlike all too many of today's courses won't put your length of drive on trial. It will, however, more than likely test every golf club in your bag. The holes are all very individual and bristle with old fashioned character. And then the accompanying atmosphere? Well, according to Sir John Betjeman even the turf finds time to rejoice in this splendidly relaxed environment. In short, St Enodoc is a sheer delight.

Doing his best to ensure that St Enodoc stays lost in this wonderful golfing time warp is the **Club's secretary, Mr L Guy**. He can be contacted by writing to the **St Enodoc Golf Club, Rock, Wadebridge, Cornwall, PL27 6LB** or by telephoning **(020 886) 3216**. Individual visitors are welcome throughout the week, although not surprisingly it is likely to be difficult to arrange a tee time for the weekend. Bookings (up to 4 days in advance) should be made through the Club's **professional, Nick Williams**, tel **(020 886) 2402**. Golfing Societies, or parties of twelve or more will need to make arrangements with the secretary.

Since 1982 there have been two 18 hole courses at St Enodoc. The main course is now named the **Church Course** and the newer (and considerably less testing)

one is called the **Holywell Course**. To play on the Church Course visitors must possess maximum handicaps of 24. Green fees in 1994 for the Church Course were set at £22 a round midweek , £35 a day with £27 per round, £40 per day payable at weekends. Fees for the Holywell Course are £12 per round, £18 per day. Junior golfers pay half rates and there are also various reductions available for those wishing to purchase weekly or fortnightly 'temporary memberships'.

St Enodoc is much less remote and more easily reached than many people imagine. Coming by road the two towns to look for on the map are Bodmin and Wadebridge. The former is linked to Exeter by the A30 and to Plymouth by the A38. Wadebridge is 7 miles north of Bodmin. At Wadebridge the B3314 should be taken to St Minver and then a left turn should be taken at this village to Rock.

The Church Course takes its name from the tiny, half-sunken church which is situated near the far end of the links. Many years ago the church was barely visible after a violent storm practically covered it in sand. It is well worth inspecting and Sir John Betjeman is buried in the graveyard. The church almost comes into play on the celebrated 10th hole, the toughest par four on the 6207 yards par 69 layout (the Holywell Course measures 4165 yards, par 62). As well as being the most difficult two shot hole on the course it is also one of the most memorable. The drive is downhill, but it must carry almost 200 yards to find a narrow, heavily contoured fairway; off to the left is a marshy area and a stream and to the right are steep sand dunes and uncompromising rough. The second shot to the green is almost as daunting as the tee shot!

Betjeman's birdie came at the 13th but the other hole that everyone talks about is the 6th; here the golfer must confront the 'Himalayas', 'the highest sand hill, to the best of my belief, I have ever seen on a golf course' remarked the famous golf writer Bernard Darwin (another who was thoroughly enchanted by St Enodoc). With holes like the 6th it isn't difficult to see why St Enodoc is so often likened to Prestwick.

The area around Padstow is most fortunate in having both St Enodoc and Trevose so close at hand. Together they make a marvellous pair and offer two very different challenges. It is difficult to imagine anyone playing St Enodoc and not relishing a return visit . . . and who knows what an unexpected birdie might inspire!

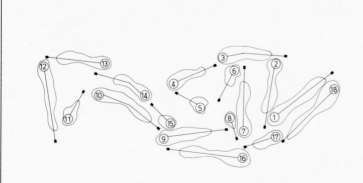

Hole	Yards	Par		Hole	Yards	Par
1	518	5		10	457	4
2	436	4		11	178	3
3	436	4		12	366	4
4	292	4		13	360	4
5	160	3		14	355	4
6	378	4		15	168	3
7	394	4		16	482	5
8	155	3		17	206	3
9	393	4		18	446	4
Out	**3,164**	**35**		**In**	**3,043**	**34**
				Out	**3,164**	**35**
				Totals	**6,207**	**69**

St Mellion Lodges & Hotel

St Mellion is a modern golf and country club situated in the Caradon District of South East Cornwall, offering a stunning variety of sporting facilities to both its members and guests. The golf at St Mellion is truly second to none with the Old Course and the Jack Nicklaus Championship Course available for all guests to enjoy. The Old Course here offers a challenging and enjoyable round to the club golfer and is in pleasant contrast to the more demanding Nicklaus course, home of the Benson and Hedges International Open.

Guests can enjoy a full range of indoor and outdoor facilities: all weather tennis courts, squash courts, indoor heated leisure pool, jacuzzi and sauna, snooker, even an archery club. Guests can also take advantage of the multi-gym and solarium. However if you just like to walk, the five hundred acre estate offers some relaxing strolls along streams and lakes. There is much to explore in the surrounding Cornish countryside, with picturesque villages and sandy beaches but a short distance away.

The St Mellion Hotel has everything to make the guest's stay enjoyable and comfortable. The bedrooms are attractively furnished with bathroom en-suite, colour television and tea/coffee making facilities. The superb restaurant in the Club house serves a first class menu of International cuisine and a wide choice of fine wines. However some may prefer the comfort and luxury of the St Mellion Lodges, beautifully equipped and furnished with all the requirements for up to eight people. Luxury fitted kitchens, en-suite bathrooms, television and video are standard and most lodges have an inbuilt sauna room.

Whether you are a keen golfer, or just looking for a relaxing break, St Mellion will reward you with the holiday of a life time. Situated only ten miles from Plymouth, St Mellion is easily accessible by road, rail or air.

St Mellion Golf and Coutry Club
Saltash
Cornwall PL12 6SD

Tel: Liskeard (0579) 50101
Fax: Liskeard (0579) 50116

St Mellion

I wonder what the golfing critics would have said if a few years ago someone had suggested that Jack Nicklaus would one day be designing a Championship course in Cornwall? 'Go tell it to the pixies', I should imagine. Well, in Cornwall myths, legends and fairy tales have a habit of turning out to be true.

St Mellion is the brainchild of farming brothers Martin and Hermon Bond. What made these charming people turn from profitable pig breeding and potato farming to golf course building remains something of a mystery; what is certain, however, is that their success has been nothing short of phenomenal.

The St Mellion story really has two parts to it. Act One commenced in the mid 1970s when the Bonds first decided to create a golf course. In short, their idea met with resounding triumph and a first class Championship course was constructed. Within a few years, tournament golf came to Cornwall (T.V. cameras and all) for the first time. Ambition swelled and Act Two was conceived: 'Let's build the best course in Europe' (well, why not!) An additional two hundred acres of adjoining woodland was purchased from the Duchy of Cornwall and an approach was made to the great man himself, Jack Nicklaus. Negotiations followed and Nicklaus came over to inspect the new land. His initial thought was that the land was far too hilly and narrow—an impossible task. But of course, like the Bond brothers, Jack could never resist a challenge...

Plans were drawn up and at least on paper the object was a simple one, namely to build, in Jack's words, 'Potentially the world's greatest galleried golf course'. Let us just say that the construction team put in a few good hours! The end result is now ready for all the world to see. Some have described it as an 'Augusta in Cornwall'; others reckon it to be the toughest course in Britain. Perhaps the best idea is to go and judge for yourself—you'll be made most welcome.

The **Director of Golf** at St Mellion is the very helpful **Mr. David Webb**. He can be contacted by telephone on **(0579) 50101**. Any written correspondence should be addressed to **The Golf Director, St Mellion Golf and Country Club, St Mellion, Saltash, Cornwall, PL12 6SD**. While there is an understandable wish to play the **Nicklaus Course**, we shouldn't forget that there are two fine courses at St Mellion. When the Nicklaus course was being built, certain changes to the old Championship course (now known as the **'Old Course'**) were necessary. However, it remains a worthy test of golf and is certainly a long way from your average 'holiday course'.

Visitors (with handicaps) are welcome to play either course between Mondays and Fridays, and teeing times can be booked through **the starter** on **(0579) 51182**. The green fee to play a round over the Nicklaus Course was £42 in 1994. On the Old Course, the cost of a game was £22. Reduced rates are available for junior golfers and groups. The **Director of Teaching** is ex Ryder Cup Player **John Garner** and the **Professionals** are **Tony Moore, Andrew Milton** and **David Moon**.

Although it nestles deep in the Cornish countryside, St Mellion is easily accessible from all directions. Travelling from afar most will come via Plymouth which is situated eight miles to the south east. Plymouth is linked to Exeter by the A38 and Exeter in turn to Bristol by the M5. On reaching Plymouth the A38 should be followed towards Liskeard and the turning for St Mellion is clearly signposted.

It is difficult to say which are the best holes on the Nicklaus Course; a few, however, do stand out and they exude the Nicklaus approach. The 3rd is an excellent hole—miss the fairway to the right and you can be facing a desperate uphill shot over a huge ravine to a heavily protected green. On the 5th, the drive is across a lake and thereafter the fairway sweeps around to the left towards the green which has a stream running in front of it. And so it goes on, but note especially the par three 11th and par five 12th which have been likened to Augusta's 12th and 13th. However, for all the comparisons with Augusta and Jack's best courses in America, the golfer only has to lift his eyes and look around to be reminded where he is. The surrounding scenery is unmistakably Cornish: the rolling green fields, the babbling brook with its kingfisher and the gnarled trees that huddle around many of the greens and look as if they've endured a million English winters.

In May 1990, Benson and Hedges brought their prestigious International Open tournament to the Nicklaus Course and victory fittingly went to one of the world's leading players, Jose-Maria Olazabal. The Spaniard was succeeded as champion by Bernhard Langer and he in turn has been followed by Peter Senior, Paul Broadhurst and Seve Ballesteros. What of the Bond brothers—ambitions fulfilled? In 1993 they released plans for the next phase of the St Mellion dream which included the building of a luxury five star hotel and a third 18 hole course. Better tell the pixies to raise the curtains on Act Three.

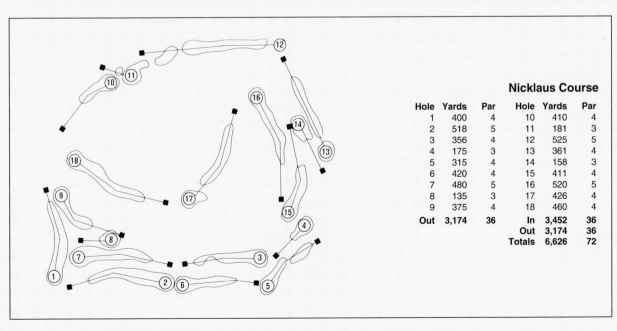

Nicklaus Course

Hole	Yards	Par	Hole	Yards	Par
1	400	4	10	410	4
2	518	5	11	181	3
3	356	4	12	525	5
4	175	3	13	361	4
5	315	4	14	158	3
6	420	4	15	411	4
7	480	5	16	520	5
8	135	3	17	426	4
9	375	4	18	460	4
Out	**3,174**	**36**	**In**	**3,452**	**36**
			Out	**3,174**	**36**
			Totals	**6,626**	**72**

This lovely old Cornish manor house, parts of which date back to the 16th century, is a rare example of a true country house hotel by the sea. Surrounded by over two acres of beautiful gardens, the hotel enjoys glorious views over the two dramatic headlands of Talland Bay.

Bedrooms are individually furnished to a high standard, many with lovely sea views. The lounges open on to a south facing terrace by a heated outdoor swimming pool.

Dinner menus are imaginative and incorporate much fresh regional produce — seafood from Looe, Cornish lamb and west country cheeses — complemented by a list of some 100 carefully selected wines.

Leisure pursuits at the hotel include: swimming (May-September), putting — some free practice! — croquet, table tennis and sauna. Nearby there is: boating, deep sea and shark fishing, riding, tennis — and of course golf.

There are several excellent golf courses within easy reach of the hotel including those at Looe, Lanhydrock and Carlyon Bay, with the championship course of St Mellion but a 40 minute drive by car. Guests at Talland Bay Hotel benefit from concessionary green fees at all these courses.

Talland Bay is a magically peaceful spot from which to explore this part of Cornwall — there are breathtaking cliff coastal walks at the hotel's doorstep, and many National Trust houses and gardens to visit locally — but most people come here just to relax and enjoy the view — why not discover it for yourself?

Talland Bay Hotel
Talland-by-Looe
Cornwall
PL13 2JB
Tel: (01503) 72667
Fax: (01503) 72940

Please note from June 1995:
Tel: (01503) 272667
Fax: (01503) 272940

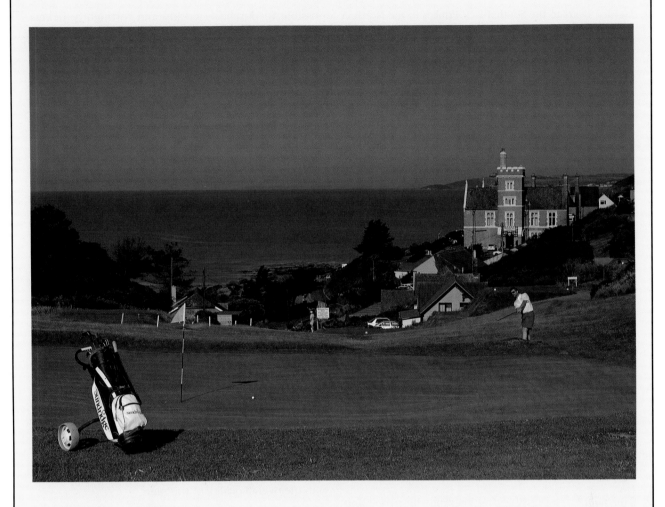

The Whitsand Bay Hotel is set in the beautiful location of Portwrinkle in Cornwall. It was originally moved, brick by brick, from Torpoint five miles away and re-erected in 1909 when it was opened as a hotel. This large cornish manor house is a superb first-class establishment, run with friendly efficiency by the Earle family who have over 30 years experience in the business. It is a matter of pride to them that their guests feel entirely at home and in good hands.

Attention to detail runs through every room in the house. The hall and elegant lounges are panelled in oak and light pours in through the unusual stained glass windows. The bedrooms vary in size from cosy beamed lodgings to a score of large family rooms, with en suite facilities and panoramic sea views. The sumptuous decor of the hotel is reflected in the stately dining rooms. Here the Earles offer a full English breakfast to start the day and, in the evening, a splendid five course dinner carefully prepared from a choice of local produce and brought to the table with panache. Good food is of the essence and guests may wish to stroll back from the beach to a healthy bar lunch and a cool drink. Cream teas are always provided in the afternoons and can be served in one of the lounges which have spectacular views of the coast .

The hotel has its own well equipped leisure complex, with an indoor swimming pool and a pool-side coffee bar. The complex also houses a sauna, solarium, Turkish bath, hairdressing and beauty salon, a games room and a toddlers room. The less energetic may simply choose to relax on the terrace overlooking the play area and watch the sun set over Whitsand Bay.

There is no shortage of activities and where better to start the day than on the **hotel's 18 hole golf course**. It is intended for everyone from beginners to low handicap players and competitions for ladies, gents and mixed couples are held weekly. This is a true golfers paradise — there are five other golf courses within a ten mile radius. There are beaches to suit every taste and nearby, at the port of Looe, guests may choose to try their hand at deep sea and shark fishing. The bustling port of Plymouth is only a short drive away and is ideal for shopping trips and sightseeing.

Whitsand Bay Hotel
Portwrinkle
nr Torpoint
Cornwall
PL11 3BU
Tel: (0503) 30276
Fax: (0503) 30329

Golden Bears to the South, Black Princes to the North. A golfing holiday in Cornwall will never be the same again.

Ten years ago it was the sand iron that battled for hegemony with the bucket and spade; nowadays it is just as likely to be the one iron or the two iron. Golfing in Cornwall used to mean golfing around Cornwall as all the biggest attractions were situated directly on the coast—either on cliffs overlooking the sea or somewhere deep amongst the sand dunes. But first St Mellion and now Bowood have caused a radical rethink.

As one who originally comes from Devon, I have always thought that the 'middle bits' of Cornwall had a slightly foreign air about them. Somehow, the scenery seems to belong to another country. My opinion was confirmed last winter when I travelled to Camelford in the north of the county to investigate a new golf course that a colleague had been raving about. A 'Valderrama in Cornwall' was his description and suddenly, as I drew near the course, I saw at least a dozen windmills; well, an extensive wind farm at any rate. Don Quixote would have felt at home here I thought, especially with Valderrama down the road.

Bowood lies just beyond the town of Camelford and the turning for the golf club is clearly signposted from the A39 Wadebridge road. The name apparently derives from the adjacent ancient woodland which, some 600 and more years ago was the Deer Park of the Black Prince—he of Crecy and The Hundred Years War fame. As King Arthur's legendary castle at Tintagel is a mere seven or eight miles away, this must have been a very turbulent place once. Today, there is a total peace and although still very young, Bowood has indeed the makings of a very special golf club.

The people responsible for keeping the peace and ensuring a decidedly warm welcome are the **proprietor and founder, Ross Cobbledick** (who like the Bonds at St Mellion is from a local farming family) and the very experienced **Director of Golf, Bryan Patterson**. Bryan manages all golfing matters at Bowood and visitors wishing to arrange a game should telephone the golf shop on **(0840) 213017**. The Club's full address is Bowood **Golf Club, Bowood Park, Lanteglos, Camelford, Cornwall, PL32 9RT**. The green fees in 1993 were set at £22 per round and £30 per day throughout the week. It is also

possible to purchase weekly and fortnightly tickets (contact the Club for details). There are no general restrictions as to the times when visitors (with handicaps) can play at Bowood although with the course becoming increasingly popular booking is advised.

Notwithstanding the very laid back ambience that pervades the Club, the 19th hole facilities seem to be forever expanding and all levels of pre and post golf sustenance can be enjoyed. Before stepping on to the first tee, however, the one 'must' is to inspect the extraordinary putting green. Beautifully landscaped in a rockery terrace style, the inspiration for the design was the famous putting green at Little Aston: this one may be better.

From the back tees, the course measures a lengthy 6,692 yards, par 72 (5,700 yards, par 72 from the ladies tees). But what about the Valderrama comparison? It is a very bold one (not to mention a mighty compliment) for the Spanish course is widely regarded as the finest in Continental Europe. In truth, it shouldn't be taken too literally, rather there is a distinct flavour of Valderrama in the shaping and the hazards on several of the holes and a certain number of visitors have in fact made comments to this effect. Certain holes are genuinely striking in their appearance and condition but it should also be said that Bowood is very much a course of two halves.

The front nine is built on much higher and more open ground; there are far fewer mature trees and hence some rather serious rough is required to give the holes greater definition. The 5th and 7th are probably the best pair and there are some marvellous views of the Cornish countryside (not to mention the wind farm) but the golfer—especially if he or she is anticipating Valderrama type quality—may be a shade disappointed with the overall quality of this nine.

The second half of the round, however, should blast any feelings of disappointment to Kingdom come! If ever a course stepped up a gear it is this one. Six good holes are mixed with three great ones; namely the 12th, 13th and 15th. It would be worth travelling a considerable distance just to photograph, never mind play these holes: they are as seductive and challenging a trio as one is likely to find on any course—including St. Mellion and, dare I say it, Valderrama.

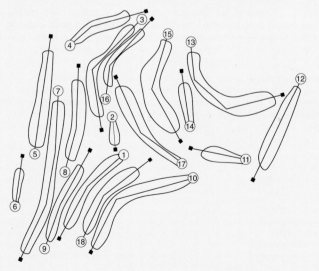

Hole	Yards	Par	Hole	Yards	Par
1	380	4	10	515	5
2	129	3	11	228	3
3	490	5	12	385	4
4	325	4	13	510	5
5	420	4	14	191	3
6	174	3	15	409	4
7	600	5	16	331	4
8	374	4	17	402	4
9	387	4	18	436	4
Out	**3,314**	**36**	**In**	**3,279**	**36**
			Out	**3,279**	**36**
			Totals	**6,692**	**72**

Cornwall Complete Golf

Key

To avoid disappointment
it is advisable to telephone
in advance

***Visitors welcome at most times
**Visitors usually allowed on
weekdays only
*Visitors not normally permitted
(Mon, Wed) No visitors
on specified days

Approximate Green Fees
A £30 plus
B £20 to £30
C £15 to £25
D £10 to £20
E under £10
F Greens fees on application

Restrictions
G Guests only
H–Handicap certificate required
H–(24) Handicap of 24 or less
L –Letter of introduction required
M–Visitor must be a member of
another recognised club.

Bowood G.C.
(0840) 213017
Lanteglos, Camelford
(18)6692 yards/***/B/H

Bude and North Cornwall G.C.
(0288) 352006
Burn View, Bude
(18)6202 yards/**/B/H

Budock Vean Hotel G.C.
(0326) 250288
Mawnan Smith, Falmouth
(9)5007 yards/***/D/L/H

Cape Cornwall G.& C.C.
(0736) 788611
St Just, Penzance
(18) 5650 yards/**/D

Carlyon Bay Hotel G.C.
(0726) 814228
Carlyon Bay, St Austell
(18)6463 yards/***/C

China Fleet C.C.
(0752) 848668
Saltash
(18)6551 yards/***/F/H

Falmouth G.C.
(0326) 311262
Swanpool Road, Falmouth
(18)5680 yards/***/B/H

Holywell Bay G.C.
(0637) 830095
Holywell Bay, Newquay
(18)2784/***/E

Isle of Scilly G.C.
(0720) 22692
St Mary's, Isles of Scilly
(9)6001 yards/***/D

Killiow Park G.C.
(0872) 70246
Killiow, Kea
(18)3500 yards/**/D

Lanhydrock G.C.
(0208) 73600
Lostwithiel Road, Bodmin
(18) 6137 yards/***/F

Launceston G.C.
(0566) 773442
St. Stephens, Launceston
(18)6407 yards/**/D/H/L

Looe G.C.
(05034) 239
Widegates, Looe

(18)5940 yards/***/D
Lostwithiel G.& C.C.
(0208) 873550
Lower Polscoe, Lostwithiel
(18)6098 yards/**/D/H

Mullion G.C.
(0326) 240276
Cury, Helston
(18)6022 yards/**/C/H

Newquay G.C.
(0637) 872091
Tower Road, Newquay
(18)6140 yards/***/D/H

Perranporth G.C.
(0872) 572454
Budnick Hill, Perranporth
(18)6286 yards/***/C/H

Porthpean G.C.
(0726) 64613
Porthpean, St Austell
(9)3266 yards/***/E

Praa Sands G.C.
(0736) 763445
Germoe Crossroads, Penzance
(9)4104 yards/***/D/H

St Austell G.C.
(0726) 72649
Tregongeeves Lane, St Austell
(18)6000 yards/***/F/M/H

St Enodoc G.C.
(0208) 863216
Rock, Wadebridge
(18)6207 yards/***/B/H(24)
(18)4142 yards/***/D

St Kew G.C.
(0208) 84500
St Kew Highway, Bodmin
(9)2204 yards/***/E
St Mellion G.& C.C.
(0579) 50101

St Mellion, Saltash
(18)6626 yards/**/A/H
(18)5927 yards/**/C

Tehidy Park G.C.
(0209) 842208
Cambourne
(18)6241 yards/***/B/H

Tregenna Castle Hotel G.C.
(0736) 795254
St Ives
(18) 3549 yards/***/F

Treloy G.C.
(0637) 878554
Treloy, Newquay
(9)2143 yards/***/E

Trethorne G.C.
(0566) 86324
Kennards House, Launceston
(9)3169 yards/***/E

Trevose G.& C.C.
(0841) 520208
Constantine Bay, Padstow
(18)6608 yards/***/E/H
(9)3000 yards/***/F
(9)1367 yards/***/F

Truro G.C.
(0872) 72640
Treliske, Truro
(18)5347 yards/***/C/H

West Cornwall G.C.
(0736) 753401
Lelant, St Ives
(18)5884 yards/***/B/H

Whitsand Bay Hotel G.C.
(0503) 30276
Portwrinkle, Torpoint
(18)5800 yards/***/D/H/L

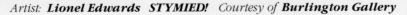

Artist: **Lionel Edwards** STYMIED! Courtesy of **Burlington Gallery**

Artist: **Robert Guy** **WESTWARD HO!** *Courtesy of:* **Burlington Gallery**

Glorious Devon' they call it—beaches to the north, beaches to the south and Dartmoor in the middle. Well, amidst all the glory are some thirty golf courses, the majority of which lie either directly on the coast or within a mile or so of it. The two most widely known are both located to the north of the county: **Royal North Devon** (or Westward Ho! as it is commonly known) and **Saunton.** The greater number of courses, however, are on the southern coast, or to put it another way, while North Devon may have the cream, most of the tees are to be found in the south.

Firstly though, what about golf in the middle? The beautiful setting of the **Manor House** Hotel Golf Course at Moretonhampstead (see feature page) is known to many. However, it is not the sole course within Dartmoor, **Okehampton** is another moorland type course and whilst not overly long, has a number of interesting holes making it well worth a visit. Away from Dartmoor, but still fairly centrally located is the parkland course at **Tiverton,** easily reached from the M5 (junction 27), and a little closer to Exeter and adjacent to Woodbury Common is the highly acclaimed new development at **Woodbury Park**, where there is a very challenging 18 hole championship course designed by Hamilton Stutt plus a shorter 9 hole course and driving range. Note the spectacular par three 18th hole here—arguably the most dramatic closing hole in the south west.

With its many Tudor buildings, historic guildhall and impressive cathedral, Exeter makes an attractive county town. Golfwise, the city has an 18 hole course at Countess Wear, south of the town off the A377. A fairly short parkland course, **Exeter** Golf and Country Club has a very grand clubhouse and the course is renowned for its beautifully maintained greens, undoubtedly among the best in Devon. There are many outstanding places in which to spend a night or two when visiting this part of the world. Exeter is a likely base and here the Royal Clarence Hotel (0392) 58464 is extremely comfortable and enjoys a splendid position overlooking Cathedral Square. Also in the city, the White Hart (0392) 79897 on South Street is a delightful old inn with good accommodation. One of the oldest and best known pubs in Exeter is the Ship on St Martins Lane—ideal unless you're over six feet tall!

On Dartmoor, the striking Manor House Hotel (0647) 40355 at Moretonhampstead is where many golfers will choose to hang up their spikes, but a number of splendid alternatives are at hand. Chagford offers the exceptional Gidleigh Park (0647) 432367 and the Mill End Hotel (0647) 432282. In nearby Frenchbeer, Teignworthy House is marvellously relaxing. In Lydford, Lydford House (0822) 82347 is pleasant, as is the Castle Inn (0822) 82242, and the Lodge Hill Farmhouse (0884) 252907 at Ashley is convenient for Tiverton. Whilst in the area, a visit to Huntsham is also in order: Huntsham Court (039 86) 365 is a rambling Gothic hotel, with many quaint touches. After a game at Manor House, two popular pubs to note are the White Hart in Moretonhampstead and the Ring of Bells in nearby historic North Bovey.

South Devon

On the east side of the River Exe and only half an hour's drive from Exeter are the courses at Sidmouth and Budleigh Salterton (**East Devon**). Both are on fairly high ground providing panoramic views out to sea. **Sidmouth** is perhaps more of a typical clifftop course with well wooded fairways and 'springy' turf, while East Devon is a cross between downland and heathland with much heather and gorse. Convenient for both courses is

the charming 18th century country house hotel, Salston Manor Hotel (0404) 815581 which also offers inclusive golf packages for Woodbury Park. East Devon's delights are detailed ahead.

To the west of the Exe estuary, the friendly **Warren** Golf Club at Dawlish offers the only true links golf in South Devon. Laid out on a narrow hook-shaped peninsula and covered in gorse and numerous natural bunkers this is Devon's answer to St Andrews—and if this sounds a little far-fetched just inspect the aerial photographs at the 19th! It is a much improved course with an interesting finishing hole that will have the wayward hitter threatening both the members in the clubhouse and/or quite possibly the passengers on a passing London to Penzance 125. A fairly near neighbour of the Warren is **Teignmouth** Golf Club. It may be near, but Teignmouth offers a totally different challenge, being situated some 900 feet above sea level on Haldon Moor. Teignmouth can become shrouded in fog during the winter, but when all is clear, it's a very pleasant course and most attractive too.

Those seeking a memorable 19th hole on their way to the south coast may have sped past Gittisham—a mistake, for Combe House (0404) 42756 provides great elegance and style. In Sidmouth, the Riviera (0395) 515201 is grand, the Torbay Hotel (0395) 513456 good value, while for a family holiday the Westcliff (0395) 513252 may be the best choice. Just east of Sidmouth, the Masons Arms at Branscombe is perfect for a relaxing dinner and a stopover if required. The Bolt Head Hotel (0548) 843751) in Salcombe also offers the highest standards of comfort. In Dawlish Warren, most convenient for the golf links is the Langstone Cliff Hotel (0626) 865155 (just roll down the hill and you're almost there). Not too far from the many courses of east Devon at Hawkchurch, near Axminster, the comfortable Fairwater Head Hotel (02977) 349 is recommended. Just to the north west of Newton Abbot in Haytor lies the Bel Alp House Country Hotel (0364) 661217, an elegant country house offering genuine tranquillity to our doubtless exhausted golfers. Another local favourite, worthy of its popularity, is the Moorland Hotel (0364) 661407 while in Teignmouth, the Monmouth Court (0626) 774229 is a small hotel offering good value breaks for golfers and also recommended is the Coombe Bank Hotel (0626) 772369 .

The three handiest courses for those holidaying in the Torbay area are probably **Churston, Torquay** and **Newton Abbot**. The first two mentioned offer typical downland/clifftop type golf and a very different game from Newton Abbot's course at Stover where abundant heather, woods and a meandering brook are likely to pose the most challenges. A word too, on the recently opened course at **Hele Park** which has a mature outlook and greens reputedly second to none. Speaking of challenges, mention must be made of the **Dartmouth** Golf and Country Club at Blackawton, Totnes.

One of the most pleasant and convenient places to stay in this area is the Orestone Manor House (0803) 328098 in Maidencombe. In Torquay itself, there are numerous fine hotels. The most famous is the Imperial (0803) 294301, which offers all manner of splendid facilities but charges for it! The Palace Hotel (0803) 200200 is less costly, but courtesy still prevails. Perhaps the best value to be found is at Homers Hotel (0803) 213456 with its first class restaurant.

Still seeking an ideal 19th hole, the Quayside Hotel (0803) 855751 in the popular resort of Brixham is charming and the town retains a much quieter atmosphere than its neighbour across the bay. In Dartmouth, two

Your hosts at Holne Chase, now in their 23rd year at the hotel have an excellent knowledge of local facilities.

GOLF: Kenneth Bromage has compiled a list of no fewer than 15 courses less than an hour away from the hotel, plus three others of international standing within about 90 minutes. Other courses recently built but said to be good are not listed as he has not yet had a chance to play them.

Small golfing parties staying at the hotel will find flexibility in meal times to help them plan their golfing tour and your host will be happy to advise the best days for playing on each chosen course, thus avoiding competitions etc.

HORSERACING: Newton Abbot is England's most westerly racecourse. National Hunt meetings run from early August through to late May. Frequently, meetings at Newton Abbot are followed /preceded by meetings at Exeter racecourse. Holne Chase is handy for both.

FISHING: The Dart is arguably one of Britain's loveliest rivers. Certainly, it is a challenge to the ardent fly fisherman. Holne Chase has a single bank beat about a mile long which is available to residents at no extra charge.

Holne Chase became an hotel in 1934. The surrounding woodlands were partly laid out as an arboretum in 1878 and so afford many interesting walks taking in an old mine shaft (c1790), an iron age fortified camp and early 20th century charcoal burners' hearths.

The woodlands abound with wildlife, including roe and red deer, badger, fox, rabbit and otter, buzzard, heron, kingfisher and even a flight of shellduck which have colonised a stretch of the river.

The Bromage family took the hotel over in 1972 and have been working on it ever since. All 14 bedrooms have bath and/or shower en suite. The hotel is classified 4 Crown 'Highly Recommended' by the English Tourist Board and has won many awards over the years, both in the kitchen and in the cellar.

Holne Chase is an exceptional place in which to relax. Deep comfy sofas and armchairs, a well stocked library, blazing fires on winter evenings make relaxation easy. Dartmoor itself is wonderful walking country and guided walks can be arranged at all times of the year. Riding can also be arranged from some of the best Stables on Dartmoor all within 20 to 30 minutes from the hotel.

Holne Chase is three miles north of the Ashburton. To find the hotel, take the Two Bridges/Princetown turning off the A38, marked Pear Tree, and follow the road for approximately three miles. The hotel turning is on the right just after the road crosses the River Dart.

Holne Chase Hotel & Restaurant
Nr Ashburton
Devon
TQ13 7NS
Tel: (03643) 471
Fax: (03643) 453

restaurants merit special comment: the Cherub Dining Rooms (0803) 832571 which has delicious seafood as a speciality, and the Carved Angel (0803) 832465. Just outside Dartmouth, in Dittisham, Fingals at Old Coombe Manor (080422) 398 is well worth the short trip and finally the Holne Chase Hotel (03643) 471 in Ashburton—a glorious setting with a restaurant to match.

Heading further down the coast, the picturesque village of **Thurlestone** has one of the most popular courses in Devon. It is a superb clifftop course with several far-reaching views along the coast. **Bigbury** lies a short distance from Thurlestone and although perhaps a little less testing it is nevertheless equally attractive and looks across to Burgh Island, a favourite (or hopefully an ex-favourite) haunt of smugglers. Both Thurlestone and Bigbury can be reached from Plymouth via the A379, or from the Torbay region via the A381. The Thurlestone Hotel (0548) 560382 is a perfect base not only for playing the two nearby courses, but also for exploring what is a delightful part of Devon. It also has its own very pleasant short 9 hole course. Buckland-Tout-Saints (0548) 853055 at Kingsbridge is also worthy of inclusion on any itinerary. For lovers of the country mansion, Holbeton offers the Alston Hall Hotel (075 530) 555 but if a good pub is sought the Pilchard on Burgh Island is one of the best—but beware the tide!

Golfers in Plymouth have probably been noting with interest the recent developments at nearby **St Mellion**, just over the border in Cornwall. Also not far from the great seafaring city, the **Elfordleigh Hotel's** (0752) 336428 9 hole golf course at Plympton is very pleasant—and not as demanding as the Nicklaus course! And towards Dartmoor, **Yelverton** is certainly one not to be missed. Designed by Herbert Fowler, the architect of Walton Heath, Yelverton lies midway between Plymouth and Tavistock on the A386. It is a classic moorland course and very attractive too, with much gorse and heather.

Tavistock is also not far from Plymouth. **Tavistock** Golf Club is perhaps not as attractive as Yelverton, but worth a visit all the same. A second golf course in Tavistock, **Hurdwick** Golf Club has recently been opened. For good places to stay, the Prince Hall Hotel is a small friendly hotel in country house style while the Moorland Links Hotel (0822) 852245 at Yelverton needs little explanation and for a place to celebrate one's birdie at the 18th the Who'd of Thought It at Milton Combe sounds highly appropriate—it really is an excellent pub and serves outstandingly good value lunches.

North Devon

From Plymouth, the north coast of Devon is about an hour and a quarter's drive - from Exeter, a little less. Unless there is some urgency a leisurely drive is recommended for the scenery is truly spectacular. A few suggestions for breaking the journey include Milton Damerel, where the Woodford Bridge (0409) 261481 is a first rate hotel, Hatherleigh for the handsome George Hotel (0409) 272219 and Clawton near Holdsworthy for the delightful Court Barn (040 927) 219. Then there is Winkleigh, where the Kings Arms is a praiseworthy pub in an attractive village. Just beyond Winkleigh, towards Barnstaple, there is a fine new 18 hole course at **Libbaton** near Umberleigh—again definitely worth breaking the journey for.

North Devon can boast one of the oldest golf clubs in England, the **Royal North Devon** Club at Westward Ho! Founded in 1864, it can also claim to have seen the low-

est known score for eighteen holes of golf. In 1936 the Woolacombe Bay professional recorded a 55 on his home course—29 out and 26 back, including a hole in one at the last! As this took place on the 1st January, one cannot help wondering quite what he did the night before! Unfortunately, this course closed long ago although there are 9 holes at **Morthoe & Woolacombe** and a very popular 18 hole test at nearby **Ilfracombe.** Situated several hundred feet above sea level, this latter course offers many outstanding views of the North Devon coastline. The best hole is the par four 13th and there is an interesting selection of par three holes, one of which, the 4th, is played across a plunging ravine but measures a mere 80 yards. Whilst in the area, two notable hotels for golfing breaks in Ilfracombe are St Brannochs House Hotel (0271) 863873 and the Seven Hills (0271) 862207 while yet another very recent addition to the county's golfing scene is the **Clovelly** Country Club near the famous 'sleepy village.'

Both **Saunton** and Westward Ho! deserve more than a fleeting visit and are featured ahead. Westward Ho! is a place for pilgrimage, but Saunton provides the more modern championship challenge. There are two fine courses at Saunton, the East (which is the championship course) and the greatly improved West. Large sandhills dominate both courses, and when the wind blows.......

Sleeping in the dunes is strictly out of bounds so here are a few ideas for the 19th. Visitors to North Devon should consider Yelden House (0237) 474400 in Bideford, whilst in Saunton Sands, the hotel of the same name is first class and popular with golfers (0271) 890212. A noted nearby eating place is Otters Restaurant (0271) 813633 in Braunton. The Preston House Hotel (0271) 890472 is also close to Saunton's links and is again very highly regarded by golfers. At Fairy Cross, near Bideford, the Portledge Hotel (0237) 451262 is for the lover of peace and quiet, as is Whitechapel Manor (0769) 573377 at South Molton, while in Northam the Durrant House Hotel (0237) 472361 is great for recuperating after an excursion to Westward Ho!

More thoughts? Recommendations are many and various: in Westward Ho! Culloden House (0237) 479421 is small but friendly and there is also the popular Buckleigh Lodge guesthouse (0237) 475988. The small town of Umberleigh provides yet more worthy country house establishments in the shape of Northcote Manor (0769) 60501 and the Highbulben Hotel (0769) 540561. Woolacombe offers the superb Woolacombe Bay Hotel (0271) 870388 and the award winning Watersmeet Hotel (0271) 870333. Then there is the Penhaven Country House (0237) 451388, a lovely old rectory transformed into a hotel at Parkham near Bideford and the elegant Halmpstone Manor (0271) 830321 at Bishop's Tawton near Barnstaple.

Among a number of good eating places in the area are Gray's Country Restaurant (0271) 812809 in Knowle and the Knoll House Hotel (0271) 882548 in Kentishbury. For those who prefer to cater for themselves in one of the many pretty cottages that abound in Devon, Country Holidays (0282) 445566, and Devon and Dorset Cottages (0626) 333678 are both worth contacting.

A final thought as we leave North Devon—should it actually happen and for some peculiar and presumably non-golfing reason (?!) you do get stranded in the dunes at Saunton, the chances are you will wake up to a glorious sunrise. If this is the case let's just hope the morning's golf is equally spectacular.

Woolacombe Bay itself, surely one of the most beautiful and magical settings for any hotel. Family run, the Woolacombe Bay Hotel with six acres of spacious lawns running down to the beach, set in a secluded valley between rolling green hills, the spectacular rugged coastline giving way to a breathtaking three mile expanse of wide golden sands with grassy dunes, rock pools and boisterous rolling surf provides the complete, the perfect, holiday setting. The views in all directions are magnificent, Lundy Island on the horizon, craggy headlands in the distance and the beautiful National Trust countryside supplying a backdrop to this outstanding elegant hotel with the mellow Devonian landscape.

This distinctive Edwardian building which is the Woolacombe Bay Hotel was built in the days of gracious living and exudes a feeling of luxury and traditional style, combining comfort and service with a range of truly modern amenities. Accommodation is available to suit all requirements single, doubles, family suites etc, every bedroom en suite, central heating, direct dial telephone, baby listening facilities, colour television (with satellite T.V), radio, tea and coffee making facilities, towelling robes, hairdriers etc. Some rooms have spa bath, exceptional sea views and balcony overlooking the bay. The hotel's public rooms are restful, generously proportioned, comfortable and welcoming.

The elegant, chandeliered restaurant provides a relaxed ambience for the serious pleasure of eating. The table decor and the unobtrusive attention of the silver service waiting staff, sets the standard for the unhurried enjoyment of full English breakfast (available for the serious golfer) and seven course dinner for which the hotel is justly famous. Many dishes comprise fresh local fish, meats and vegetables all carefully selected and expertly prepared by the chef. This supplemented with a fine wine chosen from the wine cellar makes each meal an outstanding and memorable part of a visit to this stylish, friendly hotel.

For the evenings there is no shortage of entertainment either in the bar or the hotel's magnificent ballroom ensuring enjoyment to end another eventful day.

Relaxation is easy, but for those with boundless energy there is a tremendous opportunity with unlimited use of ther extensive sporting facilities which include tennis, squash, snooker, indoor and outdoor heated pools, new health suite with steam room, sauna, spa, solarium, bowls, croquet, gym and pitch and putt. There is also a power boat for charter. Massage, hairdressing, horse riding, and clay pigeon shooting are also available. Special reduced green fees have been arranged at Saunton Sands, the nearby championship course, only six miles away. Short breaks are the hotels speciality.

Woolacombe Bay Hotel
Woolacombe
Devon
EX34 7BN
Tel: (0271) 870388
Fax: (0271) 870613.

Royal North Devon (Westward Ho!)

This is a Club truly steeped in the history of the game. Westward Ho!, as it is commonly known, was the first English links course and being founded in 1864 the Royal North Devon Golf Club lays claim to being the oldest English Club still playing over its original land. Furthermore it boasts the oldest Ladies Golf Club in the world, the Westward Ho! Ladies Golf Club which was established in 1868. Originally designed by Tom Morris, and reconstructed by Herbert Fowler, the 18 holes are situated on Northam Burrows. The Burrows is a vast, exposed and relatively flat area of common land which stretches along the coast a couple of miles north of Bideford between Westward Ho! and Appledore.

Several of Britain's historic courses, particularly those in Scotland, have fascinating ties with common land and associated local rights which have existed since 'time immemorial', but whilst the inhabitants of St Andrews no longer use their hallowed turf for practising archery upon, nor put their washing out to dry on the banks of the Swilcan Burn, the locals of Northam village still graze their sheep and horses on the Burrows. There can surely be no other Championship course in the world where you can have teed up on the first, taken a few steps backward to survey the drive ahead only to see a sheep wander up and peer inquisitively at your ball! One shouldn't get too alarmed though, the animals are well-versed in the etiquette of the game—they generally keep a respectful distance from the fairways and greens, they take care not to bleat when you putt and what's more they certainly won't contemplate stealing your golf ball as I'm told the crows do at Royal Aberdeen.

Seriously, golf at Westward Ho! is a rich experience and given the warm welcome visitors receive, definitely to be recommended. Presently responsible for continuing the tradition of friendliness is the **Secretary, John Linaker**. Mr. Linaker can be contacted via **The Royal North Devon Golf Club, Golf Links Road, Westward Ho! Bideford, Devon EX39 1H, tel: (0237) 473817**.

If you are considering a trip to the Club you may find it advisable to telephone first in order to check if any tee reservations have been made. Fine weather can make the course particularly popular during the holiday season but it is now possible to pre-book a starting time. Societies are also welcomed and bookings can be arranged with the Secretary. In 1994, a green fee of £22 entitled the visitor to a single round with £26 payable for a full day's golf. As for juniors, the green fee was a mere £5—excellent value. The Club's **professional** is **Graham Johnston** and he can be reached by telephone on **(0237) 477598**.

The course can be approached from both East and West via the A39, although travellers from the West may be able to avoid the busy town of Bideford by joining the B3236 near Abbotsham. Visitors travelling from the Dartmoor region should take the A386 road which runs from Okehampton to Bideford, whilst those coming from Exeter should follow the A377 to Barnstaple, thereafter joining the A39 as above.

From the medal tees the course measures 6449 yards (the Championship course is some 200 yards longer) and is divided into two fairly equal halves. Westward Ho! has a traditional out and back layout and there are some panoramic views across Bideford Bay, especially from the 6th tee where, on a clear day, the Isle of Lundy can be seen. In theory, the links receives a degree of protection from the elements from a large bank of shingle which separates the Burrows from the beach. I say in theory for this is surely one of Britain's most windswept courses. However, the wind is not the only factor that can make scoring extremely difficult. There are numerous ditches and hidden pot bunkers and then of course, there are the Great Sea Rushes. To the uninitiated a word of caution—these giant marshland reeds, unique to Westward Ho!, can literally impale golf balls, so do as the sheep do—stay clear!

Westward Ho! is not only known for its golf course, it has literary fame as well. The village was founded a year before the Golf Club and was named after Charles Kingsley's adventure novel about Elizabethan seafarers. A decade or so later Rudyard Kipling attended the local college and remembered his days there in Stalky and Co. Alas, there is no record to suggest that Mr. Kipling was an exceedingly good golfer but while he was studying, a young boy from Northam was out on the course caddying for sixpence a round.

The boy was destined to become Open Champion on five occasions. John H. Taylor learnt his game at Westward Ho! and his great affection for the Club remained throughout his long life. In 1957 the Club elected him their President.

In addition to a friendly and unpretentious atmosphere, the Clubhouse offers some excellent catering. It also houses the Club's museum. It is most interesting and contains a great variety of golfing memorabilia, ranging from one of Tom Watson's gloves to some near priceless art.

For the golfer who has confined himself to playing on gentle heathland fairways, sheltered from any wind by tall trees, a visit to Westward Ho! would probably create quite a shock to the system. But clearly, for those with even a moderate interest in the history of the game and, of course, who are not afraid of a stiff challenge, Westward Ho! is a golfing must.

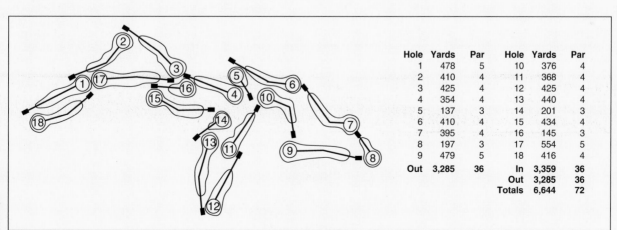

Hole	Yards	Par		Hole	Yards	Par
1	478	5		10	376	4
2	410	4		11	368	4
3	425	4		12	425	4
4	354	4		13	440	4
5	137	3		14	201	3
6	410	4		15	434	4
7	395	4		16	145	3
8	197	3		17	554	5
9	479	5		18	416	4
Out	**3,285**	**36**		**In**	**3,359**	**36**
				Out	**3,285**	**36**
				Totals	**6,644**	**72**

The Preston House is a gracious Victorian country house hotel standing in its own grounds and overlooking the ten mile sweep of Barnstaple's magnificent bay. The area is a veritable paradise for golfers who will find the Preston House ideally situated for two of the finest championship courses, Saunton and Royal North Devon. Guests of the hotel may take advantage of concessionary green fees and pre-booked tee times at both courses, and the management pride themselves on being able to cater for all golfers including beginners.

While Saunton lies less than half a mile from the hotel, and Royal North Devon is no more than a short drive away, there are many courses to be enjoyed in this part of Devon and a variety of other diversion on the doorstep. There is direct access to the beach where yachting, surfing and canoeing equipment can be hired and lessons are available if required. Riding and fishing can also be arranged close by and a leisurely stroll along the marvellous coastal walks is always a rewarding experience.

The hotel itself is immaculate and resplendent with antique furniture and crystal chandeliers, while the modern facilities are no less than one would expect from a hotel of this calibre.

All 15 bedrooms are individually designed to a very high standard, most with sea views. Guests can enjoy the spa bath, sauna, and solarium or relax around the heated outdoor swimming pool and admire the scenery. The conservatory is another favourite spot for guests to sit and take in the wonderful views out to sea over breakfast or lunch.

In the luxurious dining room overlooking the bay guests can savour the highly commended cuisine prepared from country-fresh food, and the hotel is renowned for its home-baked ham and succulent roast sirloin of beef as well as excellent service.

The Preston House with its old world charm and grand yet informal setting assures golfers of a warm welcome, tremendous hospitality and a memorable golfing break.

Preston House Hotel
Saunton
Braunton
North Devon
Tel: (0271) 890472
Fax: (0271) 890555

At a time when the likes of John H Taylor and Horace Hutchinson were striding the windswept fairways on Northam Burrows, across the Taw Estuary on the Braunton Burrows other men were busy trapping rabbits. It took more than thirty years for matters to be put right.

Saunton Golf Club was founded in 1897 some three decades after Westward Ho! In common with many great Clubs, Saunton's beginnings were rather modest. At first there were only nine holes and the original Clubhouse was a single room next to the local Post Office. Although the course was extended to 18 holes before the First World War (and a new Clubhouse acquired) it wasn't until after the War that Saunton's reputation really gained momentum. Chiefly responsible for this was golf architect Herbert Fowler, who having reshaped Westward Ho! performed a similar task at Saunton.

In 1932 the course was selected to stage the British Ladies Championship and this was followed by the English Amateur Championship of 1937. Unfortunately the links didn't fare too well during the Second World War as it was considered the perfect place for a Battle School and concrete and barbed wire covered the fairways. Reconstruction didn't begin until 1951, C.K. Cotton this time directing matters. Once restored the course quickly re-established itself as one of Britain's leading Championship links. In the early seventies a second 18 holes were added and today the two are known as the **East** (the former 'Old Course') and the **West** Course.

The **Secretary, Paul Stevens** can be reached by telephone on **(0271) 812436**, and the **professional, Jimmy McGhee**, can be contacted on **(0271) 812013**. Other than being able to provide proof of handicap there are no general restrictions on visitors—however prior telephoning is strongly recommended. Golfing Societies are equally welcome at Saunton; those wishing to make written applications to the Club should address correspondence to the Secretary at **The Saunton Golf Club, Saunton, Braunton, Devon EX33 1LG**.

The green fees for 1994 were set at £28 per day to play either the Championship East Course or the West Course, or both, with a slight increase to £33 on Saturdays, Sundays and on Bank Holidays. Juniors are offered a fifty per cent reduction.

Although on the map Saunton and Westward Ho! appear to be very neighbourly, travelling from one to the other is in fact about a 20 mile trip via Barnstaple. The Club's precise location is off the B3231 south of Saunton village. The B3231 can be picked up at Braunton, with Braunton in turn being joined to Ilfracombe in the north and Barnstaple to the south by the A361. Those travelling from further afield should aim for Barnstaple, which can be reached from Exeter by the A377 and from Tiverton on the new M5 link road, while for those approaching from the north of Cornwall the A39 is likely to prove of most assistance.

At 6703 yards, par 73 (SSS 73) from the Championship tees, the East Course is some 350 yards longer than the West (6356 yards par 71). Both, however, provide a fairly stiff challenge with large sand hills being the dominant feature on each.

The East Course could hardly be described as one of those that breaks you in gently: the first four holes all measure over 400 yards. There are several notable par fours early in the round, but perhaps the best are the 12th, with its ever-narrowing fairway, and the 16th which demands a tee shot over a vast sand hill with the second needing to be carried over a deep bunker in front of the green. The course record on the East Course stands at 66.

Since its reopening in 1951 Saunton has hosted several important Championships, both professional and amateur. On three occasions the English Open Amateur Strokeplay Championship has been played on the East Course and in 1966 the PGA Championship was held at Saunton. The St Andrews Trophy was also played here in 1984, as was the 1992 British Ladies Matchplay event.

On more than one occasion I have read that if Saunton had a different geography it would be an Open Championship venue. Maybe I'm missing the point, but I've never fully appreciated the 'geography argument'. If it's a question of remoteness, surely North Devon is no more remote than certain parts of the east and west coasts of Scotland—especially now that a motorway runs as far as Exeter (one hour's drive away). Attendance figures? Such is the popularity of golf in modern times it seems most unlikely that the crowds wouldn't flock to the area, and as for accommodation North Devon abounds with places to stay. Come to think of it, what better place for a week's holiday in July?

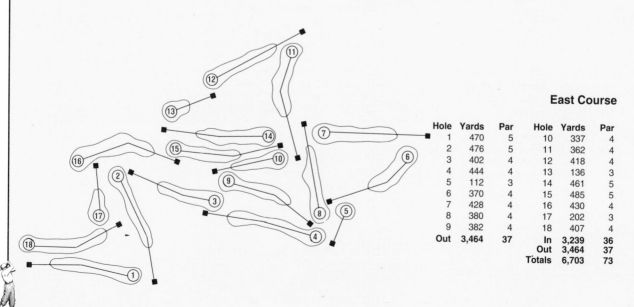

East Course

Hole	Yards	Par	Hole	Yards	Par
1	470	5	10	337	4
2	476	5	11	362	4
3	402	4	12	418	4
4	444	4	13	136	3
5	112	3	14	461	5
6	370	4	15	485	5
7	428	4	16	430	4
8	380	4	17	202	3
9	382	4	18	407	4
Out	**3,464**	**37**	**In**	**3,239**	**36**
			Out	**3,464**	**37**
			Totals	**6,703**	**73**

Alston Hall was built at the turn of the century and has retained its original Edwardian elegance whilst incorporating the highest standards of a luxury hotel. Thoughtful use of beautiful fabrics and fine antique furniture complement handsome oak panelling and large open fireplaces.

The Great Hall is quite breathtaking with its balustraded minstrels gallery and stained glass windows. It acts as an elegant drawing room in which to relax and enjoy a drink or after dinner coffee. There are 20 individually designed bedrooms, all en suite, most of which are very spacious and command stunning views of the surrounding countryside.

Dining at the hall is an occasion. Whilst relaxing in the library over an aperitif and canapes, one can linger over the menu and extensive wine list, secure in the knowledge that you are about to experience a gastronomic delight. The menu is changed daily, only fresh produce of the highest quality is used and the bread rolls are home made to perfection.

Take advantage of the Leisure Club - after an evening of overindulgence a morning dip before breakfast in either the indoor or outdoor pool is a refreshing start to the day. Other facilities include a mini-gym, solarium, sauna, croquet and all-weather tennis courts for the more energetic.

Alston Hall nestles in over four acres of lawned grounds with wide expansive views across the hills of the South Hams. Enjoy the Devonshire peace at Mothecombe Beach, which is less than a mile away, or enjoy the wealth of fascinating places to visit in the area from the isolated splendour of Dartmoor to medieval market towns and quaint thatched hamlets, to bustling harbours and seafronts with a variety of sandy beaches.

Friendly staff are attentive and willing to arrange almost any activity you wish, from a ride in a hot air balloon to a round of golf at one of several excellent golf courses which linger close by. The historic city of Plymouth is only a 20 minute car journey away.

Alston Hall is also the ideal venue for private functions, for weddings, for pleasure or for business. This fine Edwardian manor house is open to residents and visitors alike, whether it be for breakfast, lunch or dinner. It is advisable to book first and worth noting that jeans are not acceptable at dinner.

Alston Hall has retained the charm and atmosphere of a bygone age and is the perfect retreat for those seeking relaxation and self indulgence.

Alston Hall Country House Hotel
Alston
Holbeton
nr Plymouth
South Devon
PL8 1HN
Tel: (0752) 830555
Fax: (0752) 830494

The Watersmeet Hotel, only seven miles from Saunton Championship course, has a superb setting on the National Trust coastline overlooking the Atlantic. The gardens reach down to the sea and all the public rooms in the hotel command majestic views across Woolacombe Bay past Hartland Point to Lundy Island. The Devon coastal footpath goes from the hotel to Morte Point and beyond and provides some of the most spectacular walking and coastal views you will ever experience.

All the main bedrooms face the sea and have bathrooms, colour television, telephone etc. They are all individually furnished with designer fabrics with lightness and freshness in mind. We have single rooms, twin or double rooms, family room, family suites and private suites.

Perhaps our forte is the evening restaurant where every meal is made into an occasion; its octagonal shape gives every table an excellent sea view. Particular care is taken in preparing each dish and our efforts have been recognised by the AA who have awarded the Watersmeet TWO ROSETTES for "A high standard of food that demonstrates a serious, dedicated approach to cooking". When this accolade is coupled with our 76% AA three star rating this makes us the highest rated three star hotel in the area. Our two rosette rating, only matched by a very few other three star hotels in the whole of the South West of England, guarantees that all the dishes are freshly prepared and cooked to order. Each evening there is a vegetarian choice in every course.

The hotel was originally a private gentleman's residence by the sea, built and proclaimed "Fit for human habitation" in 1907. It became a hotel in 1921 and since that time it has been a much respected establishment where, as the old brochures say:- "Accommodation can be provided for guests, butlers and chauffeurs". Today we seem to be limited to occasional requests for "nanny" accommodation.

For the dedicated golfer there is a choice of four highly respected courses in the area. Firstly, there is Saunton Golf Club with its two courses. Secondly, only about 40 minutes away, there is the Royal North Devon at Westward Ho. For a full day St Mellion is about 90 minutes drive away. For the more conservative player, we have six less demanding courses within 40 minutes drive of the hotel, a veritable haven for all golfers.

Experience the magic of Watersmeet. We have the beach, the world's best rock pools and the Atlantic surf at the bottom of the garden, spectacular walks, award winning food and comfort, and above all peace and tranquillity. Guests have been returning year after year and a sequence of 20 to 30 years is not uncommon.

Activities at or near the Watersmeet include lawn tennis, croquet, swimming in our outdoor heated pool, bathing and surfing at the bottom of the garden. Nearby is a golf driving range, a nationally acclaimed shooting ground – clay –game – pistol – automatic etc, riding is arranged from the hotel, and during the season many other interests are readily available including flying instruction (Exeter), helicopter jaunts (Woolacombe), ballooning and even yachting from the south coast.

AA *** 76% Two Rosettes
RAC *** with all three Merit awards
ETB Four crowns Highly Commended

Watersmeet Hotel
Mortehoe
Devon
EX34 7EB
Tel: (01271) 870333
Fax: (01271) 870890

This charming 18th century country house is situated in the historic town of Ottery St Mary and set in one of the greenest and most attractive valleys in East Devon. Formerly the home of the Coleridge family, the hotel is set in five acres of lovely grounds overlooking the Otter Valley.

Guests are offered every comfort in the 27 light and airy bedrooms, all modernised to the highest standards. In the Otter View restaurant the finest cuisine is prepared using only the freshest ingredients.

The hotel boasts a large indoor swimming pool, a sauna, two squash courts, a croquet lawn and a putting green. Nearby, guests can visit the cathedral city of Exeter, take a stroll along some of the most beautiful beaches in the country or ramble through the hills and valleys of Exmoor and Dartmoor. There are a host of local attractions to entertain everyone.

Guests may wish to indulge in country pursuits — activities such as horse riding and clay-pigeon shooting can be arranged by the hotel. Special golf breaks are available with inclusive golf at Woodbury Park Golf and Country Club and at the Axe Vale Golf Club at Axmouth.

Salston Manor Hotel
Ottery St Mary
nr Exeter
Devon
EX11 1RQ
Tel: (0404) 815581
Fax: (0404) 815581

Artist: **H G Gandy CLEAR FAIRWAYS** *Courtesy of:* **Burlington Gallery**

Most cliff top courses are essentially downland or parkland in nature, very often they are beautifully situated but the quality of the golf offered isn't quite out of the top drawer. East Devon at Budleigh Salterton is quite a rarity, for this is where heathland golf meets the sea. Some of the holes here look as if they have been plucked from Surrey or Berkshire; the 6th and 7th for instance where a touch of Walton Heath (heather, gorse and silver birches) is followed by a touch of The Berkshire (tall pines and total seclusion.) But of course, what these famous courses cannot offer are spectacular seascapes. Laid out on cliffs some 250 to 400 feet above sea level there are breathtaking views out to sea and along the South Devon coast in both directions. The views inland, mind you, are just as expansive, with the rolling Devon countryside presenting itself in all its glory. East Devon is now beginning to sound a little like Bamburgh Castle in Northumberland, often rated as Britain's most beautiful golf course. This comparison is especially valid in that both Budleigh and Bamburgh are famed for an abundance of wild flowers including some rather rare orchids, a feature that adds even more charm and colour to the setting.

But what is really special about East Devon is that the golf course takes full advantage of the location and the natural splendour of the terrain. East Devon is not as testing as somewhere like Walton Heath; it is not as long for a start, although at 6,214 yards (par 70) it is not exactly short either, and the heather and gorse do not encroach to the point where they intimidate the golfer as on several of the south east's Championship courses; however, variety and challenge present themselves at every hole. The layout is such that the course continually rises and falls, twists and turns; there are a couple of uphill drives and many dramatic downhill tee shots and there are some fine left and right dog-leg holes. Precise shot making is well rewarded at East Devon! Finally, there is the all year round quality of the putting surfaces—the best in Devon many players reckon—and for this the Club must thank its excellent green keeper, who in turn must thank Mother Nature.

The **Secretary** at East Devon is the very able **John Tebbet** who may be contacted at **The East Devon Golf Club, North View Road, Budleigh Salterton, Devon EX9 6DR** and by telephone on **(0395) 443370**. The Club's **professional, Trevor Underwood** can be reached on **(0395) 445195**. Subject to being able to provide proof of handicap visitors are welcome most days after 10.00am. However to avoid any possible disappointment prior contact with the Secretary's office is recommended. The green fees for 1994 were £25 per round, £30 per day during the week with a slight increase to £30 per round and £35 per day at week-

ends and Bank Holidays.

Many of the country's prettiest golf courses are by definition somewhat hidden away from their nearest towns and can be rather difficult to find. This is not the case with East Devon. The entrance to the Club is clearly signposted from the main road which runs through Budleigh Salterton, the golf course being located on the Exmouth side of the town. Budleigh is linked to Exmouth by the A376 although motorists travelling from the Exeter area can avoid journeying through the heart of Exmouth (not a good idea in summer!) by picking up the B3179 at Clyst St George. If Budleigh is being approached from the north and east then the A3025 which joins Lyme Regis to Exeter is likely to be helpful (exiting just north of Sidmouth.)

As the driver pulls into the Golf Club car park, the Clubhouse and 1st tee are immediately ahead. A quick look to the right and there is the rolling countryside, to the left the view is down over the ocean which, if the sun is out, is sure to be shimmering. In between countryside and sea are great swathes of gorse and undulating fairways carved out of heather and bracken. The normal reaction to all this is a quickening pulse. Perhaps it is fortunate then that the two opening holes are the tamest on the course.

Probably the most outstanding sequence of holes at East Devon comes between the 6th and the 9th. What makes the par five 6th so spectacular is the choice facing the golfer after a good drive. The fairway narrows all the way to the green; out of bounds lurks to the right, thick woodland menaces to the left and if that isn't sufficiently fear-inducing, twenty yards short of the green is a natural gulley full of humps and hillocks. The sensible shot is to lay up but the devil-may-care golfer will not be able to resist the challenge.

After a short walk through the woods, the magnificent back tee for the 7th is reached. The tree-lined fairway dog-legs sharply to the left 50 feet below and you can't see the green as you drive. The approach is slightly uphill and the amphitheatre-like green is protected by a mischievously placed deep bunker. The next hole is a tough par three measuring over 200 yards—miss the green to the right here and a par will be a major achievement. The 9th tumbles 450 yards downhill all the way and is perhaps the best of many exhilarating downhill holes at Budleigh. In 1934, a player actually drove to the edge of the green.

Maybe 'exhilarating' is indeed the best word to sum up East Devon: if there is a more splendidly situated and more attractive golf course in England I would like to see it, and if there is a course that offers greater variety and sheer pleasure, I would like to play it.

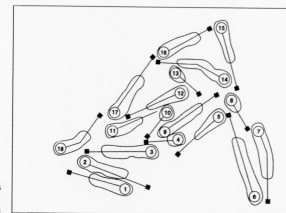

Hole	Yards	Par	Hole	Yards	Par
1	343	4	10	155	3
2	341	4	11	337	4
3	414	4	12	483	5
4	151	3	13	143	3
5	361	4	14	404	4
6	524	5	15	301	4
7	392	4	16	402	4
8	206	3	17	453	4
9	464	4	18	340	4
Out	3,196	35	In	3,018	35
			Out	3,196	35
			Totals	6,214	70

Manor House (Moretonhampstead)

Bleak and mysterious, Dartmoor may seem an unlikely setting for one of Britain's finest golfing gems but the Manor House Hotel course, near Moretonhampstead, is nothing less than that. Within howling distance of the Baskerville legends, it lies beneath a backdrop of granite tors and rolling hills.

Manor House itself is a vast and impressive Jacobean-style mansion, built between the wars as a home for the W.H. Smith family. The golf course dominates the grounds of what is now a superbly refurbished hotel and country club (part of the Principal Group). Indeed, immediately on entering the gates, the driveway will take you alongside the 13th and 14th fairways. However, it is only on reaching the mansion (clubhouse somehow doesn't seem appropriate) that the full beauty of the surroundings can be appreciated. From here, the view out across the course is quite simply stunning, and the bracing moorland air should inject a sense of joie de vivre into even the most wretched of souls!

One gentleman who would appear to have no cause to be a wretched soul is **Mr. Richard Lewis**. As **Golf Manager** he effectively runs the administrative side of things and all correspondence relating to golfing matters should be addressed to him at **The Manor House Hotel Golf and Country Club, Moretonhampstead, Devon TQ13 8RE** . Mr. Lewis is also the resident PGA professional, and can be reached by telephone on **(0647) 40355**. Golfers wishing to visit the course are always made very welcome and are permitted to play on any day of the week. During the summer months it is essential to book a starting time and although the course is often pleasantly uncrowded, a quick telephone call to check for any tee reservations is always advisable, particularly at weekends. Manor House is not surprisingly a popular meeting place for golfing societies.

In 1994 the green fee payable on weekdays is £22.50 per round or £30 for a full day, with half-rates for juniors; at weekends the fees are £28 per round and £35 per day. Unless it is impossible for some reason, a day ticket is strongly recommended and if the prospect of 36 holes is a little daunting one could always consider the merits of hiring one of the electric-powered buggies that line up outside the pro-shop.

Whilst Moretonhampstead may look somewhat remote on the map (the Hotel is 2 miles west of the town) the splendid scenery of these parts should make the journey a particularly pleasant one. The B3212 is the most direct as well as the most scenic route from Exeter—a distance of approximately 14 miles. The Club's entrance is immediately off this road and is clearly signposted. Persons approaching from the Plymouth region may also find the B3212 helpful, while those travelling from further west and from the Torbay area will probably need to use the A30/A38.

At 6016 yards the course in not particularly long by modern standards—refreshingly so, some might say—nevertheless the par of 69 is a fairly strict one and there is only one par five on the card. (From the ladies tees the course measures 5010 yards, par 70). To be frank though, length is really one of the last things the golfer should be concerned about when he comes to tackle this course—the sight from the elevated first tee should make this abundantly clear. The trout-filled River Bovey meanders its way through the centre of the course and is the dominant feature on the first seven holes. It takes a 'Seve type' to try and carry it from the tee on the 1st; it runs immediately in front of the green on the dog-leg 2nd and all the way along the right hand side of the narrow 3rd. This tricky par three, with its overhanging trees to the left is surely one of the finest short holes in the country. At the back of the green, and circling round to the left, lie a profusion of rhododendrons and azaleas which in early summer burst into a kaleidoscope of colour: pinks and purples, yellows, reds, vivid blue and peach colours—as someone aptly remarked on seeing it, 'Augusta comes to Devon' !

The 4th hole is the lone par five, and a genuine one at that with the river having to be carried from the tee, trouble all the way down the left and a raised green. The river crosses again in front of the 5th green and reappears on the 7th, where it twice cuts across the fairway. If you can reach the 8th tee without having once gotten wet you're a better man than most! The 8th itself is fairly unspectacular but the 9th, after a steep climb to the tee, gives you a chance to open the shoulders as you drive across a deep valley. Two fairly difficult par threes sandwich the 11th, the longest par four on the course. The 13th and 14th are what television commentators might describe as potential birdie holes, but the closing stretch is quite tough, particularly the challenging 18th with its acutely angled fairway and blind second. As you walk off the final green you should be left in no doubt that you've played a very special golf course.

The Hotel acts as a rather grand 19th. An excellent and very full range of catering is offered with additional light snacks being available throughout the day in the new golfer's bar. But the balcony terrace, with its extensive views over the course and surrounding Hotel gardens is a must on a warm day .... imagine sitting out there on a bright and clear day in June, with just a hint of breeze and a cool drink in your hand .... joie de vivre? I should say so!

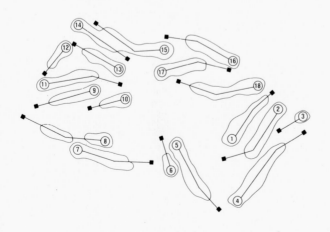

Hole	Yards	Par		Hole	Yards	Par
1	293	4		10	172	3
2	375	4		11	450	4
3	151	3		12	207	3
4	517	5		13	320	4
5	403	4		14	279	4
6	156	3		15	385	4
7	384	4		16	337	4
8	399	4		17	379	4
9	400	4		18	409	4
Out	**3,078**	**35**		**In**	**2,938**	**34**
				Out	**3,078**	**35**
				Totals	**6,016**	**69**

Devon Complete Golf

Key

*To avoid disappointment
it is advisable to telephone
in advance*

****Visitors welcome at most times*
***Visitors usually allowed on
weekdays only*
**Visitors not normally permitted
(Mon, Wed) No visitors
on specified days*

Approximate Green Fees
  A £30 plus
  B £20 to £30
  C £15 to £25
  D £10 to £20
  E under £10
  F Greens fees on application

Restrictions
  G   Guests only
H   Handicap certificate required
H   (24) Handicap of 24 or less
  L   Letter of introduction
      required
M   Visitor must be a member of
      another recognised club.

Ashbury G.C.
(0837) 55453
Fowley Cross, Okehampton
(18)5839 yards/***/D

Axe Cliff G.C.
(0297) 24371
Squires Lane, Axmouth,
(18)5057 yards/***/C/H

Bigbury G.C.
(0548) 810557
Bigbury-on-Sea, Kingsbridge
(18)6076 yards/***/C/H

Chumleigh G.C.
(0769) 80519
Leigh Road, Chumleigh
(18)1450 yards/***/E

Churston G.C.
(0803) 842218
Churston, nr Brixham
(18)6219 yards/***/B/H/M

Clovelly G.& C.C.

(0237) 431442
East Yagland, Wolsery, Bideford
(9)5641 yards/***/D
Dainton Park G.C.
(0803) 813812
Totnes Road, Newton Abbot
(18)6210 yards/***/D

Dartmouth G.& C.C.
(0803) 712686
Blackawton, Totnes
(18)7191 yards/***/B/H
(9)2583 yards/***/D/H

Dinnaton G.C.
(0752) 892512
Ivybridge
(9)4100 yards/***/D/H

Downes Crediton G.C.
(0363) 773991
Hookway, Crediton
(18)5958 yards/***/C/H/M

Easewell Farm Holiday Park
(0271) 870225
Woolacombe
(9)2426 yards/***/E

East Devon G.C.
(0395) 443370
North View Road, Budleigh
Salterton
(18)6214 yards/***/B/H

Elfordleigh Hotel G.& C.C.
(0752) 336428
Colebrook, Plympton, Plymouth
(9)5664 yards/**/C

Exeter G. & C.C.
(0392) 874139
Countess Wear, Exeter
(18)6000 yards/**/C/H

Fingle Glen G.C.
(0647) 61817
Tedburn St Mary, Exeter
(9)2466 yards/***/D

Highbullen Hotel
(0769) 540561
Chittlehamolt
(9)2210 yards/***/F

Holsworthy G.C.
(0409) 253177
Kilatree, Holsworthy
(18)6012 yards/***/D

Honiton G.C.
(0404) 44422
Middlehills, Honiton
(18)5940 yards/***/C/H/M

Hurdwick G.C.
(0822) 612746
Tavistock Hamlets, Tavistock
(18)4861 yards/***/C

Ilfracombe G.C.
(0271) 862176
Hele Bay, Ilfracombe
(18)5893 yards/***/D/H

Libbaton G.C.
(0769) 60269
High Bickington, Umberleigh
(18)5812 yards/***/D

Manor House G.& C.C.
(0647) 40355
Moretonhampstead
(18)6016 yards/***/B/H

Newton Abbot (Stover) G.C.
(0626) 52460
Bovey Road, Newton Abbot
(18)5899 yards/***/C/M

Okehampton G.C.
(0837) 52113
off Tors Road, Okehampton
(18)5300 yards/***/D/H

Padbrook Park G.C.
(0884) 38286
Cullompton
(9)6108 yards/***/E

Royal North Devon G.C.
(0237) 473824
Golf Links Road, Westward Ho!
(18)6662 yards/***/B/H

Saunton G.C.
(0271) 812436
Saunton, nr Braunton
(18)6708 yards/***/B/H/M
(18)6356 yards/***/B/H/M

Sidmouth G.C.
(0395) 513023
Peak Hill, Cotmaton Road,
(18)5109 yards/***/D

Sparkwell G.C.
(0989) 767676
Blacklands, Sparkwell, Plymouth

(9)6000 yards/***/E

Staddon Heights G.C.
(0752) 402475
Staddon Heights, Plymstock
(18)5874 yards/***/D/H

Tavistock G.C.
(0822) 612049
Down Road, Tavistock
(18)6250 yards/***/C/H

Teignmouth G.C.
(0626) 774194
Exeter Road, Teignmouth
(18)6247 yards/***/C/H

Thurlestone G.C.
(0548) 560405
Thurlestone, nr Kingsbridge
(18) 6303 yards/***/C/H/M

Tiverton G.C.
(0884) 252187
Post Hill, Tiverton
(18)6263 yards/***/B/H/M

Torquay G.C.
(0803) 314591
Petitor Road, St Mary Church
(18)6198 yards/***/C/H

Torrington G.C.
(0805) 22229
Weare Trees, Torrington
(9)4418 yards/***/D

Warren G.C.
(0626) 862255
Dawlish Warren, Dawlish
(18)5973 yards/***/C/H

Woodbury Park G.C.
(0395) 233382
Woodbury Castle, Woodbury, nr
Exeter
(18)6707 yards/***/C

Wrangaton G.C.
(0364) 73229
Golf Links Road, Wrangaton
(18)6040 yards/***/C/H

Yelverton G.C.
(0822) 852824
Golf Links Road, Yelverton
(18)6363 yards/***/F/H/M

Artist: **Major Hopkins** **LADIES GOLF** *Courtesy of* **Burlington Gallery**

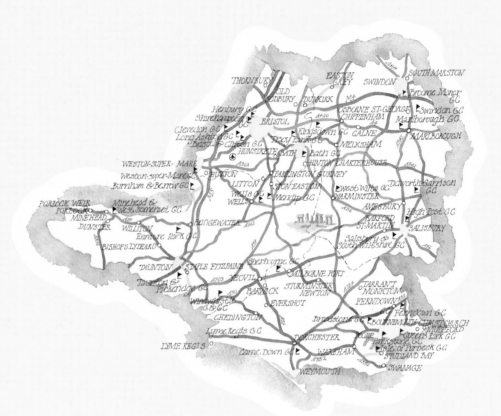

Artist: **Robert Wade** **THE CADDIE** *Courtesy of:* **Rosenstiel's**

From the wild beauty of Exmoor to the mystery of Stonehenge. The Quantocks and the Mendips; Lyme Regis and Bath; Avebury, Chesil Beach and Lulworth Cove. The West Country offers so much, no wonder those of us who do not live there are more than a little envious. The golf too can be equally spectacular. There may not be a Wentworth or a St George's here but the region offers a considerable variety and there is certainly no shortage of challenge. There is a true championship links at Burnham and Berrow and a magnificent clifftop course at the Isle of Purbeck. Excellent downland golf can be enjoyed at Long Ashton and Bath while Bournemouth offers some majestic heathland and parkland type courses. We shall tee off in Somerset.

Somerset

Burnham and Berrow (featured ahead) is without doubt the finest course in the county and the place where John H Taylor wielded his famous mashie to great effect. The two holiday towns of **Minehead** and **Weston-Super-Mare** house the region's other two links courses. The Minehead and West Somerset Golf Club has more than a hundred years of history—it therefore remembers the quieter days in the years 'Before Butlins'. A fairly flat and windy course, it is situated on the eastern side of the town. Visitors are welcome, though during the peak season a quick telephone call to the club is advisable. The same can be said of Weston—a slightly longer, well maintained course, located just off the main A370 Bristol road. Perhaps a nearby course on which it may be easier to arrange a game is the attractive new 18 hole parkland layout at the **Isle of Wedmore** Golf Club. After an arduous day's golf at Burnham, visitors can find more than adequate accommodation in the club's Dormy House. Some quite incredible steaks are served in the clubhouse, 'worth killing for!' according to one of my mashie wielding friends. Further up the scale, Weston has a number of hotels, with the Grand Atlantic situated on the seafront (0934) 626543, and bordering the resort is Hutton Court (0934) 814343, a magnificent 15th century manor house. the Gascony (0643) 705939 and the Alcombe House Hotel (0643) 705130 are also suitable resting places, whilst slightly farther afield, try the Luttrell Arms (0643) 821555 in Dunster.

Taunton's golf course is at Corfe, the **Taunton and Pickeridge** Golf Club. It is located close to the town's racetrack and is fairly undulating. In Taunton, the Castle (0823) 272671 is a super place to stay and a nearby pub of note is the Greyhound at Staple Fitzpaine. For the more energetically minded, the Cedar Falls Health Farm (0823) 433233 at Bishops Lydeard makes it all the easier to indulge elsewhere. In Yeovil, the delightful Manor Hotel (0935) 23116 is very handy for Sherborne Golf Club over the border in Dorset.

More golf is found near Bridgwater. **Enmore Park,** located to the south of the town is a very pleasant medium length affair. The course enjoys a delightful setting and nestles around the foothills of the Quantocks. The White House Hotel (0984) 632306 at Williton is convenient for the golf club. Moving from the Quantocks to the Mendips, the **Mendip** Golf Club at Gurney Slade offers possibly the most spectacular vistas of any course in the South West. From its 4th fairway, almost 1000 feet above sea level, on a clear day it is possible to sight the Cotswolds and the Quantocks, the Welsh Mountains and the Purbeck Hills, Glastonbury Tor and Westbury's White Horse....need I go on? Mendip is an enjoyable course and very visitor-friendly. An agreeable pub to note in Gurney Slade is the George Inn.

The city of Wells is always worth inspecting. The cathedral is splendid and after a round on the **Wells** golf course a pleasant lunch can be enjoyed at the Ancient Gate House. One final course to mention in Somerset is the magnificently titled **Windwhistle** Golf and Squash Club at Chard. The golf course is another laid out on high ground and offering extensive views. It's also close to the famous Cricket St Thomas Wildlife Park, where birdies and eagles abound.

Avon

The golf course at **Clevedon** stares spectacularly out across the mouth of the Severn. Clevedon is a clifftop course rather than a links and is well worth visiting. By travelling inland from Clevedon towards Bristol along the B3128, two of the city's best courses are reached before the famous suspension bridge. **Long Ashton** is actually immediately off the B3128, while to find **Bristol and Clifton** a left turn should be taken along the B3129. There is probably little to choose between the two, both being particularly attractive examples of downland golf. **Henbury** Golf Club is closer to the centre of Bristol, about three miles to the north to be precise, in the quiet suburb of Westbury-on-Trym. Henbury is a very mature parkland course with an abundance of trees making for some very attractive and challenging holes. One final club to recommend in Bristol is **Shirehampton**—always beautifully maintained.

Perhaps the most stylish hotel in Bristol is the aptly named Grand Hotel (0272) 291645 on Broad Street. Two recommended restaurants are Harveys (0272) 277665 and Restaurant Lettonie (0272) 686456 in Stoke Bishop. An excellent base to the north of the city at Thornbury is the Tudor styled Thornbury Castle (0454) 281182.

Anyone travelling from Bristol to Bath (or vice versa) is likely to pass within a few miles of the **Tracy Park** Golf and Country Club at Wick. If possible a detour is recommended. Tracy Park is a newish course, built in the mid-seventies around a 400 year old mansion which acts as a rather impressive clubhouse. Although the course can get a little soggy in winter it offers a very good test of golf. Everybody, they say, falls in love with Bath—the Romans did, the Georgians did and the Americans think it's cute. For visiting golfers, if the other half should come under the spell, the City has two attractive propositions: **Bath** Golf Club and **Lansdown** Golf Club. The former, commonly known as Sham Castle because of its situation adjacent to Bath's greatest fraud (there is a beautiful castle frontage but nothing else!) is laid out high above the city and provides tremendous views over the surrounding countryside. Lansdown occupies flatter ground adjacent to Bath Races.

Staying in Bath is a sheer delight. The hotels in the city are among some of the finest in the country. The Royal Crescent (0225) 319090 takes pride of place but the Apsley House (0225) 336966, the Paradise House Hotel (0225) 317723 and the Priory (0225) 331922 can also be recommended with confidence. The hotels themselves house excellent restaurants but other popular eating places in Bath include Popjoys, the Clos du Roy (0225) 444450 and Garlands (0225) 442283. There is no shortage of guest houses in and around Bath (the city does become incredibly busy in the summer—be warned!) while close at hand are a number of other outstanding establishments. Ston Easton Park (0761) 241631 boasts a considerable reputation as does Hunstrete House. Another gem is the Homewood Park Hotel (0225) 723731 in Hinton Charterhouse. North of Bath the marvellously

The Priory has long been regarded as one of Britain's finest country house hotels. Built in 1835 of Bath stone, the hotel is located on the western edge of Bath adjoining Victoria Park.

The hotel has twenty-one tastefully appointed bedrooms, each with its own individual style of decor, which are enhanced by their antique furniture and superb works of art. Most of the rooms have views over the beautiful garden.

The Priory restaurant has long been acclaimed internationally and has consistently received awards from the main guide books. The cuisine is predominantly French but features national and local classical dishes. Each of the rooms in the restaurant focuses on the garden and may be used separately or as a whole depending on the clients requirements.

Organisations looking for a prestigious location for senior management meetings or seminars will find The Priory an ideal venue. Its high reputation, peaceful location in idyllic surroundings make it very conducive for work or for pleasure. Recreation facilities include a heated outdoor swimming pool and a croquet lawn.

The World Heritage City of Bath offers a multitude of interesting attractions from its wonderful architecture to a wide choice of museums, art galleries and the world famous Roman Baths. There are numerous golf courses within easy distance and Bath race course, which has eight meetings a year, is only minutes away.

Bath is well served by transportation, by train from London in 80 minutes, Heathrow in 90 minutes and Bristol airport is 40 minutes.

The Priory Hotel
Weston Road
Bath
Avon
Tel: (0225) 331922
Fax: (0225) 448276

named Old Sodbury offers the charming Sodbury House Hotel (0454) 312847 and the Cross Hands Hotel (0454) 313000, and Dunkirk the Petty France Hotel (0454) 238361. Just outside Bath at Colerne is Lucknam Park (0225) 742777 a delightful early 18th century mansion converted into an hotel. Close by, near Corsham, is the stylish Rudloe Park Hotel (0225) 810555.

Wiltshire

A decade ago there were only a dozen or so golf courses in Wiltshire, now there are at least 20. Perhaps the two developments that have attracted most attention are the Dave Thomas designed championship course at **Bowood,** just off the A4 between Calne and Chippenham, and the dramatic layout at **Castle Combe** (now named the **Manor House** Golf Club) located to the north west of Chippenham, the handiwork of Peter Alliss and Clive Clark. Two very different courses, Bowood and Castle Combe are both explored ahead. Recommended places to stay naturally include for Castle Combe, the Manor House (0249) 782206, which is situated within the 'prettiest village in England' while for Bowood any of the establishments mentioned for Bath should prove convenient. There is also the outstanding Queenwood Golf Lodge (0249) 822228 which is located within the confines of the Bowood course and offers exceptional value.

In **Wooton Bassett**, just west of Swindon, Alliss and Clark have constructed another new course, thus giving Swindon's golfers three courses close to the town; the two others are **Broome Manor** and the **Swindon** Golf Club, both situated south of the town. The latter at Ogbourne St George, despite its name, is in fact closer to Marlborough than Swindon. It is an undulating, downland type course—very typical of the county's more established courses. Broome Manor is a public course and thus probably more accommodating to the visiting golfer.

Swindon is one of the fastest growing towns in the British Isles. A comfortable place to stay here is the Wiltshire (0793) 528282 and in Blunsdon is the charming Blunsdon House (0793) 721701. The Robin Hood Inn at Ogbourne St George is very handy after a game at Swindon. **Marlborough** Golf Club is a near neighbour of Swindon Golf Club, being situated to the north west of the town on the Marlborough Downs. It offers similarly wide ranging views (and is similarly breezy!). The Sun (0672) 512081 in Marlborough is an ideal 19th—it offers good food in addition to reasonably priced accommodation. Also worth a visit is the Ivy House (0672) 515333—extremely comfortable. A pleasant drive westwards will take you to Lacock near Chippenham where the Sign of the Angel (0249) 730230 is a tremendous 15th century inn and still further west there is a reasonable golf course at **Kingsdown.**

Dropping down the county, near Warminster, the **West Wilts** Golf Club is very well established, the new 'pay and play' **Erlestoke Sands** course, south west of Devizes is popular and t'other side of Stonehenge, **Tidworth Garrison** is certainly one of Wiltshire's top courses. It lies on Salisbury Plain and is owned by the Army. (Note the excellent Antrobus Arms (0980) 623163 in nearby Amesbury). Salisbury offers two fine challenges, to the north, **High Post** and to the south west **Salisbury and South Wilts**. In the days before Bowood and Castle Combe appeared on the county's ever-chang-

ing golf map High Post was generally considered to be the leading course in the county. It's another classic downland type. Salisbury and South Wilts offers some splendid views of Salisbury's cathedral. One's best base in Salisbury is probably either the Rose and Crown Hotel (0722) 327908 or the Old Bell Hotel (0722) 327958.

Dorset

The better golf courses in Dorset lie within a ten mile radius of the centre of Bournemouth. Having said that, **Sherborne** in the far north of the county is undoubtedly one of the prettiest inland courses to be found anywhere in Britain. In nearby Gillingham, you can stay at the Stock Hill House Hotel (0747) 823626 which comes with our highest recommendation and boasts an excellent restaurant to boot. Also, in Evershot, the Summer Lodge is a fine restaurant and in Sturminster Newton stands Plumber Manor (0258) 72507 a gorgeous country house.

Lyme Regis, famed for its fossils and more recently its French Lieutenant's Woman, has a fairly hilly 18 hole course which lies to the east of the town. The road between Lyme Regis and Weymouth provides dramatic views over Chesil Beach and passes through some of the most beautiful villages in England. The area north of Weymouth is Thomas Hardy country. Dorchester stands in the middle of it all and **Came Down** Golf Club is well worth noting when in these parts as is the **Mid Dorset** Golf Club at Blandford Forum. Yalbury Cottage (0305) 262382 in Dorchester offers good accommodation and the countryside has remained gloriously unspoilt. In Lyme Regis, the Fairwater Head Country House Hotel (0297) 678349 is a good bet. The excellent Chedington Court (0935) 891265 in Beaminster is also well worth a visit.

The **Isle of Purbeck** and **Ferndown** are featured ahead but **Parkstone** and **Broadstone** also fall in the 'must be visited' category. They are beautiful heathland courses with much heather, gorse and pine trees and each is kept in immaculate condition. In addition to a game on one or more of these great courses, there are a handful of other easier to play courses around Bournemouth and Poole, including the new **Bulbury Woods** Golf Club at Lytchett Matravers west of Poole and the even newer **Crane Valley** course at Verwood, north of Ferndown. Bournemouth's public courses shouldn't be overlooked either: **Meyrick Park** is very good while **Queens Park** is often described as the finest public course in England. The Bournemouth—Poole—Swanage area abounds with hotels and restaurants. Here are just a few suggestions: in Bournemouth, the Langtry Manor (0202) 553887 comes very highly recommended, the Swallow Highcliff (0202) 557702, Royal Bath (0202) 555555 and the Hotel Collingwood (0202) 557575 are all good whilst Crusts (0202) 551430 is an excellent restaurant. In Poole, the Mansion House (0202) 685666 and Barrie's Seafood restaurant are recommended. Swanage offers the Pines (0929) 425211 and Christchurch, Splinters restaurant (0202) 483454. Ferndown golfers can look to the comfortable Dormy Hotel (0202) 872121 and Parkstone players can enjoy superb food at both Isabels (0202) 747885 and the Warehouse on the quay (0202) 677238. People wishing to get away from the sea and sand, or the water hazards and bunkers should visit Tarrant Monkton. Here in the popular Langton Arms (0258) 830225, a converted stables makes for a really splendid little restaurant.

For most golfers, a great golfing break involves not just the game, but also the 'base camp', A place to relax and enjoy good company, food and drink before and after the triumphs and frustrations of the game itself.

While the very prospect automatically conjures up images of Gleneagles and St Andrews, the West Country can also lay claim to its fair share of attractions and Hutton Court is certainly one of them. This is a hotel and restaurant in classic country house style that caters for every golfer's needs.

The championship links of Burnham and Berrow are only 20 minutes away and golf there is available to residents by special arrangement as it is at five other courses equally as close to the hotel. The variety these courses provide means an itinerary can be prepared to suit golfers of all abilities and make every sortie from this accommodating base camp one of pleasurable anticipation.

At Hutton Court you sleep in bedrooms dating from the 17th century, with modern comforts added, and dine in the great hall of the 1450s. Local meat, fish, game and venison of the region are specialities. Cuisine befits the best British tradition, substantial yet refined and matched by over a hundred wines from a dozen countries, ranging from house wines to classics like Cheval Blanc and Petrus. The key to the place is its relaxed atmosphere and service that makes you a personal house guest rather than a paying customer with a room number.

At Hutton Court, we'll do everything to ensure you get the most from your stay, whether you're a glutton for action or just want a few lazy days. You can fish the trout lakes of Blagdon and Chew and there is sea angling on the Bristol Channel. Naturalists watch buzzards, sparrow hawks or even the odd peregrine or goshawk in and around the hotel grounds, which foxes and badgers visit.

The cathedral cities of Wells, Bath with its splendid shopping and Bristol are all within easy reach. You can walk or ride on the Mendips, explore Cheddar, Wookey, Glastonbury and the Somerset levels or potter around antique shops and old country pubs.

Special rates are available for individual or party breaks and we'll tailor food and drink to your requirements, form packed lunches to full scale banquets. Ring us for information: we promise you a warm West Country welcome.

Hutton Court
Church Lane
Hutton
Avon BS24 9SN
Tel: (0934) 814343
Fax: (0934) 811018

I wonder how many people have travelled along the M5 between Bristol and Exeter and wondered what lay beyond the great Iron Age fort that rises out of level ground, like something from out of 'Close Encounters', midway between Weston-Super-Mare and Bridgwater. Well, many golfers will know that a short distance behind the great hill lies one of England's finest links courses.

Burnham and Berrow appeared on the golfing map in 1891 and the first professional the Club engaged was a no lesser a man than John H. Taylor. The great man was then in fact a lad of 19 although within three years he was to win the Open Championship at Sandwich—the first of his five victories. John Henry thought very highly of what, until quite recently, had been a 'wild rabbit infested waste of sandhills' for he said it was here, at Burnham, that he was 'given the splendid opportunity of developing my mashie play' (as the course) 'necessitated very accurate approach play.'

The present day visitor to the North Somerset Club is most unlikely to confront a gathering of wild rabbits (at least of the animal variety) nor, one assumes, will he possess a mashie amongst his armoury. However, despite a number of alterations made over the years, the towering sandhills remain by far the course's most dominant feature.

Not surprisingly Burnham and Berrow is a popular course and whatever the time of year visitors would be wise to telephone the Club before setting off. **Mrs. E.L.Sloman** is the **Secretary** and she can be contacted on tel: **(0278) 785760**, fax: (0278) 795440. The Club's **professional, Mark Crowther-Smith**, can be reached on **(0278) 784545**. Persons interested in organising a Society meeting are advised to write to the Secretary, the Club's full address being, **Burnham and Berrow Golf Club, St Christopher's Way, Burnham- on-Sea, Somerset TA8 2PE.**

Green fees for 1994 were set at £30 for weekdays and £40 at weekends, fees being payable in the clubhouse. For juniors the fees were half the above rates. Persons holidaying in the vicinity (Weston-Super-Mare is less than 10 miles away) might well consider the merits of a weekly ticket (£170 in 1994) or a fortnightly ticket (£330 in 1994). Furthermore, in addition to the 18 hole Championship Course there is also an adjacent 9 hole course situated alongside the sea. Whilst not quite up to the standard of the full Championship Course, at 3275 yards, par 36, it certainly represents a fine challenge and the green fee of £8 represents excellent value. Approaching by car from both North and South the M5

is the most direct route, leaving at exit 22. Thereafter one should follow the B3140. The course is situated about a mile north of Burnham-on-Sea and is well signposted.

Right from the 1st hole the premium on accuracy becomes apparent. Anything short of a straight tee shot will leave a blind, not to mention very awkward second. At one time the layout of the course demanded the playing of several blind shots. However, today, accurate driving will largely eliminate such difficulties although on a number of holes the base of the flagstick will not be visible when playing the approach shot. As he or she stands on the 1st green, two features, in addition to the omnipresent sandhills will strike the first time visitor. The one is the condition of the greens—quite superb; the other is the surrounding tangling rough—buckthorn it's called—avoid it like the plague (if you can!) Burnham's 2nd is a good straight hole played from an elevated tee, whereas the 3rd, at least from the back, is one of those 'bite-off-as-much-as-you-dare' holes with the fairway dog-legging sharply to the left towards a sunken punch—bowl green. From the 4th tee there is the first of several panoramic views of the Bristol Channel and distant Wales as the course moves nearer the sea. There are two par threes on the front nine, the 5th and the 9th, the latter is surely one of the finest short holes to be found anywhere.

On reaching the turn anyone claiming to have mastered the large sandhills may well have to eat his words after playing the 10th: a minor mountain must be carried from the tee and there is a severe drop away to the right—be warned! If the front nine is perhaps the more interesting of the halves, the second nine is probably the more testing. The 11th is a long par four and the 12th and 13th require very precise second shots; both the short holes are exceptionally tricky and the 18th needs a couple of mighty big hits if it is to be reached in two. A good score at Burnham certainly has to be earned, but is immensely satisfying if achieved.

Visitors should find the clubhouse atmosphere pleasantly informal. The catering is of a high standard and is offered daily between the hours of 11 am and 6 pm. With prior notice both breakfast and dinner can be arranged. Visitors might also wish to note the Club's Dormy House which can sleep eight persons.

Burnham and Berrow is a friendly Club and well worth a visit. Clearly the message to all golfers who pass down the M5 oblivious to what goes on beyond the great hump is quite simply, come on over!

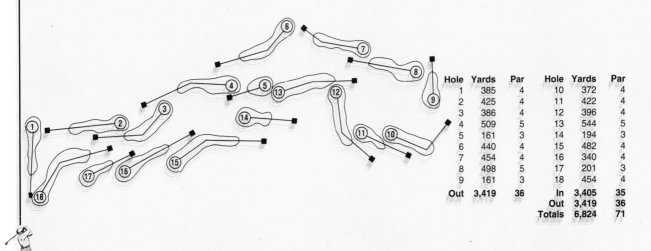

Hole	Yards	Par	Hole	Yards	Par
1	385	4	10	372	4
2	425	4	11	422	4
3	386	4	12	396	4
4	509	5	13	544	5
5	161	3	14	194	3
6	440	4	15	482	4
7	454	4	16	340	4
8	498	5	17	201	3
9	161	3	18	454	4
Out	**3,419**	**36**	**In**	**3,405**	**35**
			Out	**3,419**	**36**
			Totals	**6,824**	**71**

In a country packed with more than 10,000 hotels you might be forgiven for thinking that one is very much like another. But very occasionally you stumble upon a rare gem of an hotel where the building, food, service and history blend to form something quite exceptional. Such is the Langtry Manor Hotel, Bournemouth.

Built in 1877 by the then Prince of Wales (later King Edward VII) for his favourite, Lillie Langtry, as a love nest, this beautiful home has been lovingly restored by the Howard family in the style of the finest Country House hotels. The elegant bedrooms and suites are all individually designed for your comfort, some with a four poster or jacuzzi. You can even stay in the King's own suite.

The magnificent Dining Hall with its stained glass windows and minstrels gallery is complemented by delicious food and fine wine. Staff are chosen primarily for their ability to make you feel an honoured guest in this friendly, welcoming home.

There are about twenty golf courses in the vicinity of Bournemouth, catering for all standards of player—Langtry Manor would be pleased to make arrangements for you to be able to play at most of them. And if your partner does not share your enthusiasm for the game there is so much more to see and do—the sea—the New Forest—a beautiful shopping area—delightful gardens—stately homes—the list is endless.

Welcome weekends include the famous Edwardian banquet at which all six mouthwatering courses are displayed for your choice by staff in Edwardian dress. A short 'son et lumiere' gives a flavour of the history of this lovely house and its famous occupants.

Don't forget to tell them if you have a Birthday or Anniversary, you can be sure they will make it a celebration to remember. Seek out Langtry Manor, it is an experience to be savoured and creates a desire to return.

Price guide from £54.50 per person per night (including dinner).

Langtry Manor
Derby Road
East Cliff
Bournemouth
Dorset
Tel: (0202) 553887
Fax: (0202) 290115

Ask a group of golfers to give an example of a beautifully conditioned golf course and the chances are they'll cite the likes of Augusta National and Muirfield Village. There is little doubt that when it comes to perfectly manicured fairways and quick, ultra-true greens the American courses tend to be superior to their British counterparts. Ferndown, however, is a definite exception. Indeed the fairways and greens are often among the best kept in the whole of Britain. Someone clearly deserves a mighty large pat on the back!

There are in fact two courses at Ferndown, the **Old** and the **New**. The Old Course was originally designed in 1912 by Harold Hilton, who was twice Open Champion before the turn of the century. The shorter New Course, which has nine holes but eighteen tees, has a much more recent history being designed in 1969 by J. Hamilton-Stutt and opened two years later.

The **Secretary** at Ferndown is **Mr. Eddie Robertson**, Tel **(0202) 874602.** Visitors to the Club are welcome on any weekday provided prior permission is first obtained. Societies are limited to Tuesdays and Fridays and written applications should be addressed to the Secretary at **Ferndown Golf Club, 119 Links Road, Ferndown, Wimborne, Dorset, BH22 8BU.** All visitors and Society members must be prepared to produce a handicap certificate or alternatively a letter of introduction from their home Club.

To play the Old Course the green fee set in 1994 was £35 during the week with £40 payable at the weekend - this sum applies for a single round or a full day's golf. The green fee for the New Course is £15 during the week or £20 at weekends.

Ian Parker, the **Professional** at Ferndown, can be reached on **(0202) 873825).** A former Walker Cup player and very fine professional, I once read that in an Alliance Meeting at Ferndown he played the course in 60 strokes - enough said! Ferndown has indeed been very fortunate with its professionals; Percy Alliss served the Club for over 25 years and it was here that his son Peter learnt to play.

Located approximately six miles north of Bournemouth, Ferndown is quite easily reached from all directions. Motoring from the west of England the A35 from Dorchester, which suddenly becomes the A31 near Bere Regis passes through Ferndown very close to the Golf Club. Approaching from the east, from London the M3 runs to Southampton which in turn is linked to

Ferndown (or Trickett's Cross to be precise) by the A31. The left fork should be taken at Trickett's Cross and this leads on to Golf Links Road, the course being immediately on the left. From the north the route is via Salisbury where the A338 should be followed as far as Ringwood and thereafter the A31 as above. Finally anyone who happens to possess their own jet may wish to note that Bournemouth has a small airport at Hurn, again very close to the Golf Club.

The Old Course at Ferndown measures 6442 yards from the back tees, par and standard scratch both being 71. From the forward tees the length is reduced by a little over 200 yards. The layout is essentially one of two loops, an inner loop comprising holes one to eight and the outer containing the ninth to the eighteenth.

Ferndown's fairways are of the sandy, heathland type and are gently undulating throughout. The rough consists mainly of heather and together with the many pines and fir trees gives the course a most attractive appearance. There are a considerable number of dog-leg holes necessitating much thought from the tee. The toughest holes on the course are possibly the uphill 6th, which is normally played into the wind, the dog-leg 9th and the 11th - all fairly lengthy par fours from the back tees. One should also mention the 5th, an excellent par three where the rhododendrons provide a splash of colour in season, and the 16th named 'Hilton's Hole' after its illustrious architect. At 5604 yards (par 70) the New Course is less demanding in terms of length but it too has its challenges and is set in equally beautiful surroundings.

Ferndown's Clubhouse has a prime location grandly surveying the course from its elevated position. On a clear day there are views across the course to the Isle of Wight. The facilities are excellent with lunches being offered daily. Both breakfast and dinner can be arranged with prior notice and a jacket and tie should be worn in public rooms at all times.

In recent years, the Club has played host to many competitions and tournaments, such as the Women's English Amateur Championship in 1985 and the Hennessy Cognac Cup, a four man team competition, played over the Old Course in 1982 and 1984. The Ladies European Open visited the course in 1987, while in 1989 large crowds flocked to Ferndown to watch a most exciting Ladies British Open, won by leading American player Jane Geddes with an impressive four round total of 274.

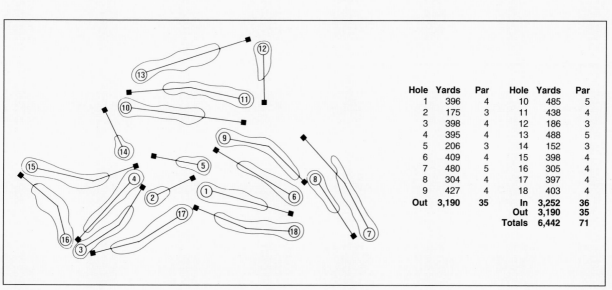

Hole	Yards	Par	Hole	Yards	Par
1	396	4	10	485	5
2	175	3	11	438	4
3	398	4	12	186	3
4	395	4	13	488	5
5	206	3	14	152	3
6	409	4	15	398	4
7	480	5	16	305	4
8	304	4	17	397	4
9	427	4	18	403	4
Out	**3,190**	**35**	**In**	**3,252**	**36**
			Out	**3,190**	**35**
			Totals	**6,442**	**71**

Chedington Court is a traditional country house hotel built in the local mellow hamstone, nestling below the leafy ridge of a Dorset hillside on the edge of Thomas Hardy country. The view from the house is one of the most spectacular in the south of England. The ten acre garden, with its terraces, balustrades, pools, some rare trees and shrubs which attract a huge variety of birdlife and butterflies, combines a subtle blend of the well tended and the wild. A reputed thousand year old yew tree is set among the tombstones in the old churchyard which forms part of the gardens, which also feature a massive sculptured yew hedge.

The welcoming interior of the house creates an atmosphere of comfortable yet distinctive informality with its old Persian rugs, stone fireplaces, fine brass fittings and antique furniture. Ten spacious bedrooms and their bathrooms, all different, feature most attractive fabrics and furniture.

The renowned restaurant offers a limited choice of French and English style cooking with carefully prepared well chosen raw materials with the accent on taste and popularity. Vegetarians and special diets are catered for. The acclaimed wine list shows over 500 wines from around the world, many half bottles, many at modest prices.

The golf course is 9 holes, par 74, built on 90 acres of parkland bisected by an ancient droveway. It measures 3295 yards and it is one of the longest 9 hole courses in the country. All the holes have very different characteristics and present their own individual challenges. Described as one of the best of the newer golf courses, it makes use of the natural features of the beautiful rolling countryside. The course is particularly attractive in the spring with the wild flowers in the rough and blossom on the hedgerows. Preservation of wildlife and the natural flora and fauna are of prime concern in the working management of the course. The surrounding wooded hills provide a sensational backdrop of changing colours throughout the year. There are plans afoot to extend the course to a full 18 holes and this will hopefully have come about by April 1995.

Anyone wishing to learn the game can start on the associated 780 yard pitch and putt course and there are two practice areas, one for chipping and one for driving.

Fly fishing, horse riding, shooting and ballooning are some of the activities that can be arranged. The many fascinating places to visit, both the well documented and the remote, offer the visitor a wonderfully worthwhile, interesting, memorable holiday.

Chedington Court
Chedington
Beaminster
Dorset
DT8 3HY
Tel: (01935) 891265
Fax: (01935) 891442

Most people are a little surprised when they learn that the Isle of Purbeck Golf Club was founded as long ago as 1892—a decade before Sunningdale and Walton Heath. They are probably even more surprised when they hear that Enid Blyton and her husband were once owners of the Club. Originally only a 9 hole course, there are now 27 holes comprising the 18 hole **Purbeck** Course and an adjacent, shorter 9 hole course, The **Dene**. In 1966 a superb new Clubhouse was built using the local Purbeck stone and it was around this time that more and more people began to consider seriously the quality of the golf here as well as the sheer beauty of the Club's setting.

Today the Club is owned and managed by the Robinson family. **Mrs Joan Robinson** is **Managing Director** and she can be contacted on **(0929) 44361.** All written communications should be addressed to her at **The Isle of Purbeck Golf Club, Swanage, Dorset, BH19 3AB.** The Club's **professional, Ian Brake** can be contacted on **(0929) 44354.**

Visitors to the Isle of Purbeck are welcome to play on both courses although those wishing to play on the Purbeck course must possess a handicap. Green fees for 1994 were set at £22.50 per round and £30 per day to play on the Purbeck course during the week, with £27.50 (£35) payable at weekends and Bank Holidays. Junior golfers pay £13 for a weekday round on the Purbeck course. The Dene course can be played for £10 during the week or £12 at the weekend, with a reduction for those teeing off after 4.30pm. Buggies are for hire at an extra £25 per round.

Swanage has become a very popular holiday centre and keen golfers might consider the merits of a temporary membership of the Club. In 1994, a week's golf on the Purbeck course was set at £165, two weeks at £240, and three at £275. There are reductions for joint membership and for those wishing to limit their golf to the Dene course. Visitors may also wish to note that the Club stages a limited number of open competitions during the summer. Information concerning these can be obtained from Mrs Robinson. Golfing Societies are encouraged to come to the Isle of Purbeck and those organising should find the Club very accommodating.

Getting to the Isle of Purbeck may present the biggest headache. This is hardly the most accessible of Britain's golf clubs—not that the Club can be blamed for that!

Anyway, the best routes are probably as follows: from the West the A35 runs from Honiton through Dorchester and joins the A351 at Lytchett Minster near Poole. The A351 should be followed as far as Corfe Castle from which the B3351 Studland road should be taken. The Club is situated just off this road. Travelling from the North the A350 also joins the A351 near Poole and from the Bournemouth/Poole area a car ferry operates between Sandbanks and Shell Bay and avoids the drive around Poole Harbour.

Any of the aforementioned headaches will surely be dispelled on arrival at the Clubhouse. The south coast possesses a number of scenic courses, but one would be very pushed to find an equal to the magnificent views provided by the Isle of Purbeck. The view from the 5th on the Purbeck Course, 'Agglestone' is particularly outstanding as you tee off from the top of an ancient Saxon burial mound. The par three 11th, Island, with its backdrop of pines and two-tier green is also an exceptional hole.

For those who find the modern day monster courses somewhat tedious with the great emphasis they place on brute force (and ignorance?) the Purbeck Course should prove rather refreshing. From the back tees it measures 6248 yards (par 71) whilst from the forward tees the course is reduced to 5823 yards (par 69). From the Ladies' tees the course measures 5648 yards (par 73).

On returning to the Clubhouse, the golfer will find that a full range of catering is offered and that the food and service are of a high standard. The Clubhouse has recently undergone total refurbishment, with a new bar, restaurant and showers. Breakfast and dinner can be arranged and lunch and high teas are offered daily. A jacket and tie must be worn for dinner and Sunday lunch. Again, some splendid views are to be enjoyed from the Clubhouse.

When in South Dorset many visitors like to take in a spot of fossil hunting. Lyme Regis and Charmouth are within easy reach, however golfers need not look beyond the four walls of the Clubhouse—it is full of old fossils. Lest I be accused of insulting the members, I should quickly explain: when the Clubhouse was built several fossilised dinosaur footprints and some massive ammonites were incorporated into the interior walls. It therefore follows—and golf historians please note—that to a limited extent the Isle of Purbeck could be said to possess the oldest Clubhouse in the world!

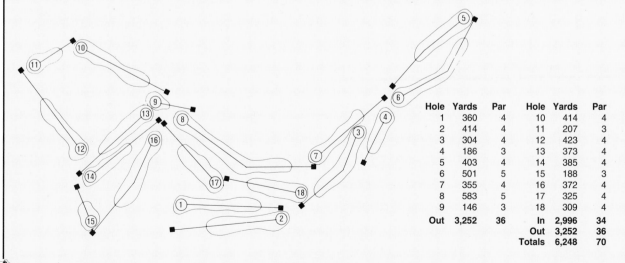

Hole	Yards	Par	Hole	Yards	Par
1	360	4	10	414	4
2	414	4	11	207	3
3	304	4	12	423	4
4	186	3	13	373	4
5	403	4	14	385	4
6	501	5	15	188	3
7	355	4	16	372	4
8	583	5	17	325	4
9	146	3	18	309	4
Out	**3,252**	**36**	**In**	**2,996**	**34**
			Out	**3,252**	**36**
			Totals	**6,248**	**70**

Bowood Golf and Country Club lies in the western corner of Capability Brown's magnificent 2000 acre park. It was laid out by the master of landscape design, Lancelot Brown, between 1762 and 1768. Hundreds of men with horses, carts and wheelbarrows shaped the features of the park and planted the thousands of trees for which Bowood is famous.

By contrast, with modern machinery David Thomas took just twelve months to design and mould this stunningly beautiful championship course. His winding fairways harmonise with Brown's landscape. His deep bunkers, which on many courses scar the countryside, are almost invisible. Indeed those who knew this area before the golf course was built agree that it is far more beautiful today than it was when it was arable fields and rough grazing.

The earliest estate maps dating back to 1754 show two buildings in the middle of the course, on the same site as the Queenwood Golf Lodge. It is a fair assumption that

the main lodge was built in the first half of the 18th century, some 20 or 30 years before the Lansdowne family bought Bowood House.

Queenwood Golf Lodge has recently been carefully restored and extended to accommodate parties of up to eight guests in unparalleled comfort. There are four double bedrooms with bathrooms en suite, hall, study, sitting room and dining room. Lady Shelburne, wife of the proprietor, has decorated and furnished the house throughout.

Guests are requested to book into the clubhouse after 3pm and are then taken to Queenwood where the lodge manager will look after every requirement. The tariff of £700 (exc VAT 1994 prices) for up to eight guests includes two free rounds of free golf, three course dinner and English breakfast cooked by the lodge chef. Where else can a party of eight enjoy supreme comfort surrounded by a championship course from £87.50 (exc VAT) per person.

Call to make a booking on : 0249 822228.

Queenwood Golf Lodge
Derry Hill
Calne
Wilts
SN11 9PQ
Tel: (0249) 822228
Fax: (0249) 822218

The Golden Gate Bridge may lead you to San Francisco but the Golden Gates will lead you to Bowood. And Bowood is everything that California is not.

Of all the great English country estates that in recent years have found the charms of the Royal and Ancient game impossible to resist, the development at Bowood seems destined to emerge as one of the best: best in terms of the quality and range of facilities and best in terms of the quality and condition of its 18 hole Championship layout.

Notwithstanding the magnificently grand entrance to the Golf and Country Club — the above mentioned Golden Gates — there is nothing exclusive, or certainly no air of exclusivity, about Bowood. The atmosphere throughout the 19th hole buildings is extremely relaxed and informal and while there are golf club members at Bowood, with the exception of Saturday and Sunday mornings visitors are actively encouraged seven days a week. These 19th hole facilities (the Clubhouse is a beautifully restored 18th century farmhouse) include an extensive golf academy, incorporating three practice holes and a driving range headed by the **Director of Golf, Nigel Blenkarne**, one of the game's leading coaches.

Bowood's proprietor Lord Shelburne, oversees all administrative matters and ensures that very high standards of service are maintained. Visitors wishing to make individual or group bookings should telephone the club on **(0249) 822228**; the address for written correspondence is **Bowood Golf and Country Club, Calne, Wiltshire, SN11 9PQ** and the club's fax number is (0249) 822218. In 1994 the green fees were as follows: £27 for 18 holes, £35 for 27 holes, £40 for 36 holes during the week and £32 per round after midday at weekends. The precise location of the golf course is 10 miles south of the M4 junction 17 (Chippenham) at the point where the A4 meets the A432.

So, after passing through the Golden Gates and entering this welcoming corner of the grounds of Bowood House, the visitor needn't feel overawed: indeed the initial impression of the golf course will in all probability confirm this mood. Bowood is something of a rarity these days — a modern Championship length golf course with a refreshingly unpretentious design. Architect Dave Thomas has not attempted to trade Wiltshire for Palm Springs, as one suspects many of his fellow designers might have tried to do. Lancelot Capability Brown was the original 'architect' of Bowood and surely he would have turned in his grave at any suggestion of deference to the American way! The best word to describe Dave Thomas' design is 'subtle'. Not too many of the holes at Bowood will astonish you when you stand on the tee but by the time you leave the green (having hopefully mastered its myriad contours) there are very few you will not relish playing again soon.

Water is a feature of the design but it doesn't lead the design, indeed it tends to frame rather than shape those holes where it is present. Each of the 18 holes certainly has an individual flavour and there is plenty of variety to accompany the subtlety of the challenge. Moreover there is a great feeling of space at Bowood — none of the holes encroaches on another and with the gentle mounding and graded rough there is considerable definition to each hole. There are some nice touches too, such as the additional putting green beside the 1st tee, and the huge double green shared by the 5th and 14th holes. Subtlety aside for a moment, if there are two holes at Bowood that could be said to 'take your breath away' then they are the par four 8th and the par four 11th where on each a downhill tee shot must be perfectly positioned to open up a sharply doglegging fairway. For my money, however, the real strength of Bowood is to be found in its outstanding quartet of par five holes, namely the 3rd, 4th, 10th and 15th, and in its superb closing hole, where a deft approach is required to find a well protected and well-contoured putting surface — a fine hole and one that personifies the character of the course.

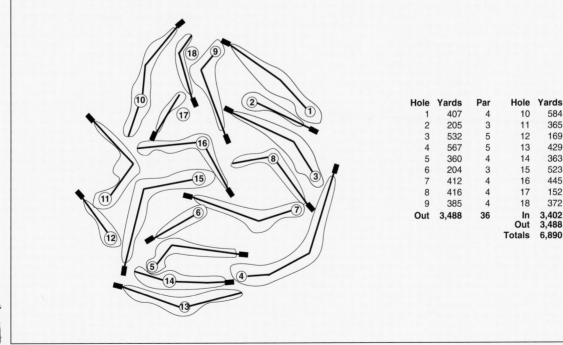

Hole	Yards	Par	Hole	Yards	Par
1	407	4	10	584	5
2	205	3	11	365	4
3	532	5	12	169	3
4	567	5	13	429	4
5	360	4	14	363	4
6	204	3	15	523	5
7	412	4	16	445	4
8	416	4	17	152	3
9	385	4	18	372	4
Out	**3,488**	**36**	**In**	**3,402**	**36**
			Out	**3,488**	**72**
			Totals	**6,890**	**72**

Time stands still in the Bybrook valley at the southern tip of the Cotswolds. Renowned as one of the prettiest villages in England, picturesque Castle Combe nestles in this delightful wooded valley where nothing has changed for the past 200 years. Rough-hewn limestone cottages, ancient market cross and a packbridge over the Bybrook, described in 1458 as 'the great town bridge', are the epitome of a peaceful English village.

Certainly there can be no lovelier approach to any village than the narrow lane winding its way down to Castle Combe through a green tunnel of interlocking branches.

To the enchantment of this hidden village, the Manor House lends an extra fairytale dimension. Steeped in history, with parts of the house dating back to the 14th century and added to by the Jacobeans in 1664, it is the quintessential English manor. A symphony of chimneys, mullioned windows and creeper covered walls and inside welcoming log fires and inviting sofas.

There is rich wood panelling, and gleaming glass and silver in the candlelit Bybrook restaurant. There are bedrooms tucked away in romantic attics, or boasting an Elizabethan fireplace and triple aspect views. They are all luxurious, some with four poster beds, others with Victorian style bathrooms. All the rooms in the main house have been restored and refurbished during the past two years to an exceptional degree, revealing hidden beams, stonework and a grain drying kiln.

Croquet, tennis and a heated outside swimming pool are all available for guests, with trout fishing on the one mile stretch of the Bybrook flowing through the 26 acres of gardens and parkland.

The Manor House is surrounded by countryside designated as an area of outstanding natural beauty. There are suggested walks through neighbouring woodland, or for the more energetic there are cycles available for visits to the many delightful nearby Cotswold villages.

Set in 200 acres of wooded valley and downland, the exceptional 18 hole championship. Manor House Golf Course, dominated by ancient oaks and beech woods, was designed by Peter Allis and Clive Clark and provides interesting and challenging golf for the average golfer and good player alike.

Guests staying at the Manor House are able to enjoy one of the most spectacular and challenging 6340 yard, par 73 golf courses in the south of England.

Although lost in the heart of the Cotswold countryside, access is not difficult. The M4 motorway is only 15 minutes away and the journey from London by road takes but one hour and 40 minutes. The intersection with the M5 is only 20 minutes away, linking the Midlands, the North and South West for ease of access.

The Manor House
Castle Combe
Chippenham
Wiltshire
SN14 7HR
Tel: (0249) 782206
Fax: (0249) 782159

The Manor House (Castle Combe)

'Invest in land' Mark Twain advised, 'they're not building any more of it.. What value then an area of dramatically rolling countryside bordering the beautiful Wiltshire village of Castle Combe? We are certainly talking about a very special place; it is the kind that if, some years ago, you were a golfer idly wandering across the land (day dreaming about your favourite pastime!) You would doubtless have sighed to yourself, 'my, what a marvellous setting this would make for a golf course!' Some day dreams can come true.

The Manor House Golf Club at Castle Combe opened in 1992, the 18 hole golf course that now winds its way through this spectacular piece of property was designed by Peter Alliss and Clive Clark. Not only does it make the most of the terrain (more of which later) but it genuinely 'accommodates' it. I choose this word because the golf course was never allowed to impose itself on the land and enormous care was taken at all stages of the development to preserve, and indeed encourage the natural flora and fauna and the abundant wildlife that inhabits the surrounding countryside.

Helping to keep the fairways green are the **General Manager, Michael Craig** and his staff. Manor House is a members' club but visitors who are able to provide proof of handicap are very welcome and can reserve tee times by contacting the club in advance of intended play. Bookings can be made by telephoning the Golf Office on **(0249) 783101**; the address for written correspondence is **The Manor House Golf Club, Castle Combe, Wiltshire SN14 7PL**. The green fees in 1994 were set at £25 per round, £35 per day midweek and £30 per round, £40 per day at weekends. Note also that a twilight green fee of £15 is available after 4.30pm, Mondays to Fridays.

The Golf Club is located directly off the B4039 road just beyond the village, between Chippenham and Bath. A leisurely drive to the Club is recommended for on reaching their destination many will exchange their car for a golf buggy, which means three or four hours of the golfing equivalent of a motor cross rally. The cart paths at Castle Combe are certainly well surfaced and well laid out but some of the routes between green and tee are guaranteed to set the pulse racing! How many golf clubs have required you to take a buggy test to prove that you can handle serious inclines? Of course, what this underlines is the fact that Castle Combe is nothing if not an extraordinarily exciting and exhilarating golf course. (You can also walk, by the way!)At 6,340 yards, par 73 from the back tees and 5,823 yards, par 71 and 5,119 yards, par 72 from the forward tees, Castle Combe is not a long course by the standards of many new 'high profile' layouts, but then added length is probably the last thing that this course needs. It opens with a relatively straightforward hole but the tempo immediately changes with the first of five really good par threes. Precision is vital at each of these short holes for the bad stroke is seriously punished. To reach the next tee, one of those amazing trips through the woods must be undertaken; but what a hole awaits! The 3rd is a classic par five, a genuine three shot hole where the terrain tumbles away from the tee in tiers to a far off island fairway; the second shot must somehow avoid a large tree, a stream and a small lake and then the approach is uphill to a green surrounded by sand. If the 3rd is the most memorable hole on the front nine then the 7th, a beautifully curving, tree lined par five is technically its equal.

The second nine at Castle Combe contains an even greater selection of hazards and outstanding holes. The sequence between the 11th (a quite stunning short hole where the tee shot must carry a little brook to find an angled green) and the par four 14th (where there are two distinct options from the tee the brave line and the very brave line) is quite sensational. Then comes the extraordinary finish with the vertigo inducing par three 17th and intimidating par four 18th with its beautifully landscaped greenside lake—a feature that would not look out of place at the Chelsea Flower Show. The inhabitants of Castle Combe can not only claim that they reside in 'the prettiest village in England' but its Golf Club Members can also justifiably boast how they now preside over 'the prettiest finish in England'.

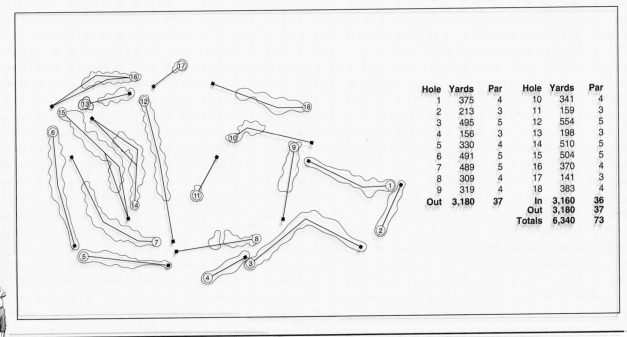

Hole	Yards	Par	Hole	Yards	Par
1	375	4	10	341	4
2	213	3	11	159	3
3	495	5	12	554	5
4	156	3	13	198	3
5	330	4	14	510	5
6	491	5	15	504	5
7	489	5	16	370	4
8	309	4	17	141	3
9	319	4	18	383	4
Out	**3,180**	**37**	**In**	**3,160**	**36**
			Out	**3,180**	**37**
			Totals	**6,340**	**73**

Key

_To avoid disappointment
it is advisable to telephone
in advance_

***_Visitors welcome at most times_
**_Visitors usually allowed on
weekdays only_
*_Visitors not normally permitted
(Mon, Wed) No visitors
on specified days_

Approximate Green Fees
A   _£30 plus_
B   _£20 to £30_
C   _£15 to £25_
D   _£10 to £20_
E   _under £10_
F   _Greens fees on application_

Restrictions
G—Guests only
H—Handicap certificate required
H—(24) Handicap of 24 or less
L—Letter of introduction required
_M—Visitor must be a member of
another recognised club._

SOMERSET

Brean G.C.
(0278) 751595
Coast Road, Brean
(18)5714 yards/**/D/H

Burnham and Berrow G.C.
(0278) 785760
St Christophers Way, Burnham-on-Sea
(18)6327 yards/***/A/M
(9)6332 yards/***/E

Cannington College G.C.
(0278) 652226
Cannington, Bridgwater
(9)5858 yards/***/D

Enmore Park G.C.
(0278) 671481
Enmore, Bridgwater
(18)6400 yards/***/C/H

Halstock G.C.
(0935) 891689
Common Lane, Halstock
(18)4000 yards/***/E

Isle of Wedmore G.C.
(0934) 712452
Lineage, Wedmore
(18)5800 yards/***/D

Kingweston G.C.
(0458) 43921
Compton Dundon, Somerton
(9)4516 yards/*/F

Longsutton G.C.
(0458) 241017
Longsutton, Langport
(18)6148 yards/***/D

Mendip G.C.
(0749) 840570
Gurney Slade, Bath
(18)6330 yards/***/B/H

Minehead and West Somerset G.C.
(0643) 702057
The Warren, Minehead
(18)6228 yards/***/B

Oake Manor G.C.
(0823) 461993
Oake, Taunton
(18)6109 yards/***/D

Taunton and Pickeridge G.C.
(0823) 421537
Corfe, Taunton
(18)5927 yards/***/F/H/L

Taunton Vale G.C.
(0823) 412220
Creech Heathfield, Taunton
(18)6072 yards/***/D
(9)2004 yards/***/E

Vivary Park G.C.
(0823) 333875
Taunton
(18)4620 yards/***/F

Wells G.C.
(0749) 675005
East Horrington Road, Wells
(18)6014 yards/***/D/H

Wincanton G.C.
(0963) 34606
Wincanton Racecourse
(9)3333 yards/***/E

Windwhistle G. & C.C.
(0460) 30231
Cricket St Thomas, Chard
(18)6500 yards/***/F

Yeovil G.C.
(0935) 22965
Sherborne Road. Yeovil
(18)6144 yards/***/B/H
(9)5016 yards/***/D/H

Weston-Super-Mare G.C.
(0934) 621360
Uphill Road North, Weston-Super-Mare
(18)6251 yards/***/B/H

Worlebury G.C.
(0934) 625789
Worlebury, Weston-Super-Mare
(18)5945 yards/***/C/H

AVON

Bath G.C.
(0225) 425182
North Road, Bath.
(18)6369 yards/***/B/H

Bristol and Clifton G.C.
(0275) 393117
Beggar Bush Lane, Failand
(18)6270 yards/**/B/H

Chipping Sodbury G.C.
(0454) 319042
Chipping Sodbury, Bristol
(18)6912 yards/***/B/H
(9)6190 yards/***/E/H

Clevedon G.C.
(0275) 874057
Castle Road, Clevedon
(18)5887 yards/***/B-A/H

Entry Hill G.C.
(0225) 834248
Entry Hill, Bath
(9)4206 yards/***/E

Farrington G.C.
(0761) 241274
Farrington Gurney, Bristol
(9)1200 yards/***/E

Filton G.C.
(0272) 694169
Golf Course Lane, Filton, Bristol
(18)6042 yards/**/B/H

Fosseway C.C.
(0761) 412214
Charlton Lane, Midsomer Norton
(9)4608 yards/***/(Wed p.m,Sat & Sun a.m)/D

Henbury G.C.
(0272) 500044
Henbury Hill, Westbury-on-Trym
(18)6039 yards/**/B/H

Knowle G.C.
(0272) 770660
Fairway, Brislington
(18)6016 yards/***/B/H/L

Lansdown G.C.
(0225) 422138
Lansdown, Bath
(18)6300 yards/***/B/H

Long Ashton G.C.
(0275) 392316
Long Ashton, Bristol
(18)6077 yards/***/B/H

Mangotsfield G.C.
(0272) 565501
Carsons Road, Mangotsfield
(18)5337 yards/***/E

Mendip Spring G.C.
(0934) 853337
Honeyhall Lane, Congresbury
(18)6328 yards/***/D
(9)2287 yards/***/E

Puxton Park G.C.
(0934) 876942
Puxton, Weston-Super-Mare
(18)6600 yards/***/E

Saltford G.C.
(0225) 873220
Golf Club Lane, Saltford
(18)6081 yards/***/B/H

Shirehampton Park G.C.
(0272) 822083
Park Hill, Shirehampton
(18)5500 yards/**/C/H

Stockwood Vale G.C.
(0272) 866505
Keynsham, Bristol
(9)2005 yards/***/E

Tall Pines G.C.
(0275) 472076
Downside, Backwell
(18) 5800 yards/***/D

Thornbury G.C.
(0454) 281144
Bristol Road, Thornbury
(18)6154 yards/***/D
(18)2195 yards/***/E

Tracy Park G.& C.C.
(0272) 372251
Bath Road, Wick, Bristol
(27)6629 yards/***/B

West Bristol G.C.
(0275) 393707
West Bristol
(18)6288 yards/***/B/H

West Country G.C.
(0275) 856626
Clevedon Road, Tickenham
(9)2000 yards/***/D

Woodlands G. & C.C.
(0454) 618121
Woodlands Lane, Almondsbury
(18)5550 yards/***/D

DORSET

Ashley Wood G.C.
(0258) 452253
Wimborne Rd, Blandford Forum
(18)6231 yards/***/C

Bridport & West Dorset G.C.
(0308) 422597
East Cliff, West Bay, Bridport
(18) 5246 yards/***/C

Broadstone G.C.
(0202) 693363
Wentworth Drive, Broadstone
(18)6300 yards/**/A/H

Bulbury Woods G.C.
(0929) 459574
Lytchett Matravers, nr Poole
(18)6020 yards/***/C

Came Down G.C.
(0305) 813494

Came Down, Dorchester
(18)6224 yards/***/B/H

Canford School G.C.
(0202) 841254
Canford School, Wimborne
(9)5918 yards/***/E/G

Chedington Court G.C.
(0935) 891413
Nr Beaminster, Dorset
(9)3500 yards/***/E

Christchurch G.C.
(0202) 473817
Iford, Christchurch
(9)4270 yards/***/E

Crane Valley G.C.
(0202) 814088
The Clubhouse, Verwood
(18)6420 yards/***/C/H
(9)2030 yards/***/E

Dudmoor Farm
(0202) 483980
Dudmoor Lane, Christchurch
(9)1562 yards/***/E

Dudsbury G.C.
(0202) 593499
Christchurch Road, Ferndown
(18)6208 yards/***/F

East Dorset G.C.
(0929) 472244
Hyde, Wareham
(18)6640 yards/***/C/H
(9)2440 yards/***/D/H

Ferndown G.C.
(0202) 874602
Golf Links Road, Ferndown
(18)6452 yards/***/A/H/L
(9)5604 yards/***/C/H/L

Highcliffe Castle G.C.
(0425) 272210
Lymington Road, Highcliffe-on-Sea
(18)4686 yards/***/B/H/M

Iford Bridge G.C.
(0202) 473817
Barrack Road, Christchurch
(9)2377 yards/***/F

Isle of Purbeck G.C.
(0929) 44361
Studland, Swanage
(18) 6295 yards/***/B/H
(9) 2022 yards/***/D

Knighton Heath G.C.
(0202) 572633
Francis Avenue, West Howe
(18)5987 yards/**/F/H

Lyme Regis G.C.
(0297) 442963
Timber Hill, Lyme Regis
(18)6220 yards/***/B/H

Lyons Gate G.C.
(0300) 345239
Lyons Gate, Dorchester
(9)2100 yards/***/E

Meyrick Park G.C.
(0202) 290307
Meyrick Park, Bournemouth
(18) 5885 yards/***/E

Mid Dorset G.C.
(0258) 861386
Belchalwell, Blandford Forum
(18)6500 yards/***/C

Moors Valley G.C.
(0425) 479776
Horton Road, Ringwood
(18)6270 yards/***/E

Parkstone G.C.
(0202) 707138
Links Road, Parkstone
(18) 6250 yards/**/A/H/M

Queen's Park G.C.
(0202) 396198
Queen's Park, Bournemouth
(18) 6505 yards/***/E

Sherbourne G.C.
(0935) 812475
Higher Clatcombe, Sherbourne
(18)5949 yards/***/B/H

Solent Meads Par Three G.C.
(0202) 420795
Hengistbury Head, Bournemouth
(18)2325 yards/***/F

Sturminster Marshall G.C.
(0258) 858444
Moor Lane, Sturminster Marshall
(9)4650 yards/***/E

Wareham G.C.
(0929) 554147
Sandford Road, Wareham
(18) 5603 yards/**/C

Weymouth G.C.
(0305) 773981
Links Road, Westham, Weymouth
(18)6030 yards/***/B/H

WILTSHIRE

Bowood G. & C.C.
(0249) 822228
Derry Hill, Calne
(18)6890 yards/***/B-A

Bradford-on-Avon G.C.
(0225) 868268
Trowbridge Road, Bradford-on-Avon
(9)2297 yards/**/E

Brinkworth G.C.
(0666) 41277
Longman's Farm, Brinkworth
(18)5900 yards/***/E

Bremhill Park G.C.
(0793) 782946
Shrivenham, Swindon
(18)5880 yards/***/E

Broome Manor G.C.
(0793) 532403
Pipers Way, Swindon
(18)6359 yards/***/E
(9)2745 yards/***/E

Castle Combe G. & C.C.
(0249) 782982
Castle Combe
(18)6300 yards/***/B-A/H

Chippenham G.C..
(0249) 652040
Malmesbury Road, Chippenham
(18)5540 yards/***/B/H/M

Cricklade Hotel G.C.
(0793) 750751
Common Hill, Cricklade
(9)1830 yards/***/D

Cumberwell Park G.C.
(0225) 863322
Bradford-on-Avon
(18)6810 yards/***/D

Erlestoke Sands G.C.
(0380) 831069
Erlestoke, Devizes
(18)6649 yards/***/D

Hamptworth G. & C.C.
(0794) 390155
Hamptworth Road, Landford
(18)6512 yards/**/F/H

High Post G.C.
(0722) 73356
Great Durnford, Salisbury
(18)6297 yards/**/B/H

Highworth Community G.C.
(0793) 766014
Swindon Road, Highworth
(9)3200 yards/***/E

Kingsdown G.C.
(0225) 742530
Kingsdown, Corsham
(18) 6445 yards/**/B/H

Marlborough G.C.
(0672) 512147
The Common, Marlborough
(18)6526 yards/***/B-A/H

Monkton Park Par Three G.C.
(0249) 653928
Chippenham, Swindon
(9)1000 yards/***/E

North Wiltshire G.C.

(0380) 860257
Bishops Cannings, Devizes
(18)6484 yards/***/F/H

Salisbury and Wiltshire G.C.
(0722) 742645
Netherhampton, Salisbury
(18)6528 yards/***/B-A/H

Shrivenham Park G.C.
(0793) 783853
Penny Hooks, Shrivenham
(18)5900 yards/***/D

Swindon G.C.
(0672) 841217
Ogbourne St George, Marlborough
(18)6226 yards/**/C/H

Thoulstone Park G.C.
(0373) 832825
Chapmanslade, Wesbury
(18)6300 yards/***/D

West Wiltshire G.C.
(0985) 212702
Elm Hill, Warminster
(18)5709 yards/***/B/H

Wootton Bassett G.C.
(0793) 849999
Wootton Bassett, Swindon
(18)6634 yards/***/B/H

Wrag Barn G.C.
(0793) 861327
Shrivenham Road, Highworth
(18)6548 yards/**/C

Upavon G.C.
(0980) 630787
Douglas Avenue, Upavon
(9)5589 yards/***/D

Artist: **Major Hopkins** *A FOURSOME AT WESTWARD HO!* *Courtesy of* **Burlington Gallery**

Artist: **C.E. Brock** **THE PUTT** *Courtesy of:* **Sotheby's**

Even if the Isle of Wight and the Channel Islands were taken away from this region it would still score top marks, both for the quality of the golf and the quality of the accompanying scenery. With the New Forest to the south, the Downs to the north and Winchester Cathedral standing proudly in the middle, Hampshire is arguably the fairest of all English counties. And amongst all this finery stand the likes of Liphook, Old Thorns, North Hants, Blackmoor and Brokenhurst Manor—five of the country's leading inland courses.

From Heathland to Links

Hampshire's traditional 'big three' of **Liphook**, **North Hants** and **Blackmoor**, lie towards the east of the county close to the boundary with Surrey. Not surprisingly they are staunch members of the heathland club—silver birch and pine, fir, heather and a dash of gorse. Liphook is possibly the pick of the three, though it's a close thing. Each measures between 6200 and 6300 yards and is maintained in superb condition. The **Army** Golf Club, just north of Aldershot is another fine and quite lengthy heathland type course with a reputation for separating the men from the boys, although it is perhaps not quite in the same league as the illustrious trio above. The final mention in this area goes to one of the county's newest recruits, the **Old Thorns** Golf and Country Club, situated just south of Liphook. Old Thorns is featured on a later page.

There's no shortage of comfortable hotels in the north of Hampshire and often quite hidden in the countryside are some delightful pubs and restaurants. Inns to ease the golfer's slumber include the Crown and Cushion in Minley and the Chequers in Well. Fleet bisects these two villages and the Lismoyne Hotel (0252) 628555 is ideally located. In Passfield, the Passfield Oak does good food and some popular real ales, while in Grayshott, Woods Place (0428) 605555 is an excellent little restaurant and it sounds perfect for golfers. In Liphook, as well as the superb Old Thorns (0428) 724555, the Links Hotel (0428) 723773 is very handy for the 9th and 10th tees on the Liphook course. An Indian restaurant nearby, the Bombay (0428) 722095 is recommended (and its celebrated curries are reputed to add 20 yards to your drive!) Basingstoke isn't Hampshire's most attractive town—too much London overspill. A very good and relatively new course nearby however is the **Sandford Springs** Golf Club at Wolverton, built on the site of a former Roman shrine, and officially opened in 1989 by Nick Faldo.

Winchester golfers, like those at Liphook, are doubly fortunate having two first class courses at hand: **Royal Winchester** and **Hockley,** which is located two miles south of the city on the A333. Both are well kept downland type courses. A recent, and most attractive addition to the Winchester/South Hampshire area is the **Botley Park** Hotel and Country Club (0489) 780888. Some excellent golfing weekend packages are offered.

In Ampfield, south of Winchester, and Romsey, also south of the cathedral town, two ideal 19th hole establishments catch the eye. In the former, Potters Heron (0703) 266611 is comfortable and convenient for the A31 and the Old White Horse (0794) 512431 is a welcoming inn located in Romsey's marketplace. In Winchester there are numerous restaurants, perhaps the best is the Old Chesil. Also in Winchester the Forte Crest (0962) 861611 is not cheap but it is particularly comfortable. North west of the city is Sparsholt, where one finds one of those exquisite English country house hotels, Lainston House (0962) 863588. More modest accommodation can be found at the Aeire Guest house (0962) 862519. In Stockbridge, the Game Larder (0264) 810414 is a first class restaurant and the Sherrif

House (0264) 810677 also offers outstanding food. People coming from, or returning to the west should note Middle Wallop—more specifically—Fifehead Manor (0264) 781565, a delightful manor house with a good restaurant. Finally, I must point pub lovers in mid-Hampshire in the direction of Ovington where the Bush is tremendous fun.

Returning to the fairways, and switching nearer to the south coast, the **Rowlands Castle** parkland course occupies a peaceful setting. The course can play fairly long, especially from the back markers. While we're on the subject of length, a hundred years ago the links at **Hayling Island** is said to have measured 7480 yards—so much for the modern-day monster courses! Today the course is less frightening but still quite a challenge and visitors are warmly received.

Another drink is needed and two fine pubs are at hand—the Old House at Home (superb name) in Havant and the Royal Oak in Langstone: both are ideally situated for Rowlands Castle. Another establishment to sample in this area is the notable Old House Hotel (0329) 833049 in Wickham and in Botley, Cobbett's (0489) 782068 is a fine French restaurant. Finally, back on Hayling Island, we recommend the Newtown House Hotel (0705) 466131 as ideal for all visitors to the area.

Southampton and the New Forest

Stoneham is without doubt the pick of the courses in the Southampton area, it is located just two miles north of the town. The venue of the first Dunlop British Masters tournament back in 1946, it is quite undulating with an ample sprinkling of gorse and heather which, though appealing to look at, is often the curse of the wayward hitter. Just outside of Portsmouth a fine 18 hole course to note is **Waterlooville,** although there are in fact a number of courses (including some very reasonable public courses, such as **Fleming Park** at **Eastleigh**) in and around Southampton and Portsmouth. Midway between Portsmouth and Southampton (M27 junction 7) is the **Meon Valley** Golf and Country Club. A relatively new parkland course, designed by J Hamilton Stutt, it too has an attractive setting, not a million miles from the New Forest. For a night's rest the Meon Valley Hotel (0329) 833455 is the obvious selection, being both comfortable and highly convenient.

I'm afraid I know very little about William the Conqueror but I understand there are at least two things we should thank him for—one is the Domesday Book and the other is the New Forest, without doubt one of the most beautiful areas in Britain. There are two real golfing treats in the New Forest, one is **Bramshaw** Golf Club which is owned and run by the owners of the charming Bell Inn (0703) 812214—two fine 18 hole courses here, the Manor and the Forest courses—and the second is **Brokenhurst Manor,** a superb heathland course. Both venues are decidedly worth inspecting. A short distance from the New Forest, **Barton-on-Sea**'s exposed clifftop course is also worth a visit if in the area—it's not long, but with enough challenges and some spectacular views across to the Isle of Wight and Christchurch Bay.

A few ideas for the 19th hole, and we make a start at Lyndhurst and the Parkhill House Hotel (0703) 282944—a pleasant spot with a good restaurant as well. Two B's now, Beaulieu and Brockenhurst. In the former, the Montagu Arms (0590) 612324 and its fine restaurant is ideal to hang up one's clubs and in the latter a number of places should be considered; two to include are Carey's Manor (0590) 23551, a great all rounder and the Forest Park. In nearby Sway, the Tower (0590) 683034 is another that can be unfailingly recommended. Further south on the A337 we

Newtown House Hotel

Situated within close proximity to Chichester, Portsmouth and the beautiful South Downs, Newtown House Hotel offers guests an ideal base from which to enjoy one of Britain's most picturesque and challenging golf courses and also to tour this attractive part of the country, with its mild climate, calm water for sailing and superb stretches of sandy beach.

Old ships beams, oak panelling, inglenook seating, and stone fireplaces all contribute to create a wonderful old world atmosphere in the bar and lounges of the hotel. During the winter season, log fires burn brightly in the fireplaces welcoming guests to this truly unique hotel.

One of the most popular features of the hotel and one of its greatest assets, is its restaurant. English and continental dishes are offered in an interesting à la carte menu which is varied regularly, and the table d'hote dining and wine list also proves most popular. The restaurant enjoys a well deserved reputation with guests and

locally, for the excellent quality of its cuisine, and the friendly, helpful and efficient service of its staff.

All bedrooms are individual and tastefully furnished, with private bath or showers en suite, radio and telephone, colour television and tea/coffee making facilities.

The New Wave Leisure Complex offers extensive facilities for sports and recreation, including heated indoor swimming pool, multi-gym, jacuzzi sauna and steam room. Tennis and swimming tuition are available from a resident instructor and there is an excellent well maintained hard tennis court. Hayling Island has an international reputation for the excellence of its sailing facilities.

The hotel has catered for businessmen and local firms over many years and the Tudor Room is available for business conferences and training seminars for up to 60 people and is also popular as a private dining room for executive luncheons or private dinner parties.

Newtown House Hotel
Manor Road
Hayling Island
Hants
PO1 1QR
Tel: (0705) 466131
Fax (0705) 461366

arrive at Lymington. In another good hotel setting stands the Passford House (0590) 682398 and for a stylish guest house, try Wheatsheaf House (0590) 679208. Among other things, the nearby the South Lawn Hotel (0590) 643911 is convenient for ferries leaving for the Isle of Wight, while Limpets, also in Lymington, is a tasty restaurant. In New Milton, we find the county's (quite probably the country's) finest country house hotel, Chewton Glen (0425) 275341.

Isle of Wight

There are no fewer than seven golf courses on the Isle of Wight. There are two 18 hole courses, **Shanklin and Sandown** is the better of the two (beautifully wooded with heather and gorse) and the other is **Freshwater Bay** (more of a downland/clifftop course.) Of the 9 holers, **Osborne** is the most scenic but a visit to any is appealing. All courses welcome visitors and green fees tend to compare favourably with those on the mainland–note that in summer, the courses can be very busy and so a pre-match telephone call is strongly advised.

In Shanklin, the Cliff Tops (0983) 863262 and Luccombe Hall stand out, though there are many good hotels on the island. Two pubs to visit in Shanklin include the Fisherman's Cottage–good food and a fine setting and the Crab–more seafood and a high street position. Elsewhere on the island, Cowes of course is busy and fun, especially during Cowes week itself, but for our purposes Bonchurch beckons, where the Peacock Vane (0983) 852019 is a delightful restaurant with some rooms. There is also a tremendous selection of moderately priced establishments on the island; suggestions include, Gambits Private Hotel (0983) 402649, Blenheim House (0983) 752858 at Freshwater, the Culver Lodge Hotel (0983) 403819 and the excellent St Catherine's Hotel (0983) 402392, both at Sandown.

The Channel Islands

If the Isle of Wight is good for golf, the Channel Islands are even better and we note that Ian Botham with his recommendation for **Alderney** is doing his bit to promote the islands' golfing reputation in the foreword to this book! **La Moye, Royal Jersey** and **Royal Guernsey** are the three outstanding 18 hole courses; although it seems the German troops didn't share this opinion during the island's four year occupation: they demolished La Moye's clubhouse and dug up the fairways at Royal Guernsey. Both have long since recovered though and all three provide tremendous holiday golf. La Moye's links, the regular venue for the Jersey Open, is featured ahead.

When it comes to hotels one is quite simply spoilt for choice. In Guernsey St Peter's Port offers a whole handful of excellent establishments, generally good value as well. The St Pierre Park (0481) 728282 is the most luxurious hotel, and for real character La Fregate Hotel (0481) 724624 is an 18th century manor house overlooking the harbour. The Old Government House (0481) 724921 is again beautifully stylish while Les Ozouets Lodge (0481) 721288 both have good restaurants to match a friendly welcome. For a good seafood restaurant try the unfortunately named Absolute End (0481) 723822 and for a cosy guest house, La Girouette (0481) 63269 near Perrelle Bay.

In Jersey, St Brelade's Bay offers the superb Atlantic Hotel (0534) 44101 (ideal for La Moye links). Other recommended hotels here are the Hotel L'Horizon (0534) 43101, La Place Hotel (0534) 44261, and the Little Grove Hotel (0534) 25321. St Helier boasts the aptly named Grand Hotel (0534) 22301–note especially the restaurant–the less expensive Almorah Hotel (0534) 21648 and St Peter, the Mermaid (0534) 41255. Perhaps the best restaurant on the island is to be found at St Saviours–Longueville Manor (0534) 25501. In Bouley Bay is the delightfully secluded Water's Edge Hotel (0534) 862777. The intrepid guest house brigade will find more than enough to please them at Millbrook House (0534) 33036 in St Helier and Bryn-y-Mor (0534) 20295 in St Aubin. Finally in Grouville Bay where the Royal Jersey Golf Club is situated is La Hougue Grange, a charming country house and one of those great treats where the words 'fore' and 'fare' can be combined so happily!

Artist: **John Goodall** **THE FIRST** *Courtesy of* Rosenstiel's

There are two reasons why we have selected Old Thorns as one of our 100 featured courses in this edition of _Following the Fairways_. Firstly, it is because a visit to Old Thorns can fairly be described as a unique experience and the purpose of this book, after all, is to illustrate the wealth and variety of golfing challenges that these islands have to offer. The second, just as important, is that Old Thorns is both exceptionally attractive and visitor-friendly. Nature, with a little help from course designers Peter Alliss and Dave Thomas, is chiefly responsible for the beauty of the situation. The visitor-friendly aspect is a direct result of the fact that Old Thorns isn't a Golf Club as such. Like The Belfry, there are no members for whom tee times must be reserved.

What about the unique experience? Old Thorns is where East meets West, not just on the Golf course but at the 19th hole. Old Thorns is owned by a large Japanese publishing company, Kosaido who acquired the course and accompanying hotel only two years after its official opening in 1982. The Japanese inherited a very English set up. The centre piece of the clubhouse and hotel is a converted 150 year old tithe barn; a delightful building. The new owners have maintained, even enhanced, its traditional 'log fires in winter' ambience, but they have also added a Japanese Centre which includes a charming Japanese garden. The buildings have been extended generally to an extent that Old Thorns now boasts a splendid range of luxury facilities. The hotel has 27 well appointed rooms and guests can enjoy a genuine Japanese Shiatsu massage!

Golfers wishing to visit Old Thorns should contact the Club in advance. The address to write to is **Old Thorns, Longmoor Road, Liphook, Hampshire GU30 7PE**. The **General Manager** is **Mr. G. Jones** but telephone enquiries of a golfing nature can usually be handled by the **Professional Philip Loxley** and his staff on **(0428) 724555,** fax: (0428) 725036.

Subject to booking a tee time visitors can play on any day of the week. In 1994, the green fees were £25 per round, £40 per day midweek and £35 per round at the weekend. Incidentally, something like two thirds of all visitors on a Sunday are either Japanese or Korean and there is a thoroughly international atmosphere. Hotel residents pay reduced green fees while golf buggies and sets of clubs can be hired from the professional.

Located approximately one hour's drive from London (less from Heathrow and Gatwick airports) and very close to the A3, Old Thorns is very easy to find. The A3 runs through neighbouring Liphook's golf course! The B2131 Longmoor Road should be joined close to the centre of Liphook village, near the Royal Anchor Hotel. Old Thorns is found about one mile down this road.

Just an hour's drive perhaps, but London can seem a world away when you arrive at the course. The surrounding countryside is some of Britain's finest; a great spread of oaks, beech trees, chestnuts and pines adorn the landscape and the golf course winds its way through the woods, gently rising and falling. Natural springs abound and much use has been made of them! Water hazards are numerous at Old Thorns; there are many streams and several times the golfer is asked to play over or across the edge of a small lake. The course is maintained in good condition all year round and the greens have a reputation for being quick.

From the back markers the course measures 6533 yards, par 72; from the forward tees it is a less daunting 6129 yards, par 72 and from the ladies tees the course measures 5342 yards, par 74. It is difficult to single out individual holes at Old Thorns but first timers often remember the holes around the turn, especially the 9th, 10th and 11th, where on each hole a miss-hit shot can cause the sight every golfer dreads—ripples on water! Avoid the water at Old Thorns though and a good score is always a possibility; the rough is rarely punishing and the bunkers not too difficult to play out of.

Old Thorns has an excellent finish with the par three 16th and the dramatic two-shot 17th being perhaps the best holes of all.

After holing out successfully on the tricky 18th green a stiff drink at the 19th may be in order—a shot of saki perhaps? A good meal may also be sought and some people reckon that this is where Old Thorns really comes into its own. There is a superb selection of European and Japanese cuisine in its very characterful restaurants. If you have never tried Japanese food before then the renowned Nippon Kan Restaurant and the Teppan Yaki Bar are the perfect places for an introduction. Old Thorns is guaranteed to charm you from the moment you arrive to the time you leave.

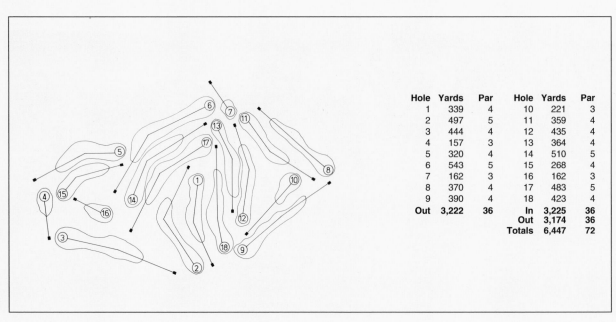

Hole	Yards	Par	Hole	Yards	Par
1	339	4	10	221	3
2	497	5	11	359	4
3	444	4	12	435	4
4	157	3	13	364	4
5	320	4	14	510	5
6	543	5	15	268	4
7	162	3	16	162	3
8	370	4	17	483	5
9	390	4	18	423	4
Out	3,222	36	In	3,225	36
			Out	3,174	36
			Totals	6,447	72

England is part of the Channel Islands. Yes, England is part of the Channel Islands—at least this is what an islander will tell you. Apparently, the islands belonged to William, Duke of Normandy some time before he came over and added England to his territories.

So what of the golf in the 'mother country', the land where the great Harry Vardon was born? In short, there are three very fine courses: Royal Guernsey, Royal Jersey and La Moye. The first two certainly offer a marvellous day's golf but the general consensus is that La Moye sneaks it as the pick of an excellent trio. Its setting alone makes the course stand out, laid out as it is two hundred and fifty feet above St Ouen's Bay, Jersey's finest beach, on the south west tip of the island. From such a vantage point there are some tremendous views to be enjoyed from the course, particularly perhaps from the 13th where the four sister islands of Guernsey, Sark, Herm and Jetou can all be seen. Add to this a warm climate and of course, the quality of the championship links itself and you can see why people want to play golf here!

La Moye Golf Club was founded in 1902 by the then headmaster of the local school, one George Boomer. A course was mapped out but it didn't really take shape until James Braid added his skilful craftsmanship. Thereafter the course was left more or less untouched, so to speak, until 1977 when major alterations were made resulting in an improved and, when played from the back tees, much longer course.

The **Secretary** at La Moye is **Mr. Chris Greetham;** he can be contacted by telephone on **(0534) 43401** or by writing to: **La Moye Golf Club, La Moye, Jersey, Channel Islands**. The Club **professional, Mike Deeley** can be reached on **(0534) 43130.**

In addition to being a superb Championship course, La Moye doubles as a very popular holiday course in the best sense of the word. Visitors are always made most welcome. The only specific requirement is that they must be members of a recognised Golf Club. It isn't essential to book a tee time but during the summer months the course can become extremely busy. Making an early start is always a good idea (whether this fits in with the holiday schedule is another matter!)

The green fees for 1994 were set at £35 per round, £55 per day (inclusive of lunch) during the week and £40 during the weekend when afternoon play only is permissable. For junior golfers a reduced fee of £17.50 is payable, or £20 at the weekend. A weekly ticket may well be preferred and can be purchased for £145.

As for finding the course, there really should be no problem. La Moye is only a mile or so from St Brelade and just five minutes by road from Jersey's Airport. The island is such a size that it shouldn't take much more than half an hour to travel between La Moye and Royal Jersey in Grouville, though of course it depends on the traffic and on how much of Jersey you want to take in along the way.

From the Championship tees, the course can be stretched to beyond 6700 yards, as it is for the Jersey Open. The medal tees however, are less exacting and the total yardage is 6464 yards, par 72: no pushover certainly, and there is often a very stiff wind. From the ladies tees the course measures 5903 yards, par 74. La Moye is a typical links type course—large sand hills, pot bunkers, the odd blind shot, gorse bushes and punishing rough (though it's not as punishing as at some). It really is full of variety with a number of dog-legs and plateau greens. Apart from the 13th and its enchanting views, many will probably remember the 17th hole best of all: it is a lengthy par four with the green dramatically set on the edge of the cliffs, rather like the famous 5th hole at Portrush.

The Jersey Open is a very popular event on the European Tour and the pros, inspired by the surroundings, have produced some very good scores—although La Moye has never been torn apart. Some well known names have won the Jersey Open here including; Sandy Lyle, Tony Jacklin, Bernard Gallacher, Howard Clark, Ian Woosnam and Sam Torrance. So some of the best golfers in the world have played at La Moye and they may soon be joined by the best golfer to have played on the moon! Alan Sheppard, now Admiral Sheppard, has recently become an honourary member at La Moye. One suspects he is a rather good bunker player!

All golfers, terrestrial and non-terrestrial are sure to enjoy the Club's excellent 19th. A spacious new Clubhouse, it is one of a series for the Club. The original burned down while the second was destroyed by German soldiers during the island's war-time occupation. Let's just wish the new one the best of British luck!

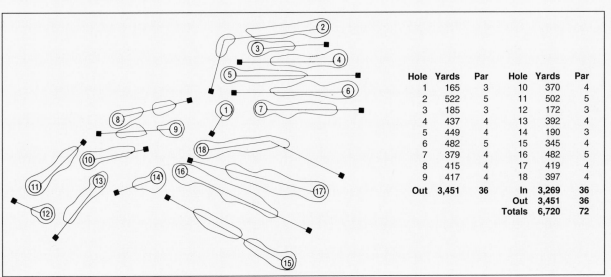

Hole	Yards	Par	Hole	Yards	Par
1	165	3	10	370	4
2	522	5	11	502	5
3	185	3	12	172	3
4	437	4	13	392	4
5	449	4	14	190	3
6	482	5	15	345	4
7	379	4	16	482	5
8	415	4	17	419	4
9	417	4	18	397	4
Out	**3,451**	**36**	**In**	**3,269**	**36**
			Out	**3,451**	**36**
			Totals	**6,720**	**72**

Hampshire and the Channel Islands Complete Golf

Key

To avoid disappointment
it is advisable to telephone
in advance

***Visitors welcome at most times
**Visitors usually allowed on
weekdays only
*Visitors not normally permitted
(Mon, Wed) No visitors
on specified days

Approximate Green Fees
A £30 plus
B £20 to £30
C £15 to £25
D £10 to £20
E under £10
F Greens fees on application

Restrictions
G—Guests only
H—Handicap certificate required
H—(24) Handicap of 24 or less
L—Letter of introduction required
M—Visitor must be a member of
another recognised club.

Alresford G.C.
(0962) 733746
Cheriton Road, Alresford
(18)6038 yards/**/C/H

Alton G.C.
(0420) 82042
Old Odiham Road, Alton
(9)5744 yards/***/D/H

Ampfield Par Three G.C.
(0794) 368480
Winchester Road, Ampfield,
Romsey
(18)2478 yards/***/D/H

Andover G.C.
(0264) 323980
Winchester Road, Andover
(9)5933/**/C/H

Army G.C.
(0252) 541104
Laffans Road, Aldershot
(18)6579 yards/**/F/H

Barton-on-Sea G.C.
(0425) 615308
Marine Drive, Barton-on-Sea, New
Milton
(18)5737 yards/***/B/H

Basingstoke G.C.
(0256) 465990
Kempshott Park, Basingstoke
(18)6350 yards/**/B/H/M

Bishopswood G.C.
(0734) 815213
Bishopswood Lane, Tadley
(9)6474 yards/**(Mon,Wed)/D/M

Blackmoor G.C.
(0420) 472775
Golf Lane, Whitehill, Bordon
(18)6232 yards/**/B/H

Blacknest G.C.
(0420) 22888
Frith End, Binstead
(9)6726 yards/***/D

Botley Park Hotel & G.C.
(0489) 780888
Winchester Road, Boorley Green
(18)6026 yards/***/C/H

Bramshaw G.C.
(0703) 813433
Brook, Lyndhurst
(18)6233 yards/**/D/H
(18)5774 yards/***/D/H

Brokenhurst Manor G.C.
(0590) 23332
Sway Road, Brockenhurst
(18)6222 yards/***/B/H(24)

Burley G.C.
(0425) 402431
Cott Lane, Burley
(9)6149 yards/***/D/H

Cams Hall G.C.
(0329) 827222
Cams Hill, Fareham
(18)5890 yards/**/B/H
(9)3059 yards/**/E/H

Chilworth G.C.
(0703) 733166
Main Road, Chilworth
(9)2347 yards/***/E

Corhampton G.C.
(0489) 877279
Sheeps Pond Lane, Droxford
(18)6088 yards/**/B/H

Dean Farm G.C.
(0420) 489478
Kingsley
(9)1350 yards/***/F

Dibden G.C.
(0703) 845596
Dibden, Southampton
(18)6206 yards/***/E
(9)1520 yards/***/E

Dummer G.C.
(0256) 397888
Dummer, Basingstoke
(18)6556 yards/**/B/H

Dunwood Manor G.C.
(0794) 340549
Shootash Hill, Romsey
(18)5885 yards/**/B/H

Fleetlands G.C.
(0705) 822351
Fareham Road, Gosport
(9)4852 yards/***/F/G

Fleming Park G.C.
(0703) 612797
Magpie Lane, Eastleigh
(18)4436 yards/***/E

Furzeley G.C.
(0705) 231180
Furzeley, Denmead
(9)1858 yards/***/E

Gosport and Stokes Bay G.C.
(0705) 527941
Off Fort Road, Haslar, Gosport
(9)5966 yards/**/D

Great Salterns G.C.
(0705) 664549
Portsmouth Golf Centre, Eastern
Road,
(18)5970 yards/***/E

The Hampshire G.C.
(0264) 357555
Winchester Road, Goodworth
Clatford
(18)6318 yards/***/D
(9)1050 yards/***/E

Hartley Wintney G.C.
(0252) 844211
London Road, Hartley Wintney
(9)6096 yards/***/D

Hayling G.C.
(0705) 464446
Links Lane, Hayling Island
(18)6489 yards/***/A/H/M/L

Hockley G.C.
(0962) 713165
Twyford, Winchester
(18)6279 yards/**/C/G

Kingsley Par Three G.C.
(0420) 476118
Main Road, Kingsley, Bordon
(9)1800 yards/***/E

Leckford and Longstock G.C.
(0264) 810320
Leckford, Stockbridge
(9)3251 yards/*/F/G

Lee-on-the-Solent G.C.

(0705) 551170
Brune Lane, Lee-on-the-Solent
(18)5959/**/B/H

Liphook G.C.
(0428) 723271
Wheatsheaf Enclosure, Liphook
(18)6250 yards/**/A/H/L

Meon Valley G.& C.C.
(0329) 833455
Sandy Lane, Shedfield,
Southampton
(18)6519 yards/***/A
(9)2885 yards/***/D

New Forest G.C.
(0703) 282752
Southampton Road, Lyndhurst
(18)5742 yards/***/D

North Hants G.C.
(0252) 616443
Minley Road, Fleet
(18)6257 yards/***/B/H/L

Old Thorns G.C.
(0428) 724555
Longmoor Road, Liphook
(18)5629 yards/***/A

Petersfield G.C.
(0730) 262386
Heath Road, Petersfield
(18)5603 yards/**/C

Portsmouth G.C.
(0705) 372210
Crookhorn Road, Widley,
Portsmouth
(18)6139 yards/***/E

Romsey G.C.
(0703) 734637
Nursling , Southampton
(18)5851 yards/**/B/H

Rowlands Castle G.C.
(0705) 412784
Links Lane, Rowlands Castle
(18)6627 yards/**/B/H

Royal Winchester G.C.
(0962) 852462
Sarum Road, Winchester
(18)6218 yards/**/B/H/M

Sandford Springs G.C.
(0635) 297881
Wolverton, Basingstoke
(27)6222 yards/**/B

Southampton G.C.
(0703) 768407
Golf Course Road, Bassett,
Southampton
(18)6218 yards/***/F
(9)2391 yards/***/F

Southsea G.C.
(0705) 660945
The Mansion, Great Salterns
(18)5900 yards/***/F

Southwick Park G.C.
(0705) 380131
Pinsley Drive, Southwick, Fareham
(18)5972 yards/**/F

South Winchester G.C.
(0962) 877800
Pitt, Winchester
(18)6697 yards/**/B/H/L

Southwood G.C.
(0252) 548700
Ively Road, Cove, Farnborough
(18)5738 yards/***/D

Stoneham G.C.
(0703) 768151
Bassett Green Road, Bassett
(18)6310 yards/**/B/H

Test Valley G.C.
(0256) 771737
Micheldever Road, Overton
(18)6811 yards/***/C

Tidworth Garrison G.C.
(0980) 42301

Bulford Road, Tidworth
(18)6075 yards/**/D

Tylney Park G.C.
(0256) 762079
Rotherwick, Basingstoke
(18)6109 yards/**/B/H

Waterlooville G.C.
(0705) 263388
Cherry Tree Avenue, Cowplain,
Portsmouth
(18)6647 yards/**/B/H

Wellow G.C.
(0794) 22872
Ryedown Lane, East Wellow
(18)5902 yards/***/D

Weybrook Park G.C.
(0256) 20347
Aldermaston Road, Basingstoke
(18)6100 yards/***/D

ISLE OF WIGHT

Cowes G.C.
(0983) 292303
Crossfield Avenue, Cowes
(9)5934 yards/***/D/H

Freshwater Bay G.C.
(0983) 752955
Afton Down, Freshwater Bay
(18)5662 yards/***/C/H
Newport G.C.
(0983) 525076
St Georges Down, Newport
(9)5704 yards/***/D/H

Osborne G.C.
(0983) 295421
Osborne House Estates, East Cowes
(9)6276 yards/**/D/H

Ryde G.C.
(0983) 614809
Binstead Road, Ryde
(9)5287 yards/***/D/H

Shanklin & Sandown G.C.
(0983) 403217
The Fairway, Lake, Sandown
(18)6000 yards/**/B/H/M

Ventnor G.C.
(0983) 853326
Steep Hill Down Road, Upper
Ventnor
(9)5752 yards/***/F

CHANNEL ISLANDS

Alderney G.C.
(0481) 822835
Route des Carrieres, Alderney
(9)2528 yards/***/D

La Moye G.C.
(0534) 43401
La Moye, St Brelade, Jersey
(18)6741 yards/***/A/H/L

Les Mielles Par Three G.C.
(0534) 81947
The Mount, Val de la Mare, St
Ouens
(12)1971 yards/***/E

Royal Guernsey G.C.
(0481) 47022
L'Ancresse Vale, Guernsey
(18)6206 yards/**/B/H

Royal Jersey G.C.
(0534) 854416
Grouville, Jersey
(18)6059 yards/***/(W/E pm)/A/H

St Clements G.C.
(0524) 21938
St Clements, Jersey
(9)3972 yards/***/(Sun pm)/F

St Pierre Park G.C.
(0481) 727039
Rohais, St Peter Port, Guernsey
(9)2511 yards/***/D

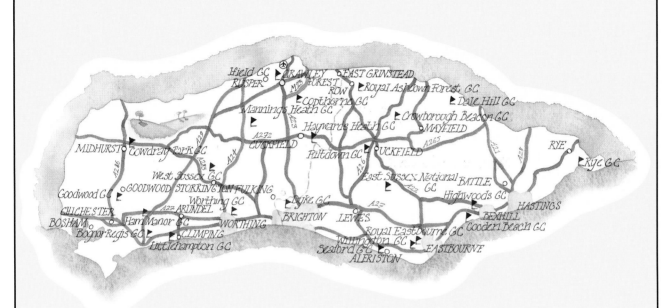

Artist: **Henry Sandham THE CLUB'S THE THING** *Courtesy of:* **Rosenstiel's**

Sussex; where the South Downs tumble gently towards spectacular chalk cliffs or as Tennyson wrote, 'green Sussex fading into blue'. Here is the county of downland and weald, of dramatic rollercoasting cliffs, the Seven Sisters and Beachy Head.

The situation in Sussex is superb. The golf is glorious as is the countryside all around, while at no time can you claim to be isolated—except perhaps when you visit the gorse at Ashdown Forest. West Sussex is as charming an area as one could find—the golf course of the same name is delightful and reflects the quality of some splendid nearby country house hotels. While in Rye, the golfer must visit with a packed wallet in order to seduce a member in a local drinking haunt and thus secure that elusive thing—a round of golf at Rye—a more spectacular day could not be wished for.

Tempting as it is to think of Sussex as one region, there are of course two counties, East and West, and between them they possess nearly fifty courses, many of which are outstandingly good. Golfers in these parts can count themselves pretty fortunate!

Close to the coast

On a selective tour of some of the better courses on or near the Sussex coast, there seems no more logical a place to commence than in the region's south west corner, and **Goodwood**—glorious Goodwood to racegoers, though the golf course is in a similarly idyllic spot, nestling in the southern foothills of the South Downs. Some four miles north of Chichester on the A286 it is in fact located just below the racecourse and has a magnificent 18th century clubhouse.

In Goodwood itself, Goodwood Park Hotel (0243) 775537 is an excellent place to stay and very convenient for the course, but the delights of Chichester are also close at hand. Here are a variety of attractions including numerous antique shops and the excellent Festival Theatre (0243) 781312. The Dolphin and Anchor (0243) 785121 opposite the cathedral near the market cross is most welcoming (great bar snacks) and a fine place for an overnight stop is Clinch's (0243) 789915. A theatre of the open air variety can be found at Bosham as can the pleasant Millstream Hotel (0243) 573234.

Staying in the south west of the region, **Bognor Regis** is worth a visit—a flattish but attractive parkland course with several testing par fours. Note the **Royal Norfolk** (0243) 826222 in town as well as the many hotels in and around Chichester. The course at **Littlehampton** lies about seven miles east of Bognor Regis off the A259. It is the nearest one gets to a true links course in West Sussex and is always kept in first class condition. Further along the A259 at Angmering is the friendly club of **Ham Manor**, like Bognor, is a parkland course with an interesting layout of two distinct loops. It also boasts a beautiful clubhouse.

This corner of West Sussex is renowned for its tremendous hotels and after a day's golf there can be no better place to visit than Arundel where the Norfolk Arms (0903) 882101, a georgian ioaching Inn has welcomed travellers for over two hundred years. Also to be found in Arundel are many pleasant guest houses and inns, among them the Arden Hotel (0903) 882544, Bridge House and the Swan Hotel (0903) 882314. South of Arundel, lies Climping: here Bailiffscourt (0903) 723511, a 13th century replica offers superb comforts and an excellent restaurant.

As a town Worthing is somewhat overshadowed by neighbouring Brighton (though apparently it inspired Oscar Wilde). Overshadowed or not, it has one of the leading clubs in Sussex. **Worthing** has two 18 hole courses, the Lower and the Upper. Both are exceptionally fine tests of golf. There is a reasonable public course too at Worthing, Hill Barn, while for a convenient 19th hole our recommendation in town is the Chatsworth Hotel (0903) 36103.

Moving into East Sussex and the town of Brighton; probably the best course in the area, and there are a number to choose from, is the **Dyke** Golf Club, located five miles north of the town centre. One of the more difficult courses in Sussex, it is on fairly high ground and provides some splendid views.

As arguably the most famous resort in Britain, it isn't surprising to find literally hundreds of hotels. Among the best are the Sheridan Hotel with its excellent sea food restaurant and the Grand Hotel (0273) 321188. Brighton naturally has accommodation to suit everyone's taste and pockets and slightly less expensive are the Allendale Hotel (0273) 675436, the Croft Hotel and the Trouville Hotel (0273) 697384. A restaurant well worth a visit is Langans Bistro (0273) 606933.

A short distance along the ubiquitous A259 is Seaford. One of the older clubs in Sussex, the **Seaford** Golf Club at East Bletchington celebrated its centenary in 1987. A fair sprinkling of gorse and hawthorn is the feature of this outstanding downland course. The views too are quite spectacular being perched high above the town and overlooking the Channel. Also worth noting is the dormy house adjacent to the course.

As we continue to trek in an easterly direction, passing near to Beachy Head we arrive at Eastbourne where there are two fine courses—**Royal Eastbourne** and **Willingdon**. The former is situated very close to the town centre with the enviable address of Paradise Drive. Willingdon, north of the town off the A22, is quite a hilly course and very tough. Its interesting design has been likened to an oyster shell with the Clubhouse as the pearl. In the area around Bexhill, both **Cooden Beach** and **Highwoods** are well established courses. Hotels in the area are less plentiful than in Brighton but Eastbourne does offer the exceptionally fine Lansdowne (0323) 725174, while in Battle, Netherfield Place (04246) 4455 is extremely elegant. Convenient guest houses include the Bay Lodge Hotel (0323) 732515 and Mowbray Hotel (0323) 20012.

Before heading inland a quick word on **Rye**. It is unquestionably one of the greatest and most natural links courses in Britain—in many people's opinion the equal of Deal and Sandwich. However, visitors are normally permitted to play only if accompanied by a Member—hence the rather flippant remark in the second paragraph! Where might such a seduction take place then? In Rye itself, the Mermaid Inn (0797) 223065 is an historic establishment standing in a steep cobbled street, while for a cosy guest house, try the Old Vicarage (0797) 222119, Little Orchard House (0797) 223831 or the listed Jeakes House (0797) 222828. A charming inn nearby is The Hayes Arms (0797) 253142 in Northiam and the Flackley Ash in Peasmarsh is a fine country house style hotel (0797) 230651

Further Inland

If the majority of the leading courses in Sussex are located either on the coast or within a few miles of it, perhaps the most attractive courses are to be found a few more miles inland. **Piltdown**, two miles to the west of Uckfield, is a good example. Piltdown is a natural heathland course with a beautiful setting and somewhat unusually, although it shares the curiosity with Royal

Ashdown, it has no bunkers–though there are certainly enough natural hazards to set the golfer thinking.

Leaving the Piltdown Men and crossing the boundary from East to West, moving from Uckfield to Cuckfield, **Haywards Heath** stands right in the middle of Sussex. A very good heathland course this, but the pride of West Sussex is undoubtedly Pulborough–the **West Sussex Golf Club**. Along with **Royal Ashdown** and **East Sussex National** it is featured on a later page–suffice to say here that its reputation extends far beyond the bounds of East and West Sussex. Not too far from Pulborough, Brian Barnes has been the driving force behind the fine new development at **West Chiltington** and where the possibility for visitors of a weekend game is a definite bonus! Still in the West three more to note are in the north of the county, and very convenient for Gatwick, The **Ifield** Golf and Country Club, **Cottesmore** and **Copthorne**. Another popular course is found at **Cowdray Park**–very pleasant and ideal should you happen to play polo as well! There is also a very reasonable course at **Mannings Heath** (parkland golf despite the name). The newest addition to the heart of Sussex of course is the magnificent **East Sussex National**.

Places to stay? For Cowdray, the Spread Eagle (0730) 816911 at Midhurst–the hotel and restaurant are both excellent, as is the Park House Hotel (0730) 812880 and the Angel (0730) 812421 is a decidedly fine hotel overlooking Cowdray Park; for Pulborough, Little Thakeham (0903) 744416 at Storrington and Abbingworth Hall (0798) 813636 at Thakeham–sounds confusing? Fear not, both are outstanding, as is the Horsted Place (0825) 750581 which is adjacent to the 9th green on the West Course at East Sussex National. The South Lodge Hotel (0403) 891711 at Lower Beeding is centrally situated for most of the above courses.

Towards the north of East Sussex, **Dale Hill** is a much improved course with a stylish new hotel (0580) 200112 attached. Considerable investment here has resulted in both a course of challenging quality and a hotel of the highest calibre. Next comes a classic pair: **Royal Ashdown Forest** (see ahead) and **Crowborough Beacon**–two wonderfully scenic courses where the heather and gorse simply run riot. Crowborough's course is situated some 800 feet above sea level and on clear days the sea can be glimpsed from the Clubhouse. Sir Arthur Conan Doyle would have taken in this view on many occasions for he lived adjacent to the course and was Captain of the Golf Club in 1910. It really is the most beautiful of courses and has in the par three 6th one of the best short holes in Britain.

Although there may be closer places, the sixteenth century Middle House Hotel (0435) 872146 at Mayfield is recommended for a stay near Crowborough. As for Royal Ashdown three ideas here: for convenience (and considerable comfort) the Ashdown Forest Hotel (0342) 824866 which has its own fine course in addition to being adjacent to the Royal club, in Forest Row the Chequers Hotel (0342) 824394 is also popular while nearer East Grinstead is glorious Gravetye Manor (0342) 810567. East Grinstead also boasts an excellent guest house in the shape of the Cranfield Lodge Hotel (0342) 321251.

In the course of our brief trip no doubt several splendid 19th hole hotels have been omitted, but such is life! In order to fit in more restaurants, please forgive this somewhat hasty appraisal of some of the best in both counties: Le Francais at Brighton is busy while Byrons (0323) 720171 at Eastbourne is fishy. In Rusper, Ghyll Manor (0293) 871571 provides a comfortable resting place. Returning to Alfriston, we see Moonrakers (0323)

870472–try a Hot Sussex Smokie! In Herstmonceux, the Sundial (0323) 832217 is French, whilst Jevington's Hungry Monk (0323) 482178 is outstanding. In Midhurst try Mida, in Pulborough plump for Stane Street Hollow (0798) 872819 while in Poynings Au Petit Normand (079156) 346 should answer your prayers. But for a finale to end this array, try Manley's (0903) 742331 in Storrington–(if you can get a table!).

No trip to the heart of Sussex would be complete either without a visit to one of the many country houses, castles, pubs or inns. Here are a few more random thoughts for life beyond the 18th green: the White Horse Inn (0243) 59215 in Chilgrove has an excellent restaurant, while the Shepherd and Dog in Fulking and the Lickfold Inn at Lickfold are also good. Aside from the antiques of Chichester–Arundel, (an excellent castle to see here) and Petworth which offers the superb Petworth House, there is a summer of unsurpassed opera at Glyndebourne. In contrast, a totally flamboyant place to spend time is Brighton. The streets in the old town offer several bargains while the Grand Pavilion is as striking as ever. Returning to the subject of castles, Bodiam in East Sussex is not too widely known, but nonetheless quite majestic. Any thoughts for the player who had trouble in the groping gorse at Ashdown? Well, Blackboys, the pub in the village of the same name is welcoming and resuscitating as is the Roebuck in Wych Cross (0342) 823811. But perhaps the best plan is to return to Alfriston where the Smugglers and the Star are both great value. Sussex, in short, is a true delight, both on and off the fairways.

H Rountree **BULLDOG BREED** Burlington Gallery

One of the best kept secrets in West Sussex, South Lodge Hotel captures the essence of Victorian style and elegance, with an atmosphere of warmth and hospitality, hidden amongst 90 acres of beautiful gardens and parkland, with views over the rolling South Downs.

Built in 1883, this grey stoned mansion, strewn with wisteria, was once the home of the Godman family; Fredrick Ducane Godman, a keen botanists and explorer, collected hundreds of rare shrubs and trees and an outstanding variety of rhododendron and camellia, which today make the gardens at the hotel such a delight.

Dining at South Lodge is always a special occasion. In the elegant wood panelled dining room guests enjoy innovative menus created by top chef Anthony Tobin, featuring local meat, game and fish, with herbs and soft fruits grown in the hotel's own walled garden.

Each of the 39 bedrooms and suites is perfectly appointed. All are individually decorated in the true country house style, sympathetically incorporating all the modern amenities one expects to find at a first class hotel.

South Lodge is an excellent base for racegoers, with Goodwood, Lingfield, Brighton, Fontwell Park and Plumpton courses all less than 45 minutes away - a pleasant drive through picturesque countryside.

Guest staying at the hotel may enjoy a variety of activities ranging from coarse fishing to tennis, croquet or petanque. It is also an ideal location for exploring the wealth of National Trust houses and gardens that Sussex has to offer; Petworth and Arundle are within easy distance, along with the charming coastal town of Brighton, with its famous 'lanes'.

South Lodge Hotel
Lower Beeding
Near Horsham
West Sussex
Tel: (0403) 891711
Fax: (0403) 891766

West Sussex (Pulborough)

'Concentrate your mind on the match until you are dormy. Then look at the surrounding scenery and expatiate on its beauties.'
(A.J. Robertson)

In the opinion of many, West Sussex, or Pulborough as it is commonly known, is quite simply the most beautiful course in England. The setting is the South Downs and seclusion is total. Commander George Hillyard founded the Club in 1930 having conceived the idea, so the story goes, as he looked out of his bathroom window one day while taking his morning shave! (His house, it should be explained, overlooked the present layout). The course was designed by Sir Guy Campbell and Major C.K. Hutchinson and opened for play in October 1930.

In a similar vein to Woodhall Spa in Lincolnshire, Pulborough has often been described as something of an oasis, the surrounding countryside being predominantly meadow and marshland with the course lying on sandy soil and heather running throughout. Heather naturally adds charm to any golf course but it is perhaps the magnificent spread of pines, oaks and silver birch trees that are most striking at Pulborough.

Mr. G.R. Martindale is the present **Club Secretary**; he may be contacted via the **West Sussex Golf Club, Pulborough, West Sussex RH20 2EN, tel: (0798) 872563.** Visitors are welcome, but strictly by appointment only; the same applies to golfing Societies. It should also be noted that three ball and four ball matches are not generally permitted—singles and foursomes being preferred. The only specific restrictions on times visitors can play are before 9.30am (throughout the week), on Fridays and at weekends. The green fees for 1994 were set at £30 for a single round or £40 for a day ticket. One final introduction: **Tim Packham** is the Club's **professional**, and he may be reached by telephone on **(0798) 872426.**

While Pulborough may enjoy a gloriously peaceful setting situated right in the heart of the Sussex countryside, it could hardly be described as remote and is easily accessible from all directions. The Club's precise location is about two miles east of Pulborough just off the A283 road to Storrington. The A283 links Pulborough to the outskirts of Brighton on the south coast and to Milford (near Guildford) to the north. For those approaching from westerly directions the A272 from Winchester is likely to help—it joins the A283 at Petworth approximately five miles from Pulborough. Motoring from the London area the quickest route is probably to take the M23 towards Gatwick joining the A264 at Crawley and travelling through Horsham. The A264 merges into the A29 near Billingshurst which in turn joins with Pulborough.

One of the features of Pulborough is its conspicuous absence of a par five beyond the first hole—a hole which in any event becomes a four when played from the tees of the day. At 6221 yards, (SSS 70) the par of 68 is a difficult one to match. With none of the par fours being overly short there aren't any really obvious birdie opportunities. Perhaps the best known hole on the course is the par three 6th; measuring 220 yards it requires an exceptionally accurate tee shot across water to a small green that has an out-of-bounds and tall trees directly behind it. Henry Longhurst, a great admirer of Pulborough, very aptly said of the 6th, 'If ever there was an all or nothing hole, this is it.' Immediately after the potential disaster of the 6th, the 7th requires a long uphill drive to carry over some thick heather and scrub not to mention an enormous sand bunker. With holes of such a nature and quality as the 6th and 7th it isn't unrealistic to draw a comparison between this corner of Pulborough and Pine Valley in New Jersey. It is a brave comparison (and an enormous compliment) because the North American course is generally considered to be the finest and perhaps most naturally beautiful inland course in the world.

The 6th and 7th are not the only outstanding holes, mind you: the 4th, 5th and 8th are equally memorable while on the back nine perhaps the 10th, 13th, 16th and 17th are worthy of special praise (even expatiation!) As for its 19th, West Sussex has a very comfortable Clubhouse offering full catering facilities including two bars. A jacket and tie should be worn in all public rooms.

Henry Longhurst is only one of a number of celebrated admirers of Pulborough and the late Bobby Locke, four times Open Champion, considered it his favourite English course. While no major professional tournament has been played over the course (again there is a parallel to be drawn with Pine Valley) the Club has hosted several national amateur championships—both men's and ladies.

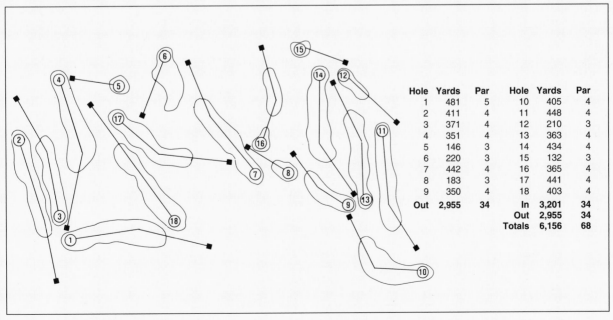

Hole	Yards	Par	Hole	Yards	Par
1	481	5	10	405	4
2	411	4	11	448	4
3	371	4	12	210	3
4	351	4	13	363	4
5	146	3	14	434	4
6	220	3	15	132	3
7	442	4	16	365	4
8	183	3	17	441	4
9	350	4	18	403	4
Out	**2,955**	**34**	**In**	**3,201**	**34**
			Out	**2,955**	**34**
			Totals	**6,156**	**68**

Occupying a majestic setting in twenty three acres of landscaped Sussex countryside, Horsted Place offers an enviable combination of modern facilities in a delightful and elegant form. Individually decorated suites, a magnificently appointed main dining room, two private Dining Rooms, executive meeting and conference facilities, a heated indoor swimming pool, a tennis court and helicopter landing area are all designed to more than cater for the needs of the modern traveller. Rated as one of the best hotels in the British Isles by the Guide Michelin and also renowned for its culinary prowess, Horsted Place provides unequalled standards of service and facilities for visitors, golfers and the business community. Over one thousand acres of rolling countryside surrounding Horsted Place have now been transformed into two golf courses which have quickly become established as two of Britain's finest inland challenges. If quality is the cornerstone of excellence, East Sussex National sets a standard that will not easily be equalled. American course designer Robert E. Cupp, has coaxed out of the beautiful Sussex countryside two layouts that offer a stern competitive challenge, as well as some memorably beautiful holes. The East course features gallery mounding for the benefit of spectators, the area of the eighteenth green alone being able to accommodate up to 30,000 spectators. The West course, meanwhile, is like the East over 7,000 yards from the gold tees and features nine holes where water comes perilously into play. The special qualities of the courses have been recognised by top players on the PGA European Tour resulting in the East course being chosen to host the 1993-1996 European Open. The momentous challenge posed by both courses is made slightly less awesome by the provision of a three hole Teaching Academy and fabulous practice facilities.

Visitors to East Sussex National and Horsted Place are immediately struck by both a glorious setting and an attention to detail that result in an ambience of all-round excellence. Every visit is guaranteed to become a memorable encounter-contact the numbers below for your own taste of a unique leisure experience.

East Sussex National Golf Club and Horsted
Place
Little Horsted
Uckfield
East Sussex, TN22 5TS
Tel: (hotel) (0825) 750581
Tel: (golf) (0825) 880088
Fax: (hotel) (0825) 750459
Fax: (golf) (0825) 880066

East Sussex National

Move over Sunningdale, Wentworth and Walton Heath! These three great championship venues, all situated in the magnificent heathland belt of Surrey and Berkshire, are now having to make room for a newcomer from the heart of rural Sussex.

So what are we getting so excited about? East Sussex National has two great golf courses, the East and West which were officially opened for play as recently as April 1990. Both were designed by the American, Robert E Cupp, formerly Jack Nicklaus' senior designer. For the first time in Great Britain, bent grasses were used throughout from tee to green and the instant result was golf course conditioning of a type never witnessed before in this country.

Both courses measure in excess of 7000 yards from their Championship tees and are similarly challenging but quite different in appearance. The East Course is the 'stadium' course and was specifically designed with a view to its staging big events, hence the gentle 'gallery mounding' very evident around the 15th and 18th greens. The West Course is more intimate than the East. The landscape rises and falls quite sharply in parts. The surrounding woodland is more dense but because of the climbs there are many spectacular views over the South Downs.

East Sussex National was first conceived in the mid 1980s when a Canadian entrepreneur purchased Horsted Place, an elegant Victorian manor house which he immediately converted into one of Britain's leading country house hotels. Various parcels of adjoining land were also acquired which, when pieced together, totalled a massive 1100 acres of prime Sussex countryside. Construction began in May 1988 on the two 18 hole Championship courses and, only 23 months later, both opened for play.

Aside from the golf courses, and of course Horsted Place, East Sussex National boasts superb golf practice facilities including three full length academy holes, one of the best golf shops in the country and a new 27,000 sq ft clubhouse.

Individuals, groups and corporate societies are welcome at East Sussex. Visitors will invariably play the East Course as the West is reserved for members. Bookings can be made by telephoning **Reservations** on **(0825) 880088.** The visitors' green fee in 1994 was £60 for 18 holes and £80 per day. Seasonal discounted rates

including lunch/brunch are also available. All membership and corporate enquiries can be dealt with through the Sales Office on the above number. The address for written correspondence is **East Sussex National Golf Club, Little Horsted, Uckfield, East Sussex TN22 5ES.**

There are many outstanding holes on the **East Course** but perhaps the par fives are especially memorable. Three of the four, the 7th, 10th and 14th are as good a trio as one is likely to find on any course, anywhere. Of these, only the 10th is realistically reachable in two shots and then only after a brave downhill second is successfully hit over water—a hole not too dissimilar to the 15th at Augusta. There is also a great finish to the East Course, with the par four 17th being perhaps the best hole on either course.

Although the challenge isn't any greater on the **West Course**, in most people's minds it has the greater number of 'pretty' holes; in fact, 'provocatively spectacular' might be the description of some. Anyone wishing to put together a 'dream nine holes' could do worse than select the 1st, 2nd, 3rd, 9th, 10th, 12th, 13th, 14th and 18th on the East Sussex National West Course. This collection would provide two outstanding short holes, on both of which the tee shot must flirt with water; a pair of genuine par fives and five two-shot holes ranging from a drive and a short iron (the dog-leg 1st) to a truly intimidating stroke one hole (the monstrous 14th). And what a dramatic finale the 18th provides! In his course notes, architect Robert Cupp gives an interesting commentary on the closing holes of the West Course. Having metaphorically walked on to the back tee at the 18th he holds his breath and surveys the view ahead:

'The player has been restricted at fourteen, tempted at fifteen, devilled at sixteen and exhausted at seventeen. Now, he stands on the elevated tee, looking across a deep chasm to a fairway lined right and left by giant oaks, and a green guarded by huge bunkers and the Clubhouse beyond. The word here is "test". The reaction in tournament conditions is clammy hands'.

In 1993 East Sussex National gained its first major event - no lesser a tournament than the European Open. It is clearly a testimony to the quality of the club's facilities that it has acquired such a prestigious championship so soon.

West Course

Hole	Yards	Par	Hole	Yards	Par
1	363	4	10	404	4
2	517	5	11	423	4
3	136	3	12	520	5
4	354	4	13	184	3
5	504	5	14	450	4
6	396	4	15	365	4
7	192	3	16	117	3
8	408	4	17	566	5
9	392	4	18	365	4
Out	**3,262**	**36**	**In**	**3,394**	**36**
			Out	**3,262**	**36**
			Totals	**6,565**	**72**

69

A French style farmhouse, thoughtfully converted over the years, lies at the centre of the Club and provides all the facilities of a luxuriously appointed country club offering the latest in sport and fitness technology, with an emphasis on corporate and family fitness. Golf, swimming, tennis, squash, a spa and sauna are all on offer at this superb club whose tranquil surroundings belie the fact that it is just minutes from Gatwick Airport and Crawley.

There are two 18 hole golf courses nestling in 247 acres of beautiful Sussex countryside. The fairways wind through rhododendrons, silver birch and chestnut trees and the colours change from dramatic purple to deep gold in autumn. The lakes add that touch of difficulty to the courses and are often covered in early morning mist, adding extra beauty to this peaceful setting.

The clubhouse offers accommodation with en suite facilities and all the rooms have patios and balconies overlooking the golf course. There are also bars, a coffee shop and restaurant within the club.

For corporate clients, the Buchan Suite has been designed to cater for seminars, corporate golf days, meetings and private functions. For convenience, there is a private entrance, bar, lounge and dining facilities. The Buchan Suite can accommodate up to 64 delegates.

The Cottesmore Country Club
Buchan Hill
Pease Pottage
Crawley
West Sussex
RH11 9AT
Tel: (0293) 528256/529196
Fax: (0293) 522819

Royal Ashdown Forest

Although it is now less than an hour's drive from the frantic chaos of Greater London, Ashdown Forest is a place of great beauty, charm and tranquillity. And so it should be, for it was here, somewhere deep in this secluded forest of pine and silver birch, that the most famous of all 'Golden Bears', Winnie The Pooh pursued his never ending quest for honey. Such is the setting for one of Britain's most fortunate golf clubs.

In 1988 Royal Ashdown Forest celebrated its centenary. It was on Christmas Eve just over a hundred years ago that the Reverend A.T. Scott teed up his ball and struck the very first shot. The course has changed little over the years, a fact which clearly speaks volumes for the original layout. The Club acquired the title Royal during Queen Victoria's reign and long before the turn of the century had established itself as one of the finest tests of golf in southern England.

Many great players have been associated with Royal Ashdown Forest over the years. The Cantelupe Club, the associate club connected to Royal Ashdown, included Abe Mitchell and Alf Padgham among its ranks and several noted amateurs have improved their technique on this most challenging course.

Casual visitors are welcomed at Royal Ashdown—rather more so, it must be said, than at some of the south east's leading courses. A recognised club handicap is, however, a requirement and it is normally advisable to telephone the Club before finalising any plans. Not surprisingly the course is very popular in the summer months.

The **Club Secretary, David Scrivens,** can be contacted via the **Royal Ashdown Forest Golf Club, Forest Row, East Sussex RH18 5LR tel: (0342) 822018.** Those wishing to organise a Society meeting should write to Mr. Scrivens at the above address. Societies can normally be accommodated during the week, Tuesday being an exception. The green fees for 1994 were set at £28 per round (£36 per day) for weekdays with £34 per round (£40 per day) payable at weekends and on Bank Holidays. Visitors should note that singles and foursomes are preferred. The club **professional** is **Martyn Landsborough** who took over in 1990 from Alf Padgham's nephew Hector, who had been the professional for over 40 years. Martyn can be reached on **(0342) 822247.**

The Club is located within Ashdown Forest, approximately 4 miles south of East Grinstead. Motoring from London and the North the A22 is by far the most direct route. This can be joined from the M25 at Junction 6. The A22 should be followed for some 4 miles beyond East Grinstead as far as Forest Row. There one should take the B2110 Hartfield road turning right after a quarter of a mile on to Chapel Lane where the Club can be found. Approaching from the South the A22 can be joined from a number of roads north of Eastbourne.

The generally held view is that Royal Ashdown Forest is a particularly difficult course. On several holes a lengthy tee shot will be required in order to find the safety of the fairway. The ever present stream and the considerable scattering of gorse and heather create a multitude of problems for the wayward golfer—and as if they were not enough, on several of the holes the fairway is exceptionally narrow and that beautiful forest will gratefully accept the result of a slice or a hook. So the message is, hit it hard and hit it straight!

Despite the variety of hazards, of all the country's leading courses Royal Ashdown Forest must surely be unique in not possessing a single bunker. Bernard Darwin is doubtless not the only golfer who failed to discover this fact until the conclusion of his game; as he put it, 'It is only at the end of a round that we realise with a pleasurable shock that there is not a single hideous rampart or so much as a pot bunker.' The Club was prevented long ago by the Forestry Commission, or the then equivalent, from creating bunkers and their absence now forms part of the character and charm of the course; furthermore, the undulating nature of the landscape produces some truly magnificent views over the Forest and beyond.

The attractive Clubhouse offers a very high standard of catering. A light lunch, such as a ploughman's, can be obtained whilst a full four course meal can also be arranged. During the months of November and December a full English breakfast is available—a welcome facility which many clubs would do well to copy: golfers, like the Forest's most famous inhabitant are hungry animals and some are more than quick to claim that the missed three footer is a result of a missed breakfast!

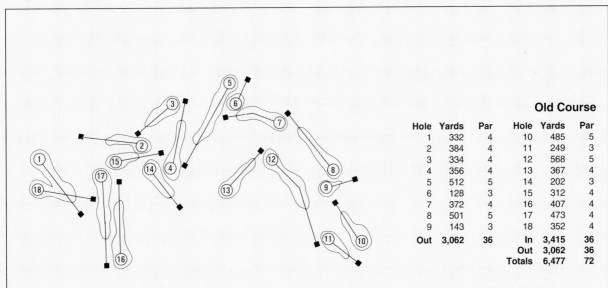

Old Course

Hole	Yards	Par	Hole	Yards	Par
1	332	4	10	485	5
2	384	4	11	249	3
3	334	4	12	568	5
4	356	4	13	367	4
5	512	5	14	202	3
6	128	3	15	312	4
7	372	4	16	407	4
8	501	5	17	473	4
9	143	3	18	352	4
Out	**3,062**	**36**	**In**	**3,415**	**36**
			Out	**3,062**	**36**
			Totals	**6,477**	**72**

Key

*To avoid disappointment
it is advisable to telephone
in advance*

****Visitors welcome at most times*
***Visitors usually allowed on
weekdays only*
**Visitors not normally permitted
(Mon, Wed) No visitors
on specified days*

Approximate Green Fees
A £30 plus
B £20 to £30
C £15 to £25
D £10 to £20
E under £10
F Greens fees on application

Restrictions
G Guests only
H Handicap certificate required
H (24) Handicap of 24 or less
L Letter of introduction required
M Visitor must be a member of
another recognised club.

WEST SUSSEX

Avisford Park Hotel & G.C.
(0243) 554611
Walberton, Arundel
(9)3009 yards/***/D

Bognor Regis G.C.
(0243) 865867
Downview Road, Felpham,
Bognor Regis
(18)6238 yards/**/B/H

Chichester Golf Centre
(0243) 533833
Hoe Farm, Hunston
(18)6177 yards/***/C

Copthorne G.C.
(0342) 712508
Bovers Arms Road, Copthorne
(18)6550 yards/**/B

Cottesmore G.C.
(0293) 528256
Buchan Hill, Pease Pottage, Crawley
(18)6113 yards/***/A
(18)5499 yards/***/B

Cowdray Park G.C.
(073 081) 3599
Midhurst
(18)6212 yards/***/B

Effingham Park G.C.
(0342) 716528
West Park Road, Copthorne
(9)1749 yards/***/D

Foxbridge G.C
(0403) 753303
Foxbridge Lane, Plaistow
(9)3015 yards/***/F/G

Gatwick Manor G.C.
(0293) 538587
Lowfield Heath
(9)2492 yards/***/F

Goodwood G.C.
(0243) 774968
Goodwood, Chichester
(18)6401 yards/***/B/H

Goodwood Park G.& C.C.
(0243) 775987
(18)6530 yards/***/D

Ham Manor G.C.
(0903) 783288
Angmering
(18)6243 yards/***/B/H

Haywards Heath G.C.
(0444) 414457
High Beech Lane, Haywards Heath
(18)6206 yards/***/B/H

Hill Barn G.C.
(0903) 237301
Hill Barn Lane, Worthing
(18)6224 yards/***/D

Horsham Golf Park
(0403) 271525
Worthing Road, Horsham
(9)2016 yards/***/E

Ifield G.& C.C.
(0293) 520222
Rusper Road, Ifield, Crawley
(18)6314 yards/**/B

Littlehampton G.C.
(0903) 717170
Rope Walk, Riverside, Littlehampton
(18)6244 yards/***/B

Mannings Heath G.C.
(0403) 210228
Goldings Lane, Mannings Heath
(18)6404 yards/**/C/H

Osiers Farm G.C.
(0798) 44097
Osiers Farm, Petworth
(9)2449 yards/***/E

Paxhill Park G.C.
(0444) 484467
Lindfield, Haywards Heath
(18) 6196 yards/***/D

Pease Pottage G.C.
(0293) 521706
Horsham Road, Pease Pottage,
Crawley
(9)3511 yards/***/E

Pycombe G.C.
(0273) 845372
Pycombe, Brighton
(18) 6234 yards/***/C

Selsey G.C.
(0243) 602203
Golf Links Lane, Selsey, Chichester
(9)5932 yards/***/D

Singing Hills G.C.
(0273) 835353
Albourne, Brighton
(9)2826 yards/***/B/H
(9)3253 yards/***/B/H
(9)3348 yards/***/B/H

Slinfold Park G.C.
(0403) 791154
Stane Street, Slinford, Horsham
(18)6450 yards/***/B

Tilgate Forest G.C.
(0293) 530103
Titmus Drive, Tilgate, Crawley
(18)6359 yards/***/D

West Chiltington G.C.
(0798) 813574
Broadford Bridge Road,
W.Chiltington

(18)6359 yards/***/D

West Sussex G.C.
(0798) 872563
Pulborough
(18)6221 yards/**/F/H/L

Worthing G.C.
(0903) 260801
Links Road, Worthing
(18)6530 yards/***/A/H/L
(18)5243 yards/***/A/H/L

EAST SUSSEX

Aldershaw G.C.
(0424) 870898
Kent Street, Sedlescombe
(18) 6218 yards/**/F/H/G

Ashdown Forest Hotel G.C.
(0342) 824866
Chapel Lane, Forest Row
(18)5510 yards/***/F

Beauport Park G.C.
(0424) 852977
St Leonards-on-Sea
(18)6033 yards/***/F

Brighton and Hove G.C.
(0273) 556482
Dyke Road, Brighton
(9)5722 yards/***/D

Cooden Beach G.C.
(0424) 842040
Cooden Sea Road, Cooden
(18)6450 yards/***/B

Crowborough Beacon G.C.
(0892) 661511
Beacon Road, Crowborough
(18)6318 yards/**/B/H/L

Dale Hill G.C.
(0580) 200112
Ticehurst, Wadhurst
(18)6150 yards/***/C

Dewlands Manor G.C.
(0892) 852266
Cottage Hill, Rotherfield
(9)3186 yards/***/B

Dyke G.C.
(0273) 857296
Dyke Road, Brighton
(18)6611 yards/***(Sun)/C

Eastbourne Downs G.C.
(0323) 720827
East Dean Road, Eastbourne
(18)6635 yards/***/D

Eastbourne Golfing Park
(0323) 520400
Lottbridge Drove, Eastbourne
(9)5046 yards/***/D

East Brighton G.C.
(0273) 604838
Roedean Road, Brighton
(18)6436 yards/***/C

East Sussex National G.C.
(0825) 880088
Little Horsted, Uckfield
(18)7138 yards/***/A
(18)7154 yards/*/F

Hastings G.C.
(0424) 852981
Battle Road, St Leonards-on-Sea
(18)6248 yards/***/F

Highwoods G.C.
(0424) 212625
Ellerslie Lane, Bexhill-on-Sea
(18)6218 yards/***/C

Hollingbury G.C.
(0273) 552010
Ditchling Road, Brighton
(18)6502 yards/***/D

Holtye G.C.
(0342) 850635
Holtye, Edenbridge
(9)5325 yards/***/C

Horam Park G.C.
(04353) 3477
Chiddingly Road, Horam, Heathfield
(9)5864/***/E

Lewes G.C.
(0273) 473245
Chapel Hill, Lewes
(18)5951 yards/**/D

Nevill G.C.
(0892) 525818
Benhall Mill Road, Tunbridge Wells
(18)6336 yards/**/A/H

Peacehaven G.C.
(0273) 514049
Brighton Road, Newhaven
(9)5305 yards/***/C/H

Piltdown G.C.
(0825) 722033
Piltdown, Uckfield
(18)6070 yards/**/B/H/L

Royal Ashdown Forest G.C.
(0342) 822018
Chapel Lane, Forest Row
(18)6439 yards/**/B/H
(18)5549 yards/**/B/H

Royal Eastbourne G.C.
(0323) 729738
Paradise Drive, Eastbourne
(18)6109 yards/***/C/M
(9)2147 yards/***/D

Rye G.C.
(0797) 225241
Camber, Rye
(18)6317 yards/*/F

Seaford G.C.
(0323) 892442
East Blatchington, Seaford
(18)6233 yards/**/F

Seaford Head G.C.
(0323) 890139
Southdown Road, Seaford
(18)5812 yards/***/D

Waterhall G.C.
(0273) 508658
Devil's Dyke Road, Brighton
(18)5775 yards/***/D

Wellhurst G.& C.C
(0435) 863636
North Street, Hellingly
(18)5717 yards/***/C

West Hove G.C.
(0273) 413411
Church Farm, Hangleton, Hove
(18)6252 yards/**/C

Willingdon G.C.
(0323) 410983
Southdown Road, Eastbourne
(18)6049 yards/**/B

Artist: **Julian Barrow ROYAL ST GEORGE'S** *Courtesy of:* **Burlington Gallery**

From the mysterious and desolate lands of Romney Marsh to the famous White Cliffs of Dover. From the rich orchards of the Garden of England to the outskirts of Greater London; a county of great contrast.. From the windswept links of Sandwich and Deal to the secluded parks of Belmont and Knole; a county of great contrast.

Kent's reputation as one of the country's greatest golfing counties has been built around a three mile stretch of links land lying midway between St Margaret's Bay and Pegwell Bay. Within this short distance lie three Open Championship courses: **Prince's** (1932), **Royal Cinque Ports** (1909 and 1920) and **Royal St George's.** Kent has a few other fine links courses but the golfer who sticks hard to the coast will be missing out on some of the most enjoyable inland golf southern England has to offer.

Golfing Inland

In common with each of the counties that borders Greater London, many of Kent's courses are gradually finding themselves more in London than in Kent. When the Blackheath golfers left their famous Common and set up base at Eltham they were doubtless surrounded by the green fields of Kent. Even Charles Darwin's village of Orpington is now feeling the pinch but happily the **West Kent** Golf Club and nearby **Lullingstone Park** provide pleasant retreats.

Enough grousing! The ancient town of Sevenoaks is categorically in Kent and a very fortunate place too with **Wildernesse** Golf Club to the north and **Knole Park** to the south. The former is rated one of the finest inland courses in the county. With narrow fairways and quite thickly wooded, it is also one of the toughest. Knole Park is very pleasant too and is one of several Kentish courses that enjoy stately surroundings, being laid out in the handsome deer park of Lord Sackville. Both Wildernesse and Knole suffered during the great hurricane of October '87 but then so did many courses in southern England.

In the south west of the county, Tunbridge Wells is a very pretty, if congested, old town. **Nevil** Golf Club is nearby and there are 36 holes at the **Edenbridge** Golf and Country Club, but the most exciting developments in this area are the new **Hever** Golf Club which is located adjacent to the famous castle and the Anglo-Japanese creation at **Moatlands** at Brenchley.

For a stopover in Sevenoaks the Royal Oak Hotel (0732) 451109 is comfortable, as is the Bull Hotel (0732) 885522 in nearby Wrotham Heath. A number of fine restaurants are also close at hand. They include La Cremaillere (0732) 851489 in Hadlow (french cooking), the Gate Inn in Hildenborough (good seafood) and the outstanding Thackeray's House (0892) 511921 in Tunbridge Wells. If you require a place to stay in Tunbridge Wells, The Royal Wells (0892) 511188 is particularly good value with a fine restaurant, and for a second place to eat try Eglantine's (0892) 524957. Finally in the south western corner of the county there is an outstanding pub—great for lunches—at Speldhurst, namely the 13th century George and Dragon.

To the north of the county, both **Mid Kent's** downland course at Gravesend and **Rochester and Cobham Park** are handy for those travelling along the A2 although neither is outstanding. Further along this road is the attractive town of Faversham and south of the town off the A251 is Belmont Park, the estate of Lord Harris and the home of **Faversham** Golf Club. Here golf is played in the most tranquil of settings and can be particularly delightful in autumn when the fairways abound with countless strolling pheasants.

Beyond the 18th green a few ideas emerge for a 19th hole. In Shorne, the Inn On The Lake (047482) 3333 is a most pleasant place to stay. An alternative for pub lovers is the Dickensian Leather Bottle (0474) 814327 in Cobham which also has some comfortable bedrooms. More expensive accommodation is located near Ash Green in the alarmingly named village of Fawkham where the Brands Hatch Place (0474) 872239 offers tremendous comfort and a good restaurant. Two pubs to note in the area are the Golden Eagle in Burham and the particularly pleasant and aptly named Little Gem in Aylesford. Close to Ash Green and Brands Hatch golfers might wish to note the new **London** Golf Club, a 36 hole multi-million pound venture including a Jack Nicklaus-designed championship course. It should be emphasised, however, that this is a very private club and visitors can only play as guests of a member. Back towards Faversham, two fine places to rest the spikes are Trowley House (0795) 539168 at Sheldwich and The Tanyard Hotel (0622) 744705 at Boughton Monchelsea. If it's just quality fare that is required, then Faversham itself houses the extremely popular Reads (0795) 535344.

Leaving Faversham, famous pheasants and all, we must make a pilgrimage. The **Canterbury** Golf Club, situated to the east of the beautiful cathedral city along the A27 is well worth a visit. Surprisingly undulating, it is a first class parkland course—one of the best in the county. South of Canterbury (via A2 and A260) at Barham is the **Broome Park** Golf and Country Club, set in the grounds of yet another famous country house—this time a beautiful 300 year old mansion, the former home of Lord Kitchener. It too is a very pleasant parkland course and quite lengthy. Whether it's the proliferation of nearby golf courses (Sandwich and Deal are just 15 miles away) or the cathedral, or even the glorious Kent countryside that attracts most, Canterbury deserves more than a short visit. Perhaps the leading hotel which also houses a commendable restaurant is the County (0227) 766266. The House of Agnes Hotel (0227) 472185 can also be recommended in Canterbury along with the Yorke Lodge Guest House (0227) 451243, the Abbot's Barton Hotel (0227) 760341 and just outside the city, Howfield Manor (0227) 738294 at Chartham Hatch is a charming small country house hotel. Ersham Lodge (0227) 463174 and Magnolia House (0227) 765121 also receive many favourable reports. The aforementioned glorious countryside is riddled with village pubs: two of note are the Duck Inn at Petts Bottom and the White Horse at Chilham Castle.

Maidstone may not have the appeal of Canterbury but to the south east of this busy commuter town is one of England's most attractive 'pay and play' golf courses, **Leeds Castle.** The castle itself was described by Lord Conway as the most beautiful in the world and the setting really is quite idyllic. There are nine very individual holes and as it's a public course (like Lullingstone Park, mentioned above, and Cobtree Manor Park on the Chatham Road) there are no general restrictions on times of play (although it can naturally get very busy). Another fairly recent golfing addition to the area is **Tudor Park** near Bearsted. Like Broome Park it is part of a country club. The golf course was designed by Donald Steel and is especially popular with golfing societies.

The golf course at **Ashford** is pretty much in the middle of the county, and is strongly worth inspecting. Ashford is a heathland type course, which in itself is fairly unique to Kent and where visitors are always made to feel welcome. We're now in the heart of the Kent Downs and a variety of fine establishments beckon. Eastwell Manor (0233) 635751 takes pride of place. Elegant and relaxing with a splendid restaurant—in fact outstanding in every way. In Wye, the Wife of Bath (0233) 812540 is a tremendous restaurant. An ideal tavern is the Compasses at Side Street and for an inn with good value accommodation the Chequers Inn (0233) 770217 at Smarden is recommended.

Back to the fairways and a word for **Cranbrook,** a very pleasant and greatly improved parkland course. This was the scene of Bing Crosby's last round in England. Apparently he was close to purchasing the course before his untimely death in Spain. Also in Cranbrook is one of Kent's most popular hotels, the Kennel Holt Hotel (0580) 712032—excellent for dinner and equally convenient for **Lamberhurst** Golf Club.

The final inland course demanding inspection is to be found at Biddenden, the Nick Faldo-Steve Smyers designed **Chart Hills** which opened for play in late 1993. We view the course on a later page.

Around the Coast

Switching from the rich countryside of Kent we now visit the coast. **Littlestone** is the first port of call, and the contrast is a stark one. Situated on the edge of the flatlands of Romney Marsh, it enjoys a very remote setting. Littlestone is a splendid links and an Open Championship qualifying course, which doesn't deserve to be overshadowed by Kent's more illustrious trio further along the coast. Littlestone's best holes are saved for near the end of the round—the par four 16th and par three 17th typify all that's best (and frightening!) about links golf.

Not too far from Littlestone is the town of Hythe where the large Hythe Imperial (0303) 267441 is a fine base, especially as there are 9 holes in the 'back garden'! North of Sandwich is the **North Foreland** Club at Broadstairs, also an Open qualifying course, although its

27 holes are more strictly clifftop than links in nature. The Royal Albion Hotel in Broadstairs is another fine place to stay, as is the intimate Rothsay Hotel. To the south of Deal is **Walmer and Kingsdown**, a downland course providing far reaching-views.

Perhaps not surprisingly, where there is one great golf links there is often another nearby: Troon, Turnberry and Prestwick in Ayrshire; Birkdale, Hillside and Formby in Lancashire. Kent's famous three, **Royal St George's, Royal Cinque Ports** and **Prince's** are all featured ahead.

Despite the great quality of golf on offer there aren't too many places along the famous three mile stretch where one can put the feet up (or the golf clubs for that matter). Anyway, in Sandwich the Bell Hotel (0304) 613388 is very comfortable and convenient: its quayside setting is also handy for the Fisherman's Wharf Restaurant (0304) 613636. St Crispin's Inn (0304) 612081 is a charming alternative. Two pubs to note in Sandwich are the King's Arms (0304) 617330 and the Fleur-de-Lis (0304) 611131. In Deal, the Black Horse Hotel (0304) 374074 and Sutherland House (0304) 362853 are popular golfing haunts. St Margaret's Bay, located on National Trust land is worth a look and the Cliffe Tavern (0304) 852749 nearby is a good place to wet one's whistle and stay if you wish. The Guildford House Hotel (0304) 375015 located on Beach Street in Deal, where there is a wider choice of accommodation is another ideal 19th hole if you're playing the famous courses nearby. As a final tip it might be a good idea to take the car on a short drive to Westcliffe, where Wallett's Court (0304) 852424 is supremely welcoming (despite its name!) As we conclude our trip another thought emerges. . . . Hardelot, Le Touquet... Why, we could nip down to Lydd where an aeroplane can whisk us off to Le Touquet...quicker than we can drive back to London. Vive le golf!

Artist: **F P Hopkins CROOKHAM** _Courtesy of:_ **Burlington Gallery**

Royal Cinque Ports (Deal)

In the year 55 B.C. Julius Caesar landed on the coast near Deal. In 1920, an American invader by the name of Walter Hagen came to Deal to play in his first Open Championship. Both came, both saw, but neither conquered. In fact both returned from whence they came, tails firmly between legs–small wonder Deal is often considered the toughest of all England's Championship links!

The Royal Cinque Ports Golf Club was founded in February 1892 by Major General J.M.Graham whilst at lunch in Deal's Black Horse Hotel. The 18 hole course was opened in 1895 and has required very few alterations during its distinguished history.

Visitors with official handicaps (maximum 20) are welcome to play the famous links, although prior booking with the club is essential. The **Secretary, Mr Hammond**, may be contacted at the **Royal Cinque Ports Golf Club, Golf Road, Deal, Kent CT14 6RF. tel (0304) 374007. Andrew Reynolds** is the **professional** and he can be reached on **(0304) 374170.** As with a number of the more traditional Clubs, three and four ball matches have no standing on the course; indeed they are rarely permitted and only by arrangement with the Secretary.

In 1994 a green fee of £45 entitles the visitor to a full day's golf, and persons arriving after 1 pm can obtain a £10 reduction. The Club also offers a twilight green fee on Mondays, Tuesdays and Thursdays where there is a 50% reduction for those teeing off after 5pm. An early start in winter with a later start in summer would appear to be the best bets. Sadly, weekend bookings are seldom possible.

The golf course is situated approximately one mile north of the town. Probably the best route from London is to take the A2/M2 as far as Dover. There, one should pick up the A258 which takes you to Deal. Also worth noting is Deal Railway Station which is on the northern side of the town near the pier.

Very often it is Mother Nature who provides the greatest challenge at Deal. Strong winds billowing in from the sea, capable of changing direction several times during a round, can turn what appear to be modest holes into monsters. The course measures 6407 yards from the medal tees (par 70) with the Championship tees extending the course to some 6785 yards (par 72). From the ladies tees the course measures 5686 yards, (par 74). The outward nine is generally considered the easier half–Michael Bonallack turned in 31 during his record ama-

teur score of 65 (a record which has stood for more than a quarter of a century). Certainly the back nine is longer and Deal is renowned for its tough finish, the classic par five 16th perhaps being the most difficult (and best) hole on the course. The fairways are humpy and hillocky and well bunkered. The rough is often thick and many of the greens stand on natural plateaux. On a clear day there are some magnificent views across the course towards the English Channel and to the distant white cliffs beyond Pegwell Bay.

Two Open Championships have been held at Deal, in 1909 and in 1920. The 1909 Championship was won by the Englishman John H. Taylor, his fourth victory in the event. The 1920 Open has already been referred to—the luckless Hagen in fact finished fifty third in a field of fifty four. Also entitled to feel somewhat peeved that year was Abe Mitchell who allowed George Duncan to come from thirteen strokes behind him to snatch victory. Plans to stage a third Championship at Deal in 1949 had to be abandoned when extensive flooding led to a temporary closure of the course.

The Royal Cinque Ports Club has also twice been selected to host the Amateur Championship, firstly in 1923 and again in 1982. In 1992 both the English Amateur and the St Andrews Trophy were staged at Deal. One of the annual highlights on the Club's calendar is the Halford Hewitt Challenge Cup. An Old Boys competition, usually played in April, the Halford Hewitt is thought to be the largest Amateur tournament in the world—over 600 players participate.

The Members of Royal Cinque Ports are doubly fortunate. Blessed with such a fine course, they also possess an excellent Clubhouse. The facilities are first class and both the early starter and our twilight golfer will be glad to find that hot and cold snacks are normally available at all times. With prior notice both breakfast and dinner can be arranged. For those just wanting a quick drink in between rounds (a stiff one may be in order!) a bar is provided.

It would not of course be fair, either to the Romans or Mr Hagen, to leave Deal without recording that both did eventually achieve their ambitions. The Romans returned a century later and conquered the Brits, and as for Walter, he didn't have to wait quite so long, for in 1922 he won the first of four Open Championships, none of which though, alas, was at Deal.

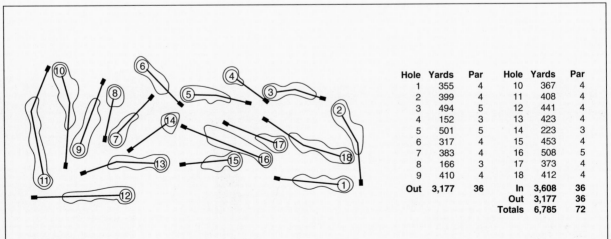

Hole	Yards	Par	Hole	Yards	Par
1	355	4	10	367	4
2	399	4	11	408	4
3	494	5	12	441	4
4	152	3	13	423	4
5	501	5	14	223	3
6	317	4	15	453	4
7	383	4	16	508	5
8	166	3	17	373	4
9	410	4	18	412	4
Out	**3,177**	**36**	**In**	**3,608**	**36**
			Out	**3,177**	**36**
			Totals	**6,785**	**72**

Prince's

One of the highlights of the magnificent 1993 Open Championship at Royal St George's was the delightful speech made at the prize presentation by the legendary American golfer, Gene Sarazen. For many years Sarazen, now in his nineties, has performed the traditional honour of hitting the first tee shot at the US Masters tournament and it is always a moving occasion. Sarazen is one of golf's greatest characters and certainly one of the finest players ever to have graced the sport. This popular American is one of only four golfers in history (Nicklaus, Hogan and Player are the others) to have won all four of golf's grand slam events, yet he will probably be remembered best for two single strokes. The first took place on the par five 15th at Augusta in the final round of the 1935 Masters. Three shots behind the leader at that stage, Sarazen holed a four wood for an albatross, or double eagle two. Needless to say, he went on to win the tournament. The second took place at Troon thirty eight years later and this time the television cameras were there to witness the 71 year old holing in one at the Postage Stamp, 8th hole. And Sarazen's link with Prince's? It was the scene of his one British Open victory in 1932 which, no thanks to Adolf Hitler, was Prince's one and only Open Championship.

Sarazen's total score of 283 was then a record for the Open Championship (just as Greg Norman's 267 total was in 1993) but today's golfer cannot properly walk in Sarazen's footsteps for the 18 hole links was dismembered during the last War (as indeed was its predecessor during the First World War)—perhaps not surprisingly given its geography and the continuous fear of invasion. For a while it looked possible that golf would never return to Prince's as there were plans to turn the links into a permanent military training site.

Fortunately for you and me, golf won the day and in 1950, Sir Guy Campbell and John Morrison were invited to restore the links. Remarkably, given the heavily scarred landscape, seventeen of the pre-war greens could still be used. Campbell and Morrison decided however, that they could best utilise the available land by creating three loops of nine holes and this layout is what greets the present day visitor to Prince's.

I'm not sure that 'greets' is actually the right terminology. Prince's may have lost its Open Championship status, but it has not lost its teeth. The three nines: the Dunes, Himalayas and Shore are each tremendously testing and, being a relatively exposed links, the golfer is at the mercy of the elements.

The Golf Club however, most definitely 'greets' the visitor. This must be one of southern England's most welcoming clubs and subject to availability, visitors with handicaps can generally play at all times. Both individuals and golfing societies (the Club can cater for over 100 persons in its spacious Clubhouse) should contact the **General Manager, Mr Bill Howie**. The address to write to is **Prince's Golf Club, Sandwich Bay, Sandwich, Kent CT13 9QB.** The telephone number is **(0304) 611118.** The club's **professional Chris Evans** can be reached on **(0304) 613797.**

For 1994, the cost of a single round (ie. 18 holes) at Prince's is £31 midweek and £35.50 at the weekend. The daily rates are £36 midweek, £41 on Saturdays and £46.50 on Sundays. These are the summer rates however and 'winter' full day packages start from as little as £25. Apart from being exceptionally good value, a full day is strongly recommended for this way all 27 holes can be tackled. Golfers playing 36 holes will play two eighteens from the following three combinations: **Dunes/Himalayas** 6506 yards, par 71; **Himalayas/Shore** 6510 yards, par 72 and **Dunes/Shore** 6690 yards, par 72. (For these composite courses the distances given are from the medal tees.) Each course is of a similarly high standard with a plethora of plateaued greens, ridges, humps and hollows but not too many bunkers. The paucity of sandtraps is a feature of golf at Prince's and unlike neighbouring St George's where there are many potential blind shots, the fairways tend to run parallel with the dunes as opposed to clambering over the top of them. There are few, if any, weak holes at Prince's, but if one were to single out a balanced 'nine of the best' from the 27 then I might venture a combination of the 2nd, 7th and 8th from the Himalayas; the 3rd, 6th and 9th from the Shore and the 3rd, 4th and 6th from the Dunes.

Situated four and a half miles from Sandwich railway station, the course is approached via St George's Road which, in turn, leads into Sandown Road, King's Avenue and finally, Prince's Drive. Sandwich is linked to Canterbury by the A257 and to Deal by the A258. Motoring from London, Canterbury can be reached by way of the A2 and M2.

Prince's most celebrated son is undoubtedly P.B.Laddie Lucas. A Walker Cup player and Captain he was also a noted war-time Fighter Pilot. Wing Commander Lucas is a son of Prince's in more ways than one for he was actually born in the old Clubhouse. Today, Prince's annually stages the Laddie Lucas Spoon, an open event for children aged between 8 and 13. Entries are received from all over Britain and France—and who knows, perhaps amongst this year's entrants there is a budding Gene Sarazen.

Himalayas			Shore			Dunes		
Hole	Yards	Par	Hole	Yards	Par	Hole	Yards	Par
1	386	4	1	430	4	1	457	4
2	415	4	2	511	5	2	167	3
3	184	3	3	176	3	3	491	5
4	355	4	4	410	4	4	414	4
5	400	4	5	386	4	5	418	4
6	580	5	6	408	4	6	498	5
7	195	3	7	562	5	7	373	4
8	415	4	8	184	3	8	208	3
9	391	4	9	425	4	9	429	4
Out	**3,321**	**35**	**In**	**3,492**	**36**	**Out**	**3,455**	**36**

Walletts Court Hotel & Restaurant

Walletts Court is an old manor house set in lovely open countryside near the white cliffs of Dover and only one mile from the sea and St Margarets Bay. It was bought and restored by the Oakley family in 1976 and with names like Bishop Odo, Queen Eleanor, Edward Gibbon and William Pitt associated with its long history, it is a house with a special atmosphere.

The main house is an attractive whitewashed 17th century manor house with black lattice window frames. The twelve bedrooms are en suite and well appointed, with television, telephone and tea and coffee making facilities. Three of the rooms are in the main house and nine are in the lovely converted outbuildings. As an hotel its rooms and facilities qualify for Four Crown Highly Commended status by the South East England Tourist Board.

The restaurant and quality of food befit the house and the period, with only fresh, seasonal dishes on a menu which changes monthly. Guests will find themselves enjoying Barbary duck served in a port wine sauce, or a fricassé of prime white fish in a brandied, creamy lobster sauce.

For those wishing to partake in some exercise after such a repast, there are numerous golf courses in the area: Walmer & Kingsdown is three miles away; Cinque Ports, four miles; Princes, six miles; Royal St George's, nine miles and Broome Park, nine miles. Alternatively guests may opt for a game of tennis on the hotel's court.

Walletts Court Hotel & Restaurant
Westcliffe
St Margarets
Dover
Kent CT15 6EW
Tel: (0304) 852424 (new STD code: 01304)
Fax: (0304) 853430

Roy Perry SEVEN IRON Rosenstiel's

Royal St George's was founded in 1887, rather ironically by two Scottish gentlemen, Dr. Laidlaw Purves and Henry Lamb after what can only be described as a rather eccentric venture. Like all good Scotsmen they had been bitten by the bug; however, both were presently living in Victorian London which meant that their golf was more or less confined to the various commons where the game was played alongside every conceivable activity imaginable. To them golf was meant to be played on a links by the sea. Hence the pair found themselves at Bournemouth setting off in an easterly direction looking for a suitable site. Having reached the eastern shore of Kent, so the story goes, they had drawn the proverbial blank (one presumes that they experienced one of those infamous Victorian pea-soupers, the day they passed through Rye); with patience no doubt wearing thin, suddenly 'land ahoy!' Doctor Purves sights a vast stretch of duneland at Sandwich. The theory is that he 'spied the land with a golfer's eye' from the tower of St Clement's Church. Quite what he was doing at the top of the tower is irrelevant—St George's had been located. Within seven short years the Open Championship had 'come south' and St George's was the first English venue.

More than one hundred years on **Gerald Watts** is the **Secretary** at St George's and he can be contacted by telephone on **(0304) 613090**. All written communication should be directed to him at **The Royal St George's Golf Club, Sandwich, Kent CT13 9PB**. As a general guide visitors are welcome between Mondays and Fridays; gentlemen must possess a handicap of no more than 18 and ladies no more than 15 and introductions are required. There are no ladies tees and other points to note are that the 1st tee is reserved daily for Members until 9.45am and between 1.15pm and 2.15pm; however, the 10th tee is usually free in the early mornings. St George's is essentially a singles and foursomes Club and three ball and four ball matches are only permissible with the agreement of the Secretary.

The green fees for 1994 were set at £50 per round, £70 per day. During the months of December, January and February the £50 fee is applicable for a full day's golf. Should there be a wish to hire golf clubs, a limited supply are for hire through the **professional, Niall Cameron**, telephone **(0304) 615236**. Finally, the services of a caddie can be booked via the **Caddiemaster** on **(0304) 617380**.

Please excuse the awful pun but finding Sandwich should be a 'piece of cake.' The town is linked to Canterbury to the west by the A257, a distance of approximately 15 miles and to Deal, 6 miles south east of Sandwich by the A258. Motoring from London, the most direct route is to head for Canterbury using a combination of the A2 and M2 and thereafter following the A257 as above. For those coming from the south coast Ashford is the place to head for: Ashford is joined to Canterbury by the A28. Sandwich can also be reached by train.

Since its first Open in 1894, won by John H. Taylor, the Championship has been held at Sandwich on eleven further occasions, most recently of course in 1993 when Australian Greg Norman won his second Championship after an epic final day's play. The visitor will not have to tackle the course from the Open Championship tees but he'll still have to confront the many dunes, the great undulations and the awkward stances that St George's is so renowned for.

Having done battle with the elements the golfer will find the Clubhouse welcoming. Excellent lunches are served daily and both breakfasts and dinners can be obtained with prior arrangement. A jacket and tie must be worn in all public rooms.

Although the 1993 Championship seems destined to be remembered as St George's greatest Open there have been many other famous happenings: Walter Hagen winning the Championship in 1922 and then promptly handing his winnings straight to his caddie; Henry Cotton's opening 67-65 in the 1934 Championship and then the Harry Bradshaw broken bottle episode of 1949. After a gap of 32 years the Open returned to St George's in 1981 when the 'forgotten' American Bill Rogers won, and again four years later when Sandy Lyle became the first British winner for sixteen years.

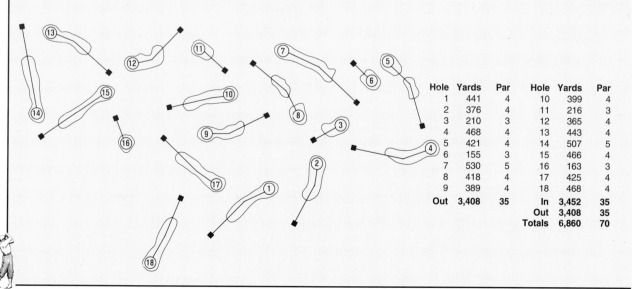

Hole	Yards	Par	Hole	Yards	Par
1	441	4	10	399	4
2	376	4	11	216	3
3	210	3	12	365	4
4	468	4	13	443	4
5	421	4	14	507	5
6	155	3	15	466	4
7	530	5	16	163	3
8	418	4	17	425	4
9	389	4	18	468	4
Out	**3,408**	**35**	**In**	**3,452**	**35**
			Out	**3,408**	**35**
			Totals	**6,860**	**70**

'Second best is unacceptable'. This is the philosophy upon which Taiyo International have built their first championship golf course in the UK. Unique in its match of Japanese design and British management, Moatlands is successful in attracting members who enjoy and take pride, not just in the facilities, but in their membership. As may also be expected of a club which incorporates a balance of British and Japanese golfing culture and expertise, there is a total commitment to detail and service. The highest standards and specifications have been employed to ensure Moatland's place as one of the top golf clubs in the UK.

Just over half an hour from South East London; twenty minutes from Maidstone, Sevenoaks and Tenterden; ten minutes from Tunbridge Wells and Tonbridge, Moatlands is situated close by the unspoilt and peaceful village of Brenchley. It is an area of outstanding natural beauty and Moatlands blends perfectly with its environment. The course itself covers the slope of Kentish Weald and is a fine example of the ultimate in environmentally friendly course design. Taking full advantage of the natural contours and individual features of the land, wildlife reserves and copses are protected and retained in their own surroundings. To this end it is worth noting over 27,000 new trees have been planted. If there is one feature of Moatlands setting it apart from most other UK courses it is the thick layer of sand used to construct the tees, greens and fairways ensuring exceptional drainage and availability of play in all weathers, except snow.

Each hole on the course offers a different challenge, one that can be enjoyed by golfers of all abilities from a selection of five tees. Also, there is a Golf Academy run by a top teaching PGA professional to cater for everyone from complete beginners to experienced players.

Every club golfer knows the importance of facilities at the 19th hole and those in the refurbished Moatlands Country Manor House are second to none. The cost of enjoying the delightful restaurant bars, deluxe changing facilities and the course as a full golfing member is remarkably modest and is reflected by the rapid growth in membership.

Seven day traditional membership requires a joining fee of £1500 with an annual subscription of £900. Alternatively seven day Gold or Silver Card Asset membership has joining fees of £1,000 and £600 respectively. They also require a deposit of £4000 and £2400 respectively but these can be the subject of spread payments and are refundable. Annual subscriptions are £680 for Silver Card and £400 for Gold Card — probably the best value for money currently on offer. Five Day, Family and Corporate Memberships are also available.

Members of this prestigious club are entitled to golf at other Taiyo International developments worldwide, including five. spectacular courses in France and one each in America, Malaysia and Singapore. Full details can be obtained from the membership office.

Moatlands Golf Club
Waterman's Lane
Brenchley
Kent TN12 6ND
Tel: (0892) 724400
Fax: (0892) 723300

Tanyard is a small medieval country house hotel with a unique and intimate atmosphere. So authentic is the higgledy, piggledy timber framed structure that, at first, you feel it can't possibly be real. Beams abound and there is scarcely a right angle in sight. Huge log fires welcome you in the winter.

All six bedrooms have en suite facilities and are furnished with antiques combined with modern comforts. The top floor suite, which is heavily beamed and has a spa bath is particularly popular.

In a truly rural setting and perched on a ridge, Tanyard has beautiful views across the Weald of Kent. There is a pond in front of the house and a stream runs through the ten acres of landscaped gardens. The surrounding area is designated as an area of outstanding natural beauty and yet Maidstone is barely 20 minutes drive away.

The recently opened 30-cover restaurant is in the oldest part of the building dating from 1350. The food on the four course menu uses the best quality local produce cooked in a modern but unpretentious style.

This is a perfect centre for touring — Leeds Castle is ten minutes and Sissinghurst 15 minutes away. Many other castles and stately homes, eg: Chartwell, Knole, Bodium, Scotney and Penshurst Place, are within easy reach. Also the historic towns of Canterbury, Rye and Tunbridge Wells are readily accessible. The ports of Dover, Folkestone and Sheerness as well as the Channel Tunnel are within one hours drive, as is Gatwick Airport.

LOCATION: From the B2163 at Boughton Monchelsea turn down Park Lane opposite the Cock pub. Take the first right down Wierton Lane, fork right down Wierton Hill and Tanyard is on the lower slopes of the hill on the left.

Tanyard Hotel
Boughton Monchelsea
Maidstone
Kent
Tel: (0622) 744705
Fax: (0622) 741998

You and I might visit Ballybunion or Royal Dornoch on a golfing pilgrimage. Our mouths water at the prospect of tackling the great sandbelt courses of Melbourne. And we would do anything to play golf at Pine Valley in New Jersey, widely acknowledged as the finest inland course in the world. For us, the stuff of dreams; for Nick Faldo, a day at the office.

It is not that Faldo is a kill-joy – quite the contrary, he has as much fun playing the great courses as anyone – it's just that nowadays whenever he makes a special visit to a famous golfing shrine he is thinking "design". Beyond the 18th green, and after his family, golf course design has become his major interest. Moreover, when his extraordinary resolve and desire to be recognised as one of the all-time greats has been satisfied (when he is confident people will tell their grandchildren 'I saw Faldo play') golf course design will take over full time. The comparison with Jack Nicklaus is striking, and since it was a vision of Nicklaus playing at Augusta back in 1971 that ignited the golfing flame, it is also rather neat.

For some years now, Faldo has been formulating his theories on course design. In the main, these ideas have been stored in the memory bank – that is until now, or rather since he met Steve Smyers. Smyers is one of America's most talented and imaginative course architects and in many ways is a kindred soul: he thinks along the same lines as Faldo. Above all, Smyers believes that you 'feel' a great golf course and that as far as possible its design should exude, even cultivate, the natural character of the landscape. Faldo and Smyers have recently joined forces to create Chart Hills.

Imagine a setting in the heart of the Kent countryside, where ancient oak trees stand proud. Imagine a golf course that has clusters of fairway bunkers reminiscent of those at Royal Melbourne; where the fairways comprise a variety of sweeping tree-lined dog-legs and island sanctuaries; where holes twist and tumble downhill in an almost links-like fashion towards huge contoured greens, and where entry to the putting surfaces is protected by winding creeks and steep riveted pot bunkers similar to Carnoustie and Muirfield. This is Chart Hills.

But one shouldn't gain the impression that Chart Hills is merely some kind of melting pot for design theories. There has been no crude imitation, rather it is the flavour of these great courses that has been incorporated and it has been done very subtlely. Indeed, the golf course doesn't so much occupy the land as seemingly melt into it. A very natural look has been achieved and,

young though it is (the course opened in October 1993), Chart Hills is developing its own special character and charm. It is a unique course; it has the hallmarks of a great course and, importantly (at least for the purposes of _Following the Fairways_!) it is a great course that visitors can play.

The club recommends that all those seeking to play should telephone in advance of arrival. The **Director of Golf**, **Roger Hyder** can be contacted on **(0580) 292148**. Handicap certificates are required and green fees in 1994 were £45 per round midweek and £48 at weekends.

The 19th hole at Chart Hills has something of an American country club atmosphere, being luxurious but not overly formal. This North American ambience starts to recede the instant you stand on the 1st tee. Not only are you staring across at the green fields of Kent but below is an extraordinary opening hole, a par five of almost 600 yards that includes elements of nearly all the design influences described earlier: a Mackenzie-like spread of fairway bunkers must be confronted with the drive; to the left of the fairway the rough is savage and there is a creek off to the right – although the shot is not too intimidating as the landing area is quite generous. The hole then dog-legs sharply to the right, sweeping down towards the green as the fairway narrows and becomes heavily contoured – a genuine links feel has been created. Fifty yards short of the green there is another nest of traps and guarding the front right entrance is a much more cavernous bunker. The green itself is very large and full of wicked borrows – a five at this hole is a good start !

And so the challenge continues, with dramatic holes being followed by more subtle ones and constant changes in direction and elevation. Among other outstanding holes at Chart Hills are the short 3rd (with its 'Redan' fortress green), the 4th (a hole that would grace Royal Melbourne), the 8th (shades of Augusta's 14th?), the 9th (a hint of Pine Valley) and on the back nine, perhaps the finest sequence of all, the 12th, 13th and 14th.

According to Smyers, a great golf course should excite, thrill and sometimes frighten. Applying this test literally, the golfer walking off the 18th green at Chart Hills is likely to be emotionally disturbed. As for Faldo, he is on record as saying that his twin ambitions in course design are to create the best inland course in Great Britain and the best links course – Nick never was one to set himself modest goals ! Play Chart Hills, though, and you may reckon him half way there already.

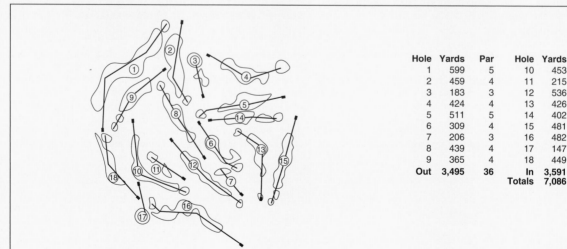

Hole	Yards	Par	Hole	Yards	Par
1	599	5	10	453	4
2	459	4	11	215	3
3	183	3	12	536	5
4	424	4	13	426	4
5	511	5	14	402	4
6	309	4	15	481	4
7	206	3	16	482	5
8	439	4	17	147	3
9	365	4	18	449	4
Out	3,495	36	In	3,591	36
			Totals	7,086	72

Key

To avoid disappointment it is advisable to telephone in advance

***Visitors welcome at most times
**Visitors usually allowed on weekdays only
Visitors not normally permitted (Mon, Wed) No visitors on specified days

Approximate Green Fees
A £30 plus
B £20 to £30
C £15 to £25
D £10 to £20
E under £10
F Greens fees on application

Restrictions
G—Guests only
H—Handicap certificate required
H—(24) Handicap of 24 or less
L—Letter of introduction required
M—Visitor must be a member of another recognised club.

Aquarius G.C.
081 693 1626
Marmora Road, Honor Oak
(9)5246 yards/**/F/M

Ashford G.C.
(0233) 622655
Sandyhurst Lane, Ashford
(18)6246 yards/***/B/H

Austin Lodge G.C.
(0322) 868944
nr Eynsford Station
(18)6600 yards/***/D

Barnehurst G.C.
(0322) 523746
Mayplace Road, East Barnehurst
(9)5320 yards/***/E

Bearsted G.C.
(0622) 738198
Ware Street, Bearsted,Maidstone
(18)6278 yards/**/B/L/M

Birchwood Park G.C.
(0322) 660554
Birchwood Road, Wilmington
(18)6364 yards/***/C

Boughton G.C.
(0227) 752277
Brickfield Lane, Boughton
(18)6452 yards/***/C

Broke Hill G.C.
(0959) 533225
Sevenoaks Road, Halstead
(18)6454 yards/***/C

Bromley G.C.
081 462 7014
Magpie Hall Lane, Bromley
(9)5538 yards/***/F

Broome Park G.& C.C.
(0227) 831701
Barham, Canterbury
(18)6610 yards/**/B/H

Canterbury G.C.
(0227) 453532
Scotland Hills, Canterbury
(18)6249 yards/**/B/H

Chart Hills G.C.
(0580) 292222
Weeks Lane, Biddenden
(18)7086 yards/***/A/H

Cherry Lodge G.C.
(0959) 572989
Jail Lane, Biggin Hill
(18)6652 yards/**/B

Chestfield G.C.

(022 779) 4411
103 Chestfield Road, Whitstable
(18)6181 yards/**/B/H

Chislehurst G.C.
081 467 3055
Camden Place, Chislehurst
(18)5128 yards/***/B/H

Cobtree Manor G.C.
(0622) 753276
Maidstone
(18)5716 yards/***/E

Corinthian G.C.
(0474) 707559
Gay Dawn Farm, Fawkham
(9)6045 yards/**/D

Cranbrook G.C.
(0580) 712833
Benenden Road, Cranbrook
(18)6351 yards/**/C

Cray Valley G.C.
(0689) 831927
Sandy Lane, St Pauls Cray, Orpington
(18)5624 yards/***/D

Darenth Valley G.C.
(0959) 522944
Station Road, Shoreham
(18)6356 yards/***/D

Dartford G.C.
(0322) 226455
Dartford Heath
(18)5914 yards/**/B/L/M

Deangate Ridge G.C.
(0634) 251180
Hoo, Rochester
(18)6300 yards/***/B

Edenbridge G.& C.C.
(0732) 865097
Crouch House Road, Edenbridge
(18)6646 yards/**/C
(18)5671 yards/**/C

Eltham Warren G.C.
081 850 1166
Bexley Road, Eltham
(9)5840 yards/***/B

Faversham G.C.
(0795) 890251
Belmont Park, Faversham
(18)6030 yards/**/C

Gillingham G.C.
(0634) 853017
Woodlands Road, Gillingham
(18)5911 yards/**/D

Hawkhurst G.C.
(0580) 752396
High Street, Hawkhurst, Cranbrook
(9)5774 yards/**/D

Herne Bay G.C.
(0227) 374097
Eddington, Herne Bay
(18)5466 yards/***/D/H

Hever G.C.
(0732) 700771
Hever
(18)7002 yards/***/A/H

Hewitts G.C.
(0689) 896266
Court Road, Orpington
(18)6077 yards/***/D

High Elms G.C.
(0689) 858175
High Elms Road, Downe
(18)6210 yards/***/F

Holtye G.C.
(0342) 850635
Holtye Common, Cowden, Edenbridge
(9)5289 yards/**/F

Hythe Imperial G.C.
(0303) 267441
Princes Parade, Hythe

(9)5560 yards/**/B

Knole Park G.C.
(0732) 452150
Seal Hollow Road, Sevenoaks
(18)6249 yards/**/B/H

Lamberhurst G.C.
(0892) 890591
Church Road, Lamberhurst
(18)6232 yards/**/B

Leeds Castle G.C.
(0622) 765400
Maidstone
(9)2880 yards/***/F

Littlestone G.C.
(0679) 63355
St Andrews Road, Littlestone, New Romney
(18)6460 yards/**/B/H

London G.C.
(0474) 879899
Stansted Lane, Ash Green
(18)7208 yards/*/F/M
(18)7005 yards/*/F/M

Lullingstone Park G.C.
(0959) 34542
Park Gate, Chelsfield, Orpington
(18)6779 yards/***/F
(9)2445 yards/***/E

Mid Kent G.C.
(0474) 568035
Singlewell Road, Gravesend
(18)6206 yards/**/F/H

Moatlands G.C.
(0892) 724400
Watermans Lane, Brenchley
(18)6460 yards/**/A/H

Nevill G.C.
(0892) 25818
Benhall Mill Road, Tunbridge Wells
(18)6336 yards/**/B/H

Nizels G.C.
(0732) 833138
Nizels Lane, Hildenborough
(18)6408 yards/***/A

North Foreland G.C.
(0843) 862140
Convent Road, Broadstairs
(18)6382 yards/**/B/H

Oastpark G.C.
(0634) 242661
Malling Road, Snodland
(18)6200 yards/***/E

Poult Wood G.C.
(0732) 364039
Higham Lane, Tonbridge
(18)5569 yards/***/E

Princes G.C.
(0304) 611118
Sandwich Bay, Sandwich
(27) (3x9)***/A/H

The Ridge G.C.
(0622) 844382
Chartway Street, East Sutton
(18)6254 yards/***/B/H

Rochester & Cobham Park G.C.
(0474) 823411
Park Dale, by Rochester
(18)6467 yards/**/B/H

Romney Warren G.C.
(0679) 62231
St Andrews Road, Littlestone
(18)5126 yards/***/E

Royal Cinque Ports G.C.
(0304) 374007
Sandwich
(18)6744 yards/**/F/H

Royal St Georges G.C.
(0304) 613090
Sandwich Bay Road, Sandwich
(18)6857 yards/**/A/H

Ruxley G.C.
(0689) 871490
Sandy Lane, St Pauls Cray, Orpington
(18)6027 yards/***/D

St Augustines G.C.
(0843) 590333
Cottingham Road, Cliffsend, Ramsgate
(18)5197 yards/***/C/H

Sene Valley G.C.
(0303) 268513
Sene, Folkestone
(18)6320 yards/***/B/H

Sheerness G.C.
(0795) 662585
Power Station Road, Sheerness
(18)6460 yards/**/D/H

Sittingbourne & Milton Regis G.C.
(0795) 842261
Wormdale, Newington, Sittingbourne
(18)6272 yards/**/D/H/L

Sweetwoods Park G.C.
(0342) 850729
Cowden, Edenbridge
(18)6400 yards/***/D

Tenterden G.C.
(0580) 763987
Woodchurch Road, Tenterden
(18)6030 yards/**/D

Tudor Park G.& C.C.
(0622) 734334
Ashford Road, Bearsted
(18)6000 yards/**/B/H

Tunbridge Wells G.C.
(0892) 523034
Langton Road, Tunbridge Wells
(9)4684 yards/**/B/H

Upchurch River Valley G.C.
(0634) 360626
Upchurch, Sittingbourne
(18)6160 yards/***/E

Walmer & Kingsdown G.C.
(0304) 373256
The Leas, Kingsdown, Deal
(18)6160 yards/***/C/H

Weald of Kent G.C.
(0622) 890866
Maidstone Road, Headcorn
(18)6169 yards/***/D

Westgate & Birchington G.C.
(0843) 831115
Canterbury Road, Westgate-on-Sea
(18)4926 yards/**/D/H/L

West Kent G.C.
(0689) 853737
West Hill, Downe, Orpington
(18)6392 yards/**/F/H/L

West Malling G.C.
(0732) 844785
London Road, Addington, Maidstone
(18)6142 yards/**/B
(18)6240 yards/**/B

Whitstable & Seasalter G.C.
(0227) 272020
Collingwood Road, Whitstable
(9)5276 yards/**/C

Wildernesse G.C.
(0732) 61526
Seal, Sevenoaks, Maidstone
(18)6478 yards/**/B/H/L

Woodlands Manor G.C.
(0959) 523805
Tinkerpot Lane, Sevenoaks
(18)5858 yards/**/F/H

Wrotham Heath
(0732) 884800
Seven Mile Lane, Comp, Sevenoaks
(9) 5959 yards/**/C/H

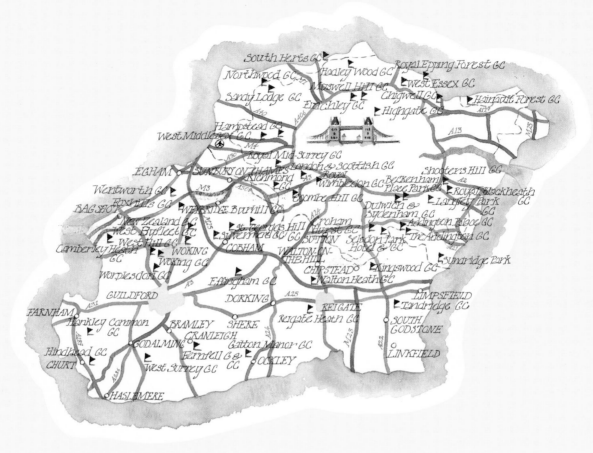

South Herts GC

Hadley Wood GC
Royal Epping Forest GC

Northwood GC
Muswell Hill GC
West Essex GC

Sandy Lodge GC
Chigwell GC
Hainault Forest GC

Finchley GC
Highgate GC

Hampstead GC
West Middlesex GC

EGHAM
Royal Mid-Surrey GC
London & Scottish GC
Shooters Hill GC

SUNBURY ON THAMES
Richmond GC
Royal Wimbledon GC
Beckenham Place Park GC
Royal Blackheath GC

Wentworth GC
Foxhills GC
Coombe Hill GC
Dulwich & Sydenham GC
Langley Park GC

BAGSHOT
WEYBRIDGE Burhill GC
New Zealand GC
St. Georges Hill GC
Croham Hurst GC
Addington Palace GC

West Byfleet GC
West Hill GC
Silvermere GC
SUTTON
Selsdon Park Hotel & GC
The Addington GC

Camberley Heath GC
WOKING
COBHAM
WALTON-ON-THE-HILL
Sundridge Park

Woking GC
Effingham GC
CHIPSTEAD
Kingswood GC

Worplesdon GC
GUILDFORD
DORKING
Walton Heath GC
LIMPSFIELD

FARNHAM
Hankley Common GC
BRAMLEY
SHERE
Reigate Heath GC
REIGATE
Tandridge GC

GODALMING
CRANLEIGH
Gatton Manor GC
SOUTH GODSTONE

Hindhead GC
Farnfell G & GC
Bramfell G & GC
OCKLEY
LINKFIELD

CHURT
West Surrey GC

HASLEMERE

Artist: **Julian Barrow WALTON HEATH** *Courtesy of:* **Burlington Gallery**

Capital Golf

Records suggest that golf was first played in England in 1608: the venue was Blackheath in London but the participants were Scottish not English. James I (James VI of Scotland) and his courtiers are generally credited with bringing the game south of the border. The exact date that the English caught the bug is unclear, certainly in the 18th century it was still pretty much an alien pastime—in his first English dictionary compiled in 1755 Dr Samuel Johnson described golf as, 'a game played with a ball and a club or bat'.

During its formative years golf in London was largely confined to the public commons such as those at Blackheath, Clapham, Chingford and Tooting Bec, the golfers having to share their rather crudely laid out courses with 'nurse-maids, dogs, horses and stubborn old ladies and gentlemen'.

Not surprisingly when the first golf clubs started to form the tendency was to retreat from the public stage. The **Royal Blackheath** Golf Club, fittingly enough the first English club to be founded (it dates from 1787) eventually moved from the Heath and now plays on a private course at Eltham. Golf is no longer played (or at least shouldn't be!) on the commons at Clapham and Tooting Bec. However, golf does survive on those at **Wimbledon** and Chingford, the latter being the home of **Royal Epping Forest** and where golfers are still required to wear red clothing in order that they can be distinguished from other users of the common.

The majority of London clubs are for obvious reasons set in deepest suburbia and with many it is often far from clear as to whether they fall within Greater London or not. In anyone's book **Muswell Hill** is in London, which for present purposes is just as well because it's an excellent course. Measuring close to 6500 yards, and quite undulating, it represents a fairly stiff test from the back tees. Other good 18 hole courses to the north of London include **Finchley** (with its elegant Victorian clubhouse), **Mill Hill** (which has something of a heathland feel to it) and **Highgate** (which is particularly pretty), while **Hampstead** has an enjoyable 9 holes.

A cluster of fine courses lie a little further to the north west of the capital. Near neighbours of one another are **Northwood** and **Sandy Lodge**. The latter could be said to be sandy by name, sandy by nature—a heathland course but it can play more like a golf links at times. Anyway, it's certainly an exceptionally fine course and hosts many top class events. Northwood is in parts parkland, in parts heathland with a very good back nine. A mention also for **West Middlesex**, one of West London's better parkland courses.

On the other side of the M1 one finds **South Herts** and **Hadley Wood**. South Herts is somewhat tucked away in Totteridge but well worth finding. The club can boast having both Harry Vardon and Dai Rees among its past professionals. Hadley Wood, near Barnet is a very beautiful course designed by Alister Mackenzie, with lovely tree-lined fairways. The clubhouse is very elegant too. Over towards Essex, Royal Epping Forest has been mentioned. Also within Epping Forest itself, **West Essex** is a very fine parkland course and there are two first rate public courses at **Hainault Forest.**

Before looking at golf in the south of the metropolis a word on some of London's better hotels. Finding real value in the capital isn't easy—local knowledge helps and it may be a case of rub of the green. The following appraisal is dedicated to the American and Japanese visitor—and to any of us who

have a generous expense account!

In Park Lane, the Inn on the Park 071 499 0888 is quite excellent and its restaurant, the Four Seasons is outstanding. Luxury of the highest order is also offered in the Dorchester 071 629 8888 as it proudly overlooks Hyde Park (alas no golf). The Grill Room and the Terrace are both restaurants of distinction. The international class of the Ritz 071 493 8181 is obvious—one can quite simply sniff the style. Nearby, Browns 071 493 6020 is contrastingly English and justifiably proud of it. A few more? Well how about the Savoy 071 836 4343, note the delightful settings of its restaurants the Grill Room and the River Restaurant. Another member of the Savoy group is Claridges 071 629 8860 traditional to a tee but still extremely popular.

For people not wishing to stay in Central London these hotels may be of some help: in Hadley Wood the West Lodge Park 081 440 8311 is a superb 19th century mansion—very convenient for the many courses of South Hertfordshire. A galleried hall is one of the features of the Mansion House at Grym's Dyke 081 954 4227. The former home of W.S.Gilbert, this hotel is located in Harrow Weald—ideal for playing (or spectating) at Moor Park. Slightly further out of town, but still only twenty miles from Central London, the five star comforts of Hanbury Manor near Ware(0920) 487722 take some beating (18 great holes of golf too) while golfers in Croydon will also find Selsdon Park Hotel very comfortable and convenient 081 657 8811. If some above are slightly out of the price range of the majority of ordinary mortals then it goes without saying that London provides a veritable feast of accommodation at vastly varying rates. Two highly recommended establishments combining comfort and value are Aston Court 071 602 9954 and the Peacehaven Hotel 081 202 9758.

Among the city's leading restaurants are the Roux Brothers Le Gavroche 071 408 0881, Rue St Jacques 071 637 0222 (very French) and the Hungarian Gay Hussar 071 437 0973. For lovers of seafood try Le Suquet 071 581 1785 or La Croisette 071 373 3694. A little less expensive than London's top restaurants but still very good are Gavvers 071 730 5983 (French), Simpsons 071 836 9112 (exceedingly English) and Leiths 071 229 4481, which sounds perfect for golf historians.

Those looking for a game in south west London might consider looking in the Wimbledon area where there are several courses. **Royal Wimbledon** is just about the best in London but golfers may find it easier to arrange a game (during the week at any rate) on the nearby course at Wimbledon Common, home of the **London Scottish** Club, located two miles from Wimbledon railway station. **Coombe Hill** is another of the capital's most prestigious clubs—its well manicured fairways are just about visible from Royal Wimbledon. A little further out at Richmond, games can be enjoyed at **Royal Mid Surrey** (two courses here, an Outer and an Inner) and at **Richmond** Golf Club with its superb Georgian clubhouse; there is also a public course at Richmond. A quick mention must be made here of Cannizaro House 081 879 1464, a truly delightful hotel on Wimbledon Common; it is perfect for the London and Surrey golfer. Due west of London, **Ealing** offers a reasonable test and there are again a number of public courses in the vicinity.

South of London the Croydon area is yet another that is thick with clubs. Althought difficult to arrange a game on, **Addington** is generally considered the best, a lovely heathland course covered in heather, pines and silver birch and has in the par three, 13th one of golf's toughest and most beautiful short holes. **Addington Palace** is also well thought of, as indeed is **Croham Hurst**. To make up a four, especially if one requires a base, **Selsdon Park** must be the selection; a pleasant parkland course set around the Selsdon escarpment. Seldson Park is very popular with societies. Not far from Croydon, the course at **Coulsdon Court** has a welcoming reputation and an extraordinary selection of trees. Two of the better courses towards the south east of London are **Langley Park** (at Beckenham)—heavily wooded with a particularly good series of holes towards the end of the round including an attractive par three finishing hole featuring a fountain and small lake, and **Sundridge Park,** where indeed there are two good courses, an East and West.

Elsewhere in the south east there is a popular public course at **Beckenham Place Park** and there are interesting layouts at **Shooters Hill** and **Dulwich** and **Sydenham**, but the final mention goes to **Royal Blackheath.** The club has a great sense of history and the course is full of character. Early in the round one may confront the famous 'Hamlet Cigar bunker' while its 18th isn't so much difficult as unusual, requiring a pitch over a hedge to the green. In some ways it's unfortunate that the club ever had to leave its famous common—Blackheath village is quite charming—but then the author of this tome may just be a little biased!

Surrey

When Providence distributed land best suited for building golf courses it wasn't done in the most democratic of spirits. Take for instance the quite ridiculous amount of majestic links land to be found along the coast of Lancashire—it's enough to make every good Yorkshireman weep. And then there's Surrey, blessed with acre upon acre of perfect inland golfing terrain—what a contrast to poor Essex!

Though very different in appearance, it is probably safe to suggest that **Walton Heath** and **Wentworth** are the county's two leading courses. (Sunningdale—at least according to the postman—being just over the border in Berkshire). But Walton and Wentworth (both featured on later pages) are only two of Surrey's famous 'W Club'—there's also **Worplesdon** and **Woking, West Hill, West Surrey, West Byfleet** and to this list we can now add **Wisley** and **Wildwood**—two of the country's newest and most exclusive developments.

Located off the A32 to the west of Woking, Worplesdon, West Hill and Woking Golf Clubs lie practically next door to one another. Indeed it might be possible to devise a few dramatic cross-course holes—though in view of the value of some of the adjacent properties that would have to be driven over it's perhaps not such a good idea! West Hill is generally considered the most difficult of the three, the fairways at times being frighteningly narrow; Worplesdon with its superb greens is probably the most widely known (largely due to its famous annual foursomes event), while Woking, founded a century ago, perhaps possesses the greatest charm. Whatever their particular merits, all three are magnificent examples of the natural heathland and heather type course.

Marginally closer to the capital and still very much in the heart of stockbroker-belt country is a second outstanding trio of courses centred around Weybridge: **St George's Hill, New Zealand** and **West Byfleet**. Once again, these are heathland type courses where golf is played amidst heavily wooded surroundings, the combination of pines, silver birch, purple heather and, at St George's Hill and New Zealand especially, a

magnificent spread of rhododendrons, making for particularly attractive settings. St George's Hill is in fact one of the more undulating courses in Surrey and calls for several spectacular shots—indeed, many people rate it on a par with Wentworth and Walton Heath. No inland course in England however, I would suggest, has a better sequence of finishing holes than those at New Zealand, the 14th, 15th and 16th being especially memorable.

Golf in Surrey isn't of course all heathland and heather. **Tandridge** is one of the best downland courses in Southern England while just a short drive from Weybridge is the delightful parkland course at **Burhill**, situated some two miles south of Walton-on-Thames. Burhill's clubhouse is a particularly grand affair—at one time it was the home of the Dowager Duchess of Wellington. Much less grand but to some of equal interest, is the Dick Turpin cottage sited on the course and reputed to have been used by the infamous highwayman. Also worth noting is a nearby public course, **Silvermere**, located midway between Byfleet and Cobham where it may be easier to arrange a game—at least in theory, as it does get very busy—and where green fees are naturally lower.

Some thoughts for the 19th hole are required. Surrey is a rich county—in more ways than one. Quality golf comes in abundance, so too do first class country houses, pubs, hotels and restaurants. Here are a few suggestions. In Walton-on-the-Hill, very convenient for Walton Heath is Ebenezer Cottage (073 781) 3166—a super restaurant. More fine fare is found at Sutton: Partners 081 644 7743 is the place, and at Chipstead where Dene Farm (0737) 552661 has a delightful country setting. Also in Egham one can stay at the superb Jacobean style Anugraha Hotel (0784) 434355 which is ideal for trips to Wentworth and Sunningdale.

After a day's golf on any of the courses in the Woking area the Wheatsheaf Hotel (0483) 773047 is a good spot to collect one's thoughts. Another relaxing hotel is the Oatlands Park Hotel (0932) 847242—centrally located and extremely pleasant. An attractive guest house in Woking is Glencourt (0483) 764154 whilst in nearby Reading, the Aeron Private Hotel (0734) 424119 will not empty your purse either. The Cricketers (0932) 862105 on Downside Common, Cobham is a sporting little pub. Two outstanding restaurants are La Bonne Franquette (0784) 39494 in Egham and Casa Romana (0932) 843470) in Weybridge, and in Reigate La Barbe (0737) 241966 also comes highly recommended. Finally, two of the county's (and the country's) finest country house hotels are in this area, again convenient for Wentworth—Pennyhill Park (0276) 471774 near Bagshot and Great Fosters (0784) 433822 near Egham.

Generally speaking golf in the Home Counties and golf in America have precious little in common. However, the **Foxhills** Club at Ottershaw (off the A320) can make a genuine claim to have married the two successfully. A Jacobean style manor house run on American country club lines including an outstanding range of leisure facilities, it has two championship length heathland type courses and 16 rooms to accommodate golfers in some style (0932) 872050. Not surprisingly, Foxhills is a very popular haunt for golfing societies. Another fairly newish set up in this area is the **Fernfell** Golf and Country Club at Cranleigh just south of Guildford.

The country club scene may not of course appeal to all types and excellent golf in an extremely sedate atmosphere can be enjoyed at **Gatton Manor** situated in

Ockley near Dorking. The course has a very scenic layout running through woods and alongside lakes. One doesn't have to look too far for a good night's rest—the Manor House is now a very relaxing hotel with golf obviously very much on the menu. Note also the Punch Bowl in nearby Oakwood Hill—an excellent country pub.

Heading towards Walton Heath, if a game cannot be arranged over one of its famous courses then there is golf of a similarly (if less challenging nature) at **Reigate Heath** and not too far away at **Kingswood** there is a fine parkland course.

The rich heathland seam runs the breadth of the county and over to the west, practically straddling the three counties of Surrey, Berkshire and Hampshire, lies the superb **Camberley Heath** course, (there is also a first rate public course in Camberley, **Pine Ridge**, which opened in 1992) while down in the south-west corner there is yet another outstanding trio of clubs: **Hindhead**, **West Surrey** and **Hankley Common**.

Hankley Common was for many years a favourite of the late South African Bobby Locke, four times Open Champion, who once owned a house adjacent to the course. Hankley Common is widely known for its spectacular 18th hole—one of the greatest closing holes in golf. A vast gulley which seems to possess magnetic powers looms in front of the green—nine out of ten first timers fail to reach the putting surface.

The south-west corner of Surrey is particularly scenic. The hustle and bustle of London seems a world away— and of course in a way it is. In Bramley, The Bramley Grange Hotel (0483) 893434 is an ideal base from which to explore the countryside. Close to the Sussex borders lies Haslemere and another fine hotel, a timbered farmhouse on this occasion, the Lythe Hill Hotel (0428) 651251 where bedrooms in the original house have great character. People who have still not found a restaurant to visit must surely do so here for Morels (0428) 51462 offers some simply splendid dishes and a most delightful atmosphere.

 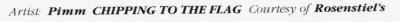

Artist: **Pimm CHIPPING TO THE FLAG** *Courtesy of* **Rosenstiel's**

It is autumn. A reddish gold leaf scurries across the 18th green. The huge gallery is silent. Fully 50 yards away to the right of the fairway, close to the trees and in the rough is the young Severiano Ballesteros. He is one hole down to the legendary Arnold Palmer and he needs a miracle. The blade flashes, and the ball flies towards the green. It pitches, it rolls and it drops ... the eagle has landed.

A stunningly beautiful place, Wentworth is set in the heart of the famous Surrey heathland belt. The name first appeared on the golfing map in the mid 1920s when Harry Colt, perhaps the greatest of all British golf architects, was commissioned to design two 18 hole courses. The East Course was the first to open in 1924, with the West Course following two years later. A third 18 hole championship course, the Edinburgh, designed by John Jacobs, Gary Player and current European Ryder Cup Captain and the Club's **professional, Bernard Gallacher** was officially opened by the eponymous Duke in 1990.

Before the War, it was the **East Course** that captured the limelight by staging the Club's first important events, in 1927 an unofficial match between British and American teams and in 1932 the inaugural Curtis Cup. In the period since 1945, the longer **West Course** has taken most of the glory with the Ryder Cup in 1953, the Canada Cup - a forerunner of the World Cup - three years later, and from 1964 the World Match Play Championship. Through the televising of the latter and the annual Volvo PGA Championship, the West has become arguably England's best known golf course.

The owners of the club, Wentworth Group Holdings, have invested substantially in both the courses and the facilities over the past five years and under Chairman, Elliott Bernard and Chief Executive, Willy Bauer standards now match the best clubs in the world. Following the completion of the Edinburgh, a computerised irrigation system was installed on the West, a new Halfway

House built serving the East and West, another on the **Edinburgh** and many other improvements to the courses and the estate.

In October 1993 a major redevelopment of the Clubhouse was completed. The golfing facilities are now all under one roof including Bernard Gallacher's proshop, the caddymaster, bagstore and splendidly equipped visitors' locker rooms. The new Club Lounge plus dining room with brasserie style and formal dining, Burma Bar, private meeting rooms and gabled ballroom offer plenty of flexibility for social and business entertainment.

In 1994 the green fees were set at £90 for the West Course with the East and Edinburgh courses at £70. Club and trolley hire and caddies may be booked in advance while special packages are available for groups of 20 or more.

Wentworth is located off the A30, between Bagshot and Egham, and may be approached via the M25 junction 13 or M4 through Bracknell or Windsor and Ascot. Heathrow Airport is only 15 minutes away.

General Manager, **Keith Williams** and his staff ensure that all visitors feel welcome. It is advisable, however, to pre-book a starting time and unless accompanied by a member, visitors are restricted to weekdays. A handicap certificate is required and men must play off 20 or less and women 30.

Enquiries should be addressed to: **Wentworth Club, Wentworth Drive, Virginia Water, Surrey GU25 4LS. Telephone (0344) 842201,** Fax(0344) 842804.

It is spring. The PGA Championship is reaching a nailbiting climax as the two players walk down the first fairway in the sudden death play off. A decade has passed and the now legendary Ballesteros hasn't won for some time. He desperately needs a victory. The blade flashes and a 5 iron is struck 220 yards towards the green. It lands, skips, rolls and finishes two feet from the pin ... El Gran Senor is back!

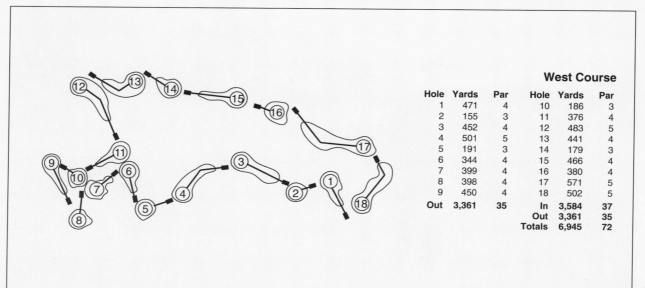

West Course

Hole	Yards	Par	Hole	Yards	Par
1	471	4	10	186	3
2	155	3	11	376	4
3	452	4	12	483	5
4	501	5	13	441	4
5	191	3	14	179	3
6	344	4	15	466	4
7	399	4	16	380	4
8	398	4	17	571	5
9	450	4	18	502	5
Out	**3,361**	**35**	**In**	**3,584**	**37**
			Out	**3,361**	**35**
			Totals	**6,945**	**72**

Gavrilo Princip may have pulled the trigger that ignited the Great War but our history books tell us that tension in Europe had sometime earlier reached boiling point. In their Palaces in St Petersburg and Berlin the Czar and the Kaiser pondered the strength of their armies. Meanwhile the great statesmen of Britain were engaged in battles of a different nature...

All square as they reach the 18th green on the Old Course at Walton Heath, Churchill turns to Lloyd-George and says, 'Now then, I will putt you for the Premiership'. Herbert Fowler once said, 'God builds golf links and the less man meddles the better for all concerned'. Herbert Fowler designed Walton Heath. However, before the opening of the Old Course in May 1904, at least a little meddling was called for. The glorious heathland through which the emerald fairways were cut was once covered, or nearly covered in thick heather, in parts as much as two feet thick (the Members will tell you it still is!) While many of Britain's leading Clubs took several years to establish their reputations, that of Walton Heath was assured months before the first stroke was even played; in January 1904 James Braid agreed to become Walton's first professional. Braid initially signed a seven year contract, his performances in the next seven Open Championships were: 2nd, 1st, 1st, 5th, 1st, 2nd and 1st, after which he became the first ever golfer to win five Opens. Hardly surprisingly his contract was extended and so indeed began an association with the Club that was to last for nearly fifty years.

In the years immediately before the First World War, Walton Heath Members included no fewer than 24 MPs (including Winston Churchill and Lloyd-George) and 21 Members of the House of Lords. Another famous Walton golfer was W.G. Grace (of whom it was once cruelly suggested that he compiled as many hundreds on the Heath as he did at the Oval). After the war a more royal flavour dominated, with the Prince of Wales becoming an Honorary Member in 1921 and Captain in 1935.

Time to leap forward to the present and introduce the **Club's Secretary: Group Captain Robbie James.** He may be contacted at **The Walton Heath Golf Club, Tadworth, Surrey KT20 7TP,** tel: **(0737) 812380.** Subject to prior arrangement with the Secretary, golfers are welcome to visit Walton Heath between Mondays and Fridays. Proof of both Club Membership and an official handicap is required. The green fees for 1994 were set at £57 for a full day's golf, with a reduced rate of £47 available if tee-

ing off after 11.30am. The hire of golf clubs can be arranged through the Club's popular **professional, Ken MacPherson,** tel: **(0737) 812152.**

Located south of London, motoring to the Club is assisted greatly by the M25. Those approaching on this motorway should leave at junction 8 turning north on to the A217. The A217 should be followed for approximately 2 miles after which a left turn should be taken on to the B2032. The Golf Club is situated a mile or so along this road. Travelling from further afield, the M25 is linked to the M23 to the South, the M20 to the East and to the North and West by the M3, M4 and M1.

There are two great courses at Walton Heath, the Old and the New (the latter first appearing as nine holes in 1907 but later extended to the full 18). Lying adjacent to one another, each possesses the same classical heathland characteristics: sandy sub-soil, heather, bracken, gorse, pines and silver birch. The finishing three holes on the Old are thought by many (including no lesser a judge than Tom Weiskopf) to be the finest on any course. The 16th is a very mild dog-leg to a raised green which slopes from left to right, with the right side of the green heavily guarded by bunkers. The par three 17th has sand traps practically encircling the green, creating a near island effect and the 18th requires a testing second to carry an enormous cross bunker.

Over the years Walton Heath has played host to many important tournaments. The major amateur championships have included the English Amateur and both the Ladies English Amateur and the Ladies British Open Amateur Championships. Among the professional events, twenty-two of the PGA Match Play Championships were staged at Walton Heath and in recent years The Ryder Cup of 1981 as well as five European Open Championships.

Walton Heath has a fine Clubhouse with an excellent restaurant and lounge. A jacket and tie should be worn in all public rooms after 11am. Lunches are served between 12.00 pm and 2.30pm.

Understandably wherever you turn in the Clubhouse you are likely to see a reminder of the long association with James Braid. One small note sent to him from the Prince of Wales conveys a message all golfers can appreciate. It relates how the Prince came to the 18th requiring a four for a 79. After explaining how his second finished just through the green he tells how, 'with the chance of breaking 80, I couldn't stand the nerve-strain and fluffed the chip and took two putts...' How the mighty fall!

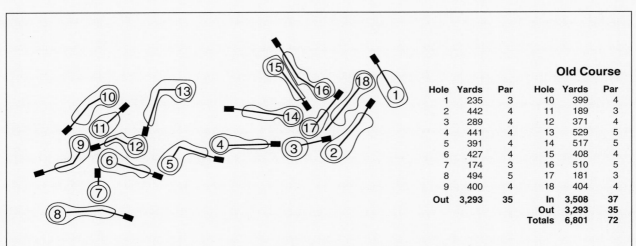

	Old Course				
Hole	Yards	Par	Hole	Yards	Par
1	235	3	10	399	4
2	442	4	11	189	3
3	289	4	12	371	4
4	441	4	13	529	5
5	391	4	14	517	5
6	427	4	15	408	4
7	174	3	16	510	5
8	494	5	17	181	3
9	400	4	18	404	4
Out	**3,293**	**35**	**In**	**3,508**	**37**
			Out	**3,293**	**35**
			Totals	**6,801**	**72**

Key

To avoid disappointment
it is advisable to telephone
in advance

***Visitors welcome at most times
**Visitors usually allowed on
weekdays only
*Visitors not normally permitted
(Mon, Wed) No visitors
on specified days

Approximate Green Fees
A £30 plus
B £20 to £30
C £15 to £25
D £10 to £20
E under £10
F Greens fees on application

Restrictions
G—Guests only
H—Handicap certificate required
H—(24) Handicap of 24 or less
L—Letter of introduction required
M—Visitor must be a member of
another recognised club.

GREATER LONDON
(including Middlesex)

Airlinks G.C.
081 561 1418
Southall Lane, Hounslow
(18)6002 yards/***/D

Arkley G.C.
081 449 0394
Rowley Green Road, Barnet
(9)6045 yards/**/C/H

Ashford Manor G.C.
(0784) 252049
Fordbridge Road, Ashford
(18)6343 yards/***/B/H/M

Beckenham Place Park G.C.
081 650 2292
Beckenham Hill Road, Beckenham
(18)5722 yards/***/E

Bexleyheath G.C.
081 303 6951
Mount Road, Bexleyheath
(9)5239 yards/**/D

Brent Valley G.C.
081 567 1287
Church Road, Hanwell
(18)5426 yards/***/F

Bushey G.& C.C.
081 950 2283
High Street, Bushey
(9)3000 yards/***(Wed)/D

Bush Hill Park G.C.
081 360 5738
Bush Hill, Winchmore Hill
(18)5809 yards/**/B/L

Chigwell G.C.
081 500 2059
High Road, Chigwell
(18)6279 yards/**/A/H/L

Chingford G.C.
081 529 2107
Station Road, Chingford
(18)6336 yards/***/F

Chislehurst G.C.
081 467 2782
Camden Park Road, Chislehurst
(18)5128 yards/**/C/H

Crews Hill G.C.
081 363 6674
Cattlegate Road, Crews Hill, Enfield
(18)6230 yards/**/F/H/M

Dulwich and Sydenham Hill G.C.
081 693 3961
Grange Lane, College Road,
(18)6610 yards/**/B/H(22)/L

Dyrham Park C.C.
081 440 3361
Galley Lane, Barnet
(18)6369 yards/*/C/G

Ealing G.C.
081 997 0937
Perivale Lane, Greenford
(18)6216 yards/**/B/H

Elstree G.C.
081 953 6115
Watling Street, Elstree
(18)6603 yards/***/D

Eltham Warren G.C.
081 850 1166
Bexley Road, Eltham
(9)5840 yards/**/B/H/M

Enfield G.C.
081 363 3970
Old Park Road South, Enfield
(18)6137 yards/**/B/H/M

Finchley G.C.
081 346 2436
Nether Court, Frith Lane, Mill Hill
(18)6411 yards/***/A

Fulwell G.C.
081 977 2733
Wellington Road, Hampton Hill
(18)6544 yards/**/A/L

Gryms Dyke G.C.
081 428 4539
Oxhey Lane, Hatch End, Pinner
(18)5600 yards/**/B/H

Hadley Wood G.C.
081 449 4486
Beech Hill, Barnet
(18)6473 yards/**/A/H/M

Hainault Forest G.C.
081 500 2097
Chigwell Row, Hainault
(18)5754 yards/***/E
(18)6600 yards/***/E

Hampstead G.C.
081 455 7089
Winnington Road, Hampstead
(9)5812 yards/***/B/H

Hartsbourne G.& C.C.
081 950 1133
Hartsbourne Avenue, Bushey Heath
(18)6305 yards/*/F/G
(9)5432 yards/*/F/G

Haste Hill G.C.
(0923) 822877
The Drive, Northwood
(18)5794 yards/***/F

Hendon G.C.
081 346 6023
Devonshire Rd, Mill Hill
(18)6266 yards/**/B/M

Highgate G.C.
081 340 3745
Denewood Road, Highgate
(18)5982 yards/**(Wed)/B/H

Hillingdon G.C.
(0895) 233956
18 Dorset Way, Hillingdon
(9)5459 yards/**(Thu)/C/H/M

The Holiday Inn
(0895) 444232
Stockley Road, West Drayton
(9)3800 yards/***/E

Home Park G.C.
081 977 2423
Hampton Wick, Richmond-upon-
Thames
(18)6610 yards/***/C

Horsenden Hill G.C.
081 902 4555
Woodland Rise, Greenford
(9)3236 yards/***/E

Hounslow Heath G.C.
081 570 5271
Staines Road, Hounslow
(18)5901 yards/**/E

Ilford G.C.
081 554 2930
Wanstead Park Road, Ilford
(18)5787 yards/**/D

Langley Park G.C.
081 650 2090
Barnfield Wood Road, Beckenham

(18)6488 yards/**/A/H

Lee Valley G.C.
081 803 3611
Picketts Lock Lane, Edmonton
(18)4902 yards/***/D

The London Golf Centre
081 841 6162
Ruislip Road, Northolt
(9)5838 yards/***/E

London Scottish G.C.
081 789 7517
Windmill Enclosure, Wimbledon
Common
(18)5436 yards/**/F/H

Magpie Hall Lane G.C.
081 462 7014
Magpie Hall Lane, Bromley
(9)2745 yards/***/F

Mill Hill G.C.
081 959 2339
Barnet Way, Mill Hill
(18)6309 yards/***/B/H

Muswell Hill G.C.
081 888 1764
Rhodes Avenue, Wood Green
(18)6474 yards/**/B/H(24)

North Middlesex G.C.
081 445 1604
Friern Barnet Lane, Whetstone
(18)5625 yards/***/B/H

Northwood G.C.
(0923) 825329
Rickmansworth Road, Northwood
(18)6553 yards/**/B/H

Old Fold Manor G.C.
081 440 9185
Hadley Green, Barnet
(18)6471 yards/**/B/H

Perivale Park G.C.
081 575 7116
Argyle Road, Greenford
(9)5267 yards/***/E

Pinner Hill G.C.
081 866 0963
Southview Road, Pinner Hill
(18)6293 yards/**/F/H

Roehampton G.C.
081 876 1621
Roehampton Lane, London
(18)6046 yards/**/F/L

Royal Blackheath G.C.
081 850 1795
Court Road, Eltham
(18)6214 yards/**/A/H/L

Royal Epping Forest G.C.
081 529 2195
Forest Approach, Chingford
(18)6620 yards/***/D/H

Royal Wimbledon G.C.
081 946 2125
Camp Road, Wimbledon
(18)6300 yards/**/A/H(18)/L

Ruislip G.C.
(0895) 638835
Ickenham Road, Ruislip
(18)5703 yards/***/D

Shooters Hill G.C.
081 854 6368
Eaglesfield Road, Shooters Hill
(18)5736 yards/**/B/H/M

Shortlands G.C.
081 460 2471
Meadow Road, Shortlands, Bromley
(9)5261 yards/*/D/G

Sidcup G.C.
081 300 2150
Hurst Road, Sidcup
(9)5722 yards/**/D/H/L

South Herts G.C.
081 445 2035
Links Drive, Totteridge
(18)6432 yards/**/F/H(24)/L

Stanmore G.C.
081 954 2599

Gordon Avenue, Stanmore
(18)5881 yards/**/E-C/H

Stockley Park G.C.
081 813 5700
Stockley Park, Uxbridge
(18)6548 yards/***/A

Strawberry Hill G.C.
081 894 0165
Wellesley Road, Twickenham
(9)2381 yards/**/C

Sudbury G.C.
081 902 3713
Bridgewater Road, Wembley
(18)6282 yards/**/F/H/M

Sunbury G.C.
(0932) 772898
Sunbury
(9)3105 yards/***/D

Sundridge Park G.C.
081 460 0278
Garden Road, Bromley
(18)6467 yards/**/A/H
(18)6007 yards/**/A/H

Trent Park G.C.
081 366 7432
Bramley Road, Southgate
(18)6008 yards/***/D

Twickenham G.C.
081 783 1698
Staines Road, Twickenham
(9)6014 yards/***/E

Uxbridge G.C.
(0895) 231169
The Drive, Harefield Place, Uxbridge
(18)5753 yards/***/D

Wanstead G.C.
081 989 3938
Overton Drive, Wanstead
(18)6262 yards/**(Wed,Thu)/B/H

West Middlesex G.C.
081 574 3450
Greenford Road, Southall
(18)6242 yards/**/C

Whitewebbs G.C.
081 363 4454
Beggars Hollow, Clay Hill, Enfield
(18)5863 yards/***/D

Wimbledon Common G.C.
081 946 7571
Camp Road, Wimbledon Common
(18)5438 yards/**/C

Wimbledon Park G.C.
081 946 1250
Home Park Road, Wimbledon
(18)5465 yards/**/B/H/L/M

Wyke Green G.C.
081 560 8777
Syon Lane, Isleworth
(18)6242 yards/**/A/H

SURREY

Addington G.C.
081 777 1055
Shirley Church Road, Croydon
(18)6242 yards/**/F/H/L

Addington Court G.C.
081 657 0281
Featherbed Lane, Addington
(18)5577 yards/***/D
(18)5513 yards/***/D
(9)1812 yards/***/E

Addington Palace G.C.
081 654 3061
Gravel Hill, Addington Park
(18)6410 yards/**/B/H/G

Banstead Downs G.C.
081 642 2284
Burdon Lane, Belmont
(18)6169 yards/**/B/H

Barrow Hills G.C.
(0932) 848117
Longcross, Chertsey
(18)3090 yards/*/F/G

Betchworth Park G.C.
(0306) 882052

Reigate Road, Dorking
(18)6266 yards/**(Tue,Wed)/A

Bletchingley G.C.
(0883) 744666
Church Lane, Bletchingley
(18)6504 yards/**/B

Bramley G.C.
(0483) 893042
Bramley, Guildford
(18)5990 yards/**/B/H

Broadwater Park G.C.
(0483) 429955
Guildford Road, Farncombe
(9)1323 yards/***/E

Burhill G.C.
(0932) 227345
Walton-on-Thames
(18)6224 yards/**/F/H/L

Camberley Heath G.C.
(0276) 23258
Golf Drive, Camberley
(18)6337 yards/**/A/H

Chessington Golf Centre
081 391 0948
Garrison Lane, Chessington
(9)1400 yards/***/E

Chiddingfold G.C.
(0428) 685888
Petsworth Road, Chiddingfold
(18)5500 yards/***/C

Chipstead G.C.
(0737) 551053
How Lane, Coulsdon
(18)5454 yards/**/B

Chobham G.C.
(0276) 855584
Chobham Road, Chobham
(18)6000 yards/*/F/G/H(from 1995)

Clandon Regis G.C.
(0483) 224888
Epsom Road, West Clandon
(18)6412 yards/**/B/H

Coombe Hill G.C.
081 942 2284
Golf Club Drive, Kingston
(18)6303 yards/**/A/H/L

Coombe Wood G.C.
081 942 3828
George Road, Kingston Hill
(18)5210 yards/**/F/H

Coulsdon Court G.C.
081 660 0468
Coulsdon Road, Coulsdon
(18)6037 yards/***/D

Croham Hurst G.C.
081 657 5581
Croham Road, South Croydon
(18)6286 yards/**/A/H/L

Cuddington G.C.
081 393 0952
Banstead Road, Banstead
(18)6394 yards/**/A/H/L

Dorking G.C.
(0306) 886917
Chart Park, Dorking
(9)5120 yards/**/D

Drift G.C.
(0483) 284641
The Drift, East Horsley
(18)6425 yards/**/B

Dunsfold Aerodrome G.C.
(0483) 265472
Dunsfold Aerodrome, Godalming
(9)6090 yards/*/E/G
Effingham G.C.
(0372) 452203
Guildford Road, Effingham
(18)6488 yards/**/A/H/G(week-ends)

Epsom G.C.
(0372) 721666
Longdown Lane South, Epsom
(18)5701 yards/**/C

Farnham G.C.
(0252) 782109
The Sands, Farnham
(18)6325 yards/**/B/H/M

Farnham Park G.C.

(0252) 715216
Folly Hill, Farnham
(9)1163 yards/***/E

Fernfell G.C.
(0483) 268855
Barhatch Lane, Cranleigh
(18)5599 yards/**/B

Foxhills G.C.
(0932) 872050
Stonehill Road, Ottershaw
(18)6680 yards/**/A
(18)6547 yards/**/A
(9)1300 yards/**/A

Gatton Manor G.C.
(0306) 627555
Ockley, Dorking
(18)6902 yards/***/D

Goal Farm G.C.
(0483) 473183
Gole Road, Pirbright
(9)1283 yards/***/E

Guildford G.C.
(0483) 63941
High Path Road, Merrow
(18)6090 yards/**/B

Hankley Common G.C.
(0252) 792493
Tilford Road, Tilford, Farnham
(18)6418 yards/**/A/H/L

Hindhead G.C.
(0428) 604614
Churt Road, Hindhead
(18)6373 yards/***/A/H

Hoebridge G.C.
(0483) 722611
Old Woking Road, Old Woking
(18)6536 yards/***/D
(18)2298 yards/***/E
(9)2294 yards/***/E

Horton Park C.C.
081 393 8400
Hook Road, Ewell
(18)5208 yards/***/D

Hurtmore G.C.
(0483) 426492
Hurtmore Road, Hurtmore
(18)5444 yards/***/D

Kingswood G.C.
(0737) 832188
Sandy Lane, Kingswood
(18)6880 yards/***/A/H

Laleham G.C.
(0932) 564211
Laleham Reach, Chertsey
(18)6203 yards/**/C

Leatherhead G.C.
(0372) 843966
Kingston Road, Leatherhead
(18)6157 yards/***/A

Limpsfield Chart G.C.
(0883) 723405
Westerham Road,Limpsfield
(9)5718 yards/**(Thu)/C/H

Lingfield Park G.C.
(0342) 834602
Racecourse Road, Lingfield
(18)6500 yards/**/B

Malden G.C.
081 942 0654
Traps Lane, New Malden
(18)6295 yards/**/F/H

Milford G.C.
(0483) 419200
Station Lane, Milford
(18)6224 yards/**/B/H

Mitcham G.C.
081 648 1508
Carshalton Road, Mitcham Junction
(18)5935 yards/**/D/H(18)

Moore Place G.C.
(0372) 463533
Portsmouth Road, Esher
(9)4186 yards/***/E

New Zealand G.C.
(0932) 345049
Woodham Lane, Addlestone
(18)6012 yards/*/A

North Downs G.C.

(0883) 653298
Northdown Road, Woldingham,
Caterham
(18)5843 yards/**/B/H

Oak Park G.C.
(0252) 850880
Crondall, nr Farnham
(18)6437 yards/***/C

Oak Sports Centre
081 643 8363
Woodmansterne Road, Carshalton
(18)6033 yards/***/D
(9)1590 yards/***/E

Pachersham Golf Centre
(0372) 843453
Oaklawn Road, Leatherhead
(9)1752 yards/***/E

Pine Ridge G.C.
(0276) 20770
Old Bisley Road, Frimley
(18)6458 yards/***/D

Purley Downs G.C.
081 657 8347
Purley Downs Road, Purley
(18)6212 yards/**/A/H/M/L

Puttenham G.C.
(0483) 810498
Heath Road, Puttenham, Guildford
(18)6204/**/C/H

Pyrford G.C.
(0483) 723555
Warren Lane, Pyrford
(18)6201 yards/**/A/H

R.A.C.Country Club
(0372) 2763111
Woodcote Park, Epsom
(18)6709 yards/*/F
(18)5598 yards/*/F

Redhill G.C.
(0737) 770204
Canada Avenue, Redhill
(9)1901 yards/***/E

Redhill and Reigate G.C.
(0737) 244626
Clarence Lodge, Pendleton Road,
Redhill
(18)5238 yards/***/D

Reigate Heath G.C.
(0737) 242610
Reigate Heath, Reigate
(9)5658 yards/**/F

Richmond G.C.
081 940 4351
Sudbrook Park, Richmond
(18)5977 yards/**/A/H

Richmond Park G.C.
081 876 3205
Roehampton Gate, Richmond Park
(18)5940 yards/***/F
(18)5969 yards/***/F

Roker Park G.C.
(0483) 236677
Holly Lane, Guildford
(9)3037 yards/***/E

Royal Mid Surrey G.C.
081 940 1894
Old Deer Park, Richmond
(18)5544 yards/***/A/H/M
(18)6343 yards/***/A/H/M

Rusper G.C.
(0293) 871456
Rusper Road, Newdigate
(9)6069 yards/**/F

St Georges Hill G.C.
(0932) 842406
St. Georges Hill, Weybridge
(18)6600 yards/**/A/H/L
(9)3000 yards/**/A/H/L

Sandown Park G.C.
(0372) 463340
More Lane, Esher
(9)5656 yards/***/D
(9)1193 yards/***/E

Selsdon Park Hotel G.C.
081 657 8811
Addington Road, Sanderstead
(18)6402 yards/***/B/H

Shillinglee Park G.C.
(0428) 653237

Chiddingfold, Godalming
(9)2500 yards/***/D

Shirley Park G.C.
081 654 1143
Addiscombe Road, Croydon
(18)6210 yards/**/B/H

Silvermere G.C.
(0932) 867275
Redhill Road, Cobham
(18)6333 yards/***/C

Springfield Park G.C.
081 871 2468
Burntwood Lane, Wandsworth
(9)4451 yards/**/E

Surbiton G.C.
081 398 3101
Woodstock Lane, Chessington
(18)6211 yards/**/A/H

Sutton Green
(0483) 766849
New Lane, Sutton Green
(18)6305 yards/***/F

Tandridge G.C.
(0883) 712273
Oxted
(18)6250 yards/**(Tue,Fri)/A/H

Thames Ditton and Esher G.C.
081 398 1551
Portsmouth Road, Esher
(9)5190 yards/***/D

Tyrrells Wood G.C.
(0372) 376025
Tyrrells Wood, Leatherhead
(18)6234 yards/**/A/H/L

Walton Heath G.C.
(0737) 812060
Tadworth
(18)6801 yards/**/A/H/L
(18)6609 yards/**/A/H/L

Wentworth G.C.
(0344) 842201
Virginia Water
(18)6945 yards/**/A/H
(18)6176 yards/**/A/H
(18)6979 yards/**/A/H

West Byfleet G.C.
(0932) 345230
Sheerwater Road, West Byfleet
(18)6211 yards/**/B

West Hill G.C.
(0483) 474365
Bagshot Road, Brookwood
(18)6368 yards/**/A/H

West Surrey G.C.
(0483) 421275
Enton Green, Godalming
(18)6300 yards/**/A/H

Wildwood G.C.
(0403) 753255
Horsham Road, Afold
(18)6650 yards/***/A/H

Windlemere G.C.
(0276) 858727
Windlesham Road, West End,
Woking
(9)5346 yards/***/D

Windlesham G.C.
(0276) 452220
Grove End, Bagshot
(18)6515 yards/A/H

Wisley G.C.
(0483) 211022
Ripley, Woking
(9)3355 yards/*/A
(9)3473 yards/*/A
(9)3385 yards/*/A

Woking G.C.
(0483) 760053
Pond Road, Hook Heath, Woking
(18)6322 yards/**/A/H/M/L

Woodcote Park G.C.
081 668 2788
Meadow Hill, Bridle Way, Coulsdon
(18)6669 yards/**/B/H

Worplesdon G.C.
(0483) 489876
Heath House Road, Woking
(18)6440 yards/**/A/H/L

Artist: **Robert Guy OPEN FAIRWAYS** *Courtesy of:* **Burlington Gallery**

Unfortunately, for all too many, the first and often lasting impression of a place can be determined by the great blue ribbons that now stretch the length and breadth of the country—Britain's ever expanding motorway network. The M1 (not to mention the M25) cuts through the heart of Hertfordshire and slices off the left ear of Bedfordshire. Between London and Luton it is a fearsome animal at the best of times and passing beyond these two counties one often draws a sigh of relief. The greater expanse of Essex fares a little better, escaping with a few nasty scratches, but in all three counties, the deeper realms are not as often explored as they might be, except needless to say by those who live there.

The golfing breed is a little more fortunate than most. In every county in Britain he, and she, can visit golf courses that are tucked away in the most secluded and tranquil of settings and even in the 'there's an open space—lets build on it 90s', Hertfordshire, Bedfordshire and Essex are not exceptions to the rule.

Hertfordshire

A glance at the map tells you that **Ashridge** in Hertfordshire isn't all that great a distance from London and the M1 but it occupies a particularly peaceful spot and the approach road which runs near **Berkhamsted** Golf Club passes through some glorious countryside—the kind that once covered much of this part of the world. Both are delightful heathland/parkland courses. Berkhamsted is best known for its conspicuous absence of bunkers, though like Royal Ashdown Forest in Sussex it has more than enough natural hazards to test the courage of any golfer, while Ashridge is perhaps most famed for its long association with Henry Cotton, for many years the club's professional. There are many fine par fours at Ashridge, the 9th and 14th being two of the best. The approach to the latter bears an uncanny resemblance to the 17th at St. Andrews—the mischievously positioned bunker front left and the road behind the green—though it's not quite as frightening! Both courses are decidedly worth a visit.

There is certainly no shortage of golf courses in Hertfordshire and several new layouts have recently opened including the impressive 18 hole course at the **Stock's Country House Hotel** (0442) 85341, situated at Aldbury, near Tring — quite close to Ashridge. In the upper realms of the county, Harpenden, convenient for those motoring along the M1, has two courses, **Harpenden** and **Harpenden Common**, the former at Hammonds End being perhaps the pick of the two. A short distance away at Wheathampstead is the **Mid Herts** Golf Club, while on the other side of the country's most famous blue ribbon lies **East Herts** near Buntingford, which is also worth noting if travelling along the A10. In the heart of Hertfordshire stands the exclusive and very impressive new **Brocket Hall** Golf Club near Welwyn. The greater concentration of courses, however, perhaps not surprisingly, is in the area just north of London. **Moor Park**, featured a few pages on, is the most widely known though nearby **Porters Park** (in the quiet of Radlett) and **West Herts** (on the edge of Watford, yet similarly peaceful) also strongly merit attention.

West Herts was once more commonly known as Cassiobury Park after its location. Bernard Darwin in his famous 'Golf Courses of the British Isles' sang its praises highly; 'Of all the race of park courses, it would scarcely be possible in point of sheer beauty, to beat Cassiobury Park near Watford.' One other course to note in Hertfordshire is the first class public course at Essendon, confusingly called the **Hatfield London Country Club.** It is possible to view the county's best courses from a London base. This isn't to say, however, that a number of excellent establishments can't be found beyond the city limits. In Thundridge, near Ware, **Hanbury Manor** (0920) 487722 is a five star country house hotel which can boast, among many things, a golf course first laid by Harry Vardon in the 1920s and recently completely redesigned by Jack Nicklaus Jnr. The course is explored on a separate page in this chapter. In **Hadley Wood**, where there is a well established 18 hole course, the West Lodge Park is an elegant mansion house 081 440 8311, while Boreham Wood carries a restaurant to note—Signor Battis.

The best bet if you are playing Moor Park and looking for nearby quality accommodation is the Mansion House at Grym's Dyke 081 954 4227 in Harrow Weald. St Albans and Harpenden, where the traffic races through, are both littered with good pubs off the busy high streets. St Albans offers its superb cathedral and the delightful St Michael's Manor (0727) 864444 which lies in its shadow. Harpenden's Moat House (05827) 64111 is a little pricey but extremely well thought of. An idea for East Herts—the Redcoats Farmhouse (0438) 729500 at Little Wymondley—very cosy.

For golfers seeking genuine excellence—a true pinnacle perhaps—the Briggens House Hotel (027979) 2416 and its elegant restaurant at Ware should serve admirably. Briggens House has its own 9 hole golf course and is only 6 miles away from Hanbury Manor.

Bedfordshire

Arguably the two leading clubs in Bedfordshire are **John O'Gaunt** at Sandy and **Beadlow Manor** near Shefford: both have more than one course. The former is more established: its two courses, the Championship John O'Gaunt course and the shorter Carthegena are curiously very different in character, the John O'Gaunt being a very pretty parkland type, the Carthegena, a heathland course. Visitors to both John O'Gaunt and Beadlow Manor can expect first class facilities and a friendly welcome and for the latter the Beadlow Manor Hotel (0525) 860800 is naturally very convenient.

Another of the better courses in Bedfordshire is **Dunstable Downs,** laid out on high ground, offering remarkably extensive views—both Surrey to the south and Warwickshire to the north west can be sighted. It is a classic downland type course.

In nearby Berkhamsted, La Fiorentina is an excellent restaurant offering fine Italian food and a knowledgeable golfing host(The town is actually in Herts, but as well as being convenient for Ashridge, it is ideal for the courses of South Bedfordshire). In Whipsnade, the zoo is excellent while the downs nearby are a good place to get rid of some energy. In Dunstable the Old Palace Lodge (0582) 662201 is well worth an overnight visit.

Elsewhere in the county, **Aspley Guise and Woburn Sands** (the more famous Woburn Golf and Country Club lies over the border in Buckinghamshire), is another that provides far-reaching views and a word also for the **Bedford and County** Golf Club, just north of the county town off the A6, and near St Neots in Cambridgeshire, but just within Bedfordshire, **Wyboston Lakes** is a pleasant pay and play course.

In Woburn some excellent hotels can be found as well as the delightful stately home and game reserve. The Paris House (0525) 290692 is an outstanding restaurant while the Bedford Arms (0525) 290441 is a welcoming Georgian coaching inn. The Black Horse and the Bell are notable pubs to visit. Outside the town, Moore Place (0908) 282000 in Aspley Guise is extremely relaxing and in Flitwick, the 17th century Flitwick Manor (0525) 712242 and its restaurant are tremendous. En route to the county town the Rose & Crown (052528) 245 in Ridgmont serves a good pint and bar snacks. In Bedford itself we could call upon the services of the Moat House group—the Bedford Moat House (0234) 355131 or the less expensive Clarenden House Hotel. For grander accommodation the Woodlands Manor (0234) 363281 in Clapham offers a delightful hotel with a quality restaurant. Finally, in the corner of Bedfordshire, Turvey offers two fine restaurants, the Three Fyshes and Laws (0234) 881 655: some accommodation is available in the latter.

Essex

Not much of Essex could be described as 'natural golfing country' yet of all England's counties this is the one witnessing perhaps the biggest explosion in golf course site applications. Strange, isn't it? Two of the top courses in the county are **Thorndon Park** (two miles South of Brentford) and **Orsett** (two miles east of Grays and in the wonderfully named area of Mucking and Fobbing). Neither is a great distance from the M25 and both can be reached via the A128. Thorndon Park, as its name suggests, is a parkland type course situated in a former deer park belonging to Thorndon Hall—a quite stunning mansion, whereas Orsett is much more of the heathland variety with sandy subsoil.

In a similar vein to neighbouring Hertfordshire, a number of the county's better courses are being gradually swallowed up by Greater London—the fine parkland course at **Abridge** with its splendidly luxurious clubhouse being one of them, now lying the wrong side of the M25 (as does the famous course at **Epping Forest.**) **Romford** is one that holds its Essex identity. A well bunkered and fairly flat course, Romford was the home of James Braid before he moved to Walton Heath. Just beyond the M25 the new Martin Gillett-designed course at Billericay, **Stock Brook Manor,** has a growing reputation.

Still further afield, both **Colchester** (the oldest town in England) and **Saffron Walden** have courses set in very pretty surroundings and for lovers of seaside golf there is a pleasant (though windy!) course at **Frinton-on-Sea.** One of the county's newest attractions is the beautifully named **Quietwaters** Club at Tolleshunt D'Arcy, not far from Maldon where there are 36 holes. Finally, for those visiting Chelmsford, both the **Chelmsford** Golf Club, to the south of the town and the **Channels** Golf Club to the north with its superb Elizabethan clubhouse can be recommended, as can the nearby **Warren** Golf Club at Woodham Walter and **The Three Rivers** Golf and Country Club in Purleigh (two courses here).

Essex is blessed with many outstanding hotels and restaurants. Dedham presents an ideal starting point. Here we find the superb La Talbooth (0206) 323150. This is a monument to good food, an ideal place to celebrate a special round of golf. Close by, the Maison Talbooth (0206) 322367 offers stylish accommodation. This delightful village with its views of the Stour also offers the Dedham Vale Hotel (0206) 322273 and its first class restaurant. All are also convenient for the many Suffolk courses. Resisting the temptation to venture further up the Stour and discover the delights of Constable's country we arrive at the coast and Harwich—heading directly for the Pier (0255) 241212, where, as you may suspect, the seafood is the speciality of the house. Golfers taking in the course at Frinton may wish to sample a local hotel, the Rock (0255) 677194. Further up the coast in Brightlingsea, a restaurant and a pub should be pointed out; Jacobs (020630) 2113 is the restaurant, the Cherry Tree is the pub.

More thoughts and in Arkesden a thatched pub, the Axe & Compasses provides good food and a cheerful hostelry. Saffron Walden offers the Saffron Hotel (0799) 522676 and the charming Newhouse Farm. Another Walden, this time a Little one, north of Saffron; in the quiet village lies The Crown—good bar food. Another Essex hotel handy for a motorway, the M11 this time, is the Green Man (0279) 442521 in Old Harlow—situated opposite the village green, the hotel totally belies the proximity of the nearby autoroute. Not particularly close to the county's best golf courses, but well worth a trip is the Whitehall Hotel (0279) 850603 in Broxted where the restaurant is excellent.

Finally we visit Great Dunmow, close to Stansted Airport and where the legendary Flitch trials take place. The Saracens Head Hotel (0371) 873901 in town is small-ish but very pleasant. If you are rushing home and cannot spend a night in the area then dinner at the Starr (0371) 874321 may still be a possibility. Incidentally for those unfamiliar with the Flitch trials, the basic idea is to test (by some rather interesting methods) the suitability of man and woman. Not apparently a necessity for selecting one's golf partner...but it's a thought!

Artist: **H Rowntree SERIOUS BRIDGER**
Courtesy of **Burlington Gallery**

I don't suppose many would dispute that the R&A Clubhouse at St Andrews is the best known 'nineteenth' in the world. However, for the title of 'most magnificent' or 'most grand' it is doubtful whether Moor Park can have many serious rivals. The Moor Park Mansion dates from the 13th century. In its illustrious history it has been the home of Earls, Dukes, Cardinals, Archbishops and even a Queen - Catherine of Aragon living there in the 16th century. During the last war the Mansion was requisitioned, becoming first the headquarters of the Territorial Army, then of the A.T.S. and later of the American 2nd Airborne Corps and it was from within Moor Park that preparations were made for the ill-fated invasion of Arnhem in 1944.

Golf first came to Moor Park in 1923, Lord Ebury founding the Golf Club just four years after the estate had been purchased by Lord Leverhulme. Leading architect Harry Colt was called in to design three golf courses, two of which remain with the Club, The High and The West courses, the third now being a public course (Rickmansworth) although it is in fact maintained by the Moor Park Club.

The Club's current **Secretary** is **Mr. John Davies;** he may be contacted by telephone on **(0923) 773146.** and by fax on (0923) 777109. The **professional, Lawrence Farmer** can also be contacted via these numbers. Visitors are welcome at Moor Park between Mondays and Fridays although it is essential to telephone the Club in advance in order to book a starting time and visitors should note that proof of handicap is required. The only general restrictions during the week are on Tuesday and Thursday mornings, when both courses are reserved for members between 8.30am and 10am. Moor Park is extremely popular with Golfing Societies and up to 110 players can normally be catered for. Those organising must make prior arrangements with the Club, written applications to be addressed to **The Secretary, Moor Park Golf Club, Rickmansworth, Herts WD3 1QN.** In 1994 the green fee for a full day's golf was priced at £50, this entitling the visitor to a round over both courses.

Situated on the north western outskirts of Greater London, Moor Park is very accessible from all parts of the country. Its precise location is off the A404 Northwood to Rickmansworth road. Those travelling from afar should find the M25 of great assistance with junctions 17 or 18 probably being the best points of exit. As for rail stations, Moor Park is the nearest at a distance of approximately three-quarters of a mile from the Golf Club (a good uphill walk mind you!) Rickmansworth station is also less than two miles away.

The major Championships staged at Moor Park are all played over the High Course. Measuring 6713 yards (par 72, SSS 72) it is some 900 yards longer than the West Course, though this at 5815 yards (par 69, SSS 68) is certainly no 'pushover'. The High Course begins with a fairly straightforward, slightly uphill 1st but the 2nd which dog-legs to the right, is one of the toughest 'fours' of the round. Towards the middle of the front nine a sliced tee shot will send a ball into some particularly pleasant properties whose gardens border the fairways (attempting to retrieve your ball is not recommended!) The back nine contains three excellent short holes including the 12th where the attractive two-tiered green is surrounded by willows and is surely one of the best par threes in the country.

Within two years of the Club being founded, Moor Park played host to the 1925 PGA Matchplay Championship, won by Archie Compston. Since then, several memorable professional tournaments and pro-ams have been played here. However, perhaps the best known game of golf at Moor Park took place back in 1928. A 72 hole challenge match was played between the American Walter Hagen, the leading professional of the day, and the aforementioned Archie Compston, one of Britain's finest players. With only one hole completed of the final round the match was all over, Hagen having been defeated 18 up with 17 to play - the greatest margin of victory ever recorded in a matchplay event. Ironically, a few weeks later Hagen won his third Open Championship at Sandwich, finishing three strokes ahead of Compston - poor Archie, he never did win the Open.

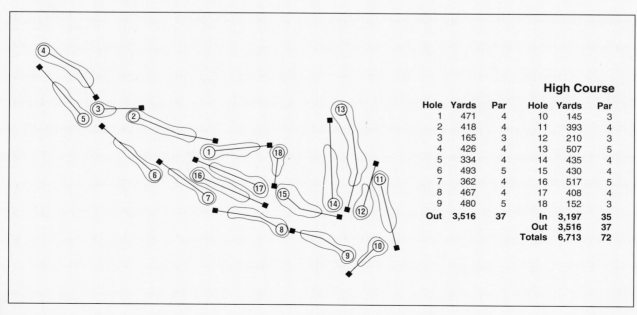

High Course

Hole	Yards	Par	Hole	Yards	Par
1	471	4	10	145	3
2	418	4	11	393	4
3	165	3	12	210	3
4	426	4	13	507	5
5	334	4	14	435	4
6	493	5	15	430	4
7	362	4	16	517	5
8	467	4	17	408	4
9	480	5	18	152	3
Out	**3,516**	**37**	**In**	**3,197**	**35**
			Out	**3,516**	**37**
			Totals	**6,713**	**72**

Hanbury Manor, awarded a much sought after 5 star rating by the AA, is a country house experience to be savoured. A lovingly restored mansion with 96 bedrooms and 10 conference suites, turn of the century charm blends with every modern comfort and service that is always friendly and courteous.

The beautiful 200 acre estate provides a vast array of amenities, including a championship golf course, tennis, squash, snooker and a fully equipped Health Club.

The perfect place to relax or to combine business with pleasure, Hanbury Manor is easily accessible, only 25 miles north of London. The elegantly appointed bedrooms spoil the most discerning traveller, whilst fine dining is available in three enticingly different restaurants including the gourmet Zodiac Restaurant and the casual Vardon Grill.

One of many highlights of a stay at Hanbury Manor will undoubtedly be the magnificent 18 hole golf course, created out of rolling Hertfordshire countryside by Jack Nicklaus II, of Golden Bear Associates. The course measures a testing 7016 yards from the championship tees, with a number of strategically placed bunkers and several picturesque water hazards providing a series of challenges for all levels of players.

The contrasting nature of the Downfield nine, beauti-fully sculpted out of existing meadowland and an old quarry site, and the inward-half - set in breathtaking parkland with mature trees provides a remarkable variety of panoramic scenery that makes for a whole series of spectacular memories. The careful design and conditioning of the course makes Hanbury Manor one of the most beautifully manicured layouts anywhere in Britain.

Whether toning up or winding down, Hanbury provides the perfect environment for relaxing after a game on the championship standard golf course. Indoors or out, the variety of freely accessible leisure activities are numerous, making Hanbury Manor a genuine resort property. The centrepiece of the magnificently equipped leisure facilities is undoubtedly the 17m x 7m swimming pool where a warm welcome is tendered to all aquaphiles under a stunning Romanesque canopy. Steam rooms, Swedish sauna, and a jacuzzi are offered as wonderful wet alternatives and vie with the Hanbury Beauty Studio and sumptuous gymnasium for guests' attention. Hanbury Manor has set out to offer guests a level of facilities and service that redefine traditional standards. Whether as a hotel guest, or as a member of our Golf and leisure sections, Hanbury Manor is quite simply an experience not to be missed.

Hanbury Manor
Thundridge
Nr Ware
Hertfordshire SG12 0SD
Tel: (0920) 487722
Fax: (0920) 487692

There can be few golfing venues in Europe where 'Old' meets and marries 'New' as successfully and interestingly as it appears to have done at Hanbury Manor in Hertfordshire.

The 'Old' is the manor itself, which since the late 19th century has been dominated by a striking Jacobean styled mansion, and its wonderful grounds which since 1918 have included a 9 hole parkland golf course. The 'New' is the very recent conversion of the estate into the Hanbury Manor Golf and Country Club including restoration and transformation of the mansion into an extremely elegant five star country house hotel and the complete redesign of the golf course into an 18 hole championship length American-style golf course.

The original Hanbury Manor course was designed by Englishman Harry Vardon. Vardon was the greatest of the 'Great Triumvirate' of Vardon, Braid and Taylor who dominated golf between 1894 and 1914. The architect of the new Hanbury course is American Jack Nicklaus II, eldest son (or chief cub) of the 'Golden Bear', the greatest of the big three of Nicklaus, Palmer and Player who dominated golf from the late 1950s until the mid 1970s.

So how new, how good and how American is the new course at Hanbury Manor? The official opening took place in the summer of 1991. Jack Jr. was present of course, and so were Tony Jacklin and Dave Stockton who played a friendly match billed as 'The Ryder Cup Captains' Challenge' and which, like the real thing, was won by Stockton. Both Stockton and Jacklin were very complimentary of both the condition of the course and its design. Stockton was also quoted as saying that it was, 'by far the best course I've played outside of the United States'. A shade rash you might think—especially given that it was uttered by someone who played in several Open Championships - but Hanbury Manor undoubtedly has great potential and while the superior conditioning of the course (it may be the best kept course in Great Britain) and the extravagant use of water hazards give the course a very American feel, the surrounding countryside is unmistakably rural England.

Hanbury Manor is located approximately 25 miles north of London, directly off the A10, just north of the Ware turn off. It is important to note that *golf is restrict-ed to hotel residents, Club members and their guests.* The residential green fees in 1994 were £35 midweek and £40 at the weekend. The hotel offers a number of 'packaged residential golf breaks' and those interested should telephone the hotel on **(0920) 487722** for details. The **Manager of Club Operations, David MacLaren** and the **professional, Peter Blaze** can also be contacted via the above number. Written correspondence should be addressed to **Hanbury Manor Golf and Country Club, Ware, Hertfordshire SG12 0SD.**

Only the very brave (or rash?) should attempt to tackle Hanbury Manor from the Championship tees: at 7016 yards it is monstrously long and many of the par fours are beyond the reach of most mortals. From the medal tees, 6622 yards (par 72) is much more realistic while the forward tees and ladies' tees reduce the course to 6057 yards and 5285 yards (par 72) respectively. As well as the mix of an American-type course in a very English setting, Hanbury Manor offers two very different challenges within an 18 hole round. The two nines are laid out on opposite sides of the mansion; the first nine has a much newer feel as here the Nicklaus team had to shape virgin golfing terrain (essentially farmland prior to its development) whereas on the back nine they built over the existing mature parkland of the Vardon layout. The degree of challenge, however, is comparable and both nines contain a number of dramatic and beautifully sculpted holes.

The threat of water looms as early as the twisting, downhill 2nd, one of two outstanding par fives on the front nine. The green at this hole has been raised and built at such an angle with fronting traps that even the biggest hitters are unlikely to attempt the water carry with their second shot. A small lake also features on the par three 6th and the very difficult par four 8th, but for my money the 7th and 9th are even better holes.

On the back nine both the 10th and 15th fairways are bordered by a splendid variety of mature trees and the 13th and 17th call for dramatic do-or-die shots over water. Respite comes at the 18th for though there is yet more water to be carried from the tee, it is not a big carry - besides, the opulent comforts of Hanbury's 19th hole are now within sight.

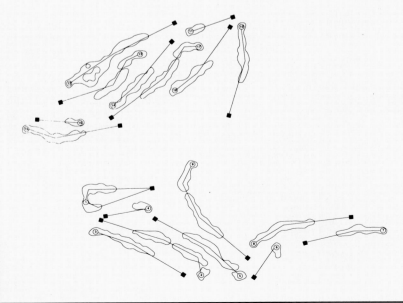

Hole	Yards	Par	Hole	Yards	Par
1	314	4	10	383	4
2	529	5	11	181	3
3	425	4	12	532	5
4	167	3	13	379	4
5	456	4	14	371	4
6	164	3	15	396	4
7	341	4	16	177	3
8	425	4	17	486	5
9	528	5	18	368	4
Out	**3,349**	**36**	**In**	**3,273**	**36**
			Out	**3,349**	**36**
			Totals	**6,622**	**72**

Stocks Hotel and Country Club

A warm and friendly welcome awaits you at Stocks.

The elegance and charm surrounding this beautiful Georgian mansion, together with high standards of food and service will make your stay unique and very special.

Stocks is located in the heart of the Chiltern Hills, set amidst 182 acres of its own picturesque grounds incorporating a new exclusive 18 hole golf course and riding stables. The course is 7100 yards long and has been skillfully designed to blend with already established parkland, using many natural features and fine old trees.

Whether for business or pleasure the unique combination of conference and leisure facilities makes Stocks an ideal venue. All 18 bedrooms including several suites are individually furnished, many with views across the gardens and parkland. The Boardroom and Drawing Room both offer natural day light and a comfortable, peaceful working environment for all levels of conferences.

Leisure facilities include the country's largest jacuzzi, sauna, steam room, solarium, putting green, croquet lawn, heated outdoor swimming pool (May to September weather permitting), golf academy, gymnasium, snooker, tennis and horse riding.

Intricate plasterwork, tapestries, crisp linen and porcelain set the tone of the Tapestry Restaurant, renowned for serving cuisine of the highest standard. The seasonal à la carte menu, though modern, does have a classic influence, with many original dishes. The table d'hote menu is changed daily and both menus utilise fresh ingredients of the finest quality. The Tapestry Restaurant is open daily for lunch and dinner.

The Conservatory is the ideal place to while away an hour or so with views of the surrounding parkland and golf course. There is also a terrace, situated beside the swimming pool, where lunch, afternoon tea and drinks can be served on warm summer days.Corporate hospitality packages are a speciality at Stocks. Golf days, off the road driving events, laser shooting and archery, are only some of the activities which can be arranged.

Stocks Hotel and Country Club
Stocks Road
Aldbury
Nr Tring
Herts
HP23 5RX
Tel: (0442) 851341
Fax: (o442) 851253

Key

*To avoid disappointment
it is advisable to telephone
in advance*

***Visitors welcome at most times
**Visitors usually allowed on
weekdays only
*Visitors not normally permitted
(Mon, Wed) No visitors
on specified days

Approximate Green Fees
A   £30 plus
B   £20 to £30
C   £15 to £25
D   £10 to £20
E   under £10
F   Greens fees on application

Restrictions
G   Guests only
H   Handicap certificate required
H   (24) Handicap of 24 or less
L   Letter of introduction required
M   Visitor must be a member of
another recognised club.

HERTFORDSHIRE

Aldenham G.& C.C.
(0923) 853929
Church Lane, Aldenham
(18)6500 yards/***/B

Arkley G.C.
081 449 0394
Rowley Green Road, Barnet
(9)6045 yards/**/D/H

Ashridge G.C.
(0442) 842244
Little Gaddesden, Berkhamsted
(18)6547 yards/**/A

Batchwood Hall G.C.
(0727) 833349
Batchwood Drive, St Albans
(18)6463 yards/**/E

Berkhamsted G.C.
(0442) 863730
The Common, Berkhamsted
(18)6605 yards/***/A/H/M

Bishops Stortford G.C.
(0279) 654027
Dunmow Road, Bishops Stortford
(18)6449 yards/**/C/H

Boxmoor G.C.
(0442) 242434
Box Lane, Hemel Hempstead
(9)4854 yards/***(Su)/D

Brickendon Grange G.C.
(0992) 511228
Brickendon, Hertford
(18)6315 yards/**/B/H

Briggens House Hotel
(0279) 793742
Briggens Park, Stanstead Abbots
(9)4600 yards/***/F

Brocket Hall G.C.
(0707) 390055
Welwyn
(18)6569 yards/*/F/G/M

Brookmans Park G.C.
(0707) 652487
Golf Club Road, Hatfield
(18)6454 yards/**/B

Bushey G.& C.C.
081 950 2283
High Street, Bushey
(9)3000 yards/**/E

Bushey Hall G.C.
(0923) 225802
Bushey Hall Drive, Bushey
(18)6099 yards/**/C/H

Chadwell Springs G.C.
(0920) 463647
Hertford Road, Ware
(9)3209 yards/**/C

Cheshunt G.C.
(0992) 24009
Park Lane, Cheshunt
(18)6608 yards/***/E

Chorleywood G.C.
(0923) 282009
Common Road, Chorleywood
(9)2838 yards/**/(Tue,Thu)/D

Danesbury Park G.C.
(0438) 840100
Codicote Road, Welwyn
(9)4150 yards/***/F/M

Dyrham Park C.C.
081 440 3361
Galley Lane, Barnet
(18)6854 yards/***/F/M

East Herts G.C.
(0920) 821923
Hamels Park, Buntingford
(18)6449 yards/**(Wed)/F/H/M

Elstree G.C.
081 953 6115
Watling Street, Elstree
(18)6603 yards/***/F

Family Golf Centre
(0462) 482929
Jack's Hill, Graveley
(18)6630 yards/***/D

Great Hadham G.C.
(0279) 843558
Great Hadham Road, Much Hadham
(18)6854 yards/***/C

Hadley Wood G.C.
081 449 4486
Beech Hill, Hadley Wood
(18)6457 yards/**(Tues)/A/H

Hanbury Manor Hotel & G.C.
(0920) 487722
Thundridge, Ware
(18)6622 yards/*/F/G/H/M

Harpenden G.C.
(0582) 712580
Redbourne Lane, Harpenden
(18)6363 yards/**/C/H

Harpenden Common G.C.
(0582) 712856
East Common, Harpenden
(18)5659 yards/**/C

Hartsbourne G.C.
081 950 1133
Hartsbourne Avenue, Bushey Heath
(18)6305 yards/*/F/G/M

Kingsway Golf Centre
(0763) 262727
Cambridge Road, Melbourn, Royston
(9)2500 yards/***/E

Knebworth G.C.
(0438) 814681
Deards End Lane, Knebworth
(18)6492 yards/**/B/H

Letchworth G.C.
(0462) 683203
Letchworth Lane, Letchworth
(18)6181 yards/**/B/H/M

Little Hay G.C.
(0442) 833798
Box Lane, Hemel Hempstead
(18)6610 yards/***/E

London Hatfield C.C.
(0707) 32624

Essendon
(18)6854 yards/***/C

Manor of Groves G.& C.C.
(0279) 722333
High Wych, Sawbridgeworth
(18)6250 yards/***/D

Mid Herts G.C.
(0582) 832242
Gustard Wood, Wheathampstead
(18)6060 yards/**/C

Mill Green G.C.
(0707) 276900
Mill Green, Welwyn Garden
(18)6470 yards/**/C/H

Moor Park G.C.
(0923) 773146
Moor Park Mansion, Rickmansworth
(18)6713 yards/**/B/H
(18)5815 yards/**/B/H

Old Ford Manor G.C.
081 440 9185
Hadley Green, Barnet
(18)6471 yards/***/F/H/M

Oxhey Park G.C.
(0923) 248312
Prestwick Road, South Oxhey
(9)1637 yards/***/E

Panshanger G.C.
(0707) 338507
Herns Lane, Welwyn Garden City
(18)6538 yards/***/F

Porters Park G.C.
(0923) 854127
Shenley Hill, Radlett
(18)6313 yards/**/A/H

Potters Bar G.C.
(0707) 652020
Darkers Lane, Potters Bar
(18)6273 yards/**/C/H/M

Redbourn G.C.
(0582) 793493
Moor Lane, Rickmansworth
(18)6407 yards/**/D
(9)1361 yards/**/E

Rickmansworth G.C.
(0923) 775278
Moor Lane, Rickmansworth
(18)4493 yards/***/E

Royston G.C.
(0763) 242696
Baldock Road, Royston
(18)6032 yards/**/C

Sandy Lodge G.C.
(0923) 825429
Sandy Lodge Lane, Northwood
(18)6340 yards/***/F/H/M

Shendish Manor G.C.
(0442) 232220
Totteridge, London
(9)6076 yards/***/C/H

South Herts G.C.
081 445 2035
Links Drive, Totteridge
(18)6470 yards/**/F/H

Stevenage G.C.
(0438) 880424
Aston Lane, Aston
(18)6451 yards/***/E

Stocks Hotel
(0442) 851341
Stocks Road, Aldbury
(18)7016 yards/***/A/H

Verulam G.C.
(0727) 853327
London Road, St Albans
(18)6457 yards/**/D/H/M

Welwyn Garden City G.C.

(0707) 325243
High Oaks Road, Welwyn
(18)6200 yards/**/B

West Herts G.C.
(0923) 224264
Cassiobury Park, Watford
(18)6488 yards/**/C/H

Whipsnade Park G.C.
(0442) 842330
Studham Lane, Dagnall
(18)6812 yards/**/B

Whitehill G.C.
(0920) 438495
Dane End, Ware
(18)6636 yards/***/D/H

BEDFORDSHIRE

Aspley Guise and Woburn Sands G.C.
(0908) 583596
West Hill, Aspley Guise
(18)6248 yards/**/C/H

Aylesbury Vale G.C.
(0525) 240196
Wing, Leighton Buzzard
(18)6711 yards/***/C/H

Beadlow Manor Hotel G. & C.C.
(0525) 860800
Beadlow, Shefford
(18)6238 yards/***/F
(9)6042 yards/***/F

Bedford and County G.C.
(0234) 352617
Green Lane, Clapham
(18)6347 yards/**/B/H

Bedfordshire G.C.
(0234) 53241
Bromham Road, Biddenham
(18)6185 yards/**/F/H

Colmworth G.C.
(0234) 378181
New Road, Colmworth
(18)6439 yards/***/D
Colworth G.C.
(0234) 781781
Unilever Research, Sharnbrook
(9)2500 yards/***/F/M

Dunstable Downs G.C.
(0582) 604472
Whipsnade Road, Dunstable
(18)6184 yards/**/F

Griffin G.C.
(0582) 415573
Chaul End Road, Caddington
(9)5516 yards/***/D

Henlow G.C.
(0462) 851515
Henlow Camp, Henlow
(9)5618 yards/***/E/M

John O'Gaunt G.C.
(0767) 260360
Sutton Park, Sandy
(18)6513 yards/***/A/H
(18)5882 yards/***/A/H

Leighton Buzzard G.C.
(0525) 373811
Plantation Road, Leighton Buzzard
(18)6101 yards/**(Tue)/C/H

Millbrook G.C.
(0525) 840252
Millbrook, Ampthill
(18)6473 yards/**(Thu)/F

Mount Pleasant G.C.
(0462) 850999
Station Road, Lower Stondon
(9)6172 yards/***/E

Mowsbury G.C.

(0234) 216374
Cleat Hill, Kimbolton Rd
(18)6514 yards/***/E

South Beds G.C.
(0582) 591500
Warden Hill Road, Luton
(18)6342 yards/**/C/H
(9)2590 yards/**/E/H

Stockwood Park G.C.
(0582) 413704
London Road, Luton
(18)5964 yards/***/E

Tilsworth G.C.
(0525) 210721
Dunstable Road, Tilsworth
(18)5443 yards/***/E

Wyboston Lakes G.C.
(0480) 212501
Wyboston Lakes, Wyboston
(18)5721 yards/***/D

ESSEX

Abridge G.& C.C.
(0708) 688396
Epping Lane, Stapleford Tawney
(18)6703 yards/**/A/H

Ballards Gore G.C.
(0702) 258917
Gore Road,Canedon
(18)7062 yards/**/C

Basildon G.C.
(0268) 533297
Clay Hill Lane, Basildon
(18)6122 yards/***/E

Belfairs Park G.C.
(0702) 525345
Eastwood Road North, Leigh-on-Sea
(18)5871 yards/***/E

Belhus Park G.C.
(0708) 854260
Belhus Park, South Ockendon
(18)5900 yards/***/E

Bentley G.C.
(0277) 373179
Ongar Road, Brentwood
(18)6709 yards/**/C/H/L

Benton Hall G.C.
(0376) 502454
Wickham Hill, Witham
(18)6520 yards/***/D

Birch Grove G.C.
(0206) 734276
Layer Road, Colchester
(9)4076 yards/***/D

Boyce Hill G.C.
(0268) 793625
Vicarage Hill, South Benfleet
(18)5882 yards/**/B

Braintree G.C.
(0376) 346079
Kings Lane, Sisted, Braintree
(18)6161 yards/**/C

Braxted Park Estate G.C.
(0621) 892305
Maldon
(9)1980 yards/**/E

Bunsay Downs G.C.
(0245) 222648
Little Baddow Road, Woodham
Walter
(9)2913 yards/***/E

Burnham-on-Crouch G.C.
(0621) 782282
Ferry Road, Burnham-on-Crouch
(9)5350 yards/**/C/M

Canons Brook G.C.
(0279) 421482
Elizabeth Way, Harlow
(18)6728 yards/**/B

Castle Point G.C.
(0268) 510830

Somnes Avenue, Canvey Island
(18)5627 yards/***/E

Channels G.C.
(0245) 440005
Belsteads Farm Lane, Little
Waltham
(18)6100 yards/**/B/H

Chelmsford G.C.
(0245) 256483
Widford Road, Chelmsford
(18)5944 yards/**/B/M

Clacton-on-Sea G.C.
(0255) 421919
West Road, Clacton-on-Sea
(18)6244 yards/***/B/H

Colchester G.C.
(0206) 853396
Braiswick, Colchester
(18)6319 yards/**/C

Colne Valley G.C.
(0787) 224233
Station Road, Earls Colne
(18)6272 yards/***/C

Earls Colne G.C.
(0787) 224466
Earls Colne, Colchester
(18)6842 yards/***/C

Fairlop Waters G.C.
081 500 9911
Barkingside, Ilford
(18)6288 yards/***/E

Forrester Park G.C.
(0621) 891406
Beckingham Road, Great Totham
(18)6073 yards/**/D

Frinton G.C.
(0255) 674618
Esplanade, Frinton-on-Sea
(18)6259 yards/**/B/H

Gosfield Lakes G.C.
(0787) 474747
(18)6512 yards/**/C/H
(9)4037 yards/**/E

Hainault Forest G.C.
081 500 2097
Chigwell Row, Hainault Forest
(18)5754 yards/***/E
(18)6600 yards/***/E

Hanover G.& C.C.
(0702) 230033
Hullbridge Road, Rayleigh
(18)6800 yards/**/B

Hartswood G.C.
(0277) 218714
King George's Playing Fields,
Brentwood
(18)6238 yards/***/F

Harwich and Dovercourt G.C.
(0255) 503616
Station Road, Parkeston
(9)5742 yards/***/F/H/L

Havering G.C.
(0708) 741429
Lower Bedfords Road, Romford
(18)5237 yards/***/D

Ilford G.C.
081 554 5174
Wanstead Park Road, Ilford
(18)5787 yards/***/D

Langdon Hills G.C.
(0268) 548444
Bulphan
(18)6485 yards/**/B/H

Loughton G.C.
081 502 2923
Clays Lane, Debden Green
(9)4700 yards/***/E

Maldon G.C.
(0621) 853212
Beeleig, Langford, Maldon
(9)6197 yards/**/C/H

Maylands G.& C.C.
(0708) 373080
Harold Park, Romford
(18)6381 yards/**/B/M

North Weald G.C.
(0992) 522118
North Weald Bassett, Epping
(18)6239 yards/**/C/H

Nazeing G.C.
(0992) 893798
Middle Street, Nazeing
(18)6598 yards/***/D

Orsett G.C.
(0375) 891352
Brentwood Road, Orsett
(18)6614 yards/**/B/H

Pipps Hill G.C.
(0268) 523456
Cranes Farm Road, Basildon
(9)2829 yards/***/F

Quietwaters Hotel & C.C.
(0621) 868888
Tolleshunt Knights, nr Maldon
(18)6194 yards/***/C
(18)6765 yards/***/A

Risebridge G.C.
(0708) 741429
Lower Befords Road, Romford
(18)6280 yards/***/E

Rochford Hundred G.C.
(0702) 544302
Hall Road, Rochford
(18)6255 yards/**/F/H

Romford G.C.
(0708) 740007
Heath Drive, Gidea Park, Romford
(18)6365 yards/**/B/H/M

Royal Epping Forest G.C.
081 529 6407
Station Road, Chingford
(18)6220 yards/***/F

Saffron Walden G.C.
(0799) 522786
Windmill Hill, Saffron Walden
(18)6608 yards/**/B/H

Skips G.C.
(0708) 348234
Tysea Hill, Stapleford
(18)6146 yards/*/F

Stapleford Abbots G.C.
(0708) 381108
Tysea Hill, Stapleford Abbots
(18)6487 yards/**/C
(18)5965 yards/**/C
(9)1140 yards/**/C

Stock Brook Manor G.C.
(0277) 653616
Queens Park Avenue, Stock,
Billericay
(18)6725 yards/***/B
(9)2977 yards/***/B

Stoke-by-Nayland G.C.
(0206) 262836
Keepers Lane, Leavenheath
(18)6516 yards/**/B/H/M
(18)6544 yards/**/B/H/M

Theydon Bois G.C.
(0992) 813054
Theydon Road, Epping
(18)5472 yards/***/B/H/M

Thorndon Park G.C.
(0277) 810345
Ingrave, Brentwood
(18)6481 yards/**/B/L

Thorpe Hall G.C.
(0702) 582205
Thorpe Hall Avenue, Thorpe Bay
(18)6286 yards/**/B/H

Three Rivers G.& C.C.
(0621) 828631
Stow Road, Purleigh
(18)6609 yards/**/C/H
(9)1071 yards/**/C/H

Toot Hill G.C.
(0277) 365523
Toot Hill, Ongar
(18)6013 yards/**/B/H

Top Meadow G.C.
(0708) 852239
Fen Lane, North Ockendon
(18)5500 yards/**/D
(9)1633 yards/**/D

Towerlands G.C.
(0376) 326802
Panfield Road, Braintree
(9)2703 yards/**/E

Upminster G.C.
(0708) 220249
Hall Lane, Upminster
(18)5926 yards/***/D/M

Wanstead G.C.
081 989 0604
Wanstead, London
(18)6262 yards/**/B/H

Warley Park G.C.
(0277) 224891
Magpie Lane, Little Warley
(27)(3 x 9)/**/B/H

Warren G.C.
(0245) 223258
Woodham Walter, Maldon
(18)6211 yards/**/B

West Essex G.C.
081 529 7558
Sewardstonebury, Chingford
(18) 6289 yards/**/B/H

Woodford G.C.
081 504 0553
Sunset Avenue, Woodford Green
(9)5806 yards/**/C

Artist: **Kenneth Reed MUIRFIELD**
Courtesy of: **Old Troon Sporting Antiques**

Please remember phone day

On 16th April 1995, all area codes starting with **0** will start **01**.
For example: Inner London changes from **071** to **0171**.
Hexham changes from **0434** to **01434**.
Five cities receive an entirely new code and an extra digit in front of the
exisiting local number:

Leeds – 0532 * * * * * *	becomes 0113 2 * * * * * *
Leicester –0533 * * * * * *	becomes 0116 2 * * * * * *
Nottingham – 0602 * * * * * *	becomes 0115 9 * * * * * *
Sheffield – 0742 * * * * * *	becomes 0114 2 * * * * * *
Bristol – 0272 * * * * * *	becomes 0117 9 * * * * * *

The International Access Code also changes from 010 to 00
From 1st August 1994 these new codes will run parallel with current codes.

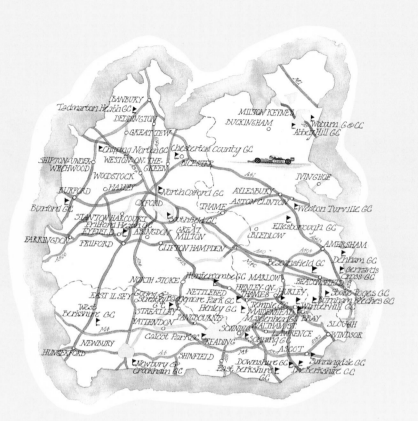

Artist: **H. Rountree STOKE POGES** *Courtesy of:* **Sarah Baddiel's Book Gallery**

Berkshire, Buckinghamshire and Oxfordshire—three very English counties, don't you think? From Burnham Beeches to Banbury Cross, the region extends from the edge of the Chilterns to the edge of the Cotswolds and occupies a very prosperous part of southern Britain.

Oxfordshire

We start at **Huntercombe,** a charming Golf Club which has enjoyed an interesting history. In the early years of the century three rather old Daimler motor cars were used to ferry members to and from the local station and later a thirty seater bus was acquired for the same purpose. The course itself has passed through various owners—at first a property company, then an insurance company (the Norwich Union) and later Viscount Nuffield before finally becoming a members club in 1963. Situated on the edge of the Chilterns at some 700 feet above sea level there are some marvellous views across the Oxford Plain. The course itself is fairly flat and is always kept in first class condition. Nearby in Henley there are two courses worth inspecting, the more established **Henley** Golf Club and **Badgemore Park**, a fairly new course but one that has settled down quickly.

A suitable 19th hole? In Henley the Red Lion (0491) 572161 is a commendable hotel. In Nettlebed, the White Hart (0491) 641245 is a pleasing inn with some good value bedrooms (very handy for Huntercombe) and North Stoke offers the excellent Springs Hotel (0491) 36687 with its first class restaurant, the Fourways (not Fairways).

So to the best golf in the county and, just as The Berkshire has a Red and Blue, so **Frilford Heath** has a Red and a Green. (Indeed, as if to outdo the Berkshire, the club will soon boast 54 holes—a Red, a Green and a Blue !). Frilford Heath is featured later in this chapter. Good food and drink can be found in nearby Fyfield at the White Hart. A short trip to Abingdon can also be recommended. Here the Upper Reaches Hotel (0235) 522311 is most welcoming.

If there is a club that may one day challenge Frilford as the county's best it is the new **Oxfordshire** Golf Club at Thame, close to the M40. Oxford is actually not all that far away either. There are two courses either side of the town—**North Oxford** and **Southfield** and although neither is in the Frilford Heath league both are certainly worth a game. The latter is the home of Oxford University. The Randolph (0865) 247481 is the pick of the Oxford hotels, and for first class restaurants, the Cherwell Boathouse (0865) 52746 is certainly among the best. Oxford, naturally, is more than a little used to visitors of all tastes and for reasonably priced accommodation try the Courtfield Hotel (0865) 242991. Outside in Cumnor, the Bear and Ragged Staff serves good food while a little further afield in Stanton Harcourt, the Harcourt Arms (0865) 310630 has a tremendous atmosphere, a good restaurant and excellent accommodation. Another fine restaurant which is near Oxford and within striking distance of Frilford is the Plough at Clanfield (036 781) 222. A final recommendation in this area is for the true golfing/culinary connoisseur and it is to visit Great Milton and Le Manoir Aux Quat' Saisons (0844) 278881—possibly the country's finest restaurant.

Back on the fairways (suitably fed one hopes!) and beyond the Oxford area, there is a flattish parkland course near Bicester, the **Chesterton** Golf Club and a much improved course at **Burford**. Inching up towards the Cotswolds there is a pleasant course at **Chipping Norton** but the best in the north of the county, although it may be a little more difficult to arrange a game upon,

is clearly **Tadmarton Heath**. At less than 6000 yards in length, it is fairly short by modern standards, but the narrow fairways and a great spread of gorse can make it a very difficult test. It also has a wonderfully remote setting. Not far away, the village of Deddington provides an admirable place to rest the heather-clad spikes, more specifically, the Holcombe Hotel (and restaurant) (0869) 38274 while Burford offers the Lamb (0993) 823155, a truly charming Cotswold inn.

Buckinghamshire

Moving into Buckinghamshire, **Woburn** stands rather alone in the far north of the county. The Golf and Country Club is featured ahead, but a brief thought on where to stay: the Flitwick Manor (0525) 712242 is a favourite with golfers of professional pedigree, and deservedly so. In Woburn Park itself, the Paris House (0525) 290692 is a highly recommended restaurant, Moore Place (0908) 282000 in nearby Aspley Guise and in Woburn village the Bedford Arms (0525) 290441 also come highly recommended. In Milton Keynes, overlooking the **Abbey Hill** public golf course, is the suitably named Friendly Hotel (0908) 561666 while the Red Lion Country Hotel (0908) 583117 is guaranteed to please.

Heading 'down the county', the new **Mentmore** Golf and Country Club boasts 36 holes of wonderfully manicured golf beneath the watchful gaze of Mentmore Towers, the magnificently grand former residence of the Rothschild family. **Ellesborough's** golf course is yet another with rather stately surroundings being located on part of the property of Chequers. Quite a hilly course and rather testing, it is well worth inspecting and not only because there are some commanding views across the Buckinghamshire countryside. Elsewhere in the centre of the county, there is a less attractive but fairly lengthy parkland course at **Weston Turville**, south of Aylesbury.

Ideas for a 19th hole in these parts include in Ivinghoe, the Kings Head (0296) 668388, a splendid restaurant in a 17th century inn, and two 'Bells', the Bell (0296) 89835 in Aylesbury's market place and the Bell (0296) 630252 in Aston Clinton (note the superb wine list here). A couple of good pubs to savour are the Rising Sun at Little Hampden and the Fox at Dunsmore.

It is in southern Buckinghamshire where most of the county's better courses are to be found. **Stoke Poges** has staged many leading amateur events, not at all surprisingly, this being one of the finest parkland courses in the south of England. We have explored Stoke Poges on a later page, but in this area note also **Farnham Park**, a nearby public course. **Denham** Golf Club is a close neighbour of Stoke Poges lying some three miles north of Uxbridge, and as an old club handbook will tell you 'half an hours drive from Marble Arch'. (Add an extra 60 minutes nowadays if you're attempting the journey during rush hour). It is worth making the escape though for Denham enjoys a beautiful setting, deeply secluded amidst some glorious countryside. It is a very good golf course and the clubhouse is a most unusual building having been built around a 16th century tithe barn.

In equally beautiful surroundings is the **Burnham Beeches** Golf Club, situated approximately four miles west of Slough. Others to note in southern Buckinghamshire include **Beaconsfield, Wycombe Heights** (an outstanding new municipal complex in the Chilterns) **Harewood Downs** (at Chalfont St Giles), **Gerrards Cross** and at Denham Court the new **Buckinghamshire** Golf Club designed by John Jacobs. And note that we now have the Berkshire, the Oxfordshire and the Buckinghamshire !

There are a number of very comfortable hotels in the south Buckinghamshire area. These include the Bellhouse Hotel (0753) 887211 just outside Beaconsfield, the Burnham Beeches Hotel (0628) 603333, a former hunting lodge—ideal for the golf course, and the Compleat Angler Hotel (0628) 484444 at Marlow Bridge—a superb riverside setting. Two good pubs are the Kings Arms in Amersham and the Lions at Bledlow.

Berkshire

Berkshire—or should one say 'Royal Berkshire'—is often described as being cigar-shaped. Now whilst this may not say much for the present day talents of cigar-makers it does serve as a fairly rough description in as much as the county is indeed peculiarly long and thin. When it comes to surveying the county's twenty or so golf courses it is tempting to adopt another cigar analogy in that one end could be said to glow rather more brightly than the other.

To the east of the county there is a famous heathland belt and it is here that the twin pearls of **Sunningdale** and the **Berkshire** are to be found. Both clubs possess two 18 hole courses which for sheer enjoyment can stand comparison with anything that golf has to offer. Sunningdale is better known than the Berkshire but it is difficult to imagine a more delightful setting than the tranquil, tree-lined fairways of the Red and the Blue Courses at the Berkshire—and so close to London too. Both clubs are featured ahead. **Swinley Forest** is the other outstanding heathland course in the area, a veritable *paradis terrestre* indeed. However this is a very private club and visitors are only permitted to play as guests of members. Still in heather and pine country is the very attractive **East Berkshire** course at Crowthorne. Also in close proximity is the popular **Downshire** public course where the green fees are naturally less expensive than the above-mentioned courses.

Windsor is where many visiting the area will choose to spend a night or two. Pride of place must go to Oakley Court (0628) 74141. Its comfortable rooms are complemented by splendid grounds and a delightful dining room, the Oak Leaf. Melrose House (0753) 865328 meanwhile, will delight those for whom money is far from no object! In the Ascot area there are a number of good establishments. The Thatched Tavern (0344) 20874 is a pleasant place to have lunch or dinner while the Berystede Hotel (0344) 23311 is an outstanding place to stay. In Sunninghill, near Ascot, the Royal Berkshire (0344) 23322 is perhaps the *crème de la crème* and admirably reflects the quality of the nearby courses. However, a night spent in Ascot does not have to be extravagantly expensive; for affordable comfort try the Highclere Hotel (0344) 25220. A good local pub is the Winkfield in Winkfield Row—a fine atmosphere and a charming restaurant. This area of Berkshire, of course, borders Surrey and we shouldn't forget its many delights. One tip is Pennyhill Park (0276) 471774 in Bagshot—a superb hotel and very convenient (not to mention appropriate) for the likes of Sunningdale.

Time for some more golf and **Temple's** fine course can be glimpsed from the main A23 Maidenhead to Henley Road. It has an interesting layout with many fine trees and lush fairways. Designed by Willie Park early this century, it was for a number of years the home of Henry Cotton. The course is always maintained in first class condition. The golf course at **Winter Hill** is on fairly high ground—apparently its name derives from the particularly chilling winds that sweep across in winter (I have no explanation for nearby Crazies Hill!) From the course there are some spectacular views over the Thames—definitely worth a visit. So for that matter is classy **Sonning**, situated further towards Reading. There is a reasonable course in (or on the outskirts of) **Maidenhead** and just beyond the boating villages of Goring and Streatly, lies the fairly tough **Goring and Streatly** course.

In Maidenhead, Fredrick's Hotel (0628) 35934 has a considerable reputation for comfort - its dining room is also highly acclaimed while in nearby Bray, the Waterside Inn (0628) 20691 is a quite outstanding restaurant. The Boulters Lock Hotel (0628) 21291 on Boulters Island, is a delightful place to stay. Again in Maidenhead, Shoppenhangers Manor (0628) 23444 is a splendid French restaurant. North of here in Hurley one finds yet another gem, Ye Olde Bell (0628) 825881, a very popular Norman inn. Meandering further down the Thames, recommended hotels must include the Great House at Sonning (0734) 692277 with its charming Elizabethan courtyard and also in Sonning, the French Horn (0734) 692204 is a super restaurant. In Streatly, the Swan Diplomat (0491) 873737 has a splendid riverside setting. In need of a pub? A visit to the Bell at Aldworth should do the trick. Another nearby local is the Crown and Horns at East Ilsley. Finally, two locations with good hotel and restaurant combinations are Pangbourne, the Copper Inn (0734) 842244 and Yattendon, the Royal Oak (0635) 201325.

On the western edge of Reading **Calcot Park** golf course poses many interesting challenges; it can boast Guinness Book of Records fame too in that one sterling fellow sprinted round the course in a motorised cart in just over 24 minutes—a more leisurely round is suggested! Recommended 19th holes around Reading include the Thames Moat House (0734) 507951 and the picturesque Bridge Cottage (0734) 713138 at Woolhampton. To the north west of Reading in the increasingly popular **Mapledurham** course and visiting golfers will find suitable accommodation at the Holiday Inn (0734) 391818.

Newbury is of course better known for its racing than its golf, but the **Newbury and Crookham** Golf Club close to Greenham Common is one of the oldest clubs in Southern England and is strongly recommended. The course is hilly and well-wooded, though not overly long. Meanwhile, at nearby Donnington there is excellent accommodation and cuisine to be had (not forgetting golf) at the **Donnington Valley** Hotel and Golf Course (0635) 551199.

Before leaving Berkshire it is worth noting one of the county's more recent additions, **West Berkshire**, situated just south of the village of Chaddleworth. It is a splendid downland course, but not exactly one for the weak-kneed—it stretches to around the 7000 yard mark with one par five measuring well over 600 yards—a hearty breakfast before playing here is a must!

Set in stunningly beautiful countryside, Mentmore Golf & Country Club aims to offer an excellent collection of facilities in tranquil surroundings. The club is overlooked by Mentmore Towers, the former family seat of the Rothschilds and Roseberys, between the Vale of Aylesbury and the Chiltern Hills.

The membership schemes, the range of golf days on offer and the Clubhouse itself are all planned to make sure that you find in Mentmore all you could possibly want from a single venue.

Apart from playing a round of golf on either of the two championship standard golf courses, members and their guests may relax over a drink and enjoy good food in the Clubhouse, set in its own landscaped grounds. Or, you may wish to take advantage of the Country Club and its leisure facilities which include a swimming pool, jacuzzi and sauna.

Business facilities include the Rothschild Suite, a private bar and lounge—ideal for board meetings, sales presentations and seminars.

If you wish to hold a small, informal function at the Club, the private rooms may be divided to suit your party. Members may enjoy unlimited access to all the facilities throughout the year.

The intention at Mentmore is to combine luxury with service and friendliness with efficiency for the very best corporate venue.

Companies of all sizes are welcome and Mentmore offer a special corporate membership package designed to be flexible enough to accommodate all individual requirements.

Mentmore's head professional, a former PGA Cup player, will be available for personalised golf clinics either prior to teeing off or after your round. This can take the form of individual tuition or a general demonstration.

Conveniently situated north west of London, just 42 miles from the centre of the capital and close to both the M1 and M25 motorways, Mentmore Golf and Country Club is easily reached from the South East, Midlands and East Anglia.

Mentmore Golf & Country
Club
Mentmore
Nr Leighton Buzzard
LU7 OUA
Tel: (0296) 662020

Stirrups Country House Hotel is situated in Royal Berkshire's rolling countryside. It is set in its own extensive grounds with pleasant and colourful gardens and terraces. The hotel is family run and provides a blend of personal attention and a truly professional approach.

Each of the 24 luxurious bedrooms has been individually designed to create its own distinctive style and charm. All have the same high level of comfort and facilities. There are ground floor bedrooms and a lift to the upper floors which enable the hotel to welcome disabled visitors. A number of adjoining rooms also link to suit family groups. The intimate candlelit restaurant has an extensive à la carte menu as well as fixed-price lunches and dinners. The wine list is well chosen. Alternatively guests can choose to dine informally and choose from a range of superb bar meals and real ales.

Stirrups achieves the winning combination of the luxury of a hotel with the warmth of a traditional inn. It is in a convenient, yet relaxing location for business meetings, conferences and training events. There are two conference rooms catering for 2-200 delegates and two dedicated syndicate rooms. The hotel can provide full audiovisual, technical and catering services.

There are a host of activities in the area to keep guests fully occupied during their stay. For racegoers the hotel is perfectly located to enjoy a day out at Ascot or Windsor racecourses and is within easy driving distance of Kempton Park. Golfers could not be more perfectly placed — surrounded by a wealth of golf courses including Wentworth, the Berkshire and Sunningdale Golf Clubs.

(Photograph — Highlight Photographers, Cleveland)

Stirrups Country House Hotel
Maidens Green
nr Bracknell
Berkshire
RG12 6LD
Tel: (0344) 882284
Fax: (0344) 882300

On seeing the spectacularly beautiful 18th hole at Killarney during one of his visits to Ireland, the late Henry Longhurst declared, 'What a lovely place to die'. Now whilst one rarely wishes to dwell on the subject of meeting our maker, golfers have been known to indulge in a considerable amount of speculation as to the type of course they might find on the arrival of such an occasion. There is a story of one heated discussion which involved, quite by chance, an Englishman, a Scotsman and an American. The latter argued with great conviction that a large number of the holes would, as sure as hell, resemble Augusta, whilst the Scotsman vehemently insisted that even the most minute deviation from the Old Course at St Andrews would constitute an act of heresy; as for the Englishman, he naturally had no doubts whatsoever that he could stroll through the Pearly Gates and meet a second Sunningdale.

Well, perhaps the heavenly blend is a mixture of all three, but in any event, the gentleman in charge of the terrestrial Sunningdale is the **Secretary, Stewart Zuill**. Mr. Zuill may be contacted on **(0344) 21681. Keith Maxwell** is the Club's resident **professional** and he can be reached on **(0344) 20128.** In common with its neighbour, The Berkshire Sunningdale has two eighteen hole courses, the **Old**, designed in 1900 by Willie Park and the **New** which was constructed by Harry Colt in 1922. Both are splendid, and many would say the leading examples of the famous Berkshire/Surrey heathland type course. The holes wind their way through glorious forests of conifer and pine with heather, bracken and gorse bordering each fairway. All around there are splashes of silver sand.

With its great reputation and close proximity to the capital, Sunningdale is not surprisingly very popular. Unless accompanied by a Member, visitors are restricted to playing between Mondays and Thursdays and must make prior arrangement with the Secretary. A letter of introduction is also required. All written communications should be addressed to Mr. Zuill at **The Sunningdale Golf Club, Ridgemount Road, Sunningdale, Berkshire SL5 9RW**. In 1994 the green fee was set at £84. This entitled the visitor to a full day's golf, enabling a round over both courses. Sets of clubs can be hired from the professional shop should the need arise. Persons keen to organise a Society meeting are also advised to approach Mr. Zuill via the above address.

Sunningdale is situated just off the A30, about 28 miles West of London. Motoring from the South and West the M3, (leaving at junction 3) and the M4 (junction 10) may be of assistance, while from the North both the A332 and the A330 pass through nearby Ascot. The Club's precise location is some 300 yards from Sunningdale Railway Station.

When golfers talk of Sunningdale, invariably it is the Old Course they have in mind, this despite the fact that a large number of people consider the New to be its equal. The former has acquired such pre-eminence largely as a result of the many major professional and amateur tournaments that have been staged there. However the Old Course is perhaps best known for a single round of golf played by the legendary Bobby Jones. In qualifying for the 1926 Open Championship, which he in fact went on to win, the great man put together what has often been described as the finest 18 holes of golf ever seen. Jones' record 66, a remarkable achievement in the 1920s, comprised twelve fours and six threes—33 for the front nine and 33 for the back nine. More amazingly Jones played only 33 shots from tee to green and took 33 putts—as Bernard Darwin put it, 'incredible and indecent'.

In more recent years Sunningdale has been repeatedly selected to host the prestigious European Open. During the 1970s the finest lady golfers assembled for the Colgate sponsored European WPGA Championship and in 1987 the Walker Cup was played at Sunningdale.

At 6586 yards (par 72) the Old Course is slightly shorter than the New (6703 yards, par 70). The respective distances from the Ladies' tees are 5825 yards and 5840 yards (both being par 74). It seems somehow wrong to single out individual holes, each course possessing its own wealth of variety and charm. The views from the 5th and 10th tees on the Old Course are, however, particularly outstanding and the 18th also provides a spectacular closing hole as it gently dog-legs towards the green and the giant spreading oak tree, very much the symbol of Sunningdale.

Sunningdale's glorious setting has been described as both 'heavenly' and 'hauntingly beautiful'. Certainly the golfer privileged to stroll up the final fairway on a summer's evening as the sun begins its leisurely dip, can be forgiven if he amends the words of Henry Longhurst and declares 'What a lovely place to be alive!'

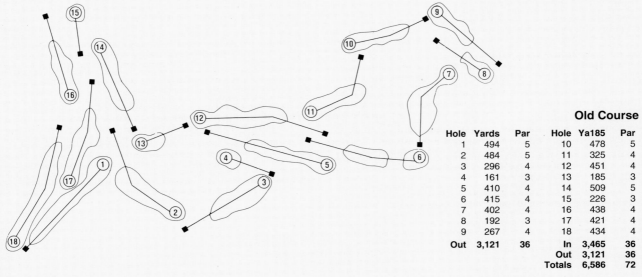

Old Course

Hole	Yards	Par	Hole	Ya185	Par
1	494	5	10	478	5
2	484	5	11	325	4
3	296	4	12	451	4
4	161	3	13	185	3
5	410	4	14	509	5
6	415	4	15	226	3
7	402	4	16	438	4
8	192	3	17	421	4
9	267	4	18	434	4
Out	**3,121**	**36**	**In**	**3,465**	**36**
			Out	**3,121**	**36**
			Totals	**6,586**	**72**

Fredrick's Hotel and Restaurant

Set in two and a half acres of attractive gardens, in the midst of beautiful Berkshire countryside, Fredrick's Hotel, which dates from just after the turn of the century has successfully managed to retain its charm and traditional style whilst at the same time offering the sophisticated modern facilities required to meet the needs of todays business and leisure traveller.

From the moment you enter the immaculate reception of this luxury Four Star Hotel with its cascading waterfall, rich furnishings, antiques and abundant flower displays, a warm and friendly welcome awaits you. 'Putting people first' is the guiding philosophy behind the running of this sumptuously equipped hotel which is indicative of the style of service that guests can expect to receive during their stay.

The hotel's thirty seven luxuriously furnished bedrooms, including five superb suites, a number of which have their own private patio or balcony, offer guests every degree of comfort and are tastefully decorated with individuality and style and provide useful features such as hairdryers, trouser presses and ironing facilities. All rooms are equipped with direct dial telephone, radio, colour TV with satellite, minibars plus ample toweling robes and slippers. On arrival, hotel guests are greeted with a choice of either champagne, white wine or sherry or a service of tea/coffee and a bowl of fresh fruit is placed in every room.

Through from the Reception is the Wintergarden overlooking the delightful patio where guests can relax and enjoy tea or just simply sit and enjoy the view of the gardens, beyond which lies the fairways and greens of Maidenhead Golf Club. In the hotel Cocktail Bar, resplendent in rich dark woods and wall hung tapestries, guests can enjoy an informal drink before sampling the culinary delights offered in Fredrick's Restaurant. Widely acknowledged and recognised by all the major guides as one of the finest restaurants in the south of England. Fredrick's offers truly outstanding cuisine. Amid the elegant decor of crystal chandeliers and crisp white linen, guests are treated to the finest gourmet cooking with imaginative and delectable dishes which are prepared from the best of fresh and seasonal ingredients under the supervision of Executive Chef, Brian Cutler.

Open daily, Fredrick's offers an extensive à La Carte and table d'hote menu plus an excellent value Sunday lunch. This combination of culinary expertise, a comprehensive wine list together with thoughtful and attentive service in delightful surroundings, ensures that every meal at Fredrick's is a special occasion.

Fredrick's Hotel and Restaurant, close to Junction 8/9 on the M4 motorway and the centre of Maidenhead, provides a highly accessible location for visitors to the Thames Valley. With a reputation for offering the best of good food, comfort and hospitality, Fredrick's is an ideal base for playing Wentworth, Sunningdale, The Berkshire and Temple and is also perfect for those attending the races at Ascot and Windsor or Henley in July.

Fredrick's Hotel and Restaurant
Shoppenhangers Road
Maidenhead
Tel: (0628) 35934
Fax: (0628) 771054

The horse racing, golf playing residents of Ascot must number among the luckiest folk in England for right on their doorsteps lie the cream of each sport. They have of course, three golfing pearls close at hand, Sunningdale, Wentworth and The Berkshire, the youngest of the illustrious trio.

The two 18 hole courses of The Berkshire, the **'Red'** and the **'Blue'**, were designed in 1928 by Herbert Fowler—a master among golf architects whose other great works include Walton Heath and Saunton. They occupy some 400 acres of Crown Land over which Queen Anne's carriage used to pass en route to the hunting in Swinley Forest.

Today, both courses give the appearance of having been hewn out of a dense forest, rather in the way that the Duke and Duchess courses were created at Woburn. This, in fact, was not the case, as much clearing of the ancient forest occurred during the First World War when the land was used for military purposes and most of the present thick woodland is of comparatively recent origin.

The Berkshire has been described as being primarily a 'Members' Club', this largely through the conspicuous absence of any big-time professional golf tournament. Perhaps the Club does not wish to have its tranquillity stirred or its rough trampled over by hordes of excited spectators, but this does not imply that the club closes its doors to the outside world, or makes visitors unwelcome. Indeed, The Berkshire is a busy and popular Club with a great number of Societies, the large majority of which choose to return year after year.

For individual visitors, no less than Societies, booking with the **Secretary** is essential and **Major P.D. Clarke** is the gentleman in question. He can be contacted at **The Berkshire Golf Club, Swinley Road, Ascot, Berkshire, SL5 8AY, tel: (0344) 21496**. It should be emphasised that unless otherwise invited, visitors are only permitted to play the course during weekdays. Green fees for 1994 were set at £50 for a single round with £65 payable for a day ticket, this securing a game on both courses—something to be strongly recommended. If clubs need to be hired the **professional, Paul Anderson** can assist—

some forewarning is advisable. He can be contacted on **(0344) 22351**.

The Berkshire can be reached easily from London. It lies just off the A332 road between Ascot and Bagshot. The A332 can be joined from Windsor to the north and Guildford to the south, while motoring from Reading and the West, the M4 should be left at junction 10 and the A329 followed to Ascot.

The two courses are of fairly similar length—the Red slightly longer, measuring 6369 yards to the Blue's 6260 yards, although the latter's par is one fewer at 71. The Red course is perhaps the better known of the two, to some extent due to its comprising an unusual six par threes, six par fours and six par fives. In any event, most people agree that there is little to choose between the two, both in terms of beauty and degree of difficulty, moreover there are many who claim that the golf at The Berkshire is as good, if not better than that offered by its more celebrated neighbours.

The Berkshire is especially famed for its glorious tree-lined fairways. There is a splendid mix of mature pines, chestnuts and silver birch and both courses are kept in the most superb condition. Much of the rough consists of heather ensuring that the wayward hitter is heavily punished.

The Club may have avoided professional tournaments, but it does play host to a number of important amateur events. The Berkshire Trophy is one of the annual highlights on the amateur calendar and before turning professional Messrs. Faldo and Lyle were both winners. It is an open event for players with a handicap limit of one. A major ladies amateur open, the Astor Salver, is also played at The Berkshire, with a handicap limit of six.

As for its 19th hole, the Club possesses one of the country's largest and grandest Clubhouses; furthermore, it has a reputation for providing the most stupendous roast lunches. A fine fellow by the name of Sam is responsible for these veritable feasts.

So then, how about 18 holes on the Blue, one of 'Sam's specials' and then 18 on the Red—can you think of a better way to spend a day?

Red Course

Hole	Yards	Par	Hole	Yards	Par
1	517	5	10	188	3
2	147	3	11	350	4
3	480	5	12	328	4
4	395	4	13	486	5
5	178	3	14	434	4
6	360	4	15	477	5
7	195	3	16	221	3
8	428	4	17	532	5
9	478	5	18	175	3
Out	**3,178**	**36**	**In**	**3,191**	**36**
			Out	**3,178**	**36**
			Totals	**6,369**	**72**

Blue Course

Hole	Yards	Par	Hole	Yards	Par
1	217	3	10	199	3
2	344	4	11	477	5
3	475	5	12	355	4
4	153	3	13	154	3
5	330	4	14	363	4
6	476	5	15	406	4
7	364	4	16	452	4
8	404	4	17	378	4
9	310	4	18	403	4
Out	**3,073**	**36**	**In**	**3,187**	**35**
			Out	**3,073**	**36**
			Totals	**6,260**	**71**

Flitwick Manor is situated in a peaceful corner of Bedfordshire's Green Sand Ridge and only five miles from Woburn Golf Club. Surrounded by 50 acres of rolling gardens extending to the picturesque English countryside, the Georgian Manor has retained much of its heritage. The old deer park, croquet lawns, Gothic grotto and 12th century ironstone church, the kitchen garden with its castellated walls and the large ornamental lake all serve to retain the tradition of years gone by.

The hotel is an exquisite blend of the comfortable and the refined, with fine paintings and period antiques perfectly complementing the deep inviting armchairs and real log fires. This is elegance and hospitality at its finest. At the heart of Flitwick Manor is undoubtedly the Regency dining room. General Manager, Sonia Banks, restaurateur by background but hotelier by training, has as head chef one the country's remarkable young talents, Duncan Poyser. Indeed such are his skills that Mrs Banks feels that the Manor would be best described as a 'first class restaurant with beautiful rooms' rather than 'a beautiful hotel with a fine restaurant'

Duncan's approach to fine cuisine is refreshingly simple: fine ingredients, prime cuts, the correct seasoning and complementary sauces, brought together with a deftness of touch and breadth of vision. Respect for the classics is apparent in the finesse of his medallions of beef gently hot smoked and set on a delicate onion fumet; in honey roast supreme duck glazed with a red wine sauce perfumed with clove; in coarse terrine of chicken and duck liver served with grilled country bread and shallot vinaigrette. His sense of adventure, infused still with a deep appreciation of tradition, is portrayed in dishes which include ravioli of monkfish and leeks glazed with a langoustine vinaigrette scented with mint and vanilla, and a salad of Mediterranean bulgar; local pigeon marinated with curry spices gently roasted, served with a dried chutney and a light cauliflower fondant; leaves of turbot steamed with lovage, resting on a bed of spinach noodles in a champagne sauce.

The luncheon menu from £18.50, (including VAT) offers a choice from four first and four main courses, with dessert, coffee and petit fours. Dinner is £37.50 for three courses, coffee and friandes (including VAT) the price being determined by the main course selected. For that special dinner party Duncan is very happy to devise a particular menu to suit your requirements.

While menus reflect seasonal changes several enthusiastic regulars have ensured that certain dishes are omitted at the chef's peril. Whatever the dish, whether it be a tried and tested formula, or some completely new creation, it is guaranteed to be another of the kitchen's culinary successes.

Whether staying the night or simply enjoying a meal, customers become guests as soon as they walk through the door at Flitwick Manor. The gracious gravelled drive, mellowed walls, green acres, period charm and superb cuisine conspire together to create a special atmosphere that, once savoured will be ever remembered.

Flitwick Manor
Bedfordshire
Tel: (0525) 712242
Fax: (0525) 718753

Amagnificent stately home housing one of the finest art collections in the world, the largest wildlife safari park in Europe and two of the finest inland golf courses in Britain—quite a place Woburn!

The stately home is of course Woburn Abbey which since the reign of Henry VIII has been the home of the Dukes of Bedford, while the wildlife park and the golf courses lie within the grounds of the great estate.

In a game that prides itself on its antiquity the Woburn Golf and Country Club might be described as a remarkably precocious youngster. It was founded as recently as 1976 and its two courses, aptly named the Duke's and Duchess, were not opened until 1977 and 1979 respectively. In such a short period of time Woburn has acquired an enviable reputation.

In charge of all golfing matters at Woburn is **Alex Hay** whose Celtic tones are well-known to millions of television viewers. Mr. Hay is the **Managing Director** and he may be contacted on **(0908) 370756**. The **professional** is **Luther Blacklock**, who can be reached on (0908) 647987. The club Fax number is (0908) 378436.

Visitors, Societies and Company Days are all welcome from Monday to Friday at Woburn, although prior booking is essential. In addition, visitors must be Members of recognised golf clubs and be able to provide proof of handicap. All written enquiries should be addressed to the Managing Director, **Woburn Golf and Country Club, Bow Brickhill, Milton Keynes, MK17 9LJ**. The green fees for 1994 were set at £95 per person per day for parties of nine and above, and £70 for parties of less than nine. This fee is inclusive of golf and lunch while dinner can also be arranged if there are 24 people or more.

Having booked a game, travelling to Woburn ought not to present too many problems. The Club is located approximately 45 miles from London and 73 miles from Birmingham and is well-served by major roads. Both the M1 (junction 13) and the A5 pass close by. For those using British Rail, Bletchley Station, some four miles away has good connections from both London and Birmingham. Luton and Heathrow Airports are also within fairly easy reach. The town of Woburn and the Abbey are both actually within the county of Bedfordshire while the Golf and Country Club lies a short distance over the boundary in Buckinghamshire;

presumably the lions amble from county to county.

Twenty years ago if someone had suggested that a Championship Course (never mind two) could have been built on the Woburn Estate, the famous lions would probably not have been the only ones to roar. The present site was then a dense forest, with giant trees and bracken restricting vision beyond a few yards. Golf architect Charles Lawrie of Cotton Pennink was called in and plans were drawn up. The bulldozers soon arrived and from amidst the pines and the chestnuts great avenues were carved. The fairways flourished on the sandy subsoil and within two years of opening, The **Duke's** Course was considered fit to stage a major professional tournament. It proved a popular decision and a succession of sponsors decided to follow suit. Following its opening the **Duchess** matured with equal rapidity and Woburn soon possessed two precious gems.

The tournaments held at Woburn have included numerous British Masters Championships, The Ford Ladies Classic and the Weetabix Women's British Open. Under the sponsorship of Dunhill, Woburn has in fact become something of a home for the British Masters event, and winners have included such great names as Trevino, McNulty, Ballesteros, Lyle and Faldo. During the 1992 event, won in such thrilling style by Christy O'Connor Jnr, Bernhard Langer was quoted as saying of the Duke's Course, 'It is as good a golf course as we play all year'.

From the back markers (or tiger tees?) the Duke's Course stretches to 6940 yards (par 72), while the Duchess measures 6641 yards (par 72). The corresponding distances for the ladies are 6060 yards (par 75) and 5831 yards (par 74). The best hole at Woburn? Not easy when there are 36 fine holes to choose from, but many people single out the picturesque short 3rd on the Duke's Course; for my money however, the 13th is one of the best par fours in the country.

As one might expect from a modern Golf and Country Club the facilities at Woburn are excellent. The newly rebuilt and refurbished Clubhouse offers a full complement of catering, though dinners must be pre-arranged. For the sporty types there is tennis and an open-air heated swimming pool. The majority of golfers, however, will probably head for one of the two bars. . . .'and toast the Duke and the Duchess.

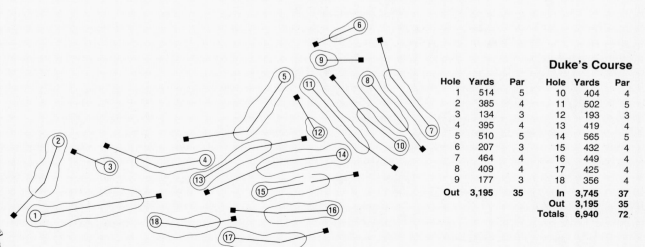

Duke's Course

Hole	Yards	Par	Hole	Yards	Par
1	514	5	10	404	4
2	385	4	11	502	5
3	134	3	12	193	3
4	395	4	13	419	4
5	510	5	14	565	5
6	207	3	15	432	4
7	464	4	16	449	4
8	409	4	17	425	4
9	177	3	18	356	4
Out	**3,195**	**35**	**In**	**3,745**	**37**
			Out	3,195	35
			Totals	**6,940**	**72**

How does it go? 'The first thing we do, let's kill all the lawyers.' Never utter this Shakespearean line at Stoke Poges. Not only will it insult some of the members but it will likely stir the former Lord of the Manor, Sir Edward Coke, the first Lord Chief Justice of England (and the judge who put paid to Guy Fawkes) once owned the estate on which Stoke Poges Golf Club now stands and his presence is still greatly felt for his towering monument can be seen from many parts of the course.

While no one seriously disputes that the best golf in the Home Counties is to be found south west of London, especially in the celebrated heathland belt of Surrey and Berkshire, to continually visit the heather and gorse can get a little frustrating at times. For this reason alone there is good cause for investigating Stoke Poges, near Slough in southern Buckinghamshire. But there are many better reasons for doing so. Stoke Poges is arguably the finest 'established' parkland course in the south of England; it is certainly one of the loveliest and its palatial mansion Clubhouse is one of the most historic and attractive that any travelling golfer is likely to come across.

Writing in 1910, just a year after golf first came to Stoke Poges, Bernard Darwin gave his opinion on the merits of the site. 'It is a beautiful spot, and there is very good golf to be played here; the club is an interesting one, moreover, as being one of the first and most ambitious attempts in England at what is called in America, a Country Club, there are plenty of things to do at Stoke besides playing golf. We may get very hot at lawn tennis or keep comparatively cool at bowls or croquet, or, coolest of all, we may sit on the terrace or in the garden and give ourselves wholly and solely to loafing'. Well, the good news is it's still a marvellously relaxing place!

Visitors who wish to play golf, as opposed to loaf, should first approach the Club's **Secretary, Mr. R.C. Pickering**. He and his very helpful staff may be contacted by telephone on **(0753) 526385**, or by writing to **The Stoke Poges Golf Club, North Drive, Park Road, Stoke Poges, Slough SL2 4PG**. Visitors (including Societies) are welcome between Mondays and Fridays with the exception of Tuesday mornings. All players must possess a handicap. Stoke Poges' **professional Tim Morrison** can be reached on **(0753) 523609**.

The green fees for 1994 are £35 per round, £50 per day. A reduced rate of £25 is payable after 5pm. Junior golfers under the age of 14 and accompanied by an adult pay £12 per round.

The precise location of the golf course is 2 miles from the centre of Slough via the B416. Travellers from London should head towards Stoke Poges using either the M4 (junction 6) or the A40 (leaving at Gerrards Cross). Approaching from the south and west the M3 (junction 3) and the M4 (junction 6) are likely to prove helpful while from the north and midlands the route is by way of the M1 (junction 8) then through Chesham, Amersham and Beaconsfield.

Stoke Poges is a fairly medium-length course: it will not wear you out but it will definitely challenge you to play some precise shots. Harry Colt planned the course, and Colt probably put more thought into the courses he designed than any other architect before or since. At Stoke Poges he made magnificent use of a very wooded landscape and some of the short holes he created here are among the most seductive in England. The 7th is the most talked about; it is not an especially long par three but the tee shot must be measured to perfection for the narrow green has been built at an angle and is fronted by a brook, surrounded by trees and has a devilishly positioned bunker at the back of the 'safest' side of the green. There are at least half a dozen very good two-shot holes, and here one might single out the 3rd, 6th, 8th, 12th, 17th and 18th.

The 19th hole at Stoke Poges is the spectacular mansion referred to in the third paragraph (a famous illustration of it by Harry Rountree is reproduced at the beginning of this chapter). 'A dazzling vision of white stone' was Darwin's description. It was built in 1775 by one of the Penn family of Pennsylvania fame and was assaulted by Odd Job after his evil master, Goldfinger, had been caught cheating by James Bond. (A pity Lord Coke didn't catch him.) Some fine refreshment is available within (phone the catering manager on (0753) 526385 before 11am to reserve an a la carte lunch) and again as we have already commented, it has a marvellously relaxed ambience. 'Begging your pardon m'Lord, what I meant to say was, The first thing we do, let's kill all the loafers!'

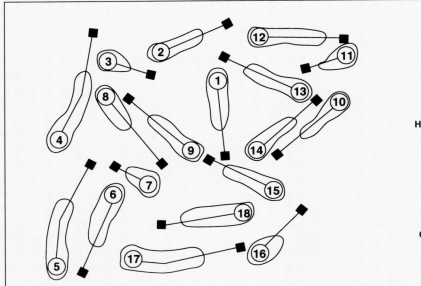

Hole	Yards	Par	Hole	Yards	Par
1	502	5	10	390	4
2	411	4	11	156	3
3	198	3	12	435	4
4	425	4	13	502	5
5	496	5	14	429	4
6	412	4	15	326	4
7	150	3	16	187	3
8	354	4	17	421	4
9	454	4	18	406	4
Out	**3,402**	**36**	**In**	**3,252**	**35**
			Out	**3,402**	**36**
			Totals	**6,654**	**72**

In 1910, just two years after the Golf Club was founded, Bernard Darwin described Frilford Heath as, 'A wonderful oasis in a desert of mud. The sand is so near the turf,' he enthused, 'that out of pure exuberance it breaks out here and there in little eruptions'.

The sand must be the only thing that has ever erupted at Frilford Heath. Peaceable and peaceful, this is one of England's most pleasant and understated golfing retreats. I would also suggest that it is one of England's most underrated venues. In Darwin's day there was only one 18 hole course, today the club has 36 holes—and indeed will have 54 when a third course presently being constructed has been completed. They are quite marvellous tests of golf and although the club has hosted a number of important championships, its reputation is still not as widespread or as great as it merits; moreover the condition and quality of the courses has improved significantly since the late 1980s. It is always pleasing to see the construction of new tees and the careful planting of indigenous trees but at Frilford additional gorse and heather have also been introduced, and of course, there is an important difference between placing new hazards and positioning new hazards. A lot of thought has gone into all the many subtle alterations and when added to the fact that the greens at Frilford have never been better and the rough really is rough (so rare these days) there is certainly much to admire.

Visitors wishing to inspect either or both of the established courses, the **Red** and the **Green** as they are known, should make arrangements with the Club's **Secretary, Mr J W Kleynhans**, preferably by telephoning in advance on **(0865) 390864**. Handicap certificates are required and play is not normally permitted before 10am. The **professional** at Frilford is **Derek Craik**, tel **(0865) 390887** and the Club's full address is **Frilford Heath Golf Club, Abingdon, Oxford OX13 5NW.** The green fees in 1994 were set at £42 for Monday to Friday with £52 payable at weekends and on Bank Holidays. A reduced fee is payable after 5pm (£26 in 1994)

The Golf Club is located three miles west of Abingdon off the A338 Oxford to Wantage road (an old Roman Road). It is only a few minutes from the A420, the A415 and the A34, the latter linking Oxford to the M4.

It is sometimes said that the Red and Green courses are very different in character: I would not use the word 'very'. It is certainly fair to say that the Red is the more exacting (for it is more than 800 yards longer) and that the Green has the greater number of 'pretty' holes, but there is a fair distribution of challenge and charm on both courses.

The **Red Course** (6843 yards, par 73 from the back markers and 6590 yards from the forward tees) opening holes have been modified to accommodate several holes of the new **Blue Course**. Arguably the best sequence on the Red comes between the 5th and the 9th. The 5th is a difficult par four with a fiendish cross bunker that often comes into play as the prevailing wind is against. If the wind is blowing then the par five, 6th is reachable in two, although its green, like most at Frilford is heavily contoured. The 7th is a difficult par four—the key here being a long and accurate drive, and the stroke one 8th has a hog's back shaped fairway, making it a veritable 'beast' of a hole. Beauty follows beast though in the form of the par three 9th where the tee shot is struck over a picturesque pond. On the back nine the golfer confronts a two-tiered green on the short 11th and a saucer-shaped green on the 13th. Two other notable holes are the 12th, with its backdrop of magnificent trees—a kaleidoscope of colours in autumn, and the 16th where a new back tee has turned the hole into a very good dog-leg.

The **Green Course** (6006 yards, par 69) begins more impressively than the Red with a heavily wooded, sweeping par five followed by a most attractive par three. The 2nd is in fact one of two outstanding short holes on the front nine, the other being the 6th. The dog-leg 12th is perhaps the most memorable of the two-shot holes on this course—the drive here is over a natural lake, and there is a trio of lengthy par fours starting at the 14th, but in the right conditions the 18th is just about driveable—thus affording the perfect opportunity to show off in front of the clubhouse!

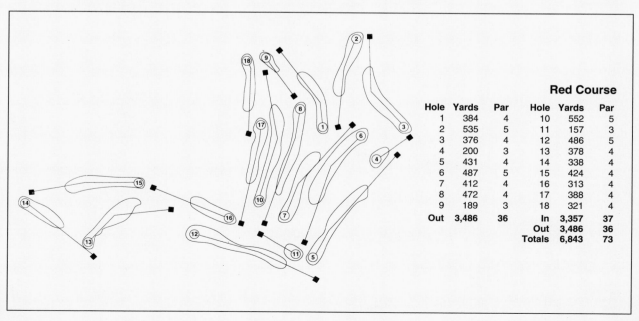

Red Course

Hole	Yards	Par	Hole	Yards	Par
1	384	4	10	552	5
2	535	5	11	157	3
3	376	4	12	486	5
4	200	3	13	378	4
5	431	4	14	338	4
6	487	5	15	424	4
7	412	4	16	313	4
8	472	4	17	388	4
9	189	3	18	321	4
Out	3,486	36	In	3,357	37
			Out	3,486	36
			Totals	6,843	73

Key

To avoid disappointment it is advisable to telephone in advance

****Visitors welcome at most times*
***Visitors usually allowed on weekdays only*
**Visitors not normally permitted (Mon, Wed) No visitors on specified days*

Approximate Green Fees
   A £30 plus
   B £20 to £30
   C £15 to £25
   D £10 to £20
   E under £10
   F Greens fees on application

Restrictions
   G Guests only
   H Handicap certificate required
   H (24) Handicap of 24 or less
   L Letter of introduction required
   M Visitor must be a member of another recognised club.

BERKSHIRE

Bearwood G.C.
(0734) 760060
Mole Road, Sindlesham
(9)5624 yards/**/E/H
The Berkshire G.C.
(0344) 21495
Swinley Road, Ascot
(18)6356 yards/**/A/L
(18)6260 yards/**/A/L

Bird Hills G.C.
(0628) 7710307
Drift Road, Hawthorn Hill
(18)6212 yards/***/D

Blue Mountain Golf Centre
(0344) 300200
Wood Lane, Binfield
(18)6097 yards/***/D
Calcot Park G.C.
(0734) 427124
Bath Road, Calcot, Reading
(18)6283 yards/**/F

Datchet G.C.
(0753) 541872
Buccleuch Road, Datchet
(9)5978 yards/**/C/H

Donnington Valley G.C.
(0635) 32488
Old Oxford Road, Donnington
(18)4002 yards/***/F

Downshire G.C.
(0344) 302030
Easthampstead Park, Wokingham
(18)6382 yards/***/E

East Berkshire G.C.
(0344) 772041
Ravenswood Avenue, Crowthorne
(18)6345 yards/**/A/H

Goring & Streatley G.C.
(0491) 873229
Rectory Road, Streatley
(18)6255 yards/**/B

Hawthorn Hill G.C.
(0628) 771030
Drift Road, Maidenhead
(18)6286 yards/***/E

Hennerton G.C.
(0734) 401000
Crazies Hill Road, Wargrave
(9)2730 yards/***/D

Hurst G.C.
(0734) 344355
Sandford Lane, Hurst, Wokingham
(9)3013 yards/***/E

Lavender Park G.C.
(0344) 884074
Swinley Road, Ascot
(9)1104 yards/***/E

Maidenhead G.C.
(0628) 24693
Shoppenhangers Road, Maidenhead
(18)6360 yards/**/B/H

Mapledurham G.C.
(0734)463353
Chazey Heath, Mapledurham
(18)5625 yards/***/D

Mill Ride G.C.
(0344) 886777
Mill Ride, North Ascot
(18)6690 yards/***/A/H

Newbury & Crookham G.C.
(0635) 40035
Burys Bank Road, Greenham, Newbury
(18)5880 yards/**/B/M

Pincents Manor G.C.
(0734) 323511
Pincents Lane, Calcot
(9)4882 yards/***/E

Reading G.C.
(0734) 472909
Kidmore End Road, Emmer Green, Reading
(18)6212 yards/**(not Friday)/B

Royal Ascot G.C.
(0344) 25175
Winkfield Road, Ascot
(18)5653 yards/**/F/M

Sand Martins G.C.
(0734) 792711
Finchampstead Road, Wokingham
(18)6297 yards/**/B

Sonning G.C.
(0734) 693332
Duffield Road, Sonning
(18)6366 yards/**/F/H

Sunningdale G.C.
(0344) 21681
Ridgemount Road, Sunningdale, Ascot
6586 yards/**/A/H/L
6676 yards/**/A/H/L

Sunningdale Ladies G.C.
(0344) 20507
Cross Road, Sunningdale
(18) 3622 yards/***/B(men extra)

Swinley Forest G.C.
(0344) 20197
Coronation Road, South Ascot
(18)6011 yards/*/A/G/H

Temple G.C.
(0628) 824248
Henley Road, Hurley, Maidenhead
(18)6206 yards/**/A/H

West Berkshire G.C.
(0488) 638574
Chaddleworth, Newbury
(18)7053 yards/**/C

Winter Hill G.C.
(0628) 527613
Grange Lane, Cookham, Maidenhead
(18)6408 yards/**/C/H

BUCKINGHAMSHIRE

Abbey Hill G.C.
(0908) 563845
Monks Way, Two Mile Ash, Stony Stratford
(18)6193 yards/***/F

Aylesbury Golf Centre
(0290) 393644
Hulcott Lane, Bierton
(9)5488 yards/***/E

Beaconsfield G.C.
(0494) 676545
Seer Green, Beaconsfield
(18)6487 yards/**/A/H

Buckingham G.C.
(0280) 815566
Tingewick Road, Buckingham
(18)6082 yards/**/B/M

Burnham Beeches G.C.
(0628) 661448
Green Lane, Burnham
(18)6449 yards/**/A/H

Chartridge Park G.C.
(0494) 791772
Chartridge, Chesham
(18)5721 yards/***/C

Chesham and Ley Hill G.C.
(0494) 784541
Ley Hill, Chesham
(9)5240 yards/**/F

Chiltern Forest G.C.
(0296) 630899
Aston Hill, Halton, Aylesbury

(18)6038 yards/**/C

Denham G.C.
(0895) 832022
Tilehouse Lane, Denham
(18)6451 yards/**(Fri)/A/L/M

Denham Court G.C.
(0895) 835777
Denham
(18)6880 yards/*/A/G

Ellesborough G.C.
(0296) 622114
Butlers Cross, Aylesbury
(18)6271 yards/**/F/H

Farnham Park G.C.
(0753) 647065
Park Road, Stoke Poges
(18)6172 yards/***/E

Flackwell Heath G.C.
(06285) 520929
Treadaway Road, Flackwell Heath
(18)6207 yards/**/B/H

Gerrards Cross G.C.
(0753) 885300
Chalfont Park, Gerrards Cross
(18)6295 yards/**/A/H

Harewood Downs G.C.
(0494) 762308
Cokes Lane, Chalfont St Giles
(18)5958 yards/**/B/H

Hazelmere G.&C.C.
(0494) 718298
Penn Road, Hazelmere, High Wycombe
(18)6039 yards/***/B

Iver G.C.
(0753) 655615
Hollow Hill Lane, Iver
(9)6214 yards/***/E

Ivinghoe G.C.
(0296) 668696
Wellcroft, Ivinghoe
(9)4508 yards/***/F

Lambourne G.C.
(0628) 666755
Dropmore Road, Burnham
(18)6746 yards/***/A/H

Little Chalfont G.C.
(0494) 764877
Lodge Lane, Little Chalfont
(9)5852 yards/***/F

Mentmore G.&C.C.
(0296) 662020
Mentmore, Leighton Buzzard
(18)6777 yards/**/B/H

Princes Risborough G.C.
(0844) 346989
Lee Road, Saunderton Lee
(9)5017 yards/***/D

Silverstone G.C.
(0280) 850005
Silverstone Road, Stowe
(18)6164 yards/***/D

Stoke Poges G.C.
(0753) 526385
Stoke Park, Park Road, Stoke Poges
(18)6654 yards/**/A/H

Stowe G.C.
(0280) 813650
Stowe, Buckingham
(9)4573 yards/**/F/G

Thorney Park G.C.
(0895) 422095
Thorney Mill Lane, Iver
(9)3000 yards/**/E

Three Locks G.C.
(0525) 270050
Great Brickhill, Milton Keynes
(9)6654 yards/***/E

Wavendon Golf Centre
(0908) 281811
Wavendon, Milton Keynes
(18)5800 yards/***/E

Weston Turville G.C.
(0296) 24084
New Road, Weston Turville
(18)6782 yards/***/D

Wrexham Park G.C.
(0753) 663271
Wrexham Street, Wrexham
(18)5836 yards/***/D
(9)2383 yards/***/E

Whiteleaf G.C.
(08444) 3097
The Clubhouse, Whiteleaf
(9)5391 yards/**/C/H

Windmill Hill G.C.
(0908) 378623
Tannenhoe Lane, Bletchley
(18)6773 yards/***/E

Woburn G. and C.C.
(0908) 370756
Bow Brickhill, Milton Keynes
(18)6913 yards/**/F/H
(18)6641 yards/**/F/H

Wycombe Heights G.C.
(0494) 816686
Rayners Avenue, Loudwater
(18)6300 yards/***/E

OXFORDSHIRE

Aspect Park G.C.
(0491) 578306
Remenham Hill, Henley on Thames
(18)6369 yards/***/C/H

Badgemore Park G.C.
(0491) 572206
Badgemore Park, Henley on Thames
(18)6112 yards/***/B/H

Braties G.C.
(0608) 685633
Sutton Lane, Brailes
(18)6270 yards/**/C/M

Burford G.C.
(0993) 822583
Burford
(18)6405 yards/**/B/H

Cherwell Edge G.C.
(0295) 711591
Chacombe, Banbury
(18)5925 yards/***/E

Chesterton G.C.
(0869) 241204
Chesterton, Bicester
(18)6224 yards/***/D/H

Chipping Norton G.C.
(0608) 2383
Southcombe, Chipping Norton
(18)6283 yards/***/C

Drayton Park G.C.
(0235) 550607
Steventon Road, Drayton
(18)6500 yards/***/D

Frilford Heath G.C.
(0865) 390864
Frilford Heath, Abingdon
(18)6768 yards/***/A/H
(18)6006 yards/***/A/H

Hadden Hill G.C.
(0235) 510410
Wallingford Road, Didcot
(18)6563 yards/***/D
Henley G.C.
(0491) 575742
Harpsden, Henley on Thames
(18)6330 yards/**/A/H

Huntercombe G.C.
(0491) 641207
Nuffield, Henley on Thames
(18)6301yards/**/A/H

Lyneham G.C.
(0993) 831841
Lyneham, Chipping Norton
(18)6669 yards/***/D

North Oxford G.C.
(0865) 54415
Banbury Road, Oxford
(18)5805 yards/**/B/H

The Oxfordshire G.C.
(0844) 278300
Rycote Lane, Milton Common, Thame
(18)7187 yards/***/F/M/L

Southfield G.C.
(0865) 242158
Hill Top Road, Oxford
(18)6230 yards/**/B/H

Tadmarton Heath G.C.
(0608) 737278
Wiggington, Banbury
(18)5917 yards/**/B/H

Waterstock G.C.
(0844) 338093
Oxford Road, Cowley
(18)6482 yards/***/D

Map labels:
KIDDERMINSTER · Kidderminster GC · BELBROUGHTON · Blackwell GC · BROMSGROVE · ABBERLEY · DROITWICH · Kington GC · KINGTON · WORCESTER · Worcester GC · WEOBLEY · Herefordshire GC · TILLINGTON · GREAT MALVERN · Worcestershire GC · COLWALL · MALVERN WELLS · EVESHAM · HEREFORD · Belmont GC · WOOLHOPE · BROADWAY · Broadway GC · TEWKESBURY · Ross-on-Wye GC · CORSE LAWN · BISHOPS CLEEVE · BUCKLAND · ROSS-ON-WYE · Tewkesbury Park Hotel GC · CLEEVE HILL · Cleeve Hill GC · MORETON-IN-MARSH · WILTON · SOUTHAM · LOWER SLAUGHTER · SYMONDS YAT WEST · SHURDINGTON · CHELTENHAM · Lilley Brook GC · GLOUCESTER · Gloucester Hotel & GC · UPTON · Cotswold Hills GC · BOURTON-ON-THE-WATER · COLEFORD · Royal Forest of Dean GC · ST LEONARDS · PAINSWICK · AMBERLEY · Cirencester GC · BIBURY · Stinchcombe GC · MINCHINHAMPTON · Minchinhampton GC · CIRENCESTER · KINGSCOTE · TETBURY · WESTONBIRT

Artist: **C.E. Brock** THE DRIVE Courtesy of: **Sotheby's**

Ahush descends as you ponder your first swing in old Worcestershire. Apple and cherry trees are in blossom and in the distance a herd of white faced Herefords appraise your stance. You're fortunate, for several hundred years ago the air in these parts was thick with the clatter of sword against sword but now there is peace. Crack! Straight down the fairway—the echo resounds and then dies—you're on your way.

Herefordshire, Worcestershire and Gloucestershire—what a lovely trio! Bordering the principality the region is arguably the most tranquil in England. It is an area of rich pastures and cider orchards, of small market towns and sleepy villages rather than crowded cities and encompasses the Cotswolds and the Malverns, the beautiful Wye Valley and the splendid Vale of Evesham. Truly a green and pleasant land!

Hereford & Worcester

Herefordshire and Worcestershire are no more—at least according to the modern county boundaries—Hereford and Worcester it is now, no doubt a compromise to the two county towns.

Golf courses aren't exactly plentiful, but those there are tend to be very scenic, often hidden away deep in the glorious countryside. To the north west of Hereford, **Kington** and **Herefordshire** are two typical examples and both clubs warmly welcome visitors. Kington is further towards Wales and is reputed to be the highest course in either country. It is a place where poor golf can always be blamed on the rarefied atmosphere. To the south of Hereford is another attractive course, **Belmont**, one of the newer courses in the region, but one that has already gained a good reputation.

Hereford is a natural base when golfing in the area and there are a number of good hotels. The Graftonbury Hotel (0432) 356411 is a charming garden hotel with easy access to Belmont Golf Club. The Green Dragon Hotel (0432) 272506 is particularly comfortable—note the many four poster beds—and in nearby Much Birch, the Pilgrim Hotel (0981) 540742 is a splendid former rectory. The Hopbine Hotel (0432) 268722 and the White Lodge Hotel offer reasonably priced accommodation near to Hereford city centre. A short drive to Weobley reveals the Red Lion (0544) 318419, a 14th century inn in the centre of a delightful village—very handy for Herefordshire Golf Club. Near the same golf course is a good pub, the Bell at Tillington, while for Belmont, the Butchers Arms is recommended (some accommodation here too). Kington has a first class restaurant, Penrhos Court (0544) 230720, and also boasts the Oxford Arms (0544) 230322, a 16th century coaching inn near to the golf course. Visitors to this pleasant area should also consider the excellent Allt-yr-ynys Hotel (0873) 890307 in Walterstone.

Ross-on-Wye is a renowned beauty spot and the town's golf course reflects the reputation. Set in the heart of the Wye Valley and surrounded by a blaze of colour, it's hard to believe that the M50 is under a mile away (junction 4). If staying a few days in the area, the Pengethley Manor Hotel (0989) 730211 is most charming, and the Peterstow Country House boasts an award winning restaurant. Alternatively, try the New Inn (0989) 730274 in St Owens Cross where you are sure to receive an equally warm welcome.

Worcester is an attractive city with a very beautiful cathedral which overlooks the famous old county cricket ground. Only a mile from the town centre off the A4103 is the **Worcester** Golf and Country Club. The oldest course in the county, and possibly the finest is the appropriately named **Worcestershire** Golf Club, situated two miles south of Great Malvern. There are extensive views from the course towards the Malverns, the Severn Valley and the Cotswolds. Elsewhere in the county, the **Vale** Golf and Country Club near Pershore has recently opened to generous acclaim and boasts 27 testing holes and a driving range. An even newer development to experience is the **Bank House** in Bransford. The final recommendations in Worcestershire are **Kidderminster** and the popular **Blackwell** Golf Club near Bromsgrove.

Near Worcester, the Elms Hotel (0299) 896666 at Abberley is an outstanding country house while Malvern Wells offers the delightful Cottage in the Wood Hotel (0684) 573487 and an excellent restaurant, the Croque-en-Bouche (0684) 565612. Worcester itself contains the stylish Fownes Hotel (0905) 613151 and the moderately priced Giffard Hotel (0905) 726262. Browns Restaurant (0905) 26263 is also well worth a visit. Great Malvern provides a charming 19th century coaching inn, the Foley Arms (0684) 573397. A highly recommended hotel in Redditch is Abbey Park (0527) 63918. A final suggestion for the area is to visit Colwall Village, here the Colwall Park Hotel (0684) 40206 is exceptionally good value.

Gloucestershire

Heading into Gloucestershire, I trust that when Doctor Foster went to Gloucester he wasn't a well travelled golfer. The county has very few courses and Gloucester itself didn't possess one at all until as recently as 1976. Neighbouring Cheltenham has been a little more fortunate but granted one or two exceptions, the quality of the golf in the county doesn't exactly match up to the undeniable quality of its scenery.

The county's two best known courses are probably **Cotswold Hills** and **Lilley Brook**, located to the north and south of Cheltenham respectively. Both offer commanding views of the Gloucestershire countryside, especially perhaps Lilley Brook, one of southern England's most undulating courses. Each is well worth a visit and the beautiful Regency manor of the Cheltenham Park Hotel (0242) 222021 is only minutes from both.

Cleeve Hill is Cheltenham's third 18 hole course. Situated on high ground to the north of the town it can get rather cold in winter. One anonymous person said that when visiting Cheltenham he enjoyed a game at Lilley Brook in the summer as half of him was mountain goat, and at Cleeve Hill in the winter because the other half of him was eskimo!

The Cheltenham area has many fine hotels, but perhaps the best known is the Queens Hotel (0242) 514724. Lypiatt House (0242) 224994 is a popular alternative. A good hotel in the surrounding hills is the simply splendid Greenway (0242) 862352 in Shurdington. This hotel offers a warm welcome, a first class menu and beautiful grounds. Also, not far out of Cheltenham at Toddington, Woodleys (0242) 621313 is a superior guesthouse. In Cleeve Hill, the Malvern View Hotel (0242) 672017 is well thought of, its name self-explanatory, and a little further north in Bishops Cleeve, Cleeveway House (0242) 672585 has a small number of rooms and an outstanding restaurant.

Outside of Cheltenham, **Minchinhampton** has perhaps the biggest golfing reputation. A club of great character, it celebrated its centenary in 1989. There are two courses here, an Old and a New, the latter constructed in the 1970s. A quick word for another course in the south of the county, **Stinchcombe Hill** which is also well thought of. A first class place to stay nearby is Burleigh Court

Allt-yr-Ynys, situated on wooded river banks in Herefordshire, and standing in an acre of well-established gardens, is an elegant country hotel with a fascinating history. Robert Cecil came to this beautiful spot in 1091, after the conquest of Glamorgan, and it is said that Elizabeth I was once a house guest here. The historical appeal of the hotel remains intact - Allt-yr-Ynys as it is today was built in 1550, and retains much fine craftsmanship of the period. Moulded ceilings, oak panelling and door pillars feature throughout the house, yet at the same time the hotel offers the very finest of modern comforts.

All the bedrooms are individually furnished - the Master Suite, for example, has a Jacobean fourposter, and each has an ensuite bathroom, telephone, colour television and radio. Ancient outbuildings have been converted to provide additional luxury accommodation.

Much attention is paid to personal service at the hotel - guest are warmly and genuinely welcomed and the staff do their utmost to meet the particular needs of every guest. The Chef is only too happy to prepare special dishes, and the hotel caters for weddings and functions of all kinds. Great care is taken with the quality and presentation of food, using only the finest cuts of meat and the freshest of vegetables and other ingredients.

Guest can enjoy the indoor heated swimming pool and jacuzzi at Allt-yr-Ynys, or perhaps the Clay Shooting Centre, ideal for corporate entertaining. Realising that nobody wants to be ankle-deep in mud in wet weather clothes and wellingtons, the stands and observation area are conveniently situated under one roof.

The setting is every bit as magnificent as the hotel. On the border between England and Wales, on the English side, the rolling wooded farmland of Herefordshire gives way to the Malvern Hills beyond. On the Welsh side the Fwddog Ridge dominates the landscape. Part of the Black Mountains, it runs north to Hay-on-Wye, all within the Brecon Beacons National Park. Houses and castles of historic interest abound in the area - just as a taster, the ancient castle at Chepstow, which looks down the River Wye, and Llanthony Abbey in the Black Mountains. If you are a keen golfer Allt-yr-Ynys is conveniently situated for Abergavenny, Monmouth, Chepstow and Hereford Golf Courses.

Allt-yr-Ynys is many things to many people: Conference Centre, country retreat, holiday hotel or activity holiday location. The common thread is the personal involvement of owners and staff - you as a guest will find that your interests are always paramount.

Allt-yr-Ynys
Walterstone
Herefordshire
Tel: (0873) 890307
Fax: (0873) 890539

The Cheltenham Park Hotel is a beautiful, recently extended Regency manor house set in nine acres of landscaped gardens with a natural trout lake and waterfalls. The hotel has superb views over the Leckhampton Hills and the adjacent Lilleybrook Golf Course.

This luxury hotel was totally refurbished and extended to 154 sumptuously appointed bedrooms. These include the Presidential Suite and executive rooms which command superb views over the attractive gardens, with their meandering walkways, gentle waterfalls, romantic arbours and classically inspired gazebo.

The Lakeside Restaurant offers the best of modern English cuisine with a choice from either the table d'hote or the à la carte menus, using only the freshest of produce. Your meal will be complemented with a selection of fine wines from the cellars.

There are two bars to choose from: the Tulip Bar with its marble fireplaces, original oak panelling and large patio overlooking the golf course, or the congenial Lakeside Bar with its terraces down to the lake.

The Cheltenham Park Hotel is only two miles from the town centre and is therefore only a short drive from the racecourse. Access to and from all parts of the country is quick and easy as Cheltenham Spa lies at the hub of the country's motorway/dual carriageway network with excellent rail and coach services as well as its own airport at Staverton.

The hotel's location lends itself to ease of access to a wide range of attractions including the famous Pittville Pump Rooms in Cheltenham where the spa waters may be taken. Cheltenham's Everyman Theatre plays host to a great variety of very popular productions throughout the year and is also only a short drive from the hotel. There are a wide range of private and National Trust Gardens to visit.

This beautiful hotel is right next door to the well known Lilleybrook Golf Course and only minutes away from Cotswold Hills Golf Course - a perfect golfing location. Alternatively, a day at the races, a luxury break away from it all, or a peaceful environment for a business meeting, the Cheltenham Park Hotel is the ideal choice.

The Cheltenham Park Hotel
Cirencester Road
Charlton Kings
Cheltenham GL53 8EA
Tel: (01242) 222021
Fax: (01242) 226935

(0453) 883804, while to the north the Amberley Inn (0453) 872565 in Amberley, with its fine views over Woodchester Valley has considerable charm. For a good pub visit **Painswick** for the the Royal Oak—a short golf course here too.

The 18 hole course at **Cirencester** is probably the nearest one gets to golf in the Cotswolds. Cirencester is certainly a pleasant enough place but to most of us the real Cotswolds are the many wonderfully named villages: Bourton-on-the-Water, Stow-on-the-Wold, Upper Slaughter and Lower Slaughter.

Gloucester's newish course lies within the grounds of the **Gloucester Hotel** (0452) 525653 at Robinswood Hill. A luxurious country club, there are in fact 27 holes here plus all manner of accompanying leisure facilities. The 18 hole course enjoys a pleasant setting and has matured very rapidly. The same can be said of **Tewkesbury Park** Hotel's golf course (0684) 295405 which is laid out on the site of the famous Roses battle of 1471. Both hotels are comfortable and their courses are open to residents and non-residents alike, although booking in advance is preferred. However, for a special occasion, we can recommend a stay at **Puckrup Hall** (0684) 296200 (previously known as Tewkesbury Hall), an elegant Regency house set in 40 acres of parkland with an adjacent new

18 hole golf course and at Upton St Leonards, near Gloucester, Hatton Court (0452) 617412 is most relaxing.

The Forest of Dean is our next port of call—another beauty spot and some good golf too at the **Royal Forest of Dean** Golf Club in Coleford. In Coleford itself, there is the lovely 16th century Poolway House (0594) 833937 which is well worth more than an overnight treat as there are some exceptional value golfing breaks available through the hotel. A notable inn nearby is the Speech House (0594) 822607. Staying a few days in the area is recommended: the countryside is splendid and just eight miles away, over the border in Wales, lies Chepstow and the delights of **St Pierre**.

Last but not least, **Broadway** Golf Club—the course being a mile and a half or so from 'the loveliest village in England'. It really is a beautiful part of the world and those wishing to do some exploring will find several superb hotels, any of which will make an ideal base. The Lygon Arms (0386) 852255 in Broadway with its outstanding frontage probably takes pride of place but for excellent value the Collin House Hotel (0386) 858354 takes some beating. Both have very fine restaurants. True to form there are again some marvellous views from the golf course—this time looking out across that splendid Vale of Evesham.

RULE·IV· If a player play when his partner should have done so · · · ·

Charles Crombie RULE IV Rosenstiel's

Glos, Hereford & Worcester Complete Golf

Key

To avoid disappointment it is advisable to telephone in advance

***Visitors welcome at most times
**Visitors usually allowed on weekdays only
*Visitors not normally permitted (Mon, Wed) No visitors on specified days

Approximate Green Fees
A £30 plus
B £20 to £30
C £15 to £25
D £10 to £20
E under £10
F Greens fees on application

Restrictions
G Guests only
H Handicap certificate required
H (24) Handicap of 24 or less
L Letter of introduction required
M Visitor must be a member of another recognised club.

GLOUCESTERSHIRE

Broadway G.C.
(0386) 858997
Willersley Hill, Broadway
(18)6216 yards/**/B/H

Cirencester G.C.
(0285) 652465
Cheltenham Road, Bagendon
(18)6000 yards/***/B/H

Cleeve Hill G.C.
(0242) 672025
Cleeve Hill, Nr. Prestbury
(18)6217 yards/***/F

Cotswold Edge G.C.
(0453) 844167
Upper Rushmire, Wotton Under Edge
(18)6000 yards/**/C/H

Cotswold Hills G.C.
(0242) 515264
Ullenwood, Cheltenham
(18)6716 yards/***/B/H/L

Forest Hills G.C.
(0594) 810620
Mile End Road, Coleford
(18)5988 yards/***/D

Gloucester Hotel G.& C.C.
(0452) 411331
Matson Lane, Robinswood Hill
(18)6135 yards/***/C/H

Lilley Brook G.C.
(0204) 526785
Cirencester Road, Charlton Kings
(18)6226 yards/**/B/H

Lydney G.C.
(0594) 842614
Lakeside Avenue, Lydney
(9)5382 yards/**/D

Minchinhampton G.C.
(0453) 833866
Minchinhampton, Stroud
(18)6675 yards/***/B/H
(18)6295 yards/***/D/H

Naunton Downs G.C.

(0451) 850090
Naunton, Cheltenham
(18)6174 yards/***/C

Painswick G.C.
(0452) 812180
Painswick, Stroud
(18)4780 yards/**/D

Puckrup Hall Hotel & G.C.
(0684) 296200
Tewkesbury
(18)6431 yards/**/B/H

Royal Forest of Dean G.C.
(0594) 832583
Lords Hill, Coleford
(18)5500 yards/***/D

Stinchcombe Hill G.C.
(0453) 542015
Stinchcombe Hill, Dursley
(18)5700 yards/**/C/H

Streamleaze G.C.
(0453) 843128
Bradley, Wotton Under Edge
(9)4582 yards/***/E

Tewkesbury Park Hotel G.C.
(0684) 295405
Lincoln Green Lane, Tewkesbury
(18)6533 yards/***/B/H

HEREFORD & WORCESTER
Abbey Park G.& C.C.
(0527) 63918
Dagnell End Road, Redditch
(18)6411 yards/**/D

Bank House Hotel & C.C.
(0886) 833551
Bransford, Worcester
(18)6175 yards/***/B

Belmont G.C.
(0432) 35266
Belmont House, Belmont
(18)6480 yards/***/F

Blackwell G.C.
021 445 1781
Blackwell, Bromsgrove
(18)6202 yards/**/A/H

Bromsgrove G.C.
(0527) 575886
Stratford Road, Bromsgrove
(9)3159 yards/***/E

Burghill Valley G.C.
(0432) 760456
Tillington Road, Burghill
(18)6239 yards/***/D
(9)3075 yards/***/E

Cadmore Lodge G.C.
(0584) 810044
Berrington Green, Tenbury Wells
(9)5130 yards/***/E

Churchill and Blakedown G.C.
(0562) 700200
Churchill Lane, Blakedown
(9)6472 yards/**/D

Droitwich G.& C.C.
(0905) 774344
Ford Lane, Droitwich
(18)6040 yards/**/B/H

Evesham G.C.
(0386) 860395
Cray Combe Links, Fladbury

(9)6415 yards/**/C/H

Fulford Heath G.C.
(0564) 822806
Tanners Green Lane, Wythall
(18)6000 yards/**/B/H

Gay Hill G.C.
021 474 6001
Alcester Road, Hollywood
(18)6532 yards/**/F

Habberley G.C.
(0562) 745756
Habberley, Kidderminster
(9)5400 yards/**/D

Herefordshire G.C.
(0432) 830219
Ravens Causeway, Wormsley
(18)6100 yards/***/D

Hereford Municipal G.C.
(0432) 278178
Holmer Road, Hereford
(9)3060 yards/***/E

Kidderminster G.C.
(0562) 822303
Russel Road, Kidderminster
(18)6405 yards/**/B/H/M

King's Norton G.C.
(0564) 826706
Brockhill Lane, Weatheroak
(27)7060 yards/**/B

Kington G.C.
(0544) 230340
Bradnor Hill, Kington,
(18)5800 yards/**/D

Leominster G.C.
(0568) 612863
Ford Bridge, Leominster
(9)6100 yards/***/C/H

Little Lakes G.& C.C.
(0299) 266385
Lye Head, Bewdley
(9)6247 yards/**/D

Ombersley G.C.
(0905) 620747
Bishops Wood Road, Ombersley
(18)6200 yards/***/E

Perdiswell Municipal G.C.
(0905) 754668
Bilford Road, Worcester
(9)6004 yards/***/E

Pitcheroak G.C.

(0527) 541054
Plymouth Road, Redditch
(9)4600 yards/***/F

Redditch G.C.
(0527) 543309
Green Lane, Callow Hill
(18)6671 yards/**/B

Ross-on-Wye G.C.
(0989) 720267
Gorsley, Ross-on-Wye
(18)6500 yards/**/B/M

Sapey G.C.
(0886) 853288
Whitley Road, Upper Sapey
(18)5900 yards/***/C

Tolladine G.C.
(0905) 21074
Tolladine Road, Worcester
(9)5134 yards/**/D/H

The Vale G.& C.C.
(0386) 462781
Hill Furze Road,Bishampton
(18)7041 yards/***/B
(9)2960 yards/***/E

Wharton Park G.C.
(0299) 405222
Longbank, Bewdley
(18)6600 yards/***/B

Worcester G.and C.C.
(0905) 422555
Boughton Park, Worcester
(18)6000 yards/**/B/H

Worcestershire G.C.
(0684) 575992
Wood Farm, Malvern Wells
(18)6449 yards/***/B/H/M

Charles Crombie RULE XXIII Rosenstiel's

120

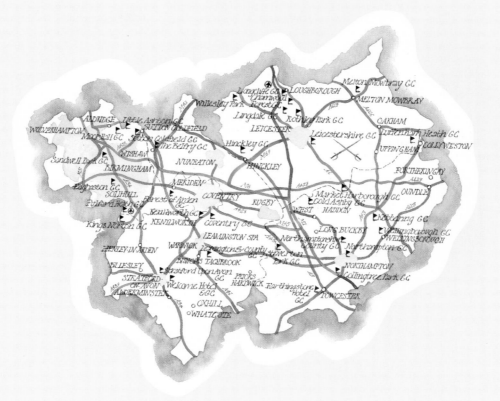

Artist: **Bill Waugh** **THE BALLESTEROS HOLE** *Courtesy of:* **Burlington Gallery**

Golfers in the City of London have often been known to get frustrated at having to travel many a mile for a decent game of golf. In 1919 one obviously disgusted individual teed up at Piccadilly Circus and proceeded to play along the Strand, through Fleet Street and Ludgate Hill firing his last shot at the Royal Exchange. Such behaviour is, as far as I'm aware, unknown in Birmingham—the Bull Ring and the NEC in their admittedly shorter existence, have never been peppered with golf balls, this I suspect may be because the needs of its golfing citizens have been properly attended to.

Within a sensible distance (ie easy access) of the town centre lie the likes of the **Belfry** and **Little Aston** to the North, **Fulford Heath, Copt Heath** and **Kings Norton** to the South, and **Sandwell Park** and **Edgbaston** lying somewhere in the middle. Golfers north of Birmingham are indeed particularly fortunate for in addition to The Belfry and Little Aston there is also **Sutton Coldfield** and **Moor Hall**. All provide extremely pleasant retreats from the noise and confusion of England's second largest city. One need hardly add that there are also a number of public courses dotted around the outskirts of Birmingham.

Despite its relative youth, the Belfry (featured ahead) has become the area's best known golfing attraction thanks largely of course to the thrilling Ryder Cup encounters staged there. However, Little Aston has long been regarded as one of Britain's finest inland courses and has hosted numerous major events—both amateur and professional. Looking in and around Birmingham for places to stay a few obvious thoughts emerge. the Belfry Hotel (0675) 470301 is most luxurious and ideal for its own two courses (as well as the plethora of golf courses in the Sutton Coldfield area). It offers practically every activity under the sun. (When does the sun ever shine in Birmingham, you ask!) As an alternative and very close by to The Belfry is the elegant Moxhull Hall 021 329 2056 which provides a more intimate atmosphere. Moor Hall 021 3083751 also provides a most comfortable and convenient 19th hole—an attractive mansion this. Still in Sutton Coldfield, Penns Hall 021 351 3111 enjoys a peaceful lakeside setting while a short distance away in Aldridge is another alternative, the Fairlawns Hotel (0922) 55122. For an inexpensive hotel in the Sutton Coldfield area, we recommend the Standbridge Hotel 021 354 3007.

Solihull to the south of Birmingham is also surrounded by good golf. The George Hotel 021 7112121 here is a modernised coaching inn and a very comfortable place in which to stay. Liaison 021 743 3993 is a pleasant spot to have dinner. Another suburb of Birmingham, on this occasion Edgbaston, provides the restaurant Sloans 021 4556697. Two pleasant and popular pubs to track down when visiting the West Midlands include the Bear at Berkswell and another beast, the White Lion in Hampton-in-Arden.

Staying more centrally in Birmingham, the Forte Crest 021 6438171 is a first rate hotel while close to the National Exhibition Centre the Birmingham Metropole (021) 780 4242 is also good. On the other side of the cost coin, the Bridge House Hotel 021 706 5900 makes for an excellent base and at Erdington there is the Willow Tree Hotel 021 373 6388, the Lyndhurst Hotel 021 373 5695 and the Cape Race Hotel 021 373 3085.

Coventry

Like Birmingham, the city of Coventry has been removed from Warwickshire and now bears the West Midlands label. **Coventry** Golf Club enjoys a decidedly peaceful setting at Finham Park, two miles south of the city along the A444. The course is good enough to have recently staged the British Seniors Championship. To the north west of Coventry at Meriden, the **Forest of Arden** Golf and Country Club offers a marvellous day's golf—36 holes to savour here with the beautiful Aylesford and Arden courses—while the leisure facilities at the Country Club Hotel (0676) 22335 are outstanding.

The major tourist attraction in Coventry is undoubtedly the spectacular cathedral. A fine piece of modern architecture sadly not reflected in the city's hotels—but then Coventry is no different from most. De Vere Hotel (0203) 633733, near the Cathedral is perhaps the best in the city, although the Coventry Hotel (0203) 402151 is also well thought of. The Hearsall Lodge Hotel (0203) 674543 offers more modest accommodation, but is perfectly pleasant and comfortable and very convenient for **Coventry Hearsall** Golf Club, just south of the city off the A46. Another recommendation is Nailcote Hall (0203) 466174, situated west of Coventry in Berkwell.

Warwickshire

Birmingham and Coventry removed, Warwickshire has been left with only a handful of courses. The county's two most popular towns (tourist-wise) are unquestionably Stratford and Warwick. Until recently **Warwick** had only a 9 hole course located inside its racetrack, but now, not far away from Warwick at Leek Wooton, (close to junction 15 of the M40) is the Warwickshire where 36 holes of American-style championship golf await. Shakespeare-spotters who've sneaked the clubs into the boot will also be well rewarded. There are two fine 18 hole courses in Stratford, **Stratford** Golf Club and the **Welcombe Hotel** Golf Course, and a little beyond the town there are plans to build a 27 hole course at Bidford-on-Avon.

The Welcombe Hotel (0789) 295252 is a beautiful mansion with comfortable rooms and a good restaurant. But there are many outstanding alternatives for those spending a night or two in the Stratford area. Pride of place must go to Billesley Manor (0789) 400888 to the west of the town: quite simply majestic—and with a superb restaurant to boot. Of the countless guest houses and B&Bs in the vicinity, two that are frequently acclaimed are Moonraker House (0789) 299346 and Oxtalls Farmhouse (0789) 205277. For pubs, a short drive towards Oxhill is recommended where the Peacock and the Royal Oak (in Whatcote village) will provide excellent sustenance.

Warwick has a famous castle, and a good restaurant to note nearby is Randolphs. **Kenilworth** also has a castle (and a pretty reasonable golf course too). Here the Clarendon House (0926) 57668 is the place to stay and a restaurant to savour is the Restaurant Bosquet (0926) 52463. Lastly we visit Leamington Spa. It may not have the attractions of a Stratford or a Warwick but it does have a very fine golf course. **Leamington and County** is a hilly parkland course, situated to the south of Leamington. After an enjoyable round at Leamington, the Lansdowne (0926) 450505 is a smallish well priced hotel in town and Crandon House a comfortable farmhouse, but if one is looking to spoil oneself then we recommend a trip to Bishops Tachbrook and Mallory Court (0926) 330214—superb rooms and a terrific restaurant await.

Leicestershire

As we move from the West to the East Midlands let us start with the best course in Leicestershire. **Luffenham Heath** lies over to the far east of the county within what was formerly Rutland and very close to the border with Lincolnshire. It is without question one of the most attractive heathland courses in England and being in a conservation area something of a haven for numerous species of wildlife. It isn't the longest of courses but then, thankfully, golf isn't always a question of how far you can belt the ball! A visit here is strongly recommended and there is no shortage of spectacular 19th holes nearby. The splendid Rutland countryside reveals many outstanding establishments. In Oakham, Hambleton Hall (0572) 756991 is quite tremendous and very convenient for the new course at Greetham, **Greetham Valley**. If you cannot spend the night here the restaurant is equally superb. By contrast, but also very enjoyable, is the Whipper Inn Hotel (0572) 75697 in Oakham's market square. A fine inn with good beers, snacks and some comfortable accommodation too. Note that this is Ruddles country and some excellent country pubs lie in wait. The King's Arms in Wing is a good example and there's a nearby maze in which to lose the children before a round of golf or a pint of County.

Rothley Park Golf Club, adjacent to the 13th century Rothley Court (0533) 374141 is one of Leicestershire's most picturesque parkland courses and is within easy access of Leicester, lying some seven miles to the north west of the city, off the A6. Leicester is well served by golf courses and there are no fewer than three 18 hole municipal courses within four miles of the centre of Leicester, **Western Park** perhaps being the best of these. **Leicestershire** Golf Club is situated just two miles from the city centre along the A6. It is one of the top courses in the county: try to avoid the ubiquitous stream that runs through it. Leicester may not be the country's most attractive city but it does have its good points. The Haymarket theatre offers a variety of productions while the art gallery includes works by English sporting artists and if you have business in town the Grand Hotel (0533) 555599 will prove the best selection. The Scotia Hotel (0533) 549200 is also popular with tourist and business people alike.

Looking further afield, in the north of the county the ancient town of Melton Mowbray has a fine 9 hole course sited on high ground to the north east of the town and Loughborough possesses an 18 hole heathland type course, Longcliffe, which is heavily wooded with a particularly testing front nine.

In the south of the county, **Market Harborough's** 9 hole course offers extensive views across the surrounding countryside. North west of Leicester, Charnwood Forest is one of the Midlands' most pleasant retreats, an area where heath and woodland confront rocky crags and granite outcrops. The village of Woodhouse Eaves lies on the eastern edge of the Forest and has two extremely pleasant courses at hand, **Lingdale** and **Charnwood Forest**. Though they are less than two miles apart they offer quite different challenges. **Lingdale** (which has recently been extended from 9 holes to 18) has a parkland setting with a trout stream flowing through it, while **Charnwood Forest** is a heathland type course—9 holes, no bunkers but several outcrops of

granite around which one must navigate.

Hinckley is linked to the centre of Leicester by the A47. Hinckley's golf course is a fairly new creation, built over the original 9 hole Burbage Common layout. Several lakes and much gorse have to be confronted making this potentially the toughest in the county. The final mention for a round in Leicestershire goes to **Willesley Park** at Ashby-de-la-Zouch. A parkland-heathland mix this and well worth a visit.

Some ideas for life beyond the 18th fairway. If a pork pie and a piece of Stilton is what you're after then Melton Mowbray is an answer to your prayers—try the George (0664) 62112—a charming inn with comfortable rooms. In the Loughborough area the Kings Head (0509) 233222 is popular and for two good restaurants, try the Old Schoolhouse (050981) 3941 in Sileby and the Cottage in the Woods (0509) 890318, Woodhouse Eaves. Finally, the Crown in Old Dalby is another good pub.

Northamptonshire

The much admired **Northamptonshire County** course is situated some five miles north of Northampton at Church Brampton, and indeed is often referred to locally as Church Brampton. Famed for its many testing par fours, it is a splendid heather and gorse type with a fair few undulations in its 6500 yards. Rather like Liphook in Hampshire a railway line bisects the course. In the past it has staged the British Youths' Championship. Though not as good as Church Brampton, **Northampton** Golf Club can also be recommended, as most certainly can **Collingtree Park**, Johnny Miller's spectacularly designed course (see feature page). One final mention for visitors to the county town is the **Delapre** Golf Complex where a game should be easily arranged.

If looking to stay overnight in Northampton, the Moat House Hotel (0604) 22441 is modern but comfortable and handy for the centre, while the Westone Moat House (0604) 406262 is a mansion with modern additions. For value and friendly service, Garenden Park Hotel (0509) 236557 is highly recommended.

Elsewhere in the county there is a reasonable course at **Kettering** and not far away there is a better course at **Wellingborough,** two miles east of the town and set around the former Horrowden Hall. Quite hilly, it has several lakes and a mass of mature trees. It is certainly one of the best courses in the county. Others include **Staverton Park** at Daventry, **Cold Ashby** (near the site of the famous Battle of Naseby of 1645) with its superb views across the Northamptonshire Uplands, the popular **Farthingstone Hotel** Golf and Leisure Centre near Towcester and **West and Park**, the new 36 hole complex at Whittlebury.

Pleasant countryside surrounds the towns of Wellingborough and Kettering. Perhaps the best bet for accommodation near the former is the Hind (0933) 222827. In the south of the county, the Crossroads (0327) 40354 at Weedon and the Saracens Head (0327) 350414 at Towcester are both welcoming, although Farthingstone Hotel (0327) 36291 must be the best bet here.

The story of Moxhull Hall begins at the turn of the century when it was built by Mr Howard Ryland, Lord Lieutenant of Warwickshire and Lord of the Manor of Moxhull and Wishaw.

It is believed that the new 'Hall' owes its origins to a series of deaths in the Ryland family from tuberculosis and that the old hall, Moxhull Park, was deliberately raised to the ground in the belief that the disease was in the woodwork.

The new hall was built to last forever on the top of an adjacent hill and the stables and the groom's quarters of the original manor now form part of the Belfry Hotel. Residents of Moxhull Hall are literally only minutes away from this famous golfing venue and are well placed to enjoy the many attractions of the area.

Matching the splendour of the building and its extensive grounds is the interior. Guests are immediately struck by the magnificence of the carved oak staircase, taken originally from Kenilworth Castle and trodden (reputedly) by Elizabeth I. The Dining Room is bedecked with fine dark oak pannelling and the Drawing Room fitted with an Adam statuary marble fireplace.

The Restaurant has become justly famous over the past few years with recommendations from all leading guides and the very best of English and French cuisine can be enjoyed in calm, elegant surroundings.

With twenty one well appointed bedrooms and the facilities for everything from small functions to large receptions, the management at Moxhull Hall pride themselves on their ability to cater for individual and corporate requirements.

Moxhull Hall
Holly Lane
Wishaw
B76 9PD
Tel: (021) 329 2056
Fax: (021) 311 1980

To adopt lawyers' jargon, it is 'beyond any reasonable doubt' that the game of golf was invented in Scotland. A handful of golfing pioneers brought the game south and today, with the exception of a few notable areas in the north, where to live is to play golf, the sport is almost as popular south of the border.

One cannot help wondering quite what those early pioneers would have made of The Belfry project... 'American-style target gowff?...'and what d'ya mean artificial burns with manmade mounds and lakes!'...'more than 7000 yards did ya say?'... 'Too many whiskies m'friend, you must be oot o'your wee mind!'

The 'Belfry project' involved not only a plan to build a Championship course on American lines where in due course the Ryder Cup could be staged, but also the siting of a new headquarters for the PGA Peter Alliss and Dave Thomas were given the task of designing the showpiece and a very great task it was, for the land they were given was flat, uninteresting and comprised one small lake, a stream and numerous acres of potato fields.

Well, the boys didn't hang about: earth mountains were moved, the potatoes disappeared and hundreds of trees were planted—the end result in fact produced two 18 hole courses, opened in June 1977. The feature course was named the **Brabazon**, after Lord Brabazon a former President of the P.G.A. and the shorter, easier course, the **Derby**.

June 1977—the month when Hubert Green survived a death threat to win the US Open and a month before Nicklaus and Watson fought out the 'Duel in the Sun' at Turnberry. So much has happened since then and to cite the history of The Belfry since its creation is almost to chart the rise of European golf—they are of course indelibly linked. Of all Europe's successes around the world the 1985 Ryder Cup triumph at The Belfry will perhaps be remembered best of all. It was, after all, the first time the Americans had been defeated in nearly 30 years, and no other single event has been more responsible for generating the golf boom that has swept right across the continent. So successfully staged was the tied match in 1989 that The Belfry was awarded the match in 1993 for the third time in succession.

A key feature of The Belfry is that it is a club without any Members. Both courses open their doors to the general public at all times all the year round, however golfers should note that a handicap of 24 or better (32 for ladies) is required to play the Brabazon course. The green fees in 1994 were £50 per round on the Brabazon and £25 per round on the Derby. The **Golf Manager**, **Robert Maxfield**, and the two resident golf **professionals**, **Peter McGovern** and **Simon Wordsworth** can be contacted on **(0675) 470301**. Special residential packages are often available and persons wishing to make reservations should contact the Sales Office on **(0675) 470033**, Fax: (0675) 470256, or write to : **The Belfry, Wishaw, N Warks B76 9PR.**

In addition to being a luxury hotel with a full complement of facilities, The Belfry has eight public bars and four restaurants open to the general public. If after a meal and a few drinks you're still not satisfied with your golf there's a final opportunity to put things right on the impressive floodlit covered driving range.

Situated close to the country's industrial heart there is surely no golfing complex in Britain better served by communication networks. The Belfry is one mile from the M42 (junction 9), five miles from the M6 (junction 4), nine miles from Birmingham city centre and less than ten minutes from Birmingham International Airport and the NEC railway station. The exact positioning of the golf club is at the apex of the A446 and A4091.

Apart from the sheer length of the Brabazon Course the many water hazards are likely to present the greatest challenge. Two of its holes are guaranteed to excite; the short par four 10th, where almost everyone tries to be famous for five seconds before spending five minutes trying to fish his or her ball out of the lake, and the thrilling 18th, where Christy O'Connor Jr hit that magnificent 2 iron in the 1989 Ryder Cup, and where Tom Watson's United States team retained the trophy in 1993, having won it in such dramatic circumstances two years earlier at Kiawah Island.

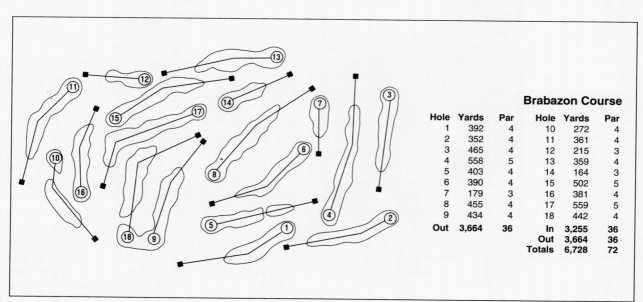

Brabazon Course

Hole	Yards	Par	Hole	Yards	Par
1	392	4	10	272	4
2	352	4	11	361	4
3	465	4	12	215	3
4	558	5	13	359	4
5	403	4	14	164	3
6	390	4	15	502	5
7	179	3	16	381	4
8	455	4	17	559	5
9	434	4	18	442	4
Out	**3,664**	**36**	**In**	**3,255**	**36**
			Out	**3,664**	**36**
			Totals	**6,728**	**72**

Johnny Miller, the former British and US Open Golf Champion, was invited to design an 18 hole golf course to be both memorable and challenging. Since then, Collingtree Park has created an enviable reputation for its high standard of service. Staff and management systems have been developed to help organise the details of a day which will be to the requirements of corporate clients.

Customers come first at Collingtree Park. Teaching professionals will offer guests step-by-step instruction and explain the fundamentals of the game. Unique academy facilities and programmes, a floodlit driving range and video swing analysis will allow even the absolute novice to play golf for the first time. Visitors can then play on three academy holes which are built to the same specification as the 18 hole course. A golf clinic can be arranged by John Cook, director of golf and a former English Amateur Champion and PGA European Tour winner.

A wide variety of special gifts are on sale and many of these can be personalised in advance with a company logo or corporate message. The restaurant at Collingtree Park serves breakfast, lunch and dinner — giving companies the opportunity to select their own special menus.

Collingtree Park is the perfect venue for a corporate golf day. It is ideally located two minutes from Junction 15 on the M1, midway between London and Birmingham. It is the perfect location for companies with a wide customer base and offers excellent value for money.

For further information please contact the corporate sales manager at:

Collingtree Park
Windingbrook Lane
Northampton
NN4 0XN
Tel: (0604) 700000
Fax: (0604) 702600

Artist: **C E Brock** **THE BUNKER** *Courtesy of:* ***Sotheby's***

Collingtree Park

In recent years we have grown accustomed to watching Australian Greg Norman tear golf courses apart: 62s at Doral and Glen Abbey; 63s at St Andrews and Turnberry and 64s at Augusta, Troon and St George's. A tournament isn't over they say, whilst Greg Norman is within seven shots of the leader. In the 1970s the man with a similar reputation for shooting extraordinary, par shattering rounds was American **Johnny Miller.** Twice in as many weeks in 1975 he returned a score of 61. That year he won the first three tournaments he entered in America, all by very large margins and he finished one shot away from catching Jack Nicklaus in the Masters after closing rounds of 65 and 66. In 1973, he stormed through the field with a final round of 63 to win the US Open; the score still stands as the lowest ever to win a major. In 1974 he won eight tournaments on the US tour and in 1976 charged around a dry and dusty Royal Birkdale in a course record equalling 66 on the final day of the Open to win by six strokes. He was a dashing champion whose hobby (like Norman's) was driving superfast cars. Johnny Miller is also the man who has designed Collingtree Park.

Opened in May 1990, it is Miller's first course in Europe; hitherto he has been responsible for impressive layouts in the United States and Japan. Without question, Miller has produced a dramatic golf course which, in time, will surely be considered one of the finest in England. It is certainly one of the most challenging with 11 acres of lakes to be negotiated and more than 72,000 imported trees and shrubbery in a layout that can be stretched to close on 7000 yards.

Collingtree Park is much more than an exciting new golf course; in addition to Miller's creation, there is a Golf Academy which includes three full length practice holes, a 16 bay floodlit driving range and an indoor video teaching room and computerised custom fitting centre. Luxury homes are being constructed around the fringes of the golf course.

Persons wishing to learn more about the grand scheme at Collingtree Park might wish to contact the Golf Club on (0604) 700000. All golf enquiries should be made to the **Golf Director**, **John Cook** and his professional staff; they may be contacted on **(0604) 700000**. The address for written correspondence is **Collingtree Park Golf Course, Windingbrook Lane, Northampton NN4 0XN**.

For individual visitors and groups of fewer than twelve players bookings can be made up to one week in advance, Handicaps are required and green fees for 1994 were set at £20 per round during the week and £30 at the weekend. Details of Corporate Day packages and tuition courses can be obtained by telephoning the above number,

Travelling to Collingtree Park should be fairly straight forward. Very centrally located in the heart of England, it is just on the outskirts of Northampton, one of Britain's fastest growing towns and very close to the M1. Junction 15 is the exit to use, immediately picking up the A5108 road to Northampton. This road should be followed for about half a mile and Collingtree Park's entrance is the second turning on the left. The golf course is sixty-five miles from London, thirty-five miles from Birmingham and about twenty miles from Milton Keynes.

When Johnny Miller first viewed the site in 1986 it is doubtful that he could have thought it the most natural setting for a golf course he had ever seen. Part meadowland, part wasteland it required a massive amount of work. With the support of Jack Nicklaus' technical services team it certainly received it. Work commenced in 1987 with the movement of over 350,000 cubic metres of earth. A positive drainage system with sixteen miles of underground piping was installed and then the course was landscaped.

'I designed the course along American lines, but not without respect for the English countryside. I wanted Collingtree to combine the best of both English and American course ideas' said Miller. At 6821 yards from the championship tees (6692 yards from the medal and 5416 yards from the ladies') it is a formidable challenge, but with the lakes, the verdant fairways and the variety of trees it is an attractive one and there are of course the special holes. There isn't a bad hole at Collingtree Park but on the front nine the par three 5th across the edge of a lake and the 9th—one of those par fives that can be reached with two good shots but where disaster awaits the failed attempt—are especially memorable and on the much more difficult back nine there is the glorious finishing hole, probably the most dramatic in Great Britain. The 18th measures close to 600 yards from the back tees and the third shot (you won't be going for this one in two) must be played to an island green—Florida comes to Northamptonshire! It is Miller's master stroke and you can guarantee that almost all conversation at the 19th hole will centre around 'how did you fare at the last?' And I dare say there will be one or two tall stories.

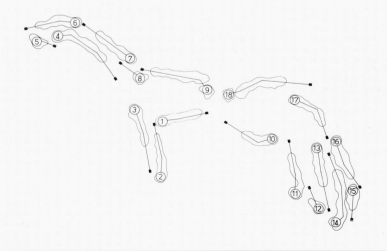

Hole	Yards	Par	Hole	Yards	Par
1	348	4	10	348	4
2	386	4	11	387	4
3	431	4	12	192	3
4	533	5	13	423	4
5	179	3	14	542	5
6	367	4	15	170	3
7	388	4	16	392	4
8	166	3	17	401	4
9	498	5	18	541	5
Out	**3,296**	**36**	**In**	**3,296**	**36**
			Out	**3,296**	**36**
			Totals	**6,692**	**72**

Nestling in some of the most beautiful countryside in Britain, while still within easy reach of the A1, this seventeenth century coaching inn retains all its country charm. The character and history of the building is reflected in the decor with plush, rich fabrics in warm hues complementing the ancient oak beams. Local links with equestrian and country pursuits are a theme carried through to the naming of the rooms and the hotel—the whipper-in is the person in charge of the hunt beagles.

The bedrooms are all beautifully restored and decorated with a unique collection of prints, paintings and antiques. Designed by internationally recognised interior decorators, each room has thick carpets, fresh flowers and sparkling luxurious bathrooms with thick fluffy towels and deep baths. Each bedroom has direct dial telephone, remote control colour television, trouser press, hairdryer and tea and coffee making facilities.

The Whipper-In Restaurant has deservedly won a reputation for providing some of the finest food available locally. Chef Carl Bontoft produces menus on a daily basis—each one reflecting the best in English and French cuisine and making full use of the abundant local natural produce. The wine cellar is well stocked with the highest calibre wines to suit all tastes and budgets.

The Whipper-In Bar is an ideal spot for a snack or an informal meal. Guests can enjoy a range of filled croissants, pies and traditional English food beside the log fire in this peaceful bar.

The two specially designed conference rooms both have natural light, easy access and offer a comprehensive meeting facility. Both rooms are equally suited to parties or private dining and can be transformed from efficient meeting rooms to sophisticated party venues in a short time.

The hotel is located in the heart of Oakham, the capital of the ancient county of Rutland and yet is only minutes away from Rutland Water, the largest man-made lake in Europe, and the endless leisure activities available there. Close by are Burghley house, Belvoir Castle and all around is the stunning Leicestershire countryside.

Whipper-In Hotel
Market Place
Oakham, Rutland
Leicestershire LE15 6DT
Tel: (0572) 796571
Fax: (0572) 757759

Key

To avoid disappointment it is advisable to telephone in advance

****Visitors welcome at most times*
***Visitors usually allowed on weekdays only*
**Visitors not normally permitted (Mon, Wed) No visitors on specified days*

Approximate Green Fees
A £30 plus
B £20 to £30
C £15 to £25
D £10 to £20
E under £10
F Greens fees on application

Restrictions
G Guests only
H Handicap certificate required
H (24) Handicap of 24 or less
L Letter of introduction required
M Visitor must be a member of another recognised club.

NORTHAMPTONSHIRE

Cold Ashby G.C.
(0604) 740548
Stanford Road, Cold Ashby
(18)6020 yards/**/C

Collingtree Park G.C.
(0604) 700000
Windingbrook Lane, Northampton
(18)6692 yards/***/A/H

Daventry and District G.C.
(0327) 702829
Norton Road, Daventry
(9)5812 yards/**/D

Delapre G.C.
(0604) 764036
Eagle Drive, Northampton
(18)6356 yards/***/D
(9)2146 yards/***/E

Embankment G.C.
(0933) 228465
The Embankment, Wellingborough
(9)3374 yards/***/E

Farthingstone Hotel G.C.
(0327) 361291
Farthingstone, Towcester
(18)6248 yards/***/C-B

Hellidon Lakes Hotel & C.C.
(0327) 62550
Hellidon
(18)6691 yards/***/B/H

Kettering G.C.
(0536) 512074
Headlands, Kettering
(18)6036 yards/**/C/H

Kingsthorpe G.C.
(0604) 710610
Kingsley Road, Northampton
(18)6006 yards/**/B/H

Northampton G.C.
(0604) 845155
Kettering Road, Northampton
(18)6534 yards/**/C/H

Northamptonshire County G.C.
(0604) 843025
Sandy Lane, Church Brampton
(18)6503 yards/***/A/H

Oundle G.C.
(0832) 273267
Benefield Road, Oundle
(18)5900 yards/**/F

Overstone Park G.C.
(0604) 671471
Billing Lane, Overstone
(18)6260 yards/***/D

Priors Hall G.C.
(0536) 60756
Stamford Road, Weldon
(18)6677 yards/***/E

Rushden and District G.C.
(0933) 312581
Kimbolton Road, Chelveston
(10)6335 yards/**/C

Staverton Park G.C.
(0327) 705911
Staverton, Daventry
(18)6204 yards/**/C/H

Wellingborough G.C.
(0933) 677234
Horrowden Hall, Great Horrowden
(18)6620 yards/**/B/H

West Park G.& C.C.
(0327) 858092
Whittlebury, Towcester
(364 x 9)7000 yards/***/C-B/H

LEICESTERSHIRE

Beedles Lake G.C.
(0533) 606759
Broome Lane, East Goscote
(18)6412 yards/***/E

Birstall G.C.
(0533) 674322
Station Road, Birstall
(18)6222 yards/***/B/H/G/L

Blaby G.C.
(0533) 784804
Lutterworth Road, Blaby
(9)2600 yards/***/E

Charnwood Forest G.C.
(0509) 890259
Breakback Lane, Woodhouse Eaves
(9)5960 yards/**/C/H/L

Cosby G.C.
(0533) 864759
Chapel Lane, Cosby
(18)6418 yards/**/B/H

Enderby G.C.
(0533) 849388
Mill Lane, Enderby
(9)4356 yards/***/E

Glen Gorse G.C.
(0533) 714159
Glen Road, Oadby
(18)6603 yards/**/B/H

Greetham Valley G.C.
(0780) 460444
Greetham, Oakham
(18) 6656 yards/***/C

Hinckley G.C.
(0455) 615124
Leicester Road, Hinckley
(18)6517 yards/**(Tue)/B/H

Humberstone Heights G.C.
(0533) 764674
Gipsy Lane, Leicester
(18)6444 yards/***/E

Kibworth G.C.
(0533) 792301
Weir Road, Kibworth Beauchamp
(18)6282 yards/**/C

Kilworth Springs G.C.
(0858) 575082
South Kilworth Road, North Kilworth
(18)6718 yards/***/D

Kirby Muxloe G.C.
(0533) 393457
Station Road, Kirby Muxloe
(18)6303 yards/**/B/H

Langton International G.C.
(0858) 545374
Langton Hall, Leicester
(18)6965 yards/***/B-A/H/L
(9)3362 yards/***/D

Leicestershire G.C.
(0533) 738825
Evington Lane, Leicester
(18)6312 yards/***/B/H

Leicestershire Forest G.C
(0455) 824800
Markfield Lane, Botcheston
(18)6111 yards/***/D

Lingdale G.C.
(0509) 890703
Joe Moores Lane, Woodhouse Eaves
(18)6545 yards/***/C

Longcliffe G.C.
(0509) 239129
Snell's Nook Lane, Nanpantan
(18)6551 yards/**/B/H

Luffenham Heath G.C.
(0780) 720205

Ketton, Stamford
(18)6254 yards/***/A/H

Lutterworth G.C.
(0455) 552532
Rugby Road, Lutterworth
(18)5570 yards/**/C/H

Market Harborough G.C.
(0858) 463684
Oxendon Road, Market Harborough
(18)6027 yards/**/D/H

Melton Mowbray G.C.
(0664) 62118
Waltham Road, Thorpe Arnold
(18)6222 yards/***/C/M/H

Oadby G.C.
(0533) 700326
Leicester Road, Oadby
(18)6228 yards/***/D

Park Hill G.C.
(0509) 815454
Park Hill, Seagrave
(9)6800 yards/***/C/H

R.A.F. North Luffenham G.C.
(0780) 720041
North Luffenham, Oakham
(9)6006 yards/*/F/G

Rothley Park G.C.
(0533) 302809
Westfield Lane, Rothley
(18)6487 yards/**(Tues)/B/H/M

Rushcliffe G.C.
(0509) 852959
East Leake, Loughborough
(18)6090 yards/***/B

Scraptoft G.C.
(0533) 418863
Beeby Road, Scraptoft
(18)6166 yards/**/B/H

Ullesthorpe G.C.
(0455) 209023
Frolesworth Road, Ullesthorpe
(18)6650 yards/***/D

Western Park G.C.
(0533) 872339
Scudmore Road, Braunstone Frith
(18)6532 yards/***/E

Whetstone G.C.
(0533) 861424
Cambridge Road, Cosby
(18)5795 yards/**/D/H

Willesley Park G.C.
(0530) 414596
Tamworth Road, Ashby-de-la-Zouch
(18)6304 yards/***/B/H/M

WEST MIDLANDS

Blackwell G.C.
021 445 1994
Blackwell, nr Bromsgrove
(18)6202 yards/**/B/H

Bloxwith G.C.
(0922) 405724
Stafford Road, Bloxwich
(18)6286 yards/**/F/H

Boldmere G.C.
021 354 3379
Monmouth Drive, Sutton Coldfield
(18)4463 yards/***/E

Brand Hall G.C.
021 552 2195
Heron Road, Oldbury, Warley
(18)5813 yards/***/D

Bromsgrove Golf Centre
(0527) 570505
Stratford Road, Bromsgrove
(9)3159 yards/**/E

Calderfields G.C.
(0922) 640540
Aldridge Road, Walsall
(18)6636 yards/***/D

City of Coventry G.C.
(Brandon Wood)
(0203) 543141
Brandon Lane, Brandon, Coventry
(18)6610 yards/***/F

Cocks Moor Woods G.C.
021 444 3584
Alcester Road South, Kings Heath
(18)5742 yards/***/F

Copt Heath G.C.
(0564) 772650
Warwick Road, Knowle, Solihull
(18)6504 yards/**/A/H/M

Coventry G.C.
(0203) 414152
Finham Park, Coventry
6613 yards/**/A/H

Coventry Hearsall G.C.
(0203) 713470
Beechwood Avenue, Coventry
(18)5983 yards/**/C/H

Dartmouth G.C.
021 588 2131
Vale Street, West Bromwich
(9)6060 yards/**/D

Druids Heath G.C.
(0922) 55595
Stonnal Road, Aldridge
(18)6914 yards/**/B/H

Edgbaston G.C. .
021 454 1736
Church Road, Edgbaston
(18)6118 yards/***/A/H

Forest of Arden G.& C.C.
(0676) 22335
Maxstoke Road, Meriden
(18)7100 yards/**/F/H
(18)6525 yards/**/F/H

Gay Hill G.C.
021 430 6523
Alcester Road, Hollywood, Birmingham
(18)6522 yards/**/B/H

Grange G.C.
(0203) 451465
Copsewood, Coventry
(9)6002 yards/**/D/H

Great Barr G.C.
021 358 4376
Chapel Lane, Great Barr, Birmingham
(18)6546 yards/**/B/H/L

Hagley G.C.
(0562) 883701
Wassell Grove, Hagley, Stourbridge
(18)6353 yards/**/B/H

Halesowen G.C.
021 501 3606
The Leasowes, Halesowen
(18)5754 yards/**/C

Handsworth G.C.
021 554 3387
Sunningdale Close, Handsworth
(18)6312 yards/**/C/H

Harborne G.C.
021 427 3058
Tennal Road, Birmingham
(18)6240 yards/**/F/H

Harborne Church Farm G.C.
021 427 1204
Vicarage Road, Harborne
(9)4914 yards/***/F

Hatchford Brook G.C.
021 743 9821
Coventry Road, Sheldon
(18)6164 yards/***/E

Hilltop G.C.
021 554 4463
Park Lane, Handsworth
(18)6114 yards/***/E

Himley Hall G.C.
(0902) 895207
Log Cabin, Himley Hall Park, Dudley
(9)3145 yards/**/E

Kings Norton G.C.
(0564) 826789
Brockhill Lane, Weatheroak
(18)7057 yards/**/B/H
(9)3300 yards/**/B/H

Ladbrook Park G.C.
(0564) 742264

Poolhead Lane, Tanworth in
Arden, Solihull
(18)6427 yards/**/B-A/H

Lickey Hills G.C.
021 453 3159
Rose Hill, Old Birmingham Road,
Rednal
(18)6010 yards/***/E

Little Aston G.C.
021 353 2066
Streetly, Sutton Coldfield
(18)6724 yards/**/F

Maxstoke Park G.C.
(0675) 464915
Castle Lane, Coleshill
(18)6437 yards/**/A

Moor Hall G.C.
021 308 6130
Moor Hall Drive, Four Oaks,
Sutton Coldfield
(18)6249 yards/**/B-A/H

Moseley G.C.
021 444 2115
Springfield Road, Kings Heath
(18)6285 yards/**/A/H/L

North Warwickshire G.C.
(0676) 22259
Hampton Lane, Meriden
(9)3186 yards/**(not Thurs)/C

North Worcestershire G.C.
021 475 1047
Frankley Beeches Road, Northfield
(18)5959 yards/**/B/H

Olton G.C.
021 705 1083
Mirfield Road, Solihull
(18)6229 yards/**(Weds)/B/H

Oxley Park G.C.
(0902) 20506
Bushbury, Wolverhampton
(18)6168 yards/***/C

Penn G.C.
(0902) 341142
Penn Common, Wolverhampton
(18)6465 yards/**/C/M

Perton Park G.C.
(0902) 380103
Wrottesley Park Road, Perton
(18)7007 yards/***/E

Pype Hayes G.C.
021 351 1014
Eaglehurst Road, Walmley
(18)5811 yards/***/E

Robin Hood G.C.
021 706 0061
St Bernards Road, Solihull
(18)6635 yards/**/F/H

Sandwell Park G.C.
021 553 4637
Birmingham Road, West
Bromwich
(18)6470 yards/**/A/H

Sedgley Golf Centre
(0902) 880503
Sandyfields Road, Sedgley
(9)3150 yards/***/E

Shirley G.C.
021 744 6001
Stratford Road, Solihull
(18)6510 yards/**/B-A/H

South Staffordshire G.C.
(0902) 751065
Tettenhall, Wolverhampton
(18)6513 yards/**(Tues)/B/H

Sphinx G.C.
(0203) 451361
Siddeley Avenue, Stoke
(9)4104 yards/***/E

Stourbridge G.C.
(0384) 395566
Worcester Lane, Pedmore
(18)6178 yards/**/C/H

Sutton Coldfield G.C.
021 353 9633
Thornhill Road, Streetly
(18)6541 yards/**/A/H

Swindon G.C.
(0902) 897031
Bridgnorth Road, Swindon,
Dudley
(18)6042 yards/**/C
(9)1135 yards/**/C

Walmley G.C.
021 373 0029
Brooks Road, Wylde Green
(18)6537 yards/**/B

Walsall G.C.
(0922) 613512
The Broadway, Walsall
(18)6243 yards/**/A/H

Wergs G.C.
(0902) 742225
Keepers Lane, Tettenhall
(18)6949 yards/***/D

Widney Manor G.C.
021 711 3646
Saintbury Drive, Widney Manor,

Solihull
(18)4709 yards/***/E

Windmill Village Hotel & G.C.
(0203) 407241
Birmingham Road, Coventry
(18)5200 yards/***/D

WARWICKSHIRE

Ansty Golf Centre
(0203) 621341
Brinklow Road, Ansty
(18)5793 yards/***/E

Atherstone G.C.
(0827) 713110
The Outwoods, Atherstone
(18)6239 yards/**/C/H

The Belfry G.C.
(0675) 470301
Lichfield Road, Wishaw, North
Warwicks
(18)6975 yards/***/A/H
(18)6186 yards/***/B

Bidford Grange G.C.
(0789) 490319
Bidford Grange, Bidford-on-Avon
(18)7233 yards/***/D

Crocketts Manor G.& C.C.
(0564) 793715
Henley-in-Arden
(18)6933 yards/***/B/H

Dudley G.C.
(0384) 233877
Turners Hill, Rowley Regis,
Warley
(18)5715 yards/**/D

Ingon Manor G.C.
(0789) 731857
Ingon Lane, Snitterfield
(18)6554 yards/***/C/H

Kenilworth G.C.
(0926) 58517
Crew Lane, Kenilworth
(18)6413 yards/***/B-A/H

Lea Marston Hotel & Leisure
Complex
(0675) 470707
Haunch Lane, Lea Marston
(9)1027 yards/***/F

Leamington & County G.C.
(0926) 425961
Golf Lane, Whitnash, Leamington
Spa
(18)6425 yards/***/B-A/H

Newbold Comyn G.C.

(0926) 421157
Newbold Terrace East, Leamington
Spa
(18)6315 yards/***/E

Nuneaton G.C.
(0203) 347810
Golf Drive, Whitestone
(18)6412 yards/**/C/H

Purley Chase G.C.
(0203) 393118
Ridge Lane, Atherstone
(18)6604 yards/***/D/H

Rugby G.C.
(0788) 542306
Clifton Road, Rugby
(18)5457 yards/**/F

Stoneleigh Deer Park G.C.
(0203) 639991
The Old Deer Park, Stoneleigh
(18)6083 yards/**/D
(9)1251 yards/**/E

Stratford Oaks G.C.
(0789) 731571
Bearley Road, Snitterfield
(18)6100 yards/***/D

Stratford-upon-Avon G.C.
(0789) 205749
Tiddington Road, Stratford-upon-
Avon
(18)6309 yards/***/F/H

Warley G.C.
021 429 2440
Lightswood Hill, Warley
(9)2606 yards/***/F

Warwick G.C.
(0926) 494396
The Racecourse, Warwick
(9)2682 yards/***(not Sundays)/E

The Warwickshire G.C.
(0926) 409409
Leek Wootton, Warwick
(18)7178 yards/***/A
(18)7154 yards/***/A

Welcombe Hotel G.C.
(0789) 295292
Warwick Road, Stratford-upon-
Avon
(18)6217 yards/**/B-A/H

Whitefields Hotel & Golf Complex
(0788) 521800
Coventry Road, Thurlaston
(18)6433 yards/***/D/H

Artist: **Charles Wagstaff GOLFERS** *Courtesy of* **Rosenstiel's**

Royal West Norfolk G.C.
Hunstanton G.C. ▶   BLAKENEY   Sheringham G.C.
OLD HUNSTANTON   BRANCASTER   WEYBOURNE   ▶ SHERINGHAM
                    STAITHE   ▶ Royal Cromer G.C.
HEACHAM ○   GREAT SNORING   CROMER
                              ALDBOROUGH ○
                         FAKENHAM
King's Lynn G.C. ▶
KING'S LYNN   ○ GRIMSTON   Royal Norwich G.C.   COLTISHALL   Great Yarmouth &
                                        ▶   NORWICH   Caister G.C.
                         Barnham Broom G.C. ▶   Great Yarmouth
Peterborough Milton G.C. ▶   BARNHAM BROOM   GORLESTON-
WANSFORD   PETERBOROUGH   ON-SEA
                                                        LOWESTOFT
Ramsey G.C. ▶   BUNWELL
                  ELY   Thetford G.G. ▶ THETFORD
                         MILDENHALL   SOUTHWOLD
HUNTINGTON   St.Ives G.C. ▶ Ely City G.C. ▶ Royal Worlington &
                              Newmarket G.C.   Thorpeness G.C.
            Cambridgeshire
            Moathouse Hotel   Bury St Edmunds G.C. ▶   Aldeburgh G.C. ▶
            & G.C.   BURY ST. EDMUNDS   ALDEBURGH
○ ST. NEOTS   ○ NEWMARKET
GRANTCHESTER   CAMBRIDGE   OTLEY   WOODBRIDGE
            The Gog   LAVENHAM   Woodbridge G.C. ▶
            Magog G.C. ▶   IPSWICH   Ipswich G.C.
MELBOURN   LONG MELFORD   HINTLESHAM   Felixstowe Ferry G.C. ▶
                                                              FELIXSTOWE

Artist: **Julian Barrow BRANCASTER** *Courtesy of:* **Burlington Gallery**

The counties of East Anglia, which for our purposes comprise Norfolk, Suffolk and Cambridgeshire, stretch from Constable Country in the south, through the Fens and the Broads to the tip of the Wash. For golfers this means it stretches from Felixstowe Ferry, through Thetford to Hunstanton. There are numerous other combinations capable of whetting the golfing appetite, for East Anglia is one of the game's richest regions; certainly for quality and variety it has few equals. It is also a corner of Britain where golf has long been a popular pastime.

Norfolk

It is doubtful whether any county in England can surpass Norfolk's great range of outstanding courses. In short it offers the golfer a bit of everything. There are the magnificent links courses at **Hunstanton** and **Brancaster**, some terrifically scenic golf along the cliffs at **Sheringham** and **Cromer** and a number of superb inland courses of which **Thetford, Barnham Broom** and **Kings Lynn** are prime examples.

However, the title of 'Oldest Club' in Norfolk goes to **Great Yarmouth and Caister**, founded in 1882. A fine seaside links, it is located to the north of Great Yarmouth close to the old Roman town of Caister-on-Sea and near to the start of the A149 coastal road. Punters may wish to note that the golf course is actually situated inside part of Great Yarmouth racecourse. Anyone who does think of combining the two might look to Gorleston on Sea for a night's rest at the Cliff Hotel (0493) 662179 or in Yarmouth itself we recommend the Imperial Hotel (0493) 851113, which is a family run hotel, and the Bradgate Hotel (0493) 842578.

Cromer, some twenty-five miles north along the A149 is apparently famed for its crabs—the town, not the golf course I hasten to add—and also for its 150 year old lighthouse. The latter is a feature of **Royal Cromer's** attractive clifftop course. The 14th, the 'Lighthouse Hole', was played by Tony Jacklin during his '18 holes at 18 different courses helicopter round'. Several elevated tees and a generous spread of gorse make for a very interesting game.

Sheringham is only five miles further along the coast and is Norfolk's other great clifftop course. Founded some three years after Cromer in 1891 it is perhaps less exacting than its neighbour but certainly no less scenic. The view from the 5th hole is particularly stunning looking out across the rugged north Norfolk coastline. We have featured Sheringham on a later page.

A glorious day's golf (followed perhaps by some early evening bird watching—don't forget the binoculars) and time to relax. Well, in Sheringham, the Beacon (0263) 822019 and the Beaumaris (0263) 822370 are handy whilst in nearby Weybourne the Swiss Restaurant (0263) 70220 is a splendid eating place and Maltings Hotel (0263) 70731 is a perfect base. On the road towards Brancaster (still the A149) the Blakeney area offers a glorious coastline and two beautifully situated hotels, the Manor (0263) 740376 and the Blakeney (0263) 740797.

And so on to **Brancaster** and **Hunstanton,** an outstanding pair to put it mildly. We have featured both courses, or both links to be precise, later in this section. Once again, there's no shortage of places in which to relax and reflect on the day's golf. In Old Hunstanton, Le Strange Arms (0485) 534411 on Golfhouse Road, is highly thought of, as is the Fieldsend Guesthouse (0485) 532593 on Homefields Road. The village of Thornham lies between Hunstanton and Brancaster and here one

might consider the Chequers Inn (0485) 512229 or the Kings Head (0485) 512213. To the south east of Brancaster the Old Rectory (0328) 820597 at Great Snoring sounds like the perfect place for a particularly long rest and a little nearer at Brancaster Staithe, the Jolly Sailors (0485) 210314 is a good pub with an accompanying restaurant. Further accommodation can be found at Titchwell, the Titchwell Manor (0485) 210221, and for two outstanding seafood restaurants we recommend the Moorings in Wells and Fishes in Burnham Market. Finally, for a really homely country house, the Holly Lodge (0485) 70790 at Heacham takes some beating.

Kings Lynn is our next port of call, and another very good golf course. Although the **Kings Lynn** Golf Club was founded back in 1923, it has played at Castle Rising to the north of the town since 1975. An Alliss-Thomas creation, it's very heavily wooded and quite a demanding test of golf. Returning to the town itself suggestions for an overnight stay might include the Dukes Head Hotel (0553) 774996 and Russett House (0553) 773098. A short journey to Grimston and one finds a real gem in Congham Hall (0485) 600250, an elegant and very well run Georgian manor house hotel.

The golfing visitor to Norwich, one of England's more attractive county towns, should have little difficulty in finding a game. **Sprowston Park** is a welcoming club on the edge of the city while for a fine combination of the old and the new try **Royal Norwich** and **Barnham Broom**. Both clubs have excellent parkland courses. Barnham Broom is part of an hotel and country club complex (0603) 759393 and has two courses with numerous accompanying leisure facilities; it is featured ahead. If Norwich is to be the base though, then the Maids Head Hotel (0603) 761111 is most comfortable. Slightly less imposing, but no less comfortable, are the Grange Hotel (0603) 34734 and the Marlborough House Hotel (0603) 628005. Amberley House is a good value guest house. Among many good restaurants are Marcos (0603) 624044, the Anchor Quay Bar (0603) 618410 and Greens Seafood (0603) 623733.

Last but not least we must visit **Thetford,** right in the very heart of East Anglia and close to the Norfolk-Suffolk boundary. Thetford is surely one of England's most beautiful inland courses. Set amid glorious oaks, pines and silver birch trees it is also a great haven for wildlife (rather like Luffenham Heath in Leicestershire). Golden pheasant abound and one can also sight red deer and even, so I'm told, Chinese Water Deer (whatever they may be!) The green fee here is always money well spent. The second place to invest the cash is at the Bell Hotel (0842) 754455 in Thetford—a jolly good place to rest the spikes.

Suffolk

Of the twenty or so golf clubs in Suffolk, about half were founded in the 19th century and the **Felixstowe Ferry** Golf Club which dates from 1880 is the fifth oldest club in England. Given its antiquity, and the fact that it was here that the 'father of golf writers' Bernard Darwin began to play his golf, Felixstowe Ferry is as good a place as any to begin our brief golfing tour of Suffolk.

The course lies about a mile to the north east of Felixstowe and is a classic test of traditional links golf. This part of Suffolk is fairly remote and at times it could easily be imagined that one was playing one of the better Scottish links courses. The greens are first class and the wind is often a major factor. Those looking to spend some time in this area (the courses at Ipswich and Woodbridge are only a short drive away) should note the Marlborough Hotel (0394) 285621 in Felixstowe.

The A45 links Felixstowe with Suffolk's largest town. The **Ipswich** Golf Club at Purdis Heath, three miles east of Ipswich, was designed by James Braid and is a fine heathland course. Always well maintained, the fairways wind their way between two large ponds and are bordered by heather and an attractive assortment of hardwood trees and silver birches. **Woodbridge** offers a similar type of challenge. Like the Ipswich course it's beautifully mature but is much more undulating. The golf club is located two miles east of Woodbridge along the B1084 Orford road.

The Ipswich-Woodbridge area is blessed with some outstanding places to stay and the seafood served in these parts is some of the best in Britain. In Woodbridge, Seckford Hall (0394) 385678 is superb while Melton Grange (0394) 384147 also appeals. A recent addition to the 'where to stay, where to play' map is provided by the new **Ufford Park** Hotel (0394) 383555 at Ufford, near Woodbridge. Here 18 holes of golf and numerous leisure facilities are offered in a pleasant country club setting. For those who enjoy their lobster Orford should be visited, more particularly the Butley-Orford Oysterage (0394) 450277. In Ipswich the Marlborough Hotel (0473) 257677 is both comfortable and good value and to the west of the town at Hintlesham is 16th century **Hintlesham Hall** (0473) 652 334, where a glorious country house with an excellent restaurant and a fairly new golf course await—gourmet golf personified! Other hotel suggestions in the Ipswich area would definitely include the good value Bentley Tower Hotel (0473) 212142.

A little further up the Suffolk coast lie two delightful holiday courses: **Thorpeness** and **Aldeburgh.** Although close to the sea both are again heather and gorse types. The town of Aldeburgh is of course famed for its annual music festival and Benjamin Britten once lived next to the club's 14th fairway. Thorpeness, yet another James Braid creation, is about two miles north of Aldeburgh and is especially scenic. One hole that everyone remembers is the par three 7th, played across an attractive pond. On the 18th an unusual water tower (the 'House in the Clouds') and a restored windmill provide a unique background. Thorpeness Golf Club has its own Golf Hotel (0728) 452176 which is naturally very convenient, but in Aldeburgh there are a number of alternatives, many of which also specialise in golfing breaks. Ideas here include the Wentworth (0728) 452312, the White Lion (0728) 452720 and the Uplands Hotel (0728) 452420. Also worth a visit is the White Horse Hotel (0728) 830694 in nearby Leiston. A final thought before moving inland is the Crown (0502) 722275 at Southwold to the north of Thorpeness—some pleasant rooms and some very good beer!

Over to the west of Suffolk the two courses that stand out are the parkland layout at **Bury St Edmunds** and the near-legendary **Royal Worlington.** Royal Worlington and Newmarket, to give its full title, is located two miles from Mildenhall, midway between Cambridge and Bury St Edmunds. A marvellous inland course with an almost links feel, it was once described as the finest 9 hole course in the world. For a night's stopover, Bury St Edmunds offers a first rate hotel in the Angel (0284) 753926 while to the south of the town two cosy establishments are the Bull at Long Melford with its 15th century frontage and the popular Swan (0787) 247477 at Lavenham. Finally the Bedford Lodge Hotel (0638) 663175 at Newmarket is renowned for its hospitality.

Cambridgeshire

Having ventured west it is time to inspect the land of the fens and the courses of Cambridgeshire. Not exactly a county renowned for its golf, the courses tend, as one might expect, to be rather flat. One great exception though is the **Gog Magog** Golf Club situated to the south east of Cambridge which offers a tremendously enjoyable test of golf. The club takes its name from the ridge of low hills on which it lies. Apparently taking a line due east from here the next range of hills one comes across is the Ural Mountains! Among many fine holes, the par four 16th stands out and is surely one of the best (and toughest!) two-shot holes in the country. A second good course, though not in the same league as Gog Magog, close to the famous University City belongs to the **Cambridgeshire Moat House Hotel** (0954) 780555. It is a particularly tough course when played from the back tees with a lake and several ditches providing the challenges. Just north of Cambridge, **Girton** Golf Club is also worth inspecting.

Cambridge with its magnificent colleges is a marvellous place to spend a day or two and the Moat House is just one of many fine hotels. Of the others the Garden House Hotel (0223) 63421 perhaps takes pride of place and is particularly welcoming. It also possesses a first class restaurant. Another good eating place in town is the Marguerite (0223) 315232. Among the less expensive hotels, both Bon Accord House (0223) 411188 and the Lensfield Hotel (0223) 355017 are recommended as are Kirkwood House (0223) 313874 and Dykelands Guest House (0223) 244300. In nearby Royston, Chiswick House (0763) 60242 has great charm and Orton Hall Hotel (0733) 391111 is one of the finest in Cambridgeshire. Some notable hostelries in the county include the Plough and Fleece at Horningsea, the Three Horse Shoes at Madingley and the Green Man at Grantchester. Other golf courses in Cambridgeshire which can be recommended include **Ramsey, St Ives** and **St Neots.** To the east of St Neots is the Abbotsley Golf Hotel (0480) 474000, situated in the grounds is the course of the same name. A duo just outside of bustling Peterborough, **Peterborough Milton** and the public course, **Thorpe Wood.** Finally, in Ely there is the attractive **Ely City** course which provides some excellent views of the stunning 12th century cathedral and where, rather interestingly, the course record is held by one Lee Trevino.

Excluding those which have staged an Open Championship, there are perhaps two courses in Britain that exude a sense of tradition, history and character above all others. One is Westward Ho! and the other is Brancaster or, to give them their correct titles, Royal North Devon and Royal West Norfolk.

Apart from their rather geographical names, they have much in common; both enjoy a wondrously remote setting yet are still fairly close to a superb Championship links (Saunton and Hunstanton); both have a unique hazard (Devon's sea rushes and Norfolk's tidal marshes) and both are particularly friendly Clubs, emphasising that tradition need not accompany aloofness.

Brancaster is something of a golfers' Camelot. Having reached the attractive little village there is every possibility that a high tide will have flooded the road that leads to the course. Indeed, many choose to leave their car in the village and walk the remainder of the journey. (Dont worry, it's not that far!) The golf course lies in a range of sand hills between marshland and sea. There is a story that the course was laid out on the suggestion of the Prince of Wales (later King Edward VII), having conceived the idea while out shooting on the land. Certainly it was he who bestowed patronage upon the Club immediately on its foundation in 1891. The Royal flavour has continued and there have been no fewer than four Royal Captains, most recently the Duke of Kent in 1981.

The **Secretary** at Brancaster is **Major Nigel Carrington Smith** and he can be contacted on **(0485) 210087**. The Club's full address is **The Royal West Norfolk Golf Club, Brancaster, Nr. Kings Lynn, Norfolk, PE31 8AX.** Individual visitors and societies are both welcome at Brancaster although all visiting parties must make prior arrangements with The Secretary—an introduction is preferred. Due to increased demand, no visitors are received at any time, unless playing with a member, during the last week in July and until the end of the first week in September.

In 1994, the green fee was £32 during the week and £42.50 at weekends and on Bank Holidays. The preferred days for golfing societies are Mondays, Wednesdays and Fridays. The **Professional** at Brancaster, **Mr. R.E. Kimber,** can be contacted on **(0485) 210616.**

The problem of being wondrously remote is that travelling to the course can be a lengthy journey. Brancaster is approximately eight miles from Hunstanton and twenty-five miles from Kings Lynn, to the south and south west respectively, and about thirty miles from Cromer to the east. Linking each to the other is the A149.

Like our friend Westward Ho!, Brancaster has the traditional out and back links layout. A quick glance at the scorecard tells us that one nine is considerably shorter than the other, the outward half measuring 3369 yards to the inward's 3059 yards. However, as at every good seaside course, wind direction is all important and on many occasions the back nine can play, or at least seem much longer. In total, the 6428 yards, par 71 represents a considerable test of golf. From the ladies tees the course measures 5927 yards, par 75.

As well as the tidal marshes which come into play around the 8th and 9th, Brancaster is famed for its great wooden sleepered bunkers. Many are cross bunkers, which as Sir Peter Allen observed: '... can be alarming to play over and frightening to play out of.' The course has received very few alterations over the years although two greens were lost to the sea in 1939 and 1940. There is no gentle beginning; the first three holes all measure over 400 yards and the great cross bunkers can come into play as early as the 3rd hole, one of the most difficult on the course. The bunker is fifty yards short of the green, which itself sits on a plateau. The 4th is a short par three but is deceptively tricky, especially into the wind. The 8th and 9th have been mentioned and the marshes must be carried twice on the 8th and from the tee on the dog-legged 9th which has a cross bunker in front of the green. The 11th and 12th are played deep amid the dunes but the 14th is perhaps the most difficult hole, with the 18th close behind—a hole with sleepered bunkers both to the front and back of the green.

The Clubhouse, which is only a year younger than the course, is decidedly comfortable and is separated from the sea only by a sea wall. This famous last line of defence had to be repaired in 1991, after high seas reaped havoc in 1990. The Clubhouse also has a lovely verandah from which there are some glorious views. The setting really is something special and nobody described it better than the late Tom Scott.

'It has a quiet and restful beauty, and when you leave the Clubhouse and drive across the marsh to the main road in the dusk of a summer evening, look back for a minute and perhaps you will be rewarded, as I have frequently been, with a view of the red sun setting over the sea with a golden glow. You will see too, the long shadows cast by the great sand hills, and you will hear the call of the many birds across the marshes, a sound to my mind typical of Norfolk.'

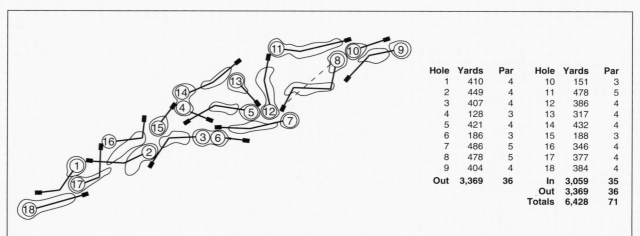

Hole	Yards	Par	Hole	Yards	Par
1	410	4	10	151	3
2	449	4	11	478	5
3	407	4	12	386	4
4	128	3	13	317	4
5	421	4	14	432	4
6	186	3	15	188	3
7	486	5	16	346	4
8	478	5	17	377	4
9	404	4	18	384	4
Out	**3,369**	**36**	**In**	**3,059**	**35**
			Out	**3,369**	**36**
			Totals	**6,428**	**71**

Imagine you are standing on the tee of a particularly diffi-cult par three hole. It is a difficult hole on a still day—188 yards long and with six deep bunkers encircling the green—but it is particularly tough on this day because the wind is dead against. You select a one iron and hit the perfect shot; so perfect that it lands a few feet from the flag and rolls into the hole. Marvellous, but what a pity this is only a practice round! A day later, in the tournament itself, you reach the 16th but this time the wind is with you. You choose a six iron and incredibly you repeat the trick—in it goes for a sec-ond hole in one. Much celebration follows at the 19th. The next day (the second of the tournament) the wind is once more at your back as you walk onto the tee of what is now your favourite hole. If a six iron was good enough yester-day, it must be good enough today you reckon. Your calcu-lations are entirely accurate and your well struck shot never really looks like missing. Three aces in three days at the same hole! Are you a liar, a dreamer... or Robert Taylor?

Taylor performed this remarkable feat in the summer of 1974 on the 16th at Hunstanton. Nobody has ever matched his extraordinary achievement and probably never will.

Founded over a hundred years ago, Hunstanton Golf Club celebrated its centenary in 1991. Although it is situ-ated on the east coast of England the course actually faces north west and looks over the Wash towards Lincolnshire. Hunstanton has the kind of geography that causes its Members to lose sleep over talk of global warming. It is a very good golf course—in the opinion of many, the east coast's finest 18 hole challenge between Sandwich and Muirfield, a distance of about 400 miles. It is a boast regularly expressed by Hunstanton's Members when a player from Brancaster happens to be within earshot. But theirs is a valid claim, for Hunstanton is a truly classic links course. Like Brancaster, the course runs out and back although not rigidly so, rather it meanders away from the Clubhouse, reaches the 8th green and meanders its way home. The outward holes have the River Hun for company, normally it is off to the right and the inward ones are closer to the shore. At first glance, the links looks very flat, and indeed there aren't any major climbs, up or down, but the course has more than its fair share of subtle undulations and there are a number of elevated tees and plateau greens, some of which offer extensive views of both sea and country.

It isn't the views though that are likely to be best remembered after a round at Hunstanton, it is the greens and bunkers. The putting surfaces are as quick (and usu-ally as well prepared) as any in Britain—including the Open Championship courses. As for the bunkers, they

are numerous, strategically (and sometimes sadistically) placed and often quite deep. Avoid the bunkers and putt well and you'll probably score well here!

The Club is very happy to receive visitors on week-days and occasionally at weekends. All must be mem-bers of Golf Clubs and have current handicaps. It is worth noting that the 1st tee is reserved on weekdays before 9.30am, but in any event it is a good idea to con-tact the club a few days prior to any visit. The **Secretary** at Hunstanton, **Mr Malcolm Whybrow** can be approached by writing to; **The Hunstanton Golf Club, Old Hunstanton, Norfolk PE36 6JQ.** Mr Whybrow can also be contacted by telephone on **(0485) 532811. Mr John Carter** is the Club's **professional** and he can be reached on **(0485) 532751**.

The green fees in 1994 were £30 per day during the week and, when available, £36 per day at weekends. Junior golfers paid half the above rates.

From the Championship tees, Hunstanton measures 6670 yards, par 72 (SSS 72); while from the medal tees it is reduced by some 350 yards to 6318 yards, although it then becomes a par 70, and for Ladies the course mea-sures 5986 yards, par 75. We have already referred to the ingenious and severe bunkering and the four par three holes emphasise this: the 4th is only 165 yards in length but has eight bunkers; the 7th is a similar length and has only one trap, but what a trap! The tee shot is an attrac-tive one over a gully to a plateau green. Anything short is almost certain to plummet into a deep, yawning bunker that almost runs the entire width of the entrance—a low runner is not the desired shot here. The 14th requires a blind tee shot of 200 yards plus and again eight bunkers are waiting to greet the player who fails to find the putting surface. The par four holes at Hunstanton offer a range of challenges. The 3rd, for instance, demands a very long approach shot if the pre-vailing wind is up to its tricks; by contrast, the 6th is a modest length hole but a deft touch is required to pitch onto the plateau green. The best hole on the course is generally considered to be the 11th which runs parallel to the shore. A high tee gives a spectacular view of both the hole and the surrounding countryside. At 439 yards it needs two perfectly hit shots along an ever narrowing valley-fairway to reach the green.

Numerous major amateur events have been staged at Hunstanton over the years, including the 1990 British Boys Amateur Championship won by the highly promis-ing Michael Welch.

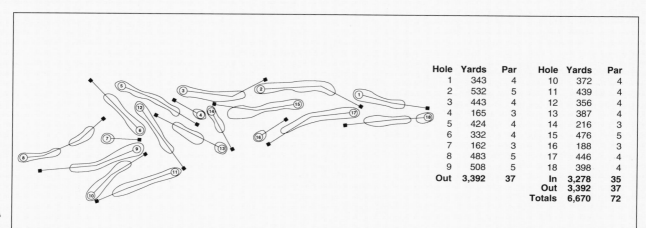

Hole	Yards	Par	Hole	Yards	Par
1	343	4	10	372	4
2	532	5	11	439	4
3	443	4	12	356	4
4	165	3	13	387	4
5	424	4	14	216	3
6	332	4	15	476	5
7	162	3	16	188	3
8	483	5	17	446	4
9	508	5	18	398	4
Out	**3,392**	**37**	**In**	**3,278**	**35**
			Out	**3,392**	**37**
			Totals	**6,670**	**72**

Hintlesham Hall's 18 hole championship standard golf course provides excellent golf in an uniquely privileged environment. Designed by well known golf course architect Martin Hawtree, the course measures 6630 yards from the medal tees with a Par of 72. Blending perfectly with the surrounding mature parkland of this prestigious location, the course was allowed the unusually long period of two full years to mature before opening for full scale use in September 1991. As a result, golfers are pleasantly surprised to find a beautifully manicured course with well defined fairways and consistently paced greens.

The Hintlesham course has been constructed to challenge the professional, while remaining enjoyable and rewarding to high handicap golfers. Practice facilities include a putting green, a short game pitching area and practice drive ground. Year round play is ensured by the quality of construction and the natural advantages of the site.

The brand new clubhouse, a bright and airy building designed with a frontage in the style of an Edwardian pavilion, includes services and facilities well above the standards of those ordinarily provided at a golf club. Large lounge, dining area and separate stud bar are bordered by a full width verandah providing extensive views over this beautiful, undulating parkland course.

Both the men's and women's changing areas are light and spacious with separate saunas, a shared steam room and large spa bath which look onto an internal courtyard.

With equal status for ladies and gentlemen, both on the course and in the clubhouse, Hintlesham Hall Golf Club provides a traditional high level of service to its members and their guests commensurate with the standards at the adjacent hotel.

Hintlesham Hall Golf Club has a growing national reputation for the total organisation of every facet of a golfing day, whether small or large scale. Alastair Spink, the club head Professional, can offer a programme of indoor and outdoor tuition and golf clinics, and is on hand to arrange tournaments and golf days. Green fee players are welcome subject to reserving tee-off times.

For further information about membership, green fee play, organised golfing days or golfing breaks, please contact the Club Secretary on (0473) 652761.

Hintlesham Hall and its Golf Club are located four miles west of Ipswich on the A1071. Hintlesham is ten minutes drive from the A14 and A12 trunk roads.

Hintlesham Hall Golf Club
Hintlesham
Ipswich
Suffolk IP8 3NS
Tel: (0473) 652761
Tel: Hotel: (0473) 652268
Fax: (0473) 652463

Hintlesham Hall, originally built in the 1570s, with a stunning Georgian facade offers the best in country house elegance and charm. Gracious living, good food and wine, attentive service and tranquil relaxation greet every guest to the hotel.

The Hall is set in over 170 acres of rolling Suffolk countryside, some of which is devoted to a beautiful 18 hole championship, full length golf course, and has 33 luxurious bedrooms and suites of differing shapes and sizes, some with four poster beds. Thoughtful attention to detail pervades the hotel and this includes the restaurant. Head Chef, Alan Ford, believes good food starts with good produce. French truffles, Scottish salmon, Cornish scallops and Suffolk lobsters are just some of the enticements of the menu which changes seasonally.

There is an award winning 300 bin wine list which ranges the world from France to Australia.

All moods are reflected in Hintlesham's fine reception rooms - the intimate book lined library, the tranquil, spacious Garden Room and the cool entrance Arcade. The Hall is just 45 minutes drive from Newmarket and is an ideal base from which to explore East Anglia, be it the medieval wool villages of Lavenham and Kersey, Long Melford and Woodbridge with their wealth of antique shops or Dedham and Flatford Mill, famous for their Constable associations. The cathedral city of Norwich and the University colleges of Cambridge are close by. However, perhaps most importantly, Hintlesham Hall is the perfect retreat for those who wish to go nowhere at all.

Hintlesham Hall
Hintlesham
Suffolk
IP8 3NS
Tel: (0473) 652268
Fax: (0473) 652463

Yes, nice place to go for a holiday, Norfolk—quaint villages, splendid country houses, Norwich Cathedral, The Norfolk Broads, a spectacular coastline... oh, and plenty of invigorating sea air.' What about a golfing holiday? 'Well yes, there are some tremendous seaside courses aren't there—Hunstanton, where the greens are faster than a marble staircase and Brancaster, a glorious reminder of how golf used to be: plus fours, sleepered bunkers, pitch and run and all that; and some fabulous cliff-top golf further along the coast at Sheringham and Cromer. Apart from Thetford though, which is almost in Suffolk anyway, there's nothing much inland is there?—too flat and too exposed I imagine.'

Barnham Broom Hotel, Golf & Country Club has shattered the illusion: thirty six marvellous holes of golf set in 250 acres of rolling parkland and a fine hotel in which to rest the weary bones overnight. As for being 'too flat and too exposed', well the two courses are called The Hill and The Valley and on both the golfer is protected from nature's worst habits by a good and varied collection of trees.

Barnham Broom actually arrived on the scene in the late 1970s at a time when the phrase 'Hotel, Golf & Country Club' was greeted somewhat suspiciously by this country's golfing fraternity. 'An American joint is it?—lots of water and 18 enormously long holes. Just like the Belfry I suppose!'

There were only 18 holes at the time—the present day Valley Course—but 1989 saw the opening of The Hill Course and they complement each other perfectly. There is a fair amount of water at Barnham Broom but it is not overdone, nor is it entirely artificial, the ubiquitous River Yare being chiefly responsible for the many watery duels. The only overtly American look to the place is the conditioning of the courses: they are beautifully maintained—unlike all too many courses these days in Britain. Certainly they deserve inspection.

Very able to assist you with your enquiries is the senior professional and **Golf Director, Peter Ballingall.** He can be approached either by writing to Barnham Broom, the full address being **Barnham Broom Golf & Country Club, Honingham Road, Barnham Broom, Norwich NR9 4DD** or by telephone on **(0603) 759393.** Also extremely helpful is golf **professional Steve Beckham** who can also be contacted via the above telephone number. In 1994, the green fees to play at Barnham Broom were set at £25 per round, £30 for a full day. These rates apply seven days per week. It is important to telephone the club in advance to book a starting time—Barnham Broom has become very popular with golf societies and hotel guests may have reserved tee times. Reduced green fees are available to hotel residents and weekend breaks are good value, especially now there are 36 holes to play.

Barnham Broom is situated 7 miles from Norwich, almost due west of the county town mid way between the A11 and the A47. The latter is likely to be the best road to take out of Norwich; an alternative is the B1108. Travelling from further afield, Norwich has been brought much closer to London by the M11 (which should be left at junction 9 for the A11). The A467 links the city with the Midlands to the west and Great Yarmouth to the east. A combination of the A45/A140/A43 should be taken from Ipswich.

The two courses are of similar length, the Valley Course measuring 6470 yards, par 71 from the back markers against the Hill Course's 6628 yards, par 72. From the tees of the day the difference in total is just 28 yards (6241 yards and 6269 yards). For ladies, each course measures a shade under 6000 yards and is a par 74. Both courses open with par fives. The 2nd on the Valley Course is a tremendous dog-leg where a mishit shot can end up in a small lake; but the challenge is even greater on the 3rd which is the stroke index one. Another fine hole on the Valley Course is the 6th although it has lost some of its sting since the January 1990 storms removed an obstructing tree.

On the Hill Course, which is maturing rapidly, the outstanding hole is probably the par five 6th which is played along a valley. Just in front of the green the river meanders severely and gives the impression of practically surrounding the golfer as he putts (hopefully) for a memorable birdie. Memorable birdies at the 6th or not, it is likely that when the golfer walks from the 18th green he will have enjoyed a memorable round.

Barnham Broom really is a delightful place to visit. The atmosphere is extremely relaxed, not at all stuffy, and the golf is par excellence. We have mentioned the hotel only briefly but it really does make a superb base and offers the sporting types a whole host of leisure facilities.

Yes, nice place for a golfing holiday, Norfolk - beside the sea - and in the heart of the country.

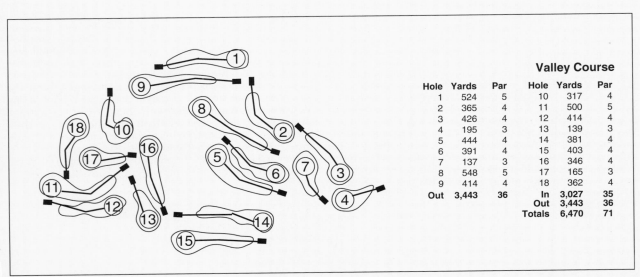

Valley Course

Hole	Yards	Par	Hole	Yards	Par
1	524	5	10	317	4
2	365	4	11	500	5
3	426	4	12	414	4
4	195	3	13	139	3
5	444	4	14	381	4
6	391	4	15	403	4
7	137	3	16	346	4
8	548	5	17	165	3
9	414	4	18	362	4
Out	**3,443**	**36**	**In**	**3,027**	**35**
			Out	**3,443**	**36**
			Totals	**6,470**	**71**

I suspect that most golfers have, at one time or another, worked out their eclectic score for the 18 holes on their home course. Recently, a friend of mine from Withington Golf Club in Cheshire, boasted after his first ever hole in one that his first four holes now ran 2-2-2-1. Not bad, I told him, but what about Ernie Riseboro. Never heard of him came the rather terse reply. Ernie Riseboro was one of the first professionals at Sheringham; the Club was founded a century ago in 1891 and he served the Club from 1907 until his retirement in 1958. Apart from longevity of service, Ernie's great claim to fame was that his best ball score for Sheringham comprised nothing higher than a 2 ....and have you seen the par fours at Sheringham!

Sheringham's splendid clifftop course is situated in one of the more remote parts of Britain, tucked away on Norfolk's northern coast, staring out across the bleak North Sea. The course has long been regarded as one of the finest on the east coast of England and as long ago as 1920 was selected to host the English Ladies Championship—more of which a little later—an event which returned in 1991 during the Club's Centenary year, when 18 year old Nicola Buxton triumphed over 17 year old Karen Stupples. Famous early members of the Club included two of Britain's greatest heroes: Robert Falcon Scott and Douglas Bader.

Today, visitors are very welcome at Sheringham, although they are required to be in possession of a Club handicap. It is always advisable to make an advance telephone call to the **Secretary, Mr. M.J. Garrett**, to check whether any tee reservations are planned. Mr Garrett may be contacted by telephone on **(0263) 823488**, and by fax on (0263) 825189. The **professional, Richard Emery**, can be reached on tel: **(0263) 822980.**

Green fees for 1995 are projected as being £29 on weekdays with £34 payable at weekends. Reduced rates are available for junior golfers. Golfing societies are also encouraged and may make weekday bookings through the Secretary, written applications to be addressed to Mr Garrett at the **Sheringham Golf Club, Weybourne Road, Sheringham, Norfolk NR26 8HG.**

Anyone approaching Sheringham should be travelling along the A149 as the course is located immediately off this road, half a mile west of the town. Coming directly from Norwich motorists should take the A140 before joining the A149 at Cromer, Sheringham being signposted off to the left on the B157 about 4 miles before Cromer is reached. A railway level crossing heralds the entrance to the Golf Club.

So having got to the 1st tee what are we confronted with? In short, from the medal tees, 6464 yards of challenging, varied and at times most spectacular golf. The par for the men is 70 (SSS 71) while for the ladies the course measures 5840 yards (SSS 73), par 73. The course has been laid out on a strip of land sandwiched between the cliffs on the one side and the North Norfolk Steam Railway line on the other. The turf is of that springy, seaside nature and there is an abundant smattering of heather and gorse. Whereas the sea can beckon on some of the front nine holes so the railway line becomes very much a feature on the home stretch.

The opening two holes, a short four followed by a par five, may well provide a solid start and dare I suggest, the chance of beginning 3-4? The next five holes run close to the cliff edges and are possibly the most enjoyable of the round; certainly the views here are tremendous. Particularly memorable is the panoramic view from the 5th fairway, looking out across the north Norfolk coastline—not a hole to be hurried. On the next seven holes the gorse becomes the most likely devil to wreck a promising card, perhaps the most testing holes being the 10th and 12th. Sheringham has an exacting finish too and with the railway line acting as a continuous boundary to the right now is not the time to suddenly develop a slice.

Special mention must be made of the 17th, a hole made famous by the great Joyce Wethered when playing in her first English Ladies Championship in 1920. Aged only 19, she reached the final to play the overwhelming favourite, Cecil Leitch. On the 17th green (which was then much closer to the railway line) Miss Wethered faced a short putt to win the match. Just as she prepared to strike the ball the 4.20 train from Sheringham thundered past- but no matter she duly sunk the putt. Questioned as to why the train hadn't put her off at all she apparently replied, 'What train?'

After her win at Sheringham Miss Wethered's career blossomed, indeed she won the next four English Ladies titles as well and was never beaten in that event. How great a player was she? According to Bobby Jones she was the best golfer in the world of either sex, but then Jones always was modest, and besides, I bet she never took on Ernie Riseboro at Sheringham.

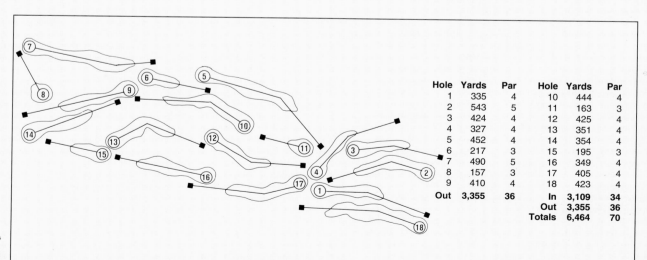

Hole	Yards	Par	Hole	Yards	Par
1	335	4	10	444	4
2	543	5	11	163	3
3	424	4	12	425	4
4	327	4	13	351	4
5	452	4	14	354	4
6	217	3	15	195	3
7	490	5	16	349	4
8	157	3	17	405	4
9	410	4	18	423	4
Out	**3,355**	**36**	**In**	**3,109**	**34**
			Out	**3,355**	**36**
			Totals	**6,464**	**70**

Key

*To avoid disappointment
it is advisable to telephone
in advance*

***Visitors welcome at most times
***Visitors usually allowed on
weekdays only*
**Visitors not normally permitted
(Mon, Wed) No visitors
on specified days*

Approximate Green Fees
A £30 plus
B £20 to £30
C £15 to £25
D £10 to £20
E under £10
F Greens fees on application

Restrictions
G Guests only
H Handicap certificate required
H (24) Handicap of 24 or less
L Letter of introduction required
M Visitor must be a member of
another recognised club.

CAMBRIDGESHIRE

Abbotsley G.C.
(0480) 215153
Eynesbury Hardwicke, St Neots
(18)6150 yards/***/C

Brampton Park G.C.
(0480) 434700
Buckden Road, Brampton
(18)6403 yards/***/B

Bourn G.C.
(0954) 718057
Toft Road, Bourn
(18)6275 yards/***/C

Cambridgeshire Moat House Hotel G.C.
(0954) 780555
Bar Hill
(18)6734 yards/***/C/L/M

Elton Furze G.C.
(0832) 280189
Bullock Road, Haddon
(18)6291 yards/*/B

Ely City G.C.
(0353) 662751
Cambridge Road, Ely
(18)6686 yards/**/B

Girton G.C.
(0223) 276169
Dodford Lane, Girton
(18)6085 yards/**/C

Gog Magog G.C.
(0223) 247626
Shelford Bottom
(18)6354 yards/**/B/H
(9)5833 yards/**/B/H

Hermingford Abbots G.C.
(0480) 495000
New Farm Lodge, Cambridge Road
(9)5468 yards/***/F

Lakeside Lodge G.C.
(0487) 740540
Fen Road, Pidley
(18)6600 yards/***/E

March G.C.
(0354) 52364
Frogs Abbey, Grange Road, March
(9)6200 yards/**/D

Old Nene G.& C.C.
(0487) 813519
Muchwood Lane, Bodsey, Ramsey
(9)5524 yards/***/E

Orton Meadows G.C.
(0733) 237478
Ham Lane, Peterborough
(18)5800 yards/***/E

Peterborough Milton G.C.
(0733) 380489
Milton Ferry, Peterborough
(18)6431 yards/**/A/H

Ramsey G.C.
(0487) 812600
Abbey Terrace, Ramsey, Huntingdon
(18)6136 yards/**/C/H

St Ives G.C.
(0480) 68392
Westwood Road, St Ives
(9)6052 yards/**/C/H

St Neots G.C.
(0480) 472363
Crosshall Road, St Neots
(18)6027 yards/**/B/H

Thorney Golf Centre
(0733) 270570
English Drove, Thorney, Peterborough
(18)6104 yards/***/E

Thorpe Wood G.C.
(0733) 267701
Thorpe Wood, Peterborough
(18)7076 yards/***/F

SUFFOLK

Aldeburgh G.C.
(0728) 452890
Saxmundham Road, Aldeburgh
(18)6330 yards/***/F/H
(9)2114 yards/***/F/H

Beccles G.C.
(0502) 712244
The Common, Beccles
(9)2696 yards/**/C

Bungay and Waveney Valley G.C.
(0986) 892337
Outney Common, Bungay
(18)6063 yards/**/C/H

Bury St Edmunds G.C.
(0284) 755979
Tuthill, Bury St Edmunds
(18)6615 yards/***/B/H

Cretingham G.C.
(0728) 685275
Cretingham, Woodridge
(9)1955 yards/***/E

Felixstowe Ferry G.C.
(0394) 286834
Ferry Road, Felixstowe
(18)6324 yards/***/C/H

Flempton G.C.
(0284) 728291
Flempton, Bury St Edmunds
(9)6240 yards/**/C/H

Fornham Park G.C.
(0284) 706777
St Johns Hill Plantation, Bury St Edmunds
(18)6212 yards/***/C

Fynn Valley G.C.
(0473) 785463
Witnesham, Ipswich
(18)5700 yards/***/D

Haverhill G.C.
(0440) 61951
Coupals Road, Haverhill
(9)5707 yards/***/C

Hintlesham Hall G.C.
(0473) 87761
Hintlesham, Ipswich
(18)6630 yards/***/B

Ipswich G.C.
(0473) 728941
Purdis Heath, Bucklesham Road
(18)6405 yards/**/B/H(18)
(9)1950 yards/***/E

Links G.C.
(0638) 663000
Cambridge Road, Newmarket
(18)6424 yards/***/B/H

Newton Green G.C.
(0787) 77217
Newton Green, Sudbury
(9)5488 yards/**/D/H

Rookery Park G.C.
(0502) 560380
Beccles Road, Carlton Coleville
(18)6649 yards/***/C/H

Royal Worlington and Newmarket G.C.
(0638) 712216
Worlington, Bury St Edmunds
(9)3105 yards/**/B/H

Rushmere G.C.
(0473) 725648

Rushmere Heath, Ipswich
(18)6287 yards/***/C/H

Seckford G.C.
(0394) 388000
Seckford Hall Road, Woodbridge
(18)5088 yards/***/E

Southwold G.C.
(0502) 723234
The Common, Southwold
(9)6001 yards/***/C/H

St Helena G.C.
(0986) 875567
Bramfield Road, Halesworth
(18)6580 yards/***/C/H
(9)3059 yards/***/C/H

Stoke-by-Nayland G.C.
(0206) 262836
Keepers Lane, Colchester
(18)6544 yards/***/B/H

Stowmarket G.C.
(0449) 736473
Lower Road, Onehouse, Stowmarket
(18)6101 yards/***/C/H

Thorpeness G.C.
(0728) 452176
Thorpeness
(18)6241 yards/***/B/H

Ufford Park Hotel & G.C,
(0394) 383555
Yarmouth Road, Ufford, Woodbridge
(18)6335 yards/***/C

Waldringfield Heath G.C.
(0473) 36768
Newbourne Road, Waldringfield
(18)6153 yards/***/C

Woodbridge G.C.
(0394) 382038
Bromeswell Heath, Woodbridge
(18)6314 yards/**/B/H
(9)2243 yards/**/B/H

Wood Valley G.C.
(0502) 712244
The Common, Beccles
(9)2781 yards/**/D/H

NORFOLK

Barnham Broom G.& C.C.
(0603) 759393
Barnham Broom, Norwich
(18)6603 yards/***/B
(18)6470 yards/***/B

Bawburgh G.C.
(0603) 746390
Long Lane, Bawburgh, Norwich
(18)6066 yards/***/D

Costessey Park G.C.
(0603) 746333
Costessey Park, Costessey
(18)5853 yards/***/C

Dereham G.C.
(0362) 695900
Quebec Road, Dereham
(9)6225 yards/**/C/H

Diss G.C.
(0379) 642847
Stutson Road, Diss
(18)6238 yards/**/C

Dunston Hall G.C.
(0508) 470178
Ipswich Road, Dunston
(9)6408 yards/***/F

Eagles G.C.
(0553) 827147
School Road, Kings Lynn
(9)4282 yards/***/E

Eaton G.C.
(0603) 51686
Newmarket Road, Norwich
(18)6135 yards/***/B

Fakenham G.C.
(0328) 862867
The Racecourse, Fakenham
(9)5879 yards/**/D

Feltwell G.C.
(0842) 827644
Thor Avenue, Feltwell, Thetford
(9)6260 yards/**/D

Gorleston G.C.
(0493) 661911
Warren Road, Gorleston
(18)6400 yards/***/C/H

Granary Hotel & G.C.
(0328) 701310
Little Dunham, Kings Lynn
(9)2132 yards/***/D

Great Yarmouth and Caister G.C.
(0493) 728699
Beach House, Caister-on-Sea
(18)6284 yards/***/B

Hunstanton G.C.
(0485) 532811
Golf Course Road, Old Hunstanton
(18)6670 yards/**/A/H

Kings Lynn G.C.
(0553) 631654
Castle Rising, Kings Lynn
(18)6646 yards/**/A/H

Links Country Park Hotel G.C.
(0263) 838383
West Runton
(9)4814 yards/***/C

Mattishall G.C.
(0362) 850464
South Green, Mattishall, Dereham
(9)6218 yards/***/E

Middleton Hall G.C.
(0553) 841800
Middleton
(9)5570 yards/***/D

Mundesley G.C.
(0263) 720279
Links Road, Mundesley
(9)5410 yards/***/C

R.A.F. Marham G.C.
(0760) 337261
RAF Marham, Kings Lynn
(9)5244 yards/*/E/G

Reymerston G.C.
(0362) 850297
Hingham Road, Reymerston
(18)6603 yards/**/C

Richmond Park G.C.
(0953) 881803
Saham Road, Watton
(18)6300 yards/***/D/H

Royal Cromer G.C.
(0263) 512884
Overstrand Road, Cromer
(18)6508 yards/***/B/H

Royal Norwich G.C.
(0603) 429928
Drayton High Road, Hellesdon
(18)6603 yards/**/B/H

Royal West Norfolk G.C.
(0485) 210087
Brancaster, Kings Lynn
(18)6428 yards/**/A/H

Ryston Park G.C.
(0366) 383834
Denver, Downham Market
(9)6292 yards/**/C

Sheringham G.C.
(0263) 823488
Weybourne Road, Sheringham
(18)6464 yards/***/B/H

Sprowston Park G.C.
(0603) 410657
Wroxham Road, Sprowston
(18)5985 yards/***/D/H

Swaffham G.C.
(0760) 721611
Cley Road, Swaffham
(9)6252 yards/**/C

Thetford G.C.
(0842) 752169
Brandon Road, Thetford
(18)6879 yards/**/B/H

Wensum Valley G.C.
(0603) 261012
Beech Avenue, Taverham
(18)6000 yards/**/D
(18)4862 yards/**/D

Weston Park G.C.
(0603) 872363
Weston Longville, Norwich
(9)3132 yards/***/C/H

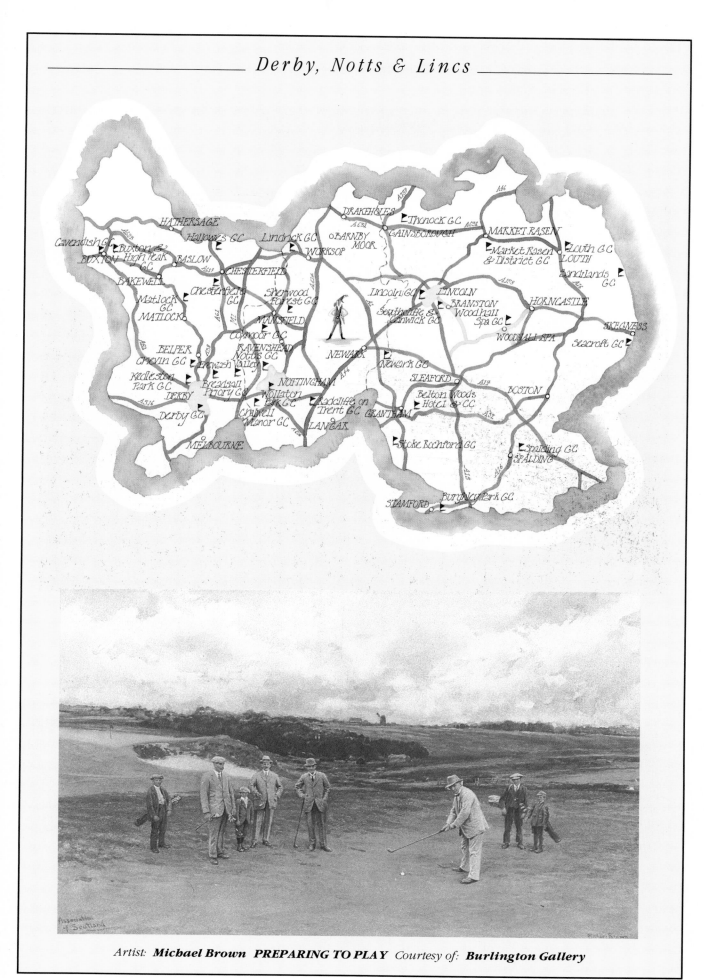

Artist: **Michael Brown PREPARING TO PLAY** *Courtesy of:* **Burlington Gallery**

Nestling in 400 acres of manicured parkland, this majestic 13th century mansion offers a combination of relaxation, elegance and comfort and yet is only minutes from Derby and motorway connections.

Breadsall Priory has been thoughtfully refurbished to provide 91 en suite bedrooms, including a number of highly individual rooms set in the Priory itself. Most rooms provide panoramic views over the mature golf course, formal gardens and ornamental lake while those in the Priory reflect the rich architectural heritage of this elegant mansion. All rooms are complemented by the facilities of the superb country club and restaurants. The Elizabethan's eye for detail and colour is clearly displayed in the Priory Restaurant, an attractive setting in which to enjoy the fine cuisine of table d'hote and à la carte menus. Lighter meals can be enjoyed in the Poolside Grill and a relaxing drink by the log fire in the cocktail bar.

The focal point of the luxuriously appointed Leisure Club is a stunning indoor pool, flanked by a spa bath, lounging area and Poolside Grill. Here you can relax and unwind or enjoy a session in the health and beauty salon or solaria. The club's gymnasium is equipped with every conceivable aid to health and fitness and there are squash and tennis courts, snooker, steam room and sauna.

The 400 acres of parkland provide scope for two challenging 18 hole golf courses; the Moorland over open moor, and the Priory, a traditional parkland course. There are also covered practice bays, tuition, a pro's shop with golf club and buggy hire.

Breadsall Priory also offers state of the art conference facilities ranging from the oak panelled library to the Oak Room accommodating up to 100 delegates.

If its 400 acres are not enough, Breadsall Priory is within easy reach of the glorious Peak District. Chatsworth and Elvaston Castle, to name just places of historical interest, are also close by.

Breadsall Priory Hotel, Country Club Resort
Moor Road
Morley
Derby
DE7 6DL
Tel: (0332) 832235
Fax : (0332) 833509

Not wishing to be unkind but Derby the town isn't one of Earth's more inspiring places—nor for that matter are most of the Midlands industrial sprawls—but Derbyshire the county is a different matter altogether. The Peak District is without question one of the most scenic regions in Britain and commencing only a short distance north of Derby, it covers the greater part of the county. The Pennine Way of course starts in Derbyshire. As well as being the beginning of all things beautiful the area just north of Derby is where three of the county's leading golf courses are to be found: Kedlestone Park, Breadsall Priory and Chevin. Located approximately four miles from Derby off the A111 (and well signposted) **Kedleston Park** golf course occupies a beautiful situation and is generally rated as the finest course in Derbyshire. Quite lengthy from the back tees, it has a variety of challenging holes. Eyeing the course from across a lake is the impressive Kedleston Hall, historic home of Lord Scarsdale.

I'm not sure what the 13th century monks would have made of the **Breadsall Priory** Golf and Country Club, three miles north east of Derby at Morley, but for heathens of the 20th century it provides an ideal setting for one of the most enjoyable games in the Midlands. Golfwise Breadsall Priory has only been on the map since 1976 but the undulating parkland course with its imported Cumberland turf greens has matured rapidly: indeed, a second 18 holes have recently been completed and they admirably complement a new plush leisure centre.

Chevin lies slightly further north off the A6 at Duffield. It has an interesting layout; the first ten holes are a steady climb towards a spectacular vantage point after which holes 11 to 18 gently bring you down to earth (or at least to Duffield!). Another course to recommend in the south of the county and over towards Nottingham is the wooded layout at **Erewash Valley**, noted for its two quarry holes.

If Derby has to be one's base then the Forte Posthouse (0332) 514933 in Littleover is comfortable enough. The Georgian House Hotel (0332) 349806 is an elegant, comfortable and reasonably priced alternative. In Belper, Remys is a very good French restaurant—a perfect place to celebrate one's closing birdie at Chevin. **Breadsall Priory** (0332) 832235 itself of course offers a most satisfying 19th hole.

Moving 'up country', the picturesque town of **Matlock** has a fairly short but pleasant course situated north of the town off the Chesterfield road, and if heading in that direction **Chesterfield's** course at Walton is also well worth a visit and there are two public courses also close to the town centre. Two recommendations for a memorable night are: Riber Hall (0629) 582795 near Matlock and the New Bath Hotel (0629) 583275 in Matlock Bath.

The town of Buxton lies in the heart of the Peak District and is for many people their idea of the perfect town. This may have something to do with the fact that some of the finest pubs in England are located round about, but it is also helped by the fact that there are two excellent golf courses either side of the town—**Buxton and High Peak** and **Cavendish**. Of similar length it is difficult to say which is the better, but in any event both warmly welcome visitors at green fees that should leave a few pennies for celebrating nearby. After a day on the fairways (not to mention an evening in a Buxton pub) a suitable hotel is required. The Old Hall Hotel (0298) 22841 is a historic hotel just one mile from the Cavendish course offering reduced green fees to golfers. There is also the Palace Hotel (0298) 22001 and the Lee Wood Hotel (0298) 23002 which overlooks the cricket ground.

Having done my bit for the Buxton tourist board another suggestion for this delightful area is in Hassop, Hassop Hall (0629) 640488.

Other good locals include the Old Bulls Head, Little Hucklow; in Hathersage, the George; and in Beeley, the Devonshire Arms which is near to Chatsworth and no trip to the area would be complete without visiting this incredible stately home, perhaps England's finest.

Nottinghamshire

Moving into Nottinghamshire, the famous **Notts** Golf Club at Hollinwell is featured separately on a later page; however, in addition to this rather splendid 'Nottingham gorse affair' those visiting the county town should strongly consider the merits of **Wollaton Park**, an attractive course set amidst the deer park of a stately home, surprisingly close to the centre of Nottingham, and the city's two 18 hole municipal courses are also fairly good. Slightly further afield but well worth noting are the parkland courses at **Chilwell Manor** (A6005) and **Radcliffe on Trent** (A52 east of the town).

Nottingham has no shortage of comfortable modern hotels and the Forte Crest (0602) 470131 and the Royal (0602) 414444 are first rate and centrally located. To the north of the city at Arnold, the Bestwood Lodge (0602) 203011 is less stylish but good value and to the south lovers of the country house scene should delight in Langar Hall (0949) 60559 at Langar (seems to have a golfing ring to it, don't you think?) The best known pub in town is probably the Olde Trip to Jerusalem—said to be the oldest in England. Mansfield is only about 15 minutes drive from Hollinwell and here Carr Bank Manor (0623) 22644 is a highly recommended hotel while a pleasant guest house is Tichfield House B&B (0623) 810356.

Two of the county's finest courses lie fairly close to one another near the centre of Nottinghamshire, **Coxmoor** and **Sherwood Forest**. The former is a moorland type course situated just south of Mansfield at Sutton in Ashfield. The Sherwood Forest course is more of a heathland type—well wooded (as one might expect given its name) with much tangling heather. Measuring over 6700 yards it is quite a test too.

Over towards the border with Lincolnshire is the attractive town of Newark with its 12th century castle and cobbled market square. **Newark** Golf Club lies four miles east of the town off the A17. Reasonably flat and quite secluded the golf is a little less testing than at some of the county's bigger clubs. An attractive place to stay is the Old Rectory, north of Newark in Kirkton. Also in town the Old Kings Arms is a fine pub (0636) 703416.

Before inspecting Lincolnshire, a brief word on **Lindrick**. Although its postal address is in Nottinghamshire the majority of the course lies in South Yorkshire. In any event, it is featured ahead. If a night's rest is required 'this side' of the border, then Ye Old Bell Hotel at Barnby Moor (0777) 705121 is a pleasant coaching inn and the Angel in Blyth is a friendly pub with some accommodation also.

Lincolnshire

Lincolnshire is a large county. It used to be even larger before Grimsby, Scunthorpe and Cleethorpes were all snatched away by that upstart Humberside. Still, by my reckoning there are at least twenty golf courses left. Woodhall Spa is of course head and shoulders above the rest but although the county as a whole is unlikely to be the venue for many golfing holidays there are certainly a handful of courses well worth a visit. **Woodhall Spa** is featured ahead. For those fortunate enough to be able to spend a few days playing the course, here are some suggestions. The appropriately named Golf Hotel (0526) 353535 (a sister to the Manor House Hotel, Moretonhampstead) is probably the most popular and convenient place in which to stay, but the Abbey Lodge (0526) 352538, Duns (0526) 352969 and the Petwood (0526) 352411 are also recommended and the Dower House (0526) 352588 is very pleasant. Lincoln of course may be a base and for those not minding a bit of a drive the George (0780) 55171 at Stamford is quite excellent—a charming atmosphere with a very fine restaurant. Stamford in fact is a delightful town: Burghley is found here, an outstandingly attractive Elizabethan house. **Burghley Park** Golf Club is noted for its greens and its links with Mark James, while just over the county boundary in Leicestershire lies **Luffenham Heath**, a truly splendid golf course.

Lincoln was briefly mentioned and it really is an attractive city—a beautiful cathedral, a castle and a wealth of history. The White Hart (0522) 526222 is a noted hotel and there are some fine restaurants—one of the best is Whites. Simpler food and a great pub can be found in the Wig and Mitre (0522) 535190. The award winning D'Isney Place Hotel (0552) 538881 will lure many and disappoint none. Outside the city in Branston, the Moor Lodge Hotel (0522) 791366 is good value. The best golf to be found in **Lincoln** is at Torksey just to the north west of the city. It's a fairly sandy, heathland type course with a lovely selection of trees. **Southcliffe and Canwick**, on the opposite side of Lincoln is a shorter parkland course, but challenging in its own way.

Three courses of note towards the north of the county are at **Gainsborough** (Thonock), **Market Rasen** and **Louth**. All are very welcoming. Thonock is a classic parkland layout, Market Rasen is a very good woodland type course while Louth has an attractive setting in a local beauty spot, the Hubbards Hills. A second course near Louth, **Kenwick Park**, recently opened and already promises to be one of the region's top courses. The Limes Country House Hotel (0673) 842357 is ideal for Market Rasen, and in Louth, the Priory (0507) 602930 offers a comfortable stop-over. (There are some fine pubs in Louth too—note especially the Wheatsheaf).

Skegness is a famous resort — perhaps not everyone's cup of tea, but a game here is certainly recommended for those who like their links golf. **Seacroft** is the place; flattish, windy and plenty of sand dunes — a most underrated course. Further up the coast, a less severe challenge is offered at **Sandilands** where the Grange and Links Hotel (0507) 441334 is adjacent to the course. The south of the county comprises much rich agricultural land but not too much in the way of golf. **Stoke Rochford** however is a popular parkland course and **Spalding** is worth inspecting particularly at the time of year when the famous bulbs have flourished. An 18 hole course here, and in the south west, the new **Belton Woods** Hotel & Country Club (0476) 593200 has a delightfully peaceful setting outside Grantham. It has two 18 hole courses, (as well as a multitude of other facilities) the Lancaster and Wellington, and there is a lot of water to be negotiated — a few Barnes Wallis type shots may be called for!

Artist: **Drummond Fish THE SECOND** *Courtesy of:* **Burlington Gallery**

Between them, Sunningdale and Walton Heath have seventy two holes, each with an Old and a New course. Many may disagree but if a composite eighteen were created, taking the best eighteen holes from the four courses I still don't think we would see a better (or more challenging) course than the round offered at Woodhall Spa—and I certainly don't view Sunningdale and Walton Heath as anything less than outstanding.

Ranked as the Number One inland course in the British Isles by Following The Fairways, Woodhall Spa Golf Club was founded in 1905. The course itself was originally laid out by Harry Vardon although substantial alterations were made firstly by Harry Colt and later by Colonel Hotchkin.

As one of the country's greatest (and most beautiful) heathland courses, Woodhall Spa is understandably extremely popular and visitors looking for a game must make prior arrangements with the Club's **Secretary**. (This applies to individual visitors and Societies alike). **Mr. B.H.Fawcett** is the very helpful gentleman in question and he may be contacted via **The Woodhall Spa Golf Club, Woodhall Spa, Lincolnshire, tel: (0526) 352511**. The Club's **professional, Campbell Elliot** can be reached on **(0526) 353229**.

The green fees at Woodhall Spa for 1994 were set at £26 per round during the week with £40 payable for a full day's golf and £30 per round at weekends, or £45 for a full day. Reduced rates are available to junior golfers, but only if accompanied by a member.

Glancing at the map, Woodhall Spa looks fairly close to Lincoln. By road the distance is in fact, at least twenty miles. Those approaching from the cathedral city should take the B1188 towards Sleaford, taking a left fork onto the B1189 towards the village of Martin. At Martin the B1191 road should be picked up and followed to Woodhall Spa, the Club being directly off this road. Those travelling from further north will probably need to use a combination of motorways before joining the A15—this road links Lincoln to the M180 (junction 4). Persons motoring from the south may have to do even more map-reading but the following is hopefully of assistance: the A1 is likely to be a good starting point; it should be left just north of Colsterworth and the B6403 then taken towards Ancaster and R.A.F. Cranwell. Just beyond RAF Cranwell the A15 can be joined. A right fork should be taken towards the wonderfully named hamlet of Ashby de la Launde on to the B1191. The B1191

takes us to Martin—remember Martin? The B1191 runs from Martin to Woodhall Spa.

The journey across Lincolnshire will have taken the traveller alongside many miles of flat agricultural land—hardly golfing country. Suddenly, everything changes as Woodhall Spa looms on the horizon like a glorious golfing mirage. Often described as the ultimate golfing oasis, Woodhall Spa has all the classic heathland characteristics; sandy subsoil, heather running riot and glorious tree lined fairways.

The course measures a lengthy 6933 yards, par 73 or, from the ladies tees, 5781 yards par 73. It is arguably most renowned for its vast cavernous bunkers and while it is almost impossible to select individual holes, perhaps those that particularly stand out are to be found towards the middle of the round, between the 9th and the 13th. Indeed, the 11th is quite possibly the finest par four in the country and certainly one of the prettiest. A plaque beside the 12th tee records how in March 1982 two Members halved the hole in one.

Another feature of Woodhall Spa is the remarkable variety of wildlife which the golfer is likely to come across (especially the more wayward hitter!) One hawkish, but obviously dedicated individual, claimed after hitting a rather poor drive to the 18th that he was 'distracted by the merry gathering of partridges and pheasants to the right of the tee and by the squirrel who was chasing a magpie across the fairway.'

Although none of the major professional tournaments has visited the course (primarily a result of its isolation) numerous major amateur events have. These have included the Youths Amateur Championship, the English Amateur Championship and the English Ladies Amateur Championship.

The Members are fortunate in having a wonderfully intimate Clubhouse. The atmosphere is both friendly and informal and there's an almost Colonial feel about the place—a Raffles in Lincolnshire perhaps? A full complement of catering is offered throughout the week with a variety of very reasonably priced meals.

I referred earlier to the often alarmingly deep bunkers; apparently a competitor in the 1974 English Amateur Championship, in his endeavours to find the exit to the Club drove his car straight into a huge bunker beside the 4th green. . . .one wonders whether this might have had a little to do with the aforementioned friendly atmosphere to be found at the 19th!

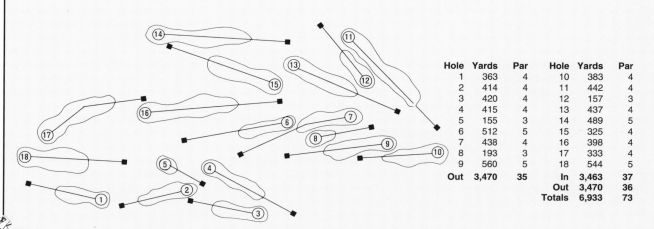

Hole	Yards	Par	Hole	Yards	Par
1	363	4	10	383	4
2	414	4	11	442	4
3	420	4	12	157	3
4	415	4	13	437	4
5	155	3	14	489	5
6	512	5	15	325	4
7	438	4	16	398	4
8	193	3	17	333	4
9	560	5	18	544	5
Out	**3,470**	**35**	**In**	**3,463**	**37**
			Out	**3,470**	**36**
			Totals	**6,933**	**73**

The Notts Golf Club was founded in 1887, although the Club's first home was in fact nearer to Nottingham itself at Bulwell Forest. Apparently the proposed move from Bulwell to Hollinwell which occurred around the turn of the century initially met with considerable opposition. Undeterred, the radicals invited Willie Park Jnr to design the new course and by the time John H Taylor had added some finishing touches, not a squeak of discontent was to be heard. Messrs. Park and Taylor had presented the members with a masterpiece.

The gentleman presently looking after the interests of the Notts golfers is the **Secretary, Mr. Stuart Goldie.** Visitors seeking a game are advised to contact him some time in advance of intended play. Mr. Goldie can be contacted by telephone on **(0623) 753225** while the address for written correspondence is **The Notts Golf Club, Hollinwell, Derby Road, Kirkby-in-Ashfield, Nottinghamshire, NG17 7QR.**

As a general guide, visitors can play between Mondays and Fridays although it should be noted that Friday is often busy, it being Ladies' Day. The first tee is reserved for members between 12.00pm and 1.00pm on Mondays and Tuesdays, and on Wednesdays and Thursdays between 12.00pm and 2.00pm or 11.30am and 1.30pm during the winter months. Societies are welcome with Mondays and Tuesdays being the favoured days. In 1994 the green fees were £33 per round or £42 per day. Another thing visitors might wish to note is the Club's popular driving range.

Since the Club's move to Hollinwell in 1900 it has had, somewhat remarkably, only four **professionals**. The present incumbent is **Brian Waites** probably our best known club pro and one who made history in 1983 by becoming the oldest British player to make his debut in the Ryder Cup. Now a very successful member of the Seniors Tour, Waites has played for the Rest Of The World Seniors against the American Seniors in the United States. He and his staff may be contacted on **(0623) 753087**. The course is located to the north west of Nottingham on the A611. Approaching from either the North or South of England, the M1 is very convenient. The motorway should be left at junction 27 at which the A608 should be followed until it joins the A611. The Club is then two miles away and is signposted off to the right.

From the Championship tees, the course is something of a minor monster stretching to a shade over 7000 yards (7030 yards, par 72). Even from the forward tees, it represents a formidable test at 6619 yards. The ladies' course measures 5882 yards, par 75. If Hollinwell is a monster, then it's a pretty one (if there can be such a creature!) with a wealth of heather and gorse lining the fairways, together with some superb oaks and silver birch trees; certainly a splendid setting in which to enjoy a day's golf.

Similar to Woodhall Spa the 1st at Hollinwell is relatively straightforward and has been described as 'ideal for the early morning top!'—something to be avoided on the lengthy 2nd, a hole famed for the huge rock which guards the back of the green known as Robin Hood's Chair. Another notable hole on the front nine is the 8th, perhaps not so intimidating from the forward tee, but from the medal tee it requires a very straight and solid drive to carry an attractive lake. Half hidden by trees to the right of the tee is the 'holy well' from which the name Hollinwell derives. Whether its waters will give you divine inspiration to tackle the back nine is debatable but it's worth a look. Actually, a prayer or two, or at least a little luck may be required when the downhill 13th is confronted. One of only three short holes, although short is hardly apt, it was once called 'an absolute terror', having 'trouble everywhere'. The 15th is another challenging hole and the round ends with a stiff par four which if achieved, will certainly earn you a drink at the club's comfortable 19th.

Championship golf regularly visits Hollinwell. Both Sandy Lyle and Nick Faldo have triumphed here, Lyle winning the 1975 English Open Stroke Play Championship (an event which returned to Hollinwell in 1992) as a precocious seventeen year old, and Faldo the European Tournament Players Championship of 1982. Arguably the most celebrated event was the 1970 John Player Classic when Christy O'Connor pocketed a cheque for £25,000, at the time a world record first prize—no doubt a few Irish eyes were smiling.

Hole	Yards	Par	Hole	Yards	Par
1	376	4	10	362	4
2	430	4	11	365	4
3	511	5	12	433	4
4	455	4	13	236	3
5	193	3	14	403	4
6	533	5	15	440	4
7	403	4	16	355	4
8	410	4	17	490	5
9	178	3	18	457	4
Out	**3,489**	**36**	**In**	**3,541**	**36**
			Out	**3,489**	**36**
			Totals	**7,030**	**72**

There are two golf courses in England whose names will be forever linked with the Ryder Cup: one is the Belfry, the other is Lindrick—and they couldn't be more different. the Belfry (perhaps one should be precise and say the Brabazon Course) is a big strapping youngster still in its teens, immature in some ways though agreeable in others. Lindrick is the seasoned campaigner. It's seen a lot in its lifetime (and in fact is old enough to have received a telegram in 1991). It is no giant but it is charming, subtle and full of challenge.

Before the Ryder Cup came to Lindrick in 1957, many golfing enthusiasts knew very little of this great course, indeed some knew nothing at all. By the end of that heady, wind-swept week in October, none present would ever forget it. It was the last time an exclusively British and Irish team would ever beat the mighty men from across the sea.

Lindrick lies close to the boundaries of Yorkshire, Nottinghamshire and Derbyshire. In fact, in places it actually forms the boundary. The majority of the course lies in Yorkshire, but some holes are in Nottinghamshire, and to the considerable annoyance of every Yorkshireman, the postal address is Lindrick, Notts!

The golf course occupies the best part of 200 acres of classic English common - Lindrick Common - and is essentially heathland in nature, lying on top of limestone rock. There is a mass of gorse which, when in bloom adds great colour (though it can be a devil if you land in it!) and a wealth of pine, oak and silver birch—a delightful setting. if ever there was one.

Visitors are very welcome to test their skills in this splendid environment, although prior arrangement with the Club is required. The **Secretary** is **Lieutenant Commander R.J.M Jack R.N.**, who may be contacted by telephone on **(0909) 475282**. Written correspondence should be addressed to **Lindrick Golf Club, Lindrick Common, Worksop, Notts, S81 8BH**. All bookings should be made through the Secretary's office, but as a general guide, visitors are not permitted to play on Tuesday mornings and the first tee is normally reserved for Members for an hour around lunchtime, but again it's best to check.

The green fees at Lindrick vary according to the season and the following are the figures for summer 1994: £40 per day during the week, or £45 for a round at the weekend. Reductions of fifty per cent are available to junior golfers if accompanied by an adult. The Club's **professional** is **Peter Cowen**, tel: **(0909) 475820**.

Although Lindrick Common may look a little isolated on the map, strangers shouldn't have too much difficulty in locating the course. Those coming from the south should find the M1 and the A1 of great assistance. The Club is actually situated just off the A57 Worksop to Sheffield road, to the west of the former and is well signposted.

From the Championship tees, the course measures 6612 yards, with the par a fairly tight 71. Quite refreshingly, it is not a long hitter's course, the fairway shots to the green being what Lindrick is all about, and there are some excellent par fours. The 2nd, with its slightly uphill approach, the 5th and the 10th, where there is a potentially punishing cross bunker, are three noted holes, others include the troublesome 12th and 13th, but perhaps the best known hole at Lindrick is the par five 4th. This requires a blind approach to a low lying green backed by trees and behind which the River Ryton flows. The green has a magnificent stage-like setting and it was here that the boundaries of Yorkshire, Derbyshire and Nottinghamshire once merged. In days of old, the stage was used for bare fist-fighting and cockfighting, contestants and spectators being able to step into a convenient county whenever unfriendly law authorities showed up. The round concludes with some very testing holes. During the 1982 Martini International tournament Greg Norman ran up a 14 at the 17th! While the par three 18th regularly ensures a climactic finish.

The Clubhouse at Lindrick provides golfers with a fine view of the 18th green and many a drama will have been witnessed; but I don't suppose there will ever be anything to equal the scenes of 1957 and the time when Dai Rees and his boys made the old campaigner smile.

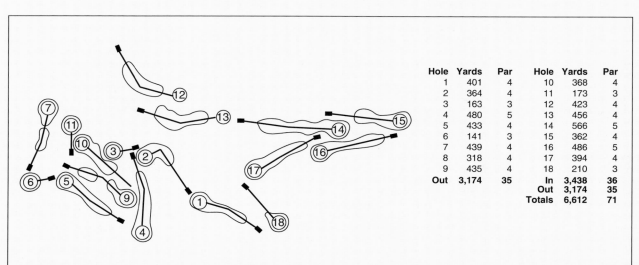

Hole	Yards	Par		Hole	Yards	Par
1	401	4		10	368	4
2	364	4		11	173	3
3	163	3		12	423	4
4	480	5		13	456	4
5	433	4		14	566	5
6	141	3		15	362	4
7	439	4		16	486	5
8	318	4		17	394	4
9	435	4		18	210	3
Out	**3,174**	**35**		**In**	**3,438**	**36**
				Out	**3,174**	**35**
				Totals	**6,612**	**71**

Key

*To avoid disappointment
it is advisable to telephone
in advance*

***Visitors welcome at most times
**Visitors usually allowed on
weekdays only
*Visitors not normally permitted
(Mon, Wed) No visitors
on specified days*

Approximate Green Fees
A £30 plus
B £20 to £30
C £15 to £25
D £10 to £20
E under £10
F Greens fees on application

Restrictions
G Guests only
H Handicap certificate required
H (24) Handicap of 24 or less
L Letter of introduction required
M Visitor must be a member of
another recognised club.

DERBYSHIRE

Alfreton G.C.
(0773) 832070
Wingfield Road, Oakerthorpe
(9)5074 yards/**/D

Allestree Park G.C.
(0332) 550616
Allestree Hall, Derbyshire
(18)5749 yards/**(Sun am)/E

Ashbourne G.C.
(0335) 342078
Clifton, Ashbourne
(9)5359 yards/***/D

Bakewell G.C.
(0629) 812307
Station Road, Bakewell
(9)5240 yards/***/D

Blue Circle G.C.
(0433) 620317
Cement Works, Hope
(9)5350 yards/*/F/G

Breadshall Priory G.& C.C.
(0332) 832235
Moor Road, Morley
(18)6201 yards/***/B/H
(18)6028 yards/***/B/H

Burton On Trent G.C.
(0283) 68708
Ashby Road East, Burton On Trent
(18)6555 yards/***/B/H/L

Buxton & High Peak G.C.
(0298) 23453
Town End, Buxton
(18)5954 yards/***/B

Cavendish G.C.
(0298) 23494
Gadley Lane, Buxton
(18)5833 yards/***/B/H

Chapel-en-le-Frith G.C.
(0298) 812118
Manchester Road, Chapel-en-le-
Frith
(18)6119 yards/***/B

Chesterfield G.C.
(0246) 279256
Walton, Chesterfield
(18)6326 yards/**/B/H

Chesterfield Municipal G.C.
(0246) 273887
Crow Lane, Chesterfield
(9)6013 yards/***/E

Chevin G.C.
(0332) 841864
Golf Lane, Duffield
(18)6057 yards/**/B

Derby G.C.
(0332) 766323
Sinfin, Derby
(18)6100 yards/***/F

Erewash Valley G.C.
(0602) 323258
Stanton by Dale, Ilkeston
(18)6492 yards/**/B/H

Glossop & District G.C.
(0457) 865247
Sheffield Road, Glossop
(18)5800 yards/***/C

Grassmoor Golf Centre
(0246) 856044
North Wingfield Road, Grassmoor
(18)5800 yards/***/E

Hallowes G.C.
(0246) 413734
Hallowes Lane, Dronfield
(18)6330 yards/**/B/H/G

Horsley Lodge G.C.
(0332) 780838
Smalley Mill Road, Horsley
(18)6434 yards/***/D

Ilkeston Borough G.C.
(0602) 307704
West End Drive, Ilkeston
(18)6636 yards/***/E

Kedleston Park G.C.
(0332) 840035
Kedleston, Quarndon, Derby
(18)6600 yards/**/B/H

Matlock G.C.
(0629) 582191
Chesterfield Road, Matlock
(18)5800 yards/**/B

Mickleover G.C.
(0332) 518662
Uttoxeter Road, Mickleover
(18)5708 yards/**/B/H

Morley Hayes G.C.
(0332) 780480
Main Road, Morley
(18)6800 yards/***/C

New Mills G.C.
(0663) 743485
Shaw Marsh, New Mills
(9)5633 yards/***/F/G

Ormonde Fields G.& C.C.
(0773) 742987
Nottingham Road, Codnor, Ripley
(18)6000 yards/***/F

Pastures G.C.
(0332) 513921
Pastures Hospital, Mickleover
(9)5005 yards/*/F

Renishaw Park G.C.
(0246) 432044
Station Road, Renishaw
(18)5949 yards/***/F

Shirland G.& C.C.
(0773) 834935
Lower Delves, Shirland
(18)6072 yards/**/C

Sickleholme G.C.
(0433) 651306
Saltergate Lane, Bamford
(18)6064 yards/***(Wed am)/B

Stanedge G.C.
(0246) 566156
Walton Hay Farm, Chesterfield
(9)4867 yards/**(pm)/D

Tapton Park G.C.
(0246) 239500
Murray House, Tapton
(18)6010 yards/***/F

NOTTINGHAMSHIRE

Beeston Fields G.C.
(0602) 257062
Beeston, Nottingham
(18)6400 yards/***/B/H

Bramcote Hills G.C.
(0602) 281880
Thoresby Road, Bramcote
(18)1500 yards/***/E

Bulwell Forest G.C.
(0602) 770576
Hucknall Road, Bulwell
(18)5700 yards/***/E

Chilwell Manor G.C.
(0602) 258958
Meadow Lane, Chilwell
(18)6379 yards/**/D/H
(18)5438 yards/**/D/H

College Pines G.C.
(0909) 501431
College Drive, Worksop
(18)6663 yards/***/D

Cotgrave Place G.& C.C.
(0602) 333344
Stragglethorpe, Radcliffe on Trent
(27)6500 yards/***/C

Coxmoor G.C.
(0623) 557359
Coxmoor Road, Sutton in Ashfield
(18)6501 yards/**/B/H

Edwalton Municipal G.C.
(0602) 234775
Wellin Lane, Edwalton
(9)3360 yards/***/E

Kilton Forest G.C.
(0909) 472488
Blyth Road, Worksop
(18)6600 yards/***(Sun)/E

Lindrick G.C.
(0909) 475282
Lindrick Common, Worksop
(18)6615 yards/***(winter)/A/H

Mansfield Woodhouse G.C.
(0623) 23521
Leeming Lane North, Mansfield
Woodhouse
(9)2446 yards/***/E

Mapperley G.C.
(0602) 265611
Mapperley, Nottingham
(18)6224 yards/***/D/H/M

Newark G.C.
(0636) 626282
Coddington, Newark
(18)6421 yards/***/B/H

Nottingham City G.C.
(0602) 278021
Bulwell, Nottingham
(18)6218 yards/***/E

Notts G.C.
(0623) 753225
Hollinwell, Kirkby in Ashfield
(18)7020 yards/**/F/H

Oakmere Park G.C.
(0602) 653545
Oaks Lane, Oxton
(18)6617 yards/***/D
(9)3216 yards/***/E

Oxton G.C.
(0602) 653545
Oxton, Southwell
(18)6630 yards/***/D

Radcliffe on Trent G.C.

(0602) 333000
Cropwell Road, Radcliffe on Trent
(18)6381 yards/***(Tues)/C/H

Ramsdale Golf Centre
(0602) 655600
Oxton Road, Calverton
(18)6546 yards/***/D

Retford G.C.
(0777) 703733
Ordsall, Retford
(9)6301 yards/**/D

Ruddington Grange G.C.
(0602) 846141
Wilford Road, Ruddington
(18)6500 yards/**/B/H

Rushcliffe G.C.
(0509) 852959
Stocking Lane, East Leake
(18)6020 yards/**/B

Serlby Park G.C.
(0777) 818268
Serlby
(9)5325 yards/***/F

Sherwood Forest G.C.
(0623) 26689
Eakring Road, Mansfield
(18)6714 yards/**/F/H/M

Southwell G.C.
(0636) 814481
Southwell Racecourse, Rolleston
(9)5500 yards/***/D

Springwater G.C.
(0602) 652129
Moor Lane, Calverton
(9)3203 yards/***/D

Stanton on the Wolds G.C.
(0602) 372044
Stanton Lane, Keyworth
(18)6437 yards/***(Tues)/B/H

Wollaton Park G.C.
(0602) 787574
Wollaton Park, Nottingham
(18)6494 yards/***/F

Worksop G.C.
(0909) 472696
Windmill Lane, Worksop
(18)6651 yards/***/C

LINCOLNSHIRE

Belton Park G.C.
(0476) 67399
Belton Lane, Grantham
(18)6420 yards/**/C/H

Belton Woods Hotel & C.C.
(0476) 593200
(18)7021 yards/***/F/H
(18)6875 yards/***/F/H
(9)1184 yards/***/F/H

Blankney G.C.
(0526) 320263
Blankney, Lincoln
(18)6402 yards/**/C/H

Boston G.C.
(0205) 350589
Horncastle Road, Boston
(18)6483 yards/**/C/H

Burghley Park G.C.
(0780) 53789
St Martins, Stamford
(18)6200 yards/**/H

Canwick Park G.C.
(0522) 522166
Canwick Park, Washingborough
Road
(18)6257 yards/**/D

Carholme G.C.
(0522) 523725
Carholme Road, Lincoln

(18)6114 yards/**(Sun)/F

Elsham G.C.
(0652) 680291
Barton Road, Elsham
(18)6411 yards/***/C/H/M

Gainsborough G.C.
(0427) 613088
Thonock, Gainsborough
(18)6620 yards/**/F/H

Gedney Hill G.C.
(0406) 330922
West Drove, Gedney Hill
(18)5450 yards/***/E

Greetham Valley G.C.
(0780) 460444
Greetham, Oakham
(18)6550 yards/***/C
(9)1472 yards/***/C

Horncastle G.C.
(0507) 526800
West Ashby, Horncastle
(18)5782 yards/***/D

Kenwick Park G.C.
(0507) 605134
Kenwick Hall, Louth

(18)6815 yards/***/B/G

Kirton Holme G.C.
(0205) 290669
Holme Road, Kirton Holme
(9)2884 yards/***/E

Lincoln G.C.
(0427) 718210
Torksey, Lincoln
(18)6438 yards/**/C/H

Louth G.C.
(0507) 603681
Crowtree Lane, Louth
(18)6477 yards/***/C

Market Rasen and District G.C.
(0673) 842416
Legsby Road, Market Rasen
(18)6043 yards/**/C/H/L

Millfield G.C.
(042771) 8255
Laughterton, Lincoln
(18)5583 yards/***/E

North Shore G.C.
(0754) 763298
North Shore Road, Skegness
(18)6134 yards/***/F/H

R.A.F. Waddington G.C.
(0552) 720271
Waddington, Lincoln
(18)5223 yards/***/F/L

Rutland County G.C.
(0780) 86330
Great Casterton, Stamford
(18)6189 yards/***/D/H

Sandilands G.C.
(0507) 441432
Sea Lane, Sandilands
(18)5995 yards/***/D

Seacroft G.C.
(0754) 763020
Drummond Road, Seacroft
(18)6501 yards/***/B/H/M

Sleaford G.C.
(0529) 488273
Willoughby Road, South Rauceby
(18)6443 yards/***/C/H

South Kyme G.C.
(0526) 861113
Skinners Lane, South Kyme
(18)6597 yards/***/D

Spalding G.C.
(0775) 680234
Surfleet, Spalding
(18)6400 yards/***/F/H

Stoke Rochford G.C.
(0476) 83275
Great North Road, Grantham
(18)6251 yards/***/B-A/H

Sudbrook Manor G.C.
(0400) 50876
Charity Lane, Grantham
(9)4566 yards/***/E

Sutton Bridge G.C.
(0406) 350323
New Road, Sutton Bridge, Spalding
(9)5804 yards/**/C/H

Woodhall Spa G.C.
(0526) 352511
The Broadway, Woodhall Spa
(18)6866 yards/***/B-A/H(20)

Woodthorpe Hall G.C.
(0507) 450294
Woodthorpe, Alford
(18)4659 yards/***/E

Artist: **Kenneth Reed** **GLORIOUS GOLF** *Courtesy of* **Old Troon Sporting Antiques**

Artist: **H. Rountree PERFECTLY PLACED** Courtesy of: **Burlington Gallery**

Choice Golf

Staffordshire, Shropshire and Cheshire: three essentially rural counties. Staffordshire shares a boundary with the West Midlands and Cheshire has two rather ill defined borders with Greater Manchester and Merseyside. As for Shropshire it enjoys a splendid peace, broken only perhaps by the mooing of cows and the cries of Fore!from the county's many lush fairways.

Each of the three has a great deal to offer the visiting golfer: in Staffordshire, Beau Desert and Whittington Barracks are two of the best (and prettiest) courses in the Midlands; Cheshire offers Tytherington, Mere, the Portal and some heathland gems (we have described Hoylake and the Wirral courses in the 'Lancashire' section) while Shropshire, in addition to possessing the likes of Hawkstone Park and Patshull Park can boast at having produced two US Masters champions—both Sandy Lyle and Ian Woosnam who were bred if not born in the county.

Staffordshire

Making a start in Staffordshire, **Whittington Barracks** and **Beau Desert** have already been mentioned. The former, located near Lichfield off the A51 is a heathland type course with fine views towards the three spires of Lichfield Cathedral — quite possibly the county's toughest challenge. Beau Desert Golf Club near Hazel Slade occupies an unlikely setting in the middle of Cannock Chase. Surrounded by fir trees and spruces it is, as its name implies, quite a haven. Perhaps a mixture of heathland and woodland, and less testing than Whittington Barracks, it is nonetheless equally enjoyable.

After a relaxing day on the golf course, some thoughts for a suitable 19th hole are in order. In Lichfield the Angel Croft (0543) 258737 is a comfortable hotel for a night's stay and Thrales (0543) 255091 is a particularly good restaurant. The George Hotel (0543) 414822, an old coaching inn, is equally recommended. (Note also the new 18 hole pay-and-play course in Lichfield, the charmingly named **Seedy Mill**.) After a round at Beau Desert, Rugeley may be the place to head for. Here the Cedar Tree Hotel (0889) 584241 is welcoming but if a restaurant is sought then nearby Armitage offers the Oakleigh House Hotel (0543) 255573. On the other side of Lichfield, in Tamworth, the Castle Hotel (0827) 57181 is recommended.

From the heart of Cannock Chase to the heart of the Potteries, there are a number of courses in and around Stoke-on-Trent. **Trentham** and **Trentham Park**, near neighbours to the south of the city, are both well worth a visit, particularly perhaps the latter where the course is well wooded and there are many delightful views. Probably the best hotel in Stoke is the North Stafford (0782) 744477, however as the recommended courses are south of the town Stone may be the most convenient place to spend a night. Two suggestions here: the Crown Hotel (0785) 813535 and the Stone House (0785) 815531, both comfortable. The Star is a good local pub. East of Stoke, the Old Beams (0538) 308254 in Waterhouses is an excellent restaurant, while in nearby Cauldon the Yew Tree is a superb hostelry.

Stafford, the county town, is pretty much in the middle of things. Once again a pair of 18 hole courses to note here: to the south of Stafford is **Brocton Hall** and to the north east, set in the grounds of the former home of the Earl of Shrewsbury is **Ingestre Park**. Both offer a very relaxing game. There is also an enjoyable 9 holer at **Stafford Castle**. If a bed is needed then Tillington Hall (0785) 53531 in Stafford is pleasant and, although a bit of a drive away, Rolleston on Dove offers the engaging

Brookhouse Inn (0283) 814188, a splendidly converted farmhouse.

Shropshire

Moving into Shropshire, many will wish to head straight for **Hawkstone Park** (0939) 200611 and its fine hotel. Hawkstone is featured ahead but Shropshire has a lot more than Hawkstone Park on the menu. **Patshull Park** (0902) 700100 makes a marvellous starter, especially considering its closeness to the Midlands—an ideal retreat in fact. As at Hawkstone golf is played amid very peaceful and picturesque surroundings and overnight accommodation is immediately at hand. The delightful setting of Patshull Park owes much to the fact that the land was originally landscaped by 'Capability' Brown.

Shrewsbury is a pleasant county town with many charming half-timbered buildings. **Shrewsbury** Golf Club is situated about five miles from the town centre off the A49. It is an interesting course with a railway track running through the middle. The Prince Rupert Hotel (0743) 236000 in Shrewsbury itself is good value for an overnight stay and the oak beams and sloping floors add character. Fieldside Hotel (0743) 353143 has no pretensions of grandeur but is extremely comfortable.

Travelling a little further down the A49 into southern Shropshire, **Church Stretton**, set amidst the Long Mynd Hills, is well worth a visit. Not the longest course in Britain but one that offers quite outstanding views. The Stretton Hall Hotel (0694) 723224 is an obvious base but the Belvedere Guest House (0694) 722232 can also be recommended and those needing to quench their thirst might note the Royal Oak in Cardington (some accommodation also).

The largest town in Shropshire is Telford. It's a strange mixture of the old and the new: a modern centre yet surrounded by a considerable amount of history—Brunel's famous Ironbridge is here. The popular **Telford Hotel** Golf and Country Club (0952) 585642 is situated near to the Ironbridge Gorge, high above it in fact, and is easily accessible from the M54 (junction 4 or 5). Full leisure facilities are offered at the hotel. Further south of Telford, towards Bridgnorth, **Lilleshall Hall** offers a pleasant game.

To the east of Telford, **Shifnal** Golf Club is set in a glorious park and an old manor house serves as an impressive clubhouse. The Park House Hotel (0952) 460128 in Shifnal is an excellent place for a stopover and the hotel's restaurant, the Idsall Rooms is particularly good.

In the middle of Shropshire, **Bridgnorth** is one of the oldest and longest courses in the county (note the distinguished Haywain (0746) 780404 restaurant in town), and in the far south is historic **Ludlow**. It's now a fairly quiet market town but in former times was the capital of the West Marches. The golf course takes you around the town's racecourse —or is it vice versa?—Anyway it's an interesting challenge and if a round of golf is being combined with a weekend's racing then the Feathers (0584) 875261 in Ludlow provides an ideal place in which to relax—note the outstanding Jacobean facade. In Brimfield, near Ludlow, you might stop at the Roebuck (0584) 872230 — a nice summer pub with a fine restaurant. Not too great a distance from Ludlow is Hopton Wafers where the Crown offers some first rate cooking and a fine drop of ale.

To the north west of Shropshire three courses are strongly recommended. **Oswestry** is one clearly to note— if only because this is where Ian Woosnam relaxes when he's not winning the Masters. Note the popular Wynnstay Hotel in town. Close to the Welsh border, **Llanymynech** (Woosie's first course) lies on high ground and is very scenic. On the 4th hole you stand on the tee in Wales and drive into England (always good for the ego). After a game here, a visit to the Bradford Arms (0691) 830582 in Llanymynech is essential as it boasts a particularly fine restaurant. Still high in the hills another 'Llany', not Wadkins but Blodwel: Llanyblodwel is where excellent refreshment can be found—the Horseshoe, with its spectacular setting. **Hill Valley** near Whitchurch, brings us down to earth. We may get wet as well with water affecting many holes on this fairly new American-style course. As well as the water there are many other challenges and it's well worth inspecting. Terrick Hall Hotel (0948) 663031 is practically adjacent to the course. In Whitchurch itself there is the Hollies Hotel (0948) 662184, ideally situated perhaps for keen golfers wanting to play both Hill Valley and Hawkstone Park.

Cheshire

Cheshire could be described as the 'Surrey of the North'. In many parts it's decidedly affluent, with a great band of commuter towns lining its northern fringes. There's also a sand belt where heathland golf is found—no Sunningdale here perhaps but **Delamere Forest** and **Sandiway** would certainly be at home in either Surrey or Berkshire. Delamere is particularly good. A creation of Herbert Fowler, who also designed Walton Heath and the Berkshire, it's a marvellous heather and gorse type course—some superb trees also. The words 'temporary green' do not exist at Delamere Forest (something winter golfers might wish to bear in mind) nor apparently does the word 'par'—the old fashioned term 'bogey' being preferred as a more realistic yardstick of a hole's difficulty—at least for the non-pro.

There are a number of first class places in which to stay in the area but pride of place must go to Rookery Hall (0270) 610016 in Worleston near Nantwich. Part Georgian, part Victorian, it's a wonderful hotel with a restaurant to match. Nantwich also offers the reasonably priced Burland Farmhouse (0270) 74210. Nearer to Sandiway in Hartford, Hartford Hall (0606) 75711 is very pleasant, whilst in Sandiway itself Nunsmere Hall (0606) 889100 is very convenient and comfortable. In Acton Bridge, the Rheingold Riverside Inn (0606) 852310 offers some really stylish food. Finally, a handy pub for Delamere is the Ring of Bells at Overton.

Mere is certainly one of the leading courses in Cheshire. Although fairly close to Sandiway and Delamere, Mere is a classic parkland course, and a beautiful one too with a testing closing stretch including the spectacular par five 18th, where a new green has been built on the edge of a small lake. After eagling the 18th at Mere the perfect place for celebration is in Lower Peeover at the Bells of Peeover (0565) 722269 (pronounced 'Peever' I'm assured).

The area around Wilmslow is fairly thick with clubs. **Wilmslow** itself and **Prestbury** have two of the better courses. For many years the former was the venue of the Greater Manchester Open. Both are extremely well kept. The popular Stanneylands Hotel (0625) 525225 at Wilmslow is convenient for both courses although again there are many fine hotels nearby to choose from, one strong recommendation being **Mottram Hall** (0625) 828135 at Mottram St Andrews—quite magnificent. The hotel now boasts a challenging 18 hole course, designed in fine style by Dave Thomas.

Stockport provides a dramatic contrast to rural Cheshire—not the prettiest of places perhaps but full of character (with a wonderful market my mother tells me). Offerton is where **Stockport** Golf Club is found. It's a good test and well worth visiting: so for that matter are the two courses at Bramhall, **Bramhall** and **Bramhall Park**. **Macclesfield's** course offers some extensive views and between Macclesfield and Prestbury is the fairly new, but highly acclaimed **Tytherington** Club which is featured ahead. **Shrigley Hall** (0625) 575757 in Pott Shrigley, again near to both Prestbury and Macclesfield, has another newish golf course in a wonderful setting with extensive views over the Cheshire Plain. Well situated for these courses (and a few more) is the Alderley Edge Hotel (0625) 583033.

Over to the far east of Cheshire, close to the Derbyshire border and the splendid Peak District is **Chapel-en-le-Frith**. A really friendly club this and some enjoyable golf too. From the far east to the far west, Chester demands inspection—a fascinating Roman city with all manner of attractions. Two of the best places to swing a club are at Upton, namely the delightful **Upton-by-Chester** Golf Club and at **Eaton**, a parkland course to the south of the city. Just 15 minutes drive from Chester an impressive Golf and Leisure Complex opened in 1994 at **Carden Park**. For a place to stay in Chester, the best hotel by far is the Chester Grosvenor (0244) 324024 (note the superb restaurant) and the Hoole Hall Hotel (0244) 350011 on the Warrington Road is not far behind. An interesting alternative though is the Blossoms Hotel (0244) 323186 where Ghost Hunting and Murder Weekends are organised! South east of Chester near Tarporley much has been happening and two courses have recently appeared on the county's ever-changing golf map, namely the highly acclaimed **Portal** Golf Club (featured ahead) and the **Oaklands** Golf and Country Club. Strongly recommended for golfers planning a trip to the golf here are the Wild Boar at Beeston (0829) 260305 and the Swan Hotel in Tarporley (0829) 733838.

In the middle of the county, **Crewe** offers a pleasant 18 holes and back towards the north of the region, **Ringway** Golf Club is a good parkland challenge, but our final visit takes us to the end of a very leafy lane in Altrincham—the impressive **Dunham Forest** Golf and Country Club. Only two miles from the M56 (junction 7) and not all that far from the whirl of Manchester it nonetheless delights in an incredibly tranquil setting. The beautifully mature tree-lined fairways are a sheer delight to play on and if you cannot enjoy your golf here, well, let's just say you've got problems!

Americans who are apt to drool at English country houses, their grounds and gardens should head for Tarporley in Cheshire; and English golfers who believe that the only good courses being built nowadays are 'American style' designs should go with them. Portal Hall in Tarporley is the kind of dwelling that would grace the front cover of Country Life magazine: the house is splendid and the gardens resplendent. Adjacent to Portal hall is the Portal Golf and Country Club and possibly the finest new golf course in the north of England.

Many of the courses constructed in Britain during the last decade tend to be either very average (due usually to the poor quality of the site or terrain) or very American - and as somebody once remarked, there's nothing wrong with American golf courses . . . in America! The reality is that Britain doesn't have America's climate and unless there is a vast amount of money behind a project to build such a course - as for example at Hanbury Manor in Hertfordshire - then achieving and maintaining the standard of conditioning required is unlikely to happen. (Interestingly, how many attempts to build a Scottish style golf links in North America have succeeded?!) Portal is very different and very special.

Like many golf clubs, it owes its existence to the dream and ambition of one man. John Lilley was the guiding force behind the creation of Portal and while he lived to see its opening (June 1991) he is no longer with us to enjoy its success. Portal is his gift to golf. The new owners, under the enthusiastic direction of Chairman, Michael Taylor are determined to enhance this legacy.

Portal has quickly developed into one of the most prestigious clubs in the area (it seems to have cornered the market in attracting sports and showbiz personalities!) and visitors are always made to feel very welcome. Tarporley is located approximately midway between Chester and Crewe off the A51. Both the M6 and M56 are within 20 minutes drive. Individuals and societies can make bookings by contacting the **Director of Golf, David Wills** on **(0829) 733933** or fax (0829) 733928. There are no specific restrictions on visitors during the week (although reserving a tee time is advisable) but week-

end golf is limited and handicap certificates are required. Telephoning to book a starting time is also essential on Saturdays and Sundays. The green fees at Portal in 1994 were £30 per round midweek and £40 per round at weekends.

The Eighteenth hole golf course was designed by British architect Donald Steel. Steel considers it to be one of his best - if not the best - and he is justifiably proud of his work. As you may have gathered from the preceding comments, he has not tried to fashion an American style course amidst this very natural and very English parkland setting. There are no Nicklaus-style mounds at Portal and Steel has no Trent-Jones-like obsession with long water carries. There are, however, plenty of sweeping elevational changes (some are dramatic as at the 3rd, 7th, 16th and 17th and some more subtle, as at the 2nd, 5th, 6th and 9th) and a huge variety of mature trees. There are lakes and ponds too, but they are not designed to terrify, indeed the purpose behind their placement is as much visual as strategic.

The visual pleasure aspect is of course where Portal gains a significant advantage over most new designs. There are many strong and challenging holes—the course measures well over 7000 yards from the championship tees but it is the stunning beauty of two in particular, the par three 15th and par five 5th that are likely to leave the most lasting impression after a visit to Portal. Stand on the stage-like green at the short 15th and you feel surrounded by cascading ponds, stately trees and rhododendron bushes - golf landscaping at its best; stand on the tee at the long 6th with its rockery banks of heather and shock of flowers and your mind may wander from golf to horticulture - dangerous as there are 600 yards of fairway and hazards to negotiate!

The 19th hole is the final treat at Portal. The Clubhouse is an extraordinary circular building; its unusual design apparently reflects the turrets of nearby Beeston and Peckforton castles. In character with the whole set up the facilities inside are first class and the atmosphere is relaxed and informal. Golf in this country has waited a long time for a club and course like Portal.

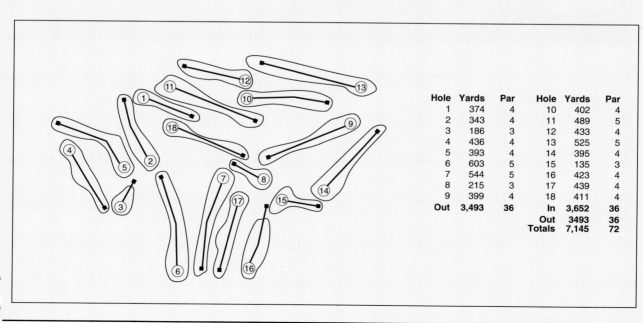

Hole	Yards	Par	Hole	Yards	Par
1	374	4	10	402	4
2	343	4	11	489	5
3	186	3	12	433	4
4	436	4	13	525	5
5	393	4	14	395	4
6	603	5	15	135	3
7	544	5	16	423	4
8	215	3	17	439	4
9	399	4	18	411	4
Out	**3,493**	**36**	**In**	**3,652**	**36**
			Out	**3493**	**36**
			Totals	**7,145**	**72**

Even a fairly detailed map is unlikely to show Weston under Redcastle, but ask a golfer for the location and it is possible he will direct you there blindfolded! The Hawkestone Park Hotel, where Sandy Lyle learned his game, is set in an exquisite 400 acre north Shropshire estate and is more than just a golfers' paradise. It features one fine 18 hole parkland golf course which is over 50 years old - the Hawkestone Course. This historical course plays around an 11th/12th century Red Castle, believed to be part of the original King Arthur legend.

The 59 bedroom en suite hotel, classified by the English Tourist Board, is a chip shot from the course and is steeped in history. It was built as an elegant and spacious hostelry in 1790, then known as the Hawkestone Inn, to cater for visitors to one of Britain's original 18th century walking centres, now designated by English Heritage as a Grade I landscape. For the first time in a

hundred years, the Park has been fully restored and allows access to residents and visitors alike who can experience unique and breathtaking cliff walks, viewing sites of historical interest which include the famous grottos, Swiss bridge, monument, Gingerbread Hall and even the modern day hermitage. The entrance to the historic park and follies provides a cafeteria, gift shop, interpretation centre and a classroom facility.

The Hawkestone Park Hotel provides banqueting suite facilities for up to 200 persons and has been successful in attaining its share of the business meeting / conference market. It offers for the golfer an excellent choice of facilities at the 19th hole. The hotel's traditional dining room offers a table d'hote menu whilst the Terrace Restaurant on the top floor of the golf centre offers daily fare or an à la carte menu. Here it is possible to enjoy views of the Hawkestone courses.

The Weston Course, now renamed the Windmill Course has been completely rebuilt and all 18 holes will be in play by summer 1995. Designed by Brian Hugget, the 6655 yard par 72 will be a challenge to all golfers. Other newly opened golfing facilities include a six hole, par 3 Academy course, a target practice range and tuition hole.

A series of residential Golf Schools is in operation covering the beginner, improver to the advanced level, all run under the guidance of top UK coach Keith Williams and his team of professionals. A fully equipped hi-tech video/computer studio is fully operational and can be used on individual, group or corporate basis.

It is atmosphere as well as the pleasantness and efficien-cy of the staff which lingers longest in the mind of the visitor who vows to return to Hawkestone annually. Kevin Brazier, Company Operations Executive, roundly declares that hotel's motto has always been 'client loving care' and this approach is apparent and continues throughout the establishment. The centre of the hotel is Grade 2 listed and it is planned to increase the size of the hotel and provide more up to date facilities whilst at the same time restoring the original house making it the centrepiece of the new proposed developments. This location is more accessible today than in the late 70s, just 25 minutes drive north of Telford from the M54 or 40 minutes south from the M6 Keele University turn off, via the A53.

Hawkestone Park Hotel
Weston under Redcastle
Shropshire
SY4 5UY
Tel: (0939) 200611
Fax: (0939) 200311

Hawkstone Park

What is a man to do when his two daughters, his pride and joy, tell him that they wish to leave home? Well, such was the dilemma facing a certain Sir William Gray in 1921. His solution you might think was an admirable one... he promised to build them a golf course. For two young ladies much bitten by the bug it proved irresistible—clearly bribery of the highest calibre. In 1921 the ingenious Sir William owned Hawkstone Park, and the golf course, the subject of this tale, grew from an original nine holes to the present day Hawkstone course.

Today probably every golfer from Land's End to John O'Groats has heard of Hawkstone Park—nothing to do with the 'golfing Grays', but one Sandy Lyle, Open Champion of 1985 and U S Masters Champion of 1988. Sandy's association with Hawkstone Park has been life-long. Whilst there is probably no truth in the rumour that he was born adjacent to the first tee he certainly grew up nearby. For many years his father Alex served as professional and in every sense it was here that Sandy learnt his game.

Hawkstone Park is, of course, much more than the birthplace of Sandy Lyle. Today there are two courses, the well established Hawkstone and the very new Windmill course (built in the main over the former Weston course which was completely redesigned and extended). Both are set in the beautiful grounds of the Hawkstone Park Hotel. The hotel itself is certainly a grand affair. In a guide book of 1824 it was described as 'more like the seat of a nobleman than an hotel' and the grounds are not only exceptionally beautiful—exotic plants and flowers abound—but they are also steeped in history and legend.

The hotel runs the golf courses and other than an early morning tee reservation for residents there are no general restrictions on visitors, but starting times must be pre-booked. This can be done by telephoning the **Golf Centre** on **(0939) 200611**, fax: (0939) 200311. Parties of twelve or more are deemed to be golfing societies, subject again to making prior arrangements. They are equally welcome and written applications may be made in writing to the **Golf Sales Administrator,** at **The Golf Centre, Hawkstone Park Hotel, Weston-under-Redcastle, Nr Shrewsbury SY4 5UY.**

It has been said that one of the reasons for Hawkstone Park enjoying such a delightfully peaceful setting is that it is 'miles from anywhere'—not strictly true: it is only seven miles south of Whitchurch, or if you prefer, twelve miles north of Shrewsbury, and is easily accessible. The A49 is the best route when approaching from either of these towns. Shrewsbury itself is linked to the West Midlands by way of the M54 and the A5, while those motoring from the north will find the M6 of assistance.

I mentioned that the Windmill course had recently been completed—all 18 holes are scheduled to be in play by April 1995; in fact a great deal has been happening of late at Hawkstone Park. The aforementioned 'Golf Centre' is itself a new building and serves as a very modern three-tiered Clubhouse, one where traditional 19th hole facilities are supplemented by a state of the art teaching academy (run by the **Head Professional, Keith Williams**—an English Golf Union coach) and an excellent all day restaurant, the Terrace, situated on the first floor. Work is also in planned to extend the hotel: an additional wing is to be added and the plan is to eventually link the hotel to the Golf Centre.

Brian Huggett is the architect responsible for completely reshaping the old Weston course, and while that was a fairly modest affair the new Windmill course measures some 6655 yards and features a series of dramatic holes where the golfer must confront do-or-die shots over and alongside water. It provides a great contrast and complement to the celebrated challenges of the Hawkstone Course.

The hotel and golf course complex provides a good level of facilities for golf meetings at a corporate or local level. A wide range of golfing breaks are offered throughout the year and many golfers regularly travel great distances to sample the delights of this Shropshire paradise. It's all come a long way since the days of Sir William Gray and his golf-mad daughters, but one suspects that they would approve.

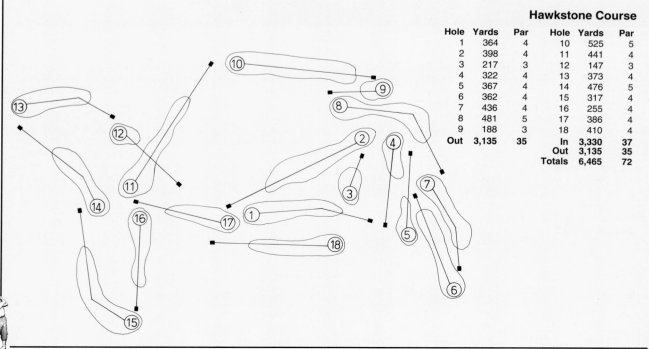

Hawkstone Course

Hole	Yards	Par	Hole	Yards	Par
1	364	4	10	525	5
2	398	4	11	441	4
3	217	3	12	147	3
4	322	4	13	373	4
5	367	4	14	476	5
6	362	4	15	317	4
7	436	4	16	255	4
8	481	5	17	386	4
9	188	3	18	410	4
Out	**3,135**	**35**	**In**	**3,330**	**37**
			Out	**3,135**	**35**
			Totals	**6,465**	**72**

Key

To avoid disappointment it is advisable to telephone in advance

****Visitors welcome at most times*
***Visitors usually allowed on weekdays only*
**Visitors not normally permitted (Mon, Wed) No visitors on specified days*

Approximate Green Fees
A   *£30 plus*
B   *£20 to £30*
C   *£15 to £25*
D   *£10 to £20*
E   *under £10*
F   *Greens fees on application*

Restrictions
G   *Guests only*
H   *Handicap certificate required*
H   *(24) Handicap of 24 or less*
L   *Letter of introduction required*
M   *Visitor must be a member of another recognised club.*

STAFFORDSHIRE

Alsager G.& C.C.
(0270) 875700
Andley Road, Alsager, Stoke-on-Trent
(18)6206 yards/**/C/M

Barlaston G.C.
(0782) 372795
Meaford Road, Barlaston, Stone
(18)5800 yards/***/C

Beau Desert G.C.
(0543) 422626
Hazelslade, Hednesford, Cannock
(18)6300 yards/**/A/H

Branston G.C.
(0283) 43207
Burton Road, Branston, Burton upon Trent
(18)6541 yards/**/C

Brocton Hall G.C.
(0785) 661901
Brocton
(18)6095 yards/***/B/H

Burslem G.C.
(0782) 837006
Wood Farm, High Lane, Tunstall
(9)5354 yards/**/D

Burton upon Trent G.C.
(0283) 44551
Ashby Road East, Burton upon Trent
(18)6555 yards/***/B/H/L/M

Cannock Park G.C.
(0543) 578850
Stafford Road, Cannock
(18)4559 yards/***/E

Craythorne G.C.
(0283) 64329
Craythorne Road, Stretton
(18)5230 yards/***/D/H

Drayton Park G.C.
(0827) 251139
Drayton Park, Tamworth
(18)6414 yards/**/B/H

Enville G.C.
(0384) 872074
Highgate Common, Kinver
(18)6217 yards/**/B/H

Golden Hill G.C.
(0782) 784715
Golden Hill, Stoke-on-Trent
(18)5957 yards/***/E

Greenway Hall G.C.
(0782) 503158
Stockton Brook, Stoke-on-Trent
(18)5676 yards/***/E

Himley Hall G.C.
(0902) 895207
School Road, Himley
(9)3125 yards/**/F

Ingestre Park G.C.
(0889) 270304
Ingestre, Stafford
(18)6334 yards/**/B/H

Lakeside G.C.
(0889) 575667
Rugeley Power Station, Rugeley
(18)5534 yards/*/F/G

Leek G.C.
(0538) 384779
Cheddleton Road, Leek
(18)6240 yards/**/B/H

Manor G.C.
(0889)563234
Leese Hill, Kingstone, Uttoxeter
(9)3523 yards/***/D

Meadow Vale G.C.
(0785) 760900
Cold Norton, Stone
(18)6500 yards/***/C

Newcastle Municipal G.C.
(0782) 627596
Keele Road, Newcastle-under-Lyme
(18)6256 yards/***/E

Newcastle-under-Lyme G.C.
(0782) 618526
Whitmore Road, Newcastle-under-Lyme
(18)6427 yards/**/B/H

Parkhall G.C.
(0782) 599584
Holme Road, Weston Coyney
(18)2335 yards/***/E

Patshull Park Hotel & G.C.
(0902) 700100
Nr Wolverhampton
(18)6400 yards/***/B/H

Perton Park G.C.
(0902) 380103
Wrottesley Park Road
(18)7036 yards/***/E

Seedy Mill G.C.
(0543) 417333
Elmshurst, Litchfield
(18)6247 yards/**/F/H

Stafford Castle G.C.
(0785) 223821
Newport Road, Stafford
(9)6347 yards/**/D

Stone G.C.
(0785) 813103
Filley Brooks, Stone
(9)6299 yards/**/C

Tamworth G.C.
(0827) 53850
Eagle Drive, Tamworth
(18)6083 yards/***/F

Trentham G.C.
(0782) 658109
Barlaston Road, Trentham
(18)6644 yards/**/B/H

Trentham Park G.C.
(0782) 658800
Trentham Park, Trentham
(18)6403 yards/***/B/H

Uttoxeter G.C.
(0889) 564884
Wood Lane, Uttoxeter
(18)5468 yards/**/D

Westwood G.C.
(0538) 398385
Newcastle Road, Walbridge, Leek
(18)6100 yards/**/C

Whiston Hall G.C.
(0538) 266260
Whiston Cheadle
(18)5724 yards/***/E

Whittington Barracks G.C.
(0543) 432317
Tamworth Road, Lichfield
(18)6457 yards/**/A/H

Wolstanton G.C.
(0782) 622413
Dimsdale Old Hall, Hassam Parade
(18)5807 yards/**/C/H

SHROPSHIRE

Arscott G.C.
(0743) 860114
Arscott, Pontesbury
(18)6035 yards/***/D/M

Bridgnorth G.C.
(0746) 763315
Stanley Lane, Bridgnorth
(18)6668 yards/***/C

Church Stretton G.C.
(0694) 722281
Trevor Hill, Church Stretton
(18)5008 yards/**/D/H

Hawkstone Park Hotel G.C.
(0939) 200611
Weston under Redcastle, Shrewsbury
(18)6465 yards/***/B
(18)6600 yards(restricted play 1994)/***/B

Hill Valley G.& C.C.
(0948) 3584
Terrick Road, Whitchurch
(18)6517 yards/***/C/H
(18)5285 yards/***/D

Lilleshall Hall G.C.
(0952) 603840
Lilleshall, Newport
(18)5906 yards/**/C/H

Llanymynech G.C.
(0691) 830983
Pant, Oswestry
(18)6114 yards/***/D/H

Ludlow G.C.
(0584) 77285
Bromfield, Ludlow
(18)6239 yards/***/C/H

Market Drayton G.C.
(0630) 652266
Sutton, Market Drayton
(18)6214 yards/**/C

Meole Brace G.C.
(0743) 364050
Meole Brace, Shrewsbury
(12)5830 yards/***/F

Mile End G.C.
(0691) 670580
Mile End, Oswestry
(9)6136 yards/***/D

Oswestry G.C.
(0691) 88535
Aston Park, Oswestry
(18)6046 yards/***/C/H/M

Severn Meadows G.C.
(0746) 862212
Highley, Bridgnorth
(9)2520 yards/***/E

Shifnal G.C.
(0952) 460330
Decker Hill, Shifnal
(18)6422 yards/**/C/H/L

Shrewsbury G.C.
(0743) 872976
Condover, Shrewsbury
(18)6212 yards/***/C/H

The Shropshire G.C.
(0952)677866
Muxton Grange, Telford
(9)3286 yards/***/D
(9)3303 yards/***/D
(9)3334 yards/***/D

Telford Hotel G.& C.C.
(0952) 585642
Great Hay, Telford
(18)6766 yards/***/B/H

Wrekin G.C.
(0952) 244032
Ercall Woods, Wellington, Telford
(18)5657 yards/***/C

CHESHIRE

Alder Root G.C.
(0925) 291919
Alder Root Lane, Winwick
(9)5564 yards/***/C

Alderley Edge G.C.
(0625) 585583
Brook Lane, Alderley Edge
(9)5839 yards/***/C/H

Alsager G.& C.C.
(0270) 875700
Audley Road, Alsager
(18)6200 yards/**/F

Astbury G.C.
(0260) 272772
Peel Lane, Astbury, Congleton
(18)6277 yards/**/B/H/M

Birchwood G.C.
(0925) 818819
Kelvin Close, Risley, Warrington
(18)6808 yards/*/C/H

Carden Park G.C.
(0829) 250325
Carden, Tilston, Chester
(18)6828 yards/***/F

Chapel-en-le-Frith G.C.
(0298) 813943
Manchester Road, Chapel-en-le Frith
(18)6065 yards/***/C/H

Chester G.C.
(0244) 677760
Curzon Park North, Chester
(18)6487 yards/***/B/H

Congleton G.C.
(0260) 273540
Biddulph Road, Congleton
(18)5103 yards/***/D

Crewe G.C.
(0270) 584099
Fields Road, Haslington, Crewe
(18)6229 yards/**/B/H

Davenport G.C.
(0625) 876951
Middlewood Road, Higher Poynton
(18)6066 yards/**/B/H

Delamere Forest G.C.
(0606) 882807
Station Road, Delamere, Northwich
(18)6305 yards/**/B

Disley G.C
(0663) 62071
Jackson's Edge
(18)6051 yards/**/F

Eaton G.C.
(0244) 680474
Eaton Park, Ecclesford
(18)6446 yards/***/F/H

Ellesmere Port G.C.

051 339 7689
Chester Road, Hooton
(18)6432 yards/***/E

Frodsham G.C.
(0928) 732159
Simons Lane, Frodsham
(18)6289 yards/***/B

Helsby G.C.
(0928) 722021
Towers Lane, Helsby, Warrington
(18)6229 yards/**/B/H

Heyrose G.C.
(0565) 733664
Budworth Road, Tabley,
Knutsford
(18)6449 yards/***/C

Knights Grange G.C.
(0606) 552780
Grange Lane, Winsford
(9)6210 yards/***/E

Knutsford G.C.
(0565) 633355
Mereheath Lane, Knutsford
(9)6288 yards/**/D

Leigh G.C.
(0925) 762943
Kenyon Hall, Broseley Lane,
Culcheth
(18)6861 yards/***/B/H

Lymn G.C.
(0925) 755020
Whitbarrow Road, Lymn
(18)6304 yards/**/C/H

Macclesfield G.C.

(0625) 423227
The Hollins, Macclesfield
(18)5625 yards/***/C/H

Malkins Bank G.C.
(0270) 765931
Betchton Road, Sandbach
(18)6071 yards/***/E

Mere G.& C.C.
(0565) 830155
Chester Road, Mere, Knutsford
(18)6817 yards/**(Wed,Fri)/A/H/L

Mottram Hall Hotel & G.C.
(0625) 828135
Mottram St Andrews
(18)6900 yards/***/A

New Mills G.C.
(0663) 743485
Shaw Marsh, New Mills, Stockport
(9)5707 yards/***(Sun)/F

Oaklands G.& C.C.
(0829) 733884
Forest Road, Tarporley
(18)6169 yards/**/C

Onneley G.C.
(0782)750577
Onneley, Crewe
(9)5584 yards/**(Tue)/C

The Portal G.C.
(0829) 733933
Cobbler's Cross Lane, Tarporley
(18)7145 yards/***/B-A

Poulton Park G.C.
(0925) 812034
Dig Lane, Cinnamon Brow,

Warrington
(9)5512 yards/***/C

Prestbury G.C.
(0625) 829388
Macclesfield Road, Prestbury
(18)6359 yards/**/B/H

Queens Park G.C.
(0270) 666724
Queens Park Gardens, Crewe
(9)5370 yards/***/E

Reaseheath College G.C.
(0270) 625131
Reaseheath, Nantwich
(9)3334 yards/***/E/M

Runcorn G.C.
(0928) 572093
Clifton Road, Runcorn
(18)6035 yards/**/C/H

Sandbach G.C.
(0270) 762117
Middlewich Road, Sandbach
(9)5614 yards/**/C/H

Sandiway G.C.
(0606) 883247
Chester Road, Sandiway,
Northwich
(18)6435 yards/***/F/H/L

Shrigley Hall G.C.
(0625) 575757
Shrigley Park, Pott Shrigley
(18)6305 yards/***/B

St. Michael Jubilee G.C.
051 424 6230
Dundark Road, Widnes

(18)5612 yards/***/F/L

Tytherington G.C.
(0625) 434562
Tytherington, nr Macclesfield
(18)6737 yards/***/B-A/H

Upton-by-Chester G.C.
(0244) 381183
Upton Lane, Upton-by-Chester
(18)5875 yards/***/C/H

Vicars Cross G.C.
(0244) 335174
Tarvin Road, Littleton
(18)6234 yards/**/C

Walton Hall G.C.
(0925) 63061
Warrington Road, Higher Walton
(18)6843 yards/***/E

Warrington G.C.
(0925) 65431
London Road, Appleton,
Warrington
(18)6305 yards/***/F/H

Widnes G.C.
051 424 2440
Highfield Road, Widnes
(18)5719 yards/**/B/H

Wilmslow G.C.
(0565) 872148
Great Warford, Mobberley,
Knutsford
(18)6607 yards/**/A

Artist: **Victor Vennor LUCKY DOG** *Courtesy of* **Rosenstiel's**

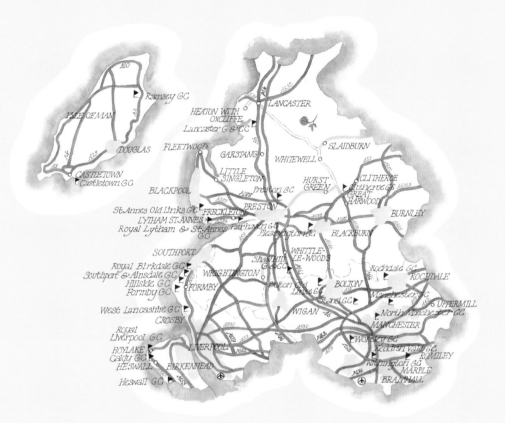

Artist: **Bill Waugh** **ROYAL LYTHAM & ST ANNES** *Courtesy of:* **Burlington Gallery**

'Caddies are not allowed on the greens when wearing clogs'—recorded in the minutes of a Lancashire golf club, 1894.

The 'Lancashire' Coast

I don't suppose they appreciate it in the slightest but the many horses that race across the sands near Southport early each morning (and the donkeys that do their best to race across the same sands) are performing within a few yards of one of the greatest stretches of golfing country in the world. On the Lancashire coast between Liverpool and Blackpool lies a magnificent collection of natural golfing links. Being more specific, between Hoylake on the Wirral Peninsula and Lytham St Annes (a distance of less than 40 miles) are to be found the likes of **Royal Liverpool, Wallasey, West Lancashire, Formby, Southport and Ainsdale, Royal Birkdale, Hillside, Royal Lytham, Fairhaven and St Annes Old Links.** A truly formidable list. Hoylake, Birkdale and Lytham have, of course, each staged the Open Championship on a number of occasions, while the Amateur Championship has been played at both Hillside and Formby, and Southport and Ainsdale has twice hosted the Ryder Cup. When the wind hammers across from the Irish Sea any of the links mentioned can become treacherously difficult and the famous Lancashire sandhills rarely provide shelter from the elements. Hoylake, Birkdale, Hillside, Formby and Lytham are each featured on later pages but a visit to any of the above will certainly not meet with disappointment (though it may result in a little damaged pride!).

Having done battle with the elements, and perhaps after visiting the treacherous Gumbley's bunker at S & A or the heather and pines at Formby, a drink will be in order. A good meal and a comfy bed for the night may also be required. Here are some suggestions. In Southport, the Scarisbrick Hotel (0704) 543000, the Prince of Wales (0704) 536688 and the Royal Clifton (0704) 533771 are probably the pick of the hotels but there are numerous others. The Metropole Hotel (0704) 536836 and the Bold Hotel (0704) 532578 are also good and amongst the less expensive options, the Ambassador Hotel (0704) 543998 and the Sunningdale Hotel (0704) 538673 will not disappoint. In Formby, the Tree Tops Motel (0704) 879651 is an ideal base.

Lytham St Annes is another golfer's paradise. It's a pleasant town and hotels to note are the Chadwick (0253) 720061 on the seafront, the Clifton Arms Hotel (0253) 739898, the Dormy House and the new Glendower Hotel (0253) 72324. Endsleigh Private Hotel (0253) 351937 and Strathmore (0253) 725478 also have good reputations. Fleetwood, to the north, has to be mentioned. The North Euston Hotel (0391) 876525 is an inexpensive base and one of the best fish restaurants here is the Trafalgar (0253) 872266.

Blackpool, famed for its 'golden mile', its great tower and impressive funfair is more of a paradise for children than golfers, but then if golf is being sneaked in on the family holiday it may be the best choice for a stay. On the North Promenade are two of the town's best hotels, the Pembroke (0253) 23434 and the Imperial (0253) 23971. Comfort here is guaranteed but there are numerous, slightly cheaper alternatives and pot luck may be the order of the day. The Sunray Private Hotel (0253) 351937, the Lynstead (0253) 351050 and the Surrey House Hotel (0253) 51743 fall into the less glamorous category but offer pleasant accommodation and on Shaftesbury Avenue, you can find the Brebyns Hotel (0253) 354263, noted for its good food. To the East, at Little Singleton,

there is a listed historic house and excellent hotel in the Mains Hall (0253) 885130.

It may be that some business in Liverpool has to be dealt with before one can put on one's plus fours and stride out onto the fairways. If you are staying in the Liver city then the Britannia Adelphi 051 709 7200 and the Atlantic Tower 051 227 4444 are both good, while first class leisure facilities can be found in the Liverpool Moat House 051 709 0181. The city has a reputation for splendid Indian and Chinese food but two European establishments are our recommendations. On the one hand the Armadillo 051 236 4123 and on the other La Grande Bouffe 051 236 3375. The nearest of the great links courses is West Lancashire, although Formby — note also the **Formby Ladies'** club here —and the Southport courses are also within easy reach. The A565 is the road to take out of Liverpool.

For the purposes of this piece **Liverpool** and **Manchester** have been included in Lancashire, a county to which they both once belonged (and still do in spirit). As the whole of **Merseyside** has been included—it's here that Royal Birkdale and Royal Liverpool are now situated—parts of former **Cheshire** are also included. Confused? Lets visit the Wirral. For such a relatively small area the peninsula is fairly thick with golf clubs. In addition to the famous links at Hoylake, **Wallasey** offers another tremendous seaside test amid some impressive sand dunes while **Heswall** offers a quite outstanding parkland challenge. Situated alongside the River Dee off the A540, it's a medium length course, beautifully maintained with views towards the distant Welsh hills. A mention also for **Caldy** which is a parkland-cum-clifftop course, and for the **Wirral Ladies'** Golf Club near Birkenhead. If an hotel and restaurant are sought on the Wirral here are some recommendations—for an hotel, the splendidly named Bowler Hat Hotel 051 652 4931 at Birkenhead is most comfortable, while Les Bougies at Heswall is a fine French restaurant. Beadles in Birkenhead is another good restaurant—ideal for a spot of lunch before playing Royal Liverpool perhaps.

Inland Golf in Lancashire

Looking to play more centrally in Lancashire, The **Shaw Hill** Golf and Country Club is most definitely one to note if travelling along the M6. Located just north of Chorley, despite its proximity to the motorway, it enjoys a very peaceful setting and is a particular favourite of golfing societies. Visitors are welcome throughout the week, and there is some high quality accommodation immediately beyond the 18th green (02572) 69221.

On the other side of the M6, **Pleasington** Golf Club enjoys similarly secluded and picturesque surroundings. The course is situated three miles west of Blackburn along the A59 and is undoubtedly one of the best parkland courses in the north of England. Still moving 'up' the country, **Preston** has a pleasantly undulating course, just north of the town. It too can easily be reached from the M6 (junction 32).

Another of the better inland courses in the county is **Clitheroe** Golf Club which is situated on the edge of the Forest of Bowland. The course lies approximately two miles south of the town with views across to Pendle Hill.

Lancashire wouldn't be complete without mentioning its county town. There are a number of clubs at hand, perhaps the best being the **Lancaster** Golf and Country Club located three miles south of the city on the A588 at Stodday. An attractive parkland course, it is laid out close to the River Lune estuary (and can be breezy!).

Well placed for many courses is the Park Hall Hotel

(0257) 452090, a popular choice for the business community for conferences and corporate events.

A few more ideas for the 19th now follow. The city of Lancaster lies west of some majestic moorland scenery. The M6 carves its way through, and near to junction 34 the Post House Hotel (0524) 65999 is ideal for travellers. Recommended alternatives include Edenbreck House (0524) 32464 and Lancaster Town House (0524) 65527. A little further north in Heaton with Oxcliffe a pub with a splendid riverside setting is the Golden Ball—well worth a visit when in these parts. In Morecambe the Midland Hotel (0524) 417180 is welcoming. At Whitewell, amid the delightful Forest of Bowland lies the Inn at Whitewell (0200) 448222 which offers excellent bar snacks, a first rate restaurant and some charming bedrooms. If you are looking for a self-catering holiday in the region, we recommend you contact either Red Rose Cottage Holidays (0200) 27310, or Country Holidays (0282) 445533. More thoughts for celebrating after a day at Preston or Clitheroe? In Hurst Green, the Shireburn Arms Hotel (0254) 826518 is well worth a visit. Not only can you enjoy the splendid Ribblesdale countryside but also some tremendous cuisine. An alternative eating establishment, a restaurant on this occasion, is Tiffany at Great Harwood, where the fish is particularly good. In Clitheroe itself, the Swan and Royal Hotel (0200) 23130 is convenient and nearby in Slaidburn is the Parrock Head Farm Hotel (0200) 446614. In Preston, both the Gibbon Bridge (0995) 61456 and Tulketh Hotel (0772) 726250 offer excellent facilities. Finally, a recommendation for the first class Mytton Fold Farm Hotel (0254) 240662 which now boasts its own course at Langho, near Blackburn.

Greater Manchester

And so to Manchester. The city itself is famed the world over for the liberal amount of rain that falls. Mancunians will tell you that this is pure poppycock (or something like that). Of course, the only time that rain can be guaranteed these days is during the five days of an Old Trafford test match. If you do happen to get caught in the rain, be it on the streets or the fairways, here are a few superior shelters. You ought to be able to find a room in the Britannia Hotel 061 228 2288 for there are 365 (one for every day of the year?) Alternatives include the Hotel Piccadilly 061 236 8414, West Lynne Hotel 061 721 4866 and the Horizon Hotel.

Outside the conurbation there are many attractive options. To the north in Egerton, the Egerton House (0204) 307171 is good value, especially at weekends, and a country setting can be enjoyed. The well respected restaurant adds appeal. Another thought is the Bramhall Moat House 061 439 8116 — it is ideal for the many courses in northern Cheshire. Altrincham has a trio to consider: the Cresta Court 061 928 8017 is modern but well equipped; the Bowdon 061 928 7121 is Victorian and comfortable; while a former coaching inn, the George and Dragon 061 928 9933 has most charm. Some of the very best restaurants in the Manchester area include: the Bonne Auberge 061 437 5701 in Heald Green, the French 061 9413355 in Altrincham, and Peppers 061 832 9393 in Bridge Street (handy for the opera).

It is probably a fair assessment to say that for golf courses, Manchester, rather like London, gets top marks for quantity but is a little shaky on the quality score. Certainly it compares unfavourably with Liverpool and Leeds — it is a shame because historically Manchester was the scene of some of the earliest golf outside Scotland. The **Old Manchester** Club was founded back in 1818. Its current status is 'temporarily without a course'—one can only hope that its members have found somewhere else to play….**North Manchester** perhaps? Only four miles from the city centre this is one of the best in the county. A close neighbour of North Manchester is the excellent **Manchester** Golf Club. Elsewhere in Greater Manchester, **Stand, Whitefield** and **Worsley** (Eccles) are fine courses, while to the north **Rochdale** is well worth travelling to. There is a cluster of courses close to the River Mersey in the Didsbury/Sale area. The best is perhaps **Withington**, and there are about ten public courses in and around the city centre. Over towards Stockport, there is a very enjoyable course at **Reddish Vale** and the area around Bolton again boasts a number of courses of which **Bolton Old Links** is probably the finest. It is a tough and interesting moorland course at which visitors are always made welcome. As for the title 'Links' it may sound a bit quaint—but there again, what are we to make of Wigan Pier?

The Isle of Man

There are five 18 hole courses on the island, with the links courses at **Castletown** and **Ramsey** particularly standing out. With fairly modest green fees and numerous relaxing places to stay the island would appear to be an ideal place for a golf holiday—ask Nigel Mansell who brought Greg Norman here! In Castletown, there are two excellent restaurants, Silverburn Lodge (0624) 822343 and La Rosette (0624) 822940, whilst the Castletown Golf Links Hotel (0624) 822201 is very comfortable and its name more than hints at what takes pride of place on the menu! Castletown golf course is featured ahead. At the other end of the island, Ramsey offers the large Grand Island Hotel (0624) 812455 and the Harbour Bistro (0624) 814182, an informal and friendly restaurant. Finally there are, of course, many places to stay in Douglas and here we can recommend the Edelweiss (0624) 833454 and the Rutland Hotel (0624) 621218, both of which are on Queen's Promenade.

Artist: **Gilroy SNOW GOLF**
Courtesy of **Burlington Gallery**

Originally built as a manor house for the keeper of the King's deer in the 14th century, the Inn at Whitewell still belongs to the Royal family as part of the Duchy of Lancaster. As a result, it still retains its associations with field sports and grouse and pheasant shooting can be arranged in season. The inn also has fishing rights to five miles of both banks of the River Hodder where you can fish for salmon and trout.

You will often find fresh fish on the menu, including local smoked salmon and game in season, black pudding and a foot long Cumberland sausage. The wine list is extensive and claims to be one of the best lists for a pub in the country as the proprietors are also wine-shippers.

Interestingly, the inn has an art gallery where you can buy works by artists from all over the country. You can also buy locally made shirts and shooting stockings, for which they have royal customers, and hand lasted shoes.

Despite all this, the inn maintains a country pub atmosphere with carved stone fireplaces, oak beams, wood panelling, oak settles and a baby grand in the corner of the lounge.

The setting is quite stunning. The inn is set in three acres of beautiful grounds and looks straight across to the Trough of Bowland. In fine weather, you can sit outside at wooden tables, high above the river, and enjoy the peace and beauty of the country.

Shooting and horse riding can be arranged and Browsholme Hall and Clitheroe Castle are nearby. For the golfer, the splendid inland course of Clitheroe Golf Club is close by. Situated on the edge of the Forest of Bowland amidst superb countryside the course looks across to Pendle Hill — a delightful setting. A short drive away lies Lancaster Golf and Country Club and the county of Lancashire is home to the famous royals:— Lytham and Birkdale, both within easy reach of the inn.

The Inn at Whitewell
Forest of Bowland
Clitheroe
Lancashire
BB7 3AT
Tel: (0200) 448222
Fax: (0200) 448298

There goes a hundred thousand bucks. . ..' the immortal words of Al Watrous after having witnessed the most magnificently outrageous stroke in golfing history. Imagine yourself in his shoes, striding down the 17th fairway, sharing the lead in the Open Championship. You have played two strokes and are safely on the edge of the green, your partner (and effectively opponent) has driven wildly into the rough and has found a small bunker—he faces a terrifying shot over sandhills, scrub and goodness knows what else—a blind shot of fully 170 yards....seconds later the impossible happens and his ball is lying a few yards from the hole, well inside your second. Minutes later you walk from the green having taken five to your opponent's four.

The occasion was, of course, the 1926 Open Championship at Royal Lytham and your opponent, the incomparable Bobby Jones.

In February 1986, Royal Lytham and St Annes proudly celebrated its one hundredth birthday. Few golf clubs in the world can have enjoyed such a rich and colourful history. There have been eight Open Championships—a ninth will be staged in 1996—four Seniors' British Opens and many other major events.

Presently in charge of all administrative matters at Royal Lytham is the Club's **Secretary, Mr L. Goodwin** and he may be contacted by telephone on **(0253) 724206**. **Eddie Birchenough** is the Club's **professional** and he may be reached on **(0253) 720094**. Visitors wishing to tread the famous fairways are asked to provide a letter of introduction from their home club, but subject to this requirement they are welcome any day between Mondays and Fridays, restrictions applying at weekends. Whilst advance booking is not essential it is clearly advisable and those wishing to write to the club should address correspondence to the Assistant Secretary, **Royal Lytham and St Annes Golf Club, Links Gate, Lytham St Annes, Lancashire FY8 3LQ.**

The green fees at Lytham were priced at £55 for a single round or £75 for a full day's golf in 1994 (both rates being inclusive of lunch). Dormy house facilities are available at the 19th hole (telephone the club for details) and Royal Lytham's Clubhouse is a marvellous Victorian building.

Golfers can enjoy the excellent catering service which is offered throughout the day.

Motoring to the course is assisted greatly by the M6 and the M61. Both northbound and southbound travellers should leave the M6 at junction 32; here the M55 can be picked up. The M55 runs out of steam at junction 4 but a left turn will take you to Lytham St Annes. The M61 links the Greater Manchester area to the outskirts of Preston. From Preston, the A583 should be followed joining the A584 which also runs to Lytham St Annes. The course is situated only a mile from the centre of the town close to St Annes railway station.

The railway line is in fact a major feature of the opening holes at Lytham, forming a continuous boundary to the right. From the back markers the course measures 6685 yards par 71 (SSS 73) with the ladies playing over 5814 yards par 75 (SSS 75). Rather unusually, Lytham opens with a par three, which at over 200 yards is quite a testing opener although the real threat of the railway looms on the 2nd and 3rd. Of the other par three holes at Lytham perhaps the 12th stands out—normally played into a prevailing wind it calls for a searching tee shot towards a raised and heavily guarded green. The back nine is generally felt to be the more difficult of the two halves although the determining factor at Lytham, as on most links courses will nearly always be the wind. The 17th has been mentioned and a plaque marks the spot from where the Jones miracle recovery shot was played. As for the 18th it of course invokes so many 'Open Championship memories': Tony Jacklin's arrow straight drive en route to winning the 1969 Championship; Gary Player putting left handed from up against the Clubhouse wall in 1974 and its two most recent Championships in 1979 and 1988, when the world twice watched Ballesteros storm home in cavalier fashion.

That 1988 Championship will always be remembered for the fantastic duel between Nick Price and the Spaniard. Price led by two shots going into the final round. He produced an almost flawless 69 yet lost by two. 'A round that happens once every 25 or 50 years' was Seve's description of his scintillating 65. Perhaps Nick Price alone can understand how Al Watrous felt.

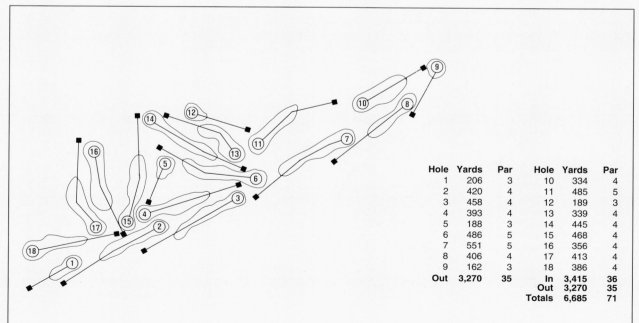

Hole	Yards	Par	Hole	Yards	Par
1	206	3	10	334	4
2	420	4	11	485	5
3	458	4	12	189	3
4	393	4	13	339	4
5	188	3	14	445	4
6	486	5	15	468	4
7	551	5	16	356	4
8	406	4	17	413	4
9	162	3	18	386	4
Out	**3,270**	**35**	**In**	**3,415**	**36**
			Out	**3,270**	**35**
			Totals	**6,685**	**71**

Back in 1889 your average J P was possibly not the most popular man in town. However, in a certain Mr. J C Barrett, Birkdale possessed a man of rare insight and one clearly cognisant of the finer things in life. Mr. Barrett was a golfer. On the 30th July, 1889, he invited eight fellow addicts to his home and together they resolved to form a golf club. One can imagine their enthusiasm as they formulated their plans, perhaps over a brandy and cigars, I know not, but very quickly a clubhouse was secured—a single room in a private residence at a four shilling per week rental! Land (at £5 per year rental) was acquired and soon a nine hole course was laid out. It all sounds rather unsophisticated, but compared with today's problems of first finding a suitable site and then obtaining planning permission, I suppose it was relatively straightforward.

Although no one could question its present day status as one of the country's leading Championship courses, historically Birkdale set off rather like the proverbial tortoise. Forced eviction in 1897 led to the Club's rerooting in its present position where a full eighteen holes were immediately available. During the 1930s a modern style clubhouse was built and John H. Taylor and Fred Hawtree were commissioned to redesign the course. As one would expect they made a splendid job of it and it was now only a question of time (and the small matter of a world war) that prevented Birkdale from staging an Open Championship. Since the War our golfing tortoise has left many of the hares behind. No fewer than seven Open Championships have now been held at Birkdale (1991 being the most recent) in addition to two Ryder Cups and numerous other major events.

Golfers wishing to play at Birkdale must belong to a recognised golf club and produce a current handicap certificate. Visitors should make prior arrangements with the **Secretary**, **Norman Crewe**. This applies to individual visitors as well as those hoping to organise a Society game. Mr Crewe can be contacted at **The Royal Birkdale Golf Club, Waterloo Road, Birkdale, Southport, Merseyside PR8 2LX. Tel: (0704) 567920** and Fax: (0704) 562327. Golf clubs may be hired from the **professional, Richard Bradbeer, (0704) 568857** and it may also be possible to obtain the services of a caddy. Individual visitors may play from Monday to Friday, green fees in 1994 being £50 per round or £70 per day. Societies are welcome on Wednesdays and Thursdays.

The Club is situated approximately two miles from the centre of Southport close to the main A565 road. From the North this road can be reached via the A59, leaving the M6 at Preston and from the South via the M62 and M57 or alternatively, as when travelling from Manchester and the East, by taking the A580 and then following the A570 into Southport.

Whilst the course possesses many of the towering sand hills so familiar with good links golf, the holes tend to wind their way between and beneath the dunes along fairly flat and narrow valleys. From the fairways the awkward stance and blind shot are the product of poor golf, not poor fortune. The greens at Royal Birkdale have recently been reconstructed (re-laid and re-designed) and the club can now claim to have some of the finest putting surfaces in the British Isles.

With its par fives the back nine is probably the easier half—at least to the longer hitter—although with the menacingly thick rough and narrow strategically bunkered fairways the wild long hitter will be severely penalised. A journey into the rough on the 16th, however, is recommended although only to visit Arnold Palmer's plaque—placed in memory of the great man's miraculous 6 iron shot when he somehow contrived to find the green after driving deep into the undergrowth.

Birkdale may have a relatively short history as an Open course, but her list of champions is as impressive a list as can be found anywhere: Peter Thomson (twice), Arnold Palmer, Lee Trevino, Johnny Miller, Tom Watson—who claimed his fifth title in nine years when winning in 1983—and Ian Baker-Finch, who set alight the 1991 championship with a brilliant front nine of 29 on the final day. The course has indeed thrown up more than its fair share of drama. Perhaps most notably in 1969 when Jack Nicklaus, ever the sportsman, conceded Tony Jacklin's very missable putt on the 18th green, so tying the Ryder Cup. In 1961, Palmer's Open, an almighty gale threatened to blow the tented village and all inside far out into the sea. In stark contrast was the 1976 Open when fire engines were close at hand as Birkdale (and all of Britain come to that) suffered in the drought. That 1976 championship saw the mercurial Miller at his brilliant best as he shook off first the challenge of Nicklaus and then of an inexperienced and unknown 19 year old who had a name no one at the time could pronounce... Severiano Ballesteros.

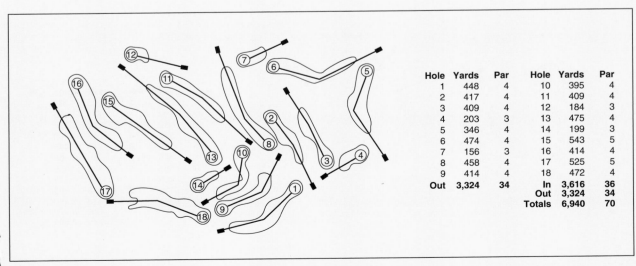

Hole	Yards	Par	Hole	Yards	Par
1	448	4	10	395	4
2	417	4	11	409	4
3	409	4	12	184	3
4	203	3	13	475	4
5	346	4	14	199	3
6	474	4	15	543	5
7	156	3	16	414	4
8	458	4	17	525	5
9	414	4	18	472	4
Out	**3,324**	**34**	**In**	**3,616**	**36**
			Out	**3,324**	**34**
			Totals	**6,940**	**70**

If Royal Birkdale is the finest golf links in England (and every modern commentator seems to think it is) then Hillside must surely be number two. Why so? Well, firstly they occupy the very same magnificent golfing country being laid out literally side by side amid a vast stretch of sandhills near Southport and, secondly, when analysing the quality of the individual golf holes people find it very difficult to separate the two courses. Perhaps it is only Birkdale's Open Championship history which accords it precedence. And why hasn't Hillside staged the 'Big One'? Presumably it's because it is only since 1967 when Hillside's back nine holes were completely reshaped that it has deserved to be ranked alongside its more illustrious neighbour. The front nine at Hillside has long been highly regarded, but the newer second nine is really outstanding and indeed very spectacular—a bit like Ballybunion minus the Atlantic Ocean.

Since 1967 Hillside has hosted a number of important championships. In the late 1970s both the British Ladies Championship and the Amateur Championship were held here and in 1982 came the European Tour's prestigious PGA Championship. A great course and a great event produced a great winner when Tony Jacklin defeated the up-and-coming Bernhard Langer in a thrilling play-off after the German had 'opened the door' by four-putting the 16th in the final round. It was Jacklin's last hurrah—thereafter he turned his attention towards winning Ryder Cups!

Golfers wishing to visit Hillside should find the Club welcoming, although arrangements are best planned some time in advance. All players must be in possession of a current handicap. The weekday green fees in 1994 were £35 per round, £45 per day. No visitors are permitted on Saturdays although occasionally it is possible to make a Sunday afternoon booking (the fee was £45 in 1994). The gentleman to approach is the **Secretary, John Graham**, tel **(0704) 567169;** fax (0704) 563192. The Club's full address is **Hillside Golf Club, Hastings Road, Hillside, Southport, Merseyside PR8 2LU.** The Club's **professional, Brian Seddon** can be contacted on **(0704) 568360.**

A quick look at the scorecard tells you that Hillside scores ten out of ten for its design balance: the two nines are of a very similar length and each comprises two par threes, two par fives and five par fours. From the back markers the links measures 6850 yards, par 72 although from the forward tees the course is a less daunting 6204 yards and from the ladies tees Hillside measures 5939 yards, par 76.

The first two holes at Hillside are fairly straightforward—provided you don't hook on to the railwayline! The 3rd is a really first class dog-leg hole where the approach must be played over a brook to a green that is well protected by deep traps: stray to the right with your second shot and you'll land in a pond. Stray to the right at the next, the short 4th and your ball will be greeted by one of three bunkers that are just as devilish as those on the 3rd. The 5th is a real teaser. It is a par five that can be reached with two good blows, and you can see everything from the tee by virtue of a gap in the dunes fifty yards short of the green, the problem is that a seemingly magnetic sleepered bunker has been placed in the gap. Three of the next four holes are difficult dog-leg par fours, all measuring in excess of 400 yards. The 7th is the breather—a lovely par three played downhill towards a generous green backed by some magnificent tall pines.

The second nine commences with another outstanding short hole, the 147 yard 10th. Distance-wise it may not sound much but it's a much tougher green to hit than most and is ringed by a series of alarmingly cavernous bunkers—yes, Hillside is inundated with them! Of the next four holes only the 12th could be described as anything less than superb, with the par five 11th, which is played from an elevated tee through a wonderful dune-lined valley, being possibly the best hole of the entire round. The 15th is where Tony Jacklin defeated Langer in the 1982 PGA play-off (there was little the German could do when Jacklin almost holed his second shot); the 16th is a big and impressive par three; the 17th, a huge par five, which some rate as good as the 11th and the 18th makes for a very demanding finishing hole, no thanks to the line of bunkers that traverse the fairway 250 yards from the tee. Langer drove into one of these traps in the final round of the 1982 PGA but still found the heart of the green with his second.

Hole	Yards	Par	Hole	Yards	Par
1	399	4	10	147	3
2	525	5	11	508	5
3	402	4	12	368	4
4	195	3	13	398	4
5	504	5	14	400	4
6	413	4	15	398	4
7	176	3	16	199	3
8	405	4	17	548	5
9	425	4	18	440	4
Out	**3,444**	**36**	**In**	**3,406**	**36**
			Out	**3,444**	**36**
			Totals	**6,850**	**72**

According to the traditionalist, as opposed to the pure pleasure-seeker, there is only one genuine form of golf and that is the sort played on a links. To this person golf might be just as enjoyable (and probably a darn sight easier when the wind blows!) on an inland course but it is not quite the real thing: Sunningdale, Gleneagles, Wentworth—all wonderful places but ..... From the pure pleasure-seeker's point of view the above mentioned courses may be more attractive, not because the challenge is probably less intimidating but because many of the best links courses tend to be fairly bleak places: Carnoustie, Lytham, Hoylake and Sandwich immediately spring to mind. Here the golfer is exposed. Trees are either very rare or non-existent; often the layout of the course is a tiresome 'straight out and straight back' and any heather doesn't seem to turn quite such a delicate shade of purple on a links as it does at Gleneagles or Sunningdale.

Formby, on the Lancashire coast (and not a million miles away from either Lytham or Hoylake) is a very rare place for it is here that the traditionalist and the pure pleasure-seeker can play a round of golf together and not fall out. Formby is a links—no question about it— firm, fast seaside greens, natural sandy bunkers and some fairly prodigious sand hills. But Formby is also blessed with a plethora of pine trees which add great beauty to the scene and often considerable shelter. Many of Formby's holes weave their way a good bit below the level of the surrounding dunes, creating a feeling of privacy, or at least occasional intimacy, so rare on a links course, and Formby certainly doesn't stretch 'out and back', in fact the bird's eye view of the links reveals eleven distinct changes of direction.

Founded over a century ago, Formby has long been one of Britain's most popular courses and visitors may find it as difficult to get a game here as at either Birkdale or Lytham. Forward planning is essential. Both individual visitors and societies are welcome on Mondays, Tuesdays, Thursdays and Fridays. The **Secretary, Mr RIF Dixon** can be contacted by telephone on **(0704) 872164** or by writing to the **Formby Golf Club, Golf Road, Formby, Liverpool L37 1LQ.** All players must hold a current golf club handicap. In 1994 the green fee to play at Formby was £45. This secured either a single round or, more attractively, a full day's golf. The **professional** at Formby is **Clive Harrison, tel: (0704) 873090.**

Formby is situated approximately 14 miles north of Liverpool and about seven miles south of Southport

(even less from Birkdale). Linking each to the other is the A565. Long distance travellers will likely use a combination of the M6 and either the M58 or the M62/M57. Both the M57 and M58 take the motorist to within two miles of the A565, just south of Formby. The M6 links with the M58 (junction 26) and with the M62 (junction 21A). There is also a train station at Formby and most who know the course well will be all too familiar with the railway line! It runs parallel to the first three fairways and is a particularly potent threat on the opening drive.

It isn't only the right hander wrestling with a slice (or the hook-happy left hander) who is likely to come to grief over the opening holes at Formby: they offer great variety and even greater challenge. Vast, gaping bunkers regularly loom in front of greens and straying from the fairways will usually be penalised heavily. If the pines don't shut you out the heather almost certainly will.

Included among most people's favourite holes at Formby are the par five 3rd and the par three 5th; the 7th with its raised green and avenue of pines and the genuinely glorious 12th. Formby's celebrated 4-3-5-4 finish calls for some very precise shot making and at the end of the round there is every chance that the golfer will have used every club in his bag. In total the course measures 6695 yards, par 72.

The 19th at Formby is very comfortable and catering facilities are provided throughout the week with the exception of Mondays. A jacket and tie must be worn in the Clubhouse.

Although the Open Championship has never visited Formby the Club regularly hosts important amateur events. Just a week after the Open was played at Royal Birkdale in 1991, the English Amateur was being staged 'down the road' at Formby. In the piece on Royal Birkdale, featured elsewhere in this chapter, we mentioned how in the Open of 1976 a raw and hitherto unknown 19 year old burst on to the scene finishing joint runner up to Johnny Miller. Arguably the high point of Ballesteros' career came in 1984 when he overcame Tom Watson to win his second Open title at St. Andrews. Later that same summer Formby, celebrating its centenary, hosted the Amateur Championship and another teenage Spaniard wrote his name into the history books: Jose-Maria Olazabal who produced some sensational golf to defeat a second future Ryder Cup star, Colin Montgomerie. Perhaps the Spanish Armada should have tried landing in Lancashire all those centuries ago.

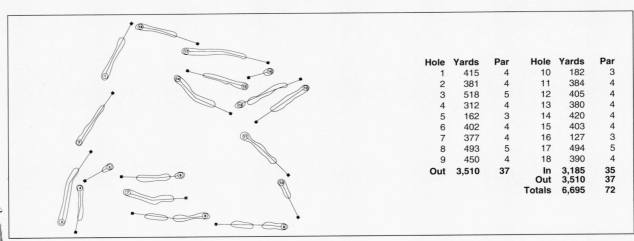

Hole	Yards	Par	Hole	Yards	Par
1	415	4	10	182	3
2	381	4	11	384	4
3	518	5	12	405	4
4	312	4	13	380	4
5	162	3	14	420	4
6	402	4	15	403	4
7	377	4	16	127	3
8	493	5	17	494	5
9	450	4	18	390	4
Out	**3,510**	**37**	**In**	**3,185**	**35**
			Out	**3,510**	**37**
			Totals	**6,695**	**72**

After an exhilarating day on the fairway, a visit to Park Hall Hotel, Leisure and Conference Centre will prove far more than par for the course and golfers staying at the hotel can take advantage of the specially discounted rates we offer for most courses in both Lancashire and Merseyside.

Set in 137 acres of grassy woodlands less than 10 minutes from Duxbury Park Golf Club, 15 minutes from Shaw Hill and convenient for many other local courses. Park Hall Hotel has a range of facilities unmatched in the area.

Smaller golfing parties may wish to make use of the superbly equipped leisure club before dining in either of the two restaurants. Guests can then relax with a drink in the welcoming lounge bar before retiring to one of ther 140 well appointed bedrooms.

On Friday and Saturday nights, the Park Nightclub provides an alternative 19th Hole.

For your corporate needs, Park Hall can offer a unique dining and entertainment package to capture the mood of any event.

The newly refurbished Lancastrian Suite can cater for up to 750 delegates; but can just as easily provide a syndicate room for as little as four people.

The hotel's extensive grounds are in great demand for team building and sporting activities (including Golf Over The Lake) and to drive home that company message your entire event can be themed to meet your individual requirements.

Whether your needs are for pleasure, leisure or business, the welcome you receive at Park Hall Hotel will suit you to a tee.

Park Hall Hotel, Leisure and Conference
Centre
Charnock Richard
Chorley
Preston PR7 5LP
Tel: (0257) 452090
Fax: (0257) 451838

The Royal Hotel at Hoylake (alas no longer with us) played a starring role in the early history of the Royal Liverpool Golf Club. In 1869 a meeting was held there which led to the famous Club's formation. Perhaps of greater significance that day, with no disrespect whatsoever to those founding Members, was the presence in the Hotel of a seven year old boy. John Ball, whose father was the Hotel proprietor, grew to become not only Hoylake's favourite son, but also the finest amateur golfer Britain has ever produced.

In the early days, golf at Hoylake must have been at times a trifle frustrating, for the Club shared the links with a racecourse and hoof prints on the fairways were a fairly common hazard. However, by 1876 the horses (doubtless equally frustrated) had found elsewhere to gallop and the golf course quickly developed into England's premier Championship test. The 1869 birthdate in fact makes Hoylake England's second oldest links course, just four years younger than Westward Ho! in Devon.

Ten Open Championships and sixteen Amateur Championships later visitors are welcome to play at Hoylake, subject to proof of handicap or letter of introduction from their home Club. The green fees in 1994 were £40 (£55 per day) during the week and £55 (£80) at weekends. The tee is reserved for members until 9.30am and between 1.00pm and 2.00pm.

On weekdays, individual bookings must be made through the **Secretary, Group Captain Christopher Moore,** tel **(051) 632 3101,** who will also authorise limited weekend bookings. Organisers should address written applications to; **The Secretary, Royal Liverpool Golf Club, Meols Drive, Hoylake, Wirral, Merseyside. L47 4AL.**

John Heggarty is the Club's **professional.** Through him, lessons can be booked, clubs hired, and caddies obtained. Mr Heggarty can be reached on **(051) 632 5868.**

Hoylake is located at the tip of the Wirral peninsula, approximately ten miles west of Liverpool and fifteen miles north of Chester. The north west of England is particularly well served by motorway connections and finding the course shouldn't be a problem. Approaching from either the north or south the M6 is likely to be of assistance; it passes midway between Manchester and

Liverpool and should be left at junction 19A. Thereafter the M56 can be followed towards Chester joining the M53 at junction 15. The M53 will then take you to the far end of the Wirral where the A553 Hoylake road should be picked up. (In a nutshell: M6—M56—M53—A553).

The course occupies fairly flat ground and is very exposed to the elements. It is most unusual for the wind not to blow. (You have been warned!) It was his mastery of the wind, a skill acquired playing at Hoylake that enabled John Ball to win many of his record eight Amateur Championships. His victories were achieved between 1888 and 1912. Ball's great rival during those years, both remarkably, and ironically, was a fellow Hoylake man, Harold Hilton. Hilton himself won four Amateur Championships. In addition both Hilton and Ball won the Open Championship, Ball in 1890 and Hilton twice, in 1892 and 1897. The great Bobby Jones is the only other Amateur golfer to have won the Open title.

Even on those very rare occasions when all is calm, Hoylake is still an exceptionally difficult test. From the medal tees the course measures 6821 yards, par 72, and it can play every inch of its length. If the most memorable and classic links-type sequence of holes occurs between the 8th and the 12th, the end of the round provides a real "sting in the tail'. Rather like Carnoustie, Hoylake is renowned for its exacting final stretch. It contains two par fives and three par fours any of which is capable of wrecking a potentially good score. The long 16th in particular can be cruelly punishing with its out of bounds to the right of the fairway.

The ten Opens held at Hoylake produced ten different Champions and among them some of the game's greatest names: Harold Hilton, John H. Taylor, Walter Hagen and Bobby Jones. The latter's victory in 1930 was the second leg of the historic grand slam.

The sole reason for the course being presently 'off the Open rota' (the last staging was in 1967 when Roberto de Vicenzo won) is that the course cannot accommodate the vast crowds that the event now attracts. Unfortunately, it is the same enthusiastic public who suffer most, for there are many who maintain that Hoylake remains the greatest of all England's Championship links.

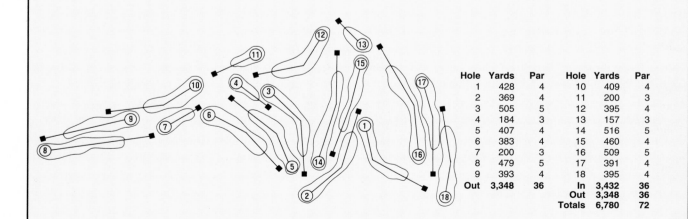

Hole	Yards	Par	Hole	Yards	Par
1	428	4	10	409	4
2	369	4	11	200	3
3	505	5	12	395	4
4	184	3	13	157	3
5	407	4	14	516	5
6	383	4	15	460	4
7	200	3	16	509	5
8	479	5	17	391	4
9	393	4	18	395	4
Out	**3,348**	**36**	**In**	**3,432**	**36**
			Out	**3,348**	**36**
			Totals	**6,780**	**72**

Was the Isle of Man ever part of the mainland? If so, which mainland? Situated almost exactly midway between Great Britain and Ireland (and roughly equidistant, as the seagull flies, from England, Scotland, Northern Ireland and the Republic, it looks as if Providence deliberately positioned it in mid-Ocean so that no-one could claim it as theirs and hence a strong spirit of independence flourished.

The Irish theory, however, has much appeal. One of the Emerald Isle's greatest heroes, Finn McCool, a legend in his own lifetime if ever there was one, and the Giant who started to build the famous Causeway was really responsible for its location. One day, Finn got out of bed the wrong side and started to have one of those days. Finn's personality problem was his temper—the only thing about him that was short. This particular day he completely lost his rag and Finn McCool became Finn Not-so-Cool. He grabbed the largest rock he could find and hurled it 50 miles into the sea. Today, that huge rock is known as the Isle of Man.

Enough about the geography and history of the island: what of the golf? Put Castletown aside for a second and it is pretty fair, add Castletown to the equation and it is pretty excellent. What really makes Castletown is its extraordinary location on the island. Like St. Andrews the course is laid out on a fairly thin strip of land but unlike St. Andrews it is surrounded by water on three sides, the golf links being laid out on a very unusual, triangular-shaped peninsula. This is the Langness Peninsula, more commonly known as Fort Island, situated right on the south eastern tip of the Isle of Man only a few minutes from the island's airport at Ronaldsway.

The extraordinary location produces some amazing seascapes and as the land 'between the sea' is more or less perfect links terrain the architect who designed Castletown was given a mighty head start by Mother Nature. Fortunately for you and I they didn't give the task to any old architect either; the original layout was prepared by 'Old' Tom Morris—he of course was the chap who reckoned that Machrihanish was 'designed by The Almighty for playing golf'. What must he have thought of this site? (Interestingly there is more than a hint of Machrihanish about some of the holes at Castletown). After the last war Castletown was reshaped and this time another celebrated architect was brought in to oversee the project: Mackenzie Ross, the man who converted Turnberry from a battle station into the majestic links it now is.

Unless one is fortunate enough to be a member of Castletown Golf Club by far the easiest way of inspecting Ross's masterpiece is to stay overnight at the adjacent Castletown Golf Links Hotel. The Hotel actually owns the golf course and booking a game is much easier for Hotel guests. Residents have priority over visitors and pay reduced green fees. Non residents can only book tee times one month in advance; this is not to say that they are unwelcome at short notice, it is just that it may be a case of pot luck. Bookings may be made through the **Golf Secretary, Carol Kaye**, tel **(0624) 822201**. Visitors who do not have a tee reservation should contact the Club's **professional, Murray Crowe**, tel **(0624) 822211**.

The green fees set for 1995 are £16 per day for Hotel residents, while visitors pay £20 per day between Monday and Thursday and £25 at all other times.
Because of the Hotel, its adjoining links and its course architect, Castletown has been called the 'Poor Man's Turnberry'. This is actually intended as a compliment; certainly there is nothing poor about the Hotel or its golf course, the quality of both is very high. In fact many people believe that in its way the golf at Castletown is just as enjoyable (if a little less testing) and scenically as enchanting as the famous Ailsa Course. From its championship tees the links can be stretched to 6713 yards, par 72. The respective lengths from the medal and forward tees being 6546 yards and 6137 yards. Among the best holes on the course are two fine par threes, the 6th and the 11th, the sharply dog-legging 7th and a truly spectacular pair, the 8th and the 17th. The former carries a famous name, 'The Road Hole.' There are no railway sheds to drive over here but terror does lurk all the way down the right side of the fairway: a sliced drive will either end up on tarmac, the beach or the sea. Take the road away and from the back tee the 8th is almost a mirror image of the 1st at Machrihanish—it is of a similar length too at 426 yards. There are no bunkers around the green but then getting there is problematical enough.

The 17th is called 'The Gully' and again a brave, long drive is needed if the direct route to the green is taken. The carry is nearly 200 yards over a deep chasm . . .rocks and frothy water await the mis-hit shot. You stand on the 17th tee at Castletown with the knowledge that your drive could finish up in England, Scotland, Ireland or even Wales. As the great Nigel would say, only the best drivers stay on the Isle of Man.

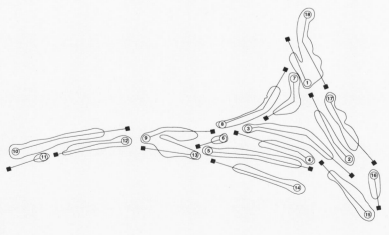

Hole	Yards	Par	Hole	Yards	Par
1	252	4	10	568	5
2	390	4	11	166	3
3	557	5	12	369	4
4	388	4	13	349	4
5	497	5	14	448	4
6	135	3	15	373	4
7	383	4	16	188	3
8	426	4	17	420	4
9	386	4	18	418	4
Out	3,414	37	In	3,299	35
			Out	3,414	37
			Totals	6,713	72

Key

*To avoid disappointment
it is advisable to telephone
in advance*

***Visitors welcome at most times*
***Visitors usually allowed on
weekdays only*
*'Visitors not normally permitted
(Mon, Wed) No visitors
on specified days*

Approximate Green Fees
A £30 plus
B £20 to £30
C £15 to £25
D £10 to £20
E under £10
F Greens fees on application

Restrictions
G Guests only
H Handicap certificate required
H (24) Handicap of 24 or less
L Letter of introduction required
*M Visitor must be a member of
another recognised club.*

GREATER MANCHESTER

Acre Gate G.C.
061 748 1226
Pennybridge Lane, Flixton
(18)4395 yards/***/E

Altrincham G.C.
061 928 0761
Stockport Road, Timperley
(18)6162 yards/***/D

Ashton-in-Makerfield G.C.
(0942) 724229
Garswood Park, Ashton-in-
Makerfield
(18)6250 yards/**(Wed)/C/M

Ashton on Mersey G.C.
061 973 3220
Church Lane, Sale
(9)6146 yards/**(Tues)/C/H

Ashton-under-Lyne G.C.
061 330 1537
Gorsey Way, Ashton-under-Lyne
(18)6209 yards/**/D

Avro G.C.
061 439 5050
Old Hall Lane, Woodford
(9)5735 yards/*/F/G

Blackley G.C.
061 643 2980
Victoria Avenue East, Blackley
(18)6237 yards/**(Thurs)/C

Bolton G.C.
(0204) 843067
Chorley New Road, Bolton
(18)6215 yards/***/B

Bolton Municipal G.C.
(0204) 842386
Links Road, Bolton
(18)6336 yards/***/F

Bolton Old Links G.C.
(0204) 843336
Monserrat, Bolton
(18)6406 yards/***/B/H

Brackley Municipal G.C.
061 790 6076
Bullows Road, Little Hulton,
Worsley
(9)3003 yards/***/E

Bramhall G.C.
061 439 4057
Ladythorn Road, Bramhall
(18)6293 yards/***(Thurs)/B/M

Bramhall Park G.C.
061 485 3119
Manor Road, Bramhall
(18)6214 yards/***/B/L

Breightmet G.C.
(0204) 827381
Red Bridge, Ainsworth, Bolton
(9)6416 yards/**/C

Brookdale G.C.
061 681 4534
Ashbridge, Woodhouses,
Failsworth
(18)6040 yards/***/C/H

Bury G.C.
061 766 4897
Unsworth Hall, Blackford Bridge
(18)5961 yards/**/C/H

Castle Hawk G.C.
(0706) 40841
Heywood Road, Castleton,
Rochdale
(18)3158 yards/***/E
(9)5398 yards/***/E

Cheadle G.C.
061 428 2160
Shiers Drive, Cheadle
(9)5006 yards/***(Tues/Sat)C/H/L

Chorlton-cum-Hardy G.C.
061 881 3139
Barlow Hall Road, Chorlton
(18)6003 yards/***/B/H

Crompton & Royton G.C.
061 624 2154
Highbarn, Royton, Oldham
(18)6222 yards/**(Tues/Wed)/B/H

Davyhulme Park G.C.
061 748 2260
Gleneagles Road, Davyhulme
(18)6237 yards/**(Wed)/B/H/L

Deane G.C.
(0204) 861944
Broadford Road, Deane, Bolton
(18)5583 yards/**/C/H/M

Denton G.C.
061 336 3218
Manchester Road, Denton
(18)6290 yards/**/B/H

Didsbury G.C.
061 998 9278
Ford Lane, Northenden
(18)6273 yards/**/B/H

Dukinfield G.C.
061 338 2340
Lyne Edge, Ashton-under-Lyne
(18)5585 yards/**/D

Dunham Forest G.C.
061 928 2605
Oldfield Lane, Altrincham
(18)6636 yards/**/B/H

Dunscar G.C.
(0204) 303321
Longworth Lane, Bromley Cross,
Bolton
(18)6085 yards/**/B/H

Ellesmere G.C.
061 790 2122
Old Clough Lane, Worsley
(18)5957 yards/**/C/H/M

Fairfield Golf & Sailing Club
061 370 2292
Booth Road, Audenshaw
(18)5654 yards/***(Wed pm/W/E
am)/C

Flixton G.C.
061 748 2116
Church Road, Flixton
(9)6410 yards/**/D

Gathurst G.C.
(0257) 252861
Miles Lane, Shevington, Wigan
(9)6308 yards/**(Wed)/D

Gatley G.C.
061 437 2091
Styal Road, Heald Green, Gatley
(9)5934 yards/**(Tues)/D

Great Lever & Farnworth G.C.
(0204) 862582
Lever Edge Lane, Bolton
(18)5859 yards/**/C/H

Greenmount G.C.
(0204) 883712
Greenmount, Bury
(9)4920 yards/**(Tues)/D/H

Haigh Hall G.C.
(0942) 831107
Haigh Country Park, Haigh, Wigan
(18)6423 yards/***/D

Hale G.C.
061 980 4225
Rappax Road, Hale
(9)5780 yards/**(Thurs)/B

Harwood G.C.
061 761 6022
Roading Brook Road, Bolton
(9)5993 yards/**/D

Hazel Grove G.C.
061 483 3978
Buxton Road, Stockport
(18)6310 yards/***/B/H

Heaton Moor G.C.
061 432 2134
Heaton Mersey, Stockport
(18)5876 yards/***(Tues)/B

Heaton Park G.C.
061 798 0295
Heaton Park, Prestwich
(18)5849 yards/***/E

Hindley Hall G.C.
(0942) 55131
Hall Lane, Hindley, Wigan
(18)5904 yards/**(Wed)/B/H/L

Horwich G.C.
(0204) 696980
Victoria Road, Horwich, Bolton
(9)5404 yards/*/F/G

Houldsworth G.C.
061 442 9611
Houldsworth Park, Reddish,
Stockport
(18)6078 yards/**/D

Lowes Park G.C.
061 764 1231
Hill Top, Bury
(9)6043 yards/**(Wed)/D/M

Manchester G.C.
061 643 3202
Hopwood Cottage, Rochdale Road,
Middleton
(18)6464 yards/**/B/H

Marple G.C.
061 427 2311
Hawk Green, Marple
(18)5700 yards/***(Thurs)/B/H

Mellor & Townscliffe G.C.
061 427 2208
Tarden, Gibb Lane, Mellor
(18)5925 yards/**(Sat)/B

North Manchester G.C.
061 643 9033
Rhodes House, Manchester Old
Road, Middleton
(18)6527 yards/***/C

Northenden G.C.
061 998 4738
Palatine Road, Northenden

(18)6469 yards/***/B/H

Oldham G.C.
061 624 4986
Lees New Road, Oldham
(18)5045 yards/***/F

Pennington G.C.
(0942) 682852
St Helens Road, Leigh
(9)2919 yards/***/F

Pike Folds G.C.
061 740 1136
Cooper Lane, Victoria Avenue,
Blackley
(9)5789 yards/**/D

Prestwich G.C.
061 773 2544
Hilton Lane, Prestwich
(18)4712 yards/**/D/H

Reddish Vale G.C.
061 480 2359
Southcliffe Road, Reddish
(18)6086 yards/**/C/H

Regent Park G.C.
(0204) 844170
Chorley New Road, Bramhall
(18)6069 yards/***/F

Ringway G.C.
061 904 9609
Hale Mount, Hale Barns,
Altrincham
(18)6494 yards/***/B/H

Romiley G.C.
061 430 2392
Goosehouse Green, Romiley
(18)6421 yards/***/B

Saddleworth G.C.
(0457) 873653
Mountain Ash, Ladcastle Road,
Uppermill
(18)5976 yards/**/B/H

Sale G.C.
061 973 3404
Sale Lodge, Golf Road, Sale
(18)6346 yards/***/B/H/M

Stamford G.C.
(0457) 832126
Oakfield House, Huddersfield
Road, Stalybridge
(18)5701 yards/**/F

Stand G.C.
061 766 2388
The Dales, Ashbourne Grove,
Whitefield
(18)6425 yards/**/B/H

Stockport G.C.
061 427 2421
Offerton Road, Offerton, Stockport
(18)6326 yards/***/B-A/M

Swinton Park G.C.
061 794 1785
East Lancashire Road, Swinton
(18)6712 yards/**/F/H

Turton G.C.
(0204) 852235
Wood End Farm, Chapeltown
Road, Bromley
(9)5894 yards/**(Wed)/D

Walmersley G.C.
061 764 1429
Garretts Close, Walmersley, Bury
(9)3057 yards/**(Tues)/D

Werneth (Oldham) G.C.
061 624 1190
Green Lane, Garden Suburb,
Oldham
(18)5363 yards/**/D

Werneth Low G.C.
061 368 2503

Werneth Low Road, Hyde
(9)5734 yards/**/C

Westhoughton G.C.
(0942) 811085
Long Island, Westhoughton,
Bolton
(9)5834 yards/**/D

Whitefield G.C.
061 766 2904
Higher Lane, Whitefield
(18)6045 yards/***/B/H/L

Whittaker G.C.
(0706) 378310
Whittaker Lane, Littleborough
(9)5576 yards/***(Tues pm/Sun)/D

William Wroe G.C.
061 748 8680
Pennybridge Lane, Flixton
(18)4395 yards/***/F

Withington G.C.
061 445 9544
Palatine Road, West Didsbury
(18)6411 yards/***(Thurs)/B/H

Worsley G.C.
061 789 4202
Stableford Avenue, Monton, Eccles
(18)6217 yards/***/B/H/L

LANCASHIRE

Accrington & District G.C.
(0254) 232734
West End, Oswaldtwistle,
Accrington
(18)5954 yards/***/D

Ashton & Lea G.C.
(0772) 726480
Tudor Avenue, Lea, Preston
(18)6289 yards/***/C

Bacup G.C.
(0706) 873170
Maden Road,Bacup
(9)5652 yards/***(Tues)/D

Baxenden & District G.C.
(0254) 234555
Top o' th' Meadow, Baxenden
(9)5740 yards/**/D

Beacon Park G.C.
(0695) 622700
Beacon Hill, Dalton, Up Holland,
Wigan
(18)5996 yards/***/F

Bentham G.C.
(0524) 261018
Robin Lane, Bentham
(9)5760 yards/***/D

Blackburn G.C.
(0254) 51122
Beardwood Brow, Blackburn
(18)6147 yards/**(Tues)/C/H

Blackpool North Shore G.C.
(0253) 351017
Devonshire Road, Blackpool
(18)6442 yards/***(Thurs/Sat)/B/H

Blackpool-Stanley Park G.C.
(0253) 393960
North Park Drive, Blackpool
(18)6192 yards/***/E

Blundells Hill G.C.
(0744) 24892
Warrington New Road, St Helens
(12) 6265 yards/*/F/G

Burnley G.C.
(0282) 421045
Glen View, Burnley
(18)5899 yards/***/C/H

Chorley G.C.
(0257) 480263
Hall o' th' Hill, Heath Charnock,
Chorley
(18)6295 yards/**/C/H/L

Clitheroe G.C.
(0200) 22292

Whalley Road, Pendleton
(18)6326 yards/***/B/H

Colne G.C.
(0282) 863391
Law Farm, Skipton Old Road
(9)5961 yards/***/D

Darwen G.C.
(0254) 701287
Winter Hill, Darwen
(18)5752 yards/***(Sat)/D

Dean Wood G.C.
(0695) 622219
Lafford Lane, Up Holland,
Skelmersdale
(18)6137 yards/**/B

Duxbury Park G.C.
(0257) 265380
Duxbury Hall Road, Chorley
(18)6390 yards/***/E

Fairhaven G.C.
(0253) 736741
Lytham Hall Park, Ansdell, Lytham
(18)6883 yards/***/B/H

Fishwick Hall G.C.
(0772) 798300
Glenluce Drive, Farringdon Park,
Preston
(18)6092 yards/**/C

Fleetwood G.C.
(0253) 873114
Princes Way, Fleetwood
(18)6723 yards/***/C/H

Ghyll G.C.
(0282) 842466
Ghyll Brow, Barnoldswick
(9)5422 yards/***(Sun)/D

Great Harwood G.C.
(0254) 884391
Whalley Road, Harwood Bar
(9)6413 yards/***/D

Green Haworth G.C.
(0254) 237580
Green Haworth, Accrington
(9)5556 yards/***/D

Herons Reach G.C.
(0253) 838866
East Park Drive, Blackpool
(18)6416 yards/***/B/H

Heysham G.C.
(0524) 851011
Trumacar Park, Middleton Road,
Heysham
(18)6258 yards/***/C/H

Hurlston Hall G.C.
(0704) 840400
Hurlston Lane, Scarisbrick
(18)6700 yards/***/C/H

Ingol Golf and Squash Club
(0772) 734556
Tanterton Hall Rd, Ingol
(18)5868 yards/***/C

Knott End G.C.
(0253) 810576
Knott End-on-Sea
(18)5789 yards/**/C/H

Lancaster G.& C.C.
(0524) 751247
Ashton Hall, Ashton-with-Stodday,
Lancaster
(18)6282 yards/**/B/H

Lansil G.C.
(0524) 39269
Caton Road, Lancaster
(9)5608 yards/***/D/H

Leyland G.C.
(0772) 421359
Wigan Road, Leyland
(18)6123 yards/**/C

Lobden G.C.
(0706) 343228
Lobden Moor, Whitworth,
Rochdale

(9)5750 yards/***/D/H

Longridge G.C.
(0772) 783291
Fell Barn, Jeffrey Hill, Longridge,
Preston
(18)5800 yards/***/C

Lytham Green Drive G.C.
(0253) 737390
Ballam Road, Lytham
(18)6175 yards/**/B/H

Marland G.C.
(0706) 49801
Springfield Park, Rochdale
(18)5237 yards/***/F

Marsden Park G.C.
(0282) 67525
Townhouse Road, Nelson
(18)5806 yards/***/F

Morecambe G.C.
(0524) 412841
Bare, Morecambe
(18)5766 yards/***/B/H

Nelson G.C.
(0282) 614583
Kings Causeway, Brierfield, Nelson
(18)5967 yards/**(Thurs/Sat)/C/H

Ormskirk G.C.
(0695) 572112
Cranes Lane, Lathom, Ormskirk
(18)6358 yards/***(Sat)/B/H/L

Penwortham G.C.
(0772) 744630
Blundell Lane, Penwortham,
Preston
(18)5915 yards/**(Tues)/B

Pleasington G.C.
(0254) 202177
Pleasington, Blackburn
(18)6417 yards/**(Tues)/B/H

Poulton-le-Fylde G.C.
(0253) 892444
Myrtle Farm, Breck Road, Poulton-
le-Fylde
(9)2979 yards/***/E

Preston G.C.
(0772) 700011
Fulwood Hall Lane, Fulwood,
Preston
(18)6233 yards/**/B/H

Rishton G.C.
(0254) 884442
Eachill Links, Blackburn
(9)6094 yards/**/D

Rochdale G.C.
(0706) 43818
Edenfield Road, Bagslate, Rochdale
(18)6002 yards/***/C

Rossendale G.C.
(0706) 213056
Ewood Lane, Haslingden,
Rossendale
(18)6267 yards/***(Sat)/B

Royal Lytham & St Annes G.C.
(0253) 724206
St Annes on Sea, Lytham
(18)6673 yards/**/A/H/L

St Annes Old Links G.C.
(0253) 723597
Highbury Road, Lytham St Annes
(18)6616 yards/**(Tues)/B-A/H

Shaw Hill G.& C.C.
(0257) 269221
Whittle-le-Woods, Chorley
(18)6467 yards/***/A/H

Silverdale G.C.
(0524) 701300
Red Bridge Lane, Silverdale,
Carnforth
(9)5417 yards/***/D

Springfield G.C.
(0706) 56401
Springfield Park, Bolton Road,

Rochdale
(18)5209 yards/***/E

Stonyhurst Park G.C.
(0254) 826478
Hurst Green, Blackburn
(9)5529 yards/***/D

Towneley G.C.
(0282) 38473
Todmorden Road, Burnley
(18)5862 yards/***/E

Tunshill G.C.
(0706) 342095
Kiln Lane, Milnrow
(9)5812 yards/**(Tues pm)/F

Whalley G.C.
(0254) 822236
Portfield Lane, Whalley, Blackburn
(9)6258 yards/***/C

Wigan G.C.
(0257) 421360
Arley Hall, Haigh, Wigan
(9)6058 yards/***(Tues/Sat)/C

Wilpshire G.C.
(0254) 48260
Whalley Road, Wilpshire,
Blackburn
(18)5911 yards/***/B/H

MERSEYSIDE

Allerton Municipal G.C.
051 428 1046
Allerton, Liverpool
(18)5494 yards/***/E
(9)1845 yards/***/E

Arrowe Park G.C.
051 677 1527
Arrowe Park, Woodchurch,
Birkenhead
(18)6377 yards/***/E

Bidston G.C.
051 638 3412
Scoresby Road, Leasowe, Moreton
(18)6207 yards/**/D

Bootle G.C.
051 928 6196
Dunnings Bridge Road, Bootle
(18)6362 yards/***/E

Bowring G.C.
051 489 1901
Bowring Park, Roby Road, Huyton
(9)5592 yards/***/F

Brackenwood G.C.
051 608 3093
Bracken Lane, Bebington
(18)6285 yards/***/F

Bromborough G.C.
051 334 2155
Raby Hall Road, Bromborough
(18)6650 yards/**/B

Caldy G.C.
051 625 5660
Links Hey Road, Caldy, Wirral
(18)6675 yards/**/F

Childwall G.C.
051 487 0654
Naylors Road, Gateacre
(18)6425 yards/***(Tues)/B/H

Eastham Lodge G.C.
051 327 3003
Ferry Road, Eastham, Wirral
(15)5813 yards/**/C/H

Formby G.C.
(0704) 872164
Golf Road, Formby
(18)6701 yards/**(Wed)/A/H/L

Formby Ladies G.C.
(0704) 873493
Golf Road, Formby
(18)5374 yards/***(Thurs)/B/H

Grange Park G.C.
(0744) 26318
Prescot Road, St Helens

(18)6429 yards/**/B/L

Haydock Park G.C.
(09252) 224389
Golbourne Park, Newton-le-Willows
(18)6043 yards/**(not Tues)/B/M

Hesketh G.C.
(0704) 536897
Cockle Dicks Lane, Southport
(18)6478 yards/**/B-A/H

Heswall G.C.
051 342 1237
Cottage Lane, Gayton, Heswall
(18)6472 yards/***/A/H

Hillside G.C.
(0704) 567169
Hastings Road, Hillside, Southport
(18)6850 yards/**/A/H/M

Hoylake Municipal G.C.
051 632 2956
Carr Lane, Hoylake
(18)6330 yards/***/E

Huyton and Prescot G.C.
051 489 3948
Hurst Park, Huyton Lane, Huyton
(18)5738 yards/**/F/L

Kirkby (Liverpool Municipal) G.C.
051 546 5435
Ingoe Lane, Kirkby
(18)6571 yards/***/F/H

Leasowe G.C.
051 677 5852
Leasowe Road, Moreton, Wirral

(18)6204 yards/***/C/H

Lee Park G.C.
051 487 3882
Childwall Valley Road, Gateacre
(18)6024 yards/***/F/L

Park G.C.
(0704) 530133
Park Road, Southport
(18)6200 yards/**/F

Prenton G.C.
051 608 1461
Golf Links Road, Prenton, Birkenhead
(18)6411 yards/***/C/H

Royal Birkdale G.C.
(0704) 567920
Waterloo Road, Birkdale, Southport
(18)6703 yards/**/A/H/L

Royal Liverpool G.C.
051 632 3101
Meols Drive, Hoylake, Wirral
(18)6780 yards/**/A/H/L

Sherdley Park Municipal G.C.
(0744) 813149
Sherdley Road, St Helens
(18)5941 yards/***/E

Southport & Ainsdale G.C.
(0704) 578000
Bradshaws Lane, Ainsdale, Southport
(18)6612 yards/**/A/H/M

Southport Municipal G.C.

(0704) 535286
Park Road West, Southport
(18)6400 yards/***/F

Southport Old Links G.C.
(0704) 28207
Moss Lane, Southport
(9)6486 yards/**(Wed)/C/H

Wallasey G.C.
051 691 1024
Bayswater Road, Wallasey
(18)6607 yards/**/B/H/M

Warren G.C.
051 639 5730
Grove Road, Wallasey
(9)5914/***/F

West Derby G.C.
051 254 1034
Yew Tree Lane, Liverpool
(18)6333 yards/**/B

West Lancashire G.C.
051 924 1076
Hall Road West, Blundellsands, Liverpool
(18)6756 yards/***/B-A/H

Wirral Ladies G.C.
051 652 1255
Bidston Road, Oxton, Birkenhead
(18)4966 yards(ladies)***(by arrangement)/F/H/L
(18)5170 yards/(men)***(by arrangement)F/H/L

Woolton G.C.
051 486 2298
Doe Park, Speke Road, Woolton

(18)5706 yards/***/B

ISLE OF MAN

Castletown G.C.
(0624) 822201
Fort Island, Derbyhaven
(18)6716 yards/***/C-B

Douglas G.C.
(0624) 675952
Pulrose Road, Douglas
(18)6080 yards/***/F

King Edward Bay G.& C.C.
(0624) 620430
Groudle Road, Onchan
(18)5457 yards/***/D

Peel G.C.
(0624) 842227
Rheast Lane, Peel
(18)5914 yards/**/D/H

Port St Mary G.C.
(0624) 834932
Kallow Road, Port St Mary
(9)2711 yards/***/F

Ramsey G.C.
(0624) 812244
Brookfield, Ramsey
(18)6019 yards/**/D/H

Rowany G.C.
(0624) 834108
Rowany Drive, Port Erin
(18)5840 yards/***/D/H

Artist: **Linda Hartough ROYAL BIRKDALE** *Courtesy of* **Old Troon Sporting Antiques**

Artist: **Roy Perry** **TO HALVE THE MATCH** *Courtesy of:* **Rosenstiel's**

The Feversham Arms Hotel

The Feversham Arms Hotel was rebuilt in 1855 by the Earl of Feversham on the site of an older hostelry known as the Board Inn. After an interesting and varied history it was purchased in 1967 by the Aragues family who have since updated the hotel facilities whilst taking care to preserve the character and charm of the old coaching inn.

Built in Yorkshire stone, the hotel has 18 bedrooms, all with private bathroom and everything you would expect of a hotel of this calibre; some even have four poster beds. The Goya restaurant, elegant and warm, and renowned for good food, specialises in shellfish and game in season. The extensive wine list includes a good selection of French grand cru classes and Spanish gran reservas. If your idea of a good break includes open fires and dinner by candlelight, you will not be disappointed by the Feversham Arms.

An acre of beautiful walled gardens is joined by a superb all-weather hard tennis court and a stunning outdoor heated swimming pool. If you are contemplating a round of golf, the hardest decision will be where to start. There are over twenty golf clubs within a radius of 35 miles, the nearest being Kirkbymoorside. Racegoers will probably find that the area needs no introduction: York, Beverley, Ripon, Thirsk, Wetherby, Pontefract and Redcar are all close to hand.

Helmsley itself is on the edge of the North York Moors National Park, which offers to the open air enthusiast over 550 square miles of panoramic views, clear waters, pine wood, steep-sided hills and rugged coastline. Villages of local stone and rich in medieval architecture with roman remains are situated within the Park.

The Feversham Arms Hotel is a must for the sport lover or for anyone visiting this beautiful and historic area.

A special BONANZA BREAKS brochure is available on request and you will not be disappointed !

The Feversham Arms Hotel
Helmsley
North Yorkshire YO6 5AG
Tel: (01439) 770766
Fax: (01439) 770346

While many consider the delights of Yorkshire to be exclusive to its northernmost area this is totally wrong. The small villages that nestle amid the southern Pennines or the Dales are delightful and the river Wharfe carves its way through south Yorkshire revealing extraordinary beauty along its trail. From the haunting howls of Haworth and the Bronte country to the jovial singing in a pub on Ilkley Moor, there is a rich tradition. Yorkshire folk are a proud breed—better reserve your best golf for the 18th fairway.

South Yorkshire

Perhaps the pick of the courses in the Sheffield area are the moorland course at **Hallamshire,** three miles west of the city off the A57, **Abbeydale**, a fine wooded parkland test to the south west and **Lees Hall**, a mix of parkland and meadowland, located south of the town centre, and occupying a lofty situation with marvellous views over the city.

Having saved your best golf for the 18th fairway a few thoughts now emerge for the 19th. The best hotel in Sheffield is probably the Grosvenor House (0742) 720041, while the Hallam Tower Post House (0742) 670067 is particularly convenient for the Hallamshire course. Sheffield also offers the comfortable Park Hall Hotel (0246) 434897. The city has many good Asian restaurants, one of the best being Nirmal's Tandoori (0742) 724054, whilst for French food enthusiasts we suggest the Restaurant Le Dauphin. Finally, we ought to recommend a good pub (the area is naturally riddled with them) but try the Cross Keys in Handsworth Road. Before noting some of the other courses in South Yorkshire, a brief word on **Lindrick** (featured separately). According to the postman it properly belongs in Nottinghamshire although the club's administrative ties are with Yorkshire and a great number of members live in the Sheffield area. Anyway, whichever side of the fence it's on (and the larger part lies in Yorkshire) it is quite superb!

Rotherham's excellent course is located at Thrybergh Park, two miles north of the town on the A630 and is well worth inspecting. Crossing the A1 we arrive at Doncaster. The **Doncaster Town Moor** Golf Club is situated very close to the famous racetrack. Like Rotherham, it's a parkland type course though not as testing. In Doncaster, the Danum (0302) 342261 and the Grand St Leger (0302) 364111 are the recommended establishments. In the countryside surrounding the busy railway town, Cadeby provides the cosy Cadeby Inn, while in Hatfield Woodhouse the Green Tree offers a warm welcome and some good snacks. The hotel with the most character in the area is the Crown at Bawtry (0302) 710341—a very pleasant high street inn. Those seeking more modern comforts should try the Moat House (0709) 364902 in Rotherham.

West Yorkshire

West Yorkshire has a greater number of golf courses. Quantity is certainly matched by quality with the area just to the north of Leeds being particularly outstanding. Within a short distance of one another are **Moortown** (featured on a later page), **Alwoodley, Sand Moor** and **Moor Allerton** all of which are of championship standard. Whilst Alwoodley, Moortown and Sand Moor are predominantly moorland in character, Moor Allerton, where there are 27 holes, is more strictly parkland. When travelling to any of the four clubs, the A61 should be taken out of Leeds itself. Moortown and Moor Allerton are probably the most widely known courses

in southern Yorkshire (if one excludes Lindrick), however, many consider Alwoodley and Sand Moor to be at least their equal. Play all four if you can! An outstanding place to stay in this area — just one mile from Moortown — is Weetwood Hall (0532) 306000; less expensive but equally welcoming is the Harewood Arms Hotel (0989) 886566 in Harewood. Other good courses to note around Leeds are **Roundhay, Leeds, Howley Hall** and **Temple Newsham.**

Following the Wharfe into the east of West Yorkshire one finds some superb countryside. This is the land of the Brontes. In Bramhope, a far cry from the romance of the Brontes but a particularly popular hotel for businessmen visiting Leeds, is the Forte Crest Hotel (0532) 842911. Visiting golfers will find plenty of good but inexpensive accommodation in Leeds, the Aragan Hotel (0532) 759306 being a fine example. The gem in this area however, is a restaurant with rooms, Pool Court (0532) 842288 in Pool-in-Wharfedale.

A second concentration of good golf courses is to be found to the north of Bradford, more particularly, **Northcliffe, Keighley** and **Shipley.** Northcliffe is probably the pick with some outstanding views of the nearby moors, but each is well worth a game. Yet another trio encircles Huddersfield, with **Bradley Park** to the north, **Woodsome Hall** to the south and **Huddersfield** Golf Club to the west. It was on the latter course that Sandy Herd learnt his game. The Open Champion of 1902, Herd finished in the first five in the Championship on no fewer than twelve occasions. He would have doubtless won on several of those but for a fellow called Vardon from Ganton across the way.

Two more courses in West Yorkshire demand to be visited — the first is **Ilkley** and the second is **Otley.** They are without question two of the county's most attractive courses. Our friend, the River Wharfe, winds its way through much of the Ilkley course and is a major hazard on several of the early holes. The equally charming course at Otley nestles majestically in the Wharfe valley. Beyond the fairways, the river and the rough, the gourmet golfer is superbly well catered for in this area. Here are some suggestions. In Ilkley, the Edwardian Breakfast at Rombalds (0943) 603201 is legendary but the hotel itself and the restaurant are both thoroughly recommended too. Elsewhere in Ilkley, a town where delightful antique shops clutter the streets, one finds the Craiglands Hotel (0943) 607676, which has a setting adjoining that famous moor and is most comfortable. Another good value establishment is the Cow and Calf (0943) 607335 one of the county's finest restaurants—book well in advance! Also, greatly renowned for its fine cuisine is the Box Tree (0943) 608484.

Continuing in the tradition of quality and class, Kildwick Hall (0756 700100) is a gorgeous Jacobean manor house which provides an outstanding place to stay and a first class restaurant too. Bradford, Bingley, Otley—all this area is riddled with enthusiastic cricket and rugby sides as well as golfers—popular pubs for one and all include the Fox at Menston, the Malt Shovel at Harden and in Ryburn, where there would seem to be a focal point, the Old Bridge and the Over the Bridge (both provide excellent lunches—perhaps in between rounds?) Finally, for a splendid restaurant visit Golcar where the George (0484) 515444 has a fine setting.

North Yorkshire

To the south and west the Yorkshire Dales, to the north and east the Yorkshire Moors. North Yorkshire is England's largest county and quite possibly

England's most beautiful.

The Dales and the Moors may not sound like great golfing country and indeed by far the greater number of Yorkshire's golf courses lie in the more populated and industrial regions of South and West Yorkshire. However, golfing visitors to North Yorkshire will not be disappointed; not only does the county boast the likes of Ganton and Fulford, two of England's greatest inland courses, but there are 25 or so others, the majority of which are set in quite glorious surroundings.

York, they say, is a city everyone should visit at least once. I recommend at least twice for there are two outstanding golf courses within three miles of York Minster: **Fulford** to the south and York Golf Club at **Strensall** to the north. Fulford (see feature page) is the better known, but York is also a championship course and has many admirers. It is a fine woodland type course, laid out on the edge of Strensall Common.

Staying in York really is a delight: there is a wealth of attractions—Shambles has some marvellous shops, the Minster itself is sensational, there are museums galore and some first class hotels in and around the city. The star of the show is Middlethorpe Hall (0904) 640241, a beautiful mansion house with an exquisite restaurant. The Mount Royale (0904) 6288565 is another well run hotel and is less expensive, while closer to the centre of town the Judges Lodging (0904) 638733 is particularly elegant. Hudson's Hotel and the equally relaxing Grasmead House Hotel (0904) 629996 are two more excellent value establishments. The town centre has many tea shops and small restaurants as well as some pleasant pubs. McCoys (0904) 612191 is a particularly fine restaurant. A noted pub outside the city can be found in Wighill—the White Swan—good value bar snacks. In Fulford village two pubs very handy for the famous course are the Saddle and the Plough and convenient accommodation can be found in Hovingham at the Worsley Arms (0653) 628234.

Next to York, Harrogate probably offers most to both sightseer and golfer. **Pannal** and **Harrogate** are the pick of the courses in the area, the former being a fairly lengthy championship challenge. It is moorland in nature and heavily wooded. Harrogate is possibly the more attractive with its lovely setting at Starbeck near Knaresborough.

The town of Harrogate is renowned for its many fine restaurants. They include the Drum and Monkey (0423) 502650 (superb seafood) and Number Six (0423) 530585. The restaurants in the town's hotels are generally particularly good, notably those at the Hotel Majestic (0423) 568972, the Russell (0423) 509866, the Studley (0423) 560425 and the Balmoral Hotel and Restaurant (0423) 508208.

Before heading towards the Dales and Moors it is worth noting **Selby** in the south of the county. Laid out over fairly sandy subsoil the course could be described as part links, part parkland. An enjoyable day's golf here might be followed by a visit to Monk Fryston and its fine hotel, Monk Fryston Hall (0977) 682369.

Skipton is known as the 'Gateway to the Dales'. The ancient market town has a fine parkland course situated only a mile or so from the town centre. The views are magnificent and a mountain stream runs through the course adding to the many challenges. An appetite created, dinner is recommended at the Devonshire Arms (075671) 0441 in Bolton Abbey. If a good drink is simply all that's required then the Angel at Helton may be preferable.

Ripon is another very charming place. There are only nine holes of golf here (at **Ripon City**) though they

offer great variety nonetheless. The surrounding countryside is quite stupendous. Jervaulx Abbey, founded in 1156 is well worth inspecting (note the outstanding Jervaulx Hall Hotel (0677) 60235), as is Fountains Abbey. For accommodation, Ripon has the Ripon Spa Hotel (0765) 602172 or the more modest Crescent Lodge (0765) 602331, and in nearby Boroughbridge, the Crown (0423) 322328 is a comfortable old inn. Lovers of Theakstons should make a pilgrimage to the White Bear at Masham. One other hotel of distinction in the area is the charming Feversham Arms at Helmsley (0439) 770766.

Two of North Yorkshire's most beautiful courses are situated fairly close to one another in the centre of the county: **Thirsk** & **Northallerton** and **Bedale**. The former lies very close to Thirsk racetrack. The views here are towards the Cleveland Hills on one side and the Hambleton Hills on another. Bedale Golf Club can be found off the A684 and is known for its beautiful spread of trees.

In the north of the county, **Richmond** Golf Club enjoys glorious surroundings. The town itself has a strange mixture of medieval, Georgian and Victorian architecture and is dominated of course by the famous castle. Fine restaurants once again abound: in Moulton, the Black Bull Inn (0325) 377289 is excellent, as is the Bridge Inn (0325) 350106 at Stapleton. Firmly recommended also are the Millers House (0969) 22630 at Middleham and the Burgogne Hotel (0428) 884292 in Reeth. Just south of Richmond, **Catterick Garrison's** Golf Club is well worth a visit.

Dropping back down in the county, **Malton and Norton** shouldn't be overlooked. It is also particularly convenient for those heading towards Ganton on the A64. **Ganton**, thought by many to be the finest inland course in the north of England, boasts a superb setting on the edge of the Vale of Pickering. It is explored fully on a later page.

Yorkshire's coast contrasts greatly with that of Lancashire, with spectacular cliffs rather than dunes dominating the shoreline. Not surprisingly, there are no true links courses to be found here. However, visitors to the resorts of **Filey** and **Scarborough** will be able to enjoy a game with sea and sand and near Flamborough Head there is a testing layout at **Bridlington.**

The splendid Royal Hotel in Scarborough caters for all tastes and the Hotel St Nicholas (0723) 364101 offers similarly fine views. Four more to note in and around Scarborough are the East Ayton Lodge, the Esplanade Hotel (0723) 360382, the Downe Arms (0723) 362471 and, midway between Scarborough and Whitby, the Raven Hall Country House Hotel (0723) 870353 with its own 9 hole course. Slightly inland at Hackness, the Hackness Grange Country Hotel (0723) 882345 enjoys a beautiful setting and makes for a pleasant stay (there's also a pitch and putt course to sneak in some early morning practice).

Humberside

To Yorkshire we must tag on Humberside, much of which once belonged to Yorkshire anyway. It has been a much maligned county and it's not fair to compare Scunthorpe and Grimsby with the likes of Harrogate and York. It has its treasures like any other county: a forty mile stretch of sand, pretty villages nestling in the Wolds and the Holderness countryside; it would be difficult to imagine a more pleasant market town than Beverley and then there's the spectacular Humber Bridge and dramatic Flamborough Head.

Unfortunately, try as I may, I cannot trot off a list of wonderful golf courses. There are enough of them about but there's no Ganton here, alas. The best in the county is arguably at **Hornsea,** famed, of course for its pottery. It is a beautiful heathland course with particularly outstanding greens. One tip—try not to kill the ducks on the 11th!

Beverley is no great distance from **Hornsea** and the Beverley Arms (0482) 869241 is a superb place for a night's rest. Tickton offers the excellent Tickton Grange (0964) 543666 and for a pleasant drink visit the White Horse in Brandesburton.

If one has crossed all 1542 yards of the Humber Bridge to reach the county's largest town then the **Hull** Golf Club at Kirk Ella is probably the best choice for a game,

although **Hessle** is now a very good course too. The Waterfront (0482) 227222 is the most attractive hotel in town. The seafood in Hull ought to be sampled and Ceruttis (0482) 28501 is one of the best places to do so.

Across the Humber, **Elsham** is well thought of (an old haunt of Tony Jacklin's this) and slightly nearer to Scunthorpe, **Holme Hall** at Bottesford is a championship length parkland course. Finally over to the Humberside coast, both **Grimsby** and **Cleethorpes** are also worth a game. Both towns are full of character (characters as well) and if you do play at Grimsby, don't miss out on the local fish and chips—they're reckoned to be the best in Britain!

Artist: **Victor Venner ADDRESSING THE BALL** _Courtesy of_ **Rosenstiel's**

This beautifully appointed country house hotel is set in three acres of its own grounds in the North Yorkshire Moors National Park close to the River Derwent. The hotel is situated in tranquil and idyllic surroundings and the historic city of York is only 38 miles away.

All bedrooms are en suite and furnished to a high standard — four of the bedrooms are honeymoon suites with traditional four poster beds. All rooms have colour televisions, radio alarms, direct dial telephones, trouser presses, hairdryers, tea and coffee making facilities.

The Victorian style restaurant is the perfect, elegant setting in which to enjoy gourmet food. Guests may choose from a comprehensive à la carte or table d'hôte menu which is complemented by an extensive and interesting wine list, ranging from house wines to chateau bottled. The restaurant's speciality is English, French and vegetarian cuisine. The dining room, which can seat up to 120 people, also has a dance floor which makes it the ideal setting for dinner dances, private parties and all types of functions.

The hotel is the perfect place to stay for those who like the countryside yet it is also only three miles from the coast. Guests can visit the coastal resorts of Scarborough and Whitby, enjoy peaceful walks at Cropton and Dalby forests or take a trip on the North Yorkshire Moors Railway. There is fishing on the River Derwent and sea fishing from Scarborough. Horse lovers may book riding sessions and pony trekking from the hotel. Theatre lovers can take advantage of special breaks, available through the hotel, at the nearby Theatre in the Round at Scarborough. For golfers there are at least six golf courses within a 20 mile radius of the hotel, including Ganton, Filey and Scarborough.

East Ayton Lodge
Moor Lane
East Ayton
Scarborough
Tel: (0723) 864227
Fax: (0723) 862680
Free Phone: 0500 131224

They used to say at Ganton that when Harry Vardon played the course twice in the same day, in his afternoon round he'd often hit his tee shots into the very divots he'd created in the morning. The chances are that this was a little bit of Yorkshire bluff but then again the Members at Ganton were fortunate to witness what were probably the very finest years of Britain's greatest ever golfer.

Vardon came to Ganton in 1896, just five years after the Club's formation. Within a few weeks of his appointment he won his first Open Championship at Muirfield defeating the hat-trick-seeking John H Taylor in a play-off. In 1900 Vardon returned from America with the US Open trophy, by which time he'd added two more Open Championships and was half way towards his record number of six victories in that event. By the time that Vardon left the Club in 1903 the name of Ganton had been firmly put on the golfing map.

Located approximately nine miles from the sea, Ganton could hardly be called a golf links in the strict sense but it is often said that it has many of the features of links golf with crisp seaside turf and sandy subsoil. Indeed, whenever new bunkers are cut, sea-shells are often discovered lying beneath the surface—it appears that the whole of the surrounding area was once an arm of the sea.

Golfers wishing to play at Ganton must make prior arrangements with the Club's **Secretary, Air Vice Marshal Price** who may be contacted via the **Ganton Golf Club, Ganton, Scarborough, North Yorkshire YO12 4PA. Tel: (0944) 710329.** The Club's **professional, Gary Brown,** can be reached on **(0944) 710260.** Subject to proof of handicap and prior arrangement, visitors are made most welcome and it is possible to pre-book starting times. The green fees for 1994 were set at £40 for a day's golf during the week with £45 payable at the weekend.

Travelling to the course is made straightforward by the A64. This road links the village directly with Scarborough to the north east (12 miles) and to both York (30 miles) and Leeds (60 miles) to the south west. If approaching from the Humberside region a combination of the A164 to Great Driffield and the B1249 will take you to within two miles of the course, while travellers from further north can avoid the city of York by heading for Thirsk and

thereafter heading for Malton by way of the A170 and the B1257. Malton lies on the A64 road and like Scarborough is approximately twelve miles from Ganton.

Ganton enjoys a beautifully peaceful setting nestling on the edge of the Vale of Pickering and the Yorkshire Moors. While the golf course is indeed beautiful, particularly when the gorse is in full bloom, it is very rarely peaceful and when the winds sweep across it can become fearsomely difficult and there are few inland courses with such cavernous bunkers—111 of them in all! In addition to the many bunkers and the great spread of gorse, there are numerous fir trees and pines which can come into play following a wayward shot, the dog-leg 18th being a notable example and one that provides a very testing finishing hole. The finest hole on the course is thought by many to be the 4th where the second has to be played across a plunging valley towards a plateau green that is heavily bunkered to the right.

The 19th at Ganton has a most welcoming atmosphere and offers an extensive range of catering. (Note the famous Ganton cake — the origins of which are unknown and the recipe a secret!) Dress is informal in the men's bar until 4pm Monday to Friday, although a jacket and tie should be worn in all other public rooms.

Inevitably Ganton's name will always be linked with Vardon's. But another great player also developed his talents on the Yorkshire course—Ted Ray, the famed long hitter who won the Open in 1912 and later found fortune in America winning their Open in 1920. In winning the latter, he ironically held off the challenge of the then 50 year old Vardon. The greatest event in Ganton's distinguished history was undoubtedly the great Ryder Cup match of 1949 when the home team led by three matches to one at the end of the first day only to lose eventually by seven to five. Ben Hogan, convalescing from his near fatal accident, led the American side as non-playing captain.

Three times since the last war the Amateur Championship has been staged at Ganton; in 1964, 1977 and most recently in 1991, the Centenary Year for the Club. The professionals have also visited Ganton with the Dunlop Masters of 1975, won by Bernard Gallacher and in 1981 the PGA Championship, resulting in a third victory in four years for Nick Faldo.

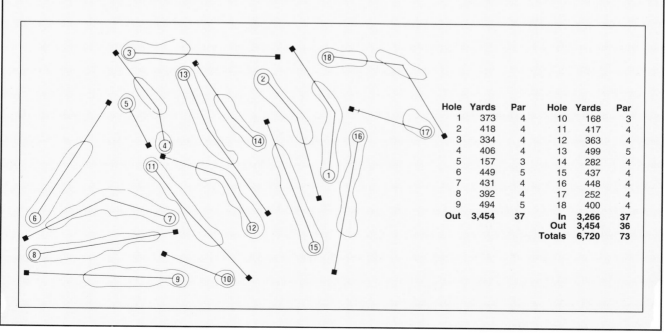

Hole	Yards	Par	Hole	Yards	Par
1	373	4	10	168	3
2	418	4	11	417	4
3	334	4	12	363	4
4	406	4	13	499	5
5	157	3	14	282	4
6	449	5	15	437	4
7	431	4	16	448	4
8	392	4	17	252	4
9	494	5	18	400	4
Out	**3,454**	**37**	**In**	**3,266**	**37**
			Out	3,454	36
			Totals	6,720	73

The hotel is the result of the tasteful blending of two beautiful William IV detatched houses. The proprietors, Richard and Christine Oxtoby, have spent a good deal of effort on restoring the former glory of these buildings and their efforts have been well rewarded.

Any traveller having an interest in English history must surely rank the fascinating city of York at least alongside London. The capital of the north and second city of the realm, it began its long and fascinating life around AD71 as a fortress to protect the Roman 9th Legion. The marauding Vikings gave the city its name, derived from Jorvik or Yorwik. This period of history has been magnificently captured in the Jorvik Viking Centre, one of the most entertaining museums in the country. The Minster or Cathedral is the largest medieval structure in Britain. There has been a Minster on the site since the 7th century, the present one is the fourth and was started about 1220, taking 250 years to complete. The city is still protected by ancient city walls, guarded by defensive bastions, working portcullis' and barbican at the Walmgate bar.

Wander around the Micklegate bar, where traitors' severed heads were displayed or visit the National Rail Museum.

Staying in York involves mixing with some of the most fascinating sights in the world. Relaxing afterwards in the intimate cocktail bar of the Mount Royale, or enjoying a delicious meal in the restaurant overlooking the delightful garden, enhances the whole experience. Enjoying the gracious beauty of the hotel, the style and antiquity of much of the furnishings, or slipping into the secluded heated swimming pool is the perfect way to pamper the body as well as the mind.

The hotel is ideal for the small conference or private dinner party, and is only a short drive from the rolling Yorkshire Dales. The perfect base, offering peace and tranquility, practically in the heart of this wonderful city.

Mount Royale Hotel
The Mount
York YO2 2DA
Tel: (0904) 628856
Fax: (0904) 611171

These days golf is not only played in every foreign field but it is also played in the most unlikely of places. In 1971 American astronaut Captain Alan Sheppard struck two golf shots from the surface of the moon, becoming in the process the only man able to shank a ball 200 yards. Not to be outdone, as ever, Arnold Palmer in 1977 hit three golf balls off the second stage of the Eiffel Tower, while in 1981 at Fulford, York, Bernhard Langer decided to take golf into further alien territory by shinning up a rather large tree and playing his chip shot to the 17th green from amidst its spreading branches.

Fulford Golf Club was founded soon after the turn of the century, but it was only as recently as 1985 that the club celebrated 50 years of playing over the present course. Televised tournament golf has undoubtedly turned the North Yorkshire Club into a 'golfing household name', but in golf's more discerning circles it has for a long time possessed the reputation of having one of the country's finest inland courses.

Golfers wishing to visit Fulford—normally possible between Mondays and Fridays—must make prior arrangements with the Club's **Secretary, Ron Bramley**. Individuals and Society Members alike are required to belong to recognised Golf Clubs and be able to provide proof of handicap. The **Secretary** can be contacted by writing to the club, the full address being, **Fulford Golf Club, Heslington Lane, Fulford, York, YO1 5DY** or by telephoning **(0904) 413579**. Green fees in 1994 were £20 per round during the week and (when available) £35 per round at weekends. Finally the Club's **professional** is **Bryan Hessay (0904) 412882**.

Fulford is situated about a mile to the south of York, just off the A19. For persons travelling from the south of England the A1 and M1 can assist as far as the Leeds area from where the A64 runs straight through to Fulford. Perhaps a more direct route though is to join the A19 near Doncaster. Those approaching York from the north should find their route a little more scenic, the most helpful roads again probably being the A19 (via Thirsk) and the A64 (via Malton—which incidentally passes Ganton further to the north east). Those journeying

from easterly directions should either use the A1099 or the A166 before joining the A64 east of York. The famous city is well served by rail connections and the Leeds/Bradford Airport is located approximately 30 miles to the west of York.

Fulford's homely looking Clubhouse is surprisingly spacious inside with a comfortable lounge and dining room. A full catering service is provided throughout the week. Jackets and ties should be worn in the Clubhouse after 6.30pm.

Measuring 6775 yards from the back tees (par 72) Fulford provides quite a stern test for the club golfer, but it is no more than a medium length course for the professionals. Much of the prodigiously low scoring achieved at Fulford during those PGA European Tour events that it has staged has had precious little to do with the length of the course. As the Members will quickly tell you, it simply reflects the superb condition in which the fairways and the putting surfaces are maintained. Fulford is especially renowned for its fast and very true greens. Certainly, Ian Woosnam found them much to his liking as he holed putt after putt during an extraordinary sequence of eight successive birdies during his final round in the 1985 Benson and Hedges International Tournament. Woosnam's score of 62 that day set a new course record but unfortunately it wasn't quite good enough to prevent Sandy Lyle from joining a distinguished list of Fulford champions. A list which includes the likes of Tony Jacklin, Greg Norman and Lee Trevino.

The 'B&H' has since gone south to St Mellion but Fulford immediately picked up another big event, the Murphy's Cup. In keeping with the tradition of eccentricity established by Bernhard Langer in 1981, the organisers announced before the 1990 event that the first player to hole in one at the 14th would receive 'one hours output of Murphy's Irish Stout' (estimated to be 13,750 pints)!

Most golfers probably won't be leaving Fulford with a 62 under their belt—nor one presumes will they have been shinning up the trees or downing Murphy's by the bucket load—but they are sure to be heading home contented souls having spent a day on what is unquestionably one of the country's most pleasurable golf courses.

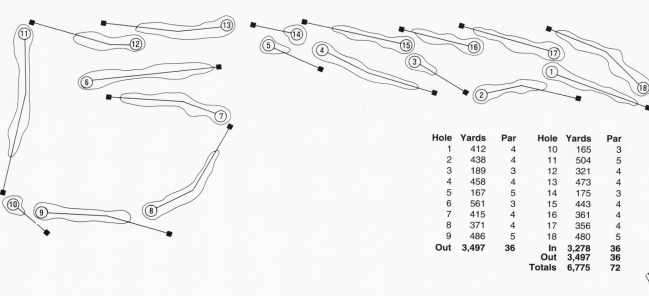

Hole	Yards	Par	Hole	Yards	Par
1	412	4	10	165	3
2	438	4	11	504	5
3	189	3	12	321	4
4	458	4	13	473	4
5	167	5	14	175	3
6	561	3	15	443	4
7	415	4	16	361	4
8	371	4	17	356	4
9	486	5	18	480	5
Out	**3,497**	**36**	**In**	**3,278**	**36**
			Out	**3,497**	**36**
			Totals	**6,775**	**72**

Moortown enjoys an enviable situation. It lies within minutes of the town centre of Leeds, yet it also lies within minutes of the Pennines and the beauty of the Yorkshire Moors. The Club was founded in the autumn of 1909 with the course being laid out by the great Alister Mackenzie. Less than twenty years after its formation Moortown was selected to host the first ever Ryder Cup to be played on British soil. It proved a momentous occasion.

The American side in 1929 was virtually identical to the one that had crushed the British team 9-2 in the inaugural staging at Worcester, Massachusetts two years previously. It included the likes of Walter Hagen, then reigning British Open Champion, Gene Sarazen, Johnny Farrel the US Open Champion, Leo Diegel the U.S.P.G.A. Champion and A1 (there goes a hundred thousand bucks) Watrous. To cut a long story short, the British side won by six matches to four. On the final day George Duncan defeated Walter Hagen by 10 and 8 and Archie Compston defeated Gene Sarazen 6 and 4. Whatever it may have done to American pride, and I note that Wall Street collapsed later that summer, it certainly secured Moortown's place in golfing lore.

Stepping forward in time, **Mr Tom Hughes** is the **Secretary** at Moortown. He may be contacted by telephone on **(0532) 686521**, while the Club's **professional Bryon Hutchinson** can be called on **(0532) 683636**.

Visitors are welcome at Moortown between Mondays and Fridays. Golfing Societies are also welcome during the week although prior arrangement with the secretary is essential. All written correspondence should be addressed to Mr Hughes at **The Moortown Golf Club, Harrogate Road, Alwoodley, Leeds LS17 7DB**. In 1994 the green fees were £35 for a single round or £40 for a full day's golf during the week, with weekend golf costing £40 for a round, or £45 for the day.

Moortown's aforementioned enviable situation is, in part, a product of the A61—the Leeds to Harrogate Road which runs from the heart of the city to within yards of Moortown's front door. For those travelling from the city centre, note that if you reach Eccup Reservoir you have gone too far! Leeds itself is well served by motorway connections, the M62 linking Leeds to Greater Manchester and the M1 joining Sheffield to Leeds. Some roads which may prove helpful include the A64 (York to Leeds) and the A65 (Skipton to Leeds). Our friend the A61 approaches from the north via Ripon, Ripley and Harrogate.

With its great spread of heather and gorse Moortown is occasionally described as heathland, although the absence of sandy sub-soil more properly makes it a moorland type course. Either way, it is always beautifully maintained and has the fine combination of being sufficiently testing yet not too severe.

From its championship tees, the course measures a lengthy 7020 yards, par 71 (SSS 73). The forward tees reduce the length to 6515 yards while for the ladies, Moortown measures 5931 yards par 75 (SSS 73). The generally held view is that the front nine is much the easier of the two halves; this may have something to do with the fact that it begins with what golfers usually term a 'birdiable hole', being a short par five to a fairly open green. Perhaps Moortown's finest hole is the 10th, a par three measuring 176 yards it calls for a shot to a plateau green built on a foundation of rock; it is called 'Gibraltar'—miss it and you're sunk. The 12th is an excellent par five, aptly titled 'The Long' for it stretches to 554 yards; the aforementioned Archie Compston once holed out here in two strokes.

Over the years Moortown has been the venue for several major events, both amateur and professional. Four English Amateur Championships have been held at Moortown, in addition to the English Ladies Amateur and the Ladies British Amateur. In recent years the Car Care professional tournament has been played over the course.

Being situated directly behind the 18th green, Moortown's Clubhouse is very much a nineteenth hole. Lunches are served daily (except Mondays) and both breakfast and dinner can be arranged with prior notice.

In concluding it seems appropriate to return to the course. The difficult, dog-leg 18th at Moortown has an alarming effect on certain people. Countless numbers, including Severiano Ballesteros, have been known to overclub and fire the ball over the green into the Clubhouse area. In the 1929 Ryder Cup during one of the foursomes matches, Joe Turnesa hooked his second behind the marquee adjoining the Clubhouse whereupon his partner promptly sailed it back over the marquee to within a yard of the hole. In the 1974 English Amateur Strokeplay tournament one player actually put his second into the Mens Bar. Opening the Clubhouse windows he played his third straight out onto the green. The Clubhouse certainly has a welcoming atmosphere but this would seem to be taking things a little too far!

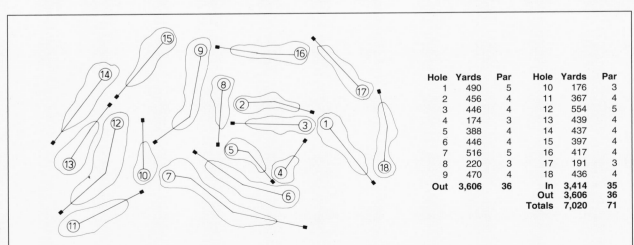

Hole	Yards	Par	Hole	Yards	Par
1	490	5	10	176	3
2	456	4	11	367	4
3	446	4	12	554	5
4	174	3	13	439	4
5	388	4	14	437	4
6	446	4	15	397	4
7	516	5	16	417	4
8	220	3	17	191	3
9	470	4	18	436	4
Out	**3,606**	**36**	**In**	**3,414**	**35**
			Out	**3,606**	**36**
			Totals	**7,020**	**71**

Key

To avoid disappointment it is advisable to telephone in advance

***Visitors welcome at most times
**Visitors usually allowed on weekdays only
*Visitors not normally permitted (Mon, Wed) No visitors on specified days

Approximate Green Fees
A £30 plus
B £20 to £30
C £15 to £25
D £10 to £20
E under £10
F Greens fees on application

Restrictions
G Guests only
H Handicap certificate required
H (24) Handicap of 24 or less
L Letter of introduction required
M Visitor must be a member of another recognised club.

NORTH YORKSHIRE

Aldwark Manor G.C.
(0347) 3353
Aldwark Alne, York
(18)6171 yards/***/C

Bedale G.C.
(0677) 422451
Leyburn Road, Bedale
(18)6565 yards/***/C

Catterick Garrison G.C.
(0748) 833268
Leyburn Road, Catterick Garrison
(18)6331 yards/***/C

Cocksford G.C.
(0937)834253
Cocksford, Stutton
(18)5518 yards/***/C

Crimple Valley G.C.
(0423) 883485
Hookstone Wood Road, Harrogate
(9)2500 yards/***(pm only)/F

Easingwold G.C.
(0347) 21964
Stillngton Road, Easingwold
(18)6262 yards/***/B/H

Filey G.C.
(0723) 513293
West Avenue, Filey
(18)6104 yards/***/C/M

Forest Park G.C.
(0904) 400425
Stockton on the Forest
(18)6211 yards/***/C

Fulford G.C.
(0904) 413579
Heslington Lane, Heslington, York
(18)6775 yards/**/B/H

Ganton G.C.
(0944) 710329
Ganton, Scarborough
(18)6720 yards/**/A/H

Ghyll G.C.
(0282) 842466
Ghyll Brow, Barnoldswick, Colne
(9)5708 yards/***(Sun)/D

Harrogate G. C.
(0423) 862999
Forest Lane Head, Starbeck, Harrogate
(18)6241 yards/***/B/M

Heworth G.C.
(0904) 424618
Muncaster House, Muncastergate, York
(11)6141 yards/***/D

Kirbymoorside G.C.
(0751) 31525
Manor Vale, Kirbymoorside
(18)5958 yards/***/C

Knaresborough G.C.
(0423) 862690
Boroughbridge Road, Knaresborough
(18)6232 yards/***/C/H

Malton and Norton G.C.
(0653) 693882
Welham Park, Malton
(18)6456 yards/***/B/H
(18)6267 yards/***/B/H

Masham G.C.
(0765) 689379
Swinton Road, Masham, Ripon
(9)5244 yards/***/D

Oakdale G.C.
(0423) 567162
Oakdale, Harrogate
(18)6456 yards/***/B/M

Pannal G.C.
(0423) 872628
Follifoot Road, Pannal, Harrogate
(18)6659 yards/**/A/M/H

Pike Hills G.C.
(0904) 706566
Tadcaster Road, Copmanthorpe, York
(18)6120 yards/**/D/M

Raven Hall Hotel & G.C.
(0723) 870353
Ravenscar
(9)1938 yards/***/D

Richmond G.C.
(0748) 825319
Band Hagg, Richmond
(18)5704 yards/***/D

Ripon City G.C.
(0765) 603640
Palace Road, Ripon
(9)5750 yards/***/C

Romanby G.C.
(0609) 779988
Yafforth Road, Northallerton
(18)6663 yards/***/D

Scarborough North Cliff G.C.
(0723) 360786
Burniston Road, Scarborough
(18)6425 yards/***/B/M

Scarborough South Cliff G.C.
(0723) 374737
Deepdale Avenue, Scarborough
(18)6085 yards/***/B/H

Selby G.C.
(0757) 228622
Mill Lane, Brayton Bariff, Selby
(18)6246 yards/**/B/H/M

Settle G.C.
(0729) 825288
Buckhaw Brow, Settle
(9)4600 yards/***(Sun)/D

Skipton G.C.
(0756) 793922
Skipton
(18)6191 yards/***(Mon)/B

Swallow Hall G.C.
(0904) 448219
Crockley Mill, York
(18)3092 yards/***/E

Thirsk & Northallerton G.C.
(0845) 522170
Thornton-le-Street, Thirsk
(9)6257 yards/***/C/M

Whitby G.C.
(0947) 602768
Low Straggpeton, Whitby
(18)5706 yards/***/C/H

York G.C.
(0904) 491840
Lords Moor Lane, Strensall, York
(18)6285 yards/***/B

SOUTH YORKSHIRE

Abbeydale G.C.
(0742) 360763
Twentywell Lane, Dore, Sheffield
(18)6419 yards/***/B

Austerfield Park G.C.
(0302) 710841
Cross Lane, Austerfield, N Bawtry, Doncaster
(18)6828 yards/***/C

Barnsley G.C.
(0226) 382856
Wakefield Road, Staincross, N.Barnsley
(18)6048 yards/***/E

Beauchief G.C.
(0742) 367274
Abbey Lane, Sheffield
(18)5423 yards/***/E

Birley Wood G.C.
(0742) 647262
Birley Lane, Sheffield
(18)5483 yards/***/E

Concord Park G.C.
(0742) 570274
Shiregreen Lane, Sheffield
(18)4321 yards/***/E

Crookhill Park G.C.
(0709) 862979
Carr Lane, Conisborough, nr Doncaster
(18)5846 yards/***/E

Doncaster G.C.
(0302) 868316
Bawtry Road, Bessacarr, Doncaster
(18)6220 yards/**/B/M/H

Doncaster Town Moor G.C.
(0302) 535286
Belle Vue, Doncaster
(18)6094 yards/***(Sun am)/D

Dore and Totley G.C.
(0742) 360492
Bradway Road, Sheffield
(18)6265 yards/***/B/H

Grange Park G.C.
(0709) 559497
Upper Wortley Road, Rotherham
(18)6461 yards/***/E

Hallamshire G.C.
(0742) 302153
Sandygate, Sheffield
(18)6396 yards/***/B

Hallowes G.C.
(0246) 413734
Hallows Lane, Dronfield, Sheffield
(18)6342 yards/***/B

Hickleton G.C.
(0709) 896081
Hickleton, Doncaster
(18)6361 yards/***/C/H/M

Hillsborough G.C.
(0742) 343608
Worall Road, Sheffield
(18)6035 yards/**/B/H

Lees Hall G.C.
(0742) 554402
Hemsworth Road, Norton, Sheffield
(18)6137 yards/***/C

Lindrick G.C.
(0909) 475282
Lindrick Common, Worksop
(18)6615 yards/***(Tues am)/A/H

Owston Park G.C.
(0302) 330821
Owston Hall, nr Carcroft
(9)6148 yards/***/E

Phoenix G.C.
(0709) 363864
Pavilion Lane, Brinsworth, Rotherham
(18)6145 yards/***/D/M

Renishaw Park G.C.
(0246) 432044
Station Road, Renishaw, Sheffield
(18)6253 yards/**/B/H/M

Rotherham G.C.
(0709) 85081
Thrybergh, Rotherham
(18)6323 yards/**/B/M

Roundwood G.C.
(0709) 523471
Rawmarsh, Rotherham
(9)5646 yards/**/D

Sandhill G.C.
(0226) 753444
Little Houghton, Barnsley
(18)6214 yards/***/E

Serlby Park G.C.
(0777) 818268
Serlby, Doncaster
(9)5370 yards/***/D/M/H

Sheffield Transport G.C.
(0742) 373216
Meadow Head, Sheffield
(18)3966 yards/***/F/M

Sickleholme G.C.
(0433) 51306
Saltergate Lane, Bamford, Sheffield
(18)6064 yards/***(Wed am)/D

Silkstone G.C.
(0226) 790328
Field Head, Silkstone, Barnsley
(18)6045 yards/***/C/H

Sitwell Park G.C.
(0709) 541046
Shrogswood Road, Rotherham
(18)6203 yards/***/B/M

Stocksbridge and District G.C.
(0742) 882003
Royd Lane, Townend, Deepcar, Sheffield
(18)5200 yards/***/C/H

Tankersley Park G.C.
(0742) 468247
High Green, Sheffield
(18)6212 yards/**/C

Thorne G.C.
(0405) 812084
Kirton Lane, Thorne
(18)5366 yards/***/E

Tinsley Park G.C.
(0742) 44237
High Hazel Park, Darnall, Sheffield
(18)6064 yards/***/E

Wath G.C.
(0709) 872149
Abdy, Blackamoor, Rotherham
(18)5857 yards/**/C

Wheatley G.C.
(0302) 831655
Armthorpe Road, Doncaster
(18)6345 yards/***/B/H/M

Wombwell Hillies G.C.
(0226) 754433
Wentworth View, Wombwell
(9)2095 yards/***/E

Wortley G.C.
(0742) 885294
Hermit Hill Lane, Wortley, Sheffield
(18)5983 yards/**/B/H/M

WEST YORKSHIRE

Alwoodley G.C.
(0532) 681680
Wigton Lane, Alwoodley, Leeds
(18)6686 yards/**/A/H/M

Baildon G.C.
(0274) 595162
Moorgate, Baildon, Shipley
(18)6225 yards/**/D

Ben Rhydding G.C.
(0943) 608759
High Wood, Ben Rhydding, Ilkley
(9)4711 yards/***(Sat/Sun am)/D

Bingley St Ives G.C.
(0274) 562436
The Mansion, St Ives Estate, Bingley
(18)6480 yards/**/B

Bradford G.C.
(0943) 875570
Hawksworth Lane, Guiseley, Leeds
(18)6259 yards/***(Sat/Sun am)/F

Bradford Moor G.C.
(0274) 638313
Scarr Hall, Pollard Lane, Bradford
(9)5854 yards/***/E

Bradley Park G.C.
(0484) 539988
Bradley Road, Huddersfield
(18)6202 yards/***/E

Branshaw G.C.
(0535) 643235
Branshaw Moor, Keighley
(18)5858 yards/**/D/H

Calverley G.C.
(0532) 569244
Woodhall Lane, Pudsey
(18)5516 yards/***(Sat/Sun am)/D

Castlefields G.C.
(0484) 712108
Rastrick Common, Brighouse

The Worsley Arms Hotel, an attractive stone built Georgian coaching inn, is situated in the heart of Hovingham near York, and has a history stretching back to Roman times. The hotel overlooks the village green and is surrounded by delightful gardens. Having been built in 1841 by Sir William Worsley, the first baronet, it is still owned and run by the Worsley family whose home, Hovingham Hall, stands nearby in wooded parkland amidst beautiful rolling countryside.

Elegant traditional furnishings and open log fires give the Worsley Arms the welcoming and restful atmosphere of a pleasant and comfortable country house. The graceful and spacious sitting rooms are havens of peace and tranquillity and are the ideal place in which to relax over morning coffee, full afternoon tea or an aperitif. There is also a congenial bar where residents can meet both local people and other guests.

The Worsley Arms Hotel often plays host to private shooting parties, and with 500 acres of picturesque nature trails and jogging paths, created entirely by Sir Marcus Worsley, it is an ideal place for an enjoyable picnic. The executive chef is happy to provide picnic hampers and champagne for guests. The Wyvern Restaurant offers an exquisite and imaginative menu. With its 18th century paintings, delightful decor, and a host of fresh flowers, the emphasis is on delicacy of preparation, with intriguing combinations of flavour and texture in the food that it serves. Specialising in local game from the estate, when in season, the carefully selected wine list has to offer quality and fine variety. The chef's own herb garden is recognised in his cooking of fine fresh herbs.

Situated on the edge of the Howardian Hills, close to the Yorkshire Dales, the Wolds and the North Yorkshire Moors National Park, the Worsley Arms Hotel and Hovingham Hall are within easy driving distance from the City of York, Castle Howard and other Heritage and National Trust properties. The hotel offers a warm and friendly personal welcome to its guests and staff will ensure that your stay in the heart of Yorkshire is both restful and memorable.

The Worsley Arms Hotel
Hovingham
York
YO6 4LA
Tel: (0653) 628234
Fax: (0653) 628130

(6)2406 yards/*/F/M

City of Wakefield G.C.
(0924) 367442
Lupset Park, Howbury Road,
Wakefield
(18)6299 yards/***/E

Clayton G.C.
(0274) 880047
Thornton View Road, Clayton,
Bradford
(9)5518 yards/***(Sun)/E

Cleckheaton and District G.C.
(0274) 851266
Bradford Road, Cleckheaton
(18)5847 yards/***/B

Crosland Heath G.C.
(0484) 653216
Felk Site Road, Crosland Heath,
Huddersfield
(18)5962 yards/***/F

Dewsbury District G.C.
(0924) 492399
The Pinnacle, Sands Lane, Mirfield
(18)6256 yards/**/C/H

East Bierley G.C.
(0274) 681023
South View Road, Bierley, Bradford
(9)4692 yards/**(Sun)/D

Elland G.C.
(0422) 72505
Hammerstones, Leach Lane, Elland
(9)5526 yards/***/D

Fulneck G.C.
(0532) 574049
Fulneck, Pudsey
(9)5564 yards/**/D

Garforth G.C.
(0532) 863308
Long Lane, Garforth, Leeds
(18)6296 yards/**/B/H/M

Gott's Park G.C.
(0532) 638232
Armley Bridge Road, Leeds
(18)4960 yards/***/E

Halifax G.C.
(0422) 244171
Union Lane, Ogden, Halifax
(18)6037 yards/***/B

Halifax Bradley Hall G.C.
(0422) 374108
Stainland Road, Holywell Green,
Halifax
(18)6213 yards/***/B

Halifax West End G.C.
(0422) 363293
Highroad Well, Halifax
(18)6003 yards/***/C/H

Hanging Heaton G.C.
(0924) 461606
White Cross Road, Bennett Lane,
Dewsbury
(9)5874 yards/**/D/M

Headingley G.C.
(0532) 679573
Back Church Lane, Adel, Leeds
(18)6298 yards/***/B/H

Headley G.C.
(0274) 833481
Headley Lane, Thornton,Bradford
(9)4914 yards/***/E

Hebden Bridge G.C.
(0422) 843733
Great Mount, Wadsworth, Hebden
Bridge
(9)5064 yards/***/D

Horsforth G.C.
(0532) 586819
Layton Road, Horsforth, Leeds
(18)6243 yards/***/B/H

Howley Hall G.C.
(0924) 472432
Scotchman Lane, Morley, Leeds
(18)6029 yards/***(Sat)/C/H

Huddersfield G.C.
(0484) 426203
Fixby Hall, Fixby, Huddersfield
(18)6424 yards/***/A

Ilkley G.C.
(0943) 600214
Middleton, Ilkley
(18)6256 yards/***/A

Keighley G.C.
(0535) 604778
Howden Park, Utley, Keighley

(18)6149 yards/**/B/H

Leeds G.C.
(0532) 659203
Elmete Lane, Leeds
(18)6097 yards/**/C/M

Lightcliffe G.C.
(0422) 202459
Knowle Top Road, Lightcliffe,
Halifax
(9)5388 yards/***(Wed/Sat)/D/M

Longley Park G.C.
(0484) 422305
Maple Street, off Somerset Road,
Huddersfield
(9)5269 yards/**(Thurs)/D

Low Laithes G.C.
(0924) 273275
Parkmill Flushdyke, Ossett
(18)6468 yards/**/B

Marsden G.C.
(0484) 844253
Mount Road, Hemplow, Marsden
(9)5702 yards/**/E

Meltham G.C.
(0484) 850227
Thick Hollins, Melton
(18)6145 yards/***(Wed/Sat)/B

Middleton Park G.C.
(0532) 700449
Middleton Park, Leeds
(18)5233 yards/***/E

Mid Yorkshire G.C.
(0977) 374762
Havercroft Lane, Darrington
(18)6500 yards/***/C/H

Moor Allerton G.C.
(0532) 661154
Coal Road, Wike, Leeds
(27)6045 yards/**/B/H
6222 yards/**/B/H
6930 yards/**/B/H

Moortown G.C.
(0532) 686521
Harrogate Road, Alwoodley, Leeds
(18)7020 yards/***/A/H

Mount Skip G.C.
(0422) 892896
Hebden Bridge
(9)5114 yards/***/F

Normanton G.C.
(0924) 892943
Snydale Road, Normanton,
Wakefield
(9)5288 yards/***(Sun)/D

Northcliffe G.C.
(0274) 596731
High Bank Lane, Shipley
(18)6104 yards/**(Sat/Tues)/B/H

Otley G.C.
(0943) 465329
West Busk Lane, Otley
(18)6235 yards/***(Sat)/B

Oulton Park G.C.
(0532) 823152
Oulton, Leeds
(18)6500 yards/***/E

Outlane G.C.
(0422) 374762
Slack Lane, Outlane, Huddersfield
(18)6003 yards/***/C

Painthorpe House G.C.
(0924) 255083
Painthorpe Lane, Crigglestone
(9)4520 yards/***(Sun)/E

Phoenix Park G.C.
(0274) 667573
Phoenix Park, Dick Lane, Thornbury
(9)4774 yards/**/F

Pontefract & District G.C.
(0977) 792241
Park Lane, Pontefract
(18)6227 yards/**/B
Pontefract Park G.C.
(0977) 702799
Park Road, Pontefract
(9)4068 yards/***/F

Queensbury G.C.
(0274) 882155
Brighouse Road, Queensbury,
Bradford
(9)5102 yards/**/D/M

Rawdon G.C.
(0532) 506040
Buckstone Drive, Rawdon, Leeds
(9)5960 yards/**/D/H

Riddlesden G.C.
(0535) 60214
Elam Wood Road, Riddlesden
(18)4185 yards/***/D

Roundhay G.C.
(0532) 662695
Park Lane, Leeds
(9)5166 yards/***/E

Ryburn G.C.
(0422) 831355
Norland, Sowerby Bridge, Halifax
(9)5002 yards/***/D/H

Sand Moor G.C.
(0532) 685180
Alwoodley Lane, Leeds
(18)6429 yards/**/B/M

Scarcroft G.C.
(0532) 892263
Syke Lane, Leeds
(18)6426 yards/***/B/H

Shipley G.C.
(0274) 568652
Beckfoot Lane,
Cottingley Bridge, Bingley
(18)6218 yards/***(Tues/Sat)/B

Silsden G.C.
(0535) 652998
High Brunthwaite, Silsden
(14)4870 yards/***/D

South Bradford G.C.
(0274) 679195
Pearson Road, Odsal, Bradford
(9)6004 yards/**/D

South Leeds G.C.
(0532) 700479
Gipsy Lane, Beeston Ring Road
(18)5890 yards/**/C/M

Temple Newsam G.C.
(0532) 645624
Temple Newsam Road, Leeds
(18)6448 yards/***/E
(18)6029 yards/***/E

Todmorden G.C.
(0706) 812986
Rive Rocks, Cross Stone, Todmorden
(9)5878 yards/***/C/H

Wakefield G.C.
(0924) 258778
Woodthorpe Lane, Sandal,
Wakefield
(18)6626 yards/***/B/H

West Bowling G.C.
(0274) 724449
Newall Hall, Rooley Lane, Bradford
(18)5770 yards/**/B/H

West Bradford G.C.
(0274) 542767
Chellow Grange, Bradford
(18)5752 yards/***/C

West End G.C.
(0422) 353608
The Racecourse, Paddock Lane,
Highroad Well
(18)6003 yards/***/C/H

Wetherby G.C.
(0937) 583375
Linton Lane, Wetherby
(18)6235 yards/***/B/H

Whitwood G.& C.C.
(0977) 512835
Altofts Lane, Whitwood, Castleford
(9)6282 yards/***/F

Woodhall Hills G.C.
(0532) 554594
Woodhall Road, Calverley, Pudsey
(18)6102 yards/***/B

Woodsome Hall G.C.
(0484) 602971
Fenay Bridge, Huddersfield
(18)6080 yards/***(Tues)/B/H

HUMBERSIDE

Beverley & East Riding G.C.
(0482) 868757
Anti Mill, The Westwood, Beverley
(18)6164 yards/***/D

Boothferry G.C.
(0430) 430364
Spaldington, Howden, Goole
(18)6651 yards/***/E

Bridlington G.C.
(0262) 606367
Belvedere Road, Bridlington
(18)6491 yards/***/D

Brough G.C.
(0482) 667374
Cave Road, Brough
(18)6159 yards/**(Wed am)/B/H

Cave Castle Hotel & G.C.
(0430) 421286)
South Cave, Brough
(18)6409 yards/***/D

Cleethorpes G.C.
(0472) 814060
Kings Road, Cleethorpes
(18)6015 yards/***/C

Driffield G.C.
(0377) 253116
Sunderlandwick, Driffield
(18)6199 yards/***/C

Elsham G.C.
(0652) 680291
Barton Road, Elsham, Brigg
(18)6411 yards/**/B/M

Flamborough Head G.C.
(0262) 850333
Lighthouse Road, Flamborough,
Bridlington
(18)5438 yards/***(Sun am)/D/M

Ganstead Park G.C.
(0482) 811280
Longdales Lane, Coniston, Hull
(18)6801 yards/***(Wed/Sun
am)/C/H

Grimsby G.C.
(0472) 342630
Littlecoates Road, Grimsby
(18)6058 yards/***/C/H

Hainsworth Park G.C.
(0964) 542362
Brandesburton, Driffield
(18)6003 yards/***/D

Hessle G.C.
(0482) 650171
Westfield Road, Cottingham, Hull
(18)6638 yards/**(Tues am)/C/H

Holme Hall G.C.
(0724) 862078
Holme Hall, Bottesford Road,
Scunthorpe
(18)6475 yards/**/C/H

Hornsea G.C.
(0964) 532020
Rolston Road, Hornsea
(18)6450 yards/***(Tues)/C

Hull G.C.
(0482) 658919
The Hall, Packman Lane, Kirk Ella
(18)6242 yards/**/B/H

Immingham G.C.
(0469) 75298
Church Lane, Immingham, Grimsby
(18)6161 yards/**/E

Kingsway G.C.
(0724) 840945
Kingsway, Scunthorpe
(9)1915 yards/***/E

Normanby Hall G.C.
(0724) 720226
Normanby Park, Normanby,
Scunthorpe
(18)6548 yards/***/D

Scunthorpe G.C.
(0724) 866561
Burringham Road, Scunthorpe
(18)6281 yards/**/B/H/M

Springhead Park G.C.
(0482) 656309
Willerby Road, Hull
(18)6439 yards/***/E

Sutton Park G.C.
(0482) 74242
Salthouse Road, Sutton, Hull
(18)6251 yards/***/E

Withernsea G.C.
(0964) 612258
Chestnut Avenue, Withernsea
(9)5112 yards/***/E/M

Artist: **Arthur Weaver THE GREEN** *Courtesy of:* **Burlington Gallery**

A gracious, stone-built Lakeland home, with a wealth of mahogany woodwork, Michaels Nook is quietly tucked away overlooking the Grasmere valley and surrounded by well-kept lawns and beautiful trees. It was opened as a hotel over twenty years ago by owner Reg Gifford, a respected antique dealer, and furnishings, enhanced by an abundance of flowers and plants, reflect his appreciation of English furniture, antique rugs, prints and porcelain. The Hotel retains the mellowness of the private home, and a hint of pleasing eccentricity, accentuated by the presence of a Great Dane and some exotic cats.

There are twelve, lovely, individually-designed bedrooms, all with en suite bathrooms, and two magnificent suites. Each room has colour television and direct dial telephone, and is provided with many thoughtful extra touches, such as fresh flowers, fruit, and mineral water. Full room service is available.

In the Restaurant, polished tables gleam, set with fine crystal and porcelain, and only the best fresh ingredients are used for dishes memorable for their delicate flavour and artistic presentation. Different choices are offered each day. A very extensive

Wine List offers selections from all the best wine-producing areas, and makes for fascinating reading, as well as excellent drinking. The panelled Oak Room, with handsome stone fireplace and gilt furnishings, hosts Director and Senior Manager meetings and private celebrations.

Spectacular excursions, by car or on foot, start from the doorstep of this delightful house, and encompass some of Britain's most impressive scenery. Dove Cottage, Wordsworth's home during his most creative period, is close at hand, and Beatrix Potter's farm at Sawrey only a short drive away.

The Hotel itself has three acres of landscaped grounds, and a further ten acres of woodland and wild fell, plus a speciality rhododendron garden covering four acres of nearby hillside. Guests are also welcome to make use of the heated swimming pool, and other health facilities of The Wordsworth Hotel, less than a mile away, and under the same ownership. Both Hotels offer special arrangements with Keswick Golf Club, and enjoy a close proximity to some of the excellent northern links courses.

Michaels Nook
Grasmere
Ambleside
Cumbria LA22 9RP
Tel: (05394) 35496
Fax: (05394) 35765

There are two things which keep people returning time and again to the beautiful market town of Appleby-in-Westmorland.

Firstly, there's the opportunity to enjoy a memorable round of golf on the 18-hole moorland course. The panoramic views which surround you are truly splendid and the course is a pleasure to play, with superb greens and just enough variety and challenge to keep you happily satisfied for all of its 5895 yards.

Secondly, there's nowhere nicer to return to after a rewarding day's golf than the relaxing and friendly three-star Appleby Manor Country House Hotel. Just a few minutes drive from the course, the hotel is set in wooded grounds overlooking Appleby Castle with views which are as equally as impressive as those on the course.

You can relax tired muscles in a variety of ways in the hotel's super indoor leisure club equipped with a heated pool, jacuzzi, sauna, solarium and steam-room. In the award winning restaurant you will be pleasantly surprised by the abundance of good food served by your talented chef.

The cocktail bar, with its impressive range of over 70 single-malt whiskies, will keep you occupied after dinner and you will find everything you need in your comfortable bedroom, including remote-control colour television with film and satellite channels, tea/coffee facilities, fully-tiled private bathroom, direct-dial telephone and hairdryer.

Great value special breaks of two days or more are available all year round at the hotel, with golf booked direct with the club. Please telephone for a full-colour brochure.

Appleby Manor Country House Hotel
Appleby-In-Westmorland
Cumbria CA16 6JB
Tel: (017683) 51571
Fax: (017683) 52888

In the very heart of English Lakeland, and the centre of one of its loveliest villages, The Wordsworth combines the sophistication of a first-class Hotel with the magnificence of the surrounding countryside. Situated in two acres of landscaped grounds next to the churchyard where William Wordsworth is buried, its name honours the memory of the area's most famous son. The scenery that so inspired the Lake Poets can be enjoyed from the peaceful lounges, furnished with fine antiques , or in the Conservatory and Cocktail Bar with the aid of a favourite aperitif or specially mixed drink.

The Hotel has 35 most attractive and comfortable bedrooms, each with private bathroom, colour TV, radio, direct-dial telephone, and intercom. Some rooms have romantic four-poster beds (a honeymoon package is offered) and there are two suites. 24-hour room service is available. The facilities of the Coleridge Room are ideal for private functions of up to 100 guests, and a marquee on the lawns is not uncommon for larger parties, especially summer weddings.

The Prelude Restaurant, named after Wordsworth's famous autobiographical poem, is the place to enjoy the best of the seasonal produce skilfully prepared by the Chef and his team. The accompanying Wine List combines familiar favourites with some pleasantly surprising 'finds', and a fine selection of claret and burgundies. The Hotel's own pub - 'The Dove and Olive Branch' -is a friendly meeting place for a traditional beer or tasty snack, and has recently received accolades from The Good Pub Guide and national newspapers.

For the energetic and those wishing to pamper themselves, the Wordsworth has an indoor heated swimming pool, opening onto a sun-trap terrace, a jacuzzi, mini-gym, sauna and solarium. In the area, the sports-minded can indulge in clay shooting, fishing and all manner of water sports.

For the golfer, the Hotel can arrange free rounds from Monday to Friday at Keswick Golf Club - par 71 - in a delightful valley setting amidst spectacular mountain scenery. It is also within easy reach of several excellent links courses, such as Silloth, as well as the famous championship courses at Royal Lytham and Royal Birkdale. The Hotel Management will do whatever it can to assist with arrangements at these courses.

The Wordsworth Hotel
Grasmere
Ambleside
Cumbria LA22 9SW
Tel: (05394) 35592
Fax: (05394) 35765

Just as Devon is often viewed by holiday-makers as a mere stepping stone to Cornwall (which as a Devonian pleases me greatly!) so the far north of England is often viewed by golfers as a mere pretty pathway to the delights of Scotland—Turnberry, Gleneagles etc. Indeed some even believe that north of Lytham there's nothing much in the way of golfing challenges until the 'Bonnie Land' is reached. To those I simply say, 'shame on you!

Our region covers Cumbria as well as the North East. Now admittedly Cumbria is hardly perfect golfing territory. A Sunningdale in the middle of the Lake District is hard to imagine (although some spectacular holes are clearly possible!) But there are a number of golf courses in between the fells and the lakes, and furthermore Cumbria comprises more than just the Lake District. Before the counties were rearranged and renamed in the early seventies, Cumberland was the most northerly county in the West of England, and home not only to the famous sausage but to the **Silloth-on-Solway** Golf Club, which is, dare I say it, as good a links as you'll find anywhere in England. As for the North East, **Seaton Carew** near Hartlepool offers championship golf of a very high calibre and **Slaley Hall** is full of Northumbrian promise, while even further north along the Northumberland coast lie a string of golfing pearls— **Alnmouth, Dunstanburgh, Bamburgh** and **Goswick**— good courses with breathtaking scenery.

Cumbria

Let us make a start in the Lake District with the hope that in addition to the picnic hamper and the climbing boots, we've left room in the back of the car for the golf clubs.

The Lake District is the land of poets, 'Where breezes are soft and skies are fair' (W C Bryant), and 'Where nature reveals herself in all her wildness, all her majesty' (S Roger).

At Keswick the golfer can meet the poet. **Keswick** Golf Club lies four miles east of the lakeland town via the A66. Whilst the course now measures well over 6000 yards, it recently held a rather dubious claim to being the shortest course in Britain—in 1976 there was a splendid clubhouse but only five holes—no doubt some remarkable scores were returned! These days scoring is a little more difficult with several streams and some dense woodland to be avoided. As one might imagine the views are quite something and a visit will never disappoint.

Still in the Lakes, we find **Kendal**, a fine parkland course, just three-quarters of a mile from the town centre and only two miles from the M6 link road. Although a fair bit shorter than Keswick its first hole is often considered to be the toughest opener in Britain—231 yards, uphill all the way, out of bounds to the left and woods to the right! Should one make it to the 2nd the holes get much easier. However there is an infamous quarry on the right of the 15th fairway which has been known to receive more than golf balls. One frustrated chap after firing ball after ball into its murky depths decided to throw in his bag for good measure. Fortunately he didn't throw himself in as well but the word is he never played golf again. Who said it was only a game!

The Golf Club at **Windermere** should prove much more relaxing. The club has recently celebrated its centenary and the course has improved considerably in the last few years. An ideal place for a game of golf while on holiday in the Lakes, we have featured Windermere on a later page. Another first class course, still within the National Park boundary is at **Penrith**, close to the A6 but a lovely setting near Ullswater and several very challenging holes.

Recommending both superior and reasonably priced establishments in the area is a difficult task, to put it mildly, simply because there are so many. But hopefully the following suggestions will prove of assistance. Grasmere is a personal favourite and here Michael's Nook (05394) 35496 is an outstanding country hotel with an excellent restaurant. The Wordsworth (05394) 35592 is a grand hotel while at White Moss House (05394) 35295—the poet's former residence—another superb restaurant can be found. Another truly first class establishment in the area is the delightful Nanny Brow Hotel near Ambleside, (05394) 32036, with views to match. Slightly nearer to Keswick, Armathwaite Hall (07687) 76551 in Bassenthwaite is charming, while for a really relaxing country inn, the Pheasant Inn (07687) 76234 in Bassenthwaite Lake can have few equals. In Keswick itself there is the Woolpack (0539) 723852.

Penrith is a bustling town with numerous hotels. As an alternative to staying in town Ullswater naturally attracts and here the Sharrow Bay Hotel (07684) 86301 and its restaurant are particularly stylish. Cheaper accommodation is available nearby in one of the area's best pubs, the Queens Head at Askham, while the Old Church Hotel at Watermillock offers spectacular views (07684) 86204. Also worth hunting out is the Brandelhow Guesthouse (0768) 64470.

Oh-so-popular Windermere offers a wealth of good hotels. Three certainly meriting attention are the Miller Howe (05394) 42536, the Langdale Chase (05394) 32201 and the moderately priced Applegarth Hotel. Rogers (05394) 44954 in the High Street is another recommended restaurant. Among other first class establishments near Windermere Golf Club we can also recommend Gilpin Lodge Country House (05394) 88818 and Linthwaite House Hotel (05394) 88600, while the Burn How Garden House Hotel (05394) 46226 offers a luxurious and rather unique style of accommodation. Other ideas for a 19th hole in the Lake District must include the Old Vicarage (05395) 52381 at Witherslack, the Mortal Man (05394) 33193 at Troutbeck (wake up to a glorious setting), the Wild Boar in Crook (05394) 45225 and for a really popular pub try the Masons Arms in Cartmel Fell.

To the south of Cumbria the highly rated **Furness** Golf Club lays claim to being the oldest in the county. A true links and being quite exposed, scoring well is often more difficult than the card suggests. An after golf thought here is the excellent Abbey House Hotel (0229) 838282, while Eccle Riggs Manor (0229) 716398 is equally recommended. Also pleasant is Bridgefield House (0229) 885239 at Spark Bridge and further inland the Uplands Country House Hotel (05395) 36248 is extremely good value.

Travelling along Cumbria's coast, **Seascale** is soon reached. Another links, and somewhat underrated. One shouldn't be put off by the thought of being close to the Seascale nuclear installations (and jokes about balls glowing in the dark are uncalled for): it's an excellent test of golf—some tremendous views too towards the Wasdale Screes and the Scafell Range. North of Workington (en route to Silloth) there is a fair course at **Maryport**. There is doubtless some convenient accommodation nearby but I'll recommend a trip inland to another personal favourite, Buttermere, one of the more westerly lakes, and where the Bridge Hotel (07687) 70252 is very comfortable.

Silloth-on-Solway has already been referred to and is again featured separately on a later page. The course certainly deserves more than a fleeting visit and two handy hotels in the town are the Queen's Hotel (06973) 31373 and the Golf Hotel (06973) 31438. Both are very

Crosby Lodge was purchased by the Sedgwick family in 1970, and has been skilfully restored and converted into the romantically beautiful country house hotel it is today.

The front door opens onto an enormous welcoming log fire, with an oak staircase leading up to the bedrooms. Each bedroom is decorated and designed individually, with en suite bathrooms. Various period pieces, such as half-tester beds, have been retained, whilst at the same time the hotel provides first class modern amenities. Crosby Lodge has an established reputation for excellence and the large spacious rooms, full of antiques and elegantly furnished, welcome guests with a comfortable and relaxed atmosphere.

Overlooking tree-lined parkland, the delightful dining room, with its beamed ceiling, gleaming cutlery and long windows, is a haven for the connoisseur of good food and wine. Deliciously exciting menus feature authentic continental cuisine alongside the very best of traditional British fare. The four course table d'hote menu has a vast choice and is complemented by a smaller a la carte menu providing such delights as steaks, scampi and Dover sole. The Crosby Lodge sweet trolley is renowned far and wide, and coffee and delicious home-made sweetmeats can be taken in the charming lounge and cocktail bar. Chef Proprietor Michael Sedgwick produces exciting dishes using fresh, mainly local ingredients, ensuring everything is to the highest standard.

The wine list, written by daughter Philippa, is exceptional offering from the very best house wines, through to the hidden cellar for the connoisseur

To the visitor, Crosby Lodge offers untold days of pleasure, with the Lake District and Scottish Lowlands so near at hand. Historic Hadrian's Wall, stunning Cumberland and Northumberland country and the ancient border city of Carlisle await the visitor. Travelling further afield, yet returning to Crosby Lodge in the evening, one can reach Edinburgh, a city steeped in history and culture. For the golfer the hotel is ideal, with arrangements easily made on the new Riverside Course, only minutes away, or indeed on a variety of courses at Carlisle, Brampton, Penrith and Silloth.

Featured in the Egon Ronay, Michelin, with three AA stars, 1 rosette, and a British Tourist Four Crown Highly Commended hotel, Crosby Lodge is fully deserving of the praise it receives. With an emphasis on comfort, relaxation, good food, traditional courtesy and old-fashioned hospitality, Michael and Patricia Sedgwick, son James and staff will ensure that you have a memorable stay and every assistance with your arrangements. Situated off the A689 between Carlisle and Brampton. Leave M6 motorway at Exit 44.

Crosby Lodge
Country House Hotel and Restaurant
Crosby-on-Eden
Carlisle
Cumbria CA6 4QZ
Tel: (0228) 573618
Fax: (0228) 573428

comfortable and specialise in golf packages, as for that matter does the nearby Skinburness Hotel (06973) 32332. Golfers in Carlisle are well catered for with two good courses in the area, **Carlisle** and **Brampton** (or Talkin' Tarn as the latter is sometimes called). Brampton is located to the east of Carlisle off the B6413 and is a beautifully kept course, laid out four hundred feet above sea level with extensive views towards the nearby hills. It is probably best described as moorland whereas Carlisle, equally well maintained, is more of a parkland type. For an overnight stop in Carlisle the Crown and Mitre (0228) 25491 is welcoming while in Brampton, Farlam Hall (06977) 46234 is an excellent hotel and the Hare and Hounds (06977) 3456 a comfortable inn. The Angus Hotel (0228) 23546 is inexpensive and convenient for the city centre. Fantails (0228) 560239 in Wetheral is possibly the best restaurant in the area and for a pleasant water setting, the Crosby Lodge at Crosby-on-Eden (0228) 573618 is recommended.

Before leaving Cumbria, a quick mention for the somewhat isolated **Appleby** Golf Club. If you are in the vicinity it's well worth a visit. A splendid combination of moorland and heathland—very colourful. Remote, perhaps but in nearby Appleby-in-Westmoreland the Appleby Manor (07683) 51571 awaits while for a nearby friendly inn note the Black Swan at Ravenstondale.

The North East

And so to the North East—and what a mixture! Durham, Cleveland, Tyne & Wear and Northumberland. An area encompassing Tyneside, Teeside and Wearside, it also includes the Cleveland Hills, the Cheviots and the wild spectacular coast of ancient Northumbria. The four modern-day counties stretch from the far end of the Yorkshire Pennines and intrude into the Scottish Borders, the greater part of Northumberland lying north of Hadrian's Wall.

The appeal of any golf course can be affected greatly by its surroundings and nowhere in Britain does the accompanying landscape seem to dictate the enjoyment of a game as much as in this part of the world. The contrast between the industrial and rural North East is dramatic to put it mildly. The golf courses in the former tend towards the uninspiring—Seaton Carew being one great exception—whilst the likes of Bamburgh Castle and Hexham offer such magnificent scenery that the quality of the golf can often be relegated to a secondary consideration.

Cleveland

Beginning in the south of the region, Cleveland is one of the smallest counties in England and not surprisingly has very few courses. **Seaton Carew** is far and away the best in the county. In fact, it is almost certainly the best links course on the East Coast of England, north of Norfolk. It is located approximately three miles south of Hartlepool and has a skyline dominated by far-off chimneys which at night appear like giant torches. Golf here is played amidst the dunes with gorse and devilishly thick rough lining the fairways. In recent years several important championships have been held here, including the British Boys Championship in 1978 and 1986.

South of the Tees, despite its name, the golf course at **Saltburn** isn't right by the sea, it's about a mile west of the town and is a well-wooded meadowland course. Quite a contrast to Seaton Carew: a trifle easier, but certainly worth a visit. Around Teeside itself there are courses at Redcar (**Cleveland**), **Middlesborough** and **Billingham** but perhaps the best or most enjoyable in

the area is found at **Eaglescliffe**, a hilly course where there are some marvellous views of the Cleveland Hills.

The top hotel in this area for golfers is undoubtedly Hardwick Hall (0740) 620253, well placed for Seaton Carew and the courses in County Durham. There are a number of other good hotels in the county, although as everywhere some of them are very modern and unfortunately rather characterless. An exception to this is the Crathorne Hall Hotel (0642) 700398 at Yarm. Also handy for Seaton Carew is probably the Grand (0429) 266345 in Hartlepool. At Saltburn an excellent pub can be recommended, namely the Ship with its splendid sea views, while a little inland at Moorsholm the Jolly Sailor offers some very good food. Those playing at Eaglescliffe can enjoy midday sustenance (or evening celebration) at the Blue Bell.

Durham

Crossing into Durham, people often talk of (some even whistle about) Old Durham Town, but of course it's very much a city with a cathedral that has been adjudged the most beautiful building in the world. Without doubt the course to visit here is **Brancepeth Castle**, four miles south west of the city and set in very beautiful surroundings. Rather like St Pierre at Chepstow the course occupies land that was formerly a deer park and a 13th century church and castle provide a magnificent backcloth. Perhaps the most convenient place to stay is at the Bridge Hotel 091 378 0524 in Croxdale but there are a number of good hotels in Durham itself including the Royal County 091 386 6821. Just north of Durham is the historic Lumley Castle 091 389 1111 which offers first class food and accommodation overlooking the course at Chester-le-Street. Lothlorien Guesthouse 091 371 0067 meanwhile, will leave plenty of spare pennies with which to explore the region's many attractions.

Further north, **Beamish Park** near Stanley is another laid out in a former deer park (belonging to Beamish Hall) and is worth a detour if heading along the A1. **Bishop Auckland** in the centre of the county is a pleasant parkland course. The land here belongs to the Church of England and one of the terms of the club's lease is that the course has to close on Good Friday and Christmas Day. Play then at your peril!

To the south west of Bishop Auckland, **Barnard Castle** enjoys yet another delightful setting. More of a moorland course than anything else, it has a stream that must be crossed seventeen times during a round! There are some fine establishments nearby in which to celebrate (or perhaps even dry out?) In Barnard Castle itself the Jersey Farm Hotel (0833) 38223 is excellent value for a night's stay while those just looking for a bar snack and a drink might visit the nearby villages of Cotherstone (The Fox and Hounds) and Ronaldkirk (The Rose and Crown.) A slightly longer drive to Eggleston, also possible from Bishop Auckland, and one finds the Three Tuns—famed for its pub lunches. Midway between Bishop Auckland and Darlington at Newton Aycliffe is the **Woodham** Golf and Country Club which has a growing reputation.

Darlington is the largest town in the county. It may not have the appeal of Durham but for golfers there's a twin attraction: to the north, **Haughton Grange** with its great selection of MacKenzie greens and to the south, **Blackwell Grange** with its fine variety of trees. Both courses are parkland and always superbly maintained. For an ideal base one doesn't really have to look further than the 17th century Blackwell Grange Moat House

Hardwick Hall enjoys a reputation as one of the most beautifully situated country house hotels in the north east of England.

Set in 120 acres of parkland, there are splendid country-side views for guests to enjoy, yet the hotel is only five minutes from the two main roads servicing the region, the A1(M) and the A19.

The very location of the hotel makes it ideal for golfers travelling from all over Britain to sample the challenge of one of the foremost links courses on the east coast, Seaton Carew. While this celebrated links has played host to many a championship over the years, it is just one of a number of excellent courses to be enjoyed in the immediate vicinity of Hardwick Hall with Brancpeth Castle to the north, Bishop Auckland to the west and Woodham to the south.

Golfers will find the rooms at the hotel appointed to a very high standard having recently been refurbished with deluxe facilities. The restaurant boasts not only first class cuisine but a magnificent oil painted ceiling while private parties can be accommodated in the lounge with a roaring log fire and tables bedecked with the best china, crystal and silver ware for that special occasion.

Hardwick Hall and its management are well known for the high standards to which they cater for all their guests and the hotel is a popular venue for conferences and corporate hospitality occasions. An exceedingly diverse range of sporting and leisure facilities can be tailormade to suit requirements and the capacity of the conference and banqueting facilities range from 15 to 230 delegates in the hotel itself, while a marquee to accommodate up to 400 guests can be erected on the lawn.

While the proximity of Sedgefield racecourse is another attraction for sporting guests and for companies indulging in corporate entertaining, the historic city of Durham and the many other attractions of this former land of the Prince Bishops have long been a draw for tourists from far and wide and few hotels are better placed to serve all visitors as Hardwick Hall.

Hardwick Hall Hotel
Sedgefield
Cleveland
TS21 1EH
Tel: (0740) 620253
Fax: (0740) 622771

(0325) 380888. However, a good French restaurant to note in the town is the Bishops House and for a drink try the Kings Head (0325) 380222.

Tyne and Wear

Tyneside is essentially a tale of two cities, Newcastle and Sunderland—home of the Geordies and where the welcome is second to none. There are plenty of golf courses in the area but the really attractive golf lies further north along the coast. The **Northumberland** (Gosforth Park) Golf Club and **Ponteland** probably have the best two courses in Tyne & Wear. The former is situated alongside Gosforth Park Racecourse and like Seaton Carew has staged several national championships. However the visitor may find it easier to arrange a game at Ponteland (at least during the week)— a particularly well-kept course this and very convenient if you happen to be flying to or from Newcastle Airport. **Whitley Bay** is another alternative. It is quite a long, windswept course with very large greens and a wide stream that can make scoring pretty difficult.

If there's one large town in England that could really do with a championship standard golf challenge it's Sunderland, a place of great character—golf architects please note! The best two courses in the area are probably **Whitburn** and **Boldon**.

Staying in and around Newcastle, the leading hotels are the Swallow Gosforth Park Hotel 091 236 4111, the Holiday Inn 091 236 5432 and the Marriott 091 493 2233, while the newly opened Copthorne on the Quayside 091 222 0333 is fast developing a good name for itself. All offer all the mod. cons. and some first class leisure facilities. Jesmond offers a multitude of less expensive hotels and guesthouses—Chirton House Hotel 091 273 0407 being but one example. In Newcastle itself, the choice is tremendous. The city now boasts a real 'Chinatown' along Stowell Street with a host of superb restaurants of which Ming Dynasty 091 261 5787 remains one of the best. For Indian (or Punjabi to be more accurate) cuisine of the highest order there can be only one selection and that is Sachins 091 261 9035 - do ring to reserve a table and get directions. An evening at 21 Queen Street 091 222 0755 on the Quayside is always a culinary experience and there are now a number of other restaurants in the immediate vicinity to suit any palate or pocket. Finally, excellent cooking can always be found at either the Fisherman's Lodge 091 281 3281 or the Fisherman's Wharf 091 232 1057.

Northumberland

Finally then, a look at Northumberland, a county with a splendid, almost mythical history. The first golf course on the way up, as it were, is **Arcot Hall**, six miles north of Newcastle and a most tranquil setting. A James Braid creation, Arcot Hall is a heathland course with a wealth of trees and a lake. The 9th here is a particularly good hole. The club has a sumptuous clubhouse but beware of the Grey Lady who ghosts in and out from time to time! If thoroughly frightened, many peaceful villages

are at hand and some very good pubs. The Highlander at Belsay is one such place (and equally convenient incidentally after a day's golf at Ponteland).

Trekking northwards again, **Morpeth** is next on the agenda. Another pleasant course designed this time by one of James Braid's old rivals—Mr. Vardon no less. One of England's finest Georgian country houses lies only a short distance away at Longhorsley—Linden Hall (0670) 516611. Also nearby is the Besom Barn at Longframlington—a good place for a drink with some splendid English cooking.

Along the rugged coast some tremendous golf lies ahead. The course at **Alnmouth** is very pleasing and in the village is the comfortable Marine House Hotel (0665) 830349. Just a little beyond are the magnificent castle courses of **Dunstanburgh** (at Embleton) and **Bamburgh.** The golf is glorious—the scenery spectacularly superb. Dunstanburgh Castle, the ruins of which were immortalised in watercolour by Turner, occupies a wondrously remote setting. The course is a genuine links, hugging close to the shore and staring out across miles of deserted beach. Bamburgh Castle is perhaps even more special, often referred to as England's most beautiful course. Not long by any means—but the setting! Holy Island and Lindisfarne, the Cheviot Hills and a majestic castle; furthermore, the fairways are bordered by a blaze of colour, with gorse, purple heather and numerous wild orchids. Bamburgh Castle is featured ahead. Not far from here is the fairly short but underrated course at **Seahouses**.

Having placated the golfing soul a few suggestions for the body include the Dunstanburgh Castle Hotel — as its name suggests, very handy for the golf course, the Lord Crewe Arms (06684) 243 in Bamburgh—good for a drink with some accommodation also. A further good resting place is to be found in Belford, the Blue Bell Hotel (0668) 213543. Among several good Northumbrian pubs are the Tankerville Arms in Wooler, the Olde Ship in Seahouses, the Jolly Fisherman in Craster and the Craster Arms in Beadnell.

For centuries the town of Berwick-upon-Tweed didn't know whether it was coming or going, passing between England and Scotland like the proverbial shuttlecock. However disorientated it has a fine links course at **Goswick**, three miles south of the town. Two thoughts for what may be one's last night in England—or maybe one's first? — are the Kings Arms Hotel (0289) 307454 and the Turret House Hotel.

Having sent the golfer north of Newcastle I am aware of having neglected **Hexham**, and the county's newest golfing gem, **Slaley Hall** which is featured ahead. Hexham Golf Club is only a short drive west of Newcastle, along either the A69 or the A695. The journey is well worth making as the course has a glorious setting and the nearby villages with their many inns — note the Hadrian, at (would you believe) Wall, the Three Wheat Heads and the Boat at Warden — cry out for inspection. Finally a restaurant of note is the Black House (0434) 604744 just south of the market town. A golfing holiday I believe is in order—and who needs Scotland!

Ideally situated for County Durham's beautiful parkland golf courses and adjacent to the Chester-le-Street Golf Club, this beautiful castle sits high above the River Wear. Although the main building was constructed in the 14th century, this magnificently preserved castle dates back to the 9th century. While sympathetically refurbished and transformed into a luxury international hotel, the hotel has retained much of its original character and historic atmosphere.

The bedrooms are individually and elegantly furnished. The sumptuous King James Suite boasts a genuine Queen Anne four poster while the courtyard rooms provide rustic charm with old beams. The hidden corridors and secret passages combine to enhance the atmosphere of a more leisurely age.

Medieval pillars support the multi-domed ceiling of the delightful candlelit restaurant which is complemented by the excellent cuisine and a fine selection of wines.

The much acclaimed Elizabethan Banquets are an ongoing feature and are held in the Baronial Hall where guests are entertained by troubadours and ladies of the court in period costume. Medieval Memories and Murder Mystery weekends are also popular events.

Lumley Castle is positioned near the ancient cities of Durham and Newcastle and is only ten minutes drive from the Gateshead Metro Centre and the contrasting outdoor museum at Beamish. It offers easy access to the North East of England's many challenging and interesting coastal and inland courses.

Lumley Castle Hotel
Chester-Le-Street
County Durham
DH3 4NX
Tel: (091) 389 1111
Fax: (091) 387 1437

The Lake District is often referred to as the most beautiful corner of England. Beloved for generations by poets and artists, the magnificent scenery forms a romantic backcloth to the bustling Lakeland villages. Mountains, lakes, hill farms and villages create the harmonious environment which make up the National Park.

Wordsworth, Coleridge, Ruskin, Southey, Beatrix Potter - all lived in the Lakes and their homes and works reflect their love of this beautiful area. Today, the arts are alive and continue to flourish in Cumbria.

Bowness on Windermere is in the heart of the Lake District on the shores of Englands largest and perhaps most beautiful lake. Surrounded by magnificent scenery it is the ideal centre for touring the whole Lake District.

Burn How is a unique combination of Victorian houses, modern chalets and family rooms. Whichever you choose you will find the same high standards throughout - all are luxuriously appointed with private bathroom, colour television, radio, hairdryer, direct dial telephone and tea and coffee facilities. Many of the rooms have private sun balconies, and for the romantically inclined, four poster beds. The family chalets have baby listening services and six ground floor rooms have been designed

with the disabled in mind. There is a children's menu and room service is available for any meal. The highly acclaimed, award winning restaurant in the main house is a tasteful combination of Victorian and Georgian furnishings, but with any restaurant it is the food that matters most and here you will find dishes best described as "English with French connections" - the finest of fresh market produce with caring service. It is evident that the owner, Michael Robinson, and his staff take pride in offering first class food and friendly service. The advantages of Burn How do not end here - there is a sauna and solarium for your enjoyment and ample car parking just by your accommodation. Above all you will enjoy the excellent meals and the obvious desire of all concerned to ensure that your stay is truly memorable.

For those wishing to swim and exercise we have membership for our residents at a nearby luxurious leisure club. In minutes you can be sailing, exploring the lakeside footpaths or walking the nearby fells. Within easy reach are all the other lakes and the spectacular mountains of Helvellyn, Skiddaw and Scafell. Nearby Windermere Golf Course, now into its second century comprises 200 acres of undulating terrain often described as a "mini" Gleneagles.

The Burn How Garden House Hotel
Bowness-on-Windermere
Cumbria LA23 3HH
Tel: (05394) 46226
Fax: (05394) 47000

Whoever first coined that atrocious phrase, 'Golf is a good walk spoiled' was more than likely an idiot. One thing's for sure, he (or she) had never visited Windermere Golf Club in the Lake District. Golf not only 'takes us to such beautiful places', as Henry Longhurst used to say, but it also regularly guides us to some beautiful vantage points. Had our idiot stood on the 8th tee at Windermere he would have assuredly been forced to revise the ill-informed comment. Golf, if nothing else, is a good walk with a good incentive. (Better not tell that idiot then that the 8th at Windermere is called 'Desolation'!)

Windermere Golf Club celebrated its centenary in 1991. Cleabarrow Fells, the land on which the course is laid out was originally leased in 1891 from the Rector of Windermere before being purchased outright by the Club in 1912. The 200 acres comprised, in addition to classically undulating lakeland terrain, a serious amount of heather, bracken and rocks. However, it was soon converted into a sporting 9 hole course and so well was this received that a further 9 holes were added before the end of 1892.

The Club's centenary booklet reveals a colourful history. In the 1920s, the course measured 4320 yards but had a par of 72 (today it is 5006 yards, par 67.) Holes had interesting pars in those days and our friend 'Desolation', though a similar length as now at 131 yards, was a par three and a half! In the 1930s, the fees for a caddy were 2s.2d. per round for a 'First Class Adult' ranging to 1s.1d. for a 'Second Class Schoolboy.'

Windermere has always been a popular course, perhaps never more so than at the present time, just as the Club enters its second century. Windermere has never had pretensions to becoming a Championship length course but it has always offered an enjoyable challenge, and with its outstanding views and the marvellous condition in which the course is currently maintained, it is easy to understand why more and more people are calling it a 'mini Gleneagles.' Windermere is probably worthy of such flattery.

Visiting golfers are very welcome to come and judge for themselves. Not too many foreigners associate the Lake District with the Royal and Ancient game but there can surely be few more delightful environments than this. Visitors should contact the Club in advance of intended play. **Mr K R Moffat** is the Club's **Secretary** and he can be approached by telephone on **(05394) 43123**; Windermere's **professional Stephen Rooke** and his staff handle all tee reservations and they can be contacted on **(05394) 43550**. The address is **Windermere Golf Club,**

Cleabarrow, Windermere, Cumbria. LA23 3NB.

As a general guide, tee times can normally be reserved between 10.00am and 12.00pm, 2.00pm and 4.30pm and before 9.00am. Players must be members of golf clubs and have official handicaps. Golf Societies (maximum 50 persons) can usually be accommodated by arrangement. The green fees in 1994 were set at £23 between Mondays and Fridays and £28 on Saturday, Sunday and Bank Holidays.

For most people travelling to the Lake District will be via the M6. The best exit point for southbound travellers is junction 37 and for northbound motorists, junction 36. The precise location of the Golf Club is a mile and a half from Bowness-on-Windermere along the Crook (Kendal) road, the B5284.

The Clubhouse is most welcoming (some excellent bar snacks are offered between Tuesdays and Saturdays) and the golf course will certainly not disappoint. With a par of 67, there are of course many par three holes and while none of the par fours is overly long the naturally rugged landscape makes up for the lack of length. As on a links type course, awkward stances and blind shots are not uncommon at Windermere, and with the greens being fairly small a well-honed short game is often the key to a good round.

We have already singled out the 8th as Windermere's 'signature hole': from the tee the green sits roughly at eye level but in between is a deep valley of gorse. The green is in fact table-shaped and can be extremely difficult to hit. Distraction is the last thing a player really needs here but over the player's shoulder is a marvellous view of Morecambe Bay while stretching ahead are the magnificent mountains of the Lake District.

Among other notable holes at Windermere one might include the 2nd, a very long par three; the 4th which is the stroke one hole with its difficult drive to an acutely angled fairway and potentially even more difficult blind approach; the 6th and 7th where you play beside an attractive little reservoir and the three closing holes, which, according to the card run 5-4-3—scores that most players will be happy to settle for!

Having introduced Windermere with a regrettable quote, it seems only appropriate to conclude with one of the more noble philosophies on life and reputedly first uttered by the legendary golfer Walter Hagen: 'You're only here for a short while; don't hurry, don't worry, but be sure to smell the flowers along the way.' Of course at Windermere, they might even be found fluttering and dancing in the breeze.

Hole	Yards	Par	Hole	Yards	Par
1	315	4	10	199	3
2	232	3	11	259	4
3	252	4	12	291	4
4	356	4	13	306	4
5	291	4	14	146	3
6	354	4	15	187	3
7	371	4	16	480	5
8	130	3	17	356	4
9	269	4	18	203	3
Out	**2,579**	**34**	**In**	**2,427**	**33**
			Out	**2,579**	**34**
			Totals	**5,006**	**67**

Eccle Riggs Manor retains the character and charm of a bygone era yet possesses the modern conveniences necessary to ensure a luxury stay at a manor house hotel. The hotel has been tastefully modernised, bringing all the benefits of contemporary comfort to this beautiful building.

The hotel is set in glorious gardens and is located in the award-winning Cumbrian village of Broughton-in-Furness. The twelve beautifully appointed bedrooms are en suite and have remote control colour television with in-house video, radio, baby listening service, tea and coffee making facilities, hairdrier and trouser press. Many of the rooms have fabulous views over the hotel's grounds giving a delightful feeling of well-being upon awakening.

The heated indoor swimming pool can be utilised by hotel guests at their convenience and is totally free of charge. Swimmers can enjoy a full range of beauty treatments and massage, by appointment. Guests can also take full advantage during their stay of the hotel's delightful private par three golf course. The hotel is easily located for guests to visit a number of golf courses on the Cumbrian coast, including the highly rated Furness Golf Club which claims to be the oldest in the country. This is a perfect base for guests to explore the surrounding Cumbrian countryside. The hotel is situated just to the south west of the Lake District which is the north's premier holiday location.

Special two day packages are available and from time to time special offers are made available to previous visitors. Whether you are travelling on business or on a family holiday, a visit to Eccle Riggs Manor will make you wish to return again and again.

Eccle Riggs Manor Hotel
Foxfield Road
Broughton-in-Furness
Cumbria
LA20 6BN
Tel: (0229) 716398 / 716780
Fax: (0229) 716958

One of the greatest ever lady golfers, Miss Cecil Leitch once said, 'If you can play Silloth you can play anywhere'. The four times British Ladies Champion and the great rival of Joyce Wethered would have been able to judge better than most for she grew up in Silloth and it was on Silloth's Championship links that she and her four golfing sisters learnt to play.

Silloth-on-Solway Golf Club celebrated its centenary in 1992. At one time there was some uncertainty as to the exact date of the Club's formation as although the first few holes were laid out in 1892, it was not until 1903 when the Club together with its 'new' Clubhouse was formally opened by the Speaker of the House of Commons, The Rt. Hon. Edward Gully.

Today, Silloth is perhaps one of Britain's lesser known Championship links, this doubtless a result of its somewhat remote situation 23 miles west of Carlisle. Hidden away it may be but it is a journey decidedly worth making, for not only is this one of Britain's greatest tests of golf but the Silloth Club is just about the most friendly one is likely to come across.

Helping to promote this welcoming atmosphere is the Club's **Secretary**, **John Proudlock**, who may be contacted by telephone on **(06973) 31304**. There are no specific restrictions on visiting golfers during the week and they can play by arrangement at almost any time. At weekends the Club restricts the number of visitors to 40 and they may play a single round subject to the tee being pre-booked for competitions etc.

The cost of a day's golf at Silloth in 1994 is priced at £22 during the week and £27 per round at weekends. The fees for juniors are half the above rates. Weekly tickets (Monday to Friday) can be purchased for £88. Golfing Societies must book starting times either by telephoning the Club or by writing to the Secretary at **The Silloth-on-Solway Golf Club, Silloth-on-Solway, Carlisle, Cumbria CA5 4BL**. Should the need arise, sets of clubs may be hired from the **professional**, **John Burns**, tel: **(06973) 31304.**

With the M6 running to Carlisle, Silloth isn't actually quite as remote as many people imagine. Golfers travelling from the south should leave the M6 at junction 41 and thereafter take the B5305 to Wigton. At Wigton the B5302 should be picked up and followed to Silloth. Those who have been sensible enough to take their golf

clubs to the Lake District may find the B5300 road helpful; it runs along the coast from Maryport to Silloth. Finally those approaching from Scotland should head for Carlisle and thereafter follow a combination of the B5307 and the B5302 to Silloth.

Measuring a modest 6357 yards, par 72 (5780 yards, par 75 for Ladies), Silloth may not sound particularly frightening, and you may just be wondering what all the fuss is about. Standing on the 1st tee with the wind hammering into your face you'll know exactly what all the fuss is about! Humbling is perhaps the best way to describe the sensation. Two shots later (hopefully!) you'll also discover why the large greens at Silloth have acquired such a marvellous reputation. The course meanders its way through and over some classic links terrain. There are occasional spectacular vantage points—the coastal views from the 4th and 6th tees being especially memorable—and the round calls for several demanding strokes, both going out and coming home. Of the many great holes however, perhaps the par five 13th stands out. Appropriately named 'Hogs Back' it has an exceptionally narrow fairway that is heather lined on either side and a plateau green. Hit a good drive and you'll be tempted to go for the green in two—miss it and you're in deep trouble!

The comfortable and recently extended Clubhouse at Silloth offers full catering until 9pm after which light snacks may be obtained from the Bar. The lunchtime menu is quite outstanding and provided some pre-warning is given, a full Cumberland breakfast can be arranged.

The Club is understandably proud of the fact that twice in recent years it has been selected to host the British Ladies Amateur Championship. However, it can also be proud of the courage some of its members displayed back in 1912; for this information I am greatly indebted to the Club's former Secretary, John Todd. On behalf of all the Clubs in the British Isles Silloth appealed against the assessment to income tax on green fees. Unfortunately for the Golf Clubs the learned judge found in favour of the Inland Revenue; this left Silloth with the task of finding £433 12s. 9d. for legal expenses. 81 Clubs promised contributions to help towards the debt and they eventually raised £140 11s. between them, leaving Silloth with a deficiency of almost £300. One very famous Club I am told subscribed one shilling—and I bet you'd like to know which!

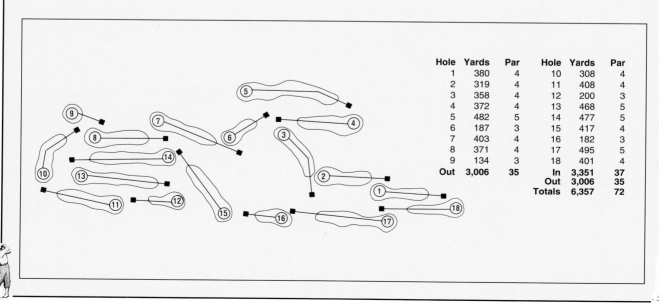

Hole	Yards	Par	Hole	Yards	Par
1	380	4	10	308	4
2	319	4	11	408	4
3	358	4	12	200	3
4	372	4	13	468	5
5	482	5	14	477	5
6	187	3	15	417	4
7	403	4	16	182	3
8	371	4	17	495	5
9	134	3	18	401	4
Out	**3,006**	**35**	**In**	**3,351**	**37**
			Out	**3,006**	**35**
			Totals	**6,357**	**72**

Despite its proximity to Scotland, the 'royal' and 'ancient' county of Northumberland has made little impact on the history of the royal and ancient game. In the future, however, this situation may change. How? The catalyst, or at least the potential catalyst may be found deep in the countryside at Slaley Hall.

Slaley Hall itself is one of those lovely old ivy-clad manors that belongs to a forgotten world. Not totally forgotten in this case it seems, for Newcastle based entrepreneurs, Seamus O'Carroll and John Rourke conceived the idea of turning the large estate into one of the world's leading golf and leisure complexes—men clearly not interested in half measures! The plan was to build an 18 hole Championship golf course around Slaley Hall and then extend the Hall by constructing an adjoining luxury hotel complete with all manner of accompanying facilities.

The Championship Golf course was designed by Dave Thomas and opened for play in July 1989. Let us at once say that Thomas has produced a masterpiece; he himself considers it his finest work. Immediately it opened, critics were describing it as 'The Woburn of the North' and with dense forest surrounding the course it doesn't need much imagination to see why.

Unfortunately things haven't progressed quite as smoothly off the course as on. At the time of writing (July 1994) the luxury hotel has yet to open its doors; however, a five star infrastructure is certainly in place, while various property developments, from holiday villas to Scandinavian—styled timeshare lodges are continuing to mushroom all over the Northumbrian landscape. Overseeing all aspects of golf at Slaley Hall is the **Director of Golf, Stuart Brown.** He can be contacted by telephone on **(0434) 673350.** For written correspondence the Club's full address is **Slaley Hall Golf and Country Club, Slaley, Hexham, Northumberland NE47 0BY.**

Visitors are always made extremely welcome at Slaley Hall. Provided they possess a recognised handicap they may play at any time during the week and can usually book a tee time for the weekend. The 1994 green fees were set at £22.50 per round, £35 per day midweek and £25 per round, £40 per day on Saturdays and Sundays. Although it genuinely is situated in deepest, rural Northumberland visitors shouldn't have too much difficulty finding Slaley Hall. Its precise location is 6 miles south of Hexham and 2 miles west of the A68 road, between Corbridge and Consett. The quickest route from Newcastle (and its Airport) is to pick up the A69 towards Hexham. From Hexham, the road to take for Slaley is the B6306. Approaching from further afield the A1/M1 is likely to be of most assistance for those motoring up from the south and the midlands, while to the north Hexham is linked to Edinburgh by the A68; the aforementioned Newcastle Airport is approximately 18 miles from the golf course.

From its Championship tees Slaley Hall weighs in at a fairly formidable 6995 yards, par 72. Less daunting are the medal tees from which the course is reduced to 6382 yards, par 72. From the ladies tees the course measures 5832 yards, par 76.

The 1st hole offers a chance to open the shoulders, for the fairway is fairly wide, but thereafter at least a little caution may be the order of the day. The 2nd and 3rd are excellent holes; the former being a swinging dog-leg where, if you're too greedy from the tee, the conifers will swallow your ball. Fir trees are ever present at Slaley Hall, lining just about every fairway and giving the course something of an alpine feel. The golfer must do battle with streams and small lakes at the 4th, 5th, 6th and 7th; the 8th is another of Slaley's swinging dog-legs and the 9th is a magnificent par four—a hint of Woodhall Spa perhaps?

On the back nine, holes 11, 12 and 13 are highly memorable; laid out close to Slaley Hall itself cherry trees abound and they are a truly spectacular sight when in bloom. Holes 14 to 17 have a distinctly moorland feel and the 18th is a classic, though very difficult, finishing hole.

Just a year after opening, the magazine Executive Golfer International featured Slaley Hall in its June 1990 edition, and had this to say: 'We feel confident in predicting that Slaley Hall will soon become a name synonymous with major golf events—in the same league as Wentworth, Gleneagles and Turnberry. But in addition, Slaley Hall will be the total resort for all reasons and all seasons—as they say, the ultimate dream.'

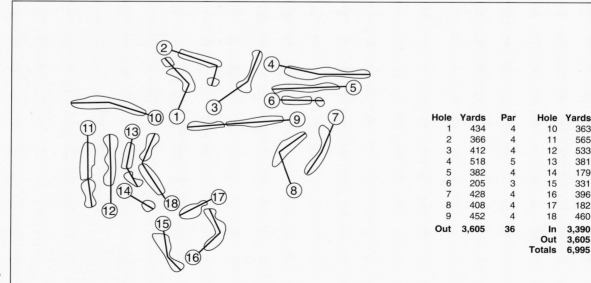

Hole	Yards	Par	Hole	Yards	Par
1	434	4	10	363	4
2	366	4	11	565	5
3	412	4	12	533	5
4	518	5	13	381	4
5	382	4	14	179	3
6	205	3	15	331	4
7	428	4	16	396	4
8	408	4	17	182	3
9	452	4	18	460	4
Out	**3,605**	**36**	**In**	**3,390**	**36**
			Out	**3,605**	**36**
			Totals	**6,995**	**72**

In an earlier piece I quoted one of Henry Longhurst's most celebrated comments, namely; 'What a lovely place to die' (referring to the 18th hole at Killarney). The golf course at Bamburgh merits another from the great man; 'Golf takes you to such beautiful places.'

The setting is quite stunning. A number of Britain's golf courses fall within the gaze of nearby castles; Royal St. David's and Harlech Castle is perhaps the best known example, Cruden Bay and Dunstanburgh are others, but none is more dramatic than the situation at Bamburgh. Standing 150 feet high on a vast, rocky crag and covering over eight acres, Bamburgh is one of Britain's most spectacular castles. It towers over the village and is visible in all its majesty from the adjoining 18 hole links.

Apparently we have to thank the Normans for the splendid keep. It was they who built it, having acquired the original castle from Matilda, Countess of Northumberland, after threatening to take out the eyes of her captive husband—charming times!

Turning to less gory subjects, **Mr. T.C. Osborne** is the **Secretary** of Bamburgh Castle Golf Club; he may be contacted by telephone on **(0668) 214321**. The Club has no golf professional but should you turn up without any balls—a fate arguably worse than that of the Count of Northumberland—fear not, a supply can be purchased in the Clubhouse.

Visitors are made extremely welcome at Bamburgh. However, they are often restricted at weekends and on Public Holidays when they must be accompanied by a Member. Handicap certificates are also required. Before setting off, golfers are advised to contact the **Steward** on **(0668) 214378**.

The green fees at Bamburgh vary according to the season. The summer fees for 1994, applicable between the 1st April and the 30th October, are as follows: £23 per day during the week (£9 for juniors) and £30 per round, £35 per day at weekends (£9 and £12 respectively for juniors). For Autumn and Winter visitors the fees are £23 during the week and £30 at weekends. Finally, five day temporary membership can be purchased for £60 during the Summer (£30 for juniors). Golfing Societies are equally welcome at Bamburgh, though pre-booking with the Secretary is essential. All written enquiries should be addressed to Mr Osborne at **The Bamburgh Castle Golf Club, The Club House, Bamburgh, Northumberland NE69 7DE.**

Bamburgh has what might be described as an 'invigo-rating climate'. Situated on the north eastern coast of Northumberland, only Berwick-upon-Tweed lies further north in England and Bamburgh is a shade closer to the North Pole than either Prestwick, Turnberry or Troon. Despite its remoteness, the journey is a fairly straightforward one and is definitely worth making. Both north and southbound travellers should pick up the A1 which runs between Berwick and Alnwick, passing Bamburgh midway. It doesn't however, pass through Bamburgh. Those approaching from the north should exit left on to the B3142 at Belford, while those approaching from the south are best leaving the A1 just north of Warenford before following the B3141 to Bamburgh. Anyone motoring across the glorious Northumberland countryside may find Wooler a useful place to head for: the B6348 connects Wooler to the A1 just north of the B1341 turn off.

By any standards, Bamburgh Castle is a short course measuring 5621 yards (par 68) from the men's tees and 5098 yards from the ladies' tees (par 70). Short it may be but it isn't without its tests; there are many whin bushes and several of the fairways are flanked with tangling heather. As with every seaside course, the moods of the wind must always be considered. In any event the golfer will not have come to Bamburgh to seek golf's toughest challenge, it is the splendour of the unique setting that is to be enjoyed. The Castle isn't the only sight that demands attention: there are magnificent views across to nearby Holy Island and Lindisfarne and the Cheviot Hills provide a glorious backdrop. As for the course itself, in addition to the great spread of purple heather, a number of fairways are lined with rare wild orchids. It is hardly surprising that Bamburgh is often described as Britain's most beautiful course. Especially memorable holes at Bamburgh include the short 8th with its tee shot over a valley, the 15th—from this tee the golfer can spy no fewer than four castles—and the 17th which is guaranteed to bring the dreaming golfer down to earth.

What about the 19th? In short, exceptionally friendly (as one comes to expect in this part of England). There are no formal dress requirements and lunches and dinners are offered daily in addition to light snacks.

There is a saying used in many sports that 'a good big'un' is always better than 'a good little'un'; the golf course at Bamburgh demonstrates that the phrase has no meaning whatsoever in the world of golf.

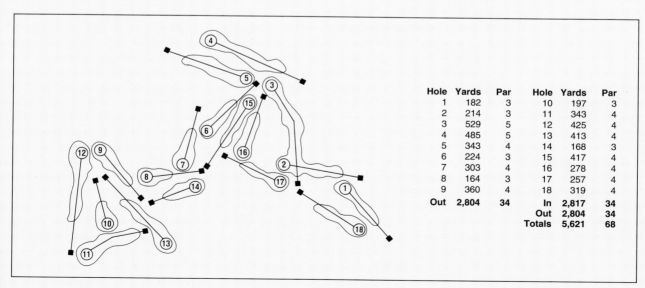

Hole	Yards	Par	Hole	Yards	Par
1	182	3	10	197	3
2	214	3	11	343	4
3	529	5	12	425	4
4	485	5	13	413	4
5	343	4	14	168	3
6	224	3	15	417	4
7	303	4	16	278	4
8	164	3	17	257	4
9	360	4	18	319	4
Out	**2,804**	**34**	**In**	**2,817**	**34**
			Out	**2,804**	**34**
			Totals	**5,621**	**68**

Key

*To avoid disappointment
it is advisable to telephone
in advance*

***Visitors welcome at most times
***Visitors usually allowed on
weekdays only*
**Visitors not normally permitted
(Mon, Wed) No visitors
on specified days*

Approximate Green Fees
A   £30 plus
B   £20 to £30
C   £15 to £25
D   £10 to £20
E   under £10
F   Greens fees on application

Restrictions
G Guests only
H Handicap certificate required
H (24) Handicap of 24 or less
L   Letter of introduction required
M Visitor must be a member of
another recognised club.

CUMBRIA

Alston Moor G.C.
(0434) 381675
The Hermitage, Alston
(9)5380 yards/***/E

Appleby G.C.
(07683) 51432
Brackenber Moor, Appleby-in-
Westmorland
(18)5895 yards/***/E

Barrow G.C.
(0229) 825444
Rakesmoor Lane, Hawcoat
(18)6209 yards/***/C/M

Brampton G.C.
(06977) 2255
Talkin Tarn, Brampton
(18)6420 yards/***/C/H

Brayton Park G.C.
(06973) 20840
Lakeside Inn, Brayton Park
(9)2521 yards/***/E

Carlisle G.C.
(0228) 513303
Aglionby, Carlisle
(18) 6278 yards/**/B/H

Casterton G.C.
(05242) 71592
Sedbergh Road, Casterton
(9)3015 yards/***/E

Cockermouth G.C.
(07687) 76223
Embleton, Cockermouth
(18)5496 yards/***/D

Dalston Hall G.C.
(0228) 710165
Dalston Hall, Dalston
(9)2667 yards/***/E

Dunnerholme G.C.
(0229) 62675
Duddon Road, Askam in Furness
(10)6181 yards/***(not Sun)/D
Eden G.C.
(0228) 23161
Crosby-on-Eden, Carlisle
(18)6975 yards/***/C

Furness G.C.
(0229) 471232
Central Drive, Walney Island,
Barrow-in-Furness
(18)6363 yards/***/D

Grange Fell G.C.
(05395) 32536
Fell Road, Grange-over-Sands
(9)4826 yards/***/D

Grange-over-Sands G.C.
(05395) 33180
Meathop Road, Grange-over-Sands
(18)5938 yards/***/C

Kendal G.C.
(0539) 724079
The Heights, Kendal
(18)5483 yards/***/C/H

Keswick G.C.
(07687) 79324
Threlkeld Hall, Keswick
(18)6175 yards/***/C

Kirkby Lonsdale G.C.
(05242) 76366
Scaleber Lane, Barbon
(18)6283 yards/***(Sun am)/D

Maryport G.C.
(0900) 812605
Bank End, Maryport
(18)6272 yards/***/C

Penrith G.C.
(0768) 62217
Salkeld Road, Penrith
(18)6026 yards/***/C/M/H

Seascale G.C.
(09467) 28202
The Banks, Seascale
(18)6416 yards/***/C

Sedbergh G.C.
(05396) 21551
Catholes Abbot Holme, Sedbergh
(9)5504 yards/***/D

Silecroft G.C.
(0229) 774250
Silecroft, Millom
(9)5712 yards/**/E

Silloth on Solway G.C.
(06973) 31304
Silloth on Solway
(18)6343 yards/***/B/H

Silverdale G.C.
(0524) 701307
Red Bridge Lane, Silverdale
(12)5417 yards/***/D

St Bees School G.C.
(0946) 812105
Rhoda Grove, Rheda, Frizington
(9)5082 yards/***/E

Stonyholme Municipal G.C.
(0228) 34856
St Aidans Road, Carlisle
(18)5783 yards/***/F

Ulverston G.C.
(0229) 52824
Bardsea Park, Ulverston
(18)6142 yards/***/D/M/H

Windermere G.C.
(05394) 43123
Cleabarrow, Windermere
(18)5006 yards/***/B/H

Workington G.C.
(0900) 603460
Branthwaite Road, Workington
(18)6200 yards/***/C/M/H

CO DURHAM

Aycliffe G.C.
(0325) 310820
School Aycliffe Lane, Newton
Aycliffe
(18)5430 yards/***/F

Barnard Castle G.C.
(0833) 38355
Harmire Road, Barnard Castle

(18)5838 yards/***/C

Beamish Park G.C.
091 370 1382
Beamish, Stanley
(18)6205 yards/***(notSun)/C/H

Birtley G.C.
091 410 2207
Portobello Road, Birtley
(9)5154 yards/**/E'

Bishop Auckland G.C.
(0388) 602198
Durham Road, Bishop Auckland
(18)6420 yards/***/D

Blackwell Grange G.C.
(0325) 464464
Briar Close, Blackwell,
(18)5587 yards/***/D

Brancepeth Castle G.C.
091 378 0075
Brancepeth, Durham
(18)6300 yards/**/B/H

Chester-le-Street G.C.
091 388 3218
Lumley Park, Chester-le-Street
(18)6054 yards/**/B/H/L

Consett and District G.C.
(0207) 502186
Elmfield Road, Consett
(18)6001 yards/**/C/H

Crook G.C.
(0388) 762429
Low Jobs Hill, Crook
(18)6016 yards/***/C

Darlington G.C.
(0325) 463936
Haughton Grange, Darlington
(18) 6032 yards/**/B/M

Dinsdale Spa G.C.
(0325) 332297
Middleton St George, Darlington
(18)6078 yards/**/D

Durham City G.C.
091 378 0069
Littleburn Farm, Langley Moor
(18)6326 yards/***/C

Hobson Municipal G.C.
(0207) 71605
Hobson, nr Burnopfield,
(18)6582 yards/***/E

Houghton le Spring G.C.
091 584 1198
Copt Hill, Houghton le Spring
(18)6450 yards/*/D/M

Mount Oswald G.C.
091 386 7527
South Road, Durham
(18)6101 yards/***/D

Roseberry Grange G.C.
091 370 0670
Grange Villa, Chester-le-Street
(18)5628 yards***/E

Ryhope G.C.
091 521 3811
Leechmere Way, Ryhope
(9)6000 yards/***/E

Seaham G.C.
091 581 2354
Dawdon, Seaham
(18)5972 yards/***/D

South Moor G.C.
(0207) 232848
The Middles, Craghead, Stanley
(18)6445 yards/***/D/M/H

Stressholme G.C.
(0325) 461002
Snipe Lane, Darlington
(18)6511 yards/***/F

Woodham G. & C.C.
(0325) 320574
Burnhill Way, Newton Aycliffe
(18)6770 yards/***/F

TYNE AND WEAR

Backworth G.C.
091 268 1048
The Hall, Backworth
(9)5930 yards/**/F

Birtley G.C.
091 536 5360
Portobello Road, Birtley
(9)5660 yards/***/D

Boldon G.C.
091 536 5360
Dipe Lane, East Boldon
(18)6348 yards/**/F

City of Newcastle G.C.
091 285 1775
Three Mile Bridge, Gosforth
(18)6508 yards/***/D

Garesfield G.C.
(0207) 561278
Chopwell, Garesfield
(18)6603 yards/***/C

George Washington G.C.
091 417 2626
Nr Washington Moat House Hotel
(18)6604 yards/***/D

Gosforth G.C.
091 285 3495
Broadway East, Gosforth
(18)6043 yards/**/C/H

Gosforth Park G.C.
091 236 4480
Gosforth, Newcastle
(18)6100 yards/***/D

Heworth G.C.
091 469 2137
Gingling Gate, Heworth
(18)6462 yards/**/D

Newcastle United G.C.
091 286 4693
Ponteland Road, Cowgate
(18)6498 yards/**/D/M

Northumberland G.C.
091 236 2009
High Gosforth Park
Newcastle upon Tyne
(18)6640 yards/**/A

Ponteland G.C.
(0661) 22689
53 Bell Villas, Ponteland
(18)6524 yards/**/B

Ravensworth G.C.
091 487 2843
Moss Heaps, Wrekenton
(18)5872 yards/***/C/H

Ryton G.C.
091 413 3737
Stanners Drive, Ryton
(18)6034 yards/**/D

South Shields G.C.
091 456 0475
Cleadon Hills, South Shields
(18)6264 yards/**/B/L

Tynemouth G.C.
091 257 4578
Spital Dene, Tynemouth
(18)6403 yards/**/C/M

Tyneside G.C.
091 413 2742
Westfield Lane, Ryton
(18)6055 yards/**/C/H

Wallsend G.C.
091 262 4231

Bigges Main, Wallsend
(18)6608 yards/***/D

Wearside G.C.
091 534 2518
Coxgreen, Sunderland
(18)6373 yards/***/C/M/H

Westerhope G.C.
091 286 9125
Whorlton Grange, Westerhope
(18)6407 yards/***/D

Whickham G.C.
091 488 7309
Hollinside Park, Whickham
(18)6129 yards/**/B

Whitburn G.C.
091 529 2144
Lizard Lane, South Shields
(18)5773 yards/***/D

Whitley Bay G.C.
091 252 0180
Claremont Road, Whitley Bay
(18)6617 yards/***/C

NORTHUMBERLAND

Allendale G.C.
091 267 587
Allendale, High Studdon
(9)5044 yards/***/E

Alnmouth G.C.
(0665) 830231
Foxton Hall, Alnmouth
(18)6414 yards/**/B/H

Alnmouth Village G.C.
(0665) 830370
Marine Road, Alnmouth
(9)6078 yards/***/D/H

Alnwick G.C.
(0665) 602632
Swansfield Park, Alnwick
(9)5379 yards/***/D

Arcot Hall G.C.
091 236 2794
Dudley, Cramlington
(18)6389 yards/***/B/H

Bamburgh Castle G.C.
(0668) 214378
The Wynding, Bamburgh
(18)5465 yards/***/B/H

Bedlingtonshire G.C.
(0670) 822457

Acorn Bank, Bedlington
(18)6224 yards/***/C

Bellingham G.C.
(0434) 220530
Boggle Hole, Bellingham
(9) 5245 yards/***/D

Berwick-upon-Tweed G.C.
(0289) 87256
Goswick, Berwick-upon-Tweed
(18)6425 yards/***/B

Blyth G.C.
(0670) 367728
New Delaval, Blyth
(18)6300 yards/**/C

Burgham Park G.& C.C.
(0670) 787898
Felton, Morpeth
(18)7139 yards/**/E

Close House G.C.
(0661) 852953
Heddon-on-the-Wall
(18)5587 yards/***/D/M

Dunstanburgh Castle G.C.
(0665) 576562
Embleton, Alnwick
(18)6038 yards/***/F

Haltwhistle G.C.
(06977) 47367
Greenhead, Haltwhistle
(18)5968 yards/***/E

Hexham G.C.
(0434) 603072
Spital Park, Hexham
(18)6272 yards/***/B/H

Magdalene Fields G.C.
(0289) 306384
Berwick-upon-Tweed
(18)6551 yards/***/C

Matfen Hall G.C.
(0434) 672285
Matfen, Hexham
(18)6732 yards/***/C

Morpeth G.C.
(0670) 519980
The Common, Morpeth
(18)6215 yards/***/B/H

Newbiggin-by-the-Sea G.C.
(0670) 817344
Newbiggin-by-the-Sea
(18)6452 yards/***/B

Ponteland G.C.
(0661) 22689
Bell Villas, Ponteland
(18)6512 yards/**/B

Prudhoe G.C.
(0661) 832466
Eastwood Park, Prudhoe
(18)5812 yards/**/D

Rothbury G.C.
(0669) 20718
Old Racecourse, Rothbury
(9) 5146 yards/***(not Sat)/D

Seahouses G.C.
(0665) 720794
Beadnell Road, Seahouses
(18)5462 yards/***/D

Slaley Hall G.& C.C.
(0434) 673350
Slaley, Hexham
(18)7021 yards/***/B

Stocksfield G.C.
(0661) 843041
New Ridley, Stocksfield
(18)5594 yards/***/D/H

Swarland Hall G.C.
(0670) 787010
Coast View, Swarland
(9)6517 yards/***/D

Tynedale G.C.
(0434) 608154
Tyne Green, Hexham
(9)5706 yards/***/D

Warkworth G.C.
(0665) 711596
The Links ,Warkworth
(9)5856 yards/***/D

Wooler G.C.
(0668) 281956
Dodd Law, Doddington, Wooler
(9)6353 yards/***/D

CLEVELAND

Billingham G.C.
(0642) 554494
Sandy Lane, Billingham
(18)6460 yards/*/B/H

Castle Eden & Peterlee G.C.
(0429) 836220
Castle Eden, Hartlepool
(18)6293 yards/***/D

Cleveland G.C.
(0642) 471798
Queen Street, Redcar
(18)6707 yards/***/D/H

Eaglescliffe G.C.
(0642) 780098
Yarm Road, Eaglescliffe
(18)6275 yards/***/D

Hartlepool G.& C.C.
(0429) 274398
Hart Warren, Hartlepool
(18)6255 yards/***(not Sun)/D/H

Hunley Hall G.C.
(0287) 76216
Brotton, Saltburn
(18)6918 yards/***/C

Knotty Hill G.C.
(0740) 620320
Sedgefield, Stockton-on-Tees
(18)6668 yards/***/D

Middlesbrough G.C.
(0642) 311515
Brass Castle Lane, Marton
(18)6106 yards/***(Tues)/B/M

Middlesbrough Municipal G.C.
(0642) 315533
Ladgate Lane, Middlesbrough
(18)6314 yards/***/E

Norton G.C.
(0642) 676385
Junction Road, Norton
(18)5870 yards/***/E

Saltburn-by-the-Sea G.C.
(0287) 622812
Guisborough Road, Hobb Hill
(18)5803 yards/***/C/M

Seaton Carew G.C.
(0429) 266249
Tees Road, Seaton Carew
(18)6855 yards/***/B

Teesside G.C.
(0642) 616516
Acklam Road, Thornaby
(18)6472 yards/***(pm only)/C

Wilton G.C.
(0642) 465265
Wilton Castle, Redcar
(18)6104 yards/***(not Sat)/C

*Artist: **F P Hopkins** A PAINSTAKING PUTT Courtesy of **Burlington Glallery***

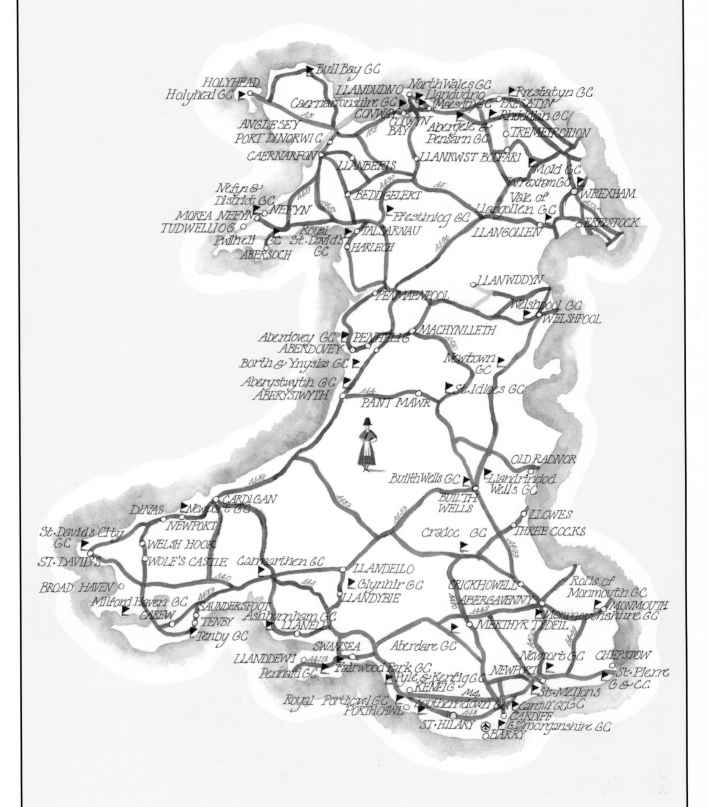

Llangoed Hall

On this site, fourteen hundred years ago, the Welsh Parliament stood — at least according to legend. Inspired by this the celebrated architect, Sir Clough Williams-Ellis, transformed the largely Jacobean mansion he found here into the great country house it is today. Llangoed Hall was completed in 1918, although parts of the South facing wing, including the panelled library, date from 1632. Inside it is the Laura Ashley genius that is most striking, that ability of interpreting the past to bring comfort and beauty to the present.

The intention of Sir Bernard Ashley, when he decided to convert the hall, was never that of the usual hotelier. Having decided to return to the idea of entertaining guests rather than patrons, he worked hard to recreate the style and atmosphere of what it once was, a great Edwardian country house where visitors could stay and enjoy the way of life it once stood for. Thoughtful luxuries abound and personal touches make all the difference: fresh fruit; a decanter of sherry or mineral water ready to pour; plenty of books in the bedrooms; fleecy robes and luxurious oils in the bathrooms; a tray of famous Welsh afternoon tea, of scones and home-made jam, shortbread and cream filled meringues and local Bara Brith served in the morning room to welcome you on your arrival.

The dining room is handsome, with yellow and corn-flower blue, a perfect complement to the menu of one of the finest young chefs in Britain, always insisting on fresh local produce: Welsh lamb, Wye salmon and traditional laverbread; vegetables and herbs collected from the hotels own gardens. All to be enjoyed with a choice from some of the 300 superb wines assembled from the greatest wine regions of the world.

For the sportsman, three superb golf courses are within easy driving distance; all 18 hole with breathtaking scenery. In addition to the hotel's own all-weather tennis court and croquet lawn, guests may fish for salmon and trout on the Upper Wye and River Irfon. The countryside, rich in wildlife, offers a variety of rough shooting and bird-watching. Riding can easily be arranged and the magnificent Brecon Beacons have much to offer both the serious and casual walker; not to mention the fascinating surrounding countryside from Wordworth's beloved Tintern Abbey to the ancient castles of Raglan and Caerphilly.

Conference facilities are, naturally, extensive with a variety of rooms available, from the panelled library to the traditional Orangery which opened in October 1994. For all guests, a chauffeur driven car is available for day-to-day touring or collection from rail and air terminals and helicopters may use the south lawn by prior arrangement.

Llangoed Hall
Llyswen
Brecon
Powys
Wales
LD3 OYP
Tel: (0874) 754525
Fax: (0874) 754545

The family home of the Weatherills, Llanwenarth House was for five centuries or more the home of the Morgan family, whose most illustrious and some would say infamous member was the privateer and Governor of Jamaica, Captain Henry. The house is situated within the Brecon Beacons National Park and is bordered on one side by the Brecon and Monmouthshire Canal, commanding views over the Vale of Usk.

The Weatherill family have carefully renovated and restored their home without altering its well proportioned rooms and character. They have maintained its elegant atmosphere and offer their guests the best of hospitality. The five rooms are en suite and individually furnished with family antiques, as one would expect to find in a country house.

Dinner is prepared by Amanda on most evenings. A cordon bleu cook, her dinner here should not be missed.

Vegetables and herbs come from the garden as well as the majority of summer fruits. Salmon and trout come from the rivers Usk and Wye and the family breed their own Welsh lamb and free range ducks and chickens.

Llanwenarth and its surrounding small estate is indeed a haven of peace and quiet, but there is much to explore beyond the mountains, historic castles and the friendly Welsh towns and villages. For those who are Travellng the Turf, this is a great place to return to after an exhausting day at Chepstow, Hereford or indeed Cheltenham. Golfers will find Llanwenarth ideally located for visits to the nearby courses of the Rolls of Monmouth at the Hendre, St Pierre at Chepstow, the Monmouthshire at Abergavenny and a number of others.

The family's pastimes include equestrian activities and they hunt with various packs, including the Monmouthshire, South Hereford, and Sennybridge.

Llanwenarth House
Govilon
Abergavenny
Gwent
NP7 9SF
Tel: Gilwern (0873) 830289
Fax: (0873) 832199.

Balls in South Wales are often large, oval-shaped and made of leather. However, those belonging to the much smaller dimpled breed—usually white, though these days sometimes shocking pink and yellow—are to be found in some particularly pleasant spots, and in a great variety of places between the Wye Valley and the Gower Peninsula. In addition to The Glamorgans and Gwent our region takes in Mid Wales as well, that is the larger, less inhabited counties of Dyfed and Powys—'the real Wales', they'll tell you there.

Gwent

For many travellers their first sample of golf in South Wales will be the impressive **St Pierre** Golf and Country Club at Chepstow (see feature page). Unfortunately, far too great a number make St Pierre their one and only stop. Further up the Wye Valley both **Monmouthshire** and the **Rolls of Monmouth** offer an outstanding game in delightful surroundings. Bounded by the River Usk, the Monmouthshire Golf Club lies half a mile west of Abergavenny at Llanfoist. In 1992 the club celebrated its centenary—quite an achievement when one considers its unusual beginnings. Laid out on ground formerly used for polo and later for horseracing, golf was started here in 1892, as the club handbook tells you, 'the result of a bet as to whether such a venture could be run successfully at Abergavenny!' Clearly the golfers backed a winner. Golf at 'The Rolls' is explored on a later page.

The St Pierre Hotel (0291) 625261 is a 14th century mansion providing a whole range of facilities. However, those not wishing to wake up next to the famous 18th green should note the Castle View Hotel (0291) 620349, also in Chepstow and very comfortable. In Abergavenny, the Walnut Tree (0873) 852797 is without doubt one of the finest restaurants in Wales and Llanwenarth House (0873) 830289 at Govilon to the west of Abergavenny makes an excellent base for golfing visitors.. Monmouth provides the Kings Head Hotel (0600) 712177 while the nearby Crown at Whitebrook (0600) 860254 offers award winning cuisine and good accommodation.

One other golf course in Gwent which is well worth a visit is **Newport** at Rogerstone. It is a very fine downland course and decidedly handy when travelling along the M4 (junction 27)—en route to Porthcawl perhaps? Undoubtedly the place to stay in Newport is the Celtic Manor Hotel where a Robert Trent Jones course is being built with a future Ryder Cup bid in mind.

The Glamorgans

Golfers in Cardiff (or Caerdydd) are quite fortunate having a number of well established courses close at hand. Not surprisingly they tend to be busier than the majority of Welsh courses and therefore before setting off it is especially important to contact the particular club in question. The **Cardiff** Golf Club is a superior parkland course situated some three miles from the city centre at Cyncoed. **St Mellons,** north east of the city, within easy access of the M4, is another popular parkland course—quite challenging, with several interesting holes. To the south west of Cardiff, **Wenvoe Castle**, one of the more hilly courses in South Glamorgan can be recommended as can the **Glamorganshire** course, located to the west of Penarth.

Perhaps the best three hotels in Cardiff are the Park Hotel (0222) 383471, the Angel Hotel (0222) 232633 and the very modern Cardiff Moat House (0222) 732520. Among the better restaurants, Noble House (0222) 388430 is well thought of, while the Blas-Ar Cymru

(0222) 382132 offers a delightful taste of Wales. Another good eating place is found in Penarth, the Caprice (0222) 702424, where excellent seafood accompanies fine views over the Bristol Channel. Also in Penarth, the Captain's Wife is recommended (a pub it should be added!). More pubs, and to the north and south of Cardiff are the Maenllwyd at Rudry and the beautifully thatched Bush at St Hilary. Still further south is the popular Blue Anchor at East Aberthan (superb lunches).

A short distance to the north of Cardiff, the town of Caerphilly is more famous for its castle and its cheese than for its golf; however there is some good golf in the area, **Mountain Lakes** Golf and Country Club being particularly noteworthy. Before heading off to the glorious coastal strip around Porthcawl a course certainly deserving a mention is **Aberdare**—an excellent woodland course, undoubtedly the finest in 'the Valleys'.

One would have to travel many a mile to find a course the equal of **Royal Porthcawl** (also featured later this chapter) but its near neighbour to the east, **Southerndown** gets closer than most. Situated on high ground it is an outstandingly scenic downland type course measuring a little over 6600 yards (par 70). Even closer to Porthcawl is the fine links of **Pyle and Kenfig,** on more than one occasion the venue for the Welsh Amateur Stroke Play Championship. It is a very tough challenge, being open to the elements, and boasts some very large sand dunes.

Some ideas for a well earned night's rest in the area include in Porthcawl, the Atlantic Hotel (0656) 785011 and The Fairways (0656) 782085. In Nottage, the Rose and Crown (0656) 784850 is an excellent pub serving good food and with some accommodation, while another notable drinking establishment is the Prince of Wales in Kenfig. As a base for covering the whole region in style, the historic Great House at Laleston (0656) 657644 and the elegant Egerton Grey (0446) 711666 are hard to beat.

Beyond Pyle and Kenfig the M4 heads into West Glamorgan passing through Port Talbot towards Swansea, and beyond Swansea is the beautifully secluded Gower Peninsula. If you are fortunate enough to be visiting these parts, three courses that can be strongly recommended are **Fairwood Park, Clyne** and **Pennard**. Fairwood Park, situated close to Swansea Airport, is a second course over which racehorses once galloped. It is a much improved course and has several long par fours. Clyne offers a moorland challenge while from Pennard's clifftop course there are some splendid views out across the Bristol Channel.

A hotel for the night? In Swansea, the Forte Crest Hotel (0792) 651074 is very good and in nearby Mumbles, the Norton House Hotel (0792) 404891 is most relaxing. On the Gower, Fairyhill Country House (0792) 390139 is recommended, especially for its cuisine. No less restful is Langrove Lodge. As for a drink there are numerous pubs. Here are two suggestions: the Joiners Arms in Bishopston and the Welcome to Town in Lanrhidian.

Mid Wales

For every person in New Zealand there are twenty sheep. Regrettably, I don't have the figures for Dyfed and Powys but I suspect they're fairly similar. The bad news is that the lack of human beings is unfortunately reflected by a low number of top class golf courses (unlike in New Zealand it should be said). However, the good news is that even during the summer months most of the courses remain relatively uncrowded, visitors are made very welcome and the green fees tend to be a lot cheaper than in most parts of Britain.

Dyfed

The two championship courses in this region lie on Dyfed's southern coast, some 30 miles apart. Both **Ashburnham** and **Tenby** were founded before the turn of the century and each has staged more than one Welsh Amateur Championship, Ashburnham in fact being a regular venue.

Located one mile west of Burry Port, Ashburnham's links is fairly close to industrial South Wales which, I suppose, extends as far as Llanelli, or at least to where the M4 from London fizzles out. The course measures 7000 yards from the championship tees and 6686 yards from the medal tees—certainly not a course for the inexperienced! Connoisseurs of the game, however, should find it an excellent challenge. There are more glorious sandy beaches around Tenby than one could care to count. As well as being a haven for the bucket and spade it is also a wonderful place for a round of golf. Tenby is a true links course with natural sand hazards and fast greens.

In Llanelli, the Diplomat (0554) 756156 is convenient for Ashburnham, but for a really relaxing 19th hole, golfers may prefer to stay in Tenby with its stylish Georgian harbour. Here the Imperial (0834) 843737 is recommended. The Tall Ships (0834) 842055 also enjoys a suitably convenient location. A local favourite is the St Brides Hotel (0834) 812304 which enjoys superb views of Carmarthen Bay and its restaurant makes the best use of locally captured lobster. Equally impressive in this respect is the magnificent Penally Abbey (0834) 843033, ideally situated for Tenby Golf Club. To the north, nestling in the foothills of the Black Mountains, is the town of Llandeilo and a stay at the delightful 18th century coaching inn of the Cawdor Arms Hotel (0558) 823500 is highly recommended. Another good hotel which also offers excellent seafood can be found in Broadhaven—the Druidstone Hotel (0437) 781221.

Moving westwards along the Dyfed coast, the next 18 holes are to be found at **Milford Haven**, a medium-length parkland course to the west of the town. In days of old the former whaling town may well have been a 'haven' but the present day 'landscape in oils' isn't everyone's cup of tea. More attractive is **St Davids** with its beautiful cathedral making it the smallest city in Britain. Unfortunately for golfing visitors there is only a modest 9 hole golf course 20 miles away at **Newport**. Although again only a 9 holer, this is a very fine golf course, and one which offers some tremendous sea views.

St Davids has many pleasing hotels, and Warpool Court (0437) 720300 is particularly good. Should one tire for some reason of the coast then the Wolfscastle Country Hotel (043 787) 225, in Wolfscastle is very welcoming (even though it may not sound like it). The 17th century Hotel Merineth (0437) 763353 in Haverford West is another comfortable hotel in this area. Perhaps the most appropriate place for golfers who have played somewhat waywardly is the village of Welsh Hook — Stone Hall (0348) 840212 is the establishment recommended. Good places for a drink include the contradictory Sailors Safety and the Ship Aground, both at Dinas and the Golden Lion in Newport. If you are still hungry then the best tip is to visit Cardigan and the Pantry (0239) 820420. Failing the Pantry, try the kitchen—the Castle Kitchen (0239) 615055, an informal but well run restaurant nearby.

Leaving 'Little England beyond Wales' and heading still further up the coast, the University town of **Aberystwyth** has an 18 hole course that looks out over Cardigan Bay. Try the Belle Vue Royal Hotel (0970) 617558 for a 19th hole here—a lovely hotel with seafront views over Cardigan Bay. A more impressive golf course though is **Borth and Ynyslas,** one of the oldest clubs in Wales. Borth is a superbly maintained seaside links. The B4353 road runs right alongside much of the course and is often peppered by golf balls. Taking out insurance before playing Borth is recommended.

Whether you've peppered the road or the flagsticks the Cliff Haven Hotel (0970) 871659 in Borth may be the most convenient place for a good sleep, however, further north at Eglwysfach, 16th century Ynyshir Hall (0654) 781209 is well worth inspecting (note the nearby bird sanctuary) and in Machynlleth, the Wynnstay Arms (0654) 70294 is a cosy former coaching inn. Back in Borth, the Victoria Inn is a good pub and finally a great example of friendly local hospitality in an elegant setting is the Conrah Country Hotel (0970) 617941.

Inland, there is precious little golf to speak of in Dyfed, though there is a fairly testing hilltop course at **Carmarthen**—one which is decidedly better in summer than in winter and an attractive parkland course, **Glynhir,** near the foothills of the Black Mountain Range. The latter is a particularly friendly club situated close to the Glynhir Mansion where the first news of Wellington's victory at Waterloo is reputed to have been received by carrier pigeon. (Must have been a pretty sharp pigeon!) One doesn't have to look far for a night's stay either: in Llandybie, the Mill at Glynhir (0269) 850672 overlooks the 14th green.

Powys

The golf courses in Powys are few and far between, but those that there are tend to be set amidst some splendid scenery. There is an 18 hole course at **Welshpool** up in the hills near the English border (do try to visit Powys Castle and its superb gardens if you're in the area) and two interesting 9 hole courses at Newton (**St Giles**) and at Llanidloes (**St Idloes**) in the quiet of the Cambrian Mountains (note the very fine Glansevern Arms (05515) 240 in Pant Mawr). Two of the region's best courses are situated right in the centre of Wales, **Llandrindod Wells** and **Builth Wells**. Both are attractive courses, but Llandrindod in particular offers spectacular views. For Builth Wells there can be no finer base to play from than the Lake Country House (05912) 202 while in the town itself is the Lion Hotel (0982) 553670, an historic inn and very pleasant too. In Llandrindod the large Metropole Hotel (0597) 823700 is very convenient, the Harp at Old Radnor is an ideal place for a drink and a snack after a round at Llandrindod, but for a real overnight treat a visit to either Llangoed Hall (0874) 754525 or to a Welsh Rarebits property (0686) 668030 is recommended.

One final course to mention, and one good enough to have held the Welsh Amateur Stroke Play Championship is **Cradoc** near Brecon. A lovely course this, and again, very scenic being within the Brecon Beacons National Park. Here's another tip: a drink at the White Swan in Llanfrynach followed by dinner and a relaxing stay at Gliffaes (0874) 730371 in Crickhowell. This hotel ranks among the best and is an ideal base from which to play many courses.

By common consent Royal Porthcawl is not only the finest course in Wales, it is also one of the greatest Championship links in the British Isles; yet like many famous Clubs, Porthcawl's beginnings were rather humble. The Club was founded in June 1891 and the following year a nine hole course was laid out on a patch of common land known as Lock's Common, consent having been given by the local parish vestry. Having to share the course with, amongst other things cattle, soon frustrated the Members and a second nine holes were sought. These they found on the present site closer to the shore. By 1898 Lock's Common was abandoned altogether and the 'favoured' second nine holes were extended to a full eighteen. Once settled the Club prospered and in 1909 patronage was bestowed. Royal Porthcawl had well and truly arrived.

The Members were extremely fortunate in finding this new home for today Royal Porthcawl is not only considered to be one of Britain's finest golfing challenges but also one of the most beautifully situated. Every hole on the course provides a sight of the sea and from many points there are spectacular views across the Bristol Channel to the distant hills of Somerset and North Devon.

Presently presiding over the Royal domain is the Club's helpful **Secretary, Mr. Tony Woolcott.** He may be contacted by telephone on **(0656) 782251.** The **professional, Peter Evans,** can be reached on **(0656) 773702.** Golfers wishing to visit Royal Porthcawl can expect a warm welcome. Subject to possessing a Golf Club handicap there are no general restrictions; however, being an understandably popular Club prior telephoning is advisable. Those wishing to organise Golf Society Meetings should either telephone or preferably address a written application to the Secretary at **The Royal Porthcawl Golf Club, Porthcawl, Mid Glamorgan, Wales, CF36 3UW.** Tuesdays and Thursdays are the usual Society days.

The green fees at Royal Porthcawl for 1994 were set at £35 per day during the week with £45 payable at weekends. A rather novel and most encouraging policy is adopted towards junior golfers. Junior Members of the Club can introduce an outside junior for a green fee of just £1 during weekdays.

The course is situated approximately 15 miles east of Swansea and about 20 miles west of Cardiff. The M4 makes travelling to Porthcawl fairly straightforward. Approaching from either east or west the motorway should be left at junction 37; thereafter the A4229 can be followed into Porthcawl. The course's precise location is towards the northern end of the town.

In the opening paragraph Porthcawl was described as a 'links'. This isn't perhaps entirely accurate for although much of the course is certainly of a links nature, some parts are more strictly downland and heathland in character and there aren't the massive sandhills that feature so prominently on the great Championship links of Lancashire, and which are indeed to be found at neighbouring Pyle and Kenfig. The absence of sandhills means there is no real protection from the elements on stormy days and when the winds blow fiercely Porthcawl can be as tough a challenge as one is likely to meet.

From its Championship tees the course stretches to 6691 yards (par 72, SSS 74) while from the medal tees it measures 6409 yards (par 72) with the ladies playing over 5714 yards (par 75). Good scores at Porthcawl (the course record stands at 65) are likely to be fashioned on the first ten holes; from the tough par three 11th inwards there are some very difficult holes. The second shot from the fairway on the dog-leg 13th is one not to be hurried though, the views out across the course are quite breathtaking. The 15th and 16th are two quite lengthy par fours and the round ends with a glorious downhill finishing hole.

As for its 19th Porthcawl has a splendid Clubhouse. There is an informal Men's Bar where spikes may be worn, a mixed lounge (jacket and tie after 7pm) and a Dining Room (jacket and tie at all times). Both lunches and dinners can be arranged with prior notice, and light snacks are offered at all times except on Sundays.

One final thought for those wishing to explore the delights of Royal Porthcawl, I beg you to consider carefully before deciding to visit late on a November's afternoon for as the light fades and a mist starts to descend upon the links the ghost of the Maid of Sker walks the 17th fairway—don't say you haven't been warned!

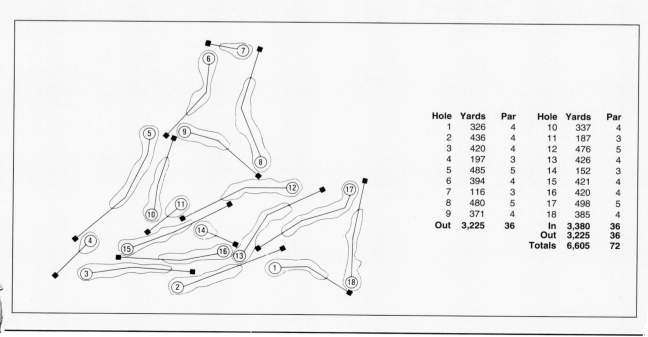

Hole	Yards	Par	Hole	Yards	Par
1	326	4	10	337	4
2	436	4	11	187	3
3	420	4	12	476	5
4	197	3	13	426	4
5	485	5	14	152	3
6	394	4	15	421	4
7	116	3	16	420	4
8	480	5	17	498	5
9	371	4	18	385	4
Out	**3,225**	**36**	**In**	**3,380**	**36**
			Out	**3,225**	**36**
			Totals	**6,605**	**72**

The hotel is set in 400 acres of beautiful parkland and even has its own eleven acre lake. This is an ideal place to escape the pressures of everyday life and seek sanctuary in the countryside. The heart of the hotel is a beautiful stone 14th century mansion.

Situated in Chepstow, and just two miles from Junction 22 of the M4 motorway, and only minutes from the M5, this is a truly luxurious hotel. A £3.5 million refurbishment, the first phase completed in March 1994, ensures that the 143 bedrooms and public areas at St Pierre provide all that is expected of a 4 star hotel.

Guests will find that the hotel is equipped with all the leisure facilities you could ever hope to need. Enjoy a dip in the beautifully designed indoor heated swimming pool or relax with a sauna and jacuzzi. For the less energetic, pamper yourself in the health and beauty salon or try your hand at Crown Green Bowling!

The hotel is also an ideal venue for business meetings and conferences, from the large scale proportions of the chandeliered St Pierre Suite, to smaller syndicate rooms.

The St Pierre Hotel is also famous for Championship golf. With its two 18 hole golf courses it is renowned as a European Tour venue. St Pierre has hosted the Dunlop Masters Golf Tournament and the Epson Grand Prix of Europe. Golfers will appreciate the Old Course with its 18th drive across the lake and the Mathern Course which has a brook running through it to provide a challenge to golfers of all abilities.

For those who have any spare time during their stay, the hotel is close to the glorious Wye Valley and any racegoers might want to visit the nearby Chepstow races.

St Pierre Hotel, Country Club Resort
St Pierre Park
Chepstow
Gwent
Tel: (0291) 625261
Fax: (0291) 629975

One of the first jokes that an English Schoolboy learns is, 'How do you get two whales in a mini?'—(Answer) 'Cross the Severn Bridge!' For golfers the act of crossing the famous bridge usually means one thing—The St Pierre Golf and Country Club at Chepstow.

St Pierre has been in existence for over thirty years. Mr Bill Graham founded the Club in 1961 and the Ken Cotton designed **Old Course** opened the following May. The first thing to strike one at St Pierre is the setting: quite simply, magnificent. The golf course occupies land that was originally a deer park and it has an abundance and great variety of mature trees. There is also a lake covering eleven acres situated in the heart of the course. Whilst the Old Course is understandably St Pierre's pride and joy, there are in fact 36 holes, as a second eighteen, the **Mathern Course** opened in 1975.

Visitors wishing to arrange a game at St Pierre must book starting times in advance. The club's **professional, Renton Doig** and his staff can be contacted by telephone on (0291) 65261; all written correspondence should be addressed to: **The St Pierre Hotel, Golf and Country Club, St Pierre Park, Chepstow, Gwent NP6 6YA.**

Other than proof of handicap there are no general restrictions on times of play. The 1994 Summer green fees are as follows: £40 for a round over the Old Course during the week, £45 at the weekend, with £25 payable for a game on the Mathern Course. For junior golfers a single round on the Old Course is priced at £22 with £15 purchasing a game on the Mathern. Societies are normally only received during the week unless they are resident at the hotel, in which case they may also play at weekends.

Travelling to St Pierre ought to present few problems. The Golf Club is located to the South of Chepstow off the A48. The M4 links Chepstow to Cardiff and Swansea in the west and to London and Bristol in the east. The M4 should be left at exit 22, the A446 then taken into Chepstow where the A48 can be joined and followed to St Pierre. The best route for those approaching from Birmingham and the north of England is probably to travel south on the M5 leaving at exit 8, thereafter picking up the M50 to Ross-on-Wye. From Ross-on-Wye a

combination of the A40 and A466 provides a pleasant drive through the Wye Valley to Chepstow.

The Old and the Mathern Course differ quite considerably in length. The Old is the Championship Course and from the back tees it measures 6748 yards (par 71). The forward tees reduce the length to 6492 yards, while for the ladies it measures 5950 yards (par 75). The respective distances for the Mathern Course are 5762 yards (par 68), 5593 yards and 5204 yards (par 70).

Despite its relative youth, the Old Course has been the venue for a remarkable number of professional events. The Dunlop Masters and Silk Cut Masters were staged regularly here; illustrious winners included Tony Jacklin, Bernhard Langer and Greg Norman. The latter on his way to a seven stroke victory in 1982 drove the 362 yard 10th with a three wood. In recent years the Epson Grand Prix tournament was also held at St Pierre. In 1989 Seve Ballesteros produced easily his best golf of the year to win his first title in Wales; in 1990 the tournament changed its format from match play to stroke play and resulted in a popular home victory for the Welsh Wizard Ian Woosnam and a year later Jose Maria Olazabal strolled home nine shots ahead of the field.

Perhaps the most famous hole on the Old Course is the 18th, surely one of the most dramatic finishing holes in golf. A par three of 237 yards, it requires a brave tee shot across the edge of the lake with large trees lining the left hand side of the fairway. Standing proudly behind the green is the St Pierre Hotel.

The hotel is in fact a former 14th century country mansion and it serves the golfer as a particularly impressive 19th. In addition to an excellent restaurant which offers breakfast, lunch and dinner, there are four bars. Celebrating at the end of a round is always to be recommended—particularly if the 18th hole has been tackled successfully. Share a thought though for a person by the name of Arwyn Griffiths who came to the 18th needing a three for a gross 63. A few minutes later he walked off the green having taken eleven strokes—but even he found cause for celebration, for Arwyn still won the competition!

Old Course

Hole	Yards	Par	Hole	Yards	Par
1	576	5	10	362	4
2	388	4	11	393	4
3	135	3	12	545	5
4	379	4	13	219	3
5	420	4	14	521	5
6	165	3	15	375	4
7	442	4	16	426	4
8	309	4	17	412	4
9	444	4	18	237	3
Out	3,258	35	In	3,490	36
			Out	3,258	35
			Totals	6,748	71

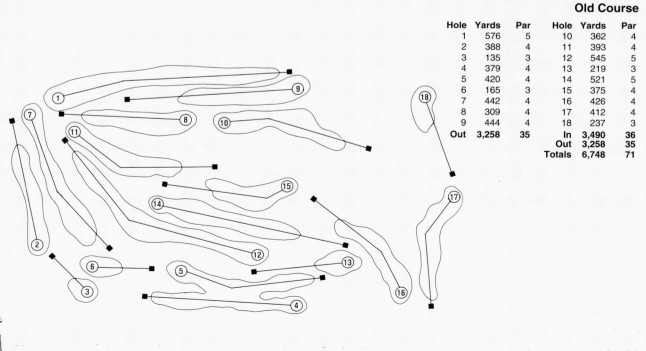

A thoroughly charming Victorian country house hotel, Gliffaes boasts fine gardens and parkland, situated in the National Park yet only one mile off the main A40 road. It offers peace and tranquillity as well as being easily accessible.

The hotel's location makes it ideal for visiting golfers. The championship course of the Rolls of Monmouth is only 30 minutes away, while top courses such as Cradoc and Abergavenny lie within ten miles of the hotel. St Pierre, Builth Wells and Llandrindod Wells are also in reasonable proximity.

The house, which faces due south, stands in its own 29 acres in the beautiful valley of the River Usk, midway between the Brecon Beacons and the Black Mountains. Built in 1885 as a private residence, it has been ideally adapted to provide spacious comfort in the country house tradition. There are 22 bedrooms with private bathrooms or showers and all are individual in decor and furnishing, including three in the converted lodge.

The downstairs rooms include a large, comfortable panelled sitting room which leads into an elegant Regency style drawing room. From here, french windows open into a large conservatory with double doors onto the terrace. The dining room and comfortable bar also open onto the terrace, with glorious views of the surrounding hills and River Usk some 150 feet below. The billiard room has a full sized table and provides an additional sitting room with something of a club atmosphere.

Breakfast is served from a sideboard, lunch is a cold buffet with soup and a hot dish. Dinner is either table d'hote or a la carte. In fact, country house standards of the old order are carefully maintained by the resident owners: the Brabner family have held sway here since 1948.

External facilities include fishing for salmon and trout in the part of the Usk which the hotel overlooks, tennis, bowls, putting and croquet. There is an extensive range of short walks in the vicinity and a nearby riding and pony trekking establishment where horses and ponies can be hired.

The hotel is justly proud of its in-house cooking and remains open from the middle of March to the end of the year.

Gliffaes Country House
Crickhowell
Powys
Wales NP8 1RH
Tel: (0874) 730371
Fax: (0874) 730463

If this golf course didn't already have such a splendid name it would be necessary to invent one. 'Tranquillity Golf Club' might suffice. OK maybe that's a bit naff, but it wouldn't be in breach of the Trade Descriptions Act. The Rolls of Monmouth enjoys one of the most peaceful and secluded settings in Britain. The golf course is relatively young—it opened in 1982—but the accompanying countryside of gentle, circling hills and far off mountains cannot have altered greatly in hundreds of years. Indeed the 20th century seems strangely to have passed it by.

The actual name is no mystery at all for the golf course lies within the grounds of the Rolls Estate, the former country home of Charles Stewart Rolls, who, together with Henry Royce, founded the famous Rolls Royce company. The imposing mansion which dominates the grounds and is visible from several parts of the course was largely built in the 18th century. Fortunately for we present day golfers the Rolls family were rather keen on landscaping and the grounds are blessed with a wonderful variety of trees and shrubs. Given such a setting and the fact that the Rolls course was laid out to championship specifications, incorporating several small lakes and streams, it isn't difficult to see why it has quickly established itself as one of the finest parkland tests in Britain.

The precise location of the club is four miles west of Monmouth, immediately off the B4233 Monmouth to Abergavenny road. The attractive market town is itself linked to Chepstow and Hereford by the scenic A466 and to Ross-on-Wye by the A40.

Individual visitors and societies are equally welcome at The Rolls and can make bookings seven days per week. Tee reservations should be made by contacting the **Booking Secretary, Mrs Sandra Orton** by telephone on **(0600) 715353** or by fax on (0600) 713115. The Club's full address is **The Rolls of Monmouth Golf Club, The Hendre, Monmouth, Gwent NP5 4HG**. Handicap certificates are not essential but as this is a serious test of golf, all players should have attained a reasonable level of competence. The green fees in 1994 were £30 per day during the week with £35 payable at weekends.

Both the Clubhouse and golf shop are adjacent to the mansion and full catering is available in the former throughout the week. The Club has recently received planning permission to build a second course, hotel and conference centre, and to convert the mansion, a listed building, into what promises to be a superb 'new' Clubhouse.

From its back markers the existing course measures a lengthy 6723 yards, par 72, although many are likely to play from the forward tees which reduce the length to a more modest 6283 yards. The Rolls is very much a course of two halves, the two nines being laid out on opposite sides of the estate (this of course enables groups to start from either the 1st or the 10th tee with minimal fuss).

The front nine opens fairly tamely (though prettily enough) with three gentle par fours all requiring slightly downhill approaches and the short 4th which has an attractive lake just behind the green and a semi-concealed bunker to the left. Then comes probably the most difficult series of holes in the round. The 5th has a deep ravine in front of the green and the only saving grace for the golfer is that it is a par five; the 6th is the stroke one hole and requires two very accurate shots across a severley contoured fairway and the 7th dramatically curls, tumbles and twists its way downhill for all of 500 yards until it meets a lake and a little stream—as for the green it's still another thirty yards the other side of the stream. The 8th is one of four very good par three holes at The Rolls, and the 9th, a short par four played from a spectacular high tee is a real 'open the shoulders' type!

Among the more memorable holes on the back nine are the 11th, a lovely sweeping downhill par four, the sharply dog-legging 15th at the far end of the course (some splendid mountain views here) and the two par threes, the 13th and the 18th. The former has been described as 'an absolute beauty' and the latter 'an absolute horror'! Water features on both holes, but while it merely helps to shape the 13th and make it a very picturesque one-shotter, it turns the 18th into a very intimidating closing hole. 'Tranquillity'? Tell that to the match waiting on the 18th tee with all bets in the balance!

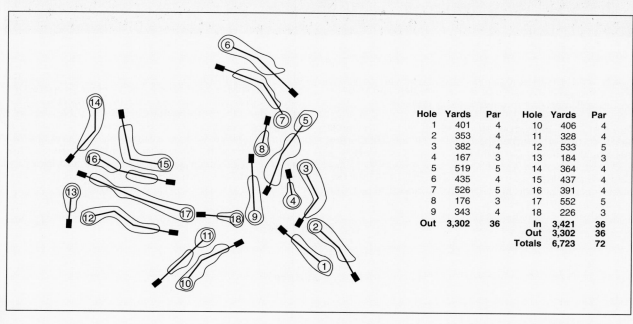

Hole	Yards	Par	Hole	Yards	Par
1	401	4	10	406	4
2	353	4	11	328	4
3	382	4	12	533	5
4	167	3	13	184	3
5	519	5	14	364	4
6	435	4	15	437	4
7	526	5	16	391	4
8	176	3	17	552	5
9	343	4	18	226	3
Out	**3,302**	**36**	**In**	**3,421**	**36**
			Out	**3,302**	**36**
			Totals	**6,723**	**72**

A real treat awaits golfers in the south west corner of Wales; it is called Tenby and it is where genuine championship golf meets memorable holiday golf head on.

Tenby and its immediate surrounds is one of the most beautiful, peaceful and unspoiled areas of the British Isles; it is an unashamedly old fashioned seaside golf course.

Tenby is the oldest golf club in Wales and its 18 hole layout is a classic seaside links—plenty of sand dunes; undulating, windswept fairways; the occasional blind shot and awkward stance and firm, fast greens prepared by Mother Nature. Long enough and good enough to have staged several championships, Tenby doubles up as a very welcoming holiday course. There are a number of outstanding holes with many people selecting the 3rd, 4th, 12th, 16th and 18th among their favourites, while some truly spectacular views of the coast add greatly to the enjoyment of a round. In short, Tenby is a delight—whether you play on of off the fairways.

Tenby Golf Club
The Burrows
Tenby
Dyfed SA70 7NP
Te;l: (0834) 842787

Penally Abbey is quite simply one of Pembrokeshire's loveliest country houses. From the elegant lounge and dining room guests can enjoy spectacular views across Carmarthen Bay and the challenging links of Tenby Golf Course. The proximity of the Abbey to the club and the concessionary rates available to golfing guests are just two factors that make this elegant gothic style mansion an ideal base for the itinerant golfer.

Set in five acres of gardens and woodland in the picturesque floral village of Penally there is an air of tranquillity to the Abbey and an emphasis on relaxation.

Whatever the weather Penally Abbey is a haven of comfort and cheerful ambience. Every season brings with it a variety of outdoor pursuits; spring and autumn are the perfect time for horse-riding and sailing, summer brings surfing and swimming as well as Eistedfodds, pageants, concerts and country shows galore. In winter you can walk the coastal path in appreciation of Pembrokeshire's incomparable beautiful coastline.

With the ruined chapel now the last surviving link to its monastic past, guests are assured of a more traditional but no less hospitable welcome than visitors to the Abbey in bygone years. Crackling log fires and candle-lit dinners, mouthwatering dishes of seasonal delicacies are the order of the day. As is the care the management take to accommodate individual preferences with vegetarian meals and special diets prepared to order.

The bedrooms are perfect for that special occasion, anniversary or honeymoon. Exquisitely furnished and decorated with antiques and period furniture, many have four poster beds. All are centrally heated, have en suite bathrooms, tea and coffee making facilities, telephones, colour television and hairdriers. Whether in the main building or in the adjoining converted coach house you will be delighted with their old world charm.

Penally Abbey
Pembrokeshire
Tel: (0834) 843033
Fax: (0834) 844714

The Lake is a riverside country house set in 50 acres of beautiful grounds with sweeping lawns, woods, riverside walks and a large well stocked lake. The hotel offers spacious and luxurious accommodation, enhanced by log fires and antiques. Excellent, imaginative food prepared from fresh local produce is served in the elegant dining room, accompanied by one of the finest wine lists in Wales. The Lake was awarded the Restaurant of the Year by Johansens for 1991 and had also received a Rosette for food from the AA for the last two years. The Lake offers all that is best in country house hospitality and satisfied guests return again and again.

For the golf enthusiast, The Lake is ideally situated for the region's top three courses: Llandrindod Wells, Cradoc and Builth Wells whose attractive parkland course is only ten minutes from the hotel and guests enjoy concessionary green fees.

This part of Wales is also a fisherman's paradise with a lake covering $2\frac{1}{2}$ acres within the grounds and a $4\frac{1}{2}$ mile stretch of the River Irfon running through the extensive parkland of the hotel. The trout in the river are mostly wild fish and run up to 5lb, with some larger. The water is divided into six beats, a maximum of two rods allowed on each. The Wye provides good trout fishing and the Irfon is likely to produce salmon almost anytime in the season, but really comes into its own in the latter part. There are also a number of Welsh Water Authorities Reservoirs within easy reach.

The region is well known to birdwatchers and is an ideal centre for walkers and a haven for wildlife, including badgers and red kite. There are spectacular drives in all directions . Clay pigeon shooting and horse riding are available.

AA and RAC 3 stars and Merit Award. Children welcome. Dogs by arrangement.

The Lake Country House
Llangammarch Wells
Powys
Wales LD4 4BS
Tel: (05912) 202/474
Fax: (05912) 457

One's first thoughts of North Wales are often of lakes, great castles and even greater mountains, or as a fine fellow by the name of Hywell ap Owain, 12th century Prince of Gwynedd, put it (I offer it in translation):

I love its sea-marsh and its mountains,
And its fortress by its forest and its bright lands,
And its meadows and its water and its valleys,
And its white seagulls and its lovely women.

A man who had obviously seen much of the world! Of course in the 12th century the Welsh didn't play golf, or at least if they did they kept it pretty quiet and in any case you can be pretty confident that Hywell ap Owain would have told us about it. Well, what about the golf in North Wales then? In a word, marvellous. Inland it tends to get hilly to put it mildly, and should you wish to venture up into 'them thar hills' as well as the climbing gear, don't forget to bring the waterproofs! But there again, leave room for the camera (hope you've got a large golf bag).

In the main though, it is to the coast that the travelling golfer will wish to head. Between Flint to the east of Clwyd and Aberdovey in southern Gwynedd are the impressive championship links of Prestatyn, Maesdu, North Wales, Conwy, Royal St Davids and of course Aberdovey itself. In addition, there are several with spectacular locations, Nefyn on the Lleyn Peninsula being an outstanding example.

Clwyd

Before journeying around the coast though, a brief mention for some of the inland courses, with a few thoughts as to where one might stop off in order to eat, drink, be merry or simply rest the weary golf clubs. Away from the sea and sand probably the best two challenges are to be found at Wrexham and Llangollen. **Wrexham**, located just off the A53, is fairly close to the English border and indeed the views here are across the Cheshire plain. Two good holes to look out for are the 4th and 14th. Llangollen's splendid course, the **Vale of Llangollen**, is set out alongside the banks of the River Dee. There are some truly excellent holes, notably the 9th. Appropriately named the River Hole it is a really tough par four of 425 yards. The golfer who likes a spot of fishing (or perhaps even the golfing fisherman) would be in his element here and on a good day should see a few of the famous Dee salmon being landed—probably easier than netting a birdie. One name to watch in the future is the spectacular new **Chirk Golf and Country Club**, south of Wrexham on the A483. Over 7000 yards of manicured fairways are to be complemented by a much less taxing par three course and driving range. North west of Wrexham on the road to Flint can be found the St Davids Park Hotel (0352) 840440 and **Northop Country Park** Golf Club complex. Excellent accommodation and a course now attracting PGA events make this well worth a visit.

As host to the famous International Eisteddfod Festival Llangollen has long been a popular tourist centre and there are a number of fine hotels in the town including the Hand (0978) 860303 and the Royal (0978) 860202. Also in Llangollen, Gales Wine Bar is well recommended as is Caesars restaurant (0978) 860133 with its enterprising menu. Practically midway between Llangollen and Wrexham with a beautiful Deeside setting is the Boat Inn (0978) 780143 at Erbistock—not quite the first (or is it the last) inn in Wales, but one of the best—especially appealing when floodlit at night. In Wrexham itself, the Crest Hotel offers a comfortable forty winks.

Remaining in Clwyd and the unfortunately named town of **Mold**. A pleasant parkland challenge here, while still further north and getting nearer the coast is the **Rhuddlan** Golf Club. They say you should never rush a round at Rhuddlan. If you are heading for the tougher links courses on the coast then this is the ideal place to groove the swing. The course is laid out close to one of North Wales' famous massive fortresses in the grounds of Bodrhydden estate and overlooks the Vale of Clwyd. Just a couple of thoughts for golfers wishing to wet the whistle: The Dinorben Arms at Bodfari and the Salisbury Arms at Tremeirchion—two fine hostelries.

Golfwise there is not a great deal more in the deeper realms of North Wales. **Ffestiniog**, (in Gwynedd) famed for its mountain railway, has a short nine holes of the moorland variety but the scenery in these parts may prove a little too distracting. Ffestiniog nestles in the heart of Snowdonia and the encircling mountains are quite awe-inspiring. Exploring the countryside is a delight and there is a plentiful supply of country houses and inns to entice the traveller. Somewhat isolated, though quite outstanding, is Pale Hall (06783) 285 at Llandderfel near Bala (off the B4401). Lake Bala is actually not that far away and those who enjoy watersports should take note. Another charming place to rest is the 16th century Hand Hotel (069176) 666 at Llanarmon Dyffryn Ceiriog—all wooden beams and roaring fires—wonderful! Time to tear oneself away. The coast beckons and it's time to put that grooved swing into practice. **Prestatyn** warrants first attention. Close to Pontin's holiday camp (or is it village nowadays?) it is a genuine links and when the prevailing westerly blows, can play very long (the championship tees stretch the course to 6714 yards). If a day at Pontin's isn't your cup of tea then the Sands Hotel located in the town is convenient. Thirsty golfers might also find the time to drive over the hill to the village of Gwaenysgor and the Eagle and Child pub—good food and good ale.

The A55 is the coastal road that should be followed to find our next port of call, the **Abergele and Pensarn** Golf Club, just west of Abergele. This course is a fairly new parkland layout (the bulldozer having removed the former) and it lies beneath the walls of fairytale Gwyrch Castle. Games are often won or lost on the last three holes at Abergele. The round is supposed to finish five, three, five—but not many scorecards seem to!

Gwynedd

A trio of championship courses are to be found a little further along the coast and just over the county border in Gwynedd. Golfers in Llandudno are more fortunate than most, having two fine courses to choose from: **North Wales** and **Llandudno (Maesdu)**. Both are of a high standard and each offers superb views across the Conwy estuary towards Anglesey.

The **Caernarvonshire** Golf Club lies the other side of the estuary—yet another spectacular siting between the sea and mountains and another course where the wind can blow fiercely. A regular venue for the important Welsh Championships, Conwy is a long course and is generally considered second only to Royal St Davids in terms of golfing challenges in North Wales. It possesses everything that makes links golf so difficult—gorse, rushes, sandhills and more gorse, rushes and sandhills—quite frightening!

The Llandudno-Conwy-Colwyn Bay area is riddled with places of interest and places to stay. Indeed it offers a veritable feast for the golfing gourmet. Here are a few thoughts. In Llandudno, famed for its Great Orme, are four excellent hotels, the Empire (0492) 860555, St Tudno (0492) 874411, St Georges (0492) 877544 and the Marine Hotel, while slightly inland at Deganwy is the renowned 17th century Bodysgallen Hall (0492) 584466. Set amid quite idyllic grounds, the hotel offers great style as well as sumptuous cuisine. Less expensive accommodation of good quality can be found at the Bryn Cregin Garden Hotel (0492) 585266 also in Deganwy and very highly recommended. Returning to Llandudno the Floral restaurant has a gregarious atmosphere and is most pleasing while a pair of pubs whose names you should have little difficulty in remembering are the Kings Head and the Queens Head, the latter a little to the south of the town at Llandudno Junction. Nearby in Conwy a liquid round can be enjoyed at the Liverpool Arms on the quay. There are many attractions in the area: the great castle of course and the town walls, Bodnant Gardens in the Conwy Valley and even the smallest house in Great Britain. Finally in Colwyn Bay among the many hotels two that merit attention are the Norfolk House Motel (0492) 531757 and the interestingly named Hotel Seventy Degrees (0492) 516555.

Heading for the golf courses of the Lleyn Peninsular, many may wish to break their journey at Caernarvon. The castle is splendid and well worth inspecting. Those staying in the area might note that one of the best restaurants in Wales is to be found here —the Seahorse (0248) 670546 at Port Dinorwic. I suppose every golfer has at one time or another drawn up a mental listing of favourite golf courses. Anyone who has made the trip to **Nefyn** is almost certain to have the course high on such a list. A sheer delight to play on (see feature page) Nefyn was a regular haunt of Lloyd-George, as was neighbouring **Pwllheli,** which was in fact opened by him in 1909 when he was the Chancellor of the Exchequer. Not far from Pwllheli there is a good golf course at **Aberscoch.** Handy hotels for Nefyn include the Linksway (0758) 720258, Woodland Hall (0758) 720425 and the Caeau Capel Hotel (0758) 720240. There are numerous pubs, including the Ty Coch Inn (almost on the course itself), and the Sportsman. Close by, situated right on the cliffs is the Dive Inn (0758) 877246 at Tudweilog, which has an excellent restaurant. Another pleasant establishment is the lively Bryncyann Inn (0758) 720879 in Morfa Nefyn. In Pwllheli the Tower Hotel (0758) 612822, the Bel-Air Restaurant (0758) 613198 and Porth Tocyn Hotel (0758) 7113303 can also be thoroughly recommended.

A trip to the north west of Wales wouldn't be complete without a visit to Harlech, another great castle and certainly a great golf links, home of course, of the **Royal St Davids** Golf Club (it too is explored on a later page). On the culinary side in Harlech there are two good restaurants, the Castle Cottage (0766) 780479 (some accommodation) and the Cemlyn (0766) 780425, while not far off in Talsarnau is the excellent Maes-y-Neuadd (0766) 780200 hotel and restaurant, extremely convenient for Royal St Davids, as is St Davids Hotel (0766) 780366. Finally in Harlech, Alexa House and Stable Cottages offer charming accommodation at a charming price. In Porthmadoc is another good hotel, the Royal Sportsman (0766) 512015. Lastly, you cannot miss out on visiting Portmeirion, Cluff Williams Ellis' attempt at creating the Italian Riviera on the coast of Wales. We recommend you stay at the Hotel Portmeirion (0766) 770228.

Heading further south and passing the splendid George III Hotel (0341) 422525 at Penmaenpool, **Aberdovey** is soon reached. The subject of favourite courses has been raised and Aberdovey was the choice

of the celebrated golf writer Bernard Darwin, 'the course that my soul loves best of all the courses in the world.' It has an interesting layout, sandwiched between the sand dunes on the one side and a railway line on the other, (the railway line in fact links Aberdovey to Harlech and is a pretty good service).

Golfers looking to play Aberdovey should find the Trefeddian Hotel (0654) 762213 is exceptionally convenient for the course and the Corbett Arms (0923) 822388 ideally situated for their requirements. As an alternative there is the attractive Hotel Plas Penhelig (0654) 767676 which overlooks the Dovey estuary.

Isle of Anglesey

The Isle of Anglesey is linked by a road bridge to the mainland across the Menai Straits. There is a choice of four golf courses with plans in the pipeline for extending this number. Perhaps the best two games to be found are at **Bull Bay**, near Amlwch, and at **Holyhead (Trearddur Bay)** on Holy Island. Both courses are very scenic and we have featured Holyhead separately. Bull Bay enjoys a fairly remote, and certainly spectacular setting on the island's northern coast. It is a hilly course with much gorse and several rocks to confront and when the wind blows it can be very tricky. The club handbook relates how in an exhibition match to mark the opening of the course, featuring John H. Taylor and James Braid, the latter tangled with the gorse on the short third hole and finished up with an eight! There's hope for us all. Two convenient resting places are the Bull Bay Hotel (0407) 830223 at Amlwch and the impressive Trearddur Bay Hotel (0407) 860301 which lies adjacent to the Holyhead Golf Club. In addition there are not surprisingly a vast number of reasonably priced guest houses on Anglesey—contact the Welsh Tourist Board for details—and for a real treat we recommend the Tre-Ysgawen Country House (0248) 750750 at Capel Coch near Llangefni.

Artist: **Lance Thackery A LONG DRIVE**
Courtesy of the **Burlington Gallery**

Providing a Mecca for golfing societies and individual golfers, the Corbett Arms has an ideal location for players choosing Aberdovey Golf Course. On offer is that rarely found combination of very reasonable accommodation prices, attractive cuisine, warm and friendly service and quality accommodation standards.

Nestling as it does on the edge of Snowdonia National Park there are beautiful views of the mountains. Much of the original character of this Grade 2 listed building (a former coaching inn) has been retained in what has been from time immemorial a location of hospitality and cheer for travellers.

All the bedrooms are individually furnished, several with traditional four poster beds and each has its own en suite bathroom, telephone, colour television and beverage making facilities.

Within the three bars a selection of real ales is available, together with a fine and sometimes unusual selection of malts. An ideal location for that relaxing drink must be the beautifully maintained beer garden offering magnificent views of the surrounding countryside. The hotel restaurant offers a traditional choice of local cuisine and fine wines whilst top quality snacks may be obtained from the bars.

Aberdovey Golf Club

The possibility of playing golf at Aberdovey was first recognised by a Col Arthur Ruck, a member of Formby golf club. Legend has it that he used flower pots or jam jars sunk into the grounds for holes, forming a 9 hole course. Major General R M Ruck, brother of the founder, and later knighted, was a powerful force in Welsh golf and became President of the Welsh Golfing Union from 1932 to 1935.

The Rucks had a nephew, the celebrated golf writer Bernard Darwin, who became the Times golf correspondent. Darwin fell head over heels in love with Aberdovey and travelled there by train regularly. Many of his writings feature the course and his journeys northwards to the Cambrian coast.

Darwin was a major factor in Aberdovey's initial success and still accounts for many visitors, particularly those from across the Atlantic, where his writings are widely read and collected. Aberdovey will remain his "best loved place in all the world".

The now 18 hole course at Aberdovey has an interesting layout, sandwiched between the sand dunes on the one side and a railway line on the other.

Corbett Arms Hotel
Corbett Square
Tywyn
Gwynedd
Wales
Tel : (01654) 710264
Fax: (01654) 710359

The Bryn Cregin Hotel

The Bryn Cregin hotel was originally built in the 1890s as a fine house for a retiring ship's captain. The good fellow obviously knew what he was doing as he set his home in its own beautiful gardens with panoramic views over the Conwy Estuary, Conwy Castle and the Snowdonia mountains.

We must assume that he was also a keen golfer as the hotel is within two miles of three of North Wales' finest championship golf courses. Llandudno (Maesdu) and North Wales are on the east shore of the estuary and are kept to a very high standard. Both offer superb views over the water to Anglesey. Opposite, on the west shore, is the famous and sometimes daunting Caernarvonshire course (Conwy). A classic links course an ample supply of gorse and rushes. Leave your woods in the bag on a windy day.

Today, after extensions in the 30s and a complete refurbishment in the mid 80s, the Bryn Cregin is one of the most finely appointed and comfortable hotels in the area. The hotel has 16 bedrooms all with private bath and shower. Each room has remote control colour TV, direct dial telephone, radio and tea and coffee making facilities. All rooms are individually furnished and decorated to a very high standard and most over look the estuary and garden.

After a testing day on the course what better than to sit on the terrace, drink in hand, watch the sun set over Anglesey and Puffin Island. Then bathe and change and down to splendid dinner in the intimate restaurant. A bottle of fine wine from the celler to accompany the meal and a snifter or two with coffee afterwards,why not!

The opening of the North Wales expressway (A55) as dual carriageway as far as Conwy has made getting to this beautiful part of the world very much easier. Well under two hours from most parts of Cheshire, Lancashire, the West Midlands and the Yorkshires. Journey time from the home countries is about four hours.

The Bryn Cregin welcomes golfers all year round and can cater for parties up to 30.The basic package is for two nights dinner, bed and breakfast and two glorious days of golf (green fees not included). The three courses are featured so you can try them all or master just one. If you want to stay longer that's no problem and you will find welcome reductions for extended holidays.

For longer suffering non-golfers there is ample to do and see in the local area. Riding,hill walking, visiting the wealth of National Trust properties and gardens or just taking the wonderful scenery.

Please write or call for a free illustrated brochure.
The Bryn Cregin Hotel
Ty Mawr Road
Deganwy
Nr Conwy
GwyneddLL31 9UR
Tel: (0492) 585266
Fax: (0492) 596203

Royal St David's (Harlech)

With a St Andrews in Scotland and a St George's in England, it seems only right that there should be a St David's in Wales. Along with Royal Porthcawl in the South, the Royal St David's Golf Club at Harlech is one of the Principality's two greatest Championship links.

The Club was founded in 1894 by the Hon. Harold Finch-Hatton together with Mr. W.H. More who for twenty years acted as Honourary Secretary. The course itself was open for play at the end of 1894 and the opening competition was fittingly won by the greatest golfer of the day and the then reigning Amateur Champion, John Ball. St David's became Royal St David's early this century and in 1935 The Duke of Windsor (then Prince of Wales) became the Club's captain.

Of its many attributes St David's is perhaps best known for its glorious setting: on the one side stretch the blue waters of Tremedog Bay, and on the other the imperious Snowdon and the other great mountains of Snowdonia National Park; while surveying all from its lofty perch is the almost forbidding presence of Harlech Castle. The massive fortress built by Edward I has known a particularly turbulent past. It played a prominent role in the War of the Roses when a great seige took place eventually ending in surrender. The seige is commemorated in the famous song 'Men of Harlech'.

The present 'Men of Harlech' to whom I should introduce you are the **Secretary, Mr R I Jones (tel. (0766) 780361** and the Club's **professional John Barnett** who may be contacted by telephone on **(0766) 780857.** The Club has the simple address of **Royal St David's Golf Club, Harlech, Gwynedd, LL46 2UB.**

St David's has a reputation for being one of Britain's friendliest Clubs; subject to being Members of Golf Clubs visitors and Golfing Societies are welcome at all times although those wishing to make party bookings must do so by written application to the Secretary. The cost of a day's golf in 1994 was set at £24 during the week with £30 payable at the weekend and on Bank Holidays.

The setting is indeed superb but the journey to get there can be a lengthy one—Harlech alas isn't like the proverbial Rome and there is just one road that travellers must join, namely the A496. From the North this road approaches from Blaenau Ffestiniog via Maentwrog (east of Porthmadog) and from the South via Dolgellau and Barmouth. Those coming from further afield may find Bala (if travelling from the north) and Welshpool (if motoring from the south) useful towns to head for. Bala links with Maentwrog by way of the A4212 and the A487, while the A458 and A470 link Welshpool to Barmouth. Finally, for those not travelling by car, the train station at Harlech may prove of assistance.

Measuring less than 6500 yards from the Championship tees, St David's may not at first glance seem overly testing. However the general consensus is that the course, to adopt golfers' terminology, 'plays long'. Par is a very tight 69 and there are only two par fives on the card. Furthermore the rough can be very punishing (not to mention frustrating) and it is very rare for there not to be a stiff westerly wind.

Perhaps the most difficult holes on the course are the 10th, a long par four into the prevailing wind, and the classic 15th which requires a lengthy, angled drive followed by a precise approach. The round finishes with, to adopt another curious golfing expression, 'a nasty long short hole.'

The nineteenth at St David's matches the high standards set by the previous eighteen. There is an excellent bar for celebration or recuperation and light snacks, lunches and dinners are all offered. With prior warning a full Anglo/Welsh breakfast can also be arranged.

As one might imagine, each of the major Welsh Championships is staged regularly at St David's; in addition the British Ladies Championship, (won for the fourth time by Cecil Leitch in 1926) and both Mens and Ladies Home International Matches have also been played at Harlech.

The conviviality of the Club atmosphere has already been mentioned; unfortunately there are some English who consider the Welsh a little insular—a visit to Royal St David's makes one realise that Welsh Golf Clubs could teach many of their English counterparts a thing or two about hospitality...and on that controversial note, I wish you good golfing!

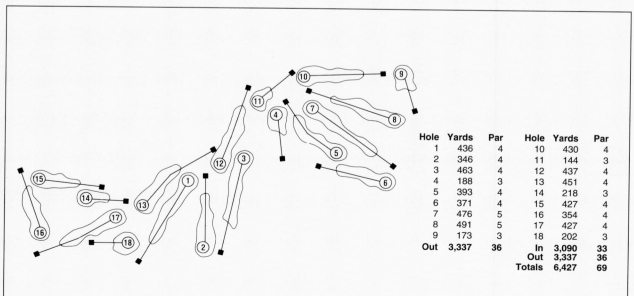

Hole	Yards	Par	Hole	Yards	Par
1	436	4	10	430	4
2	346	4	11	144	3
3	463	4	12	437	4
4	188	3	13	451	4
5	393	4	14	218	3
6	371	4	15	427	4
7	476	5	16	354	4
8	491	5	17	427	4
9	173	3	18	202	3
Out	**3,337**	**36**	**In**	**3,090**	**33**
			Out	**3,337**	**36**
			Totals	**6,427**	**69**

Anglesey has long been popular as a peaceful retreat and the Trearddur Bay Hotel, with its magnificent location, has proved to be one of its most prized assets. Step outside the hotel and the bay beckons with scenic walks, miles of golden sandy beaches and the ideal haven for watersports.

Few hotels are able to offer guests such striking, varied accommodation; but then few hotels boast such panoramic views from so many rooms. There are 31 rooms, nine being studio suites, including the four-poster 'Shearwater': with authentic oak beams and all the facilities of a first class hotel. Every one of them provides the perfect home away from home.

Before dinner why not enjoy a cocktail or your favourite aperitif in a quiet corner of the bar before set-tling down to the superb cuisine of the restaurant to savour a meal chosen from table d'hote and à la carte menus. Besides the breathtaking views another advantage of the hotel's location is the sheer range of fresh, locally caught seafood that is so readily available, accompanied, perhaps, by a fine wine from the extensive cellars.

There are many activities available to guests at Trearddur Bay, from the indoor heated swimming pool to pool in the games room; while outside the whole of the Isle awaits with a range of sports, including tennis and golf, to the fascinating historical sites sites of Beaumaris Castle and Bryn Celli Ddu.

Naturally a hotel of such stature offers the finest in conference and function facilities where nothing is too much trouble.

Trearddur Bay Hotel
Holyhead
Anglesey
North Wales
Tel: (0407) 860301
Fax: (0407) 861181

Holyhead (Trearddur Bay)

'**W**hich do you reckon are the best holes at Holyhead?' I asked a Mancunian friend who plays the course every summer without fail. 'They're all real crackers down there', he replied. 'In fact, it's a cracking course full stop'. And he's right.

Holyhead, or Trearddur Bay as many people call it, is one of two superb golf courses on the Isle of Anglesey, the other being Bull Bay on the island's northerly tip at Amlwch. There are other courses on Anglesey, making it an ideal place for a week's golfing holiday, but these two are the best—a couple of crackers in fact! Arguments as to which is the better frequently dominate 19th hole discussions in pubs around the island. Bull Bay's clifftop setting is certainly spectacular and the course provides a real test, but maybe Trearddur Bay offers the greater variety of challenge and its location on Holy Island, if not quite as stunning as Bull Bay, is sufficiently invigorating for most golfing souls.

A glance at the scorecard tells you that the course measures only just over 6000 yards in length from the back tees, moreover, from a distance, it looks relatively tame with only one serious hill to negotiate. Look a little closer however, and you will soon realise that not only are the fairways extremely narrow and quite undulating but the rough comprises much gorse, heather, bracken and, as my friend puts it, 'all kinds of horror stories'—the words of one who has been thrilled too often—and then there is the wind which whips across from the Irish Sea. Yes, a real challenge and, thanks to architect James Braid, 18 very different holes to savour.

The course can get fairly busy during the peak summer months but the Club is very welcoming and does its best to cater for parties of all sizes. The **Secretary** at Trearddur Bay is **David Entwistle;** visitors should make prior arrangements with him, either by telephone on **(0407) 763279** or in writing to The Secretary, **Holyhead Golf Club, Lon Garreg Fawr, Trearddur Bay, Anglesey, LL65 2YG**. The club's **professional Stephen Elliot** can be reached on **(0407) 762022.**

In 1994 the green fees were set at £17 per round, £20 per day during the week with £20 per round, £25 per day payable at weekends and Bank Holidays. Juniors pay half the above rates. There is a very relaxed atmosphere in the

Clubhouse and some fine refreshment is usually available throughout the day. Visitors might also note that between the months of March and September full board facilities are offered in the Club's Dormy House.

Being wide awake on the 1st tee however is strongly recommended. You had been licking your lips contemplating a very short, straightforward par four to open proceedings but you survey the scene ahead and suddenly there is the feeling you are looking down a gun barrel. The fearless big hitter will hope to fire one up the middle and perhaps even reach the green; most golfers however, could only feel really comfortable playing this and the next few holes wearing blinkers.

The 2nd is a very tricky par three. Clammy hands is the sensation here: go left and you must visit the local farmer (not recommended)—stray right and you may tumble down the edge of a cliff on to an adjacent fairway from which the pitch to the green is less than inviting. The next is a tremendous hole—a par four from the front tees but the 3rd is a genuine five from the back markers. Here the drive is hit straight into the crest of a hill. Once over the hill, there is then a gentle climb to the green; two good straight hits—usually into the wind—will be needed to set up any chance of a birdie. Then comes the shortest hole on the course, the 4th, played directly towards the sea. Very exposed to the elements, this hole can play anything from a long iron to a sand iron. If the wind is against you, as it usually is, the only good news is that it's going to be at your back for the next few holes.

Whether the wind is with you or against you, the challenge continues throughout the round with the Stroke One 9th and the 10th being two especially memorable holes. It also culminates with a glorious, if fiendish finishing hole where to the right of the fairway the gorse and bracken have been permitted to run rampant. 'Can't remember the last time I hit the 18th green in two' my friend tells me', in fact, I can't remember the last time I parred it—it's far too tough for me' he says. Perhaps you should give Anglesey a miss this summer, I dare to suggest. Go to Spain perhaps? 'What! Five hours for a round under a blazing hot sun instead of playing golf here... you must be crackers. Absolute crackers.'

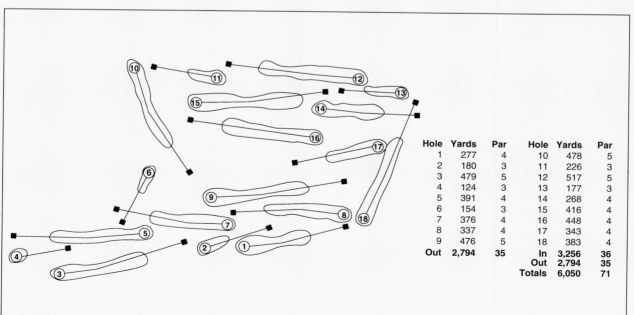

Hole	Yards	Par	Hole	Yards	Par
1	277	4	10	478	5
2	180	3	11	226	3
3	479	5	12	517	5
4	124	3	13	177	3
5	391	4	14	268	4
6	154	3	15	416	4
7	376	4	16	448	4
8	337	4	17	343	4
9	476	5	18	383	4
Out	**2,794**	**35**	**In**	**3,256**	**36**
			Out	**2,794**	**35**
			Totals	**6,050**	**71**

The wonderful parkland setting could have inspired a Constable masterpiece and had much the same effect on course designer, John Jacobs!

Created with championships in mind, the course is a real test for golfers of all abilities, with no two holes the same. Thanks to its high specification, particularly on the greens, winter golf will be as enjoyable as a game in high summer.

Significant advice and coaching can be arranged through the professional team, led by former world champion, David Llewellyn. Full and varied practice facilities are available, including a video swing analysis room within the clubhouse.

Ever mindful of the increasing participation of ladies playing golf, Northop Country Park have an attached lady professional on the WPGE Tour. Locally based golfer, Sara Robinson, views Northop as an excellent venue for improving her all-round game.

The clubhouse features first class facilities and a superb restaurant which specialises in local dishes and food from around the world. Additionally, the clubhouse offers saunas, a gymnasium and tennis courts to its members and visitors.

Just five minutes away and operationally linked to the course is the four star St Davids Park Hotel.

The hotel is the perfect combination of superb modern facilities and traditional comfort. Designed in Georgian style, around an inner courtyard, the hotel offers 121 luxuriously appointed bedrooms, the award winning Fountains Restaurant and a range of fully equipped private rooms. The hotel also offers a full leisure club including an indoor swimming pool, snooker room, beautician, sauna, steam room and gymnasium.

At St Davids Park, you will find that the era of hospitality and service has not gone completely!

A full range of exciting golf and leisure packages is available through the hotel and for guests, free transfer to the golf club can be provided.

St Davids Park Hotel
St Davids
Clewy
Wales
Tel: (0244) 520800
Fax: (0244) 520930

Set amidst a dramatically picturesque 247 acres of North Wales parkland landscape, the course was designed by John Jacobs Golf Associates, led by the renowned John Jacobs, together with chief executive David Pottage.

Extending over 6735 yards from the championship tees. The layout is non punitive and varied in its direction, with no two consecutive holes reversing. Bunkers are strictly strategic and are placed to catch only the wayward shot. Teeing grounds are large with a minimum of four separated tees per hole. The sand greens at Northop have been built to the true USGA specification which ensures consistent all year round playability. Extensive drainage and irrigation systems are also a feature.

The large well contoured greens make for an endless variety of pin positions. The bunkers, which are shaped to suit their precise location, are of different depths and gradients. Adding to this the moulded fairways and unrestricted lines of play make Northop Country Park a true and testing challenge for golfers of all abilities.

The course comprises four par 3s, four par 5s and ten par 4s with twelve changes of par in the round. The par 3s range in length from 156 yards for the well bunkered 17th to 203 yards for the difficult and slightly uphill 5th with its three tiered McKenzian green. The second is a tricky 180 yards to an elevated green whilst the final par 3 is the idyllically situated 192 yard 14th.

Of the four par 5s the most daunting is the awesome 559 yard 11th. Appropriately named 'Wooden Heartache', this double dog-leg is sentried by some of the most magnificent mature native trees (along with the odd import) to be seen anywhere. A good drive down the right hand side is needed if good position for the green approach is to be achieved. A solitary bunker guards the left side of the green. Despite its parkland setting few birdies are ever seen or heard of on the 11th! Of the remaining par 5s the first at 541 yards represents the next greatest challenge to the player. Rising gently and bunkered left and right with out of bounds ever present along the entire right side making club and shot selection vitally impor-

tant. The remaining par 5s, the 505 yard 8th and the 522 yard 15th are birdiable in the right conditions.

Notable par 4s on the front nine are the 355 yard 4th, the 428 yard 7th and the tricky 390 yard 9th. The 9th green in particular is superbly shaped with many subtle yet visible borrows. It is indeed a fine example of its designers skill.

On the back nine the tenth hole, reminiscent of the 10th at the Belfry offers a 'Do I,Don't I?' challenge to the player. The 349 yard 12th, surrounded by ancient oak trees, shares the distinction along with the 13th of being completely unbunkered. The putting surfaces of these particular holes, especially that of the 12th, akin to the classical links style and offer the best defence of the hole. Water comes into play for the first and only time on the tough 378 yard 16th. Two ornamental ponds connected by a running stream will trap the unwary or over-ambitious player every time. Last but no means least is the potential `card wrecking' 440 yard 18th. This is a right to left dog-leg to a slightly raised green. The 18th above all requires nerve and conviction if the round at Northop is to be successfully concluded.

Incidentally, testimony to the course`s challenge is clearly demonstrated by the fact that August `94 sees Northop hosting the Redrow Welsh Open Championship, when the event will return to North Wales after 25 years. The tournament will be staged here for at least three years.

So to the 19th! The spacious and opulently appointed clubhouse offers every amenity the discerning golfer could wish for.

A visit to Northop Country Park would not be complete without a chat with resident Head Professional David `Lulu' Llewellyn. David, apart from being an all round good egg, is an innovative teacher and a remarkable player.

Society, corporate golfers and non members are welcome but only by prior arrangement. Tee booking times are mandatory, so a call to the pro shop is essential before playing.

Northop Country Park,
Northop,
Chester,
Clwyd CH7 6WA
Tel: (0352) 840440,
Fax: (0352)840445.

We golfers in Britain are doubly fortunate—not only do we have an infinite variety of courses to play upon (contrast for instance the Surrey heathland with the Scottish links), but we also possess a wealth of outstandingly scenic courses. Perhaps one of our lesser known treasures is perched on the cliffs of North Wales' western tip. Nefyn, or more precisely Nefyn and District, was founded in 1907, although the course really came into its own in 1920 when an extension was opened by James Braid and John H. Taylor (where was Harry you ask!)

I suppose Nefyn could be described as a classic holiday course: there is a very pleasant drive to the Club; the course is always well maintained with particularly pleasing fairways; whilst the golf is by no means easy, it is never too severe or unfair (indeed, unless the wind blows fiercely, good scores should definitely appear on the cards); the views as mentioned are quite stupendous and Good Lord to cap it all, there is even a pub two thirds of the way round! Well, what more could a golfer ask for?

Visitors to Nefyn must be prepared to produce a handicap certificate and be a member of a recognised Club. Should there be a wish to contact the Club before setting off then the **Secretary, T.G. Owen** can be reached via **The Nefyn & District Golf Club, Morfa Nefyn, Pwllheli, Gwynedd LL53 6DA tel. (0758) 720966** and fax: (0758) 720476). The **steward** can be contacted on **(0758) 720218** and the **professional, John Froom** can be reached on **(0758) 720102.** Green fees for 1994 were priced at £20 per round, £25 per day for weekdays with £25 per round, £35 per day payable at weekends and on Bank Holidays. Those holidaying close by may well be interested in a weekly ticket (please telephone for details). Keen competitors should be pleased to hear that the Club stages open events annually during the first fortnight in August. Societies are welcome at Nefyn although prior arrangement with the secretary is necessary. One final thing to note is that two motorised buggies can be hired from the pro-shop.

As for directions visitors approaching from afar are more than likely to have planned some kind of golfing holiday and so it is assumed that the traveller is already in North Wales. Coming from the Colwyn Bay, Llandudno area one should take the A55 towards Bangor. Then at Bangor, head for Caernafon on the A487 and just beyond Caernafon take the A499 and the B4417 roads through Nefyn to Morfa Nefyn. From the South the A497 connects Pwllheli with Nefyn.

From the back markers Nefyn stretches to 6332 yards and has a par of 72. Ian Woosnam, the 1991 US Masters Champion, holds the professional course record of 67. I am reliably informed that another model of Welsh consistency, Lloyd-George, was a frequent visitor to Nefyn and that this trend was in turn followed by Clement Attlee—who doubtless found the golf here a welcome diversion from the pressures of No. 10.

After a lengthy opener which certainly invites a hearty belt from the tee (sorry, controlled power) the course moves out along by the cliff edges for a number of spectacular holes. It then turns back on itself before heading in a different direction out on to a headland where arguably the best holes on the course, numbers 11 to 18 are found.

There is no real place on the course where you lose sight of the sea and you may just encounter the occasional sunbather who has lost his or her way. If the holiday mood really takes you, then down in a cove by the 12th green is the Ty Coch Inn. Yes, it is accessible from the course and on a really hot summer's day can doubtless be mistaken for a heavenly mirage. One cannot help wondering how many steady score cards have suddenly taken on erratic proportions from the 13th hole in!

Returning to the Clubhouse you will find that full catering facilities are offered. There is a snooker room and a genuinely pleasant atmosphere in which to relax and reflect on your day. Well, if you have not enjoyed your golf at Nefyn then I must venture to suggest that you are an extremely difficult person to please!

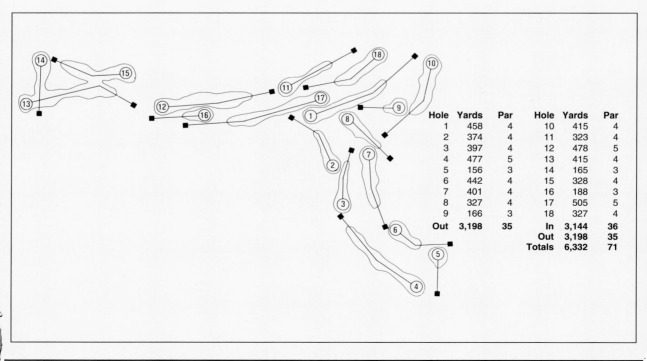

Hole	Yards	Par		Hole	Yards	Par
1	458	4		10	415	4
2	374	4		11	323	4
3	397	4		12	478	5
4	477	5		13	415	4
5	156	3		14	165	3
6	442	4		15	328	4
7	401	4		16	188	3
8	327	4		17	505	5
9	166	3		18	327	4
Out	**3,198**	**35**		**In**	**3,144**	**36**
				Out	**3,198**	**35**
				Totals	**6,332**	**71**

Key

*To avoid disappointment
it is advisable to telephone
in advance*

****Visitors welcome at most times
**Visitors usually allowed on
weekdays only
*Visitors not normally permitted
(Mon, Wed) No visitors
on specified days*

*Approximate Green Fees
A £30 plus
B £20 to £30
C £15 to £25
D £10 to £20
E under £10
F Greens fees on application*

*Restrictions
G Guests only
H Handicap certificate required
H (24) Handicap of 24 or less
L Letter of introduction required
M Visitor must be a member of
another recognised club.*

SOUTH & MID WALES

GWENT

Alice Springs G.C.
(0873) 880772
Bettws-Newydd, Usk
(18)6041 yards/***/D
(18)6400 yards/***/D

Blackwood G.C.
(0495) 223152
Cwmgelli, Blackwood
(9)5300 yards/**/D/H

Caerleon G.C.
(0633) 420342
Broadway, Caerleon
(9)3092 yards/***/E

Dewstow G.C.
(0291) 430444
Caerwent, Newport
(18)6100 yards/***/D

Greenmeadow G.C.
(06333) 69321
Treherbert Road, Croesyceiliog,
Cwmbran
(18)5587 yards/***/F

Llanwern G.C.
(0633) 412029
Tennyson Avenue, Llanwern
(18)6115 yards/**/B/H/M
(9)5239 yards/**/B/H/M

Monmouth G.C.
(0600) 712212
Leasebrook Lane, Monmouth
(18)5698 yards/***/D

Monmouthshire G.C.
(0873) 2606
Llanfoist, Abergavenny
(18)6054 yards/**/B/H/G

Newport G.C.
(0633) 892643
Great Oak, Rogerstone, Newport
(18)6431 yards/**/A/H/M

Oakdale G.C.
(0495) 220044
Llwynon Lane, Oakdale
(9)1235 yards/***/E

Parc G.C.
(0633) 680933
Church Lane, Coedkernew
(18)5136 yards/***/D

Pontnewydd G.C.
(06333) 482170
Maesgwyn Farm, West
Pontnewydd
(10)5353 yards/**/F

Pontypool G.C.
(0495) 763655
Lasgarn Lane, Trevethin
(18)6046 yards/***/C/H/L

The Rolls of Monmouth G.C.
(0600) 715353
The Hendre, Monmouth
(18)6733 yards/***/A

St Mellons G.C.
(0633) 680101
St Mellons, Cardiff
(18)6275 yards/**/B/H

St Pierre G.& C.C.
(0291) 625261
St Pierre Park, Chepstow
(18)6700 yards/***/F/H
(18)5762 yards/***/F/H

Tredegar Park G.C.
(0633) 895219
Bassaleg Road, Newport
(18)5575 yards/***/B/H

Tredegar & Rhymney G.C.
(0685) 840743
Tredegar, Rhymney
(9)5500 yards/***/D

West Monmouthshire G.C.
(0495) 310233
Pond Road, Nantyglo
(18)6118 yards/***(Sun)/D

Woodlake Park G.C.
(0291) 673933
Glascoed, Pontypool
(18)6300 yards/***/C/H

THE GLAMORGANS

Aberdare G.C.
(0685) 871188
Abernant, Aberdare, Mid
(18)5874 yards/***(Sat)/D/H

Bargoed G.C.
(0443) 830143
Heolddu, Bargoed, Mid
(18)6000 yards/**/D

Bryn Meadows Hotel & G.C.
(0495) 225590
The Bryn, Hengoed, Mid
(18)6200 yards/***/D

Brynhill G.C.
(0446) 720277
Port Road, Barry, South
(18)6000 yards/**/B/H

Caerphilly G.C.
(0222) 883481
Mountain Road, Caerphilly, Mid
(14)6000 yards/**/B/H

Cardiff G.C.
(0222) 753320
Sherborne Avenue, Cincoed, South
(18)6016 yards/**/B/H

Castell Heights G.C.
(0222) 886666
Blaengwynlais, Caerphilly, Mid
(18)7000 yards/***/F
(9)2670 yards/***/F

Clyne G.C.
(0792) 401989

Owls Lodge Lane, Mayals, West
(18)6312 yards/***/B/H

Creigiau G.C.
(0222) 890263
Creigiau, Cardiff, Mid
(18)5900 yards/**/B/M

Dinas Powis G.C.
(0222) 512727
Old Highwalls, Dinas Powis, South
(18)5377 yards/***/F/L

Fairwood Park G.C.
(0792) 203648
Upper Killay, Swansea, West
(18)6741 yards/***/B

Glamorganshire G.C.
(0222) 701185
Lavernock Road, Penarth, South
(18)6181 yards/***/B/H

Glynneath G.C.
(0639) 720452
Penycraig, Pontneathvaughan, West
(18)5499 yards/**/D/H

Inco G.C.
(0792) 844216
Clydach, Swansea, West
(12)6230 yards/***/F

Langland Bay G.C.
(0792) 366023
Llangland Bay, Swansea, West
(18)5830 yards/***/B

Llanishen G.C.
(0222) 752205
Cwm, Lisvane, South
(18)5296 yards/**/B/H

Llantrisant and Pontyclun G.C.
(0443) 222148
Llanelry Road, Talbot Green, Mid
(12)5712 yards/**/F/H/M

Maesteg G.C.
(0656) 732037
Neath Road, Maesteg, Mid
(18)5900 yards/***/C/H

Merthyr Tydfil G.C.
(0685) 723308
Cilsanws Mt, nr Merthyr Tydfil,
Mid
(11)5900 yards/***/F

Morlais Castle G.C.
(0685) 722822
Pant, Dowlais, Merthyr Tydfil, Mid
(18)6320 yards/**/D

Morriston G.C.
(0792) 771079
Clasemont Road, Morriston, West
(18)5800 yards/***/C/H

Mountain Ash G.C.
(0443) 472265
Cefnpennar, Mountain Ash, Mid
(18)5500 yards/**/D/H

Mountain Lakes G.C.
(0222) 861128
Blaengwynlais, Caerphilly, Mid
(18)5700 yards/***/C

Neath G.C.
(0639) 643615
Cadoxton, Neath, West
(18)6465 yards/**/C

Palleg G.C.
(0639) 842193
Lower Cwmtwrch, Swansea, West
(9)3260 yards/**/D

Pennard G.C.
(0792) 233131
Southgate, Swansea, West
(18)6266 yards/***/C/H

Peterstone G.C.
(0633) 680009
Peterstone Wentlooge, South
(18)6600 yards/***/C/H/M

Pontardawe G.C.
(0792) 863118
Cefn Llan, Pontardawe, West
(18)6061 yards/**/C

Pontypridd G.C.
(0443) 402359
Ty Gywn Road, Pontypridd, Mid
(18)5650 yards/***/C/H

Pyle and Kenfig G.C.
(0656) 783093
Waun-y-Mer, Kenfig, Mid
(18)6640 yards/**/B-A/H

R.A.F. St Athan G.C.
(0446) 751043
Barry, Cardiff, South
(9)5957 yards/***(Sun am)/D

Radyr G.C.
(0222) 842408
Radyr, Cardiff, South
(18)6031 yards/**/F/H/L

Rhondda G.C.
(0443) 433204
Penrhys, Rhondda, Mid
(18)6428 yards/***/C/H

Royal Porthcawl G.C.
(0656) 782251
Porthcawl, Mid
(18)6600 yards/**/A/H

St Andrews Major G.C.
(0446) 722227
Cadoxton, Barry, South
(9)2931 yards/***/E

St Marys Hotel & C.C.
(0656) 860280
St Marys Hill, Pencoed, South
(18)5236 yards/***/D/H
(9)2426 yards/***/E/H

Southerndown G.C.
(0656) 880326
Ewenny, Bridgend, Mid
(18)6613 yards/**/C-A/H

Swansea Bay G.C.
(0792) 814153
Jersey Marine, Neath, West
(18)6302 yards/***/F

Wenvoe Castle G.C.
(0222) 594371
Wenvoe, Cardiff, South
(18)6411 yards/***/F/H/M

Whitchurch G.C.
(0222) 620125
Whitchurch, Cardiff, South
(18)6319 yards/**/B/H

Whitehall G.C.
(0443) 740245
Nelson, Treharris, Mid
(9)5750 yards/**/F

DYFED

Aberystwyth G.C.
(0970) 615104
Bryn-y-Mor, Aberystywth
(18)6100 yards/***/F

Ashburnham G.C.

(0554) 832466
Cliffe Terrace, Burry Port
(18)6916 yards/***/B/H

Borth and Ynyslas G.C.
(0970) 871202
Borth, Aberystwyth
(18)6000 yards/***/C/H

Cardigan G.C.
(0293) 612035
Gwbert-on-Sea, Cardigan
(18)6600 yards/***/C/H

Carmarthen G.C.
(0267) 87214
Blaen-y-Coed Road, Carmarthen
(18)6212 yards/***/C

Cilgwyn G.C.
(0570) 45286
Llangybi, Lampeter
(9)5318 yards/***/D

Glynhir G.C.
(0269) 850472
Glynhir Road, Llandybie,
Ammanford
(18)5900 yards/***(Sun)/D

Haverfordwest G.C.
(0437) 764523
Narberth Road, Haverfordwest
(18)6005 yards/***/C

Llansteffan G.C.
(0267) 83526
Llansteffan
(9)2165 yards/***/E

Milford Haven G.C.
(0646) 692368
Hubberston, Milford Haven
(18)6071 yards/***/D

Newport (Pembs) G.C.
(0239) 820244
Newport
(9)5815 yards/***/D

Penrhos G.& C.C.
(0974) 202999
Llanrhystud, Aberystwyth
(18)6641 yards/***/D

St Davids City G.C.
(0437) 721751
Whitesands Bay, St Davids
(9)5693 yards/***/D

South Pembrokeshire G.C.
(0646) 683817
Defensible Barracks, Pembroke
Dock
(9)5804 yards/***/D

Tenby G.C.
(0834) 842978
The Burrows, Tenby
(18)6232 yards/***/C/H

POWYS

Brecon G.C.
(0874) 622004
Newton Park, Llanfaes, Brecon
(9)5218 yards/***/F

Builth Wells G.C.
(0982) 553296
Golf Club Road, Builth Wells
(18)5376 yards/***/C/H

Cradoc G.C.
(0874) 623658
Penoyre Park, Cradoc, Brecon
(18)6301 yards/***(Sun)/C

Knighton G.C.
(0547) 528646
Little Ffrydd Wood, Knighton
(9)5320 yards/***/E

Llandrindod Wells G.C.
(0597) 823873
Llandrindod Wells
(18)5749 yards/***/D

Machynlleth G.C.
(0654) 702000
Fford Drenewydd, Machynlleth
(9)5726 yards/***/D

Maesmawr G.C.
(0686) 688303
Caersws, Newtown
(9)2554 yards/***/E

Old Rectory G.C.
(0873) 810373
Llangattock, Crickhowell
(9)2878 yards/***/F

Rhosgoch G.C.
(0497) 851251
Rhosgoch, Builth Wells
(9)4842 yards/***/F

St Giles Newtown G.C.
(0686) 625844
Pool Road, Newtown
(9)5936 yards/***/D/H/L

St Idloes G.C.
(05512) 2559
Penrhallt, Llanidloes
(9)5428 yards/***/D/H

Welsh Border Golf Complex
(0743) 884247
Bulthy, Middletown
(9)3250 yards/***/E

Welshpool G.C.
(0938) 83249
Golfa Hill, Welshpool
(18)5708 yards/***/D

NORTH WALES

CLWYD

Abergele & Pensarn G.C.
(0745) 824034
Tan-y-Goppa Road, Abergele
(18)6520 yards/***/B

Bryn Morfydd Hotel & G.C.
(0745) 78280
Llanrhaeadr, Denbigh
(18)5601 yards/***/F
(9) 1190 yards/***/F

Caerwys G.C.
(0352) 720692
Caerwys, Mold
(9)3080 yards/***/E

Chirk G. & C.C
(0691) 774407
Chirk, nr Wrexham
(18)6800 yards/***/C

Denbigh G.C.
(0745) 814159
Henllan Road, Denbigh
(18)5650 yards/***/C

Flint G.C.
(0352) 732327
Cornist Park, Flint
(9)5953 yards/***/D

Hawarden G.C.
(0244) 531447
Groomsdale Lane, Hawarden
(9)5620 yards/***/C/G

Holywell G.C.
(0352) 710040
Brynford, Holywell
(9)6484 yards/***/D

Mold G.C.
(0352) 740318

Clicain Road, Pant-y-Mwyn, Mold
(18)5545 yards/***/C

Old Colwyn G.C.
(0492) 515581
Woodland Avenue, Old Colwyn
(9)5800 yards/**(Tues,Wed,Sat
pm)/D

Old Padeswood G.C.
(0244) 547401
Station Road, Padeswood, Mold
(18)6639 yards/***/C

Padeswood and Buckley G.C.
(0244) 550537
Station Lane, Padeswood, Mold
(18)5775 yards/***(Sun)/B

Prestatyn G.C.
(0745) 854320
Marine Road East, Prestatyn
(18)6764 yards/***(Sat & Tues
am)/C/H

Rhuddlan G.C.
(0745) 590217
Meliden Road, Rhuddlan
(18)6045 yards/***(Sun)/B/H

Rhyl G.C.
(0745) 353171
Coast Road, Rhyl
(9)6185 yards/***/D

Ruthin Pwllglas G.C.
(0824) 702296
Ruthin Pwllglas, Ruthin
(10)5418 yards/***/D

St Melyd G.C.
(0745) 854405
Meliden Road, Prestatyn
(9)5857 yards/***/C

Vale of Llangollen G.C.
(0978) 860040
Holyhead Road, Llangollen
(18)6461 yards/***/F

Wrexham G.C.
(0978) 261033
Holt Road, Wrexham
(18)6078 yards/***/F/H

GWYNEDD

Aberdovey G.C.
(0654) 767210
Aberdovey
(18)6445 yards/***/C

Abersoch G.C.
(0758) 712622
Abersoch
(18)5910 yards/***/D/H

Bala G.C.
(0678) 520359
Penlan, Bala
(10)4962 yards/***/D

Betws-y-Coed G.C.
(0690) 710556
Betws-y-coed
(18)4996 yards/***/F

Caernarfon G.C.
(0286) 673783
Llanfaglan, Caernarfon
(9)5860 yards/***/C

Conwy G.C.
(0492) 592423
Morfa, Conwy
(18)6901 yards/***/B/H

Criccieth G.C.
(0766) 522154
Ednyfed Hill, Criccieth
(18)5787 yards/***/D

Dolgellau G.C.
(0341) 422603
Pencefn Road, Dolgellau
(9)4512 yards/***/D

Ffestiniog G.C.
(0766) 762637
Y Cefn, Ffestiniog
(9)5032 yards/***/F

Llandudno (Maesdu) G.C.
(0492) 876450
Hospital Road, Llandudno
(18)6513 yards/***/B/H/M

Llanfairfechan G.C.
(0248) 680144
Llannerch Road, Llanfairfechan
(9)3119 yards/***/D

Nefyn and District G.C.
(0758) 720966
Morfa Nefyn, Pwllheli
(18)6335 yards/***/B/H

North Wales G.C.
(0492) 875325
Bryniau Road, West Shore,
Llandudno
(18)6132 yards/***/B/H

Penmaenmawr G.C.
(0492) 623330
Conwy Old Road, Penmaenmawr
(9)5031 yards/***/C

Porthmadog G.C.
(0766) 512037
Morfa Bychan, Porthmadog
(18)5838 yards/***/C/H

Pwllheli G.C.
(0758) 701644
Golf Road, Pwllheli
(18)6110 yards/***/F

Rhos-on-Sea G.C.
(0492) 549641
Penrhyn Bay, Llandudno
(18)6064 yards/***/F

Royal St David's G.C.
(0766) 780361
Harlech
(18)6427 yards/***/B/H

St Deniol G.C.
(0248) 353098
Penybryn, Bangor
(18)5048 yards/***/E

ANGLESEY

Anglesey G.C.
(0407) 810219
Station Road, Rhosneigr
(18)5713 yards/***/D

Baron Hill G.C.
(0248) 810231
Beaumaris
(9)5564 yards/***/D

Bull Bay G.C.
(0407) 830960
Bull Bay Road, Amlwch
(18)6160 yards/***/C/H

Holyhead G.C.
(0407) 763279
Trearddur Bay, Holyhead
(18)6058 yards/***/C/H

Llangefni G.C.
(0248) 722193
Llangefni
(9)1467 yards/***/F

W.Linton GC

EDDLESTON
Innerleithen
GC
Peebles GC
PEEBLES

LAUDER
Lauder GC
GREENLAW
A697
Galashields GC
GATTONSIDE
Melrose GC
MELROSE
A698
Kelso GC
KELSO
SELKIRK
Selkirk
GC

TWEEDSMUIR
St.Mary's
Loch
ETTRICKBRIDGE

A76

HAWICK
Minto GC
Hawick GC

Moffat
MOFFAT
GC
BEATTOCK

A702
A701
Dumfries &
County GC
Lochmaben
GC
A75
Thornhill
GC
DUMFRIES
LOCKERBIE
CANONBIE

A712
Newton Stewart GC
NEWTON STEWART
NEW
ABBEY
Powfoot GC
POWFOOT

A714
Stranraer GC
STRANRAER
A75
DALBEATTIE
KIPPFORD
COLVEND
Southerness GC
ROCKLIFFE

PORTPATRICK
Portpatrick GC

Wigtown &
Bladnoch GC
PORT
WILLIAM

Artist: **Sam Garratt PEEBLES** *Courtesy of:* **Burlington Gallery**

The two modern counties of Dumfries & Galloway and Borders encompass most of the Scottish Lowlands. A beautiful area of Britain—as of course is most of Scotland—but surely not one terribly renowned for its golf? It may not be renowned but there is still certainly no shortage of exciting and challenging courses in the area. Indeed, the very fact that the great hordes head for the more famous venues further north means that Scotland's southerly golfing gems remain by and large marvellously uncrowded.

Dumfries & Galloway

The one true championship test in this region is found at **Southerness.** Of all Scotland's great links courses this is perhaps the least widely known. We have featured MacKenzie Ross's masterpiece on a separate page.

Powfoot is a fairly close neighbour of Southerness (at least as the crow flies) the course lying five miles west of Annan off the B724. A semi-links with plenty of heather and gorse, it offers a tremendous test of golf and is an admirable companion to Southerness. Adding to the enjoyment of a round at Powfoot is the setting—the course provides extensive views towards the Cumberland Hills to the south and the Galloway Hills to the west. The Isle of Man is also visible on a clear day.

Two convenient resting places after a game at Southerness are in Rockliffe, the Baron's Craig Hotel (0556) 630225 and a little closer in Colvend, the Clonyard House (0556) 630372. Good eating places include, the Criffel Inn (038785) 244, in New Abbey, and the Pheasant in Dalbeattie. Powfoot has the Golf Hotel (0461) 700254 whilst a little further away is Canonbie and an exceptional restaurant at the Riverside Inn (03873) 71512.

Nearby there are two good 18 hole courses at Dumfries, **Dumfries and County**, to the north of the town being the pick of the two, but golfers travelling north would do well to pay **Lochmaben** a visit as well. It is a very friendly Club with an interesting 9 hole course designed by James Braid. The setting around the Kirk Loch is most picturesque and the course is famed for its many beautiful old trees.

When inspecting any of the above courses, Dumfries, the county's largest town is a likely base and here the Cairndale Hotel (0387) 54111 is most pleasant. Other recommended establishments in the area include the Dryfesdale (0576) 202427 in Lockerbie, the Lockerbie Manor Country Hotel (0576) 202610, 14th century Comlongon Castle (038 787) 283 and Allanton House (038774) 509 with its resident farm. Also note the Barjarg Tower (0848) 331545 at Auldgirth, a first class 16th century country house hotel.

Towards the western corner of Dumfries and Galloway there is more fine golf. Two 9 hole courses well worth playing are at Wigtown, **Wigtown and Bladnoch** to be precise, and at **Newton Stewart**. Still further west, **Stranraer**, the ferry terminal for Larne, has a fine parkland course north of the town overlooking Loch Ryan. But the clifftop course at **Portpatrick** is surely the major golfing attraction; rated by many to be one of the most beautiful courses in Britain. Apparently for many years in the last century the town was Ireland's Gretna Green—couples sailing across the Irish Sea to get hitched in Portpatrick's tiny church. The golf course provides some breathtaking scenery, particularly outstanding is the view from the 13th fairway. It can often get quite breezy and although only 5644 yards in length, the course is certainly no pushover.

Superb golf is accompanied by an exceptionally high number of first rate hotels in the area. In Castle Douglas, Milton Park (06443) 286 is a recurring favourite while in Newton Stewart, the Kirroughtree Hotel (0671) 402141 is excellent. More modest but still welcoming is the Bruce (0671) 402294. Port William offers the very fine Corsemalzie House Hotel (0988) 600254. Cally Palace (0559) 814341 in Gatehouse of Fleet — a beautiful 18th century mansion — has its own golf course while a number of alternatives are found at Portpatrick. Pick of the bunch is the Knockinaam Lodge Hotel (0776) 810471 which has a glorious setting and a tremendous restaurant. Others to note here are the Fernhill (0776) 810220, the Portpatrick Hotel (0776) 810333 and the North West Castle (0776) 704413.

Having sampled the delights of the coast of Southern Scotland one may head inland to the delights of the Border towns. En route one could slip 18 holes in at **Thornhill** or perhaps visit **Moffat**. The town has a very enjoyable moorland course with a marvellous setting in the valley of Annandale. The Black Bull is a welcoming hostelry after a round at Moffat and a recommended place to spend an evening is the Beechwood Country House Hotel (0683) 20210.

Borders

The Border towns offer castles aplenty, some superb woollens and some excellent rugby. Golfwise, no course here could claim to be of championship proportions, however, the majority can boast spectacular settings, visitors are always encouraged and the green fees in these parts are just about the cheapest in Britain.

A cluster of courses are to be found in the centre of the county. The town of **Melrose** is famed for its ruined Abbey where the heart of Robert the Bruce is said to have been buried (gruesome stuff!) It has a fine 9 hole course and there are others equally pleasant at **Selkirk, Hawick, Lauder, St Boswells, Innerliethen** and **West Linton.** Kelso has an interesting layout being inside Kelso racecourse. Finally well worth noting are **Peebles** and **Galashiels** — both are public courses, well maintained and true to form set amidst magnificent countryside.

Walter Scott's land really does deserve a lengthy inspection. This alas isn't the place but whether one is golfing in the Borders or simply breaking a journey, here are some ideas for places to stay. In Peebles, two choice hotels can be found: Cringletie House Hotel (0721) 730233 and the Peebles Hotel Hydro (0721) 720602. Good guest houses are also plentiful, with Lindores (0721) 720441 and Whitestone House (0721) 720337 among the best. Golfers who like a spot of fishing should also note the Tweed Valley Hotel (0896) 870636 in nearby Walkerburn. St Mary's Loch offers the Tibbie Shiels Inn (0750) 42231, Selkirk the Woodburn House Hotel (0750) 20815 and Tweedsmuir the cosy Crook Inn (08997) 272. Ettrickshaws Hotel (0750) 52229 in Ettrickbridge, Sunlaws House Hotel (0573) 450331 and the Cross Keys Hotel (0573) 223303 in Kelso are three outstanding places, and the Tilmouth Park (0890) 882255 is also ideal for both the borders and courses such as Goswick on the Northumberland coast.

Baron's Craig Hotel

The Baron's Craig Hotel stands in wooded countryside overlooking the expanse of the Solway and Rough Firth. The hotel has its own twelve acre wooded area with beautiful lawns and gardens abounding in colour, especially in spring and early summer.

The hotel was built in 1880 and has been extended for comfort and convenience whilst still retaining its original character and interest. The 22 bedrooms, all en suite, are spacious and airy. Furnishing is in keeping with the quality evident throughout the hotel while the atmosphere is friendly and relaxed.

Preparation and serving of food is under the personal supervision of the resident owner and his staff. Guests are treated to tempting and interesting menus while selected wines can be chosen from the comprehensive wine list.

The hotel is situated in the picturesque village of Rockcliffe. There is excellent bathing from the beach, only three minutes away from the hotel, while boating is available at Kippford, a sailing centre a mile further inland. For golfing enthusiasts there are six courses within easy reach of this imposing hotel.

Baron's Craig Hotel
Rockcliffe
by Dalbeattie
Kircudbrightshire
DG5 4QF
Tel: (0556) 630225
Fax: (0556) 630328

Cringletie House Hotel

Cringletie is a distinguished mansion which has retained the warm atmosphere of a private country house. It is set well back from the Peebles/Edinburgh road (A703) in twenty-eight acres of garden and woodland, in peaceful surroundings. Only twenty miles from Edinburgh, it is an excellent centre.

All rooms are tastefully decorated and furnished to a high standard of comfort, with colour televisions, direct dial telephones and en-suite facilities. There are magnificent views from all rooms. The restaurant has been consistently recommended since 1971.

Recommended by Johansen; Egon Ronay; The AA; The RAC; Signpost; Ashley Courtenay and other guide books.

Cringletie House Hotel
Peebles EH45 8PL
Tel: (0721) 730 233
Fax: (0721) 730 244

The Cally Palace Hotel

An impressive establishment offering the very best of service in a totally secluded location. This splendid old country mansion set in 150 acres of forest and parkland offers the relaxed elegance of the eighteenth century in addition to the most modern standards of comfort.

On entering the hotel you are struck by the sheer grandness of the interior. Two huge marble pillars support the original moulded ceiling. The two public lounges, restored to their original splendour, reflect the opulence of the bygone age, with their spaciousness, marble fireplaces and decorative beauty. The small cocktail bar creates a convivial ambience in which to have pre dinner drinks.

The restaurant is renowned for its top quality cuisine, using, as far as possible fresh Scottish produce. Add to this friendly but professional service (and an extensive wine list!) and you have a recipe for a never to be forgotten meal.

All fifty-six bedrooms and suites, as you would expect, are fitted to the highest standard with television, tea and coffee making facilities, direct dial telephone, trouser press and hair dryer. Within the hotel there is a leisure centre with fifteen metre pool, sauna, solarium and jacuzzi. The hotel's policies stretch to 150 acres. Outdoors there is an all weather tennis court, putting and croquet. Exclusive to residents of the hotel is an 18 hole, par 70, golf course. Length 5444 yards. The course uses natural undulating contours, mature parkland and Cally Lake to provide an exciting and fair test for any golfer.

The Cally Palace Hotel
Gatehouse Of Fleet
Dumfries & Galloway
DG7 2DL
Tel: (0557) 814341
Fax: (0557) 814522

Two of Britain's greatest (and least explored) links courses stare at one another across the Solway Firth—one is on the English side at Silloth and the other lies north of the border at Southerness. As close as they appear on the map, the only way of travelling from one to the other is by a fairly lengthy drive around the coast via Gretna Green. Before the war a bridge crossed the Solway, but before the war Southerness didn't have a golf course.

Situated 16 miles south of Dumfries, in an almost forgotten corner of southern Scotland, Southerness is the only true Championship links in Great Britain to have been built since 1945. (Quite a contrast to Ireland where the likes of Waterville, Tralee, Connemara and Ballybunion New have all been constructed within the last 20 years.)

So golf came to Southerness about 500 years after it came to St. Andrews but one cannot help wondering why it took so long—after all, the much more remote golfing outposts of Dornoch and Machrihanish took root in the dim and distant past and a more natural and pleasanter site for the links it is hard to imagine. Wild dunes, rampant heather, dense bracken and prickly golden gorse all present themselves in abundance here; as for that matter do twisting, tumbling fairways and firm, fast greens—yes, Southerness is as every truly traditional Scottish links should be - terrifyingly wonderful! In fact the golf at Southerness is probably more terrifying and more wonderful than at most.

If Mother Nature created the wonder of the setting then Mackenzie Ross (the architect of modern Turnberry) must be credited with the production of a genuine thriller. Golf at Southerness is nothing if not exhilarating. From the Championship tees the links can be stretched to 7000 yards; most mortal golfers will still find the 6564 yards, par 69 from the white tees (or 6093 yards from the yellow tees) an awesome challenge. The course's Standard Scratch is as high as 73; several of the par fours measure in excess of 400 yards (with prodigious carries to match) and two of the par threes are well over 200 yards long. A visit to Southerness is certainly recommended but pray that your long game is in fine fettle!

Before approaching the 1st tee, consultation with the Club's **Secretary, Mr W.D. Ramage** is advisable. Visitors can book tee times beween 10.00–12.00 and 2.00–5.00 midweek and between 10.00–11.30 and 2.30–5.00 at weekends. Mr Ramage can be contacted by telephone on **(0387) 88677** or by addressing a letter to **The Secretary,**

Southerness Golf Club, Southerness, Dumfries DG2 8AZ. Golfing Societies are equally welcome but must contact the Secretary in advance. Southerness does not have a golf professional.

The green fees at Southerness compare favourably with those at many of Scotland's more celebrated Championship courses. A full day's golf in 1994 cost £23 per day during the week and £30 at weekends. Junior visitors can play midweek for a green fee of just £6.

Southerness's situation is quiet rather than remote. Golfers from England, heading to or from Turnberry, Troon and Prestwick will likely drive through the town of Dumfries on the A75/A76 and Southerness is just half an hour's detour from Dumfries along the A710; a pretty drive via New Abbey. From the west the A710 approaches via Dalbeattie while Dumfries is linked to Glasgow by the A74/M74, and to Edinburgh by the A702 and the A74.

Unless the weather is frightful none will regret making that detour. Catch Southerness on a glorious morning with the sun reflecting off the dancing waters of the Solway Firth and we may just wonder why we were heading for the Ayrshire coast in the first place!

Southerness opens with three dog-legged holes, the 2nd being a classic par four and a half hole—in length strictly a par four but into the prevailing wind, in reality a par five; certainly a 4-5-4 start at Southerness is an accomplishment. After the short 4th the course doubles back on itself, then turns towards the sea. The views become more distracting but the challenge in no way diminishes. The 7th is the first of two long par threes and you aim your tee shot directly at the Solway but the best run of holes are arguably those between the 10th, a par three surrounded by a sea of heather and the 13th, the longest par four on the card. The 12th is generally considered to be the best hole of all; here a well positioned drive (avoiding the deviously positioned fairway bunkers) is essential as the second shot must be fired towards a narrow green which sits on a plateau and looks down over a beautiful beach; deep bunkers guard the green front right and a pond will gleefully swallow any shot that strays left of centre.

The toughest hole on the closing stretch is yet another of Southerness's cunning dog-legs, the 16th which is normally played into the teeth of the wind; a four here may prove more elusive than at the par five 18th, where with the wind finally at our backs we have the chance of finding the green with two good blows. Shall we go for it? Why not, Southerness is that kind of course.

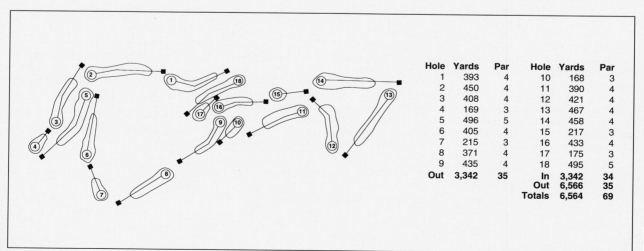

Hole	Yards	Par	Hole	Yards	Par
1	393	4	10	168	3
2	450	4	11	390	4
3	408	4	12	421	4
4	169	3	13	467	4
5	496	5	14	458	4
6	405	4	15	217	3
7	215	3	16	433	4
8	371	4	17	175	3
9	435	4	18	495	5
Out	**3,342**	**35**	**In**	**3,342**	**34**
			Out	**6,566**	**35**
			Totals	**6,564**	**69**

Built in 1882 by the famous architect Charles Barry, using stones from nearby Twizel Castle, Tillmouth typifies a more leisured age. A secluded mansion, set in fifteen acres of mature parkland and gardens, you'll feel yourself relax into it's atmosphere of a bygone age.

All of our thirteen en suite bedrooms are generous in size and individually furnished to the highest standard. The spacious public rooms are furnished with the same attention to detail and open log fires create a relaxing ambience.

Tillmouth Park is an ideal centre for country pursuits - fishing, shooting, riding and of course, golf. Spring fishing packages can be arranged on the river Tweed with all the fisherman's requirements catered for. There is

also an abundance of excellent shooting in the Borders within 30 minutes drive of the hotel. Berwick-upon-Tweed and the Hirsel at Coldstream are just two excellent golf courses nearby. There are many stately homes to visit such as Floors Castle, Manderston and Paxton, ruined abbeys, Flodden Field and Holy Island are all within easy reach.

Our Library Restaurant offers fresh local produce imaginatively prepared and presented by our Head Chef David Jeffries. To match the superb food there is an extensive wine list and comprehensive range of over 100 malt whiskies.

You can be assured of a warm welcome in the Borders when you come to Tillmouth Park.

Tillmouth Park Hotel
Cornhill-On-Tweed
Northumberland
TD12 4UU
Tel: (0890) 882255
Fax: (0890) 882540

Dumfries & Galloway & Borders Complete Golf

Key

To avoid disappointment it is advisable to telephone in advance

***Visitors welcome at most times
**Visitors usually allowed on weekdays only
*Visitors not normally permitted (Mon, Wed) No visitors on specified days

Approximate Green Fees
A £30 plus
B £20 to £30
C £15 to £25
D £10 to £20
E under £10
F Greens fees on application

Restrictions
G Guests only
H Handicap certificate required
H (24) Handicap of 24 or less
L Letter of introduction required
M Visitor must be a member of another recognised club.

BORDERS

Duns G.C.
(0361) 882717
Hardens Road, Duns
(9)5754 yards/***/D

Eyemouth G.C.
(08907) 50551
Gunsgreen House, Eyemouth
(9)4608 yards/***/E

Galashiels G.C.
(0896) 753724
Ladhope Recreation Ground, Galashiels
(18)5309 yards/***/E

Gatehouse G.C.
(0557) 814734
Laurieston Road, Gatehouse
(9)2398 yards/***/E

Hawick G.C.
(0450) 372293
Vertish Hill, Hawick
(18)5929 yards/**/E

Hirsel G.C.
(0890) 882678

Kelso Road, Coldstream
(18)5830 yards/**/D

Innerleithen G.C.
(0896) 830951
Leithen Road, Innerleithen
(9)5984 yards/***/E

Jedburgh G.C.
(0835) 863587
Dunion Road, Jedburgh
(9)5522 yards/***/F

Kelso G.C.
(0573) 223009
Racecourse Road, Kelso
(18)6066 yards/**/D

Lauder G.C.
(0578) 722526
Galashiels Road, Lauder
(9)3001 yards/**/E

Melrose G.C.
(089682) 2855
Dingleton, Melrose
(9)5464 yards/**/D

Minto G.C.
(0450) 870220
Minto Village, by Denholme, Hawick
(18)5460 yards/**/D

Newcastleton G.C.
(03873) 75257
Holm Hill, Newcastleton
(9)5748 yards/***/E

Peebles G.C.
(0721) 720197
Kirkland Street, Peebles
(18)6137 yards/***/D

St Boswells G.C.
(0835) 822359
St Boswells, Roxburghshire
(9)2625 yards/***/D

Selkirk G.C.
(0750) 20621
The Hill, Selkirk
(9)5640 yards/***/D

Torwoodlee G.C.
(0896) 752260
Edinburgh Road, Galashiels
(9)5800 yards/***(Thurs)/D

West Linton G.C.
(0968) 660970
West Linton, Peebleshire
(18)6024 yards/***/D

DUMFRIES & GALLOWAY

Castle Douglas G.C.
(0556) 502801
Abercromby Road, Castle Douglas
(9)5400 yards/***(Thurs pm)/D

Colvend G.C.
(0556) 630398
Sandyhills, by Dalbeattie
(9)2322 yards/***/D

Crichton Royal G.C.
(0387) 41122
Bankend Road, Dumfries
(9)3084 yards/**/E

Dalbeattie G.C.
(0556) 611421
Dalbeattie
(9)4200 yards/***/F

Dumfries & County G.C.
(0387) 53585
Edinburgh Road, Dumfries
(18)5928 yards/***(Sat)/C

Dumfries & Galloway G.C.
(0387) 53582
Laurieston Avenue, Dumfries
(18)5782 yards/***/D

Gatehouse of Fleet G.C.
(0557) 814734
Gatehouse of Fleet
(9)2398 yards/***/F

Gretna G.C.
(0461) 338464
Gretna
(9)3215 yards/***/D

Kirkcudbright G.C.
(0557) 330314
Stirling Crescent, Kirkcudbright
(18)5598 yards/***/D

Langholm G.C.
(03873) 80559
Langholm, Dumfriesshire
(9)5744 yards/***/D

Lochmaben G.C.
(0387) 810552
Castlehill Gate, Lochmaben
(9)5304 yards/***/D

Lockerbie G.C.
(0576) 203363
Currie Road, Lockerbie
(18)5228 yards/***(Sat)/D

Moffat G.C.
(0683) 20020
Coatshill, Moffat
(18)5218 yards/***(Wed pm)/D

New Galloway G.C.
(06442) 737
Castle Douglas, Kircudbright
(9)5058 yards/***/D

Newton Stewart G.C.
(0671) 402172
Kirroughtree Avenue, Minnigaff
(9)5500 yards/***/D

Portpatrick (Dunskey) G.C.
(0776) 810273
Portpatrick, Stranraer
(18)5644 yards/***/D/H

Powfoot G.C.
(0461) 700227
Cummertrees, Annan
(18)6266 yards/**/F

St Medan G.C.
(0988) 700358
Monreith, Port William
(9)2277 yards/***/D

Sanquhar G.C.
(0659) 50577
Old Barr Road, Sanquhar
(9)5630 yards/***/F

Southerness G.C.
(0387) 88677
Southerness, Dumfries
(18)6554 yards/***/B

Stranraer G.C.
(0776) 706359
Crechmore, Stranraer
(18)6300 yards/***/D

Thornhill G.C.
(0848) 330546
Blacknest, Thornhill
(18)6011 yards/***/F

Wigtown and Bladnoch G.C.
(0988) 403354
Lightlands Avenue, Wigtown
(9)2732 yards/***/E

Wigtownshire County G.C.
(0581) 300420
Mains of Park, Glenluce
(18)5715 yards/***/D

Artist: **J Hassall 'A DRIVE'** *Courtesy of* **Burlington Gallery**

Artist: **John Lavery** **NORTH BERWICK** _Courtesy of:_ **Sotheby's**

'Hard by in the fields called the links, the citizens of Edinburgh divert themselves at a game called golf, in which they use a curious kind of bat tipt with horn and a small elastic ball of leather stuffed with feathers rather less than tennis balls, but out of a much harder consistency and this they strike with such force and dexterity that it will fly to an incredible distance.'

When Tobias Smollett wrote these words in 1771 golf had already been played in the 'fields' around Edinburgh for at least three hundred years. The seemingly harmless pastime wasn't always popular with the authorities. In 1593 the Town Council of Edinburgh deplored the fact that a great number of its inhabitants chose to spend the Sabbath in the town of Leith where 'in tyme of sermons' many were 'sene in the streets, drynking in taverns, or otherwise at Golf'. Shame on them! Today the east coast of Scotland is famous the world over, not only because it was here that it all began, but also because its many courses remain among the very finest the game has to offer. In a 30 mile coastal stretch between the courses of **Royal Burgess** and **Dunbar** lie the likes of **Muirfield, Gullane, North Berwick, Luffness New** and **Longniddry**—truly a magnificent seven—and there are many others.

Edinburgh

Visitors to the beautiful city of Edinburgh, the so called 'Athens of the North', should have little trouble getting a game. There are numerous first class courses in and around the capital; regrettably we only have space to mention a handful of the best. To the west of the city lie a particularly historic pair—**Bruntsfield Links** and **Royal Burgess**: between them they have witnessed nearly 500 years of golfing history. The latter club in fact claims to be the world's oldest. (A claim hotly disputed I might add by Muirfield's 'Honourable Company'!) These more prestigious courses are of course difficult to play, but with advance preparation it is possible; another Edinburgh gem not to be missed is **Braid Hills**; in fact two fine public courses here, just south of the city. The **Dalmahoy** Hotel Golf and Country Club situated to the south west of the city nestles at the base of the Pentland Hills and has two excellent 18 hole courses. Dalmahoy, like Muirfield and Dunbar is featured ahead. Towards the east side of Edinburgh is Musselburgh. The old Open championship links is not what it was, alas, although you can still play the nine holes adjacent to Musselburgh racecourse for history's sake. However, perhaps the best place for a game is at **Royal Musselburgh,** a beautiful parkland course and a little further out of the city the course at **Newbattle** can be recommended.

Spending a few days in Edinburgh is a real treat whether one is a golfer or not. The city's leading hotels include the magnificent Balmoral Hotel 031 556 2414, re-opened in 1991 to great acclaim, and the Caledonian Hotel 031 225 2433. The latter's Pompadour Restaurant is quite superb. Among the many other hotels, the Sheraton 031 229 9131 is almost on a par with the city's best while the George 031 225 1251 has a most impressive edifice and is a great favourite for post-rugby celebrations. Johnstounburn House (0875) 833696 at nearby Humbie offers an out of town alternative.

Edinburgh is as well blessed with restaurants as it is with hotels. These are some of the many worth considering: La Caveau 031 556 5707 and L'Auberge 031 556 5888 will delight lovers of French food, while those who pre-

fer pasta should sample Cosmo 031 226 6743, or for an Indian try the Kalpna 031 667 9890. In Leith two noted restaurants are Oysters 031 553 6363 and Skippers 031 554 1018. To work off the excesses caused by such culinary delights, Channings 031 315 2226 is a sophisticated and elegant hotel with excellent leisure facilities.

The courses of West Lothian are not as well known as their eastern counterparts. However, two are particularly worth considering, **Bathgate,** a fine moorland course and the **Deer Park** Golf and Country Club at Livingston. Both lie within easy access of Edinburgh.

Links Golf

Travellers wishing to explore the delights of the East Coast should aim to pick up the A198 at Prestonpans near Musselburgh. Before it reaches Longniddry the road passes through Seton, where Mary Queen of Scots is known to have sharpened up her golf swing more than 400 years ago. At 13 miles east of Edinburgh, **Longniddry** ought not to be considered as merely a stopping place en route to **Muirfield**. It is a superb course, part links part parkland, with every hole having a view of the sea. **Kilspindie** Golf Club is also worth a little detour while **Luffness New** and the three neighbouring courses of **Gullane,** lie only a short distance further along the coast. Each is outstanding in its way though if you only have time to play two then Luffness New and Gullane Number One are probably the pick, although the former can be difficult to get on! The panoramic view from the top of Gullane Hill on the latter's 7th hole is one of the most famous in golf. The West Links at **North Berwick** has a wealth of charm and tradition; it is one of the most natural courses one is likely to come across and several blind shots must be encountered. Two of its holes, the 14th 'Perfection' and the 15th 'Redan' have been imitated by golf architects all over the world. As at **Dunbar** there are some splendid views across to Bass Rock.

Time for a 19th hole. Hotels are numerous, as indeed are good restaurants. In Gullane, Greywalls (0620) 842144 has gained an enviable reputation and is literally on the doorstep of Muirfield and the three links of Gullane, while La Potiniere (0620) 843214 is a restaurant to savour when in these parts. Gullane is also resplendent with guest houses; the Golf Tavern (0620) 843259 is but one recommended illustration. In Aberlady the Kilspindie House Hotel (0875) 870682 and the Wagon (0875) 870319 are both welcoming as is clearly the Open Arms (0620) 85241 in the pretty village of Dirleton. The Marine Hotel (0620) 892406 is convenient for North Berwick while other well priced alternatives include the Mallard (0620) 843228, the Royal (0620) 892401, the Point Garry Hotel (0620) 892380 and the Golf Hotel (0620) 2202. Towards Dunbar, in the town itself, the Bellevue (0368) 862322 and the Bayswell (0368) 862225 are both comfortable hotels, while the Courtyard (0368) 864169) at Woodrush Brae offers award winning cuisine to its many golfing guests. Many super establishments are to be found a little inland. Note especially the Harvesters Hotel (0620) 860395 at East Linton and the Tweedale Arms (0620) 810240 at Gifford. Travelling back westwards, 15th century Borthwick Castle (0875) 820514 at Gorebridge is another first class establishment. For the touring golfer in Scotland, a country cottage can serve as an ideal base, and both Blakes Country Cottages (0603) 783227 and Mackays 031 225 3539 offer a range of self-catering accommodation.

The Johnstounburn House Hotel

Scotland is the home of golf, and Johnstounburn offers the golfer an opportunity of staying in one of Scotland's original homes. The earliest reference to the estate goes back to 1260, and the house dates to certainly the early 17th century. Since those distant days, Johnstounburn has been cared for and enhanced by influential Scottish families - Borthwick, Broun and Usher - with most of the building on the estate having been effected in the nineteenth century.

The house sits proudly, surrounded by spacious lawns, gardens and unspoilt countryside overlooking the Lammermuir hills. The eleven bedrooms in the main house are rich in individuality and have been decorated to achieve the standard of comfort required by discerning travellers. Each has a private bathroom (only one is not ensuite), colour television and direct dial telephone. A further nine bedrooms were added when the coach house (circa 1840), some 300 yards through the gardens, was converted in 1986.

The 'Piece De Resistance' is the dining room with ornate hand

carved wood panelling from floor to ceiling, created in the mid eighteenth century. After a sumptuous meal from the table d'hote menu featuring the finest fresh local produce, and served by candlelight in traditional style, you can retire to the Cedar lounge and enjoy your coffee in front of an open hearth. Or, if the night is kind, you can stroll in the gardens and experience the tranquillity of the surrounds.

The famous golf courses of East Lothian - Muirfield, Gullane, North Berwick, Dunbar - are all within thirty minutes drive. There are more than a dozen courses from which to choose. For those not playing (or just taking the day off), Edinburgh City centre is thirty minutes away. To the south lies the beautiful Border region, with many historic castles, houses and gardens scattered about its rolling hills.

Johnstounburn offers comfort and friendly hospitality in a truly outstanding setting, with fine food carefully presented. Most of all, here you have the opportunity to savour the tradition of Scotland in a house that feels like home.

Johnstounburn House
Humbie
Nr. Edinburgh
East Lothian EH36 5PL
Tel: (0875) 833696
Fax: (0875) 833626

Muirfield is of course much more than one of the world's greatest golf links, it is also the home of the world's oldest Golf Club. The Honourable Company of Edinburgh Golfers are the direct descendants of the Gentlemen Golfers who played at Leith Links from at least as early as the 15th century. On 7th March 1744 several Gentlemen of Honour, skilful in the ancient and healthful exercise of Golf, petitioned the city fathers of Edinburgh to provide a silver club to be played for annually on the links at Leith. The winner of this competition became Captain of Golf and the club was paraded through the city. In 1744 the Edinburgh Golfers formulated the game's first code of rules, The Thirteen Articles, which were adopted almost word for word ten years later by the Royal and Ancient Club at St Andrews.

The Company played over the five holes at Leith for almost a hundred years before overcrowding forced the decision to move to the nine hole course at Musselburgh, to the east of the city. Long before they had left Leith the Members had begun to dine and play in the famous red uniform; failure to wear this usually resulted in a fine. A minute from the 1830s records how one member was fined two tappit hens for playing golf without his red coat! The Open Championship first came to Musselburgh in 1874 and was held there every third year until 1889. Meanwhile Musselburgh, like Leith, had become terribly crowded and the Company decided that the time had come for a second move. Again, they looked to the east and almost twenty miles from Edinburgh, under the lee of Gullane Hill, they discovered Muirfield. The course was designed by 'Old' Tom Morris and opened for play on 3rd May 1891. In its early years the course received much criticism. One professional described it as 'nothing but an auld watter meddie' but it appears that this had more to do with jealousy, owing to the fact that when the Honourable Company left Musselburgh it took the Open Championship with it. It was held at Muirfield in 1892 and never again returned to Musselburgh. Following the success of the 1892 Championship, Muirfield's reputation grew rapidly and today it is widely considered to be the fairest, if not the finest test in golf.

Visitors wishing to play at Muirfield must make prior arrangements with the **Secretary, Group Captain J A Prideaux**, who may be contacted by telephone on **(0620) 842123.** For gentlemen golfers there is a requirement that they belong to a recognised Golf Club and carry a handicap of 18 or less, while for lady golfers (who may only play if accompanied by a gentleman player) the handi-

cap limit is 24. The days on which visitors are welcome are Tuesdays and Thursdays. It should also be noted that by tradition foursome matches are strongly favoured at Muirfield and four ball games will only be permitted in the mornings. Golfing Societies (limited to 12 players) are also received on the usual visiting days and arrangements may be made with the Secretary. All written correspondence should be addressed to **The Secretary, The Honourable Company of Edinburgh Golfers, Muirfield, Gullane, East Lothian, EH31 2EG.** The green fees for 1994 were set at £50 for a single round with £70 entitling the visitor to a full day's golf. All fees should be paid to the cashier in the Clubhouse Dining Room.

Travelling to Muirfield (or Gullane) will often be by way of Edinburgh. Gullane is connected to the capital city by the A198. Northbound travellers can avoid Edinburgh by approaching on the A1 which runs to Dunbar to the east of Gullane. From Dunbar the A198 can be picked up. Those coming from the north and west of Scotland will need to travel via Edinburgh. The M8 links Glasgow to Edinburgh, while the M9 should be taken from Stirling and the M90 from Perth.

One of the unique features of Muirfield (or at least unique in terms of a Scottish Championship links) is its layout of two separate loops, an outer and an inner. This ensures that the golfer will not have to play several successive holes into or against the same wind direction. Although occasionally quite undulating, the course doesn't require blind shots and this contributes much to Muirfield's fairness tag. From the Championship tees the links stretch to 6941 yards, and with the often prodigiously thick rough and deep, cavernous bunkers, it can be a very severe test of golf. From the medal tees Muirfield still measures a fairly lengthy 6601 yards, par 70.

Since 1892 the Open Championship has been played at Muirfield on 14 occasions. Before the last War winners included Harry Vardon, James Braid and Walter Hagen. The first Open to be held at Muirfield after the War was in 1948, when Henry Cotton won his third title. Gary Player won in 1959 and Jack Nicklaus in 1966. Perhaps the most dramatic Open in Muirfield's history came in 1972 when Lee Trevino holed his famous chip shot from the edge of the 17th green and in the process stole the title from Tony Jacklin. In recent times British fortunes have revived dramatically however with Nick Faldo winning in 1987, and again in 1992, when he so memorably produced 'the best four holes of my life' to deny the unfortunate John Cook.

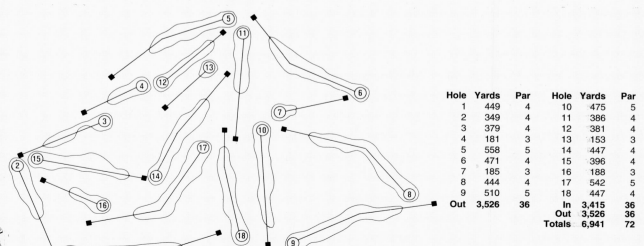

Hole	Yards	Par	Hole	Yards	Par
1	449	4	10	475	5
2	349	4	11	386	4
3	379	4	12	381	4
4	181	3	13	153	3
5	558	5	14	447	4
6	471	4	15	396	4
7	185	3	16	188	3
8	444	4	17	542	5
9	510	5	18	447	4
Out	**3,526**	**36**	**In**	**3,415**	**36**
			Out	**3,526**	**36**
			Totals	**6,941**	**72**

239

Dalmahoy resort hotel offers a wonderful choice of leisure activities. Set in acres of rolling parkland, it boasts two excellent golf courses. The championship East course is particularly challenging and has been tackled over the years by some of the world's leading players including Lyle, Faldo, Ballesteros and many more. A number of major events have been staged at Dalmahoy, including the Solheim Cup when the Women's European Tour recorded their historic victory over the USA. Through the years other events, such as the Senior Service Tournament, the Tournament Players Championship and the Scottish Professional Championship have been played.

The West course, although shorter, offers a sporting challenge and is an ideal foil for the East course. Golfers who visit Dalmahoy will find the courses reach into their games, testing all aspects of skill and control.

Complementing golf are the extensive leisure facilities including heated indoor swimming pool and jet pool, steam room and sauna poolside.

There are two squash courts, two all-weather floodlit tennis courts, gymnasium with modern cv equipment and two full size snooker tables.

There is also an excellent health and beauty salon offering a wide range of treatments.

The modern golf and leisure shop caters for all the needs of the golfer with an extensive range of hire equipment and golf merchandise.

The Terrace Restaurant within the country club offers fine food in a casual atmosphere.

Dalmahoy Hotel, Country Club Resort
Kirknewton
Midlothian
EH27 8EB
Tel: 031 333 1845
Fax: 031 333 1433

Dalmahoy near Edinburgh—the successful venue of the 1992 Solheim Cup—has a lot in common with Moor Park, near London. Apart from being an easy drive from its country's capital (although it is much easier to escape from central Edinburgh than central London) both have two parkland courses—the one being much more testing than the other; both have staged televised professional tournaments over their championship course and most immediately striking of all is that the courses of Dalmahoy and Moor park are each overlooked by magnificent mansion houses which act as extraordinarily elegant 19th holes.

Dalmahoy's mansion is a three storey Georgian building, originally designed for the Earl of Morton in 1735. To wander around its interior is an experience itself; many magnificent paintings adorn the walls and a wonderful sense of wellbeing pervades the building. The mansion has in fact been the focal point of a considerable amount of activity in recent times. The Georgian building has been sympathetically restored and is now the centrepiece of a 116 bedroomed luxury hotel and country club. The whole development plan comprised an investment of some £14 million. Lord knows what the Earl of Morton would have thought of it all! It certainly gives Dalmahoy an advantage over Moor Park where it has never been possible to stay overnight immediately behind the 18th green.

Golf has been played at Dalmahoy since the 1920s, five times Open Champion James Braid designing both courses, the championship **East** and the **West**, in 1927. From the day the very first ball was struck they have been held in extremely high esteem. The courses exemplify all that is best in parkland golf and offer a very real contrast to the nearby challenges of Muirfield, Gullane, Dunbar and the other great links courses that lie like a string of pearls along Lothian's coast. Again, like Moor Park, Dalmahoy's fairways are quite undulating and provide some far reaching views; Edinburgh Castle sits proudly on the horizon.

Casual visitors are normally only received at Dalmahoy on weekdays, the courses being reserved at weekends for members and hotel residents. There are some exceptions to the rule however, and it is always best to check with the Club. **Advance Bookings** (i.e. more than 7 days prior to intended play) can be made

by telephoning **031 333 1845;** in other cases it will be necessary to contact **Reservations** on **031 333 4105** where the professional team is headed by the **Director of Golf, Brian Anderson.** The Club's full address is; **The Dalmahoy Hotel, Golf and Country Club, Kirknewton, Midlothian EH27 8EB.**

In 1994 green fees at Dalmahoy were as follows: £24 to play a round on the West Course midweek, £34 at weekends and £34 for a midweek round on the East Course and £46 at weekends. Reduced fees are available for junior golfers and a current handicap certificate is preferred.

Dalmahoy's precise location is 7 miles south west of Edinburgh off the A71 Kilmarnock Road. It is approximately 3 miles from the City's ring road. Travelling from the Glasgow region the M8 should be left at junction 3, the A899 linking the M8 with the A71. South of Glasgow the A71 itself is a fairly quick route while travellers approaching from the north are likely to find the M9 of most assistance. Finally, it is worth noting that Edinburgh's airport is only about 6 miles from Dalmahoy and is on the 'right side' of the city.

Measuring 6677 yards, par 72, the East Course is considerably longer than the West at 5185 yards, par 68. Both however are maintained in the same superb condition all year round. Due to the recent works at Dalmahoy the East Course front and back nines have been reversed, in other words, what was formerly the 10th is now played as the opening hole. This isn't the first time this has happened. The course was played 'this way round' in 1981 during the televised Haig Tournament Players Championship.

That 1981 Tournament Players Championship witnessed some outstanding golf. On the final day, Scotland's Brian Barnes, cheered on by a partisan crowd, stormed around the course in an unbelievable 62 strokes; most unbelievable was his inward nine of just 28. This score enabled him to catch Brian Waites and inevitably, Barnes went on to win the playoff. It was perhaps the giant Scot's greatest hour, although history will doubtless remember him as the man who twice defeated Jack Nicklaus on the same day during the 1975 Ryder Cup matches in America. As for Dalmahoy, it is now indelibly linked with the Solheim Cup and that memorable week in October 1992 when the world of women's golf was so dramatically turned on its head.

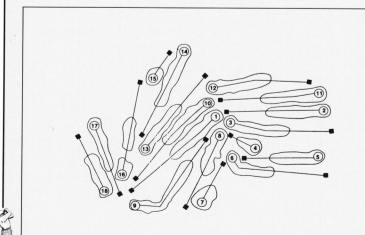

East Course

Hole	Yards	Par	Hole	Yards	Par
1	495	5	10	505	5
2	406	4	11	435	4
3	431	4	12	416	4
4	145	3	13	430	4
5	306	4	14	461	4
6	390	4	15	149	3
7	206	3	16	423	4
8	356	4	17	309	4
9	480	5	18	334	4
Out	**3,215**	**36**	**In**	**3,462**	**36**
			Out	**3,215**	**36**
			Totals	**6,677**	**72**

In common with much of eastern Scotland it isn't entirely clear when golf was first played at Dunbar. Whilst the Dunbar Golf Club was founded in 1856 following a meeting in the Town Hall, The Dunbar Golfing Society had been instituted in 1794. Furthermore, records suggest that some cruder form of golf had been played in the area at least as early as the beginning of the 17th century. In 1616 two men of the parish of Tyninghame were censured by the Kirk Session for 'playing at ye nyne holis' on the Lord's Day and in 1640 an Assistant Minister of Dunbar was disgraced 'for playing at gouff'. Times, as they say, change and 350 years later 'gouff' is still played at Dunbar, although no one is likely to be censured or disgraced for doing so and there are now 18 splendid holes.

Presently in charge of the famous links is the Club's **Secretary, Mr. Don Thompson.** He may be contacted on **(0368) 862317**. Very much a welcoming golf club, Dunbar receives visitors at all times except on Thursdays (which is members' day). Societies are equally catered for although pre-booking is not surprisingly required. Those organising Societies should write to Mr. Thompson at **The Dunbar Golf Club, East Links, Dunbar, East Lothian.** In 1994 the green fee for either a single round or a full day's golf was priced at £25 during the week and £40 at weekends. One final introduction— **Derek Small** is the Club's **professional,** he may be reached on **(0368) 862086.**

Having spent countless hours poring over maps trying to work out the best routes to a particular Golf Club it is with great pleasure that I turn to Dunbar: from the west, approach via the A1; from the south east approach via the A1! Less flippantly, the A1 runs from Berwick-upon-Tweed to Edinburgh and passes through Dunbar. Those travelling from the Borders region of Melrose and Galashiels may find helpful a combination of the A68 and the A6137 to Haddington, thereafter picking up the A1 to Dunbar.

Dunbar is very much a natural links, laid out on a fairly narrow tract of land closely following the contours of the shoreline. It is bounded by a stone wall which runs the full length of the course. While Dunbar is by no means the longest of Scottish links, when the winds blow it can prove to be one of the most difficult—this may have something to do with the fact that there is an 'out of bounds' on the 3rd, 4th, 5th, 6th, 7th, 8th, 9th, 16th, 17th and 18th holes, and the beach can come in to play on the 4th, 5th, 6th, 7th, 12th, 14th, 15th, 16th and 17th—straight hitting would appear to be called for!

Dunbar is without doubt one of the east coast's most attractive links with some splendid views out across the sea towards Bass Rock. The first three holes are played fairly close to the Clubhouse, the opening two being relatively tame par fives and the 3rd a spectacular short hole played from an elevated tee. The 4th then takes you alongside the beach as the course begins to move away from the Clubhouse. Perhaps the most testing holes occur around the turn, the 9th to the 12th, and there is no let-up either on the closing stretch with the beach readily receiving the mildest of slices. The 18th can also be a card-wrecker with the stone wall out of bounds running the entire length of the fairway to the right.

All the major Scottish Championships have been played at Dunbar, including the Scottish Amateur and Scottish Professional Championships. The Club has also staged the British Boys Championship and has become something of a home in recent years for the Scottish Boys title.

Dunbar's 19th is a comfortable building with views from the lounge across much of the course. Lunches and snacks are available seven days a week and with prior arrangement both breakfasts and dinners are also offered. One final thought as you relax in the Clubhouse—one of the Regulations of the Dunbar Golfing Society dated 1794 reads as follows: 'When the expense of each Member for dinner amounts to two shillings and sixpence, the Club shall be dissolved'— times, as they say, most certainly change!

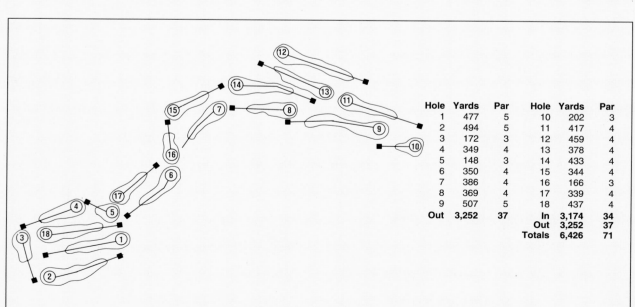

Hole	Yards	Par		Hole	Yards	Par
1	477	5		10	202	3
2	494	5		11	417	4
3	172	3		12	459	4
4	349	4		13	378	4
5	148	3		14	433	4
6	350	4		15	344	4
7	386	4		16	166	3
8	369	4		17	339	4
9	507	5		18	437	4
Out	**3,252**	**37**		**In**	**3,174**	**34**
				Out	**3,252**	**37**
				Totals	**6,426**	**71**

Lothian Complete Golf

Key

To avoid disappointment it is advisable to telephone in advance

****Visitors welcome at most times*
***Visitors usually allowed on weekdays only*
**Visitors not normally permitted (Mon, Wed) No visitors on specified days*

Approximate Green Fees

A £30 plus
B £20 to £30
C £15 to £25
D £10 to £20
E under £10
F Greens fees on application

Restrictions

G Guests only
H Handicap certificate required
H (24) Handicap of 24 or less
L Letter of introduction required
M Visitor must be a member of another recognised club.

Baberton G.C.
031 453 4911
Baberton Avenue, Juniper Green, Edinburgh
(18) 6098 yards/***/F

Bathgate G.C.
(0506) 630505
Edinburgh Road, Bathgate, West Lothian
(18) 6328 yards/***/D

Braid Hills G.C.
031 447 6666
Braid Hill Road,Edinburgh
(18) 6172 yards/***/E
(18) 4832 yards/***/E

Broomieknowe G.C.
031 663 9317
Golf Course Road, Bonnyrigg, Midlothian
(18) 6046 yards/**/C

Bruntsfield Links G.C.
031 336 1479
Barton Avenue, Davidsons Mains, Edinburgh
(18) 6407 yards/**/F/H

Carrick Knowe G.C.
031 337 1096
Glendevon Park, Edinburgh
(18) 6299 yards/***/E

Carrickvale G.C.
031 337 1096
Glendevon Park, Edinburgh
(18) 6299 yards/***/F/H

Craigentinny G.C.
031 554 7501
Craigentinny Avenue, Edinburgh
(18) 5418 yards/***/E

Craigmillar Park G.C.
031 667 2837
Observatory Road, Edinburgh
(18) 5846 yards/***/D/H or L

Dalmahoy G.C.
031 333 1845
Dalmahoy, Kirknewton, Midlothian
(18) 6664 yards/***/F
(18) 5121 yards/***/F

Deer Park G.C.
(0506) 38843
Carmondean, Livingston, West Lothian
(18) 6636 yards/***/D

Duddingston G.C.
031 661 7688
Duddingston Road, Edinburgh
(18) 6647 yards/**/D

Dunbar G.C.
(0368) 862317
East Links, Dunbar
(18) 6426 yards/***/C

Dundas Park G.C.
031 331 5603
Hope Cottage,Loch Road, South Queensferry
(9) 5510 yards/***/E/M

Gifford G.C.
(0620) 810267
Gifford
(9) 5613 yards/***(Tues/Wed W/E pm)/D

Glen G.C.
(0620) 892221
Tantallon Terrace, North Berwick, East Lothian
(18) 6098 yards/***/D

Glencorse G.C.
(0968) 677189
Milton Bridge, Penicuik, Midlothian
(18) 5205 yards/***/D

Greenburn G.C.
(0501) 770292
Fauldhouse, West Lothian
(18) 6210 yards/**/E/H

Gullane G.C.
(0620) 843115
Gullane, East Lothian
(18)6466 yards/**/F
(18)6127 yards/***/F
(18)5128 yards/***/F

Haddington G.C.
(0620) 8233627
Amisfield Park, Haddington, East Lothian
(18) 6280 yards/**(pm)/E

Harburn G.C.
(0506) 871256
West Calder, West Lothian
(18) 5843 yards/***/D

Honourable Company Of Edinburgh Golfers
(0620) 842123
Muirfield, Gullane, East Lothian
(18) 6601 yards/(Tues, Thurs only)/A/H (18)/M/L

Kilspindie G.C.
(08751) 870216
Aberlady, East Lothian
(18) 5410 yards/***/F

Kingsknowe G.C.
031 441 1144
Lanark Road, Edinburgh
(18) 5979 yards/**/E/H

Liberton G.C.
031 664 8580
Gilmerton Road, Edinburgh
(18) 5299 yards/***/D

Linlithgow G.C.
(0506) 842585
Braehead, Linlithgow, West Lothian
(18) 5858 yards/***(Wed/Sat)/D

Longniddry G.C.
(0875) 852141
Links Road, Longniddry, East Lothian
(18) 6210 yards/***/F

Lothian Burn G.C.
031 445 2206
Biggar Road, Fairmilehead
(18) 5750 yards/***/C

Luffness New G.C.
(0620) 843114
Aberlady, East Lothian
(18) 6122 yards/**/B

Merchants of Edinburgh G.C.
031 447 1219
Craighill Gardens, Edinburgh
(18) 4889 yards/***/D

Mortonhall G.C.
031 447 2411
Braid Road, Edinburgh
(18) 6557 yards/**/D

Murrayfield G.C.
031 337 1009
Murrayfield Road, Edinburgh
(18) 5727 yards/***/D

Musselburgh G.C.
031 665 2005
Monktonhall, Musselburgh, Midlothian
(18) 6623 yards/***/D

Newbattle G.C.
031 663 2123
Abbey Road, Dalkeith, Midlothian
(18) 6012 yards/**/D

Niddry Castle & G.C.
(0506) 891097
Castle Road, Winchurch
(9) 5476 yards/***/E

North Berwick G.C.
(0620) 892135
West Links, Beach Road North Berwick
(18) 6317 yards/***/C-B

Polkemmet G.C.

(0501) 743905
Whitburn, Bathgate
(9) 2967 yards/***/E

Portobello G.C.
031 669 4361
Stanley Road, Portobello, Edinburgh
(9) 2400 yards/***/E

Prestonfield G.C.
031 667 1273
6 Prestonfield Road North, Edinburgh
(18) 6216 yards/**(Sat, Sun pm)/D

Pumpherston G.C.
(0506) 32869
Drumshoreland Road, Pumpherston, Livingston
(9) 5154 yards/*/F/G

Ratho Park G.C.
031 333 1252
Ratho, Newbridge, Midlothian
(18) 6028 yards/***/C

Ravelston G.C.
031 315 2486
24 Ravelston Dykes Road, Blackhall, Edinburgh
(9) 5200 yards/*/D/G

Royal Burgess G.C.
031 339 2075
Whitehouse Road, Edinburgh
(18) 6604 yards/**/F/L

Royal Musselburgh G.C.
(0875) 810276
Preston Grange House, Prestonpans, East Lothian
(18) 6237 yards/***/C/H

Silverknowes G.C.
031 336 3843
Silverknowes, Parkway, Edinburgh
(18) 6210 yards/***/E

Swanston G.C.
031 445 2239
Swanston Road, Edinburgh
(18) 5024 yards/***/D

Torphin Hill G.C.
031 441 1100
Torphin Road, Colinton, Edinburgh
(18) 5024 yards/***/D

Turnhouse G.C.
031 339 1014
Turnhouse Road, Edinburgh
(18) 6171 yards/**/D

Uphall G.C.
(0506) 856404
Uphall, West Lothian
(18)6250 yards/***/D

West Lothian G.C.
(0506) 826030
Airngarth Hill, Linlithgow, West Lothian
(18) 6578 yards/**/D

Winterfield G.C.
(0368) 86562
St Margarets,North Road,Dunbar
(18) 5053 yards/***/F

Artist: E A Pettitt THE MARINE, NORTH BERWICK *Courtesy of* **Burlington Gallery**

Strathclyde

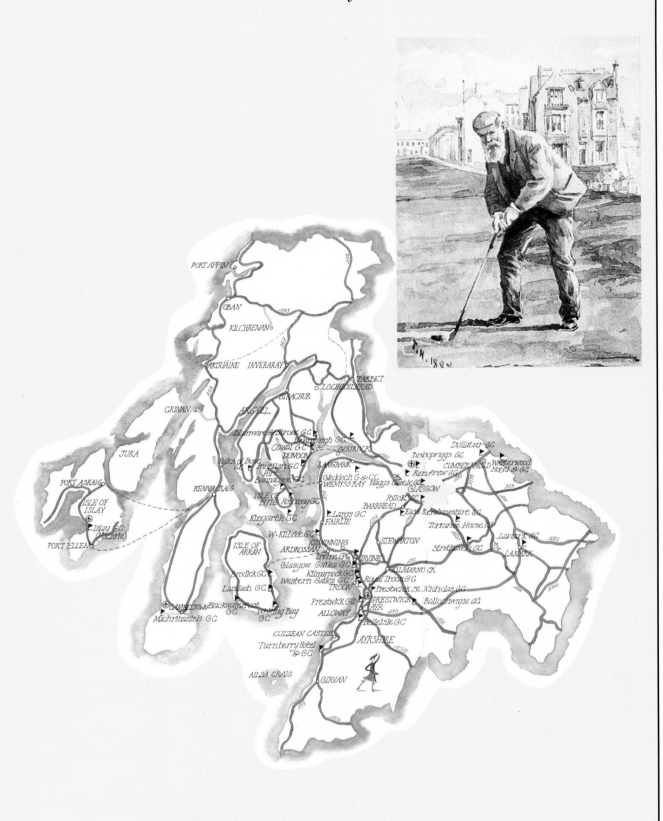

Map labels (from the illustration):

PORT APPIN

OBAN

KILCHRENAN

ARDUAINE   INVERARAY

CRINAN

ARGYLL

STRACHUR

TARBET

LOCHGOILHEAD

Blairmore & Strone GC   Benmuagh GC

JURA   Cowal GC   GOUROCK

Kyles of Bute GC   DUNOON   Dullatur GC

Innellan GC   LANGBANK   Bishopriggs GC   CUMBERNAULD   Westerwood Hotel & GC

PORT ASKAIG   Bennnehrae GC   Gladdoch G & CC   Renfrew GC

KENNACRAIG   WEMYSS BAY   Haggs Castle GC   GLASGOW

ISLE OF ISLAY   ISLE OF BUTE   Rothesay GC   Pollok GC

Islay GC (Machrie)   BARRHEAD   East Renfrewshire GC

Kingarth GC   Largs GC   Tarinaire House GC   Lanark GC

PORT ELLEN   FAIRLIE

W. Kilbride GC   Strathaven GC   LANARK

ISLE OF ARRAN   KILWINNING   STEWARTON

ARDROSSAN   Irvine GC   IRVINE

Brodick GC   Glasgow Gailes GC   KILMARNOCK

Kilmarnock GC   Royal Troon GC

Lamlash GC   Western Gailes GC   TROON

CAMPBELTOWN   Blackwaterfoot   Prestwick GC   Prestwick St. Nicholas GC   Balloonyle GC

Machrihanish GC   Whiting Bay GC   ALLOWAY   AYR   PRESTWICK

Belleisle GC

CULZEAN CASTLE

Turnberry Hotel & GC   AYRSHIRE

AILSA CRAIG   GIRVAN

Artist: **T. Hodge TOM MORRIS** *Courtesy of:* **Sotheby's**

The Ayrshire Coast

An ancient golfing rhyme from the land of Burns runs:
'Troon and Prestwick, old and classy,
Bogside, Dundonald, Glasgow Gailes, Barassie,
Prestwick St Nicholas, Western Gailes,
St Cuthbert, Portland—memory fails,
Troon Municipal (three links there)
Prestwick Municipal, Irvine, Ayr,
They faced the list with delighted smiles -
Sixteen courses within ten miles'.

Even without Turnberry, that 'little corner of heaven on earth', some 15 miles south of Ayr, an extraordinarily impressive list, and little wonder that this small region of Scotland's coast has become nothing short of a Mecca for golfers the world over.

Prestwick, Troon and **Turnberry** have of course each staged the Open Championship. Prestwick was the birthplace of the event back in 1860 and is probably the most classical test of traditional links golf—penal the American architects would describe it, on account of the many blind shots. The Open is no longer held at Prestwick but the history of the place is overwhelming and quite magnetic. Troon and Turnberry are both firmly on the 'Open' rota. It was last played over the latter's Ailsa course in 1986 (Norman's great victory) and was last held at Troon in 1989 (Norman's near victory); in 1994 Norman will be defending at Turnberry. Understandably the golfer making a pilgrimage to the Ayrshire coast will be drawn towards this famous trio. However, if time isn't, as they say, of the essence, it would be bordering on a disgrace not to sample as many of the nearby delights as possible. As the old rhyme relates, within short distance of one another lie a number of outstanding courses and where at any of which it may be easier to arrange a game.

For those making the pilgrimage north from England, an excellent choice for an overnight break (or longer) would be Farlam Hall (06977) 46234 one of Cumbria's top hotels. While not all roads lead to Ayr, as the largest town on the coast, it's probably as good a starting point as any. Here we find a belle—**Belleisle** to be precise and a most attractive parkland course. Considered by many to be the finest public course outside of St Andrews and Carnoustie and, being somewhat sheltered, it's an admirable retreat from the more windswept links nearby. Furthermore as a municipal course the green fees are very cheap.

Just north of Ayr lie a series of outstanding links courses, all within a mile or two of one another. Prestwick and Troon are featured on later pages (as is Turnberry) but also in this area one finds first class courses at **Prestwick St Nicholas, Barassie, Western Gailes, Glasgow (Gailes)** and **Irvine** (also known somewhat unfortunately as Bogside). Each warmly welcomes visitors and, although they are less busy than the big three, prior telephoning is strongly recommended, especially during the peak summer months. Weekdays are inevitably the best times for a visit.

Just as there is a proliferation of golf courses, so the area is inundated with all manner of hotels, guest houses, pubs and restaurants. A few thoughts follow. To start at a pinnacle, undoubtedly one of the best hotels in Britain is the Turnberry Hotel (0655) 31000, the first ever purpose-built hotel and golf course. Both hotel and restaurant are truly outstanding in every way. Guests enjoy reduced green fees and more importantly have priority on the golf courses. For beautiful views over the Isle of Arran, we also recommend nearby Malin Court (0655) 31457. If staying in this area, Culzean Castle (open between April and October) is well worth a visit and in nearby **Girvan** where there is an underrated municipal course, an excellent place for liquid refreshment is the King's Arms (0465) 3322. and golfers may also find the Bardrochat (0465) 88232 here ideal for their accommodation needs. If you've food on your mind we suggest you forget about calories and go for a slap up meal in Splinters! (0465) 3481. Perhaps the most popular, and certainly the most convenient hotel for Royal Troon is the Marine Highland (0292) 314444. It proudly overlooks the Old Course Championship links. Two other splendid hotels in Troon are Piersland House (0292) 314747 and the Ardneil (0292) 311611. The two best known hotels in Ayr are the Caledonian (0292) 269331 and the Pickwick (0292) 260111 while close by in Alloway is the excellent Balgarth Hotel (0292) 42441 and in Maybole, the Ladyburn Hotel (06554) 585 is good value. On to Prestwick, which if you've arrived by plane may well be your first port of call. Here, the Carlton (0292) 76811 and the Parkstone (0292) 77286 stand out from the crowd as does the Prestwick Old Course Hotel with its Thai Restaurant and there are numerous B&Bs and small hotels. The Fairways Hotel (0292) 70396 and Fernbank Guest House (0292) 75027 are always popular retreats. Kilmarnock is now a busy industrial centre yet it was here that Robbie Burns' first collection of poems was published. Just to the north of the town at Irvine is the Hospitality Inn (0294) 274272 which in keeping with its name is most welcoming. If an escape to the countryside is sought then a trip to Stewarton is highly recommended. Here, set in glorious surroundings, is the redoubtable Chapeltoun House (0560) 482696—quiet and very comfortable with a first class restaurant. Kilwinning is a final recommendation for this area, the Montgreenan Mansion House (0294) 557733 is superbly situated with excellent facilities including some practice holes to warm up before sallying forth.

To the north of the famous golfing stretch there is plenty of less testing golf to be found. This may well be necessary in order to restore battered pride! **West Kilbride** (another links type) and **Largs** (a wellwooded parkland course) should suit admirably. Both also offer some magnificent views across to Argyll and the Isle of Arran where there are no fewer than seven golf courses, and an ideal base to play them from is the Auchrannie Country House Hotel (0770) 302234. Also roughly due east of Ayr, close to the A76 there is a very good course at **Ballochmyle.**

Glasgow

Glasgow is Britain's third largest city after London and Birmingham and, being Scottish to boot, not surprisingly has a huge number of golf courses. Indeed some wag once said of Glasgow that there was a pub in every street with a golf club around each corner. One interesting statistic is that between 1880 and 1910 more than 80 golf courses were built in the Greater Glasgow area—so much for today's golf boom! Unfortunately the problem for the golfing stranger to Glasgow is that many of the city's leading clubs permit visitors to play only if accompanied by a member. Among the city's more traditional courses—and where arranging a game can be difficult—are **Haggs Castle, Pollok** and **Glasgow Killermont.** Other suggestions include **Renfrew** and **East Renfrewshire,** to the north west and south west respectively and **Bishopriggs** to the north of Glasgow. There are a number of public courses in Glasgow so the visiting golfer confined to Glasgow need not get too depressed. The pick of the municipals is probably **Lethamhill** and **Little Hill**—a game on either is remarkably inexpensive.

Forgetting the golf for a moment, it came as something of a surprise for many south of the border when Glasgow was chosen as European City of Culture for 1990, in succession to Athens and Paris, among other cities. Of course those familiar with the city will know that it has changed out of all recognition in the past decade or so. Good hotels are not as thick on the ground as golf courses but a list of the best would include the Glynhill Leisure Hotel 041 886 9555 which caters equally well for individuals and groups and offers various golfing packages. Others to note are the Holiday Inn 041 226 5577, the Hospitality Inn 041 332 3311 and the less modern (and with a much more attractive exterior) Stakis Grosvenor 041 339 8811. One Devonshire Gardens 041 339 2001 also combines old-fashioned elegance and service. Glasgow Airport, actually situated eight miles away in Paisley, offers a choice between the Stakis Normandy Hotel, 041 886 4100, complete with driving range and the Forte Crest 041 887 1212. As for restaurants, Glasgow is pretty well endowed. Fish lovers will adore Rogano's Oyster Bar 041 248 4055 in Exchange Square while those seeking first class French cuisine should head for the Buttery 041 221 8188 on Argyle Street. High quality Chinese and Indian restaurants also abound, with the Amber 041 339 6121 and Balbir's Ashoka Tandoori 041 221 1761 both well worth seeking out. For a sample of Glasgow's culture the Theatre Royal 041 332 9000 offers distinguished ballet, opera and drama and the Burrell Collection in Pollok Park is Scotland's leading art gallery.

Time for a spot more golf, and the **Gleddoch House** Hotel Golf and Country Club (0475) 540711 provides the solution. Located at Langbank it is close to the Clyde Estuary and offers views of the Lombard Hills. It is easily accessible from Glasgow by way of the M8 and in a nutshell could be described as a darn good hotel with a darn good restaurant and a darn good golf course! Further north, the course at **Helensburgh** is also worth a visit.

From Glasgow, the great challenges of Troon, Turnberry and Prestwick lie to the south west (the A77 is incidentally the most convenient route), but championship golf can also be found to the north and east — **Dullatur** is one such venue, **Lanark** another. The former is a parkland course whereas Lanark is essentially moorland. For Dullatur a hotel to note is Crow Wood House 041 77 3861 and an excellent restaurant, La Campagnola 041 779 3405—both are in Muirhead. The Cartland Bridge Hotel (0555) 664426 is recommended for the course at Lanark. twenty miles or so east of Glasgow near Cumbernauld the **Westerwood Hotel** (0236) 457171 and its golf course have only recently appeared on the map. An inspection is strongly recommended — the golf course is very challenging and calls for many daring shots, which is not altogether surprising since Seve Ballesteros had a hand in its design (Westerwood is featured later in this section).

Further Afield

Before heading for the more distant corners of Strathclyde a quick mention for two courses lying due south of Glasgow; **Torrance House** and **Strathaven** are the pair in question. Both are very easily reached by way of the A726, although Strathaven is quite a bit of a way from the city and by the time you arrive at the course you'll have climbed 700 feet above sea level. But a lovely setting, and a most convenient hotel, the Strathaven (0357) 20421 await.

What of the more remote outposts then? Strathclyde is

a vast region extending well into the Highlands. There's not a great deal in the way of golfing challenges here— the landscape precludes it—but the countryside is quite glorious and there are some extremely fine hotels and country houses nestling in and around the hills, all making splendid bases for exploring the magnificent scenery of these parts. North of Loch Lomond one finds Stonefield Castle (0880) 820836 at Tarbet alongside Loch Fyne. If inspecting the delights of Oban a detour to Kilchrenan is highly recommende.; The Ardanaiseig (08663) 333 is the place—outstandingly relaxing. Still nearer to Oban at Knipoch, the Knipoch Hotel (0852) 6251 offers great comfort together with all manner of country pursuits.

Two great courses still remain to be charted—those magical 'M's'—**Machrie** and **Machrihanish.** Each enjoys a kind of splendid isolation and is a superb test of traditional links golf. Machrie is to be found on the distant Isle of Islay at Port Ellen. As it can now be reached by plane from Glasgow there can be no excuse for not making the trip - besides right on the course is the excellent Machrie Hotel (0496) 2085. Many have already made the pilgrimage to Machrihanish and as it too is reachable by air a large number are certain to follow. Following The Fairways has also succumbed to its charms and Machrihanish is explored on a later page. There are a number of hotels and guest houses nearby, both in Machrihanish itself and in Campbeltown, and it's well worth spending a few days here. The Putechan Lodge (05832) 323 can be highly recommended and offers special golfing breaks. Before you leave the area a mellow tune may come to mind—Mull of Kintyre by one Paul McCartney. The music inspired millions: the golf course and its surrounds will almost certainly give equal satisfaction.

Artist: **Arthur Weaver WILLIE PARK JNR**
Courtesy of **Burlington Gallery**

Bardrochat was built in 1893 by the famous Scottish architect Robert Lorimer. This large, private, country house stands high on the south side of the beautiful Stinchar Valley overlooking the River Stinchar and the village of Colmonell in south west Ayrshire. Glasgow airport is only one and a half hours by road.

Staying at Bardrochat as a guest of the owners is a chance to enjoy a completely different experience from the normal impersonal hotel. The house can sleep six couples, all bedrooms are en suite and four have their own dressing rooms. The large drawing room has beautiful views over the valley and the dining room can seat up to 20 people.

On the west side of the house is a large croquet lawn and below that is a walled garden and tennis court. Bardrochat is the perfect base from which to play the courses of Ayrshire and the south west of Scotland. As well as the three Turnberry courses, there are many more local and championship courses in the area, including Prestwick, Troon and Barrassie. There are at least eight golf courses within a radius of 25 miles of the house.

In May and the beginning of June guests can combine golf with the great gardens of the area - the gardens at Lochinch are only 35 minutes from the house. In October guests can also try their hand at salmon fishing as the estate has one mile of single bank fishing for four rods on the River Stinchar.

Featured in Architectural Digest of January 1993 and English Vogue of March 1994, Bardrochat offers a unique opportunity to sample the atmosphere and comfort of a country home with delicious food and famous Scottish hospitality. Prices and directions are available on application.

Bardrochat
Colmonell
Ayrshire
KA26 0SG
Tel: (0465) 88232
Fax: (0465) 88330

Turnberry Hotel Golf Courses and Spa

Recently awarded the Automobile Association's most prestigious accolade , five red stars, closely followed by 'Hotel of the Year' award*, Turnberry is located on the west coast of Scotland, set in 360 acres overlooking the islands of Arran and Ailsa Craig.

The two championship links golf courses, owned and managed by the hotel, make it a year round Mecca for golfers. The Ailsa course was the venue for the 123rd British Open in July 1994 and was universally acclaimed for its outstanding condition.

A superb clubhouse was opened in June 1993 by HRH the Duke of York. It has been designed to complement the traditional style of the hotel and offers a clubhouse restaurant and lounge, both with outstanding views over both the Ailsa and Arran courses. In addition there are two traditionally furnished hospitality suites and an imposing first floor gallery.

The Turnberry Spa, unrivalled in Britain and described as being 'a decade ahead of its time', is an additional amenity for the golfer and non golfer alike. The Spa includes a 20 metre deck level pool with underwater music, spa bath and bio sauna, two squash courts, cardio-vascular and muscular gymnasium and aqua and floor aerobics. The nine treatment rooms offer a range of 25 treatments, including hydrotherapy and aromatherapy.

Nearby are riding stables and fishing, rough and clay shooting are available. Culzean Castle, Robert Burns country and the Burrell Collection are also of interest.

The hotel was built at the turn of the century and the tradition of elegance and comfort is retained throughout. At Turnberry, living is indeed comfortable and relaxed; every bedroom has its own individual character.

The Turnberry Restaurant, under the direction of executive chef Stewart Cameron, specialises in an alliance of traditional Scottish and French cooking. Entertainment is provided each evening by resident musicians and the atmosphere is very much that of the grand country house.

The Bay at Turnberry enjoys spectacular views of Turnberry Bay towards Arran and Ailsa Craig. The focus is on a lighter style of cooking both at lunch and dinner, in an informal setting. The Clubhouse restaurant is open for all day dining.

Whilst staying at Turnberry, guests will enjoy warm hospitality, the constant concern and those little formalities and gracious touches that make all the difference. Perhaps it is because of this that so many guests and their families choose to return year after year.

* The Caterer and Hotelkeeper

Turnberry Hotel, Golf Courses and Spa
Ayrshire
Scotland
KA26 9LT
Tel: (0655) 31000
Fax: (0655) 31706

Turnberry

Not so many years ago it was said that the golfing visitor to Scotland journeyed to St. Andrews for the history and to Turnberry for the beauty. Incomparable is a word often used to describe Turnberry's setting, magnificent and majestic are two others. Quite what causes Ailsa Craig to be so mesmerising is a mystery, but mesmerising it is and the views towards the distant Isle of Arran and the Mull of Kintyre can be equally captivating and enchanting. Since 1977, Turnberry has possessed history as well as beauty.

The Open Championship of 1977, Turnberry's first, is generally considered to have been the greatest of all Championships. Nicklaus and Watson, the two finest golfers of the day, turned the tournament into a titanic, head-to-head confrontation—the 'Duel in the Sun' as it came to be known. On the final day, both having pulled along way clear of the field, Nicklaus held a two stroke advantage as they left the 12th green. Who in the world can give Jack Nicklaus two shots over six holes and beat him? asked Peter Alliss—the rest, as they say, is history.

There are two Championship courses at Turnberry: the better known **Ailsa** Course, to which the Open returned for a third time in 1994, and the **Arran** Course. Both are owned and run by the Turnberry Hotel. Visitors with handicaps are welcome to play on either course although written prior arrangements must be made with the **Golf Operations Manager, Mr. Ewen Bowman.** Mr. Bowman and his staff can be contacted via **The Turnberry Hotel, Turnberry, Strathclyde, KA26 9LT, telephone (0655) 31000.**

In 1994 the summer green fees were set at £85 for a day's golf consisting of one round on each course. A single round on the Arran is priced at £30. Reduced rates of £50 for a round on both courses is available to Hotel residents (they pay £20 for a single round on the Arran Course) and further reductions are available to all golfers during the winter months. Turnberry's **professional Robert Jamieson** can also be contacted on **(0655) 31000.** Caddies and hire of clubs are best arranged by telephoning in advance.

The Hotel and golf courses lie approximately 17 miles south of the town of Ayr off the A77. For those travelling from the Glasgow region, the A77 runs direct from Glasgow to Turnberry and is dual carriageway for much of the journey. Motoring from Edinburgh the A71 is the best route, picking up the A77 at Kilmarnock. Approaching from England, Carlisle is likely to be a

starting point (M6 to Carlisle). The distance from Carlisle to Turnberry is one of just under 120 miles, and although there are two choices, the quickest route is to head north on the A74 leaving (in what appears to be no man's land) and joining the A70 towards Ayr. Finally, Prestwick Airport is situated just to the north of Ayr.

From its elevated perch, the red-roofed Turnberry Hotel enjoys a commanding view over both courses. It will have witnessed much of Turnberry's rather turbulent past. During the War the rolling expanse of links had been used as an air base and a vast runway had been constructed. Much levelling of the ground had also taken place and in 1945 the last thing Turnberry must have looked was the setting for two Championship courses. Mackenzie Ross is the architect we all have to thank. From its medal tees, the Ailsa Course isn't a great deal longer than the Arran, their respective distances being 6440 yards, par 69, and 6014 yards, par 68. The same from the ladies tees are 5757 yards, par 75 and 5501 yards par 72. When Turnberry's second Open was staged in 1986 the Ailsa course weighed in at 6950 yards, par 70 and the fairways had been narrowed to alarming proportions. Greg Norman's second round 63, achieved in far from perfect weather conditions, was a remarkable feat.

After three holes 'inland' as it were, the Ailsa course hugs the shore tightly for a series of dramatic holes between the 4th and the 11th. The 6th, named Tappie Toorie, is possibly the most difficult par three on the course; the shot is to a heavily guarded green across a valley (play it into the wind and you may be short with a driver). The 9th and the 10th, though, are the holes most likely to be remembered. The 9th 'Bruce's Castle', is played alongside the famous Turnberry lighthouse, built over the remains of Turnberry Castle, birthplace of Robert the Bruce. The Championship tee for this hole is perched on a pinnacle of rock with the sea crashing below. Stand on this tee and you can appreciate why parallels have often been drawn between Turnberry and Pebble Beach. Following the par three 11th, the holes turn inland and if the scenery is a little less spectacular the challenge in no way diminishes.

The closing holes in fact produced a marvellous climax to the 1994 Open when Jesper Parnevik birdied five of his final eight holes yet was still overtaken by Nick Price. The popular Zimbabwian birdied the 16th and then eagled the 17th with a putt of fully 60 feet. Watson, Norman and Price... Tunberry's great triumvirate.

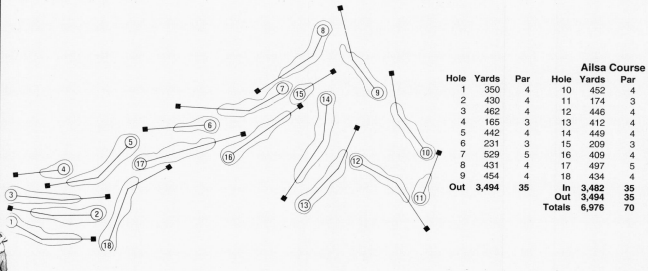

Hole	Yards	Par	Hole	Yards	Par
1	350	4	10	452	4
2	430	4	11	174	3
3	462	4	12	446	4
4	165	3	13	412	4
5	442	4	14	449	4
6	231	3	15	209	3
7	529	5	16	409	4
8	431	4	17	497	5
9	454	4	18	434	4
Out	**3,494**	**35**	**In**	**3,482**	**35**
			Out	**3,494**	**35**
			Totals	**6,976**	**70**

Ailsa Course

Montgreenan Mansion House Hotel

The Mansion House at Montgreenan was built by Dr Robert Glasgow in 1817 as a family home and so it remains today, with all the period features including the attractive marble and brass fireplaces, decorative ceiling and plasterwork having been carefully retained. Indeed, the traveller who visits Montgreenan may be forgiven for feeling he has made a journey back in time. Where better to relax and enjoy the peaceful setting and magnificent view of the distant Ailsa Craig and Arran Hills, or to stroll through the 50 acres of beautiful gardens and secluded parklands. Montgreenan prides itself on its high standards of personal service and warm hospitality.

Whatever the occasion, Montgreenan is the ideal venue offering spacious rooms, a secluded setting and quiet, attentive service. The comfortable bedrooms are finished to a deluxe standard with antique and reproduction furniture and offer a choice of luxurious beds including a king size round bed and four posters. .

Relax and enjoy the culinary skill of award winning chef Alan McCall. Seasonal specialities are incorporated into Alan's menus and fresh Scottish fare is always available, making dining at Montgreenan an experience not to be missed. The wine cellar has one of the finest selections of fine wines available in Ayrshire and offers something for every taste, including Montgreenan's own specially selected Bordeaux.

Enjoy the challenge of playing the finest links courses in Ayrshire including Turnberry, venue for the British Open in 1994 and the magnificent Prestwick Golf Club where the original Open was held in 1860. There are also many interesting courses inland. In fact, there are over 30 courses within 45 minutes of Montgreenan. In addition, Montgreenan has its own 5 hole practice course which allows guests to play at their leisure.

Montgreenan Mansion House Hotel
Montgreenan Estate
Kilwinning
Strathclyde
KA13 7QZ
Tel: (01294) 557733
Fax: (01294) 850397

O'a the links where I hae golfed
Frae Ayr to Aberdeen,
On Prestwick or Carnoustie and mony mair I ween
What tho' the bents are rough and bunkers yawn aroun'
I dearly lo'e the breezy links, the breezy links o' Troon.
(Gilmour)

When the golfing mind focuses on Troon it invariably thinks of the Postage Stamp, the par three 8th on the Old Course, unquestionably the world's most celebrated short hole. During the 1973 Open Championship, Gene Sarazen, then at the mature age of 71, holed out with his punched five iron shot in front of the watching television cameras. Sarazen declared that he would take with him to heaven a copy of the film to show to Walter Hagen and Co. Legend has it, that on hearing of Sarazen's feat, an American flew to Britain and travelled to Troon. He strode to the 8th tee and proceeded to strike 500 balls in succession towards the green. Not surprisingly he failed to equal Sarazen's achievement whereupon he left the course and duly flew home to America. Who said it was only mad dogs and Englishmen?

Anyone contemplating the above ought at least to consult the **Secretary** first, **Mr. J.D. Montgomerie** being the gentleman in question. He can be contacted at the **Royal Troon Golf Club, Craigend Road, Troon, Ayrshire KA10 6EP: tel. (0292) 311555.** (Fax. (0292) 318204.)

The Royal Troon Club Golf possesses two 18 hole courses, **The Old** and **The Portland**. Gentlemen visitors are welcome to play both courses between Mondays and Thursdays provided prior arrangement is made with the Secretary. Lady golfers are also welcome, although they are limited to playing on the Portland Course. All visitors must be members of a recognised club and be able to produce a certificate of handicap (maximum 18). Society games may be arranged but organisers should note that their numbers must not exceed 24. In 1994 a green fee of £78 entitled the visitor to a round on each course, while a fee of £48 secured a full day's golf on the Portland Course; both fees are inclusive of lunch. There are no concessionary rates for junior golfers who, in any event, must have attained the age of eighteen before they will be permitted to play over the Old Course. Sets of clubs and trolleys may be hired from the Club's **professional, Brian Anderson (tel: 0292 313281)**. A caddy can also usually be obtained.

Troon lies just to the north of Prestwick and Ayr. The town can be reached from Glasgow and the north via the A77, which also runs from near Stranraer in the south. The A78 is the coastal road, running from Largs through Irvine to Loans just east of Troon. Travelling from Edinburgh, the A71 should be taken, whilst from the North of England the best route is probably via the A74 and the A71. Finally, Prestwick Airport is no more than two miles away. Located as it is, bordering the Firth of Clyde, the wind often blows very fiercely across the links and Troon is hardly a place for the faint-hearted golfer.

The Old Course at Troon has both the longest hole of any Open Championship course—the 6th at 577 yards and the shortest—the Postage Stamp, which measures a mere 126 yards. In the 11th it also possesses one of the toughest, with its railway out-of-bounds, thick gorse and painfully narrow fairway. At 6274 yards the Portland Course represents a more modest test but it is none-the-less a very fine course and although in parts closely resembles a moorland-type course, has all the challenges of traditional links golf.

The Club is naturally proud of its great history. When it was founded in 1878 by twenty-four local enthusiasts there were originally only five holes—by 1923 it had staged its first Open Championship. Since then the Club has held five Opens; in 1950, 1962 (when a rampant Palmer stormed to a six stroke victory), 1973 and 1982 (both bringing popular triumphs for Americans Weiskopf and Watson) and of course most recently the Championship of 1989, where a dramatic playoff concluded an unforgettable final day's play.

Mark Calcavecchia had the luck of a Sarazen to hole out from the deep rough on the 12th during the final round. It helped him catch Greg Norman whose 64, highlighted by six straight birdies from the 1st, is likely to stand as the course record for a long time. The Gods of Troon seem to have little difficulty in smiling on an American golfer, but we shouldn't take anything away from Calcavecchia for it takes more than just a little skill to birdie the 18th hole twice in an afternoon.

If you have played all 36 holes at Troon and waged a successful war against the elements you will have earned your drink at the 19th. The Clubhouse provides all the usual facilities and the catering has a very good reputation. When you leave you will probably not have a video to take to heaven, but you will at least know that you have visited one of the earth's greatest golfing shrines.

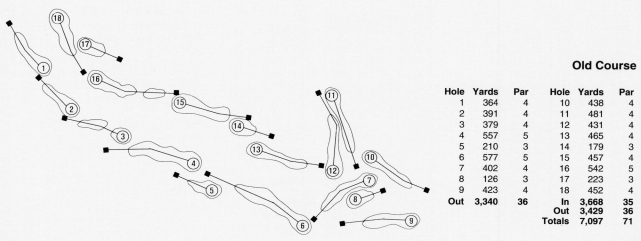

Old Course

Hole	Yards	Par	Hole	Yards	Par
1	364	4	10	438	4
2	391	4	11	481	4
3	379	4	12	431	4
4	557	5	13	465	4
5	210	3	14	179	3
6	577	5	15	457	4
7	402	4	16	542	5
8	126	3	17	223	3
9	423	4	18	452	4
Out	**3,340**	**36**	**In**	**3,668**	**35**
			Out	**3,429**	**36**
			Totals	**7,097**	**71**

Farlam Hall

Farlam Hall was opened in 1975 by the Quinion and Stevenson families who over the years have achieved and maintained consistently high standards of food, service and comfort. These standards have been internationally recognised by all the major guides with three red stars and two rosettes from the AA, Three Stars and Blue Ribbon from the RAC and membership of The Relais and Chateaux.

This old border house, dating in parts back to the seventeenth century was extended to its present size in Victorian times and is now set in acres of mature landscaped gardens which can be seen from the elegant lounges and dining room.

The fine silver, crystal and starched white linen, all combine to create the feeling of a more elegant era and complement the quality of the English country house style of cooking produced by Barry Quinion and his team of experienced chefs. Attentive service from the family and their local staff add the finishing touch.

There are only thirteen bedrooms in this large house which allows some of the rooms to be on rather a grand scale, while the rooms designed originally for lesser family members are of a more conventional size. This variation in room size permits a wide price range in the tariff. No matter what size or shape, the same care and quality has been applied and, as with the whole house, antique and fine furniture has been used wherever possible.

This area offers a wealth of different attractions - miles of unspoilt country for walking, eight golf courses within thirty minutes of the hotel, and close by are Hadrian's Wall, Lanercost Priory and Carlisle with the Castle, Cathedral and Museum. The Lake District, Scottish Borders and Yorkshire Dales provide an ideal day's touring. The hotel's proximity to the M6 also makes it an ideal overnight stop when travelling to or from Scotland.

Dogs are welcome. Closed at Christmas. Directions: Farlam Hall is two and a half miles south east of Brampton on the A689, not in Farlam Village.

Farlam Hall Hotel
Brampton
Cumbria CA8 2NG
Tel: (06977) 46234
Fax: (06977) 46683

One could be forgiven for thinking that they take their golf a little too seriously at Prestwick—especially when one hears of such apparently true stories like the one about the monk from a nearby monastery who played a match against the Lord of Culzean to settle a deadly feud: at stake was the monk's nose!

The truth more likely is that Prestwick folk are a competitive breed. Only nine years after the formation of their Club in 1851 the Members got together and decided to stage an annual Open competition. The winner of the event was to receive an elegant red belt subscribed for by the Members. Whilst there may have been only eight entrants, the 1860 Open marks the birth of the world's most prestigious Championship.

Willie Park of Musselburgh (a 'foreigner from the east coast') won the 1860 Open and it was decided that if anyone should win the event three years in succession they would win the Belt outright. 'Young' Tom Morris (somehow Tom Morris Junior doesn't seem quite appropriate) was the greatest player of his day and fittingly enough in 1870 won his third title in as many years. Whereas Tom may have kept the Belt, Prestwick didn't keep the Open, or at least not the sole rights, as St. Andrews and Muirfield now joined Prestwick in the dawning of a new era.

In those early days the combatants played over a twelve hole course; today there are eighteen holes though the distinctive flavour remains (in fact seven of the original greens are in the same place). The modern day golfer must still play over the humps and hillocks, face blind shots and tackle the numerous deep sleeper-faced bunkers that are so much the charm of Prestwick.

Visitors wishing to play the historic course are advised to approach **Mr. D. E. Donaldson**, the Club's **Secretary**, in order to book a starting time. Mr. Donaldson can be contacted at **The Prestwick Golf Club, 2 Links Road, Prestwick, Ayrshire, KA9 1QG, Tel. (0292) 77404.** Visitors should note that they will not be permitted to play at weekends or after 11am on Thursdays, and that the first tee will usually be reserved for Members between the hours of 9am-10am and 1230pm and 2.45pm. Furthermore, three ball and four ball matches are not allowed prior to 9.00am.

In 1994 the summer green fee was set at £55 per day; however, for those arriving after 2.45pm the green fee is reduced to £40. The winter green fee is also £40 per day. Sets of golf clubs and caddies can be hired through the **professional, Frank Rennie, tel. (0292) 79483.**

I suppose, like most things at Prestwick, the Clubhouse could be described as having a traditional atmosphere. Ladies are not permitted in the Dining and Smoking Rooms where jackets and ties must be worn at all times, but all may enter the Cardinal Room where some fine light lunches are offered. Dinners can also be arranged though some prior warning is necessary.

At one time Prestwick was a fairly remote place. However, improved roads and the opening of an International Airport has made the area much more accessible from all directions. More immediately, the A77 runs directly from Glasgow in the North and along the coast from Stranraer in the South. Those travelling from Edinburgh should use the A71, before joining the A77 at Kilmarnock.

From the back markers Prestwick measures 6544 yards and has a par of 71. Perhaps not overly long by modern Championship standards, it is nonetheless extremely challenging and local knowledge (not to mention rub of the green) can make a considerable difference. At 346 yards the opening hole is small beer in comparison to the first on the original twelve hole layout—that one measured a lengthy 578 yards and in an age of hickory shafts and gutty balls no doubt proved a stiff bogey six. One can only wonder as to how in the 1870 Open, en route to his aforementioned hat trick, 'Young' Tom Morris managed to hole out in three strokes! Another of Tom's notable achievements at Prestwick occurred in the 1868 Open when he scored the first ever recorded hole in one. The 3rd hole at Prestwick is probably the most famous: here the golfer must carry the vast Cardinal bunker which stretches the entire width of the fairway right at the point of the dog-leg. Later on in his round he must also confront the legendary 'Himalayas' (5th) and the 'Alps' (17th). The course is not actually quite so mountainous as some of the names suggest and the American who arrived at the airport saying he was going to take thirteen clubs and a pick-axe was himself going a little 'over the top'. If the golfer does find himself getting frustrated with his game he should at least enjoy the marvellous views of Ailsa Craig and the Isle of Arran.

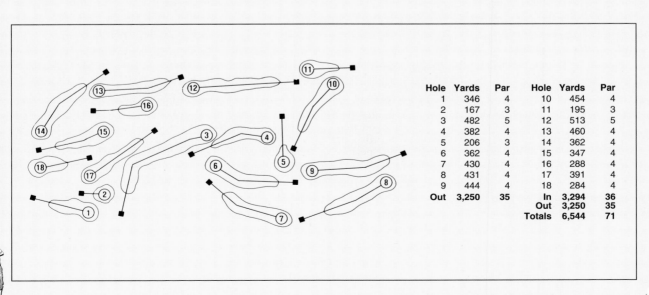

Hole	Yards	Par	Hole	Yards	Par
1	346	4	10	454	4
2	167	3	11	195	3
3	482	5	12	513	5
4	382	4	13	460	4
5	206	3	14	362	4
6	362	4	15	347	4
7	430	4	16	288	4
8	431	4	17	391	4
9	444	4	18	284	4
Out	3,250	35	In	3,294	36
			Out	3,250	35
			Totals	6,544	71

Once the home of a Glasgow shipping baron, Gleddoch House stands in its own 360 acre estate with dramatic views across the River Clyde to Loch Lomond and the hills beyond. The estate is conveniently situated only ten minutes drive from Glasgow airport and 20 minutes from the city centre.

The 39 bedrooms have en suite facilities, each has its own individual character and many offer picturesque views of the gardens and surrounding estate. Executive rooms and suites are available on request. Within the estate there are also refurbished self-catering lodges available for rent. The Garden restaurant has achieved international recognition for its award winning Scottish cuisine. The morning room and conservatory offer spectacular views over the Clyde Estuary and Gleddoch estate, a splendid setting in which to relax and enjoy the comfort and tranquillity of a by-gone era.

Gleddoch House is the exclusive venue for conferences and meetings. Conference facilities are comprised of five stylish rooms which can be used for meetings, product launches, seminars and conferences for up to 120 delegates.

Guests may use the Gleddoch Golf and Country Club which is adjacent to the hotel. The magnificent 18 hole, par 72, golf course provides a unique challenge to all golfers. A resident golf professional is available for golf clinics, tuition and coaching on an individual or group basis. On the estate a series of activities are available such as clay-pigeon shooting, archery, off the road driving and falconry. The equestrian centre offers guests of all ages and abilities the opportunity to explore the wealth of attractions throughout the estate, taking in the miles of unspoilt countryside far removed from the stress of city life.

Gleddoch House Hotel & Country Estate
Langbank
Renfrewshire
PA14 6YE
Tel: (0475) 540711
Fax: (0475) 540201

Originally built at the turn of the century, this red sandstone mansion house was bought by the Nicholas family in 1967. Since then the property has gradually been extended and transformed into a prestigious 125 bedroom hotel renowned for its excellent cuisine, all round comfort, service and superb leisure facilities.

The hotel's situation close to the airport and just seven miles from Glasgow city centre on the M8 motorway, makes it perfect for visitors to the area. Golfers can enjoy access to many of the first class courses around Glasgow such as Gleddoch and Ranfarly Castle, while the hotel prides itself on the number of golfers who also elect to use the hotel as a base for exploring Prestwick, Troon and Turnberry and other such delights on the Ayrshire coast.

The growing reputation of Glynhill's Le Gourmet restaurant and Palm Court Carvery has played no small part in establishing the hotel as a firm favourite with tourists and business men alike. No matter how large or small the party, diners are ensured first class service and a wide selection of excellent food from the extensive table d'hote and à la carte menus.

As befits an hotel with four crowns commendation from the Scottish Tourist Board the rooms are appointed to a very high standard, all are en suite with colour television, satellite, direct dial telephone, hairdrier, tea/coffee tray and fresh fruit. Special accommodation for families is available in spacious rooms with all the comforts of home (and more), and the hotel now also boasts 50 executive bedroom/suites.

Leisure facilities are included in the overnight tariff and amongst those at the disposal of guests are a good size heated indoor swimming pool, spa bath, steam room, sauna, drench and impulse showers, snooker room and a well equipped gymnasium.

Small wonder then that the Glynhill Leisure Hotel is proving so popular with its guests, be they golfers taking advantage of the hotel's location and contacts or companies making full use of the wide ranging meeting and conference facilities.

The Glynhill Leisure Hotel
Paisley Road
Renfrew
PA4 8XB
Tel: 041 886 5555
Fax: 041 885 2838

Westerwood Hotel, Golf and Country Club is located in Cumbernauld 13 miles from Glasgow city centre. Its location on the A80 makes Westerwood within easy access of the key road networks and both Glasgow and Edinburgh Airports.

The hotel has 49 bedrooms, comprising of standard and executive rooms and both one and two bedroomed suites. All rooms are furnished in a traditional style with modern fabrics and many have scenic views over the golf course to the Campsie Hills.

Dining at Westerwood offers a choice of a light snack, an informal meal in the clubhouse overlooking the course or an à la carte menu in the Old Masters Restaurant, where a pianist plays nightly.

Set in ideal golfing country, the 18 hole, par 73 course designed by Seve Ballesteros and Dave Thomas offers an exciting challenge to all golfers. The most spectacular hole is the 15th, aptly named the Waterfall, set against a 40 foot rock face. Each hole meanders through the silver birches, firs, heaths and heathers which are natural to this area of countryside, each offering a different and exciting challenge to every class of golfer.

Standing on the first tee, the player sees the fairway sweep away to the left and two very well struck shots will be required to reach the well guarded green tucked away amongst the trees. This sets the scene for the round and before the majestic 18th is reached, there are another 16 golfing delights to savour. These include the

difficult 4th with its two water hazards, Seve's trap, the 6th, with Seve's cunningly placed bunker in front of the green, the tantalising 9th with its small undulating green, the 15th (the Waterfall) - a fabulous par 3 - and finally the 18th, possibly one of the finest finishing holes in golf.

The resident Golf Professional offers both individual and group tuition. There is also a range of golfing breaks and golf schools throughout the year. In inclement weather the indoor golf facility will be used for all tuition. There are various types of membership available to the course including a competitively priced overseas and country membership to golfers residing more than 50 miles/80 kms from Westerwood Golf Course.

After your golf relax in the Country Club which has a range of facilities including swimming pool, jacuzzi, tennis, snooker, and gymnasium to name but a few.

Westerwood is one of a group of three courses, the other two being Murrayshall and Fernfell. Murrayshall is at Scone, Perth and boasts a country house hotel with award winning cuisine. Fernfell Golf and Country Club is located just out of Cranleigh, eight miles from Guildford, Surrey. For details of these courses please refer to their entries in this guide. Corporate golf packages are offered at all three courses with the opportunity to place your company name and logo on a tee, and reserve the course for your company golf day. Golf societies and green fee players are welcome.

Westerwood Hotel, Golf and Country Club
St Andrew's Drive
Cumbernauld
Glasgow
G68 0EW
Tel: (0236) 457171
Fax: (0236) 738478
Pro shop: (0236) 725281

If your regular golfing partner is getting a bit cocky, a little bit too big for his golf shoes then it may be an idea to take him to Westerwood on a cold and blustery day and make him play off the back tees. If he scores under his handicap then you have every justification for shooting him, or at least drowning him in the pond beside the 18th green. You see, Westerwood is a golf course that doesn't take prisoners.

Less than 20 miles to the east of Glasgow and 30 miles west of Edinburgh at Cumbernauld, Westerwood is a new Championship golf course designed by Seve Ballesteros in conjunction with Dave Thomas, and, to a lesser extent, Laura Davies. Ballesteros, Thomas and Davies have at least two things in common: firstly, each hits the ball the proverbial country mile and secondly each has a reputation for playing attacking, devil-may-care golf. Westerwood was never destined to be a tame golf course! Of course one doesn't have to play Westerwood from the back tees (nor pick a cold and blustery day) but anyone who does, and scores below their handicap, is a bigger bandit than Ned Kelly. This course is one of the most challenging one is likely to come across. It is also one of the most thrilling.

Westerwood is set amid pretty countryside, with three distinct ranges of hills, the Kilsyth, Ochil and Campsie Hills forming the backdrop to the golf course. It is the first course in Britain that Seve has put his signature to and like Jack Nicklaus and Johnny Miller's first designs in England it has opened to great acclaim.

The golf course is the centre piece attraction of an impressive hotel and leisure complex, however, as with the Club's sister course in Scotland, Murrayshall, and unlike many new grand schemes in Great Britain, there is nothing exclusive about Westerwood. Non resident golfing visitors are very welcome to play the course although they do pay higher green fees. Tee reservations can be made by telephoning the Club on **(0236 452772)**. The Club's full address is **The Westerwood Hotel, Golf and Country Club, St. Andrews Drive, Cumbernauld G68 0EW.** Green fees for 1994 were, for non residents, £22.50 per round, £35 per day midweek and £27.50 per round, £45 per day at weekends. Hotel guests paid just £17.50. Golf societies and company days are encouraged and details of special golfing breaks can be obtained by telephoning the hotel. The club has recently added an indoor golf facility and the hotel offers a range of golf schools throughout the year for all levels of golfer.

The possibility of playing golf on a Championship course at the weekend is extremely attractive to nomadic golfers from Glasgow and Edinburgh, where it can prove difficult to arrange a game on the more traditional, established courses. Travelling from both cities is very straightforward (and quick). Westerwood is located just off the A80 which runs through Cumbernauld; in Cumbernauld the Dullatur road should be taken and Westerwood is off to the right. The A80 links Cumbernauld to Glasgow. Those approaching from Perth and further north should travel on the M9 before joining the M80 just south of Stirling; the M80 becomes the A80 only 3 miles from Cumbernauld. A combination of motorways (M9, M876, M80) should also prove the best bet from the Edinburgh region.

What makes Westerwood such a demanding course? First of all it is pretty long—6721 yards from the back tees (6429 from the forward tees and 5883 yards from the ladies tees—many of which were positioned on the advice of Laura Davies). Secondly, the terrain is fairly rugged: there are some steep climbs and several very undulating, twisting fairways, often creating blind shots. Then there are the natural hazards—heather, bracken, firs and silver birch trees—all very pretty and colourful but they haven't exactly been asked to make way for the golf course. And finally, there are the many water hazards, the cunningly placed bunkers and the often severely contoured greens.

The challenge is present from the outset: stand on the 1st tee and you are confronted by a swinging, tumbling dog-leg of 500 yards—a very good opening hole. The 2nd is an enormously long par three: 231 yards from the tiger tees! And so it continues. Other memorable holes on the front nine include the 6th, called Seve's Trap because of the bunker fronting the green which even the maestro might find difficult to get up and down from, and the par five 9th.

On the back nine, the 13th, 14th and 15th provide a spectacular sequence of holes with the 15th, 'Waterfall' being easily the most dramatic on the course. The waterfall itself doesn't actually come into play (or shouldn't!) but it does provide a charming backdrop and in any event a brook runs in front of the green and meets up with the waterfall in a pond beside the green! The round ends, as it began, with an excellent par five, one of half a dozen in total at Westerwood … and I bet even your cocky friend won't be able to keep a six off his card!

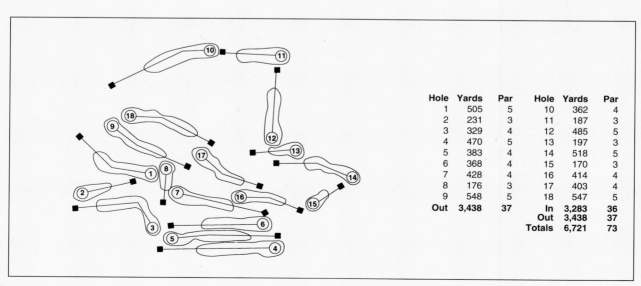

Hole	Yards	Par	Hole	Yards	Par
1	505	5	10	362	4
2	231	3	11	187	3
3	329	4	12	485	5
4	470	5	13	197	3
5	383	4	14	518	5
6	368	4	15	170	3
7	428	4	16	414	4
8	176	3	17	403	4
9	548	5	18	547	5
Out	**3,438**	**37**	**In**	**3,283**	**36**
			Out	**3,438**	**37**
			Totals	**6,721**	**73**

The chief purpose of *Following the Fairways* is to guide the golfer around the counties of Great Britain and Ireland seeking out the finest golfing challenges (not to mention some of the most welcoming 19th hole establishments). Let us imagine, for once, that we are only allowed to play 18 holes but that we may assemble these 18 from any course in Great Britain and Ireland—a dream round if you like.

If there is any romance in our souls we will conclude this round on the 18th green of the Mahony's Point Course at Killarney, no doubt lining up a twenty footer for a two in the lengthening shadows of the encircling pines, and with the gentle lapping of Lough Leane in the background. And if we are bold we will step on to the 18th tee after tackling the Road Hole 17th at St. Andrews. But what do we choose for our opening hole? Well, if we are both romantic and bold we will select the 1st at Machrihanish. Let us hope that we have picked a mild day and that any wind is at our backs .....

Machrihanish—the very name borders on the mystical—was founded in 1876 (although it was in fact originally named the Kintyre Golf Club). Situated on the south western tip of the Mull of Kintyre, Machrihanish is perhaps the most geographically remote of all the great courses in the British Isles. Fortunately for golfers however, Machrihanish is actually only half an hour's flying time from Glasgow; there is an alternative—a three hour drive (each way) along the A82\A83 which admittedly passes through some magnificent countryside. **Loganair (041) 889 3181** are the people to talk to for anyone contemplating the aerial route.

Pilgrims have always been made very welcome at Machrihanish though one shouldn't assume that the course will be deserted. Machrihanish has never been golf's greatest secret. Old Tom Morris first let the cat out of the bag when he visited the links to advise on any alterations to the layout. Old Tom declared that 'The Almighty had designed Machrihanish for playing golf'. Before the First World War Machrihanish had already hosted a number of important amateur events. In those pre-1914 days a journey to Machrihanish must have been quite a trek, but then every Briton fancied himself as an intrepid explorer and on arrival doubtless some approached the first elderly bearded man they came across with the greeting, 'Tom Morris, I presume.'

Today, visitors are requested to book starting times

with the Club's **professional, Ken Campbell.** The address for written correspondence is **The Machrihanish Golf Club, Machrihanish by Campbeltown, Argyll PA28 6PT.** Mr Campbell can also be contacted by telephone on **0586 810277.** The Club's **Secretary, Mrs Anderson** can be reached on **0586 810213.**

The green fees for 1994 are £16 per round, £22 per day midweek with a single weekend green fee of £22. Anyone planning to spend a few days in the area—there are plenty of convenient guest houses and hotels nearby, many offering golfing packages—might consider a weekly ticket, available for £88 in 1994.

If the situation is exhilarating and invigorating in itself the golf course will in no way disappoint; certainly for the lover of traditional links golf, Machrihanish has everything. The layout has altered quite a bit since Tom Morris' day but the natural character of the course remains: awkward stances and blind shots are very much a feature of Machrihanish.

There is nothing blind however about the 1st hole; from the tee the challenge ahead is a very visible one. It is a long par four of 423 yards and the only way of ensuring that the green can be reached in two shots is by hitting a full-blooded drive across the waters of Machrihanish Bay. From the back tees a 200 yard carry is called for. 'Intimidating' is the description; 'Death or Glory' is the result.

After the 1st the rest must be easy? Not a chance! If the opening hole tests the drive, several of the following holes will test the approach shot, particularly perhaps at the 3rd, 6th, and 7th. Machrihanish has its own 'Postage Stamp' hole, the 4th which measures just 123 yards, and on the back nine there are successive short holes at the 15th and 16th, although the latter is hardly short being almost twice the length of the 4th. The course starts to wind down at the 17th and pars here are frequently followed by birdies at the 18th and considerable celebration at the 19th ...

So there we are, on our dream round, standing bewitched on the 1st tee at Machrihanish. The Atlantic rollers are crashing below and, just as the song told us it would, the mist is about to roll in from the sea. Dare we smash one across the Bay? Or do we play safe out to the right? A famous golfing phrase is whispered in our ear: 'If you can't take golf you can't take life'. Of course we have no option ...

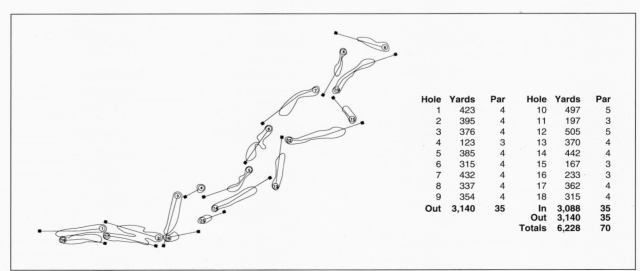

Hole	Yards	Par	Hole	Yards	Par
1	423	4	10	497	5
2	395	4	11	197	3
3	376	4	12	505	5
4	123	3	13	370	4
5	385	4	14	442	4
6	315	4	15	167	3
7	432	4	16	233	3
8	337	4	17	362	4
9	354	4	18	315	4
Out	**3,140**	**35**	**In**	**3,088**	**35**
			Out	**3,140**	**35**
			Totals	**6,228**	**70**

Key

*To avoid disappointment
it is advisable to telephone
in advance*

***Visitors welcome at most times
**Visitors usually allowed on
weekdays only
*Visitors not normally permitted
(Mon, Wed) No visitors
on specified days

Approximate Green Fees
A £30 plus
B £20 to £30
C £15 to £25
D £10 to £20
E under £10
F Greens fees on application

Restrictions
G Guests only
H Handicap certificate required
H (24) Handicap of 24 or less
L Letter of introduction required
M Visitor must be a member of
another recognised club.

Airdrie G.C.
(0236) 62195
Rochsoles, Airdrie
(18)6004 yards/***/F/L

Alexandra G.C.
041 556 3711
Sannox Gardens, Glasgow
(9)2800 yards/***/E

Annanhill G.C.
(0563) 21644
Irvine Road, Kilmarnock
(18)6270 yards/***(Sat)/F

Ardeer G.C.
(0294) 64542
Greenhead, Stevenston
(18)6630 yards/***(Sat)/E/H

Auchen Harvie G.C.
(0292) 603103
Moor Park Road, Saltcoats
(9)5300 yards/***/F

Ayr Belleisle G.C.
(0292) 441258
Doonfoot Road, Ayr
(18)6550 yards/***/F

Ayr Dalmilling G.C.
(0292) 263893
Westwood Avenue, Ayr
(18)5752 yards/***/D

Ayr Seafield G.C.
(0292) 441258
Belleisle Park, Doonfoot Road
(18)5498 yards/***/F/H

Ballochmyle G.C.
(0290) 50469
Ballochmyle, Mauchline
(18)5952 yards/**/F/H

Balmore G.C.
(0360) 620240
Golf Course Road, Balmore
(18)5516 yards/***/F

Barshaw G.C.
041 889 2908
Glasgow Road, Paisley
(18)5673 yards/***/F

Bearsden G.C.
041 942 2351
Thorn Road, Bearsden, Glasgow
(9)6014 yards/***/F/L

Beith G.C.
(05055) 3166
Threepwood Road, Beith
(9)2559 yards/**/E/H

Bellshill G.C.
(0698) 745124
Motherwell Road, Orbiston

(18)6205 yards/***/F/H

Biggar G.C.
(0899) 20618
Broughton Road, Biggar
(18)5416 yards/***/E

Bishopbriggs G.C.
041 772 1810
Brackanbrae Road, Glasgow
(18)6041 yards/*/F/H

Blairbeth G.C.
041 634 3355
Burnside, Rutherglen, Glasgow
(18)5448 yards/*/F

Blairmore & Strone G.C.
(036984) 676
High Road, Strone, by Dunoon
(9)2112 yards/***/E

Bonnyton G.C.
(03553) 2781
Eaglesham, Glasgow
(18)6252 yards/**/B

Bothwell Castle G.C.
(0698) 853177
Blantyre Road, Bothwell
(18)6243 yards/**/B/H

Brodick G.C.
(0770) 2349
Brodick, Isle of Arran
(18)4404 yards/***/D

Brunston Castle G.C.
(0465) 81471
Dailly, Girvan
(18)6792 yards/*/B

Calderbraes G.C.
(0698) 813425
Roundknowe Road, Uddingston
(9)5046 yards/*/D

Caldwell G.C.
(0505) 850329
Uplawmoor, Renfrewshire
(18)6102 yards/**/F

Cambuslang G.C.
041 641 3130
Westburn Drive, Cambuslang
(9)6072 yards/*/G/F/L

Campsie G.C.
(0360) 310244
Crow Road, Lennoxtown
(18)5517 yards/***/F

Caprington G.C.
(0563) 23702
Ayr Road, Kilmarnock
(18)5718 yards/***/F/L

Cardross G.C.
(0389) 841213
Main Road, Cardross
(18)6466 yards/**/F

Carluke G.C.
(0555) 771070
 Mauldslie Road, Hallcraig (18)5805
yards/**/C/H

Carnwath G.C.
(0555) 840251
Main Street, Carnwath
(18)5955 yards/***(Sat)/D/H

Carradale G.C.
(05833) 387
Carradale, Campbeltown, Argyll
(9)2387 yards/***/E

Cathcart G.C.
041 638 9449
Mearns Road, Clarkston
(18)5832 yards/*(intro by member)/F/H

Cathkin Braes G.C.
041 634 6605
Cathkin Road, Rutherglen, Glasgow
(18)6266 yards/**/C/H

Cawder G.C.
041 772 7101
Cadder Road, Bishopbriggs
(18)6229 yards/**(prior arrangement)/F/H
(18)5877 yards/**(prior arrangement)/F/H

Clober G.C.
041 956 1685
Craigton Road, Milngavie
(18)5068 yards/*/E

Clydebank & District G.C.
(0389) 73289
GlasgowRoad, Hardgate
(18)5825 yards/**/D/H

Clydebank Overtoun G.C.
041 952 6372
Overtoun Road, Dalmur
(18)5349 yards/***/F

Coatbridge G.C.
(0236) 28975
Townhead Road, Coatbridge
(18)6020 yards/***/F

Cochrane Castle G.C.
(0505) 20146
Scott Avenue, Craigston
(18)6226 yards/*/C/H

Colonsay G.C.
(09512) 316
Scalasaig, Isle of Colonsay
(18)4775 yards/***/F

Colville Park G.C.
(0698) 263017
Jerviston Estate, Motherwell
(18)6265 yards/*/G/C

Corrie G.C.
(077081) 223
Sannox, Isle of Arran
(9)1948 yards/***/E/H

Cowal G.C.
(0369) 5673
Ardenslate Road, Kirn, Dunoon
(18)6250 yards/***/B/H/M

Cowglen G.C.
041 632 0556
Barrhead Road, Glasgow
(18)6006 yards/***/F/L/H

Craignure G.C.
(06802) 370
Scallastle, Isle of Mull
(9)4436 yards/***/E

Crow Wood G.C.
041 779 4954
Garnkirk Estate, Muirhead
(18)6249 yards/*/C/H

Cumbernauld G.C.
(0236) 734969
Palacerigg Country Park, Cumbernauld
(18)6412 yards/**/E

Dalmally G.C.
(08382) 216
Old Saw Mill, Dalmally
(9)2277 yards/***/F

Deaconsbank G.C.
041 638 7044
Stewarton Road, Eastwood
(18)4800 yards/***/F

Dalmilling G.C.
(0292) 263893
Westwood Avenue, Ayr
(18)5752 yards/*/E

Doon Valley G.C.
(0292) 531607
Hillside, Patna
(9)5654 yards/***/E

Dougalston G.C.
041 956 5750
Strathblane Road, Milngavie

(18)6683 yards/***/F

Douglas Park G.C.
041 942 2220
Hillfoot, Bearsden
(18)5957 yards/*

Douglas Water G.C.
(055588) 361
Ayr Road, Rigside, Lanark
(9)2947 yards/***/E

Drumpellier G.C.
(0236) 724139
Drumpellier Avenue, Coatbridge
(18)6227 yards/**/B

Dullatur G.C.
(0236) 723230
Dullatur, Glasgow
(18)6195 yards/**/F

Dumbarton G.C.
(0389) 32830
Broadmeadows, Dumbarton
(18)5992 yards/**/D

Dunaverty G.C.
(0586) 83677
Southend, Campbeltown, Argyll
(18)4799 yards/***/E

Easter Moffat G.C.
(0236) 842289
Mansion House, Plains
(18)6221 yards/**/F/H

East Kilbride G.C.
(03552) 20913
Chapelside, Nerston
(18)6419 yards/*/F/M

East Renfrewshire G.C.
(03555) 258
Loganswell, Pilmuir
(18)6100 yards/*/F

Eastwood G.C.
(03555) 261
Muirshield, Loganswell
(18)5886 yards/*/C

Elderslie G.C.
(0505) 22835
 Main Road, Elderslie
(18)6004 yards/**/F/H

Erskine G.C.
(0505) 863327
Bishopston, Renfrewshire
(18)6287 yards/*/G/C

Ferenze G.C.
041 881 1519
Ferenze Avenue, Barrhead
(18)5821 yards/**/C

Girvan G.C.
(0465) 4272
Girvan
(18)5078 yards/***/F

Glasgow (Gailes) G.C.
(0294) 311347
Gailes, by Irvine
(18)6500 yards/***/A/H

Glasgow (Killermont) G.C.
041 942 2011
Killermont, Bearsden
(18)5968 yards/***/A/H

Gleddoch G.& C.C.
(0475) 540304
Langbank, Renfrewshire
(18)6333 yards/***/F

Glencruitten G.C.
(0631) 62868
Glencruitten Road, Oban
(18)4250 yards/***/F/M

Gourock G.C.
(0475) 31001
Cowal View, Gourock
(18)6492 yards/**/F/H/L

Greenock G.C.
(0475) 20793
Forsyth Street, Greenock
(18)5838 yards/***(Sat)/F/H

Haggs Castle G.C.
041 427 1157
Dumbreck Road, Glasgow
(18)6464 yards/*/B/H

Hamilton G.C.
(0698) 282872
Riccarton, Firniegair, Hamilton
(18)6264 yards/*/F

Hayston G.C.
041 776 1244
Campsie Road, Kirkintilloch
(18)6042 yards/**/B

Helensburgh G.C.
(0436) 74173
East Abercromby Street,
Helensburgh
(18)6053 yards/**/D/H

Hilton Park G.C.
041 956 5124
Auldmarroch Estate, Milnagavie
(18)6707 yards/**/D
(18)5374 yards/**/D

Hollandbush G.C.
(0555) 893484
Acretophead, Lesmahagow
(18)6100 yards/***/F

Innellan G.C.
(0369) 3546
Knockmillie Road, Innellan
(9)4878 yards/***/E

Irvine G.C.
(0294) 78139
Bogside, Irvine
(18)6434 yards/**/B

Irvine Ravenspark G.C.
(0294) 271293
Kidsneuk, Irvine
(18)6429 yards/**/D

Kilbirnie Place G.C.
(0505) 683398
Largs Road, Kilbirnie
(18)5411 yards/***(Sat)/F

Kilmacolm G.C.
(050587) 2139
Portafield Road, Kilmacolm
(18)5890 yards/**/B

Kilmarnock (Barassie) G.C.
(0292) 313920
Hillhouse Road, Barassie,Troon
(18)6473 yards/*(Wed)/B/G

Kilmarnock Municipal G.C.
(0563) 21915
Ayr Road, Caprington
(18)5460 yards/**/F/G

Kilsyth Lennox G.C.
(0236) 822190
Tak-Ma-Doon Road, Kilsyth,
Glasgow
(9)5944 yards/***(W/E am)/E/H

Kingarth G.C.
(070083) 648
Kilchattan Bay, Isle of Bute
(9)2497 yards/**/E

Kirkhill G.C.
041 641 3083
Greenless Road, Cambuslang
(18)5862 yards/***/H

Kirkintilloch G.C.
041 776 1256
Campsie Road, Kirkintilloch
(18)5269 yards/*/G/D/H/L

Knightswood G.C.
041 959 2131
Lincoln Avenue, Knightswood
(9)2717 yards/***/F

Kyles of Bute G.C.
(0700) 811601
Tighnabruaich, Argyll
(9)4778 yards/***(Sun am)/F

Lamlash G.C.
(07706) 296
Lamlash, Brodick, Isle of Arran
(18)4611 yards/***/E

Lanark G.C.
(0555) 663219
Whitelees Road, Lanark
(18)6423 yards/**/C/H

Largs G.C.
(0475) 673594
Irvine Road, Largs
(18)6220 yards/**/F/H

Larkhall G.C.
(0698) 881113
Burnhead Road, Larkhall
(9)6700 yards/**/F

Leadhills G.C.
(0659) 74222
Leadhills, Biggar
(9)4354 yards/***/E

Lenzie G.C.
041 776 1535
Crosshill Road, Lenzie
(18)5982 yards/*/D

Lethamhill G.C.
041 770 6220
Cumbernauld Road, Millerston
(18)5859 yards/***/F/L

Linn Park G.C.
041 637 5871
Simshill Road, Glasgow
(18)4592 yards/***/F/H

Littlehill G.C.
041 772 1916
Auchinairn Road, Bishopbriggs
(18)6228 yards/***/E

Lochgilphead G.C.
(0546) 602340
Blarbuie Road, Lochgilphead
(9)4484 yards/***/E

Lochranza G.C.
(077083) 273
Lochranza, Isle of Arran
(9)5600 yards/***/E

Lochwinnoch G.C.
(0505) 842153
Burnfoot Road, Lochwinnoch
(18)6202 yards/**/C/H

Loudoun G.C.
(0563) 821993
Galston, Ayrshire
(18)5600 yards/**/F

Machrie G.C.
(0496) 2310
Machrie Hotel, Port Ellen, Isle of
Islay
(18)6226 yards/***/B/H

Machrie Bay G.C.
(0770) 850261
Machrie, Isle of Arran
(9)2123 yards/***/E

Machrihanish G.C.
(058681) 213
Machrihanish, Campbeltown
(18)6228 yards/***/C/H

Millport G.C.
(0475) 530311
Golf Road, Millport, Isle of
Cumbrae
(18)5831 yards/***/F/H

Milngavie G.C.
041 956 1619
Laighpark, Milngavie, Glasgow
(18)5818 yards/*/G/F

Mount Ellen G.C.
(0236) 872277
Johnston Road, Gartcosh
(18)5526 yards/***/D

New Cumnock G.C.
(0290) 32037
Lochill, New Cumnock
(9)5176 yards/**/E

Old Ranfurly G.C.
(0505) 613612
Ranfurly Place, Bridge of Weir
(18)6089 yards/**/F/L/H

Paisley G.C.
041 884 3903
Braehead, Paisley
(18)6220 yards/*/C/H/L

Pollok G.C.
041 632 1080
Barrhead Road, Glasgow
(18)6257 yards/**/B/H

Port Bannatyne G.C.
(0700) 502009
Mains Road, Port Bannatyne, Isle
of Bute
(13)4730 yards/***/E

Port Glasgow G.C.
(0475) 704181
Devol Farm Industrial Estate, Port
Glasgow
(18)5712 yards/**/F

Prestwick G.C.
(0292) 77404
Links Road, Prestwick
(18)6544 yards/**/A/M/L

Prestwick St Cuthbert G.C.
(0292) 77101
East Road, Prestwick
(18)6470 yards/**/C

Prestwick St Nicholas G.C.
(0292) 77608
Grangemuir Road, Prestwick
(18)5926 yards/**/C/H

Ralston G.C.
041 882 1349
Strathmore Avenue, Ralston
(18)6100 yards/*/G/F

Ranfurly Castle G.C.
(0505) 612609
Golf Road, Bridge of Weir
(18)6284 yards/**/B/L/H

Renfrew G.C.
041 886 6692
Inchinnan Road, Renfrew
(18)6818 yards/**/G/F/H/L

Rothesay G.C.
(0700) 502244
Canada Hill, Rothesay, Isle of Bute
(18)5358 yards/***/D/H

Routenburn G.C.
(0475) 673230
Greenock Road, Largs, Ayrshire
(18)5650 yards/**/E/H

Royal Troon G.C.
(0292) 311555
Craigend Road, Troon
(18)7067 yards/**/A/H/L
(18)6386 yards/**/B/H/L

Sandyhills G.C.
041 778 1179
Sandyhills Road, Glasgow
(18)6253 yards/***/D/H

Sconser G.C.
(0478) 3235
Isle of Skye
(9)4796 yards/***/F

Shiskine G.C.
(077086) 226
Blackwaterfoot, Isle of Arran
(12)3000 yards/***/D

Shotts G.C.
(0501) 820431
Blairhead, Shotts
(18)6125 yards/**/D

Skelmorlie G.C.
(0475) 520152
Skelmorlie, Ayrshire
(13)5056 yards/***(Sat)/C

Stornoway G.C.
(0851) 702240
Stornoway, Isle of Lewis

(18)5178 yards/**/D

Strathaven G.C.
(0357) 20421
Overton Avenue, Glasgow Road
(18)6226 yards/**/B

Strathclyde Park G.C.
(0698) 266155
Mote Hill, Hamilton
(9)3147 yards/***/F

Tarbert G.C.
(0880) 820565
Kilberry Road, Tarbert
(9)4460 yards/***/E

Tobermory G.C.
(0688) 2020
Tobermory, Isle of Mull
(9)2460 yards/***/E

Torrance House G.C.
(03352) 48638
Strathaven Road, East Kilbride
(18)6640 yards/***/D/H

Troon Municipal G.C.
(0292) 312464
Harling Drive, Troon
(18)6785 yards/***/F
(18)6501 yards/***/F
(18)4822 yards/***/F

Turnberrry Hotel G.C.
(0655) 31000
Turnberry Hotel, Turnberry
(18)6950 yards/***/A/H
(18)6014 yards/***/A/H
(Reduced fees for hotel guests)

Vale of Leven G.C.
(0389) 52351
Northfield Road, Bonhill,
Alexandria
(18)5156 yards/**/D

Vaul G.C.
(08792) 399
Scarinish, Isle of Tiree
(9)2911yards/***/F

Westerwood Hotel & G.C.
(0236) 457171
St Andrews Drive, Cumbernauld
(18)6800 yards/***/B

Western Gailes G.C.
(0294) 311649
Gailes, by Irvine
(18)6664 yards/**(Thurs)/F/H

West Kilbride G.C.
(0294) 823911
Fullerton Drive, Seamill
(18)5974 yards/**/F/L/H

Whinhill G.C.
(0475) 724694
Beith Road, Greenock
(18)5454 yards/*/F

Whitecraigs G.C.
041 639 1681
Ayr Road, Giffnock
(18)6230 yards/*/F/H

Whiting Bay G.C.
(07707) 487
Whiting Bay, Arran
(18)4405 yards/***/F

Williamwood G.C.
041 637 1783
Clarkston Road, Netherlee
(18)5808 yards/***/H

Windyhill G.C.
041 942 2349
Bal Jaffray Road, Bearsden
(18)6254 yards/**/F

Wishaw G.C.
(0698) 372869
Cleland Road, Wishaw
(18)6051 yards/***(Sat)/D

Artist: **Cecil Aldin THE 5TH & 13TH GREENS** *Courtesy of:* **Burlington Gallery**

Rescobie is a 1920s country house set in two acres of grounds on the edge of the old village of Leslie, which adjoins the new industrial town of Glenrothes. The house, whose gardens contain a functional herb garden and a wild flower meadow, was converted in the 70s and 80s to a fully licensed hotel; all of its ten individually decorated bedrooms now have private bath or shower, direct dial telephone, colour television, radio/alarm, room bar, etc. The furnishings are comfortable, old village photographs adorn the walls of the bar and in cooler months a log fire burns in the lounge.

Perfectly positioned for golfers in the heart of an area rich in golf courses - St Andrews, Dalmahoy, Carnoustie and Gleneagles to name but a few - Rescobie is only half an hour's drive away from Perth and Dundee and forty five minutes from the centre of Edinburgh.

The owners take great pains to run the hotel as a traditional country house. There is no formal reception area; guests will find a bell in the hall and other public rooms to summon waitresses, who are dressed smartly but informally in tartan skirt and blouse in preference to the customary black and white. The owners, Tony and Wendy Hughes-Lewis, make a point of meeting all of their guests, and if Wendy does not actually welcome you into hotel one of them will meet you later on.

There are four full-time chefs, which is a large brigade for a small hotel, but they make by hand what most other catering establishments buy in. In addition to producing stocks, soups and sauces, the chefs make all of the sweets and petits fours, roll their own pasta and even cut their own chips. Tony himself makes marmalade with Seville oranges in the spring and jellies with crab apples and elderberries in the Autunm, and tends the herb garden, where the chefs can be seen in the summer gathering their daily requirements.

The effort the owners make to preserve the atmosphere of a country house is reflected in their personal attention to the well-being of their guests, the conduct of their staff and the quality of their cuisine. Such high standards are expected in a four star establishment; to find them at two star level makes the Rescobie Hotel a rare find and excellent value for money.

The Rescobie Hotel and Restaurant
Valley Drive
Leslie
Fife
KY6 3BQ
Tel: (0592) 742143
Fax: (0592) 620231

Many years ago, watching an England versus Scotland soccer game at Wembley, I remember being amused by one of the banners carried by a group of Scottish supporters which boldly declared, 'Remember Bannockburn'. Being a pigheaded Englishman I thought to myself, they ought to remember it—it was just about the only battle they won in centuries. Of course, all is now abundantly clear—the Scots were far too busy priming their golfing skills to bother themselves fighting the Sassenachs.

As long ago as 1457 the Scottish Parliament, unimpressed by the performance of its sharpshooters, felt that too much golf and football were to blame for the lack-lustre performances on the battlefields. An act was passed stating that because of their interference with the practice of archery, the 'fute-ball and golf be utterly cryit down and nocht usit'. History would seem to suggest that the Scots didn't take a blind bit of notice, and golf steadily grew in popularity. Juggle the figures that make up 1457 and we have 1754, perhaps the most significant date in golf's history—the year the Society of St Andrews golfers drew up its written rules of golf.

Today **St Andrews**, deep in the Kingdom of Fife, is the place every golfer in the world wants to visit. Even if you have only swung a club at the local municipal you'll be itching to do the same at St Andrews. However, for those contemplating a pilgrimage to the centre of the golfing world it should be said that St Andrews has several near neighbours that warrant the most discerning attention. Between Dunfermline, to the west of Fife, and St Andrews, lie what are undoubtedly some of the finest courses in Scotland.

Travelling Around the Coast

For six hundred years Dunfermline was the country's capital and the body of its most famous king, Robert the Bruce, lies buried in Dunfermline Abbey (minus his heart, apparently, which is in Melrose Abbey). The town has two courses, **Dunfermline** and **Pitreavie.** Both are parkland courses at which visitors are welcome provided some prior arrangement is made. Neither is unduly hard on the pocket. For those wishing to spend a day or two in the old royal town, the appropriately named King Malcolm Thistle Hotel (0383) 722611 provides convenient comfort.

East of Dunfermline there is a testing links at **Burntisland** with fine views over the Firth of Forth and there are again two courses in Kirkcaldy, the **Dunnikier Park** and **Kirkcaldy** golf clubs, (and make sure you pronounce it Ker-coddy!) Dunnikier Park is a public course. One other good golf club to note in the area is **Aberdour**. A peaceful night's sleep can be found at the Long Boat Inn (0592) 890625 in Kinghorn and good fare is abundantly available at the Old Rectory Inn (0592) 51211 in Dysart. Beyond Kirkcaldy, out along a glorious stretch of spectacular coast are Fife's famous five—**Leven Links, Lundin Links, Elie, Balcomie** and of course **St Andrews**. The first two are often considered as a pair, probably on account of there being very little land in between (an old stone wall serves as the boundary). Two proud clubs share the 6433 yards links at Leven, the Leven Golfing Society and Leven Thistle, however, the visitor is always made to feel welcome—as indeed he, or she is at the more hilly Lundin—an excellent course, which although very much a links has an abundance of trees on the back nine.

Elie, or the Golf House Club, lies a short distance from the two across Largo Bay, the A917 linking the town with Leven. Elie is famed for its unique periscope by the first tee and for the fact that it was here that James Braid fashioned many of the skills that won him five Open Championships. A charming and very natural links—you won't see trees anywhere here—and not too demanding in length, several of the holes are laid out right alongside a rocky shoreline. A ballot system operates at Elie during the summer but otherwise there are no general restrictions on times visitors can play.

Following the aforementioned A917 eastwards from Elie, the town of Crail is soon reached. Just beyond the town at Fifeness is the magnificent Balcomie links, home of the two hundred year old **Crail Golfing Society.** Together with St Andrews it is featured a few pages on. Incidentally, when visiting St Andrews, or if just passing by, try to visit the **British Golf Museum**—it's right next to the 1st tee on the **Old Course.**

In addition to the numerous hotels in St Andrews, there is plenty of accommodation near to the other great links courses of Fife and it is generally inexpensive. A great number are geared almost solely towards the interests of the golfing community and are situated within pitching distance of the nearest fairway. Here are a few thoughts. In Lundin Links, the Old Manor Hotel (0333) 320368 is highly thought of with a particularly good restaurant while less grand accommodation can be enjoyed at the Lundin Links Hotel (0333) 320207, an especially popular retreat for golfers. The Golf Hotel (0333) 330209 in Elie is self explanatory, and just a short distance away in Anstruther is the popular Craws Nest Hotel (0333) 310691—located midway between Elie and Crail it's an excellent base. In Anstruther one might also visit the Smugglers Inn, a cosy 300 year old tavern. Crail is a delightful fishing village and here the Golf Hotel (0333) 450206 is another obvious choice. It's a place of great character and is one of Scotland's oldest licensed inns. Still in Crail, the Caiplie Guest House (0333) 450564 is good value. Two restaurants that can be strongly recommended for the area are found a little inland, namely, Ostlers Close (0334) 655574 at Cupar and the exceptional Peat Inn (0334) 840206 on the road to Cupar.

It isn't an overstatement to say that **St Andrews** is the centre of the golfing world. As early as 1691 it was described as the 'Metropolis of Golfing'. With pilgrims today making the trip from all corners of the globe the number of hotels and guest houses is understandably considerable. The St Andrews Old Course Hotel (0334) 474371, sumptuously refurbished, is unquestionably one of Scotland's leading hotels, and overlooking the most famous hole in golf, the Road Hole 17th on the Old Course, couldn't be better positioned. More aesthetically pleasing than prior to its restoration, it now oozes class both within and without. Rufflets Hotel (0334) 472594 just outside the town is an excellent base while another room with a view can be booked at the Rusacks Marine Hotel (0334) 474321, formerly the Golf Inn, which oozes golfing history (the restaurant is also good and rather appropriately named the Niblick). The other hotels which might just hint at a round of the good old game include the St Andrews Golf Hotel (0334) 472611 and the Scores Hotel (0334) 472451 — both are good value and pleasant. There is also any number of comfortable guest houses and B&Bs in town; noteworthy examples include the Albany (0334) 477737, Arran House (0334) 474724 and the Amberside (0334) 474644. While golf clearly takes centre stage one should not forget the pleasant coastline nearby (scenes from Chariots of Fire were filmed on St Andrews' vast sands), nor the 12th century cathedral or Scotland's oldest university. One final thought for hungry souls is the popular Grange Inn

(0334) 472670 in Grange Village—an excellent eating place.

Inland Golf

Just as the leading courses of Surrey aren't all heathland and gorse, neither are those of Fife all seaviews and sandhills. **Ladybank** is actually only a few miles north of Leven but is completely different in character with heathland fairways and much pine and heather—a very beautiful course and well worth a visit. North of Ladybank lies **Cupar,** one of the oldest 9 hole golf courses in Scotland and a clubhouse that has to be approached through a cemetery (slightly older even than the golf course!)

In an area steeped in history, **Glenrothes** is a relative newcomer to the scene. Young, perhaps, but an excellent course nonetheless. Situated to the west of the town it is a fairly hilly parkland type, offering many superb views. A friendly welcome awaits but the names of two of the holes worry me a little—the 11th, titled 'Satan's Gateway' and the 18th 'Hells End'! A restful 19th is clearly in order and fortunately in Glenrothes quality places abound. The Balgeddie House (0592) 742511 is superbly

secluded and most relaxing, while the charming Rescobie Hotel (0592) 742143 at Leslie and the Rothes Arms (0592) 753701 should also placate the soul. Letham is only a short distance from Ladybank and here Fernie Castle (0337) 810381 is decidedly recommended. Equally convenient and comfortable is the Lomond Hills Hotel at Freuchie (0337) 857329. Not to be forgotten either is the classical mansion, Balbirnie House (0592) 610066, a luxury hotel set in over 400 acres of landscaped woodland and situated adjacent to **Balbirnie Park** Golf Club.

Two other courses that are well worth visiting if journeying inland in Fife are at **Thornton,** where the River Ore makes for some challenging holes, and at **Lochgelly**—convenient if travelling between Dunfermline and Kirkcaldy. The final mention though goes to **Scotscraig,** an Open Championship qualifying course at Tayport. Although close to the sea it is actually a downland type course rather than a true links, but is an admirable test of golf...and following that testing game at Scotscraig one is likely to be left with a difficult decision: to the north, Carnoustie and many other great challenges await — but then no golfer who has experienced the pleasures of the Kingdom of Fife ever left easily.

Artist: **Shortspoon IN THE BURN** *Courtesy of* **Burlington Gallery**

Balbirnie House

Balbirnie House is a privately owned country house hotel. It is situated by Markinch, equi-distant from Edinburgh and St Andrews in the Heart of the Ancient Kingdom of Fife. Under the personal supervision of Alan, Elizabeth and Nicholas Russell, this wonderful Georgian Mansion, recognised as one of Scotland's finest Grade A listed houses, maintains the warmth ands friendliness of its old days combined with the needs of today's house guests. The emphasis is on a personal service, once a home to few Balbirnie is now a home, from home to many. The house itself is the centrepiece of a 416 acre park which is landscaped in the style of Capability Brown. The estate includes specimen trees and one of the most imporant rhododendron collections in Scotland.

Views from the house extend to the golf course over fine lawns, trimmed yew hedges and interesting flowering borders. For the golf enthusiast the hotel is ideally situated just a short chip from the first tee of Balbirnie Park Golf Course, a challenging and beautifully landscaped 18 hole 6210 yard par 71 parkland course. Locally, the cham-pionship courses of Leven Links and Ladybank offer the opportunity to sample Scottish golf at its very best. The mecca of St Andrews is only half an hour by car and possibly the hardest test of all, Carnoustie, is forty-five minutes. All in all there are over a hundred golf courses within one hour of Balbirnie.

Within the perimeter of the park itself extensive recreational and leisure pursuits are available. Doorstep golf, horse riding (horses can be brought to the front door of the hotel ready to ride around the three mile bridle path within the park), jogging and woodland walking. The park is the home to an abundance of wild life. A charming craft centre is located close to the hotel and incorporates a leather workshop, a goldsmith and jewellers and a pottery workshop.

Balbirnie has many special arrangements for sporting pursuits with local operators near the park, all with high quality facilities and the hotel is happy to tailor a package to the individual's bespoke requirements and budget.

A Scottish representative of 'Small Luxury Hotels of the World'

Balbirnie House
Balbirnie Park
Markinch
Fife KY7 6NE
Tel: (0592) 610066
Fax: (0592) 610529

St Andrews Golf Hotel is a tastefully modernised Victorian house situated on the cliffs above St Andrews Bay, some 200 yards from the 18th tee of the 'Old Course'.

There are 23 bedrooms all with private bath and shower and all furnished individually to a high degree of comfort, with telephone, radio, television, tea/coffee maker, trouser press and hairdrier. A nice touch is the fresh flowers and welcoming fruit basket.

There is a quiet front lounge for residents and a most intersting golfer's cocktail bar featuring pictures and photographs of Open champions past and present. This gives out onto a small south-facing patio garden.

With a separate entrance is 'Ma Bell's' bar and daytime restaurant — popular with students and visitors alike. Tasty food, hot and cold and reasonably priced is served from noon to 6.00 pm. A main attraction is the selection of more than 80 bottled beers from all over the world, and no fewer than 14 on draught, including cask-conditioned ales.

The central feature of the hotel is the candlelit, oak-panelled restaurant with its magnificent sea view. A la carte and table d'hote menus both feature the best of local produce — fish, shellfish, beef, lamb, game and vegetables — conjured into delightful dishes by chef Adam Harrow. The food is well complemented by an interesting and comprehensive list of wines selected personally by owner, Brian Hughes.

Golf of course, is the speciality of the hotel, and you can find either prepared golf packages and golf weeks or have something tailored to your particular requirements, using any of the 30 or so courses within 45 minutes of St Andrews.

St Andrews Golf Hotel
40 The Scores
St Andrews
KY16 9AS
Tel: (0334) 472611
Fax: (0334) 472188

If there is such a thing as a truly global sport then it has to be golf. From parochial beginnings on the east coast of Scotland it is now played on every continent, in every conceivable corner. Not only are there golf courses on the exotic islands of Tahiti and Bali but there is one in the Himalayas and there is one in the Arctic; golf has even been played on the Moon. For all this there remains but one home—St. Andrews.

Whilst we will never be able to put an exact date on the time golf was first played on the famous links, several documents refer to a crude form of the game being played as early as the mid 1400s. As for the right to play at St. Andrews, which, of course, the whole world enjoys, the origins are embodied in a licence dated 1552 drawn up by the Archbishop of St. Andrews. It permitted the community to breed rabbits on the links and to 'play at golf, futeball, schueting, at all gamis with all uther, as ever they pleis and in ony time'. Furthermore, the proprietor was bound 'not to plough up any part of the said golf links in all time coming.' Organised golf came to St. Andrews in 1754 when twenty-two Noblemen and Gentlemen formed the St. Andrews Society of Golfers. In 1834 the Society became the Royal and Ancient Golf Club.

Not only can all the world play at St. Andrews, but all the world wants to and arranging a game on the **Old Course** can be a little difficult. The St. Andrews Links Management Committee handles all matters relating to times of play and they should be contacted well in advance. The summer months are naturally the busiest period and it is best to write to the Committee two to three months prior to intended play, offering if possible a number of alternative dates. The address to write to is **The St. Andrews Links Management Committee, Golf Place, St. Andrews, Fife, KY16 9JA.** The **Secretary, Mr. D. N. James** and his staff can be contacted by telephone on **(0334) 475757** and by fax on (0334) 477036. There are no handicap limits to play over the Old Course but a handicap certificate or letter of introduction is required. It should also be noted that there is no Sunday golf on the Old Course. In 1994 the green fee for a round was priced at £50.

In addition to the Old Course there are four other eighteen hole links at St. Andrews, the **New Course,** which dates from 1896, the **Jubilee** (1897)—recently lengthened and improved by Donald Steel—the **Eden** (1914) and the new **Strathtyrum Course.** No handicap certificate is required to play over any of the above four courses and the green fees for 1994 on each were £25, £25, £18 and £14 respectively. A 9 hole course, the Balgove, is also available (at a modest green fee of £6 for 18 holes), together with a driving range and extensive practice facilities.

St. Andrews is situated 57 miles north east of Edinburgh. For northbound travellers the most direct route to take is the M90 after crossing the Forth Road Bridge. The A91 should be joined at junction 8. This road can be followed to St. Andrews. Southbound travellers should head for Perth which is linked in turn to Dundee by the A85 and to the north of Scotland by the A9. From Perth a combination of the A90 and the A913 takes one to Cupar where the A91 can be picked up.

It was nature that fashioned St. Andrews and over the centuries the Old Course has seen little change. Its myriad tiny pot bunkers remain both a fascination and a frustration—providing just enough room as Bernard Darwin put it, 'for an angry man and his niblick'. Laid out on a narrow strip of land ranging from 50 to 100 yards in width, St. Andrews is famed for its enormous double greens. There are seven in all and some are more than an acre in size. With little definition between the fairways there tends to be no standard way of playing a particular hole and as a rule the wind direction will determine the preferred line. Individual holes are not likely to be easily remembered the first time of playing, especially as one will probably be walking the course in a semi-trance. History is everywhere and on the first hole as you cross the bridge over the Swilcan Burn a voice from somewhere says 'they've all walked this bridge'—and of course they have, just as they've all passed through the Elysian Fields, tackled Hell's Bunker, the Beardies and the Principal's Nose. And then of course they've all faced the Road Hole with its desperate drive and even more desperate approach and then finally strolled over the great expanse of the 18th fairway towards the Valley of Sin and the famous R & A Clubhouse beyond.

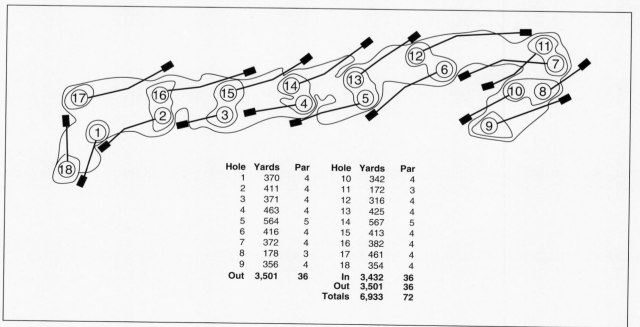

Hole	Yards	Par	Hole	Yards	Par
1	370	4	10	342	4
2	411	4	11	172	3
3	371	4	12	316	4
4	463	4	13	425	4
5	564	5	14	567	5
6	416	4	15	413	4
7	372	4	16	382	4
8	178	3	17	461	4
9	356	4	18	354	4
Out	**3,501**	**36**	**In**	**3,432**	**36**
			Out	**3,501**	**36**
			Totals	**6,933**	**72**

Standing proud on a hilltop overlooking Lundin Golf Course and with St Andrews just 12 miles distant, the Old Manor Hotel is at the heart of some of the finest golfing country in Scotland. Lundin and the adjacent links of Leven have both been used as Open qualifying courses and other such famous names as Crail, Elie , Ladybank and Scotscraig are to be found within a short distance of the hotel. Itineraries arranged for guests by the Clark family, all keen golfers with a wealth of knowledge of the game, also include Carnoustie and Rosemount which are within easy travelling distance as well as many other courses.

Lessons too can be arranged along with tee times and the Clark family pride themselves on being able to cater for golfers of every level.

As for the hotel itself, add to the unique charm, friendly atmosphere and the Clark's many years experience chef Alan Brunt's imaginative cuisine and you have all one would expect of a well managed country house hotel,

In the Prince Charlie Restaurant, with panoramic views over Largo Bay and the River Forth, the chef's modern presentation of classical dishes and the outstanding a la carte menu have earned an enviable reputation and mention in several food guides. An excellent and extensive wine list compliments the food.

The adjacent cocktail bar also overlooking the bay has a selection of nearly 100 malt whiskies. Relax there with an aperitif or, after dinner, try Islay or Speyside's finest in a most convivial atmosphere.

The Coachmans Grill and Ale House in the old coachman's cottage in the grounds, offers lunch, dinner, supper and snacks. The menu features interesting starters, succulent steaks and choice East Neuk seafood, all chargrilled to order. There is a carefully selected wine list and for the ale connoisseur, a selection of hand pulled guest beers.

As well as unrivalled golfing opportunities there are leisure parks, museums, castles, houses and gardens all within easy reach. The charming town of St Andrews - the home of golf, beautiful beaches and Scotland's oldest university, attracts visitors from all over the world. The coastal villages of the East Neuk - Lower Largo, St Monans, Pittenweem, Anstruther and Crail are full of character and are outstandingly picturesque.

The Old Manor is in the village of Lundin Links, 30 minutes drive from Edinburgh Airport and 45 minutes from Edinburgh city centre.

The Old Manor Hotel
Leven Road
Lundin Links
Nr St Andrews
Fife
Tel: (0333) 320369
Fax: (0333) 320911

On 23rd February 1986 the seventh oldest Golf Club in the world celebrated its bicentenary. Some three years before the Bastille was stormed a group of eleven gentlemen met at the Golf Inn in Crail and together formed the Crail Golfing Society. The records of that historic day are still preserved; indeed remarkably the Society possesses a complete set of minutes from the date of its inception. In those early days the Society members wore scarlet jackets with yellow buttons and dined at the Golf Inn after a day on the links. The local punch flowed and a good time was doubtless had by all—now those were the days!

Since 1895 the Club has played over the Balcomie Links which is located approximately two miles north east of Crail at Fifeness. Earlier the Society had used a narrow strip of land at Sauchope, slightly closer to Crail (and of course to the Golf Inn).

The atmosphere is still jovial and visitors are made most welcome. With the exception of a few competition days there are no general restrictions on times of play. However, individual visitors are advised to telephone the **professional, Graeme Lennie** the day before playing. He can be contacted on **(0333) 450278** or **(0333) 450960**. Societies, or golfing parties, are equally welcome and advance bookings can be made at all times apart from during the peak summer period. Written enquiries should be addressed to **The Secretary, Crail Golfing Society, Balcomie Clubhouse, Crail, Fife KY10 3XN**. The Secretary, **Mrs Cynthia Penhale**, can be reached by telephone on **(0333) 450686**.

The green fees for 1994 are pitched at £17 per round, £25 per day during weekdays or £22 per round and £33 per day at weekends. Juniors can obtain a weekday round for £9 though at other times full fees are charged. In addition short Temporary Membership is offered: examples include £51 for three consecutive weekdays and £140 for a fortnightly ticket (excluding Sundays).

The Balcomie Links is in fact ideal for 'holiday golf'. Without being overly long (5720 yards, par 69)—though the wind can affect distances greatly—it offers some exceptionally spectacular scenery and similar to Cruden

Bay further north, a nearby Castle casts a watchful eye. Balcomie Castle, where Mary of Guise, mother-to-be of Mary Queen of Scots, spent her first few days in Scotland, comes complete with ghost.

The course is always well maintained and the greens especially have acquired an enviable reputation. The holes have been laid out so that each provides a view of the sea. There is an unusual balance to the round with the front nine containing seven par fours and the back nine only two; as for par three holes, there are none on the front nine after the 3rd but the second nine boasts five short holes including the 18th. There are some rather interesting names too: 'Fluke Dub' (4th) 'Hell's Hole' (5th) 'Castle Yetts' (9th) and 'Lang Whang' (11th).

From all points south, travelling to Crail will be by way of the Forth Road Bridge and thereafter following a combination of 'A' roads. However, the M90 may also be used if St. Andrews is to be taken in en route. The A915/A917 approaches Crail from along the coast via Lundin Links and Elie, while from Cupar and St Andrews the A91/A917 should be taken. As stated the course is situated two miles from Crail in the direction of Fifeness and is well-signposted.

The 19th at Crail is as it should be, right next to the 18th green and provides commanding views over much of the course and out across the North Sea. Smart casual dress is acceptable in the Clubhouse, though presumably today if you strolled in wearing a bright scarlet jacket with yellow buttons you might raise a few eyebrows! A full complement of catering is offered at all times but for those wishing to make advanced arrangements, a quick telephone call to the Steward is never a bad idea. Mr New is the gentleman in question and he can be contacted on **(0333) 450278**.

The temptation for many on crossing the Forth Road Bridge is of course to head straight for the Royal and Ancient. Although St. Andrews may be the undisputed sovereign in the so-called Kingdom of Fife, there are also a number of handsome Princes. Balcomie stands comparison with the best and is a course of which the two hundred year old Society can justifiably be proud.

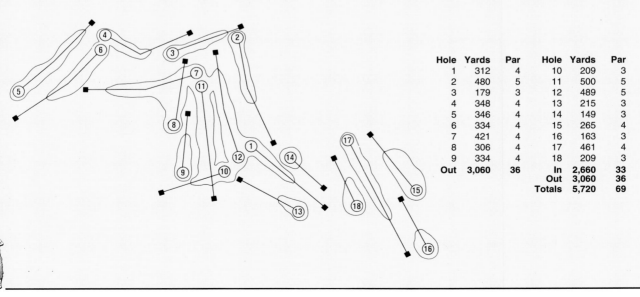

Hole	Yards	Par	Hole	Yards	Par
1	312	4	10	209	3
2	480	5	11	500	5
3	179	3	12	489	5
4	348	4	13	215	3
5	346	4	14	149	3
6	334	4	15	265	4
7	421	4	16	163	3
8	306	4	17	461	4
9	334	4	18	209	3
Out	**3,060**	**36**	**In**	**2,660**	**33**
			Out	**3,060**	**36**
			Totals	**5,720**	**69**

The Lomond Hills Hotel is situated in the picturesque village of Freuchie in the heart of Fife. Years ago it was the place to which courtiers out of favour at nearby Falkland Palace were banished. Even today the derisory saying `Awa tae Freuchie and eat mice' is used in some parts of Scotland .

The Kingdom of Fife is rich farming country, and although noblemen in the last century used to hunt wild boar, today the area lends itself to the more relaxing pursuits of hill or forest walking. Visitors may prefer to visit the numerous museums, castles and National Trust properties in the area, or enjoy the sporting delights that Fife can offer, sailing, gliding and pony trekking and some thirty golf courses are all within easy reach. Fishermen will find a wealth of rivers and reservoirs: there is truly something for everyone.

Atmosphere and comfort are two features of the Lomond Hills Hotel which make every guest's stay as enjoyable. Candlelight and simple but courteous service will enhance every meal, with a large choice of wines, sherries and liqueurs, a small selection of Scottish specialities together with popular French flambe dishes create an appetising à la carte menu and fresh produce is used wherever possible.

All bedrooms have en suite facilities, plus all the usual refinements expected of a 4 crown hotel, with comfortable lounges with grand pianos.

Start the day pleasantly with a traditional Scottish breakfast and relax in the well appointed residents lounge after a busy day, or perhaps pay a visit to the swimming pool, leisure centre or roof terrace.

The Lomond Hills Hotel
Freuchie
Fife
Tel: (0337) 857329/857498
Fax: (0337) 857329

Key

*To avoid disappointment
it is advisable to telephone
in advance*

***Visitors welcome at most times*
***Visitors usually allowed on
weekdays only*
**Visitors not normally permitted
(Mon, Wed) No visitors
on specified days*

Approximate Green Fees
A £30 plus
B £20 to £30
C £15 to £25
D £10 to £20
E under £10
F Greens fees on application

Restrictions
G Guests only
H Handicap certificate required
H (24) Handicap of 24 or less
L Letter of introduction required
M Visitor must be a member of
another recognised club.

Aberdour G.C.
(0383) 860256
Seaside Place, Aberdour
(18)5469 yards/**/D

Anstruther G.C.
(0333) 310956
Shore Road, Anstruther
(9)4120 yards/***/D

Auchterderran G.C.
(0592) 721579
Woodend Road, Cardenden
(9)5400 yards/***/F

Balbirnie Park G.C.
(0592) 752006
Markinch, Glenrothes
(18)6210 yards/***/C

Ballingry G.C.
(0592) 860086
Crosshill, Lochgelly
(9)6482 yards/***/F

Burntisland G.C.
(0592) 874093
Dodhead, Burntisland
(18)5871 yards/***/D/H

Canmore G.C.
(0383) 724969
Venturefair Avenue, Dunfermline
(18)5474 yards/**/D

Cowdenbeath G.C.
(0383) 611918
Cowdenbeath
(9)6552 yards/***/E

Crail G.S.
(0333) 50960
Fifeness, Crail
(18)5720 yards/***/C-B

Cupar G.C.
(0334) 653549
Hilltarvit, Cupar
(9)5300 yards/***/D

Dunfermline G.C.
(0383) 723534
Pitfirrane, Crossford, Dunfermline
(18) 6244 yards/**/D

Dunnikier Park G.C.
(0592) 261599
Dunnikier Way, Kirkcaldy
(18)6601 yards/***/D

Elie G.C.
(0333) 330301

Golf Club House, Elie, Leven
(18)6241 yards/***/F

Falkland G.C.
(0337) 857404
The Myre, Falkland
(9)2622 yards/***/F

Glenrothes G.C.
(0592) 754561
Golf Course Road, Glenrothes
(18)6449 yards/***/E-D

Kinghorn G.C.
(0592) 890345
Macduff Crescent, Kinghorn
(18)5246 yards/***/E

Kirkcaldy G.C.
(0592) 260370
Balwearie Road, Kirkcaldy
(18)6004 yards/***(Sat)/D

Ladybank G.C.
(0337) 830814
Annesmuir, Ladybank
(18)6617 yards/***/C-B

Leslie G.C.
(0592) 620040
Balsillie, Leslie
(9)4940 yards/***/E

Leven Links
(0333) 421390
The Promenade, Leven
(18)6434 yards/***/F

Lochgelly G.C.
(0592) 780174
Cartmore Road, Lochgelly
(18)5491 yards/***/D

Lundin Links
(0333) 320202
Golf Road, Lundin Links
(18)6377 yards/**(+Sat pm)/C/H

Pitreavie (Dunfermline) G.C.
(0383) 722591
Queensferry Road, Dunfermline
(18)6086 yards/***/D

St Andrews
(0334) 475757
St Andrews
(18)6933 yards/**(Sun)/A/H/L(Old)
(18)6604 yards/***/F(New)
(18)6500 yards/***/F(Strathtyrum)
(18)6284 yards/***/F(Jubilee)
(18)5971 yards/***/F(Eden)
(9)1754 yards/***/F(Balgove)

St Michaels G.C.
(0334) 839365
Leuchars, St Andrews
(9)5510 yards/***(Sun am)/E

Saline G.C.
(0383) 852591
Kinneddar Hill, Saline
(9)5302 yards/***(Sat)/E

Scoonie G.C.
(0333) 427057
North Links, Leven
(18)5500 yards/***/F

Scotscraig G.C.
(0382) 552515
Golf Road, Tayport
(18)6496 yards/***/F/M

Thornton G.C.
(0592) 771111
Station Road, Thornton Village
(18)6177 yards/***/D

Tulliallan G.C.
(0259) 730396
Alloa Road, Tullliallan, Kincardine
(18)5982 yards/**/F

Artist: **Kenneth Reed THE OLD COURSE, ST ANDREWS** Courtesy of: **Old Troon Sporting Antiques**

Artist: **Arthur Weaver GLENEAGLES** Courtesy of: **Burlington Gallery**

Set on a hillside overlooking the Vale of Strathmore to the Sidlaw Hills beyond, are 10 acres of tiered and rambling gardens, at the heart of which lies the 'Lands of Loyal'.

This impressive Victorian Mansion was built in the 1830s, commissioned by Sir William Ogilvy, who, on his return from Waterloo, chose Loyal Hill as the site for this magnificent home.

The Lands of Loyal was subsequently owned by a succession of families until being converted into a Hotel in 1945.

It has since been very prominent in the area, holding fond memories for the oldest generations. It is also highly regarded as a second home to country sportsmen who have remained loyal for many years. More recently, an extensive refurbishment programme, carried out in the public rooms, has further enhanced the unique atmosphere of this much respected country house hotel.

A highly acclaimed restaurant in its own right, our style of cuisine is traditional and imaginative, making full use of local fish and game.

An extensive wine list, featuring several wines and madeiras, some over 150 years old, is available to complement your meal.

The Lands of Loyal makes an ideal base for the ambitious golfer. Perthshire has 30 golf courses in total with remarkable variety. All courses are within an hour's drive of the hotel with some of the most famous and desirable spots only a few minutes away.

As fundamentally a sportsman's hotel, The Lands of Loyal appreciates the needs of the golfer. Very early breakfasts and unusually flexible dining arrangements, quality packed lunches etc., are offered courteously. Private rooms for parties can be requested in advance.

The Hotel management are delighted to arrange a complete itinerary for the golfer, whether an individual or a group. Tee times can be arranged and green fees paid. Any correspondence with golf clubs will gladly be undertaken by us.

The Lands of Loyal provides a complete and competitive golfing package. A full colour brochure and tariff is available on request.

Karl-Peter & Patricia Howell
The Lands of Loyal Hotel
Alyth
Perthshire
Scotland PH11 8JQ
Tel: (08283) 3151
Fax: (08283) 3313

Westlands of Pitlochry

Westlands is situated in the centre of the highland town of Pitlochry and enjoys stunning scenic views of the Vale of Atholl and the highland hills. The hotel is a new experience for the discerning visitor and its aim is to provide and maintain the highest possible standard of comfort without losing any of the traditional friendly atmosphere for which the hotel has long been noted.

Westlands is personally supervised by the resident proprietors who know exactly what guests require to ensure a perfect holiday. A new wing has been added in traditional grey and pink Scottish stone providing six extra large bedrooms of deluxe quality. All fifteen bedrooms are en suite with colour television, radio, tea/coffee tray, telephone and central heating.

The new Garden Room restaurant has its own dance floor and enjoys stunning scenic views of the surrounding countryside. The head chef has a first class reputation for fine cuisine, especially seafood, game and meat dishes. Only fresh produce is used and the exciting menu ranges from traditional Scottish fare to delicious international dishes. Guests can retire to the elegant cocktail bar and enjoy an after dinner coffee or drink.

Westlands is an ideal base from which to explore the surrounding highland countryside and is situated just two minutes from the excellent Pitlochry Golf Course. Several other golf courses are within easy reach of the hotel such as Kenmore, Blairgowrie and St Andrews. Golfers are particularly welcome at Westlands.

Westlands of Pitlochry
160 Atholl Road
Pitlochry
Perthshire
PH16 5AR
Tel: (0796) 472266
Fax: (0796) 473994

Glenfarg Hotel

Ideally situated for St Andrews, Gleneagles, Rosemount, Ladybank, Dalmahoy and a host of other superb and varied courses, the Glenfarg Hotel enjoys a well-earned reputation for golfing breaks, including a variety of inclusive packages to suit all budgets. This comfortable and friendly hotel is managed by a keen and active golfer and offers a comprehensive golf booking service.

The period candlelit restaurant offers an excellent selection of dishes, prepared by the hotel's award-winning chef, or if you prefer a more informal atmosphere, you can enjoy a glass of real ale and a delicious range of home-cooked bar meals in the lounge bar.

For a brochure, telephone or write to:

The Glenfarg Hotel
Glenfarg
Perthshire
PH12 9NU
Tel: (0577) 830241

Inland Gems

If, as the song says, the streams of the mountains please you more than the sea then it is to the likes of **Gleneagles**, **Pitlochry** and **Murrayshall** you will head. If you are one of the diehards who think there is but one form of golf then you will probably set course for **Carnoustie**, **Monifieth** and **Montrose**. Then again if it is felt that variety is the spice of golf a nice combination of the two can be devised. The heart of Scotland has much to offer of everything.

While there is an inevitable temptation to head for the 'bigger clubs', the Gleneagles and the Carnousties, the region boasts a staggering number of smaller clubs where golf can be equally enjoyable. **Taymouth Castle** and **Callander** are perhaps two of Scotland's lesser known courses, at least to many south of the border, yet they are two of the most scenic courses one is likely to find anywhere. At Callander in early spring the deer come down from the Perthshire hills to forage, a glorious sight, while the course at Taymouth Castle is situated in a conservation area surrounded by beautiful woods.

For golfers travelling northwards, before Gleneagles is reached some excellent golf is to be found at **Falkirk Tryst**, **Glenbervie** (Larbert), **Braehead** and **Alloa,** while over to the west of the Central region and somewhat isolated is picturesque **Buchanan Castle**. The town of **Stirling** is known as the 'Gateway to the Highlands' and Stirling's golf course has a beautiful setting beneath the Ochil Hills and in the shadow of Stirling Castle.

The world renowned **Gleneagles Hotel** (0764) 662231 near Auchterarder is a superb base, not only to secure a game on one or more of its own magnificent courses (see feature page) but also for exploring the many fine golf courses nearby. However, there is certainly no shortage of very good alternatives for a night's stay. Three miles away the Auchterarder House Hotel (0764) 663646 is excellent and is set amid beautiful gardens. In Cleish, Nivingston House (0577) 850 216 is a small, very pleasant family-run hotel—ideal for the M90 (exit 5), while at Dunblane set in its own 5000 acre estate is the celebrated Cromlix House (0786) 822125 (note especially the marvellous restaurant). Stirling, with its splendid castle offers the Park Lodge (0786) 474862, Fintry the outstanding Culcreuch Castle (036086) 228, Callander the Roman Camp Hotel (0877) 330003, and Drymen the Buchanan Arms (0360) 60588.

After Gleneagles, **Blairgowrie** is probably the best known inland course and it too is featured on a later page. However, the golfer should undoubtedly pay a visit to the 'fair city of Perth'. The **King James VI** Golf Club on Moncrieffe Island is steeped in history while nearby at Scone—former crowning place of Kings—is the **Murrayshall** Country House Hotel and its superb golf course (see ahead). A round at each is strongly recommended, and the above mentioned hotel (0738) 551171 offers some of Scotland's best accommodation and cuisine. To the south of Perth at Glenfarg is the Bein Inn (0577) 830 216, set in the most beautiful surroundings and the lovely Glenfarg Hotel (0577) 830241, ideal for Carnoustie, Gleneagles or even St Andrews. Visitors tackling Blairgowrie should look no further than Dupplin Castle (0738) 623224 a magnificent country house well situated for all the area's attractions..

Those wishing to stay in Blairgowrie itself should consider the Rosemount Golf Hotel (0250) 2604. A little distance to the west of Perth there is more fine golf at **Crieff** where there are 27 holes (note the Crieff Hydro (0764) 2401 and Galvelmore House (0764) 2277) and a

very pretty 9 hole course even further west at **St Fillans** where the Four Seasons (076485) 333 is a charming place to stay. To the north of our region and tucked away amid some breathtaking scenery, **Dalmunzie House** (0250885) 224 should not be forgotten either; situated at Spittal O'Glenshee, the hotel has its own spectacular 9 hole golf course where drives are said to travel further in the rarified atmosphere! The Ardeonaig Hotel (0567) 820 400 in Killin combines splendid views with distinguished accommodation, and in this respect the Kinnaird Estate (0796) 482440 can also never be too highly praised.

Returning to Blairgowrie, if a game cannot be arranged on either of the club's outstanding courses, then the heathland course at **Alyth** is very nearby and certainly won't disappoint. The Lands Of Loyal (08283) 3151 is a comfortable hotel close to the course and the nearby Losset Inn (08283) 2393 is more modest but equally accommodating. Perth's delights as mentioned are at hand to the south, while to the west is **Taymouth Castle** and to the north along the A9 stands **Pitlochry**. The latter is another course many will choose to play, for this is one of the most attractive in Britain—a veritable 'theatre in the hills'. Green fees at all these courses are relatively inexpensive and certainly very good value. Still further north the scenic 9 holer at **Blair Atholl** is also well worth a visit. In Strathtay, near Pitlochry a recommended 19th hole is the Grantully Hotel (0887) 840 207, while Westlands of Pitlochry (0796) 472266 is another to offer good quality and exceptional value.

More ideas for a relaxing stay include the Kenmore Hotel (0887) 830 205 in Kenmore, Scotland's oldest inn, Killiecrankie Hotel (0796) 473 220 in Killiecrankie (north of Pitlochry), the sporty Ballathie House (0250) 883 268 at Kinclave by Stanley, Kinloch House (04713) 214 at Kinloch Rannoch and the Log Cabin (0250) 881 288 at Kirkmichael. Indeed, the list is almost endless, such is the popularity of this magnificent area.

Closer to the Coast

Some of Scotland's greatest links courses are to be found between Dundee and Montrose on the Tayside coast. However, just to the north west of Dundee lies **Downfield** one of the country's finest inland courses. Indeed, five times Open Champion Peter Thomson rates this heavily wooded parkland course as one of the best inland courses in the world. It is said that Downfield is very popular with American visitors because it reminds them of some of their better courses 'back home'.

East of Dundee, the Medal Course at **Monifieth** has staged the Scottish Amateur Championship, while **Panmure** at Barry has in the past hosted the Seniors' Championship. Both are classic links courses and fairly inexpensive to play over. **Carnoustie** is, of course, one of Scotland's greatest golfing shrines and along with Montrose, Gleneagles, Letham Grange, Murrayshall and Blairgowrie is featured ahead. **Montrose,** like Monifieth, is a public links (two courses at each in fact) and when the winds blow can be extremely difficult. As earlier noted, green fees along this great coastal stretch are relatively cheap and provided some forward planning is done a game is possible at most times.

A brief word on staying in the area. In Carnoustie, the Glencoe Hotel (0241) 853 273 is very convenient as are the Park Hotel (0674) 763 415 and the George Hotel (0674) 675 050, both in Montrose. Perhaps the pick of the many hotels in Dundee is the Angus Thistle Hotel (0382) 26874, and in nearby Broughty Ferry, L'Auberge (0382) 730890 is a fine restaurant. The Castleton House (0307) 840340 by Glamis is another establishment few golfers will find fault with, and for those seeking excellent value, the Kingsley Guesthouse (0241) 873 933 in Arbroath provides exactly that. Moorfield House (0828) 27303 in Cupar Angus is also well worth trying. There are plans afoot to build a major new hotel in Carnoustie, and if these finally come to fruition there are hopes that the Open might one day return to the great links.

Finally, two inland courses to the north east of Tayside which strongly merit attention are **Edzell** and **Letham Grange**. The former, just north of Brechin,

and in a charming village is a beautiful heathland course where some marvellous mountain views can be enjoyed. The Glenesk Hotel (0356) 648 319 is but a par four away. Letham Grange is in fact a hotel and country club (0241) 890 373 and is situated at Colliston near Arbroath. The hotel is a splendidly restored Victorian mansion and, with 36 holes of golf now on offer is well worth a visit — we make such an inspection later in this chapter.

Artist: **Robert Turnbull GLEANEAGLES** *Courtesy of* **Private Collection**

There is a vast oil painting that hangs in the Tate Gallery in London; the artist is John Martin and the painting is titled 'The Plains Of Heaven'. Some may know it well, others will wonder what on earth I'm gibbering on about—suffice to say that it depicts in the most vivid colours imaginable the artist's impression of Paradise. I suspect that John Martin wasn't a golfer. Blasphemy isn't intended but for many of us who stalk the fairways of the world, Gleneagles is just about our best idea of how heaven might look—give or take a couple of angels.

The **Gleneagles Hotel** and its golf courses are set in the heart of some of the most glorious Perthshire countryside. Surrounded by the foothills of the Grampian Mountain range, everywhere one turns there is a shock of colour. The mountains themselves often appear wrapped in purples and blues. Heather, silver birch and rowan cover the crisp moorland turf. With so much around one could be forgiven for losing a little concentration, yet the golf too is glorious and for those wishing to enjoy their golf in leisurely five star surroundings there really is nothing quite like Gleneagles.

The land was first surveyed with a view to designing one or more golf courses before the first World War and James Braid was called in to direct affairs. By 1919 the **King's** and **Queen's** courses were both open for play. Braid's work met with instant acclaim and in 1921 the forerunner of the Ryder Cup was staged at Gleneagles, when a team of British professionals played a team from America.

Until quite recently The Gleneagles Hotel maintained four 18 hole golf courses, the Prince's and Glendevon courses being opened in 1974 and 1980 respectively. Subject to making a booking through the Golf Office all were open to the general public. Golf became so popular at Gleneagles that at times it came close to resembling a fairways version of Piccadilly Circus and *since 1st January 1990 golf at Gleneagles has been restricted to Hotel Residents and Gleneagles Golf Club members.*

The Prince's and Glendevon courses no longer exist either—but for a very good reason: in May 1993 a Jack Nicklaus-designed championship course opened for play. It is Nicklaus' first course in Scotland and, like his first ventures in England (St Mellion) and Ireland (Mount Juliet), it has generated an enormous amount of interest.

Laid out on land previously utilised by the Prince's and Glendevon courses, plus adjacent acquired land, the **Monarch's** Course measures in excess of 7000 yards from the Championship tees.

Things are certainly happening apace at Gleneagles and a sparkling new clubhouse has recently been constructed. Its architectural style is in keeping with the Edwardian hotel. From April 1994 the green fee for hotel residents was set at £50 per round (on any of the three courses). **Greg Schofield** Gleneagles' golf **professional** can be reached on **(0764) 662231.**

Located approximately midway between Perth and Stirling and half a mile west of Auchterarder, Gleneagles is easily reached by road. The A9, which in fact links Perth to Stirling is likely to prove of most assistance. Travelling from the Glasgow region a combination of the A80 and the M80 should be taken to Stirling. Those approaching from further south can avoid Glasgow by following the A74 and the M74/M73 joining the A80 below Stirling. Motoring from Edinburgh the best route is to cross the Forth Road Bridge via the A90 heading for Dunfermline and thereafter taking the A823 road to Auchterarder. Southbound travellers will find the A9 helpful if coming from the Highlands via Blair Atholl and Pitlochry. Motoring from Aberdeen and the north east of Scotland, the A92 links Aberdeen to Dundee and Dundee is in turn linked to Perth by the A85 (dual carriageway all the way). The Gleneagles Hotel can also be reached by rail, with a bus meeting trains from Gleneagles station.

Measuring 6471 yards, par 70, the King's course is some 500 yards longer that the Queen's at 5965 yards, par 68. Perhaps the best known hole at Gleneagles is Braid's Brawest, the 13th on the King's Course—a tough par four which requires a long straight drive to carry a ridge and a second to a raised and heavily guarded sloping green.

Many will have first viewed the glories of Gleneagles through the medium of television—the BBC Pro-Celebrity series being staged on several occasions over the King's Course during the 1970s. In the mid 1980s the European Tour brought the Scottish Open to Gleneagles and now golfing addicts have a wonderful prospect to look forward to each July—the Scottish Open at Gleneagles, followed immediately by the Open Championship... Paradise indeed!

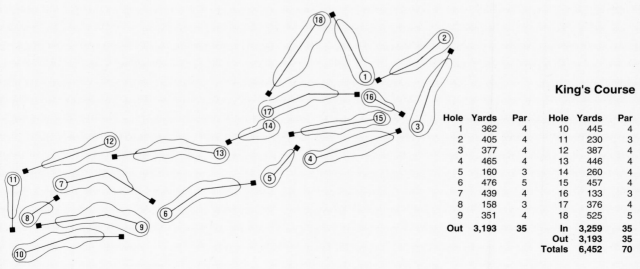

King's Course

Hole	Yards	Par	Hole	Yards	Par
1	362	4	10	445	4
2	405	4	11	230	3
3	377	4	12	387	4
4	465	4	13	446	4
5	160	3	14	260	4
6	476	5	15	457	4
7	439	4	16	133	3
8	158	3	17	376	4
9	351	4	18	525	5
Out	**3,193**	**35**	**In**	**3,259**	**35**
			Out	**3,193**	**35**
			Totals	**6,452**	**70**

Dupplin, a rare mid 20th century Scottish mansion, stands in 30 acres of private parkland, with sweeping lawns and mature woodlands. The original edifice was razed by fire and its 19th century successor was replaced by the present building, completed in 1969, to the design of one of Scotland's leading architects, Schomber Scott, and has now been upgraded to the comfort and luxury expected by today's discerning guests. Although the house is in the centre of a large estate, Perth is only 10 minutes away.

Ideal for the discerning racegoer and golfer, offering accommodation on a par with the quality of golf to be enjoyed in the area, guests are assured of hospitality and service in the tradition of gracious country house living. The old balustraded terrace and rose garden face South with stunning views over the River Earn valley.

Dupplin is not a hotel, it is a private country house of the highest quality, with all the sophistication and relaxed informality of an old fashioned house party with guests dining round the table dinner party style.

Shooting, roe-stalking, fishing on the Tay and golf are all within easy reach of Dupplin. These can be arranged for guests, but only with prior notice. For golfers, little introduction will be necessary to the area's many courses including the old course of Rosemount at Blairgowrie, Carnoustie and St Andrews. While the ballot system is to be endured for golfers wishing to play the old course at St Andrews, the demand for fishing and shooting in the Tay valley is such that up to one year in advance is necessary to salmon fish on some beats and shoot on driven partridge/pheasant days.

Dupplin is ideal for those wishing to take the whole house and can cater for up to a maximum of twelve people having six double/twin bedrooms, all with luxurious en suite facilities. Dupplin can also cater for small business/training meetings suitable for senior executives. Off-road driving, quad racing, archery & falconry can be arranged as a break during the meetings. Large functions may be catered for by using marquees on the lawns.

Transportation from Glasgow or Edinburgh can be arranged. Both Edinburgh and Glasgow are only one hour's drive from Dupplin.

Dupplin Castle
by Perth
Perthshire
PH1 OPY
Tel (01738) 623224
Fax (01738) 444140

With so many outstanding courses to choose from, all within fairly close proximity of one another, even the most blinkered of diehard Englishmen would be forced to concede that Scotland is just about the finest place on earth for a week's golfing holiday. Given seven precious days a large number of would-be travellers on opening their maps of Scotland are likely to plan a trip thus: three days on the west coast playing Prestwick, Turnberry and Troon; a day in the middle visiting Gleneagles, finishing with three on the east coast taking in Carnoustie, St Andrews and Muirfield. Marvellous stuff of course, but many of the golfing sages hold the opinion that such an itinerary misses out the greatest gem of all—the Rosemount course at Blairgowrie.

There are in fact two 18 hole courses at Blairgowrie, the older and more celebrated **Rosemount,** designed by James Braid and the **Lansdowne** course, a fairly recent addition, the work of Peter Alliss and Dave Thomas. On each, golf is played over beautiful moorland fairways, lined by forests of pine, larch and silver birch. A liberal sprinkling of purple heather and gorse add considerable colour to an already majestic setting—as one bewitched observer put it, 'somebody seems to have gone mad with a paint brush!'

Persons wishing to sample the delights of either course are advised to book starting times through the **Starter's Office** on tel: **(0250) 872594.** Visitors are welcome at Blairgowrie on Mondays, Tuesdays, Thursdays and, to a limited extent, on Fridays and occasionally at weekends. Fourball matches, it should be noted, are not normally allowed before 10 a.m. on the Rosemount course. Furthermore all visitors must be able to provide proof of handicap. Golfing parties are also welcome during the week (except on Wednesdays) though teeing off will not be permitted between 12pm and 2pm nor after 4 pm. Those wishing to organise golfing parties should address written applications to the Club's **Secretary, Mr. J. N. Simpson**, the Club's full address being, **Blairgowrie Golf Club, Golf Course Road, Blairgowrie, Perthshire PH10 6LG**. Mr. Simpson can be contacted by telephone on **(0250) 872622.** and by fax on (0250) 875451, while the club's **professional, Gordon Kinnoch** can be reached on **(0250) 873116.** In 1994 the midweek green fee for a single round on either course was set at £32 with £45 securing

a day ticket. At weekends, when available, a single round green fee cost £34.

Having metaphorically chastised the golfer who doesn't make Blairgowrie a 'must' on any golfing tour I had better detail the best routes to reach it. Hopefully the following will prove of assistance: approaching from the south the A93 Braemar road runs directly from Perth, Perth being linked to Edinburgh by the A90/M90. From easterly directions, Blairgowrie (Rosemount is just south of the town) is connected to Dundee by the A923 and to Forfar by the A926. Anyone motoring down from the north will probably travel either on the A9 (via Aviemore and Pitlochry) or on the A93 passing through Ballater and Braemar. Blairgowrie is 15 miles from Perth and 18 miles from Dundee. Gleneagles (via Perth) and Carnoustie and St Andrews (both via Dundee) are all approximately 30 miles away.

Measuring 6588 yards, par 72 from the medal tees (6239 yards, par 70 from the forward tees) the Rosemount Course may not be the toughest challenge one is likely to face but it must rank among the most enchanting. The course and surrounding landscape abound with wildlife, from pheasants and partridge to deer and winter geese, but the golfer who lifts his head too much is likely to suffer over the closing stretch; 16, 17 and 18 are all difficult holes, especially the 16th where the golfer must twice confront the infamous Black Loch.

The official course record at Rosemount stands at 64, though in 1973, during a practice round for the Sumrie Better-Ball tournament, professional Lionel Platts achieved an amazing ten consecutive birdies between the 8th and 17th—quite obscene don't you think?! The Lansdowne course is slightly longer than its older brother, and many would say a much sterner test—either way a game on each is strongly recommended.

It need hardly be added that Blairgowrie with its two courses—three if one includes the aptly named Wee Course, a short nine-holer—has a more than adequate 19th. Lunches, high teas, dinners and light snacks are all offered. There are also two bars - comfortable places where many will choose to go and celebrate a magnificent day's golfing in one of the most glorious settings the game has to offer. Planning a week's golf?....

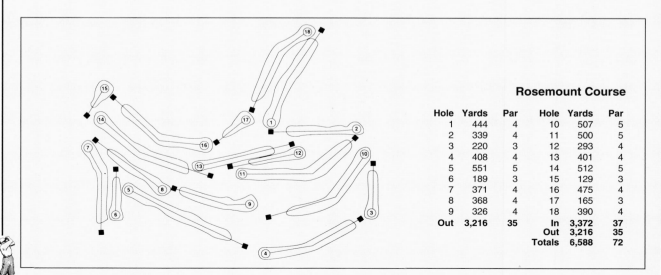

Rosemount Course

Hole	Yards	Par	Hole	Yards	Par
1	444	4	10	507	5
2	339	4	11	500	5
3	220	3	12	293	4
4	408	4	13	401	4
5	551	5	14	512	5
6	189	3	15	129	3
7	371	4	16	475	4
8	368	4	17	165	3
9	326	4	18	390	4
Out	**3,216**	**35**	**In**	**3,372**	**37**
			Out	**3,216**	**35**
			Totals	**6,588**	**72**

Dalmunzie House enjoys a glorious position in the mountains of the Scottish Highlands. The hotel stands in its own 6000 acre mountain estate. It is owned and run by the Winton family who have been in the glen for a number of decades and have years of experience looking after guests. Good home cooking, attention to detail and unobtrusive service ensure a comfortable stay at all times.

The house itself is cosy, the atmosphere is homely and the welcome both genuine and warm, the emphasis being on friendliness rather than pomp and splendour. All the bedrooms have en suite facilities, are of individual character centrally heated. Their charming decor and restful tranquillity reflect the ambience found elsewhere at Dalmunzie.

Many activities can be pursued here. The hotel has its own private 9 hole golf course, and in addition there is a tennis court and games room for the family complete with bar billiard table. River and loch fishing as well as shooting and stalking can all be easily arranged. Some of Scotland's finest mountains surround the hotel and for cross country and alpine skiers the Glenshee Ski Centre is only a few minutes drive away.

Dalmunzie House Hotel
Spittal O' Glenshee
Blairgowrie
Perthshire
Scotland PH10 7QG
Tel : (01250) 885224
Fax: (01250) 885225

Mrs Constance Ward invites you to Kinnaird, a splendid country house dating in part from 1770, set in its own estate with lovely views over the Tay Valley. With glorious gardens, open fires, a genuinely warm welcome and bedrooms of great charm and comfort, Kinnaird is a delightful spot for a relaxing break and is ideally situated for visiting the many beauty spots and places of interest in Perthshire.

Golfers will find Kinnaird the ideal base from which to visit the plethora of golf courses in the region. The nearby course at Taymouth Castle is situated in a conservation area and the King James VI Golf Course at Perth is steeped in history. Other courses within driving distance of the Estate include: Pitlochry, Alyth, Blairgowrie and Crieff.

The Estate offers a variety of sporting activities which include $2\frac{1}{2}$ miles of high quality fishing on the River Tay, superb pheasant shooting for groups of eight guns, duck flighting and roe stalking.

Less taxing perhaps are the lovely walks that are available , from a gentle stroll round the garden to longer walks on the hill and moor. The outdoor tennis court and a croquet lawn provide entertainment for summer afternoons, although should the weather prove inclement, the cedar panelled sitting room provides a selection of amusements including bridge, backgammon, billiards or simply good conversation.

The award-winning restaurant, directed by chef John Webber, offers modern cuisine of the highest standard. There is an extensive and detailed wine list partnered with a comprehensive selection of malt whisky. Both dining rooms enjoy magnificent views, while the former drawing room features exquisite painted panels of figures and landscapes. These superb surroundings provide a stunning setting for a menu of carefully chosen dishes, imaginatively prepared and beautifully presented. In addition to table reservations, private luncheons, dinners and meetings may be reserved. Lunch and dinner are always available for both resident and non-resident guests and booking is appreciated.

On the Kinnaird Estate, as well as the hotel, there are at present seven country cottages, fully equipped and refurbished, available for let. For more information please contact:

Kinnaird
Kinnaird Estate
by Dunkeld
Perthshire
PH8 0LB
Tel: (0796) 482440
Fax: (0796) 482289

The Murrayshall Country House Hotel and Golf Course is only four miles from Perth, set in 300 acres of parkland. The hotel has been refurbished to portray a traditional country house style and the bedrooms offer en suite facilities, direct dial telephones and televisions.

Guests dine in the Old Masters Restaurant, which offers a wide selection of dishes with the emphasis on good wholesome fayre. Adjacent to the hotel is the clubhouse, open from April through October, which provides informal dining.

The 6420 yard, 18 hole, par 73 course is interspersed with magnificent specimen trees lining the fairways, water hazards and white sanded bunkers to offer a challenge to all golfers. Buggies and sets of clubs are available for hire. There are various types of membership available to the course including a competitively priced overseas and country membership to golfers residing more than 50miles/80kms from Murrayshall Golf Course. Neil Mackintosh, our resident professional, is pleased to give tuition from half an hour to a week's course. Should the weather be inclement, tuition takes place in our indoor golf facility. There is a range of golf breaks and golf schools available throughout the year.

Other sporting activities include tennis, croquet and bowls. However, situated only a few miles from the famous Salmon Waters in the River Tay, even closer to Perth Race Course, Murrayshall is uniquely placed to make it an attractive venue for whatever might bring you to this area of Scotland.

Private dining and conference facilities are available in both the hotel and club house. Conference organisers, requiring the best of service and attention for their senior delegates, will find Murrayshall the ideal conference haven.

Murrayshall is one of three group golf courses, the other two are Westerwood and Fernfell. Westerwood Golf Course was designed by Seve Ballesteros and Dave Thomas and is located at Cumbernauld, near Glasgow. Fernfell Golf and Country Club is located just out of Cranleigh, eight miles from Guildford in Surrey. Corporate golf packages are offered at all three courses with the opportunity to place your company name and logo on a tee and to reserve the course for your Company Golf Day. Golf Societies and Green Fee Players are welcome

Murrayshall Country House Hotel and Golf Course
Scone
Perthshire PH2 7PH
Tel: (0738) 51171
Fax: (0738) 52595
Pro shop: (0738) 52784

Perth is a legendary place, a city steeped in history and one surrounded by stunning natural beauty. Perthshire the county evokes thoughts of everything Scottish. To North Americans, mention of the very word 'Perthshire' is enough to send them drooling. It is arguably one of the most romantic places in the world and for golfers, whether from the New World or the Old, the contemplation of a game of golf in the heart of Scotland is enough to make us forget a tweaked three footer (well almost).

It is often said that a person's golfing education is incomplete until he or she has swung a club in Scotland. And how can you visit Scotland without visiting Perth, the ancient crowning place of Kings? To the south west of Perth, and half an hour's drive away is Gleneagles which, along with St. Andrews and Augusta, is surely one of the three best known golfing centres in the world. Almost due north of Perth and again about 30 minutes by road is Blairgowrie and the delights of the Rosemount and Lansdowne courses. A little further, but still no more than an hour, are St. Andrews and Carnoustie; Perth cannot be a bad place sitting amidst all this finery! But there is more. Right on the city's doorstep, not 4 miles from the town centre, is a comparatively modern golfing jewel: Murrayshall, or to give it its full name, The Murrayshall Country House Hotel and Golf Course.

Golfwise, Murrayshall has only been on the map since the early 1980s (the course, designed by renowned architect J Hamilton Stutt, opened in 1981). The country house however, is much older and has that unmistakeable air of Scotchness. A house of great character with wonderful grounds is an ideal setting for a golf course anywhere—but on Perth's doorstep too! Murrayshall is where the peacocks strut, the pheasants call and the deer run freely in the woods. The golf course is set in 300 acres of truly rolling parkland and the holes weave their way in and out of the copses and alongside ponds. In fact, there is quite a lot of water at Murrayshall: little lakes, ponds and streams—but the golfer is guided over and around them via quaint stone bridges. Some 200,000 tulips adorn the hotel grounds and golf course ... yes Murrayshall makes folks drool and perhaps at least smile after that missed three foot putt.

Those wishing to look a little closer should approach the **Golf Manager, Neil MacKintosh**. He and his staff han-

dle all golf enquiries and bookings should be made through him. Mr MacKintosh, who is also Murrayshall's professional can be contacted on **(0738) 552784**. The address to write to is **Murrayshall Country House Hotel and Golf Course, Murrayshall, Scone, Perthshire PH2 7PH**.

Subject to players being of a reasonable golfing standard, visitors are welcome at all times. In 1994 the green fees for 18 holes were £20 midweek and £25 at weekends. A full day ticket could be purchased for £30 midweek and £40 at weekends. Reduced fees are available for Hotel residents (just £15 per round) and for junior golfers (£10). Golf societies and corporate golf days are very popular at Murrayshall and all enquiries should be directed to the Golf Manager.

Finding Murrayshall from Perth should not be too difficult. The road to take is the A94 towards New Scone; two miles out of Perth, Murrayshall is signposted off to the right. Perth itself is easily reached from all directions. It is linked to Edinburgh by the M90 and the Forth Road Bridge; to the Highlands via the wonderfully scenic A9 and to Dundee by the A35. To the south west, Perth is joined to Stirling by the A9 and anyone coming from the Glasgow area is likely to travel via Stirling. Finally, the A93 links Perth with Blairgowrie to the north east.

From the back markers, Murrayshall measures 6446 yards, par 73. The forward tees reduce the course to around the 6,000 yards mark. It isn't a long course by any means but is both attractive and challenging and certainly full of interest. Many of the fairways are bordered by magnificent oaks, copper beeches and chestnuts—not to mention those marvellous tulips. There are also some wonderful views from the higher parts of the course.

Notable holes include the 3rd, one of those par four and a half holes; the short 4th, where if you miss-hit you will land in the pond; the severely dog-legged 7th—so severe that it is known as the 'dog's grave'—and most people's favourite, the short par four 10th where the approach is played over water to a raised green.

If possible, try to stay overnight in the Hotel. The bedrooms are superbly furnished and most have views over the course and towards the distant Grampian Mountains. Perhaps a final mention for Murrayshall's Old Masters Restaurant; it has won many awards for outstanding cuisine and its name is most fitting. As with everything at Murrayshall, it oozes class.

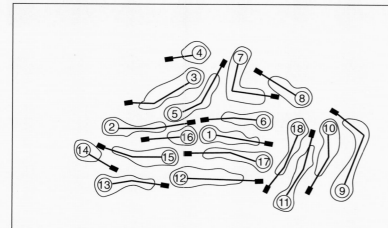

Hole	Yards	Par	Hole	Yards	Par
1	400	4	10	309	4
2	490	5	11	354	4
3	478	5	12	494	5
4	167	4	13	416	4
5	367	3	14	179	3
6	317	4	15	512	5
7	379	4	16	217	3
8	198	3	17	472	5
9	498	5	18	199	3
Out	**3,294**	**37**	**In**	**3,152**	**36**
			Out	**3,294**	**37**
			Totals	**6,446**	**73**

In the heartland of golf lies the superb new Letham Grange Hotel and Golf Courses. The magnificent Victorian Mansion nestles with the panoramic Letham Grange Estate. The Mansion has been restored to its former glory as a top quality, 3 star hotel with 20 bedrooms, offering a style and standard of living which is both traditional and sumptuous.

36 Holes of magnificent golf! Widely acclaimed as one of the premier courses in Scotland, the Old Course provides a blend of tree lined parkland and open rolling fairways. With water playing a major role, the Course is both scenic and dramatic. The New Course, although slightly shorter - and without the water hazards, offers golfers a more relaxed and less arduous round. However, it can be deceptive!

Letham Grange Hotel
Colliston
by Arbroath
DD11 4RL
Tel: (0241) 89 373
Fax: (0241) 89 414

There are 'dreamers' and there are 'doers'. Once in every blue moon—thank heavens—the two combine.

Soon after the late Sir Henry Cotton officially opened Letham Grange in 1987, Malcolm Campbell, the then editor of *Golf Monthly* bravely announced, 'We now have the "Augusta of Scotland"'. In a generally critical article a second leading UK golf magazine later lambasted this judgement saying it was, 'a bit like trying to sell blended whisky as a twelve year old malt.' But then we are a nation of 'knockers' aren't we? Of course Letham Grange isn't the equal of Augusta, where the azaleas and dogwoods run riot, but it is a wonderfully enjoyable place to play golf nonetheless and there is at least one parallel in the manner of its creation. Like Augusta, Letham Grange is the result of one man's dream. Down in Georgia the guiding force was a man named Jones: up in Angus it was a man called Smith. Letham Grange was Ken Smith's dream and aside from the quality of the end product I wouldn't be quick to criticise Letham Grange for the very fact that Ken Smith had the guts, vision and determination to do something about his dream.

It is an extraordinary place. Located inland, four miles north of Arbroath, and roughly midway between Montrose and Carnoustie, Letham Grange is where a typical and, until recently, 'oh so timeless' Scottish country estate confronts 20th century 'hotel and country club golf' head on. In fact the Victorian mansion which presides over the heavily wooded and rolling estate had become derelict by the mid 1970s, before the golfing dream was conceived. This same mansion is now one of Scotland's most luxurious 19th hole retreats. Moreover time no longer stands still at Letham Grange for since 1991 the estate has boasted two 18 hole courses—the slightly revised 1987 layout now being called the **Old Course**(!)

At 5528 yards, par 68, the **New Course** is more than 1000 yards shorter than its older sister (6614 yards, par 73) and there are none of the water hazards that make the Old Course at once potentially treacherous and positively spectacular. The green fees at Letham Grange reflect this. In the summer of 1994 a round on the Old Course cost the visitor £20 midweek and £25 at the weekend: on the New Course the fees were £12 and £15 respectively. Special rates are available for juniors, for those playing 'out of season' and for golfers wishing to play more than one round in a day. Tee reservations can be made by telephoning the club on **(0241) 890373**. **Pamela Ogilvie** is the **Golf Administrator**, she can be contacted via this number, while the **professional, David Scott** can be reached on **(0241) 890377**. All written correspondence should be addressed to **Letham Grange Hotel and Golf Courses, Colliston, by Arbroath, Angus, DD11 4RL.** The only specific restriction on visitors is before 10.30am on Tuesdays (both courses) and before 10.30am (Old Course) and 9.00am (New Course) at weekends. Bookings can normally be made for all other times.

When the New Course was constructed two holes from the original Letham Grange course were incorporated in the design, namely the old 9th and 10th. The Old Course has thus acquired two new holes.

In a nut shell the changes mean that many of the most dramatic holes at Letham Grange must be confronted midway round the Old course. The 8th, 9th and 10th for instance—a par three, par five and par four are as memorable and as challenging a sequence as the celebrated 10th, 11th and 12th at St Mellion. The pick of these is probably the two-shot 10th where the player drives from an elevated tee (usually with an iron), threading it along an ever-narrowing fairway and then fires an approach across the corner of an encroaching lake to a stage-like green. Another superb hole is the par three 15th: here the green is once again the 'wrong side' of water and is set at such an angle that only the very bold, precisely struck tee shot will be rewarded. Not a hole for the nit-picking 'knockers'.

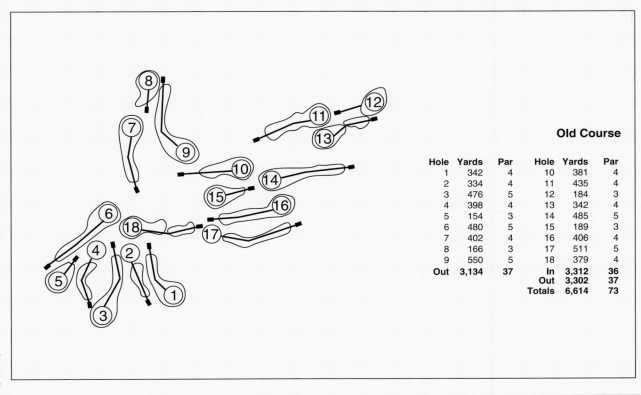

Old Course

Hole	Yards	Par	Hole	Yards	Par
1	342	4	10	381	4
2	334	4	11	435	4
3	476	5	12	184	3
4	398	4	13	342	4
5	154	3	14	485	5
6	480	5	15	189	3
7	402	4	16	406	4
8	166	3	17	511	5
9	550	5	18	379	4
Out	**3,134**	**37**	**In**	**3,312**	**36**
			Out	**3,302**	**37**
			Totals	**6,614**	**73**

The Roman Camp Hotel sits on the north bank of the River Tieth amongst 20 acres of mature and secluded gardens which nestle by the picturesque village of Callander, the Gateway to the Trossachs and the Highlands of Scotland.

The house was originally built as a hunting lodge for the Dukes of Perth in 1625 and was given its name from the conspicuous earth mounds believed to be the site of a Roman Fort which are visible across the meadow to the east of the walled garden.

The building has grown over many years as each consecutive family has added their own embellishments to this lovely home. The most obvious of these are the towers, one of which contains a tiny chapel.

Today, under the guidance of Eric and Marion Brown, the traditional country house atmosphere still evokes its alluring charm. As you enter, you will notice the abundance of freshly cut flowers, their scent lingering in the air, and be greeted by great log fires.

The library and drawing room are of grand proportions with an atmosphere of warmth and relaxation and are places to enjoy and reflect on the days sport, especially after dinner in the company of friends and a fine malt.

The tapestry hung dining room is crowned by a richly painted 16th century style ceiling. Here, dinner is served at candlelit tables, laid with fine silver and crystal, while you choose from menus of local game and fish, prepared by the chef and accompanied by vegetables and herbs from the hotel's gardens.

Each of the bedrooms has its own distinctive style and character and is equipped with all the little thoughtful extras to make your stay as comfortable as possible.

At the Roman Camp Country House you are within easy reach of many championship and picturesque golf courses and the hotel can arrange tee times at the local course, just two minutes walk from the hotel.

A stretch of river, three quarters of a mile long runs through the gardens, enabling guests to fish for wild brown trout and salmon on the private beat at no extra charge. There is also the opportunity for the hotel to arrange fishing on the many lochs and other private beats surrounding Callander.

The Roman Camp is the perfect country house hotel to make your favourite country retreat.

The Roman Camp
Callander
FK17 8BG
Tel: (01877) 330003
Fax: (01877) 331533

Walter Hagen—a shrewd judge you might think— once described Carnoustie as the greatest course in the British Isles. There are many who would agree with the great man, though doubtless the disciples of St. Andrews and several honourable gentlemen at Muirfield would beg to differ. Greatest or not, very few would dispute that when the winds blow—as they invariably do in these parts—Carnoustie is the toughest of all our Championship links.

In the days when the Campbells and the MacDonalds were busy slaughtering each other up in the Highlands, down at Carnoustie more civilised pursuits were taking place. Records suggest that golf was being played on the adjoining Barry Links, as early as the 16th century. The first official Club at Carnoustie—today there are six—was founded in 1842 and golf was played over a ten hole course laid out by Allan Robertson. Later, 'Old' Tom Morris came on the scene and extended the links to a full 18 holes, but the present Championship course didn't really take shape until James Braid made several alterations in 1926. By 1931 Carnoustie was ready to stage its first Open Championship.

As previously mentioned there are presently six Clubs at Carnoustie and play is now over three 18 hole courses; the **Championship**, the **Burnside** and the **Buddon**. Administrative matters are in the hands of the Carnoustie Golf Links Management Committee and persons wishing to visit Carnoustie should direct correspondence to the Committee's **Secretary, Mr. E.J.C. Smith.** Their full address is **The Carnoustie Golf Links Management Committee, Links Parade, Carnoustie, Tayside, DD7 7JE.** Contact by telephone can be made on **(0241) 853789** and by fax on (0241) 852720. Starting times must be booked in advance.

In 1994, the green fees to play at Carnoustie were £36 for a single round on the Championship course (£63 for a day ticket) with £43 securing a round over both the Championship and Burnside courses. Fees to play just the Burnside or Buddon courses are good value and it is also possible to obtain a three day and five day pass enabling up to three or five rounds over the Championship course. Details can be obtained by phoning the above number (caddies can also be arranged.)

The cluster of Clubs that go to make up Carnoustie's permanent golfing village provide all the ususal amenities for the visiting golfer—golf shops for clothing, equipment and club hire and of course a more than adequate

19th hole. Travelling to Carnoustie shouldn't present too many problems. The Forth Road Bridge and the M90 link the Edinburgh region with Perth; Perth in turn is linked to Dundee by the A85 (dual carriageway all the way) and Dundee to Carnoustie by the A390. Those on golfing tours will quite likely be coming via St. Andrews: the A91 (A919) runs from St. Andrews towards Dundee; it picks up the A92 just before the Tay Road Bridge and on crossing the Bridge the A930 should immediately be joined. Approaching from northerly directions, the A92 runs from Aberdeen (and beyond) to within a couple of miles of Carnoustie at Muirdrum, while the A958 links the town with Forfar. Carnoustie can also be reached by train with connections from Perth, Dundee and Aberdeen.

It isn't only the wind of course that makes Carnoustie such a difficult test. When the Championship tees are in use the course stretches close to 7200 yards making it the longest of our Open courses. From the Club medal tees, 6936 yards is still a formidable proposition.

Scotland is the land of Burns. It is also the land of burns—streams or little rivers anywhere else in the English-speaking world—and Carnoustie is famous for them. The ubiquitous Barry Burn and its wee brother Jocky's Burn traverse the fairways in the most unfriendly of places, often in front of greens and across the spot you'd ideally like to drive to. More than anything else though, Carnoustie is renowned for its incredibly tough finishing stretch. The 16th is an exceptionally long short hole and Jack Nicklaus is said to have once needed a driver followed by an 8 iron to get up! The 17th has the Barry Burn meandering across its fairway, making it a particularly difficult driving hole and at the 18th the Burn crosses in front of the green necessitating one of the most exciting (or nerve-racking) closing shots in golf.

Each of the five Opens held at Carnoustie has produced great champions: Tommy Armour (1931), Henry Cotton (1937), Ben Hogan (1953), Gary Player (1968) and Tom Watson (1975). Many consider Hogan's victory in 1953—he won by four strokes with ever decreasing rounds of 73-71-70-68—to be the greatest ever performance in a Major Championship. There are also those who feel that his final round of 68 represents the true course record. The wind blew that day and Carnoustie's teeth were gnashing. Twenty two years later when Jack Newton scored his 65 Carnoustie was smiling. It was the only Open Hogan ever played in.

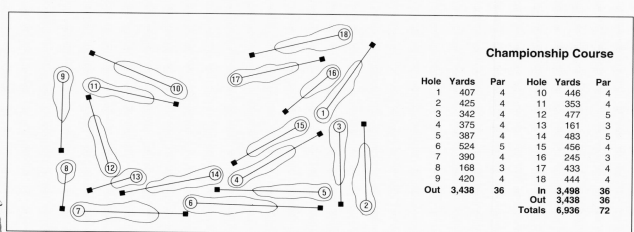

Championship Course

Hole	Yards	Par	Hole	Yards	Par
1	407	4	10	446	4
2	425	4	11	353	4
3	342	4	12	477	5
4	375	4	13	161	3
5	387	4	14	483	5
6	524	5	15	456	4
7	390	4	16	245	3
8	168	3	17	433	4
9	420	4	18	444	4
Out	**3,438**	**36**	**In**	**3,498**	**36**
			Out	3,438	36
			Totals	6,936	72

Situated in eleven acres of garden and woodland Castleton House is still surrounded by a moat constructed in 1296 when Edward Ist of England chose this prominent position as a fortress.

Woodland glens and tranquil lochs contribute to the beauty of the area and breathtaking views keep the hillwalker going forever.

For the sportsman we can arrange fishing, shooting, stalking and with over 50 excellent golf courses, including Rosemount and Carnoustie, all within one hours drive, you are offered a wealth of activity. Special golf packages including tuition by local professional.

After an exhilarating day in the open air relax in either our restaurant or less formal conservatory and enjoy fine cuisine prepared with fresh local ingredients complemented by excellent wine to suit every palate.

Castleton House Hotel
by Glamis
Forfar
Angus
DD8 1SJ
Tel: (0307) 840340
Fax: (0307) 840506

Perhaps there are two things that strike you most when you arrive at one of the famous golfing links on the east coast of Scotland: the first will almost certainly be the thought, 'So this is where it all started' - a feeling that can often leave one slightly numb. The second, and equally numbing is likely to be the thought, 'Will this wretched wind ever die down?' The famous links at Montrose is just such a place.

Golf has been played on Montrose links since the 16th century and according to the best records it is the fifth oldest course in the world. By course is meant the **Medal** Course, for there are two 18 hole links at Montrose, the Medal and the shorter **Broomfield** Course, the former having altered surprisingly little through the ages. One interesting fact is that in the 1800s, at a time when one or two more famous clubs had only 5 holes, The Medal Course at Montrose boasted 25! All of which were played in a unique tournament in 1866 won by a Mr T Doleman from Glasgow who played the 25 holes in 112 strokes; Willie Park, winner of the first Open Championship in 1860, finished 2nd scoring a 115.

In common with St Andrews and Carnoustie, Montrose is a public links and although three golf clubs play over the two courses, namely, the Royal Montrose, Caledonian and Mercantile Clubs, both are effectively managed by the Montrose Links Trust who handle all administrative matters. Any written correspondence should be addressed to this body care of **The Secretary, Traill Drive, Montrose, Angus DD10 8SW**. Mrs **Margaret Stewart** is in fact the Secretary and she may be contacted by telephone on **(0674) 672932** and by fax on **(0674) 671800**. Also most helpful is the **professional Kevin Stables**; he can be reached on **(0674) 672634**.

Being a public links there are few restrictions on the times visitors can play; indeed the only one as such is that visitors cannot play on Saturdays or tee off before 10.00am on Sundays. It should also be noted that visitors wishing to play the Medal Course are requested to produce a handicap certificate.

In 1994 a day ticket to play on the Medal Course was priced at £24 during the week and £33 at weekends with a single round costing £14 midweek and £21 at weekends. To play a round over the Broomfield Course the fee is £9 midweek and £13 at the weekend with a day

ticket available for £13 and £20 repectively). Those staying in the area might consider a weekly ticket; in 1994 these were priced at £76 for the Medal Course and £50 for the Broomfield Course. Reductions of up to fifty per cent are usually available to junior golfers.

Apart from their length, (the Medal Course measures 6443 yards (par 71) and the Broomfield 4815 yards (par 66), the two courses differ in other respects. The Broomfield is laid out on the landward side of the Medal and is considerably flatter. With its many subtle - and many not-so-subtle - undulations the Medal is by far the more testing and it is not surprisingly over this links that the major Championships are held; these have included the Scottish Professional Championship, the Scottish Amateur Championship, and the British Boys Championship and Internationals.

For twelve of its eighteen holes, the Medal Course follows closely the line of the dunes, with the 4th and 6th being especially memorable. However, some of the best holes appear at the end of the round: the 16th (Gully) being a particularly long par three and the 17th (Rashes) with its raised green, one of those par fours requiring, as a caddy once put it, three damned good shots to get up in two!

As the crow flies Montrose lies approximately midway between St Andrews and Aberdeen. For those of us without wings the A92 is likely to be of most assistance. Those travelling from the St Andrews region, or indeed from all points south, should head for Dundee. The A92 runs from Dundee to Aberdeen passing though the centre of Montrose. Montrose links lies to the north of the town, east off the A92 and is well signposted. Anyone approaching from the west, including Blairgowrie (in golf course terms a world away) can avoid Dundee by heading for Brechin and thereafter following the A935 into Montrose, passing Montrose Basin (where in winter you may sight a few rare pink-footed Arctic geese - quite possibly the only birdies you'll see all day).

As for a 19th hole, the catering requirements of visitors are more than adequately met by the golf clubs mentioned above, each having clubhouses adjacent to the links.

There are no airs and graces about Montrose; it is what might be described as a good honest links. But if you've come to Scotland to admire the golf, then Montrose is clearly one that shouldn't be missed.

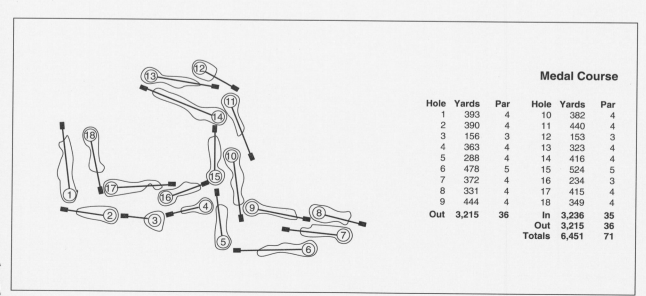

Medal Course

Hole	Yards	Par	Hole	Yards	Par
1	393	4	10	382	4
2	390	4	11	440	4
3	156	3	12	153	3
4	363	4	13	323	4
5	288	4	14	416	4
6	478	5	15	524	5
7	372	4	16	234	3
8	331	4	17	415	4
9	444	4	18	349	4
Out	**3,215**	**36**	**In**	**3,236**	**35**
			Out	**3,215**	**36**
			Totals	**6,451**	**71**

Key

To avoid disappointment
it is advisable to telephone
in advance

***Visitors welcome at most times
**Visitors usually allowed on
weekdays only
*Visitors not normally permitted
(Mon, Wed) No visitors
on specified days

Approximate Green Fees
A £30 plus
B £20 to £30
C £15 to £25
D £10 to £20
E under £10
F Greens fees on application

Restrictions
G Guests only
H Handicap certificate required
H (24) Handicap of 24 or less
L Letter of introduction required
M Visitor must be a member of
another recognised club.

TAYSIDE

Aberfeldy G.C.
(0887) 820535
Taybridge Road, Aberfeldy
(9)2733 yards/***/D

Alyth G.C.
(08283) 2268
Pitcrocknie, Alyth
(18)6226 yards/***/F

Arbroath G.C.
(0241) 875837
Elliot, Arbroath, Angus
(18)6078 yards/***/D

Auchterarder G.C.
(0764) 662804
Orchil Road, Auchterarder
(18)5737 yards/***/D

Bishopshire G.C.
(0592) 780203
Kinnesswood, Kinross
(10)4700 metres/***/E

Blair Atholl G.C.
(079681) 274
Blair Atholl, Perthshire
(9)5710 yards/***/D

Blairgowrie G.C.
(0250) 872594
Rosemount, Blairgowrie
(18)6588 yards/***(Wed)/H
(18)6895 yards/***(Wed)/H

Brechin G.C.
(0356) 622383
Trinity, by Brechin, Angus
(18)5267 yards/***/D

Caird Park G.C.
(0382) 453606
Mains Loan, Dundee
(18)6303 yards/***/F

Callander G.C.
(0877) 330090
Aveland Road, Callander
(18)5125 yards/***/F/H

Camperdown G.C.

(0382) 623398
Camperdown Park, Dundee
(18)6561 yards/***/E

Carnoustie
(0241) 853789
Links Parade, Carnoustie, Angus
(18)6931 yards/***/F/H
(18)6020 yards/***/F/H
(18)5732 yards/***/F/H

Comrie G.C.
(0764) 670055
Polinard, Comrie
(9)5966/***/E

Craigie Hill G.C.
(0738) 624377
Cherrybank, Perth
(18)5739 yards/***/D

Crieff G.C.
(0764) 652909
Perth Road, Crieff
(18)6402 yards/***/C
(9)4772 yards/***/D

Dalmunzie Hotel & G.C.
(0250) 885226
Spittal of Glenshee, Blairgowrie
(9)2035/***/E

Downfield G.C.
(0382) 825595
Turnberry Avenue, Dundee
(18)6804 yards/***/C-B

Dunblane New G.C.
(0786) 823711
Perth Road, Dunblane
(18)6876 yards/**/D

Dunkeld and Birnam G.C.
(0350) 727524
Fungarth, Dunkeld
(9)5264 yards/***/F

Dunning G.C.
(0764) 684747
Rollo Park, Dunning, Perth
(9)4836 yards/***/E

Edzell G.C.
(0356) 648235
High Street, Edzell, by Brechin
(18)6299 yards/***/D

Forfar G.C.
(0307) 463733
Arbroath Road, by Forfar
(18)6255 yards/***/D

Gleneagles Hotel & G.C.
(0764) 663543
Auchterarder
(18)6471 yards/*/F/G
(18)6964 yards/*/F/G

Green Hotel G.C.
(0577) 863407
Beeches Park, Kinross
(18)6111 yards/***/F

Kenmore G.C.
(0887) 830226
Kenmore, Aberfeldy
(9)6052 yards/***(Thurs pm)/D

Killin G.C.
(0567) 820312
Killin
(9)2508 yards/***/F

King James VI G.C.
(0738) 625170
Moncreiffe Island, Perth
(18)6026 yards/***(Sat)/D

Kirriemuir G.C.
(0575) 573317
Kirriemuir, Angus
(18)5591 yards/**/D

Letham Grange G.C.
(0241) 89377
Letham Grange, Colliston
(18)6614 yards/***/F
(18)5528 yards/***/F

Milnathort G.C.
(0577) 864069
South Street, Milnathort
(9)5411 yards/***/D

Monifieth Links G.C.
(0382) 532767
Dundee, Angus
(18)6657 yards/***(Sat)/F/H
(18)5123 yards/***(Sat)/F

Montrose Links Trust
(0674) 672932
Trail Drive, Montrose, Angus
(18)6451 yards/***/C
(18)4815 yards/***/D

Murrayshall Hotel & G.C.
(0738) 551171
Murrayshall by Scone
(18)6416 yards/***/F/H

Muthill G.C.
(0764) 681523
Peat Road, Muthill, Crieff
(18)5877 yards/***/F

North Inch G.C.
(0738) 63648
Perth
(18)4736 yards/***/F

Panmure G.C.
(0241) 853120
Barry, Angus
(18)6317 yards/***(Sat)/C

Pitlochry G.C.
(0796) 472792
Golf Course Road, Pitlochry
(18)5811 yards/***/D

St Fillans G.C.
(0764) 685312
St Fillans, Perthshire
(9)5268 yards/***/F

Strathtay G.C.
(0887) 840367
Tighanoisinn, Grandtully
(9)4980 yards/***/E

Taymouth Castle G.C.
(0887) 830228
Kenmore, by Aberfeldy
(18)6066 yards/***/D/H

CENTRAL

Aberfoyle G.C.
(0877) 382493
Braeval, Aberfoyle
(18)5205 yards/***/D

Alloa G.C.
(0259) 722745
Schawpark, Sauchie

(18)6230 yards/***/D

Alva G.C.
(0259) 760431
Beauclerc Street, Alva
(9)2407 yards/***/F

Bonnybridge G.C.
(0324) 812822
Larbert Road, Bonnybridge
(9)6060 yards/***/F

Braehead G.C.
(0259) 722078
Cambus, by Alloa
(18)6013 yards/***/D/H

Bridge of Allan G.C.
(0786) 832332
Sunlaw, Bridge of Allan, Stirling
(9)4932 yards/***(Sat)/E

Buchanan Castle G.C.
(0360) 60307
Drymen
(18)6015 yards/***/F

Campsie G.C.
(0360) 310920
Crow Road, Lennoxtown
(18)5517 yards/**/D

Dollar G.C.
(0259) 742400
Brewlands House, Dollar
(18)5144 yards/**/F

Falkirk G.C.
(0324) 611061
Stirling Road, Cumlins, Falkirk
(18)6202 yards/**/D

Falkirk Tryst G.C.
(0324) 562091
Burnhead Road, Larbert
(18)6053 yards/***/D

Glenbervie G.C.
(0324) 562605
Stirling Road, Larbert
(18)6469 yards/***/C/I

Grangemouth Municipal G.C.
(0324) 711500
Polmont Hill, Polmont, Falkirk
(18)6314 yards/***/F/H

Muckhart G.C.
(0259) 781423
Drumburn Road, Muckhart, Dollar
(18)6115 yards/***/E

Polmont G.C.
(0324) 711277
Maddiston, by Falkirk
(9)3044 yards/**/E

Stirling G.C.
(0786) 471490
Queens Road, Stirling
(18)6409 yards/**/D

Tillicoultry G.C.
(0259) 750124
Alva Road, Tillicoultry
(9)2528 yards/***/E

Tulliallan G.C.
(0259) 730396
Alloa Road, Kincardine on Forth
(18)5982 yards/***/F

Artist: **Bill Waugh ROYAL DORNOCH** *Courtesy of:* **Burlington Gallery**

Ardoe House Hotel is a Scottish baronial style mansion with commanding views over beautiful Royal Deeside. Within easy reach of many of the north east of Scotland's golf courses, the hotel is also conveniently situated close to Aberdeen, only a few minutes drive from the city centre. Set in seventeen acres of its own grounds, the stunning exterior of the hotel is matched by an equally impressive interior. Features include ornate mouldings, wood panelling and log fires with delightful public rooms providing areas for rest and relaxation.

A complete refurbishment of this Victorian House took place in the late 1980s with additions in the early 90s sympathetic to the original building. The result is a superb venue for business or pleasure with seventy-one bedrooms displaying a high level of excellence, both for their generous proportions and luxuriousness. Bedrooms have all the facilities necessary to ensure a most comfortable stay, including a hospitality tray and fresh fruit. The hallmarks of Ardoe House are our committment to maintaining high standards of comfort, fine cuisine and service which is attentive yet unobtrusive and a warmth of hospitality unrivalled anywhere.

The hotel is presently a popular base for golf parties playing the many challenging courses of the North East, in particular, Deeside and the coast, both of which are readily accessible from the hotel.

The restaurant at Ardoe House is very popular with both guests and the local community. An excellent reputation is enjoyed due, in the main, to the consistently high standards of cuisine achieved by using the best and freshest of ingredients prepared into mouth watering dishes by a team of dedicated award winning chefs eager to maintain and enhance this reputation.

Golf packages, which include accommodation in a deluxe room with a full Scottish breakfast, four course dinner and packed lunch are available all year round. Details are available on request from the manager.

Ardoe House Hotel
Blairs
South Deeside Road
Aberdeen
AB1 5YP
Tel: (0224) 867355
Fax: (0224) 861283

Mist-covered mountains and bottomless lochs, bagpipes, whisky and haggis. I doubt whether there is a more romantic place in the world than the Highlands of Scotland. I doubt also that there is a place quite so shatteringly beautiful. For our purposes 'the Highlands' covers the administrative regions of Grampian and Highland. The latter extends from the Cairngorms northwards, encompassing the Great Glen and the Western Isles. Grampian covers a similarly vast area, the entirety of north eastern Scotland. The area was at one time covered by a dense forest of pine broken only by the soaring granite peaks of the Grampian mountain range. It was the home of the savage Caledonian tribe, a land where wolves hunted in packs. Nowadays very little of the forest remains. As for the wolves, most of them were killed by the Caledonians, but then unfortunately most of the Caledonians were killed by the Romans. No wonder they called life 'nasty, brutish and short'!

Grampian

Let us make a start in Grampian. Forgetting the wolves, the savages and the Romans, what we need is a good 18 holes—and, of course, a suitable 19th. Aberdeen is a fine place to begin. Balgownie and Murcar lie right on the town's doorstep and are unquestionably two of the finest courses in Scotland. Balgownie links is the home of the **Royal Aberdeen** Golf Club and is featured ahead but **Murcar** is certainly not overshadowed and is a true championship test. It is a classic Scottish links with plenty of sandhills and a meandering burn and is quite a bit more undulating than Balgownie.

If the above are the best two courses around Aberdeen, (there are dozens in the area) and they are to the north of the city then perhaps the most spectacular is to the south at **Stonehaven**, laid out right alongside the lashing North Sea. And in total contrast to Stonehaven—and indeed to Aberdeen's great links layouts is the new 'American-style' course at **Newmachar,** north west of the city.

There are even more hotels in Aberdeen than golf courses but a large number are modern and somewhat unattractive and many may prefer to stay outside the town where establishments such as the magnificent Ardoe House (0224) 867355 can be found. Anyway some of the best hotels in central Aberdeen include the Holiday Inn (0224) 713911 and the Skean Dhu Hotel (0224) 725252. One other hotel strongly recommended by the golfing fraternity is the Atholl (0224) 23505 in Kings Gate. Many of the city's innumerable guest houses provide a more friendly ambience then their larger counterparts with Cedars Private Hotel (0224) 583225 a prominent example. An excellent seafood restaurant to visit is the Atlantis (0224) 591403 while Gerrard's (0224) 639500 is also highly thought of.

North of Aberdeen, the popular Udny Arms (03586) 89444 at Newburgh enjoys a peaceful situation overlooking the Ythan Estuary and is a total contrast to the many modern hotels of Aberdeen. Due west of the city another striking location is found at Kildrummy by Alford. Here the Kildrummy Castle (09755) 71288 is a first class establishment. To the north west, the Pittodrie House Hotel (0467) 681444 at Pitcaple enjoys glorious surroundings and in Old Meldrum one finds the similarly splendid Meldrum House Hotel (0651) 872294, which is convenient for the **Old Meldrum** course, and the many championship courses in the area.

Looking to play outside Aberdeen, the golfer is faced with two equally appealing choices—one can either head north along the coast towards Cruden Bay, or alternatively head inland along the A93. The latter choice broadly involves following the path of the River Dee and will take the traveller through some truly magnificent scenery. The 18 hole courses at **Banchory, Aboyne, Ballater** and **Braemar** all lie along this road and not surprisingly boast spectacular settings. There are several superb places in which to stay as you golf your way along the Dee. In Banchory, Raemoir House (0330) 024884 is outstanding and the Tor-na-Coille (0330) 822242 has excellent facilities, as does the Banchory Lodge Hotel (0330) 822625. Aboyne offers the Birse Lodge Hotel (03398) 86253 while the especially attractive town of Ballater boasts a number of fine establishments. Tullich Lodge (0338) 55406 is one of the leading mansion houses in Scotland but also note the Craigendarroch Hotel (03397) 55858 with its fine restaurant and Darroch Learg (03397) 55443. Should you time it right then Braemar boasts that magnificent spectacle, the Highland Games.

Journeying due northwards from Aberdeen, **Cruden Bay** is clearly the first stopping point. A truly splendid golf links this, situated some 23 miles north of Aberdeen on Scotland's Buchan Coast. It is detailed on a later page. The old fishing and whaling town of **Peterhead** has an interesting seaside course where fierce sea winds can make scoring tricky.

From fishing port to Georgian elegance—the **Duff House Royal** Golf Club at Macduff is overlooked by an impressive baroque-style mansion. The course too has a touch of class being designed by Alister Mackenzie immediately prior to his constructing the legendary Augusta National course in America—note the many two-tiered greens. Although not far from the sea, Duff House is very much a parkland type challenge. Nearby **Royal Tarlair** at Banff is well worth a visit and like Duff House is always beautifully maintained. To the south of Banff, along the A947, **Turriff** can also be recommended while even further inland (but a marvellous drive anyway) from the Banff/ Macduff area on the A97, is the charming little course at **Huntly** and the very relaxing Castle Hotel (0466) 792696. West of Huntly lies the well run Craigellachie Hotel (0340) 881204. Returning to Macduff, the Fire Arms Hotel (0261) 32408 is convenient and in Banff's High Street, the Country Hotel (0261) 815353 is another to note. Also to be found in Banff is the charming Carmelite House Hotel (0261) 812152, while nearby Cullen Bay has the welcoming Cullen Bay Hotel (0542) 840432.

Crossing the salmon-filled River Spey at Fochabers the City of **Elgin** is soon reached. There aren't too many cathedrals in this part of the world but Elgin, the capital of Morayshire, has a beautiful one that dates from the 13th century. It also possesses one of the finest inland golf courses in the north of Scotland. A mile or so south of the city and some distance away from the often fierce coastal winds, the course is sheltered by many pines and silver birch trees. Inevitably, it occupies a glorious setting with distant purple hills forming a spectacular horizon.

Inland from Elgin, a drive through the Glen of Rothes will lead the golfer to **Dufftown** where there is a pleasant and not too difficult course but if a coastal challenge is sought then Lossiemouth is the place to head for. Here, the **Moray** Golf Club has two outstanding links courses, the 'Old Course' which is more than a hundred years old and the 'New Course', a little over ten years old. Whilst the fighter aircraft from nearby RAF Lossiemouth may occasionally irritate, it would be difficult to find a finer combination of superb natural golf and scenic splendour. Moray is another club featured later in this section. In Elgin two hotels, the Mansion

House (0343) 548811 and the Eight Acres (0343) 543077 are recommended and in Rothes, the Rothes Glen (0340) 831254 is superbly relaxing. In Forres, the Knockomie Hotel (0309) 673146 is very accommodating. Finally in Lossiemouth, ideal for golf at Moray, is the adjacent Stotfield Hotel (0343) 812011.

Highland

In Scotland, where there is land there is golf and although the Highland region may be a wild and somewhat remote part of the country it nonetheless has its share of golfing gems—and more than that, in the minds of many, it has in **Royal Dornoch** the finest of them all.

As well as its gems, the region has a number of golf's genuine outposts, none more so than the **Gairloch** Golf Club situated in the far west of Scotland with views across to the Isle of Skye. There are 9 holes at Gairloch, each wonderfully named. The 6th, however, baffles me—'Westward Ho!' is its title?! The 9th though has more of a Celtic ring to it—'Mo Dhachaidh'. There is no Sunday golf at Gairloch though visitors can play at all other times. Others in the 'lonely category' include **Fort Augustus** on the edge of Loch Ness and **Fort William**, a moorland course, laid out in the shadows of Ben Nevis. In addition the very intrepid golfer will find a number of courses to play in the Western Isles and the Hebrides although the scenery may cause many to lift their heads too quickly.

In the south of Highland, the area around Aviemore has become an increasingly popular holiday retreat, particularly for winter sports enthusiasts. However, whilst the skis must go on the roof, the golf clubs can fit in the boot, and there are five or six courses at hand each of which possesses a truly glorious setting. Picking two of the best, the **Kingussie** and **Boat of Garten** Golf Clubs lie either side of Aviemore close to the A9. Both have spectacular courses at which visitors are always made welcome. Neither is particularly long, though the hills at Kingussie and the narrow fairways and small greens at Boat of Garten can make scoring extremely difficult and you are more likely to see eagles than score one! At Boat of Garten you may also catch a glimpse of one of the famous ospreys.

Some thoughts for the 19th include in the Newtonmore-Kingussie area, the Highlander (0540) 673341 and the Osprey (0540) 661510, both pleasant hotels, and the Cross (0540) 661166 is an outstanding restaurant in Kingussie. In Fort William one finds the Inverlochy Castle (0397) 702177, one of the country's finest hotels and restaurants, while two other gems are the remote Arisaig House (06875) 622 on the western coast and in Ballachulish, the Ballachulish Hotel (08552) 606. In Boat of Garten, the Boat (0479) 831258 is exceptionally convenient overlooking the golf course (note the special 'golf weeks'). The Dalrachney Lodge (0479) 841252 at Carrbridge caters exceptionally well for golfing and fishing guests. Both Seafield Lodge (0479) 872152 and the Grant Arms Hotel (0479) 872526 in Grantown-on-Spey are comfortable and good value, whilst nearer the coast at Advie is the extremely gracious Tulchan Lodge (0807) 510200.

Inverness, as the so-called 'Capital of the Highlands', is where many may choose to spend a day or two—the Loch Ness monster lives nearby and the famous fields of destruction at Culloden Moor are only a few miles to the east. Golfers may wish to note the city's 18 hole course situated just south of the town centre. However, many are likely to be drawn towards **Nairn** (16 miles away) where in addition to the magnificent championship links—see feature page—there is an excellent second course, **Nairn Dunbar**.

Both Inverness and Nairn have a number of good hotels. In the former, the Dunain Park Hotel (0463) 230512 and the 18th century Kingsmills (0463) 237166 are ideal, and near to the famous battlefield is the impressive Culloden House Hotel (0463) 790461 where a portrait of the Bonnie Prince will welcome you. Relaxation and comfort can also be found at Glenruidh House (0463) 226499 and Ballifeary House Hotel (0463) 235572. In Nairn the Golf View Hotel (0667) 452301 is situated right alongside the famous championship course but there are strong recommendations also for the Claymore House Hotel (0667) 53731, the Newton Hotel (0667) 453144, Lochloy House (0667) 455355, the Alton Burn Hotel (0667) 53325 and the Clifton Hotel (0667) 453119, all in Nairn.

On the Chanonry Peninsula, linked to Inverness by way of the Kessock Bridge, the A9 and the A832, is the flattish links course of **Fortrose** and **Rosemarkie**—surrounded by sea and well worth a visit. **Strathpeffer Spa**, a moorland course, is the prettiest of stepping stones for those heading north of Inverness along the A9 and Craigdarroch Lodge Hotel (0997) 421265 will provide comfortable respite. This road passes through **Tain**, home of the famous Glenmorangie whisky, and where there is another outstanding 18 holes—but by now most will be itching to reach Dornoch.

Royal Dornoch is regularly ranked among the top ten golf courses in Britain. For those wishing to reflect on their day's golf the Dornoch Castle (0862) 810216, the Royal Golf Hotel (0862) 810283 and the Burghfield House (0862) 810212 can all be highly recommended and there are a number of more modest B&B type places.

Having played Royal Dornoch, many find it difficult to tear themselves away, but there are two fine courses a short distance to the north, namely, **Golspie** and **Brora**. Both are testing links courses set in the most majestic surroundings with views to distant hills and along what is a truly spectacular coast. Brora (where the greens are reputed to be the equal of those at Royal Dornoch and are ringed by electric fences to keep the sheep out!) stretches out right alongside three miles of deserted sandy beach. Being so far north golf can be played at absurdly late hours and at both, the green fees are very inexpensive. In Brora, the Royal Marine (0408) 621252 and the Links (0408) 621225 hotels are both strategically placed on the aptly named Golf Road, while another well titled hotel can be found at Golspie, the Golf Links Hotel (0408) 633408.

Beyond Brora we really are getting remote! However, the A9 makes it all the way to John O'Groats. There are 18 hole courses at **Wick** and **Reay**, but the furthest north is **Thurso**, not too far from the Dounreay Power Station and if you do make it there, excellent accommodation in true country house style is available at the Melvich Hotel (0641) 3206. I should imagine it gets pretty cold up there, but if you are looking for fresh challenges then there is always the golf club in the Arctic—fittingly called the 'Polar Bear Club'—and which, I suppose it goes without saying, was founded by Scotsmen!

One of the most beautiful villages in Moray, Craigellachie lies at the confluence of the Fiddich and Spey rivers in a picturesque setting equal only to the sumptuous and elegant Victorian hotel itself. Only one hours drive from the airports of Aberdeen and Inverness, the Craigellachie is a haven of highland hospitality set in a spectacular countryside — unspoilt, wild and beautiful and ideal for all kinds of modern sporting activities.

According to the season you can play tennis, ski, ride horseback, or mountain bike along forest and mountain trails and fish for salmon or brown trout.

And then there's the golf. The Craigellachie offers a unique opportunity to enjoy a holiday in the land where golf was born, with a choice of links, moor or parkland courses all within a short drive of the hotel. Whatever your handicap, there is a course here to challenge your skill. We can arrange golf club hire and private tuition by professionals at selected clubs.

After sampling the variety of outdoor pursuits or one of the many golf courses in this beautiful part of Scotland, it is always a pleasure to return to the Craigellachie and sit beside the glowing embers of a real log fire in the hall or one of the comfortable lounges. An equally warm welcome will await you in the Quaich cocktail bar and when it's time to dine, the Ben Aigan restaurant offers a tempting menu in the hearty tradition of the finest Scottish cuisine. Here, you can savour the delights of our culinary excellence (which, according to season, feature prime local produce from sea and countryside) and then linger over coffee in the drawing room, before retiring to the comfort and luxury of one of the splendidly appointed bedrooms. Each has its own en suite bath/shower, direct-dial telephone, remote control colour television and special hospitality features. And for your further enjoyment you can make use of our library, billiards room, exercise room, sauna, solarium and rod room.

Here, at the Craigellachie, all the amenities of an international class hotel have been tastefully incorporated to retain all the original charm of a delightful Scottish country house.

Craigellachie Hotel
Craigellachie
Speyside
Banffshire
AB38 9SR
Tel: (01340) 881204
Fax: (01340) 881253

Meldrum House dates from the 13th century and originally took the form of a Z plan tower house, built on a outcrop of rock.

This part of the house has formed the nucleus for later additions in the 17th and 19th centuries. The most significant additions being the 17th stone staircase, completed in 1625 by William Seton and built over the original entrance, and the stable block with its own impressive gatehouse.

Set in acres of fields and garden, the house lies beside a small lake stocked with rainbow trout which may be fished by residents. Meldrum House enjoys an atmosphere closer to that of a private country home rather than a hotel , with a fine collection of antique furniture and paintings dating from many different periods.

Personally run by Douglas and Eileen Pearson, the house offers every comfort. The en suite bedrooms are enormous with large beds and superb antique furniture. The Dining Room offers high quality Scottish cooking featuring the very best of local produce and complemented by an extensive wine list and large selection of malt whiskies.

The hotel is ideally situated for golfing parties with a great number of golf courses in the vicinity, including the top class courses of Royal Aberdeen and Cruden Bay to the east, Newmachar to the west and Royal Duff House and Royal Tarclair to the north.

Meldrum House
Oldmeldrum
Aberdeenshire
AB51 OAE
Tel: (0651) 872294
Fax: (0651) 872484

Founded in 1780, Royal Aberdeen is the sixth oldest Golf Club in the world. For the first thirty five years of its existence the Club was known as The Society of Golfers at Aberdeen with membership of the Society being determined by ballot. They were clearly a meticulous group of gentlemen for in 1783 they became the first to introduce the five minute limit on searching for golf balls. A sensible idea you may think, but one that has caused the modern day Aberdeen Golfer much distress—a subject to which I shall return in due course.

In 1815, on the eve of the Battle of Waterloo, the Society changed its name to the Aberdeen Golf Club and in 1903 the Royal prefix was bestowed on the Club. Originally the members played over a strip of common land between the Rivers Don and Dee but in the second half of the 19th century the Club acquired its own course at Balgownie on the northern side of the River Don. Today Balgownie Links is regarded as one of Scotland's greatest Championship courses.

Ron MacAskill is both the **General Manager** and PGA **professional** at Royal Aberdeen and he may be contacted by telephone on **(0224) 702221** or **(0224) 702571**. All written correspondence should be addressed to him at **The Royal Aberdeen Golf Club, Balgownie, Bridge of Don, Aberdeen, AB2 8AT.**

Visitors are made extremely welcome at Royal Aberdeen and they may play at Balgownie on any day subject to making a tee reservation with the professional. The green fees for 1994 were set at £35 per round or £45 per day during the week with a £45 fee for a single round at the weekend. Travelling to Aberdeen is made fairly straightforward by the A92. From the south this road passes along the coast from Dundee via Arbroath, Montrose and Stonehaven to Aberdeen. It also connects the town to Fraserburgh in the north. Those approaching from the north west should find the A96 helpful (it in fact runs directly from Inverness.) Other roads which may prove of assistance are the A947 from Oldmeldrum and the A93 which links Aberdeen to Perth and passes through Blairgowrie. The links itself is situated two miles north of Aberdeen and can be sighted immediately to the right after crossing the River Don.

From its medal tees, Balgownie measures 6372 yards, par 70 (SSS 71) with the forward tees reducing the length to 6104 yards, par 69. Although perhaps not overly long, the course is very exposed to the elements and the wind can often make a mockery of some of the distances. There is also a considerable spread of gorse and the rough can be very punishing. It should be added that there are no fewer than ninety-two bunkers—ten of which appear on the short par three 8th! Balgownie has the traditional out and back links layout, the front nine hugging the shore and the back nine returning on the landside towards the Clubhouse.

The outward nine is perhaps the more interesting of the two halves; the eminent golf writer Sam McKinlay was moved to say: 'There are few courses in these islands with a better, more testing, more picturesque outward nine than Balgownie'. However, the most difficult hole on the course is possibly the last hole, a lengthy par four, well bunkered and usually played into the teeth of the prevailing wind.

Golfers may also wish to investigate the Club's second course, the shorter Silverburn Course which measures 4066 yards, par 60.

Royal Aberdeen has played host to a number of major events including the British Youth's Championship, the Scottish Amateur Championship and the Northern Open Championship. In 1993, the British Seniors Championship was played over the Balgownie links. Numerous exhibition matches have also taken place; participants have included Tom Morris Junior, Harry Vardon, James Braid, John H. Taylor, Walter Hagen and Henry Cotton.

I now return to the matter of the five minute rule. In the opening paragraph, I mentioned how in 1783 the Aberdeen Golfers had introduced the five minute limit on searching for lost balls. Well somebody somewhere it seems didn't approve and 200 years later a plague of crows was sent to deliver retribution. Throughout the long summers of 1983 and 1984 the crows determined that no one should search for his ball. They descended on the links stealing Titleists and Top-Flites, Pinnacles and Penfolds. Several Members had more than one ball stolen in a round. Numerous suggestions were put forward as to how to rid the links of this turbulent pest but alas to no avail. Even a crow trap was built but still they plundered. Then just as suddenly as they came, they left, never it is presumed to return. Sanity restored, Balgownie became once more one of Britain's friendliest links.

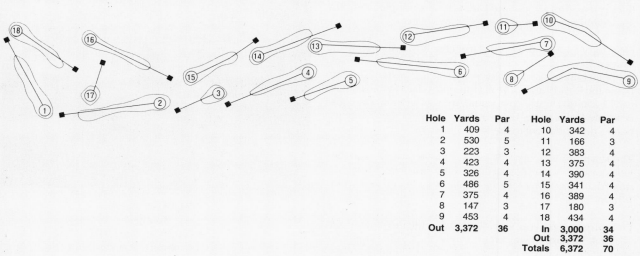

Hole	Yards	Par	Hole	Yards	Par
1	409	4	10	342	4
2	530	5	11	166	3
3	223	3	12	383	4
4	423	4	13	375	4
5	326	4	14	390	4
6	486	5	15	341	4
7	375	4	16	389	4
8	147	3	17	180	3
9	453	4	18	434	4
Out	**3,372**	**36**	**In**	**3,000**	**34**
			Out	**3,372**	**36**
			Totals	**6,372**	**70**

Dalrachney Lodge Hotel

Country House Hotel located in the centre of the Scottish Highlands just off the A9 and ideally located for fast access to eleven excellent courses. Rise early, walk over to the Carrbridge course and have nine holes prior to breakfast. A few minutes drive to Boat of Garten course in the morning then ten minutes further to Granton-on-Spey course in the afternoon. Local mini bus hire can be arranged for groups.

Completely restored former Hunting Lodge complex set in 16 acres of partly Scots pine wooded gardens directly by our own stretch of the Dulnain river which borders the grounds. We offer 28 bedrooms in five separate buildings ranging from suites and standard rooms to self-catering cottages with kitchens. The Main Lodge offers all the facilities expected of a three star, highly commended four crown Hotel. There are panoramic views of the Dulnain Valley and the Cairngorms beyond.

Accent on the finest food with three menus, table d'hote, à la Carte and bar, available daily in Stalkers Bar and the traditional Lodge Restaurant. Range of over 150 malts, wines and liqueurs.

Our golfing guests generally arrange their own schedules but if you are unfamiliar with our area we can advise and provide course information and driving times from Carrbridge.

It is not surprising that much more exists in our area for the sportsman. Dalrachney Lodge was, in the Victorian and Edwardian periods, central to one of the principal sporting estates in Scotland. Queen Victoria referred to Carrbridge as "the jewel of the north" and other royalty were regular in residence. There is no finer area for Roe Buck, Deer Stalking and Grouse. Also a bird watchers paradise with Eagles and Osprey seen from the Hotel. We can arrange fishing on 30 miles of the Rivers Spey, Findhorn and Dulnain with Ghillie, tuition and rod hire as required.

Under the personal supervision of resident owners Helen and Grant Swanney. Please telephone, fax or write for brochure and group rate details. We shall be happy to assist in any way we can.

Dalrachney Lodge Hotel
Carrbridge
Inverness-shire
PH23 3AT
Tel: (0479) 841252
Fax: (0479) 841382

The Castle Hotel

The Castle Hotel is a magnificent eighteenth-century stone building, standing in its own grounds above the ruins of Huntly Castle, on the banks of the River Deveron. Sandston as it was originally known was built as a family home to the Dukes of Gordon.

Run by a keen hotel family, the Castle Hotel has recently been refurbished providing good comfortable accommodation with en suite facilities. Good traditional food using local fresh produce is served in our spacious Dining Room, complemented by a selection from the well stocked wine cellar.

Only forty minutes drive away from the Royal Aberdeen and Cruden Bay Golf courses (listed in the U.K. top fifty courses) the hotel is ideally situated for your Golfing holiday. Closer to home the Royal Tarlour, Duff House Royal and Elgin courses can be found. Huntly's own attractive and well laid out eighteen hole Golf course, Cooper Park, lies at the bottom of the hotel's drive adjacent to the River Deveron.

The town lies in Scotland's famous Castle Country and provides an abundance of leisure and sporting activities. Not to be missed are the many famous distilleries which make up the Whisky Trail.

Our aim is to make your stay an enjoyable and memorable one. We look forward to welcoming you to the Castle Hotel. Situated on the main A96 between Aberdeen (45 minutes away) and Inverness the hotel is easily reached by road, rail and air.

The Castle Hotel
Huntly
Aberdeenshire AB54 4SH
Tel: (0466) 792696
Fax: (0466) 792641

Cruden Bay

 One often reads of famous Golf Clubs having been founded in local hostelries: Deal (The Black Horse), Crail (The Golf Inn) and Hoylake (The Royal) to name but three. Well, the birth of Cruden Bay apparently took place during a meeting in the North of Scotland Bank—one presumes a much more sober affair! The precise date of the meeting was 16th June 1898 and in March the following year the Cruden Bay Hotel and Golf Course were opened.

The Hotel (long since demolished) and the 18 hole golf course were originally both owned by the Great North of Scotland Railway Company. Within a month of their opening the company staged a professional tournament which attracted many of the day's leading players including Harry Vardon (then Open Champion), James Braid and Ben Sayers. The event proved an outstanding success with Vardon taking the first prize of £30.

Today the Club's full address is the **Cruden Bay Golf Club, Aulton Road, Cruden Bay, Peterhead, Aberdeenshire AB42 7NN.** In addition to the 18 hole Championship Course there is also a well-kept 9 hole short course, the St Olaf.

The present **Secretary** is **Mr George Donald MBE.** He may be contacted via the above address and by telephone on **(0779) 812285**, and fax:(0779) 812945. The Club's **PGA professional and club administrator, Robbie Stewart**, can be reached on **(0779) 812414**. Casual visitors are welcome at Cruden Bay, although not surprisingly certain restrictions apply during Saturdays and Sundays. It is generally advisable to telephone the Club to make an advance reservation, particularly as a starting sheet is in operation daily from April to September. Visitors should also note that they are not permitted to play the 18 hole course between 4.30 pm and 6.30 pm on Wednesdays and that at weekends, unless accompanied by a Member, handicap certificates must be provided. No specific restrictions relate to the St Olaf course.

In 1994 the green fee to play on the Championship course was priced at £20 for a weekday ticket, with £28 payable at weekends. A week's golf could be purchased for £85 and a full fortnight for £140. For juniors (under 18) the respective rates were £10, £14, £40 and £70. A day's golf on the St Olaf course could be obtained for £10 during the week and £15 at weekends (£5 and £7.50 for juniors).

Cruden Bay is situated on Scotland's Buchan Coast, some 23 miles north of Aberdeen and seven miles south of the old whaling port of Peterhead. The course itself has a dramatic setting with nearby Slains Castle providing a rather eerie backdrop. Bram Stoker, who spent some time in these parts is reputed to have been inspired by the castle when writing his Dracula stories. Fortunately the rest of the surrounding countryside bears little resemblance to Transylvania and strangers should find travelling in the area a pleasant experience. The best route when journeying from the south is probably by way of the A92 coastal road which runs from Dundee via Montrose and through Aberdeen. One should leave the A92 near Newburgh and follow the A975 direct to Cruden Bay. The A92 approaches from the North via Fraserburgh and Peterhead.

Originally laid out by Thomas Simpson, Cruden Bay is very much a traditional Scottish links and there are a number of blind and semi-blind shots. Par is a fairly tight 70 (SSS. 71). From the ladies' tees the course measures 5761 yards (par 74). A good old Scottish burn is a predominant feature of the course affecting several of the holes, there are a number of vast sand dunes and hills to be negotiated while the beach too (if one is a little wayward) can come into play around the 14th and 15th. As one might expect given its geography the wind is often a major factor and the golfer that can master the low run-up shot to the subtly contoured greens will be on to a winner. The views over the Bay of Cruden naturally add to the pleasure of the round, and it isn't difficult to comprehend why *Golf World* magazine ranks Cruden Bay amongst its top 50 courses in the British Isles.

The magnificently appointed Clubhouse has the kind of atmosphere one comes to expect in this part of the world—very friendly— and casual dress may be worn at all times. Meals are served throughout the day with lunches, high teas, dinners and some delightful steak suppers being offered in addition to bar snacks.

South of Hadrian's Wall, Cruden Bay is probably not as well known as it ought to be. The legions who arrange their golfing trips around the more traditional favourites often miss out on some of Scotland's finest courses. Cruden Bay should be included in anyone's itinerary—it is a genuinely spectacular course and perhaps of equal importance, a place where the warmest of welcomes can be guaranteed.

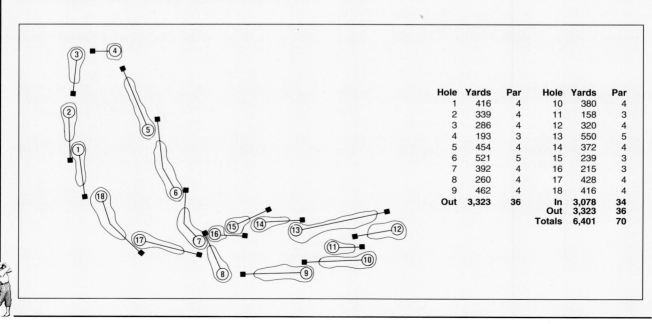

Hole	Yards	Par	Hole	Yards	Par
1	416	4	10	380	4
2	339	4	11	158	3
3	286	4	12	320	4
4	193	3	13	550	5
5	454	4	14	372	4
6	521	5	15	239	3
7	392	4	16	215	3
8	260	4	17	428	4
9	462	4	18	416	4
Out	**3,323**	**36**	**In**	**3,078**	**34**
			Out	**3,323**	**36**
			Totals	**6,401**	**70**

Stotfield Hotel

The Stotfield Hotel is situated overlooking the superb championship golf course of the Moray Golf Club - a true links course. For the less accomplished golfer there is a second 18 hole course alongside of which is the sandy beach of Moray Firth and in the distance lie the Sutherland Hills.

The Stotfield Hotel is privately owned by Mike and Patricia Warnes who, with the assistance of their son Damon, enjoy an enviable reputation for personal supervision. The hotel will celebrate its centenary very shortly and combines modern amenities with traditional charm. It has the comfortable and friendly atmosphere of a family run hotel, with 50 en suite bedrooms all equipped with colour television, direct dial telephone, alarm clock radio, and tea and coffee making facilities. The superior rooms which overlook the golf gourse also have trouser presses and hairdriers.

A high standard of services and cuisine is offered with menus ranging from 'sizzler' steaks served in the Firth Bar, table d'hote dinner and traditional Sunday lunch served in the main dining room, or for those wishing to enjoy a more specialised cuisine one may choose from the a la carte menu which is served in the sun lounge overlooking the sparkling water of the Moray Firth which reflects the magnificent Lossiemouth sunsets.

The head chef Mr Derek Roy, places special emphasis on using fresh local produce of which salmon smoked in oak chippings from the Macallan distillery, seafood crepes, fillet de boeuf Balmoral are amongst his specialities. To enhance the menus an extensive wine list is available which includes organic wines. A new attraction for a relaxed style of eating is the ' Bourbon Street Bar and Grill', specialising in American-style barbecued cuisine with imported beers.

For those interested in the Whisky Trail one may commence at the Forth Bar with its cosy relaxing atmosphere, sampling the extensive range of 120 malt whiskies.

As well as the Moray Golf Club, the Stotfield Hotel is surrounded by numerous golf courses, many of them championship status and all within a short distance. Golf parties are catered for with specialised golfing packages available. Hotel guests playing the Moray Golf Courses enjoy a 100% discount on green fees.

Your hosts Mike, Patricia and Damon Warnes, together with their staff will endeavour to make your Scottish golfing holiday a memorable one.

Stotfield Hotel
Stotfield Road
Lossiemouth
Moray IV31 6QS
Tel:(0343) 812011
Fax:(0343) 814820
AA***
STB 4 Crowns Commended

300

For a relatively small nation, the Scots have given the world much to savour; two of its greatest gifts are golf and whisky. The origins of each are shrouded in mystery, lost in the murky depths of time, yet both have never been more popular—especially it seems among the Americans and Japanese! There can surely be few better places to enjoy a combination of golf and whisky than in Lossiemouth in Morayshire. Within a short drive of some of the finest whisky distilleries in the world is one of the greatest links courses in Scotland. As the Moray Golf Club has its own ten year old single malt whisky, it would seem a perfect place in which to while away a few days—there is certainly an added allure here to a drink at the 19th!

I've no idea when whisky was first consumed in Morayshire but records indicate that golf was being played in the area from at least the late 16th century. In 1596, Walter Hay (presumably no relation to Walter Hagen) an Elgin goldsmith, found himself in hot water with the local authorities for 'playing at the boulis and golff on Sundaye'. The first Moray Golf Club at Lossiemouth was formed in 1875 but lapsed after some years and the present Club was founded in 1889. The initial 16 holes soon became 18 and as golf mushroomed in popularity, Lossiemouth became one of Scotland's most fashionable golfing resorts. Indeed, the popularity of Lossiemouth grew to such an extent that in 1905 an additional nine hole course was constructed to relieve the congestion on the Old Course. Bringing us up to the present, the late Sir Henry Cotton was called in as a golf architect in 1970 and a second 18 holes was opened for play in 1976.

The current **Secretary** at the Moray Golf Club is **James Hamilton** who may be contacted by telephone on **(0343) 812018**. All correspondence should be addressed to **The Secretary, The Moray Golf Club, Lossiemouth, Moray IV31 6QS. Alistair Thomson**, the club's helpful **professional** can be contacted by telephone on **(0343) 813330**, and by fax on (0343) 815102. Visitors are welcome at Lossiemouth seven days a week but it is advisable to book by telephone to avoid disappointment in the summer months. The cost of a day's golf on the Old Course in 1994 was pitched at £26 on weekdays with £35 payable at weekends and on the New Course at £20 on weekdays and £25 at weekends. Again in 1994, weekly tickets were available on the Old for £80 and on the New for £60. Visitors may be

required to produce handicap certificates.

Travelling to Lossiemouth is fairly straightforward. The main road from Aberdeen to Inverness is the A96 which passes through Elgin, where the well signposted A941 will take the motorist the five miles to Lossiemouth. We have already mentioned one of the pleasures of the 19th hole and, as one might imagine, the atmosphere in the clubhouse is decidedly relaxed and friendly. Casual dress may be worn at all times. Meals are served throughout the day but visitors are encouraged to make their arrangements with the catering manager before starting their round.

The **New Course** at Lossiemouth is now well established and, if a little less testing than the Old at 6,005 yards, par 69, is still a worthy challenge and a troublesome ditch comes into play at no fewer than five holes. However, after a day's golf at Lossiemouth, it is the Old Course that most first time visitors will relish a return to—if only to get even with it! Measuring 6,643 yards from the medal tees, with a demanding par of 71 (6,131 yards, par 75 for the ladies) it has many outstanding holes and like St Andrews it starts and finishes in the town.

The most celebrated sequence of holes on the **Old Course** at Lossiemouth comes towards the end of the round. The 14th, appropriately called 'Sea' for it is played directly towards it, is a fine par four and is immediately followed by a most attractive par three. The best, however, is saved for the very end. The 18th, a par four measuring 423 yards, has been described as 'the noblest finishing hole in Scotland'. With the gardens of the Stotfield houses on the right and several bunkers patrolling the left side of the fairway, the second shot has to be played to an elevated plateau green which sits in a natural amphitheatre in front of the handsome old clubhouse. The green is also beside the main street of the town and as a small critical crowd often gathers to watch players 'come home' there is no more appropriate place to register one's first birdie of the day!

Since 1912, the Scottish Ladies Amateur Championship has been played on four occasions at Lossiemouth, and the Club played host to both men's and ladies' Scottish Amateur Championships during its centenary year in 1989. The Northern Scottish Open was played at Moray in May 1991 for the eighth time, a fitting tribute to a golf course which is regarded as one of the finest tests on the Scottish Tartan Tour circuit.

Old Course

Hole	Yards	Par	Hole	Yards	Par
1	333	4	10	314	4
2	493	5	11	415	4
3	400	4	12	402	4
4	203	3	13	422	4
5	419	4	14	417	4
6	141	3	15	190	3
7	439	4	16	359	4
8	460	4	17	497	5
9	316	4	18	423	4
Out	**3,204**	**35**	**In**	**3,439**	**36**
			Out	3,204	35
			Totals	6,643	71

Culloden House is a handsome Georgian mansion with a tradition of lavish hospitality stretching back hundreds of years. Among its famous visitors was Bonnie Prince Charlie who fought his last battle by the park walls. The house stands in 40 acres of elegant lawns and parkland, enhanced by stately oaks and beech trees.

The resident proprietors, Ian and Marjory McKenzie, extend a warm welcome to all visitors to their hotel. Culloden House is decorated to the highest standard, particularly the comfortable drawing room which is decorated with magnificent Adam-style plasterwork.

Every bedroom is individually decorated and has direct dial telephone, television , trouser press, bath and shower. Guests can choose from four poster rooms, standard rooms or a room with a jacuzzi. The garden mansion also has non-smoking garden suites. Dining is a memorable experience at Culloden House; the emphasis in the Adam style dining room is on friendly and unobtrusive service matched by the highest standards of cuisine. The wine cellars hold a superb range of wines from the great vineyards of the world and there is a wide selection of aged malt whiskies.

Leisure facilities include a hard tennis court, sauna and solarium. There is so much to visit in the area - golf, fishing and shooting can be arranged and the Highlands, Loch Ness and Inverness are just waiting to be explored. Also nearby are Cawdor Castle, the Clava Cairns and Culloden Battlefield.

Situated three miles from the centre of Inverness, off the A96, Inverness - Nairn Road, Culloden House extends the best of Scottish hospitality to all its guests.

Culloden House
Inverness
IV1 2NZ
Tel: (01463) 790461
Fax: (01463) 792181
Toll Free Fax: (USA) 1800 3737987

Aglorious setting, a superb Championship course and a warm welcome to visiting golfers—that, in the proverbial nutshell, is Nairn. In 1987 the Club celebrated its centenary and played host to both men's and ladies' Scottish Amateur Championships; in 1994 the Club staged the British Amateur Championship.

Originally designed by Archie Simpson, and modified two years later by 'Old' Tom Morris, the present layout owes much to the work of James Braid, arguably the greatest of all Scottish golf architects.

Nairn is very much a traditional links with the opening holes stretching out along the shoreline. At the 10th comes the inevitable about-turn, and the head for home. It is a fine test of golf and with the abundant heather, the great sea of gorse and the distant mountains providing a spectacular backdrop, this is a veritable haven.

Being so far north on the golfing map Nairn has probably not received the recognition it must surely deserve—at least in terms of attracting professional tournaments. Yet with an airport (Inverness) a mere 8 miles away and an adequate road and rail network Nairn ought not to be considered too remote in the way that Royal Dornoch traditionally is.

A refreshing atmosphere prevails throughout the Club. Visitors to the area are actively encouraged to play on the links and there is no requirement for a handicap certificate. Except during peak hours at weekends, visitors may play when they choose, though early starters should note that fourballs are not permitted before 9.30am.

For a genuine Championship course the green fees at Nairn are fairly reasonable. In 1994 (summer) the Club is charging £26 for a weekday round with £32 payable at weekends. For £10 extra, a day ticket can be purchased. Junior golfers should find Nairn extremely welcoming—in 1994 their daily green fee is £13.

The Club's **Secretary** is **Mr. Jim Somerville**; anyone wishing to arrange a Society game should contact him via **Nairn Golf Club, Seabank Road, Nairn, Highland IV12 4HB** either by telephone on **(0667) 453208** or by fax on (0667) 456328. Both clubs and caddy carts can be hired from the **professional, Robin Fyfe, tel. (0667) 452787.**

Unless the long distance traveller has made use of Inverness airport (80 minutes flying time from London and 40 minutes from Glasgow) he is sure to have taken in some wonderfully spectacular scenery. Motoring from the south the A9 runs from Perth to Inverness via Pitlochry, Blair Atholl and Aviemore—over the mountains, through the valleys, beside forests and lochs—breathtaking stuff! The A96 links Inverness with Nairn, a journey of some 15 miles passing Culloden Moor—scene of that rather nasty skirmish. An alternative route from Glasgow is to follow the A82 which runs to the west of Loch Lomond, through Glencoe and along the shores of Loch Ness all the way to Inverness, an equally beautiful road. From the east, the A96 is the main Aberdeen to Inverness road, passing through Nairn. The golf course is located on the town's west shore.

From the medal tees the course measures 6452 yards and has a par of 71 (the Championship tees extend the course by a further 270 yards) whilst the ladies play over 5755 yards, par being 75. Nairn is certainly no monster and accuracy rather than length should determine the quality of scoring. The front nine is the shorter of the two although the prevailing south-westerly may well cause this to be the tougher half. Anyone suffering a bout of the dreaded sliced tee-shot is likely to find himself doing battle with the Moray Firth—the early holes really do run very close to the sea. The Scottish golf writer Sam McKinlay clearly relished the early challenge for he once said 'There is no more attractive 1st tee in all Scotland.' (It's amazing what a good opening drive can inspire!)

Perhaps the best series of holes, however, are found on the back nine, namely holes 12, 13 and 14. Anyone who can manage three pars here can call himself a golfer. Staying out of the gorse and avoiding the numerous well-positioned bunkers is undoubtedly the key to a good round, for with the magnificent, and not overly large greens, there is no excuse for poor putting at Nairn. And so, as they say, to the nineteenth and at Nairn that means entering one of the newest and most relaxing clubhouses in Britain. During summer the Club hosts a number of open competitions and these are invariably well supported. It isn't difficult to imagine why. For those of us who enjoy our golf in pleasant and dramatic surroundings and who occasionally feel the urge to get away from it all, there can surely be no finer place to visit than Nairn.

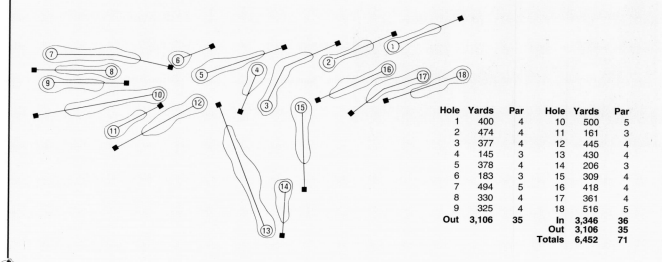

Hole	Yards	Par	Hole	Yards	Par
1	400	4	10	500	5
2	474	4	11	161	3
3	377	4	12	445	4
4	145	3	13	430	4
5	378	4	14	206	3
6	183	3	15	309	4
7	494	5	16	418	4
8	330	4	17	361	4
9	325	4	18	516	5
Out	**3,106**	**35**	**In**	**3,346**	**36**
			Out	**3,106**	**35**
			Totals	**6,452**	**71**

The Links Hotel

The Links Hotel has a magnificent situation overlooking the 18 hole Links Golf Course at Brora. Set just off the main A9, about one hours drive North of Inverness, this privately owned hotel combines old fashioned values with the thoroughly modern needs of today's traveller.

All bedrooms have a sea or mountain view, private bathroom, radio, direct dial telephone, colour television, tea and coffee making facilities.

Diners can enjoy one of the finest views in the North of Scotland from the hotel's Seaforth Restaurant. Here, the Chef prepares the finest cuisine using only the very best of local ingredients. For a spot of relaxation guests might like to sample one of the many malt whiskies that are on offer in one of the two lounge bars.

Golfers need venture no further than the hotel's terrace for a challenging game on Brora Links Course. Royal Dornoch, Golspie and Tain courses are all within easy travelling distance and provide interesting and varied alternatives.

The Links Hotel
Golf Road,
Brora,
Sutherland, KW9 6QS.
Tel: (01408) 621225
Fax: (01408) 621383.

The Royal Marine

Oiginally designed in 1910 as a private country house by the renowned Scottish architect Sir Robert Lorimer, The Royal Marine has recently undergone major refurbishment, accomplished without losing the natural character and charm of the original building.

Original antique furniture and wood panelling glow with the warmth of log fires and convivial company. All eleven individually designed bedrooms have been redecorated to a high standard without losing the charm and comfort of the past. The traditional dining room serves a 'Taste of Scotland' menu using the best local produce,fresh fish, meat and game.

For a less formal, more relaxed occasion, guests may wish to try a bar lunch or supper in the Hunter's lounge. In keeping with the country house ambience the hotel offers residents a range of leisure and sporting facilities. After dinner guests can enjoy snooker or croquet and there is also an indoor heated swimming pool and sauna. The hotel offers golfing breaks on Broras own wonderful links course and there are three other championship courses within 30 minutes of the hotel.

The Royal Marine Hotel,
Golf Road,
Brora,
Sutherland.
Tel: (01408) 621252
Fax: (01408) 621181.

Usually when a person describes his first visit to a golf course as 'the most fun I've had playing golf in my whole life,' very little is thought of it. However, when that person happens to be Tom Watson, five times Open Champion, one tends to sit up and take notice. Like Ben Crenshaw and Greg Norman who have also made the pilgrimage, Watson was enchanted by the 'Star of the North'.

There are two words that are normally associated with Royal Dornoch; one is 'greatness' and the other is 'remoteness'. Situated fifty miles north of Inverness, Dornoch enjoys a kind of splendid isolation. It is often described as the course every golfer wants to play but the one that very few actually do.

So what is the charm of Dornoch? Firstly, there's the setting (this is when people forgive its remoteness!) Bordered by the Dornoch Firth and a glorious stretch of sand, distant hills with their ever-changing moods fill the horizon creating a feeling that one is playing on a stage. And then of course, there's the history: Royal Dornoch Golf Club dates from 1877 but mention is made of golf being played on the links at least as early as 1616. Writing in the 17th century Sir Robert Gordon wrote of Dornoch: 'About this town are the fairest and largest links on any part of Scotland, fit for Archery, Golfing, Ryding and all other exercises; they doe surpasse the fields of Montrose and St Andrews.' Finally, and most importantly, there's the very links itself described on more than one occasion as the most natural golf course in the world; to quote Tom Watson again, 'One of the great courses of the five continents.'

At the time of writing a new Golf Secretary or Manager was in the process of being appointed, however the office may be contacted by telephone on **(0862) 810219** and by fax on **(0862) 810792**. All written correspondence should be addressed to **The Manager, Royal Dornoch Golf Club, Golf Road, Dornoch IV25 3LW Sutherland. William Skinner** is the Club's **professional**; he may be reached on **(0862) 810902**.

Visitors are welcome at Royal Dornoch seven days a week. However, it is probably wise to telephone the Club prior to setting off to check if any tee reservations have been made—an ever-growing number of people are now making the trip and during the months of July and August the links can get busy. The cost of a single round on the Championship course in 1994 was set at £35. A three day (Monday, Tuesday and Wednesday) ticket is available, priced at £75 in 1994. There is now a second eighteen hole course at Dornoch, the Struie Course measuring 5242 yards, par 68. A day ticket, enabling a round over both courses was available in 1994 at a cost of £45. A day ticket for the Struie Course alone could be purchased for £15 during the week (£10 per round) with £60 securing a full week's golf.

Travelling to Dornoch gets ever easier. The A9 runs from Perth to John O'Groats, Perth being linked to Edinburgh by the M90. There are regular flights from London and other parts of the country to Inverness Airport and the links itself has an adjacent landing strip for light aircraft; moreover there is now a road bridge over the Dornoch Firth and this reduces the motoring time from Inverness to 40 minutes. By today's standards Dornoch could probably be described as being of only medium length, the links measuring 6577 yards, par 70 (SSS 72). However, the last thing in the world that Dornoch is, is an easy course. It has been said that the prevailing wind at Dornoch comes from every direction but even when the winds don't thunder in from across the Firth or down from the hills, the links can be the proverbial 'smiler with the knife'.

Although the club was founded in 1877, ten years later when 'Old' Tom Morris was brought from St. Andrews to survey the links there was still only a rather crude nine hole layout. The master craftsman set to work and not only completely redesigned the nine but extended the course to a full eighteen holes. By using the natural contours of the terrain many magnificent plateau greens were created and despite major alterations made to the links by John Sutherland thirty years later, it is the plateau greens that remain the hallmark of Dornoch, the classic example perhaps being the celebrated 14th, Foxy, a double dog-leg hole. Donald Ross, considered by many to be the greatest of all golf architects was for many years the professional and head green keeper at Dornoch and several of the great American courses he later designed incorporate many of Dornoch's features. Today there are signs that Dornoch is at last shedding its remoteness tag. In 1985 the Club staged the Amateur Championship for the first time in its history—this being in the minds of many alarmingly overdue. It may be to indulge in pure fantasy but one cannot help wondering what it would be like if the hallowed links were ever visited by the greatest of all compliments.

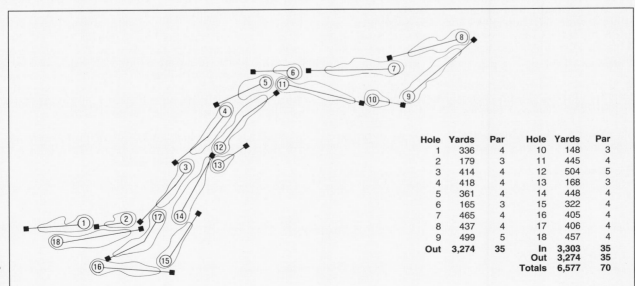

Hole	Yards	Par	Hole	Yards	Par
1	336	4	10	148	3
2	179	3	11	445	4
3	414	4	12	504	5
4	418	4	13	168	3
5	361	4	14	448	4
6	165	3	15	322	4
7	465	4	16	405	4
8	437	4	17	406	4
9	499	5	18	457	4
Out	**3,274**	**35**	**In**	**3,303**	**35**
			Out	**3,274**	**35**
			Totals	**6,577**	**70**

Knockomie Hotel

Knockomie lies well off the road with views over the Royal Burgh of Forres and on towards Findhorn and is a rare Scottish example of the Arts and Crafts house. The hotel stands amid twenty-five acres of grounds. Part of the house dates back 150 years.

As you enter by the front door you are immediately welcomed by the panelled hallway with its beamed ceiling. To your right is our Cocktail Bar where you can relax in the warm friendly atmosphere. Our well stocked bar offers a wide selection of Liquors and Spirits and we pride ourselves on an enviable collection of Malt Whiskies. Superb Bar Lunches are available at reasonable prices.

In the Fully Licensed Restaurant, which caters for up to thirty-five people, the hotel endeavours to produce culinary art with flair and imagination, whilst utilising the very best of Scottish produce. Set and A La Carte Menus are offered. The Wine Cellar boasts an extensive Selection of wines from various countries.

The Flower Room is a small area within the main restaurant. It is ideal for parties of ten—creating an atmosphere of privacy and intimacy. The walls feature fine watercolours and silks of flowers.

Fourteen tastefully decorated bedrooms are individually named after local Distilleries. All offer en suite shower/bathroom, tea and coffee making facilities, direct dialling telephones, 24hr laundry service, television and room service menus. Hairdryer, trouser press and ironing facilities are also available.

The hotel has just completed an extension, with another panelled Lounge area with fire place, overlooking the garden towards Forres. There are a further seven en suite bedrooms and one suite with four rooms on the ground floor, one with additional facilities for the disabled. Some rooms feature half tester beds, some rooms four-posters. Two rooms have patio doors opening on to the gardens.

The hotel has books, magazines and games to help you relax. Enjoy a stroll around the gardens. Practice on our Croquet Lawn or learn to play Boules.

Grantown Road,
Forres
Moray
IV36 0SG
Tel: (0709) 673146
Fax: (0309) 673290

Key

To avoid disappointment
it is advisable to telephone
in advance

***Visitors welcome at most times
**Visitors usually allowed on
weekdays only
*Visitors not normally permitted
(Mon, Wed) No visitors
on specified days

Approximate Green Fees
A   £30 plus
B   £20 to £30
C   £15 to £25
D   £10 to £20
E   under £10
F   Greens fees on application

Restrictions
G   Guests only
H   Handicap certificate required
H (24) Handicap of 24 or less
L   Letter of introduction required
M   Visitor must be a member of
another recognised club.

GRAMPIAN

Aboyne G.C.
(03398) 86328
Formaston Park, Aboyne
(18)5910 yards/***/D

Alford G.C.
(09755) 62178
Montgarry Road, Alford
(18)5290 yards/***/D

Auchenblae G.C.
(0561) 378869
Auchenblae, Laurencekirk
(9)2174 yards/***/E

Auchmill G.C.
(0224) 714577
Auchmill, Aberdeen
(18)5439 yards/***/F

Ballater G.C.
(03397) 55567
Ballater, Aberdeenshire
(18)6109 yards/***/D

Banchory G.C.
(0330) 822365
Kinneskie, Banchory
(18)5305 yards/***/D

Balnagask G.C.
(0224) 876407
St Fitticks Road, Aberdeen
(18)5468 yards/***/F

Bon-Accord G.C.
(0224) 633464
Golf Course Road, Aberdeen
(18)6384 yards/***/F

Braemar G.C.
(03397) 41618
Cluniebank, Braemar
(18)4916 yards/***/D

Buckpool G.C.
(0542) 832236
Barhill Road, Buckie
(18)6259 yards/***/D

Caledonian G.C.
(0224) 632 443
Golf Road, Aberdeen
(18)6384 yards/***/F

Cruden Bay G.C.
(0779) 812285
Aulton Road, Cruden Bay
(9)4710 yards/***/D
(18)6370 yards/***/B

Cullen G.C.
(0542) 840685
The Links, Cullen, Buckie
(18)4610 yards/***/D

Deeside G.C.
(0224) 869457
Bieldside, Aberdeen
(18)5972 yards/***/D/H

Duff House Royal G.C.
(0261) 812062
Barnyards, Banff
(18)6161 yards/***/D/H

Dufftown G.C.
(0340) 820325
Dufftown
(18)5308 yards/***/(Tues/Wed
pm)/D

Dunecht House G.C.
(0330) 860404
Dunecht, Skene
(9)3135 yards/***/F

Elgin G.C.
(0343) 542338
Hardhillock, Elgin
(18)6401 yards/***/D-C

Forres G.C.
(0309) 672949
Muiryshade, Forres
(18)6240 yards/***/D/H

Fraserburgh G.C.
(0346) 518287
Philorth, Fraserburgh
(18)6217 yards/***/F

Garmouth and Kingston G.C.
(034387) 388
Garmouth, Fochabers, Moray
(18)5649 yards/***/D

Hazelhead G.C.
(0224) 321830
Hazelhead Park, Aberdeen
(18)5303 yards/***/F
(18)5673 yards/***/F
(9)2531 yards/***/F

Hopeman G.C.
(0343) 830578
Hopeman, Moray
(18)5439 yards/***/D

Huntly G.C.
(0466) 792643
Cooper Park, Huntly
(18)5399 yards/***/(Wed/Thur)/D

Insch G.C.
(0464) 20291
Golf Terrace, Insch
(18)5632 yards/***/(Mon/Tues/Wed
pm)/D

Inverallochy G.C.
(0346) 582000
Inverallochy, Nr Fraserburgh
(18)5137 yards/***/E

Inverurie G.C.
(0467) 620207

Blackhall Road, Inverurie
(18)5711 yards/***/D

Keith G.C.
(0542) 882469
Fife Park, Keith
(18)5811 yards/***/D

Kemnay G.C.
(0467) 642225
Monymusk Road, Kemnay
(9)5502 yards/***/(Mon/Tues/Thurs
pm)/E

Kings Links G.C.
(0224) 632269
Golf Road, Kings Links, Aberdeen
(18)5838 metres/***/E-D

Kintore G.C.
(0467) 632631
Balbithan Road, Kintore, Inverurie
(18)5985 yards/***/F

Macdonald G.C.
(0358) 720576
Hospital Road, Ellon
(18)5986 yards/***/F

Moray G.C.
(0434) 812018
Stotfield Road, Lossiemouth
(18)6643 yards/***/B/H
(18)6005 yards/***/C/H

Murcar G.C.
(0224) 704345
Bridge of Don, Aberdeen
(18)6240 yards/**/C

Newburgh-on-Ythan G.C.
(0358) 789438
Newburgh, Aberdeenshire
(9)6404 yards/***/(Tues pm)/D

Newmachar G.C.
(0651) 863002
Swailend, Newmachar
(18)6605 yards/**/C/H

Nigg Bay G.C.
(0224) 871286
St Fitticks Road, Balnagask,
Aberdeen
(18)5984 yards/***/F/G

Old Meldrum G.C.
(0651) 872648
Kirkisrae, Old Meldrum
(18)5442 yards/***/D

Peterhead G.C.
(0779) 472149
Craigewan Links, Peterhead
(18)6182 yards/***/D
(9)2237 yards/***/D

Portlethen G.C.
(0224) 782572
Badentoy Road, Portlethen
(18)6735 yards/***/(Sat am)/D

Rothes G.C.
(0340) 831443
Blackhall, Rothes
(9)4956 yards/***/E

Royal Aberdeen G.C.
(0224) 702571
Balgownie, Bridge of Don,
Aberdeen
(18)6372 yards/**/B/H
(18)4033 yards/**/E/H

Royal Tarlair G.C.
(0261) 832897
Buchan Street, Macduff
(18)5866 yards/***/D

Spey Bay G.C.
(0343) 820424
Spey Bay, Fochabers, Moray
(18)6059 yards/***/F/H

Stonehaven G.C.
(0569) 762124
Cowie, Stonehaven
(18)5103 yards/***/(Sat/Sun am)/D

Strathlene G.C.
(0542) 831798
Portessie, Buckie
(18)6180 yards/***/D

Tarland G.C.
(03398) 81413
Tarland, Aboyne
(9)5812 yards/***/E

Torphins G.C.
(03398) 82115
Golf Road, Torphins, Banchory
(9)2330 yards/***/D

Turriff G.C.
(0888) 562982
Rosehall, Turriff
(18)6105 yards/***/D

Westhill G.C.
(0224) 740159
Westhill Heights, Westhill, Skene
(18)5866 yards/***/(Sat/Sun
pm)/D/H

HIGHLAND

Abernethy G.C.
(0479) 821305
Nethybridge
(9)2484 yards/***/E

Alness G.C.
(0349) 883877
Ardross Road, Alness
(9)2606 yards/***/F

Askernish G.C.
(08784) 541
Askernish, Lochboisdale, South Uist
(9)5114 yards/***/E

Boat of Garten G.C.
(0479) 831282
Boat of Garten
(18)5720 yards/***/F

Bonar Bridge G.C.
(0863) 766750
Bonar Bridge, Ardgay
(9)4626 yards/***/E

Brora G.C.
(0408) 621417
Golf Road, Brora, Sutherland
(18)6110 yards/***/D

Carrbridge G.C.
(0479) 841623
Carbridge
(9)2623 yards/***/C

Durness G.C.
(0971) 511364
Balnakeil, Durness
(9)5545 yards/***/(Sun am)/E

Fort Augustus G.C.
(0320) 366460
Markethill, Fort Augustus
(9)5454 yards/***/F

Fortrose and Rosemarkie G.C.
(0381) 620529
Ness Road East, Fortrose
(18)5973 yards/***/D

Fort William G.C.
(0397) 704464
North Road, Turlundy, Fort
William
(18)5686 yards/***/F

Gairloch G.C.
(0445) 2407
Gairloch
(9)2093 yards/***(Sun)/E

Golspie G.C.
(0408) 633266
Ferry Road, Golspie, Sutherland
(18)5900 yards/***/D

Grantown-on-Spey G.C.
(0479) 872079
Golf Course Road, Grantown-on-
Spey
(18)5745 yards/***/D

Helmsdale G.C.
(0431) 821240
Golf Road, Helmsdale
(9)1825 yards/***/F

Isle of Skye G.C.
(0478) 3235
Sligachan, Skye
(9)4796 yards/***/E

Invergordon G.C.
(0349) 852715
Cromlet Drive, Invergordon
(9)6028 yards/***/F

Inverness G.C.
(0463) 239882
Culcabock Road, Inverness
(18)6226 yards/***/D/H

Kingussie G.C.
(0540) 661374
Gynack Road, Kingussie
(18)5504 yards/***/D

Lochcarron G.C.
(05202) 257
Lochcarron, Strathcarron
(9)3578 yards/***/E

Lybster G.C.
(05932) 215
Main Street, Lybster, Caithness
(9)1898 yards/***/F

Muir of Ord G.C.
(0463) 870825
Great Northern Road, Muir of Ord
(18)5129 yards/***/D

Nairn G.C.
(0667) 453208
Seabank Road, Nairn
(18)6556 yards/***/B

Nairn Dunbar G.C.
(0667) 452741
Lochloy Road, Nairn
(18)6431 yards/***/D/H

Newtonmore G.C.
(05403) 673328

Golf Course Road, Newtonmore
(18)5890 yards/***/F

Reay G.C.
(084 781) 288
By Thurso, Caithness
(18)5865 yards/***/E

Royal Dornoch G.C.
(0862) 810219
Golf Road, Dornoch, Sutherland
(18)6577 yards/***/A
(18)5242 yards/***/D

Sconser G.C.
(0478) 613235
Sconser, Isle of Skye
(9)4796 yards/***/E

Spean Bridge G.C.
(0397) 704954
Spean Bridge, Fort William
(9)/***/F

Stornoway G.C.
(0851) 702240
Castle Grounds, Stornoway, Isle of
Lewis
(18)5119 yards/***(Sun)/D/H

Strathpeffer Spa G.C.
(0997) 421219
Strathpeffer
(18)4792 yards/***/D

Tain G.C.
(0862) 892314
Tain, Ross-shire
(18)6222 yards/***/D

Tarbat G.C.
(086287) 236

Portmahomack
(9)2329 yards***(Sun)/E

Thurso G.C.
(0847) 63807
Newlands of Geise, Thurso
(18)5818 yards/***/E

Torvean G.C.
(0463) 711434
Glenurquhart Road, Inverness
(18)5784 yards/***/E

Traigh G.C.
(06875) 234
Back of Kewppoch, Arisaig
(9)2100 yards/***/F

Wick G.C.
(0955) 2726
Reiss, Wick, Caithness
(18)5976 yards/***/F

**ORKNEY AND SHETLAND
ISLES**

Orkney G.C.
(0856) 2457
Grainbank, St Ola, by Kirkwall,
Orkney
(18)5406 yards/***/E

Shetland G.C.
(0595) 12691
Dale, PO Box 18, Lerwick
(18)5776 yards/***/E

Stromness G.C.
(0856) 850772
Ness, Stromness, Orkney
(18)4600 yards/***/E

Artist: **Linda Hartough ROYAL DORNOCH** *Courtesy of* **Old Troon Sporting Antiques**

Artist: **Douglas Adams** **THE LINKS** *Courtesy of:* **Burlington Gallery**

It is no secret that Northern Ireland has experienced a turbulent history; what is less widely known, however, is that it is a stunningly beautiful place. It is a land of forests and lakes, of mountains and glens. It boasts some of the most spectacular coastal scenery in the British Isles and where else can you view the handiwork of a giant? So much in a country no larger than Yorkshire.

The quality of golf is equally outstanding. There are approximately sixty courses in all, a large number of which are to be found close to the aforementioned coast enjoying some quite splendid isolation. Belfast, which is about the size of Bristol, has no shortage of good courses, and not just parkland types either, and then, of course, there are the two jewels in the crown—Portrush and Newcastle, or if you prefer, **Royal Portrush** and **Royal County Down.**

Belfast and County Down

Belfast is a likely starting point and getting there should be fairly straightforward. Approaching from Dublin it is a case of following the N1 and the A1, while from Britain car ferries run regularly from Stranraer. And travelling by air is even simpler should you be thinking of hiring a car when you arrive.

Having declared nothing but your urge to break 80, resist at all costs the temptation to zoom off northwards to Portrush or southwards to Newcastle - Belfast offers much more than you probably imagine. The best known golf course immediately at hand is the appropriately named **Royal Belfast**. It is situated just outside the city on the north coast alongside Belfast Lough and is a classic example of well manicured parkland golf. A number of holes here are very scenic, particularly around the turn and there is considerable challenge to combine with the charm. Royal Belfast is the oldest golf club in Ireland having been founded in 1881. It is therefore older than either Royal Lytham or Royal Birkdale just across the Irish Sea. The course is understandably very popular but with a little forward planning the visitor should be able to arrange a game. The clubhouse by the way is a magnificent 19th century building.

Remaining in Belfast, **Malone** Golf Club at Dunmurry is one of the leading inland courses in all Ireland—a visit is therefore strongly recommended—and two 'Parks' are also decidedly worth inspecting. The first is Belvoir (pronounce it Beever) and the second is Shandon. **Belvoir Park** lies about five miles south of the city centre, **Shandon Park** just to the north: both are championship courses. The former is definitely the pick of the two with its magnificent tree-lined fairways, however Shandon has the advantage of offering some interesting views over historical Stormont. **Clandeboye** Golf Club, not too far from Royal Belfast along the Bangor Road offers a different test of golf. Clandeboye is more wooded and 'heathy' with a considerable splash of gorse. There are two courses, the more difficult Dufferin and the Ava. Very close by golfers should note the new **Blackwood** Golf Course, a 36 hole development which promises to be quite special.

To the south of Newtownards, **Scrabo** Golf Club is worth an inspection—its opening hole is reckoned to be the toughest in Ireland—and circling back towards Belfast, **Lisburn** is almost in the same league as Malone and Belvoir Park.

A good base is required. In Belfast itself, the Wellington Park Hotel (0232) 381111 offers comfortable rooms and a thriving nightlife, particularly at weekends. Alternatively, the Europa Hotel (0232) 327000 is both modern and very comfortable but the most popular choice for golfers will probably be the Culloden Hotel (0232) 425223 at Holywood (very convenient for Royal Belfast). The Culloden is an impressive looking building, a baronial styled Victorian mansion. Its restaurant is particularly recommended. Another good eating place in Holywood is the Iona Restaurant and on the subject of sumptuous fare, Belfast offers the Strand (0232) 682266 and Restaurant 44 (0232) 244844. Belfast in fact is becoming renowned for its eating places and Roscoff (0232) 331532 and Manor House (0232) 238739 are two further places that offer particularly appealing fare. Whatever you do though don't forget to sample one or two of the local pubs - in most the atmosphere is tremendous. The Marine Court Hotel (0247) 451100 is recommended for those wishing to stay in Bangor, but for a really cosy inn, however, the best bet is to head towards Crawfordsburn where the Old Inn (0247) 853255 is a superb hostelry; full of character, its food is first class and there are some delightful bedrooms. Finally, the new Blackwood Golf Course has been mentioned and adjacent to it (and obviously convenient for Clandeboye Golf Club as well) is the elegant Clandeboye Lodge Hotel (0247) 853311.

Relaxed, well fed, well lubricated and swing nicely grooved, the next golf course to play is **Kirkistown Castle**. It lies near the foot of the Ards Peninsula (once described somewhat alarmingly as the proboscis of Ulster!) Kirkistown is a real old-fashioned gem. James Braid assisted in the design of the course and is reputed to have commented wistfully 'If only I had this within 50 miles of London'. The town of Portaferry is no great distance away and the Portaferry Hotel (02477) 28231 is a marvellous place to spend the night. It is another of those cosy inns (note the splendid seafood here).

If you're not in a rush it is worth spending some time on the Ards Peninsula. It is a remote and very beautiful corner of Ireland and Lough Strangford is one giant bird sanctuary and wildlife reserve. From Portaferry, a ferry can be taken to Strangford and from here a short drive will take you to **Ardglass** on the coast. Perched on craggy rocks the layout here is reminiscent of some of the better seaside courses in Cornwall. A perfect holiday course, we have featured Ardglass on a separate page ahead.

Beyond St John's Point and around Dundrum Bay, a journey of approximately twelve miles lies Newcastle, an attractive seaside town and where, as the famous song tells you, 'the mountains of Mourne sweep down to the sea'. For golfers it is a paradise. **Royal County Down** Golf Club is quite simply one of the greatest courses in the world and it too is featured on a later page. For those lucky people who are able to enjoy a few days here, the Burrendale Hotel (03967) 22599 on Castlewellan Road is very popular with golfers (and only about a five minute drive from the course). Equally recommended is the Slieve Donard Hotel (03967) 23681 which practically adjoins the famous links - in fact you'll be aiming a couple of drives at its spires. There are, alas, fewer and fewer hotels nowadays able to combine old-fashioned elegance with modern comforts but the Slieve Donard is a memorable example. Newcastle is a holiday town and good quality guest houses and bed and breakfasts are plentiful. If one is staying in the area some sightseeing is strongly advised. To the south and west the mountain scenery is quite magnificent while the southern coastal road takes in some very different but beautiful views. It is an area where smuggling was once notorious and before reaching the border we recommend that you smuggle in a quick 18 holes at **Warrenpoint**, where Ronan Rafferty learnt to play.

The Causeway Coast

Our journey now takes us back northwards, past Belfast to the Antrim coast. Here there is perhaps the most spectacular scenery of all and, equally important, yet more glorious golf.

Now, what kind of being can pick thorns out of his heels whilst running and can rip up a vast chunk of rock and hurl it fifty miles into the sea? Who on earth could perform such staggering feats? The answer is Finn McCool (who, alas is not eligible for Ryder Cup selection). Finn was the great warrior giant who commanded the armies of the King of all Ireland. He inhabited an Antrim headland, probably not far from Portrush in fact. Having fallen madly in love with a lady giant who lived on the Hebridian Island of Staffa, Finn began building a giant bridge to bring her across the water. Either Finn grew fickle or the lady blew him out but the bridge was never completed; still the Giants Causeway remains a great monument to one Finn McCool.

Royal Portrush is a monument to the Royal and Ancient game. Like County Down, Ardglass and Portstewart it is featured separately. However, don't limit your golf to Portrush, there are three other superb 18 hole courses nearby. To the east of Portrush, **Ballycastle** has an attractive situation overlooking an inviting stretch of sand and, if it didn't look so cold, the sea would be equally inviting. It is nothing like as tough as Portrush, more of a holiday course really, but tremendously enjoyable all the same.

Midway between Ballycastle and Portrush there is a pleasant nine holes at Bushfoot in Portballintrae where the Bayview Hotel (02657) 31453 provides a comfortable base. One should visit the famous **Bushmills Distillery** nearby. It is the oldest distillery in the world and whiskey has been produced here since 1608—just think

what Finn might have done after a magnum of Black Bush. Equally popular the world over with golfers it would appear is the Hillcrest Country House (0261) 731577 which offers exceptional value golf packages out of Bushmills. Another popular place to stay is the excellent Bushmills Inn (02657) 32339—ideal for those who wish to avoid both kinds of drinking and driving! Portrush's most celebrated eating place is Ramores on the quay, where there is a top class restaurant (0265) 824313 and a casual wine bar (0265) 823444. Those who have overindulged in Portrush and are seeking a comforting bed for the night should look (or stumble) no further than the excellent Magherabuoy House (0265) 823507. Alternatively we can recommend the Royal Court Hotel (0265) 822236, whose location high above the famous links is the envy of every hotel in Ireland.

Four miles west of Portrush and further along the coast is the fishing town of **Portstewart.** It has another very fine golf course (see feature page). The Edgewater Hotel (026583) 3314 in town is convenient and adequate, although more stylish accommodation and good food can be found at Blackheath House (0265) 868433 at Gurvagh five miles from Coleraine, and only a mile out of Portstewart. Also convenient for both Portrush and Portstewart, Maddybenny Farm (0265) 823394 is one of the finest guest houses in the country.

One final course remains to be played on this splendid Causeway coast and that is **Castlerock,** just a few miles across the River Bann from Portstewart. Once again it is a classic links set amid towering sand dunes and a game here will test every department of your game!

There are many golfing delights in Northern Ireland that we have not explored, however should Castlerock be your last port of call you'll have no excuses for not leaving Ireland a very contented soul.

Artist: Nick Jones PORTSTEWART Courtesy of Shades of Golf

Approximately thirty miles to the south of Belfast and beneath the spectacular gaze of the Mountains of Mourne there lies the most beautiful golf course in the world. A daring statement perhaps, but will anyone who has visited disagree?

Royal County Down is situated in Newcastle and the course stretches out along the shores of Dundrum Bay. It was laid out in 1889 by 'Old' Tom Morris from St. Andrews, who for his labours we are told, was paid the princely sum of four pounds. In a way though, there was little that Old Tom had to do, for Royal County Down is also one of the world's most natural golfing links.

Within four years of the first ball being struck the course was considered good enough to stage the Irish Open Amateur Championship which was duly won by the greatest amateur of the day, John Ball. Before the 20th century had dawned, County Down was already being considered as the finest course in all Ireland and some were even extending the accolade further.

Beautiful and natural, what next? Degree of difficulty. 'It was in fact the sternest examination in golf I had ever taken', the words of the very knowledgeable and well travelled golf writer Herbert Warren Wind. From its Championship tees, County Down measures 6968 yards, par 71. The fairways are often desperately narrow, the greens small, slick and not at all easy to hold; there are a number of blind shots amid the dunes and the rough can be, as someone once put it, 'knee-high to a giant'. Imagine what it's like in a fierce wind! Royal County Down is one of the toughest courses in the world.

Those wishing to pay homage should telephone the Club well in advance of intended play. Visitors are certainly welcome, but the course can naturally only accommodate so many. Weekends are best avoided as indeed are Wednesdays, but Mondays, Tuesdays and Fridays are relatively easy for visitors; a letter of introduction from the golfer's home Club is helpful. The **Secretary, Mr Peter Rolph** can be approached by telephone on **(03967) 23314** and by fax on (03967) 26281. while the address to write to is **Royal County Down Golf Club, Newcastle, Co. Down. BT33 0AN**. The Club's **professional, Kevan Whitson**, can be contacted on **(03967) 22419**. In summer 1994 the green fees were set at £43 per day during the week with £55 payable at the weekend.

Visitors looking for a more sedate challenge might wish to take note of the No. 2 Course at Royal County Down, which measures 4087 yards, par 65. This course is open to visiting golfers all week, with green fees currently set at £8 per day during the week and £12 at weekends.

The thirty mile journey from Belfast is via Ballynahinch along the A24 and the A2. The road is a good one and it should take less than an hour. From Dublin to the south the distance is about ninety miles and here the route to follow is the N1 to Newry and then again the A24, this time approaching Newcastle from the west. On a very clear day the Mountains of Mourne are just visible from Portmarnock's Championship links.

Unlike many of the great natural links courses, County Down doesn't have the traditional out and back type of layout; rather there are two distinct loops of nine. The outward loop, or half, is closer to the sea and hence is more sandy in nature and the dunes are consistently larger. You can hear the breaking of the waves as you play down the 1st fairway and your first blind tee shot comes as early as the par four 2nd. It is said that you can always spot the first time visitor to Newcastle for he walks up the 1st fairway backwards so enchanting is the view behind!

Among the finest holes on the front nine are the short 4th; here the tee shot must carry over a vast sea of gorse directly towards the majestic peak of Slieve Donard, the dog-legged 5th, and the 9th where an uphill drive must be targeted at the red spire of the Slieve Donard Hotel and followed (assuming the drive has successfully flown the hill and descended into the valley below) by a long second shot to a well guarded plateau green—a particularly memorable hole to conclude what many people consider to be the finest nine holes in golf.

The back nine may not have so many great sandhills, but there is still a plentiful supply of heather and gorse. Of the better holes perhaps the 13th, where the fairway curves its way through a beautiful heather lined valley and the very difficult 15th stand out.

Given its rather remote situation and the lack of facilities or space to cope with a vast crowd of spectators the Open could sadly never be staged at Royal County Down. The Amateur Championship has been played here though, Michael Bonallack completing a hat trick of victories in 1970. The Irish Amateur Championship visits County Down regularly and there have been some truly memorable finals. In 1933, Eric Fiddian playing against Jack McLean, holed in one at the 7th in the morning round and then again at the 14th in the afternoon. A magical moment in a magical setting—and I don't suppose Fiddian felt too sore when McLean eventually won the match.

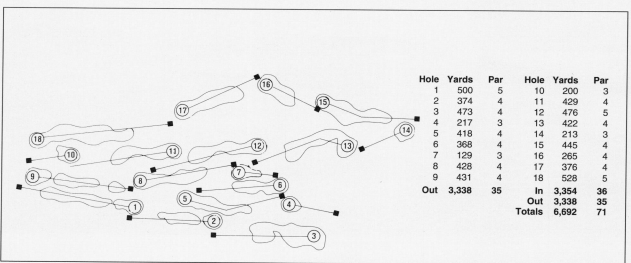

Hole	Yards	Par	Hole	Yards	Par
1	500	5	10	200	3
2	374	4	11	429	4
3	473	4	12	476	5
4	217	3	13	422	4
5	418	4	14	213	3
6	368	4	15	445	4
7	129	3	16	265	4
8	428	4	17	376	4
9	431	4	18	528	5
Out	**3,338**	**35**	**In**	**3,354**	**36**
			Out	3,338	35
			Totals	6,692	71

The golfer in a hurry—or the golfer without a soul—will travel to Portrush from Belfast by journeying inland, by driving through the heart of Northern Ireland after picking up the A26 at Ballymena; he or she, will bypass the Causeway Coast. That same person will head speedily for Newcastle, travelling due south via Ballynahinch. A bally idiot, you might think.

The route to Newcastle we recommend (for those travelling from Belfast, anyway) is a very leisurely trip around the Ards Peninsula and in this instance the first town to head for is Newtownards. Such a route will please the birdwatcher, for the road runs alongside Strangford Lough - one of the finest and largest bird sanctuaries in Europe - the country house enthusiast and historian, as the road passes near several magnificent houses (including Mount Stewart, famed for its wonderful gardens) as well as numerous castles, abbeys and monuments, and it will interest the golfer for a game could be sneaked in at Kirkistown Castle. On reaching Portaferry the traveller takes a quick ferry ride and then heads for Ardglass, just seven scenic miles away along the coast of Co. Down. The mountains of Mourne loom on the horizon and Newcastle is just 12 miles beyond Ardglass. Now we suggest that all and sundry make a decent length pit stop.

Ardglass is an historic little town. It has a great seafaring tradition and was once, though it's hard to believe now, the busiest port in Ulster. It is particularly famous for its collection of 14th to 16th century castles (there are about half a dozen of them in various states of ruin) and is apparently celebrated for its herrings, though I cannot recall ever having sampled any. Perhaps they are a speciality at the 19th hole of Ardglass Golf Club? 18 holes of golf here will certainly create an appetite, though my guess is that the first time visitor will be even more keen on getting back out and playing a second round on what is unquestionably one of the most spectacular courses in Ireland.

Let us not pretend that Ardglass is a Royal Co. Down or a Royal Portrush: we are talking about a sporting holiday course not an Open Championship type challenge.

From its back tees the course measures 5498 metres (or a little under 6100 yards) and from the ladies' tees, 4819 metres (about 5200 yards). What makes Ardglass so enjoyable is the dramatic layout of the course with several tees and greens overlooking the ocean; it has a really rugged feel and is part links part clifftop in nature. Much of the course is overrun with thick, wiry rough and vast swathes of purple heather.

Although the club was founded almost a century ago in 1896, it was not until 1971 that Ardglass could boast 18 holes. Today the club is run efficiently by the **secretary, Alan Cannon,** tel **(0396) 841219,** Fax (0396) 841841 and the **professional Kevin Dorrian, (0396) 841022.** Visitors are welcomed by arrangement throughout the week, 1994 green fees being £15 midweek and £20 at the weekend. Weekly and fortnightly tickets are also available, and the full address for written correspondence is **Ardglass Golf Club, Castle Place, Ardglass, Co. Down, BT30 7TP.**

Essentially the course meanders its way out on to a headland and then meanders its way back. The front nine holes are the more memorable, especially the first five which all run right alongside the sea. The par three 2nd is many people's favourite—and many people's undoing—with its tee shot needing to be fired across a rocky inlet: a real death-or-glory hole and somewhat reminiscent of the 3rd at Tralee. A second magnificent par three is tackled early on the back nine, the short, downhill 11th which is at the far end of the course. Whilst it is the ball hit short and left that will find the Irish Sea on the 2nd, it is the overhit shot to the right that is similarly punished on the 11th. Often this latter hole is just the proverbial 'flick with a wedge' but when the wind is dead against it can be truly intimidating. Some pretty demanding shots are called for between the 12th and 15th, and the 17th, yet another good par three, can be deceptively tricky, but the 18th offers a good chance of a closing birdie. Then of course it is off to the 19th which, being Ardglass, is a converted ancient castle and time to relax with a drink or two—unless, that is, you are a golfer in a hurry, or a golfer without a soul.

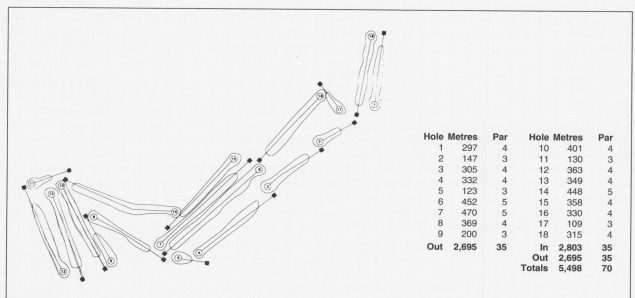

Hole	Metres	Par	Hole	Metres	Par
1	297	4	10	401	4
2	147	3	11	130	3
3	305	4	12	363	4
4	332	4	13	349	4
5	123	3	14	448	5
6	452	5	15	358	4
7	470	5	16	330	4
8	369	4	17	109	3
9	200	3	18	315	4
Out	**2,695**	**35**	**In**	**2,803**	**35**
			Out	**2,695**	**35**
			Totals	**5,498**	**70**

On the Causeway Coast in Northern Ireland, stone walls blend into green fields and sweeping cliffs roll towards the sea. This is also natural golfing country, and it is difficult to find anywhere that surpasses this natural coastal setting or a hotel that offers such a delightful base for exploring surrounding golf courses. Stand on the steps of the Magherabuoy House Hotel and you can breathe in the fresh salt air of the Atlantic Ocean.

The Magherabuoy House Hotel incorporates the period home of the former Minister of Home Affairs and has been carefully restored and extended, providing modern comforts in a majestic setting. Opulence is the key note, the elegant reception area creating a warm, sophisticated atmosphere, reflecting the standard and quality of service throughout. There are 38 luxurious bedrooms, all with private bathrooms, colour T.V. and tea and coffee making facilities. Guests can enjoy delicious a la carte meals in the Lanyon Room after a day on the golf course.

The jewel in the crown is undoubtedly the famous fairways of the championship course of Royal Portrush. Barely five minutes from the hotel, the links of Portrush set a challenge to players of every standard. There are three excellent courses: the Dunluce Course on which the Championships are played; the Valley Course on which the Ladies mainly play and the nine hole pitch and putt course at the end of the links nearest the town known as the Skerries. Throughout the years more than forty national championships, British and Irish, have been decided on these links.

Exhilarating rounds of golf in a stunning setting are available at five other courses in the area. The recently improved Portstewart can offer a challenge almost on a par with Royal Portrush; and Rathmore, Castlerock, Bushfoot, and Ballycastle all provide varied and testing golf.

The Hotel is situated only an hour's drive from the airport and docks, and guests can be collected from the airport in the hotel's own courtesy transport. For a really unusual golfing holiday you can be assured of a warm welcome.

The Magherabuoy House Hotel
41 Magheraboy Road
Portrush BT56 8NX
Tel: (0265) 823507
Fax: (0265) 824687

In May 1988, Royal Portrush celebrated its one hundredth birthday. One could say that this famous Club was born with a golfing silver spoon in its mouth. Within four years of its foundation patronage was bestowed, and there could never be a finer natural setting for a Championship links. The course is laid out amid huge sand dunes which occupy slightly elevated ground providing commanding views over the Atlantic. And what views! The Antrim coast is at its most spectacular between The Giant's Causeway and Portrush and overlooking the links are the proud ruins of a magnificent castle, Dunluce, from which the Championship Course takes its name. The first professional the Club employed was Sandy Herd, who went on to win the Open Championship in 1902, and as if by way of a final blessing, in 1951, Portrush became the first (and to this day the only) Club in Ireland to stage The Open Championship.

There are in fact two Championship Courses at Portrush. When people talk of 'the Championship links' they are invariably referring to the **Dunluce** links—this is where the Open and the 1993 Amateur Championship were staged—but there is also The **Valley** links which can stretch to 6278 yards and is used for many important events; somewhat surprisingly it has only twenty bunkers. Visitors are made very welcome at Portrush and can play either course on any day of the week except Wednesday afternoons; the Valley course is also closed to visitors on Sunday mornings. It is always wise to telephone the Club in advance as the tees may have been reserved and Portrush is extremely popular in the summer.

In 1994 the green fees to play over the Dunluce links were set at £37.50 per day between Monday and Friday, £45 on weekends and bank holidays (when available) and £15 for the Valley course during the week (£20 at the weekend). On both courses, weekly tickets are available and are excellent value for those staying in the area. Golfing Societies are equally welcome, subject of course to prior arrangement with the **Secretary, Wilma Erskine**. She may be contacted by writing to the **Royal Portrush Golf Club, Portrush, Co. Antrim. BT56 8JQ. Tel: (0265) 822311** or fax. (0265) 823139; the club's **professional, Dai Stevenson**, can be reached on **(0265) 823335**.

The Golf Club lies about half a mile from Portrush

town. Portrush itself is easily accessible as it is linked by coastal road to Portstewart and Ballycastle, and to Belfast by major road — a distance of approximately sixty miles. Londonderry is about thirty-five miles to the west. The Club is located immediately off Bushmills Road and don't forget to visit the famous distillery when you're in the area—it's less than 10 minutes from the links and is guaranteed to do wonders for your golf!

Although the game has now been played at Portrush for a hundred years, the Dunluce links in fact bears little resemblance to the original Championship course. Harry Colt is responsible for the present layout and we all owe him a great debt. Work was carried out between 1929 and 1932 and on completion he is said to have considered it his masterpiece—and Harry Colt built many a great course. Bernard Darwin wrote in *'The Times'* after viewing the links during the 1951 Open: 'It is truly magnificent and Mr. H.S. Colt, who designed it in its present form, has thereby built himself a monument more enduring than brass'.

Portrush's most celebrated holes are the 5th and the 14th. The 5th, 'White Rocks', is one of the most exhilarating two-shot holes in golf. From the tee, there is a splendid view of the Antrim Coast towards The White Rocks and The Giant's Causeway beyond. However spellbound, considerable care is required with both the drive and the approach. The hole is properly a dog-leg and although a brave drive can cut the angle, failure will result in a trip into the deep, deep rough; over-hit your second and you're in the Atlantic. The green here nearly fell into the sea some years ago but a retaining wall was built and it has been saved. The 14th is titled 'Calamity', and not without good reason—a par three of over 200 yards in length, the direct line to the pin requires a very precise shot to carry an enormous ravine—mis-hit this one and you can be playing your next shot from at least fifty feet below the hole.

As with most of the great links courses, the greens at Portrush are very large and the bunkers often deep. The course poses a considerable challenge but it's a fair one nonetheless. In the 1951 Open only twice during the entire tournament did a player break 70. Silver spoon or not, you can be sure my good friend Finn McCool would have been mightily impressed.

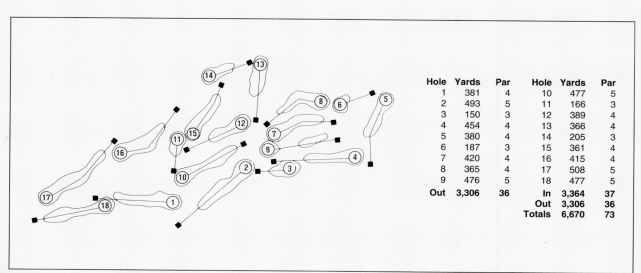

Hole	Yards	Par	Hole	Yards	Par
1	381	4	10	477	5
2	493	5	11	166	3
3	150	3	12	389	4
4	454	4	13	366	4
5	380	4	14	205	3
6	187	3	15	361	4
7	420	4	16	415	4
8	365	4	17	508	5
9	476	5	18	477	5
Out	**3,306**	**36**	**In**	**3,364**	**37**
			Out	**3,306**	**36**
			Totals	**6,670**	**73**

Blackheath House is a fine old Rectory built by Frederick Harvey, the Earl of Bristol in 1791 for the Parish of Aghadowey. It is a listed building with an interesting history set in two acres of landscaped gardens.

Once the home of Archbishop William Alexander, whose wife Cecil the poetess wrote 'There is a green hill far away' and 'All things bright and beautiful'.

In Winter, residents can enjoy a glass of hot punch in the drawing room by a welcoming fire and in the Summer can have a cool drink in the gardens.

Each of the spacious bedrooms is individually styled for comfort with bathrooms, colour television and tea/coffee making facilities.

Blackheath House is situated in the beautiful countryside of Aghadowey, once the centre of flax growing for the linen industry, whose rivers are famous for salmon and trout. Shooting and fishing can be arranged and there are excellent equestrian facilities nearby.

Aghadowey is only 7 miles from Coleraine and 11 miles from the Causeway Coast with its magnificent coastline, sandy beaches, picturesque seaside resorts and eight golf courses. We have special rates with local Golf Courses and can arrange sea fishing.

There are many interesting places to visit in the area including the Giants Causeway, Carrick-a-Rede Rope Bridge, Dunluce Castle and Old Bushmills Distillery - the home of the oldest whiskey in the world.

MACDUFF'S RESTAURANT - The Restaurant situated in the cellars of the house is renowned for its excellent food, friendly service and warm and intimate atmosphere.

Macduff's offers Country House cooking at its best using freshly grown produce, local game, salmon and seafood.

From an extensive and interesting wine list you can choose a wine from the original wine vault.

Blackheath House
112, Killeague Road
Blackhill
Coleraine
Co. Londonderry BT51 4HH
Tel: (0265) 868433

The Causeway Coast of Northern Ireland—essentially the coast of Antrim with a bit of County Londonderry stuck on—has long been regarded as a fine place for a golfing break with three very good courses and one outstanding championship links to play. The last-mentioned is of course Royal Portrush, the only golf links in Ireland to have staged the Open Championship; the three supporting courses being Ballycastle, Portstewart and Castlerock. In the last few years all this has changed. It is not the opening of a new course (although some might describe it as such) but rather the extraordinary transformation of one of the supporting cast. Portstewart now ranks among the greatest courses in Ireland. How come? Two words will suffice, Thistly Hollow.

Visitors to Portstewart have always marvelled at the magnificent 425 yards par four 1st hole. 'The best opening hole in Ireland' is the proud boast, and only the Members at Portrush seem to grumble loudly. Of course the difficulty of having such a spectacular starter is that the main course has got a lot to live up to. Although the following seventeen holes at Portstewart are considered well above average, they have not been able to sustain the sensation of wonder—that is until now. After playing the glorious 1st, golfers used to gaze up into the nearby range of sand hills, known as Thistly Hollow, and ruminate on how fantastic it would be if only they could build some golf holes amidst those towering dunes. Well now they have … and that is why Portstewart is such a fantastic golf course.

One of the people best able to tell you how this came about—for he presided over much of it—is the Club's enthusiastic **Secretary, Michael Moss**. Visitors wishing to explore the awesome sand hills and the rest of the links are advised to contact the Club a little in advance. The full address is **Portstewart Golf Club, Strand Head, Portstewart, Co. Londonderry, BT55 7PG**. Mr Moss can also be contacted by telephone on **(0265) 832015**, while Portstewart's **professional, Alan Hunter** can be reached on **(0265) 832601**.

Although it is easy to get carried away with the major reshaping of the Championship course it should be pointed out that there are now 45 holes of golf to enjoy at Portstewart. The short 18 hole Town Course has been around for a little while but a new nine hole course, the 'Riverside 9' has evolved following the aforementioned reshaping of the Championship links. Broadly speaking, what has happened is that much of the former back nine at Portstewart has become the Riverside 9 and the new holes have been 'inserted' to immediately follow the famous 1st. This is only roughly what has happened for the 'new' 18th is still more or less the 'old' 18th—confused? The best bet is to pay a visit!

Portstewart welcomes visitors at most times, although a round on the Championship course is not normally possible on Saturdays and only limited times are available on Sundays. The green fee in 1994 for the Championship course was £25 during the week and £30 at the weekend. A full eighteen holes on the Riverside 9 is priced at £10 midweek and £15 at weekends, while at similar times the green fee for the Town Course is £7 and £11 respectively.

Portstewart is situated right on the coast, some 4 miles from Coleraine and no greater a distance from Portrush which is to the east of Portstewart. The road that links each to the other is the A2. Belfast is approximately 65 miles away, though its airport is a little nearer and from which one doesn't have to journey through the capital to get to the Causeway Coast: the A26 is a very direct route. Londonderry is about 30 miles to the west and there is a second airport here.

So having played the splendid dog-leg 1st with its superbly elevated tee (every bit as exhilarating as the 5th at Portrush) and amphitheatre-like green, instead of gazing up into the sand hills the golfer playing the Championship links must now get amongst them. The 'new' front nine holes at Portstewart are being compared favourably with the back nine holes at Tralee Golf Club in County Kerry—and anyone who has played that exceptional links, designed by Arnold Palmer, will know that this is a mighty compliment. The views that these holes afford are also quite breathtaking and at times quite terrifying! The sight from the back tee at the 2nd, a stunning par four, provides an early example of both sensations. There are two tremendous short holes, the 3rd and the 6th, but perhaps even better are the long dune-fringed, sweeping par five 4th, and the classic stroke index one 5th. The golfer may feel in a world of his own as he plays these holes but then that's Portstewart — a quite extraordinary golf course.

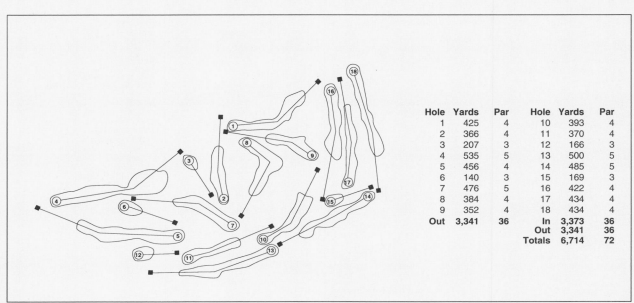

Hole	Yards	Par	Hole	Yards	Par
1	425	4	10	393	4
2	366	4	11	370	4
3	207	3	12	166	3
4	535	5	13	500	5
5	456	4	14	485	5
6	140	3	15	169	3
7	476	5	16	422	4
8	384	4	17	434	4
9	352	4	18	434	4
Out	3,341	36	In	3,373	36
			Out	3,341	36
			Totals	6,714	72

Key

To avoid disappointment it is advisable to telephone in advance

***Visitors welcome at most times
**Visitors usually allowed on weekdays only
*Visitors not normally permitted (Mon, Wed) No visitors on specified days

Approximate Green Fees
A £30 plus
B £20 to £30
C £15 to £25
D £10 to £20
E under £10
F Greens fees on application

Restrictions
G Guests only
H Handicap certificate required
H (24) Handicap of 24 or less
L Letter of introduction required
M Visitor must be a member of another recognised club.

CO ANTRIM

Ballycastle G.C.
(02657) 62536
Cushendall Road, Ballycastle
(18)5882 yards/***/D

Ballyclare G.C.
(09603) 22696
Springvale Road, Ballyclare
(18)6200 yards/**(Thur)/D/H

Ballymena G.C.
(0266) 861487
Raceview Road, Broughshane, Ballymena
(18)5245 metres/***/D/H

Bushfoot G.C.
(02657) 31317
Bushfoot Road, Portballintrae, Bushmills
(9)5572 yards/***/D/H

Cairndhu G.C.
(0574) 583324
Coast Road, Ballygally, Larne
(18)6112 yards/***(Sat)/D

Carrickfergus G.C.
(09603) 63713
North Road, Carrickfergus
(18)5752 yards/***(Sat)/D

Cushendall G.C.
(02667) 71318
Shore Road, Cushendall, Ballymena
(9)4678 yards/***/E

Dunmurry G.C.
(0232) 610834
Dunmurry Lane, Belfast
(18)5832 yards/**(Tues/Thurs pm)/D

Greenisland G.C.
(0232) 862236
Upper Road, Greenisland
(9)5887 yards/***(Sat)/D

Lambeg G.C.
(0846) 662738
Bells Lane, Lambeg, Lisburn
(9)4583 yards/***/E

Larne G.C.
(09603) 82228
Ferris Bay Road, Islandmagee, Larne
(9)6082 yards/***(Sat)/E

Lisburn G.C.
(0846) 677216
Eglantine Road, Lisburn
(18)6700 yards/***/B

Masserene G.C.
(08494) 28096

Lough Road, Antrim
(18)6614 yards/***(Sat)/C

Royal Portrush G.C.
(0265) 822311
Bushmills Road, Portrush
(18)6784 yards/***/A/H
(18)6273 yards/***/C/H

Whitehead G.C.
(09603) 53631
McCraes Brae, Whitehead
(18)6426 yards/***(Sat)/D

CO ARMAGH

Ashfield G.C.
(0693) 868180
Freeduff, Cullyhana
(18)5616 yards/***/E

County Armagh G.C.
(0861) 522501
Newry Road, Armagh
(18)6184 yards/***/D

Craigavon Golf & Ski Centre
(0762) 326606
Silverwood, Lurgan
(18)6496 yards/***/E

Lurgan G.C.
(0762) 322087
The Demesne, Lurgan
(18)6836 yards/***/C

Portadown G.C.
(0762) 355356
Carrickblacker, Portadown
(18)6119 yards/**(Tues/Sat)/C

Silverwood G.C.
(0762)326606
Turmoyra Lane, Lurgan
(18)6496 yards/***/E

Trandragee G.C.
(0762) 841272
Trandragee, Craigavon
(18)6084 yards/***/D

BELFAST

Ballyearl G.C.
(0232) 848287
Doagh Road, Newtonabbey
(9)2362 yards/***/E

Balmoral G.C.
(0232) 381514
Lisburn Road, Belfast
(18)6250 yards/***(Sat)/C

Belvoir Park G.C.
(0232) 491693
Newtownbreda, Belfast
(18)6501 yards/***(Sat)/B-A

Cliftonville G.C.
(0232) 744158
Westland Road, Belfast
(9)6240 yards/***(Sat)/D

Fortwilliam G.C.
(0232) 370770
Downview Avenue, Belfast
(18)5642 yards/***(Sat)/D

Gilnahirk G.C.
(0232) 448477
Manns Corner, Upper Brawiel Road
(9)2699 yards/***/F

The Knock G.C.
(0232) 483251
Summerfield, Dundonald
(18)6407 yards/***(Sat)/B

Knockbracken G.& C.C.
(0232) 792108
Ballymaconaghy Road, Knockbracken
(18)5312 yards/***/E

Malone G.C.
(0232) 612758
Upper Malone Road, Dunmurry

(18)6642 yards/***(Sat/Wed pm)/B

Ormeau G.C.
(0232) 641069
Park Road, Belfast
(9)5306 yards/***/E

Shandon Park G.C.
(0232) 793730
Shandon Park, Belfast
(18)6252 yards/***/B

CO DOWN

Ardglass G.C.
(0396) 841219
Castle Place, Ardglass
(18)6000 yards/***/D

Banbridge G.C.
(08206) 22342
Huntly Road, Banbridge
(18)5003 yards/***/E

Bangor G.C.
(0247) 270922
Broadway, Bangor
(18)6450 yards/**/C

Blackwood G.C.
(0247) 853311
Clandeboye
(36)/***/F

Bright Castle G.C.
(0396) 841319
Bright, Downpatrick
(18)7000 yards/***/C

Carnalea G.C.
(0247) 270368
Station Road, Bangor
(18)5584 yards/***/D

Clandeboye G.C.
(0247) 271767
Conlig, Newtownards
(18)6650 yards/***(Sat)/C
(18)5634 yards/***(Sat)/C

Donaghadee G.C.
(0247) 883624
Warren Road, Donaghadee
(18)6099 yards/***(Sat)/D

Downpatrick G.C.
(0396) 612152
Saul Road, Downpatrick
(18)6196 yards/***/C

Helens Bay G.C.
(0247) 852601
Helens Bay, Bangor
(9)5176 metres/***(Sat)/F

Holywood G.C.
(0232) 423135
Nuns Walk, Demesne Road, Holywood
(18)5885 yards/***(Sat)/C

Kilkeel G.C.
(069) 3762296
Mourne Park, Ballyardle
(9)6625 yards/***(Tues,Sat)/C

Kirkistown Castle G.C.
(02477) 71233
Cloughey, Newtownards
(18)6157 yards/**/C

Mahee Island G.C.
(0238) 541234
Comber
Mahee Island
(9)5580 yards/***/E

Royal Belfast G.C.
(0232) 428165
Holywood, Craigavad
(18)6205 yards/***/B

Royal County Down G.C.
(03967) 23314
Newcastle
(18)6968 yards/***/A/H
(18)4100 yards/***/F

Scrabo G.C.
(0247) 812355
Scrabo Road, Newtownards
(18)5699 metres/***(Wed)/D

The Spa G.C.
(0238) 562365
Grove Road, Ballynahinch
(9)5938 yards/***(Sun)/D

Warrenpoint G.C.
(06937) 52219
Lower Dromore Road, Warrenpoint
(18)6215 yards/***(Sun/Wed)/D

CO FERMANAGH

Enniskillen G.C.
(0365) 325250
Enniskillen
(18) 5476 metres/***/D

CO LONDONDERRY

Brown Trout G.& C.C.
(0265) 868209
Agivey Road, Aghadovey, Coleraine
(9)2800 yards/***/E

Castlerock G.C.
(0265) 848314
Circular Road, Castlerock
(18)6687 yards/***/C
(9)4708 yards/***/F

City of Derry G.C.
(0504) 46369
Prehan, Londonderry
(18)6450 yards/***/D

Kilrea G.C.
(0265) 834738
Drumagarner Road, Kilrea
(9)4326 yards/*(Tues/Wed/Sat)/E

Moyola Park G.C.
(0648) 68468
Shanemullagh, Castledawson
(18)6517 yards/***/D

Portstewart G.C.
(0265) 832015
Strand Road, Portstewart
(18)6800 yards/***/B
(18)4733 yards/***/D
(9)2662 yards/***/E

CO TYRONE

Dungannon G.C.
(08687) 22098
Mullaghmore, Dungannon
(18)5914 yards/***/D

Fintona G.C.
(0662) 841480
Fintona
(9)6250 yards/***/F

Killymoon G.C.
(06487) 62254
Killymoon, Cookstown
(18)6000 yards/***(Sat)/D

Newtownstewart G.C.
(06626) 61466
Golf Course Road, Newtownstewart
(18)6100 yards/***/E

Omagh G.C.
(0662) 243160
Dublin Road, Omagh
(18)5800/***/D

Strabane G.C.
(0504) 382271
Ballycolman, Strabane
(18)6100 yards/***/E

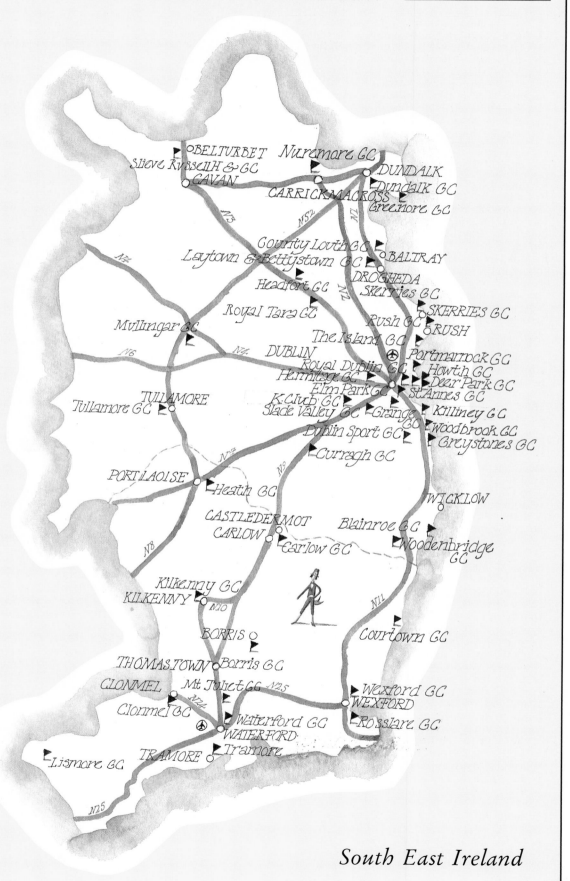

BELTURBET
Nuremore GC
Slieve Russelh & GC
CAVAN
DUNDALK
Dundalk GC
CARRICKMACROSS
Greenore GC
N3
N52
N1

County Louth GC
BALTRAY
Laytown & Bettystown GC
DROGHEDA
N4
Headfort GC
Skerries GC
N2
Royal Tara GC
SKERRIES GC
Mullingar GC
Rush GC
RUSH
The Island GC
N6
N4
DUBLIN
Portmarnock GG
Royal Dublin GC
Howth GC
Hermitage GC
Deer Park GC
Elm Park GC
St Annes GC
K.Club GC
TULLAMORE
Slade Valley GC
Grange
Killiney GC
Tullamore GC
GC
Woodbrook GC
Dublin Sport GC
Greystones GC
N7
Curragh GC

PORTLAOISE
WICKLOW
Heath GC
Blainroe GC
CASTLEDERMOT
Woodenbridge
CARLOW
GC
N8
Carlow GC

Kilkenny GC
Courtown GC
KILKENNY
N11
N10

BORRIS
Borris GC
THOMASTOWN
Mt Juliet GG
N25
Wexford GC
CLONMEL
WEXFORD
Clonmel GC
N24
Waterford GC
Rosslare GC
WATERFORD
Lismore GC
TRAMORE
Tramore
N25

From the time you arrive in Ireland and crack your first drive straight down the middle, to the time you leave, having holed that tricky putt on the final green (and then drained your last drop of Guinness at the 19th), you cannot fail to be impressed by the natural charm and helpfulness of the Irish people. Nowhere is it more immediately apparent than in Dublin—what a contrast to many of the world's capital cities! Nothing seems rushed and nothing seems too much trouble. You see, the welcome from these folk is quite simply second to none.

Dublin

Within ten miles of the city centre there are two great championship links and at least twenty other courses, the majority of which are of a very high standard. **Portmarnock** is the most celebrated, and indeed is one of the great golf links of the world. It is explored on a later page. **Royal Dublin** is said to be the only championship course located within the boundaries of a capital city. It lies just to the north of Dublin's centre on Bull Island in the charmingly named area of Dollymount. It is generally considered less severe than Portmarnock, (although the wind can blow just as fiercely!) for it is not as long and the rough isn't quite so punishing. It makes an ideal place for us to crack that first one straight down the middle.

The two best known holes on the course are probably the 5th and the 18th. The former is one of the most intimidating holes to be found anywhere. There is a story that when Danny Kaye visited the course he took one look at the 5th and turned to his caddy to ask for a rifle! The 18th is a shortish par five, reachable with two good hits but only if the 2nd is carried over a dog-leg out of bounds—an all or nothing finish. The Irish Open Championship has been played here on a number of occasions. In 1966 Christy O'Connor came to the 16th needing three birdies to tie Eric Brown—he finished eagle-birdie-eagle! Another memorable finish occurred in 1985 when Seve Ballesteros defeated Bernhard Langer in a thrilling playoff to win his second Irish title.

Portmarnock lies to the north of Royal Dublin, and a short distance to the north of Portmarnock on a tiny peninsula is the **Island** golf links. Until the mid 1970s the course could only be reached by rowing boat from the village of Malahide and the fare paid was included within the green fee. It is a delightful, often spectacular, very old-fashioned type of course, not overly long but deceptively tough with a number of semi-blind holes—something of an Irish Prestwick perhaps.

Not too far from Malahide (and close to Dublin Airport) is the impressive **St Margaret's** Golf & Country Club; we investigate the course later in this chapter.

In Malahide the Grand Hotel (010 353) 1 8450633 provides a perfect place to base oneself when playing the North Dublin courses. It is particularly handy for the Island and Portmarnock and is less expensive (and certainly more attractive) than the majority of the capital's more centrally located hotels and it also goes without saying that the Portmarnock Country Club (010 353) 1 8460611 is well worth considering. However, if one does wish to be more in the middle of things then among the better hotels in Dublin are the Shelbourne (010 353) 1 6766471 (which is attractive), the Berkeley Court (010 353) 1 6601711 (which is possibly the best), the Burlington (010 353) 1 6605222, Mont Clare (010 353) 1 6616799 and Jury's (010 353) 1 6605000. A recommended hotel for St Margaret's is the Forte Crest Hotel (010 353) 1 8444211. Also well worth noting is the Victor Hotel in Dun Laoghaire (010 353) 1 2853555. In Howth, the King

Sitric (010 353) 1 326729 is an excellent seafood restaurant, and again particularly convenient for the courses to the north of Dublin. Good restaurants abound in the centre of Dublin and suggestions could include La Stampa (010 353) 1 6778611, Patrick Guilbaud (010 353) 1 6764192, the Grey Door (010 353) 1 6763286, Le Coq Hardi (010 353) 1 6689070 and Locks (010 353) 1 6543391. Visiting a Dublin bar is an experience in itself and ought not to be missed. Take your pick, but when you do venture in be prepared for a good sing-song.

If most of the celebrated golf courses are found to the north of Dublin there are many more to the south and west of the capital, indeed, the city is practically encircled by golf courses—what a marvellous prospect! Noted 18 hole courses worthy of mention here include; **Hermitage, Howth, Deer Park,** the **Grange** and **Slade Valley**; while a good 9 hole course not far from Dun Laoghaire is found at **Killiney**. Without question the most talked about inland course in the Dublin area is the Arnold-Palmer-designed course at the **Kildare Country Club** (010 353) 1 6273333 at Straffan; the 'K' club, as it is known, is featured ahead together with Dublin's newest parkland gem, **Luttrellstown Castle**. which also boasts a first rate hotel (010 353) 1 8213237.

The leading club to the south of Dublin is **Woodbrook**. It too has played host to the Irish Open, in addition to many other important tournaments. Woodbrook offers a mixture of semi-links and parkland golf and although not the most challenging of courses is always immaculately kept. At Brittas Bay, Pat Ruddy's dramatic new links course the **European Club** has very recently opened (see feature page) and we strongly recommend an overnight stay at the outstanding Marlfield House (010 353) 55 21125 in Gorey. A few miles further down the coast is the pleasant course at **Greystones**, from the back nine of which there are some marvellous views of the Wicklow Mountains, and a nearby new 18 hole golf and hotel complex, the attractively priced **Charlesland** Golf and Country Club Hotel (010 353) 1 2876764—more great views. Near the town of Wicklow, **Blainroe** Golf Club has a much improved—and pretty demanding—championship length layout. Finally there is a very scenic 9 hole course at **Woodenbridge**. It's a bit of a drive from Dublin, but well worth it.

Following a round in South Dublin, Roly's (010 353) 1 6682611 restaurant in Ballsbridge is highly recommended. The Stillorgin Park Hotel (010 353) 1 2881681 is very lively, while in Bray, not far from Greystones or Killiney an evening spent at the Tree of Idleness (010 353) 1 2863498 should be extremely relaxing. The Wicklow area is well served by **Rathsallagh House** (010 353) 45 53112 at Dunlavin where there is another very good new course, and at Rathnew where both Tinakilly House (010 353) 404 69274 and Hunter's Hotel (010 353) 404 40106 are highly recommended.

North of Dublin

Thirty miles north of Dublin in the charming village of Baltray near Drogheda is the **County Louth** Golf Club. In the opinion of many this is the most attractive links on the east coast. **Baltray**, as the course is known, enjoys a wonderfully remote setting, but while it may be a peaceful place the course will test your game to the full. Baltray is featured ahead. One needn't look far for a bed as the club offers its own accommodation and meals are available (telephone (010 353) 41 22329 for details). However, if there's no room at the 19th the best bet is either the Boyne Valley Hotel (010 353) 41 37737 in Drogheda, or the Neptune (010 353) 41 27107 in nearby

Bettystown. This latter hotel is very close to the **Laytown and Bettystown** links which while not in the same class as Baltray certainly poses enough problems. It is the home club of the former Ryder Cup player Des Smyth. Just north of Baltray (in fact visible just beyond the 14th tee at Co. Louth) is the newly opened **Seapoint** Golf Club at Termonfeckin.

Further north the course at **Dundalk** deserves inspection. Again it's not in the same league as Baltray, but then very few are. Still, it's definitely worth visiting if only for the tremendous scenery it offers. Although very much a parkland type challenge, the course is set out alongside the shores of Dundalk Bay with the Mountains of Mourne and the Cooley Mountains providing a spectacular backdrop. The Ballymascanlon House (010 353) 42 71124 in Dundalk is very good value if a night's stopover is required while for an outstanding restaurant try Quaglinos (010 353) 42 38567.

Dundalk in fact provides a fine base for playing our final recommendation in the north east, the course at **Greenore** where a more dramatic location couldn't be wished for. Laid out alongside Carlingford Lough, Greenore golfers have recently built three new holes which are destined to be the envy of every golf course in Ireland. You don't believe it? Then go and visit, you'll be made most welcome!

Travelling Inland

For those who enjoy horseracing as well as golf (this must include near enough every Irishman), a good route to take out of Dublin is the N7. Given a clear road the Curragh is little more than half an hour's drive away. This is the Epsom of Ireland. Golf has been played on the great stretch of heathland since the 1850s and the **Curragh** Golf Club was founded in 1883 making it the oldest golf club in the Republic. Rather like England's senior links, Westward Ho!, the fairways are shared with the local farmer's sheep. There's also a nearby army range—one presumes golf is rarely uneventful at the Curragh! It's actually a very good course and the green fees are typically modest. Barberstown Castle (010 353) 62 88157 at Celbridge is an excellent place to head for after a day on the heath, especially if a game of golf has been combined with a day at the races.

Venturing further inland, **Mullingar** in County Westmeath has long rivalled Carlow as Ireland's top inland course; it again is featured ahead. **Headfort** near Kells, and **Royal Tara** at Navan, both in County Meath are two more of the region's better parkland courses, and in County Offaly, **Tullamore** is of a similar nature although it perhaps has a little more variety. All three enjoy delightful locations and welcome visitors at most times.

Finally, two hotel golf courses that are not exactly close to Dublin, but decidedly worth inspecting nonetheless are at the **Nuremore** Hotel (010 353) 42 61438 near Carrickmacross, in Co. Monaghan and one of Ireland's newest gems, the spectacular **Slieve Russell** Hotel course (010 353) 49 264444 at Ballyconnell in Co. Cavan. Slieve Russell is featured ahead.

Artist: **H Rowntree PORTMARNOCK** _Courtesy of_ **Sarah Baddiel's Book Diary**

The Nuremore Hotel is located fifty miles north-west of Dublin, and is beautifully situated within 200 acres of woods and parkland in the rolling countryside of Co Monaghan. Originally a Victorian country house, the Nuremore has, over the years, been skillfully converted and extended into a magnificent luxury hotel. Each of its seventy bedrooms has been individually designed and beautifully appointed.

The Nuremore offers its guests an unrivalled range of sports and leisure facilities, including an eighteen metre swimming pool, whirlpool, steamroom, sauna, gymnasium, tennis courts, squash courts and an 18 hole championship golf course in the hotel grounds.

The golf course, with its total length of 6246 metres and a par of 73, nestles snugly among the drumlins and lakes for which this part of Ireland is justly famous. The course designer, Eddie Hackett, has managed to carve out of the Monaghan hillside a layout that will present a challenging test of golf for the low hadicapper when played off the back tees, or a round of enjoyment for the average golfer, when played from the forward tees. In 1992 the Nuremore was the venue for the PGA Ulster Open professional championship, which is set to become an annual event at the course, providing professionals from all over Ireland with an opportunity of playing a 72 hole competition.

In addition to its own course, there are many excellent courses within easy reach of the Nuremore Hotel, including the championship courses at Baltray and Headfort, both within thirty minutes of the hotel, and Portmarnock, Royal Dublin and Royal Co Down, each no more than an hour and a half away.

For those who want to improve their game during their stay at the Nuremore, the course professional, Maurice Cassidy, is available to give tuition and golf clinics.

Situated just and hour and a half from Dublin, the Nuremore Hotel is an ideal venue for a relaxing break, and, as extensive conference facilities are provided, it is also ideal as a location for working breaks.

Nuremore Hotel
Carrickmacross
Co Monaghan
Ireland
Tel: (010 353 42) 61438
Fax: (010 353 42) 61853

County Louth (Baltray)

Golfing visitors to the east coast of Ireland can almost be forgiven if having arrived in Dublin they fail to travel any real distance beyond the fair city. Dotted around the fringes of Ireland's capital are numerous first rate challenges, something like 20 courses within 10 miles (or half an hour's drive) of O'Connell Street (How many within thirty minutes of Piccadilly Circus?)

There is great variety too with classic links courses to the north, including world famous Portmarnock and Royal Dublin and some very pleasant, well manicured parkland courses to the south and west of the city; and the quality of golf isn't the only reason why so many decide not to venture away from Dublin—the city and its people have much to offer. But I did say at the beginning, 'can almost be forgiven', this is because one of the greatest courses in Ireland lies no more than 40 miles north of Dublin (and about an hour's drive) just beyond Drogheda in the small fishing village of Baltray. This is where County Louth Golf Club is situated, and a truly magnificent and totally natural golf links.

Baltray, as everyone calls it, is one of the least widely known of Ireland's great championship links; give the Club a major professional tournament and all this would probably change, but for the moment Baltray retains a fairly low profile, which doubtless suits many of the members! Not that they won't welcome you, mind you, for this must be one of the most friendly and informal clubs around. A genuinely relaxed Saturday afternoon atmosphere prevails throughout the week.

One gentleman who helps maintain the marvellous mood is the **secretary, Michael Delany**; visitors wishing to arrange a game at Baltray should contact him in advance of intended play either by writing to him at **County Louth Golf Club, Baltray, Co. Louth** or by telephoning **(041) 22329** (010 353 41 22329 from Great Britain). Green fees are good value; in 1994 they were £27 during the week and £35 at the weekend with reduced rates for juniors. Club competitions may make it difficult to arrange a game for the weekend but usually the only other day to try to avoid is Tuesday. Golf Societies normally visit Baltray on Mondays and Thursdays. One other person you may wish to consult before striding out on to the links is the Club's affable **professional, Paddy McGuirk, tel. (041) 22444.**

As already mentioned, Baltray is about an hour's drive from Dublin; it is less from the city's airport which is located 8 miles north of the capital. The road to pick up, both from Dublin and the airport is the N1. It links the city with Drogheda (and indeed carries on towards

Belfast) and is well signposted—if you follow the course of the River Boyne towards the sea you cannot go far wrong, but make sure you journey north of the river.

We were about to stride out onto the links, and tackle all 6567 yards, par 73 from the medal tees (6783 yards, par 73 from the back markers). The first two holes tempt us to open the shoulders (after all the rough doesn't look too menacing), but on both holes a wayward drive can easily find a bunker, and this is the story all the way around. Architect Tom Simpson may have been presented with a wonderful piece of golfing terrain to work with when he designed the course in the 1930s, but he clearly put an enormous amount of thought into the positioning of bunkers and other hazards. The good shot at Baltray, however, is always rewarded, no more so than at the par five 3rd where the second must be played blind over a rise in the fairway to a narrow green. The 4th is only a drive and a pitch but it is a classic links hole with a tumbling, folding, dune-lined fairway. The 5th green is actually perched high in these dunes; it is a splendid short hole, one of Baltray's 'four little gems'.

For many the most exciting holes appear between the 12th and 16th at the far end of the links, the part closest to the sea and where nature presents the dunes at their wildest. The entire 12th fairway looks as if it has been carved out of the surrounding towering sandhills. The shot to the green has to be targeted through a gap in the dunes and only a perfect long iron will suffice; spray it to the left or right and disaster awaits. The 13th is almost as difficult but the far reaching views from the elevated 14th tee will placate most wounded souls. This is a beautiful and historic part of the world and as you smash your drive at the 14th (well it's almost reachable with a mighty blow) the broad estuary of the River Boyne, famed for its 17th century battle, stretches out ahead while over your shoulder are the far off romantic Mountains of Mourne. Another fine par four comes at the 16th where the angled approach is played into an amphitheatre green. It is a superb dog-leg hole, and again one of several at Baltray. A new championship tee has added considerable teeth to the par five 18th; however from the forward tees it still offers a real chance of a finishing birdie.

The way to celebrate such a feat at Baltray is with a drop of the famous black and white stuff, almost, but not quite obligatory. Good food and overnight accommodation in the Clubhouse can also be arranged. Like every good Irish Golf Club, Baltray has 19 splendid holes.

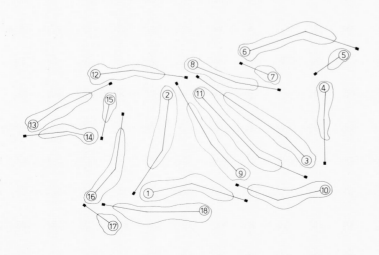

Hole	Yards	Par	Hole	Yards	Par
1	433	4	10	398	4
2	482	5	11	481	5
3	544	5	12	410	4
4	344	4	13	421	4
5	158	3	14	332	4
6	531	5	15	152	3
7	163	3	16	388	4
8	407	4	17	179	3
9	419	4	18	541	5
Out	**3,481**	**37**	**In**	**3,302**	**36**
			Out	**3,481**	**37**
			Totals	**6,783**	**73**

One day in 1893, a Scot domiciled in Dublin named W.C. Pickman was riding his bicycle along the road from Baldoyle to Portmarnock when, so the story goes, looking across the estuary it occurred to him that he was looking at magnificent golfing terrain. . . .

Portmarnock is located to the North of Dublin and lying on a peninsula is surrounded by water on three sides. It can be as tough a challenge as any in the world—more than 7000 yards from the back tees with the rough often mercilessly punishing (knee-high in parts!) But Portmarnock, rather like Muirfield, offers a genuinely fair challenge. There are no blind shots, no hidden traps and the greens are among the finest in the world. As for that rough, well, as an obviously straight-hitter once remarked, you've no business being there in the first place and you cannot really argue with that! Portmarnock has its beauty too: to the south, the Hill of Howth and the great sweep of Dublin Bay and to the north west, Drogheda and the distant Mountains of Mourne. On a fine day the links provides the player with a spectacular 360 degree vista; all in all it is a truly wonderful place to pursue the Royal and Ancient game.

The **Secretary** at Portmarnock is the very helpful **Mr. John J. Quigley.** He may be contacted by writing to **The Secretary, Portmarnock Golf Club, Portmarnock, Co. Dublin** and by telephone on **(01) 8462968** (the code is **(010 353 1)** from the UK) The Club's **professional** is **Joey Purcell**, he can be reached on **(01) 8462634.**

Providing visitors possess a handicap of 24 or less they are very welcome to play the famous links; however, ladies cannot play at weekends or on Bank Holidays. It seems that half of Dublin wants to play Portmarnock (not to mention you and me) and the course can be extremely popular. The wisest move is to telephone the Club before you set off. The green fees as set in 1994 are, for gentlemen £40 midweek, £50 at the weekend, and for lady visitors, £30 midweek. As a bit of a tip, Mondays and Tuesdays are the quietest days. Golfing Societies are equally welcome subject to prior arrangement with the Secretary.

It is far easier to travel to Portmarnock than to many of the country's other great golfing attractions. The capital is very well served by international flights and Dublin's airport is only six miles from the links. From Britain, it is also worth noting that both B&I and Sealink sail regularly to Dublin. As mentioned, Portmarnock lies to the north of the capital, a distance of about eight

miles. By road it's essentially a case of heading for Portmarnock village and then looking out for signs: from Dublin the course should be signposted off to the right, and from Malahide, look to your left.

The casual visitor will not have to attempt the full 7000 yards plus, but he's still likely to be facing a good 6600 yards so he'd better have his game in fine fettle! Happily there is a relatively gentle break-in with three holes measuring less than 400 yards. The course then changes direction and the 4th, the stroke one hole confronts you. Normally, the wind will be with you, but don't bank on it! A number of second shots will be played to plateau greens which can be very difficult to hold and a good Irish pitch-and-run may be needed frequently. The most celebrated holes are probably the 14th and the 15th. The former has been described by Henry Cotton as one of the greatest par fours in golf and it's easy to see why. The hole is played towards the sea along a gently curving fairway; the narrow green sits on a plateau and is protected by two bunkers set into the rise of the green with many humps and hillocks surrounding the putting surface—nothing but a precise second shot will do. As for the 15th, Ben Crenshaw has called it, 'one of the greatest short holes on earth'. Out of bounds in the form of the beach lurks the length of the hole to the right. Even then there is no let up and the five-four-four finish is one of the toughest around.

The gentle wind down of course begins at the 19th. Portmarnock has a splendid Clubhouse, though not the original, which unfortunately burned down. The atmosphere is tremendous and some very good value snacks are offered daily with dinner also possible during the week.

The Club has staged many great Championships in the past including, somewhat surprisingly, the (British) Amateur Championship which was won—it goes without saying—by an Irishman. The World Cup was played at Portmarnock in 1960, Palmer and Snead winning for the United States, while winners of the Irish Open on this links have included Americans Crenshaw and Hubert Green and an illustrious quartet of European stars: Ballesteros, Langer, Woosnam and Olazabal—proving the old adage that a great course will always produce a great champion.

In 1991 Portmarnock successfully hosted the Walker Cup and there are many who consider it a travesty that the Ryder Cup matches did not come here in 1993.

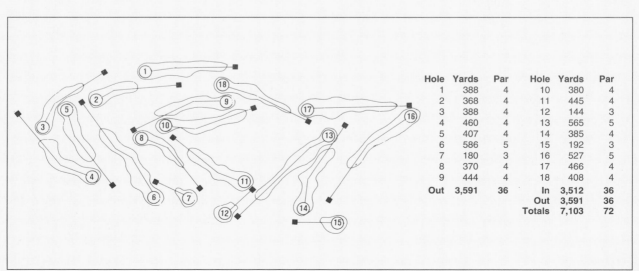

Hole	Yards	Par	Hole	Yards	Par
1	388	4	10	380	4
2	368	4	11	445	4
3	388	4	12	144	3
4	460	4	13	565	5
5	407	4	14	385	4
6	586	5	15	192	3
7	180	3	16	527	5
8	370	4	17	466	4
9	444	4	18	408	4
Out	**3,591**	**36**	**In**	**3,512**	**36**
			Out	**3,591**	**36**
			Totals	**7,103**	**72**

Mullingar

*'St. Patrick was a gentleman
Who through strategy and stealth
Drove all the snakes from Ireland,
Here's a toasting to his health;
But not too many toastings
Lest you lose yourself and then
Forget the good St Patrick
And see all those snakes again.'*

So, reading between the lines, golfers who restrain themselves at the 19th hole have about as much chance of bumping into an Irish snake as they have of meeting the Man in the Moon. But just suppose we've been less than restrained....now, we will direct the Man in the Moon towards Connemara or the New Course at Ballybunion where he should feel very much at home, and as for the snakes, we'll send them anywhere but Mullingar. Why? Well, Mullingar may not resemble The Seychelles but it must be about the nearest thing in Ireland to a golfing Garden of Eden.

'Sylvan' is an adjective commonly used to describe the setting at Mullingar and when one adds the indisputable quality of the golf course and the friendliness of the welcome to the equation it is easy to see why this has become one of Ireland's most popular Clubs to visit. Yet before the war the most accurate word to describe the Mullingar golfer might well have been 'pernickety', or 'restless' at best. This is because by the mid 1930s, less than 50 years after their Club's foundation, the golfers were already searching for a fifth home. Pernicketiness obviously paid off though for when they 'discovered' the site at Belvedere to the south of Mullingar (off the N52), and close to the peace and beauty of Lough Ennell, they knew at once that they had struck gold. And of course the obvious person to design their new layout was James Braid, architect of the majestic King's Course at Gleneagles. Braid came, advised and left; the 18 hole course at Belvedere opened for play; the Mullingar golfer stopped being pernickety and the Club hasn't looked back since. In fact the course has attracted top class tournaments and generous praise in equal abundance.

Today the best interests of the Mullingar golfer, and all visitors to this wonderful 'out in the country' location, are in the capable hands of the Club's **secretary Anne Scully.** She may be contacted by telephone on **(044) 48366**, while the **professional, John Burns** can be reached on **(044) 40085**. Visitors, preferably with official handicaps can make advance bookings, indeed this is recommended although there are no general tee restrictions. In 1994 the green fees were £16 on weekdays with £22 payable at weekends. As a rule the best days to arrange a game are Tuesdays, Thursdays and Fridays and unless one is an exceptionally good golfer (or avid spectator) the August Bank Holiday—always the first Sunday/Monday of the month—should be avoided: this is when the Club hosts the highly prestigious Mullingar Scratch Cup, an annual event first staged in 1963, and with an impressive list of winners including the likes of Joe Carr, Peter Townsend, Des Smyth and the course record holder (with an astonishing 63), Philip Walton.

From the Championship tees, Mullingar measures 6451 yards, par 72. Ballybunion was mentioned above and just as it is the massive dunes that fashion and frame the holes on this glorious seaside links, so it is the spectacular collection (and enormous variety) of trees that shape the rolling parkland fairways at Mullingar.

The most celebrated hole on the course is probably the 2nd, a long and difficult par three where the pin sits on a small, slippery table of a green flanked either side by several magnetic little pot bunkers. None of the four par fives at Mullingar is especially frightening, indeed each represents an obvious birdie opportunity for the good, straight hitter but to my mind it is the par fours that are the real strength of Mullingar. Picking out five of these I would select the 7th (the most testing two-shot hole of the round); the 8th (a severe dog-leg right with an elevated tee and an uphill approach; the 10th (again a downhill drive to a fairway bordered by some magnificent pine trees); the 11th (shades of Wentworth here) and the 17th (a sweeping dog-leg left to yet another raised and well guarded green).

The closing hole at Mullingar is one of those 'birdieable' par fives (providing you successfully carry the watery ditch that fronts the green) and the 19th is where first class sustenance can be found. Recently refurbished, the clubhouse is a fine place in which to relax, unwind and reflect on your visit to Jimmy Braid's Garden of Eden—just go easy on the toastings!

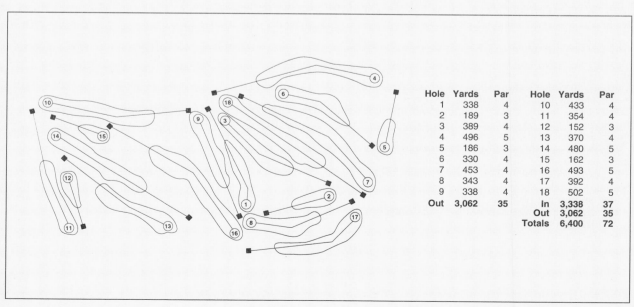

Hole	Yards	Par		Hole	Yards	Par
1	338	4		10	433	4
2	189	3		11	354	4
3	389	4		12	152	3
4	496	5		13	370	4
5	186	3		14	480	5
6	330	4		15	162	3
7	453	4		16	493	5
8	343	4		17	392	4
9	338	4		18	502	5
Out	**3,062**	**35**		**In**	**3,338**	**37**
				Out	**3,062**	**35**
				Totals	**6,400**	**72**

Surrounded by 560 acres of beautiful undulating parkland, Luttrellstown Castle evokes the enchanting atmosphere of the grand house parties of an earlier age.

Only six miles from Dublin's city centre and international airport, Luttrellstown offers one of Europe's most prestigious settings for exclusive corporate or private entertaining, visits by private groups, or select company meetings and conferences. It is unique in being the only complete estate in the Republic of Ireland, and possibly Europe, available to private individuals or corporations.

The imposing Gothic castle, part of which dates back to 1436, has recently been lavishly restored and modernised . Its sixty rooms include the magnificent ballroom, four other elegant main reception rooms, the billiard room and fourteen luxurious individually furnished double bedrooms, each with its own stylish bathroom.

The castle is run by a charming and attentive staff, whole-heartedly dedicated to its guests' comfort and enjoyment. Its cuisine is some of Ireland's finest.

The estate's picturesque grounds, with its gardens, four lakes, its waterfalls and eccentric follies, provide delightful opportunities for walking, horse-riding, shooting, and fishing. Luttrellstown also has its own tennis court and heated swimming pool.

The magnificent Championship Golf Course threads its way through the 18th century landscape.

Business facilities include a well-equipped executive office, international telephone and fax, and full secretarial services. Additional meeting facilities can be arranged on request.

Luttrellstown has a long history of entertaining royalty. Queen Victoria stayed twice in 1849 and 1900. More recent guests have been the King and Queen of Denmark, The Grand Duke of Luxembourg, Prince Ranier and Princess Grace of Monaco and a variety of Hollywood stars, including Fred Astaire, Douglas Fairbanks, Jr, Ronald Reagan, James Mason and David Niven. The estate was acquired from the Guinness family in 1984 by the Primwest group, which is intent on keeping alive Luttrellstown's reputation for unrivalled hospitality.

Luttrellstown is available on a weekly basis, or by the week-end, from Friday until Sunday night. Shorter visits or functions may be arranged, subject to availability.

There is also a limited number of 2 double bedroom apartments in the old coach yard, ideal for the Golfing Fourball.

The castle and estate is managed by Nicholas and Heather Bielenberg, who supervised all the internal and external restoration of the property. Enquiries for additional information and bookings should be addressed to Heather Bielenberg at Luttrellstown Castle.

Luttrellstown Castle
Clonsilla
County Dublin
Republic of Ireland
Tel: (010 353 1) 8213237

'I love it over here' said the great Seve Ballesteros to his Irish host. 'You have a wonderfully relaxed way of doing things. Surely there's an Irish word for our "Mañana"? Good heavens, no', replied the stunned host, 'nothing quite so urgent!'

An apocryphal story perhaps, but you understand the point. Go to Luttrellstown Castle and you'll experience the feeling. Luttrellstown is situated at Clonsilla, near Lucan, just seven miles from the centre of Dublin yet it seems a world apart. It is not as if the spectacular castle and its splendid grounds are caught in a time warp - a great deal has happened here of late - but there is an air of timelessness about the place and, yes, it is wonderfully relaxing. Moreover, for golfers it has a special appeal since the opening in July 1993 of the Luttrellstown Castle Golf and Country Club.

As far as I am aware, 'the great Seve' (a three time winer of the Irish Open) has never been to Luttrellstown but an equally legendary figure has, namely the American, Gene Sarazen. At a sprightly 91 years of age, golf's 'Oldest Member' recently visited Luttrellstown Castle and took a buggy ride out to view the pristinely new golf course. He didn't play but as he journeyed around the layout he was heard to declare, 'this is one of the finest parkland courses I have ever seen'. A spellbound Sarazen had no doubt been charmed by the majesty of the surroundings but as one who has played golf all over the world for some 80 odd years, he must know a really good course when he sees one.

Despite his Italian ancestry, Sarazen is an American through-and-through and he lives in Florida where fine golf courses are two a penny. What I suspect Sarazen liked about Luttrellstown, however, is that it is a thoroughly Irish parkland course in a thoroughly Irish setting. Had he been given a guided tour around the nearby K Club he might have imagined he was back in Florida, with all its vast man made mounds, its beach like bunkers and plethora of do-or-die shots across water.

Luttrellstown is very different . There is no shortage of water, mind you, indeed there are several dramatic water carries to be confronted during the 18 holes, but this is what the purists would describe as a very natural parkland course. The beautifully landscaped ponds and lakes exist primarily for the benefit of wildlife not golfers; there is no overt mounding but with gently undulating terrain and a glorious assortment of trees (ancient oaks, limes, beeches and a sprinkling of cedar and pine) there is plenty of definition to the holes and no need to frame the fairways with huge hills. And who in any event would wish to hide away the many delightful vistas: the serenity of the Dublin Mountains, the glimpses of an adjoining wooded glen with its waterfalls and cascades, and an ancient bridge, a Doric Temple and an ivy-clad castle?

With thoughtful positioning of the tees and greens - there are many exhilarating downhill drives and precise approach shots will always be rewarded - the golf course at Luttrellstown Castle has been designed to accommodate and take advantage of its natural inheritance. From the Championship markers it measures over 7,000 yards (par 72) although from the forward and ladies tees the challenge is less daunting. There are several highly memorable holes, with a particularly strong sequence between the 7th and 12th (the par three 10th is Sarazen's favourite) and none that could be described as dull. The putting surfaces are among the best conditioned in Ireland and the Clubhouse - built in Finnish pine and due to be opened in late 1994 promises to be one of the country's most stylish . . .yes, Luttrellstown has charmed this writer as well! But I am sure no visitor will be disappointed by a trip to Luttrellstown Castle. With 1994 green fees set at £30 during the week and £35 at weekends (with group discounts available on request) there can be few more enjoyable places to while away the hours. Tee reservations can be made by telephoning the Club's **Secretary, Maura O'Riordan** on **(01) 8208210.**

One of the most popular times to visit Luttrellstown Castle is on Wednesdays when the Club invariably stages an open fourball competition. So then, find yourself three soulmates, head on down to Luttrellstown and let yourself be thoroughly charmed.

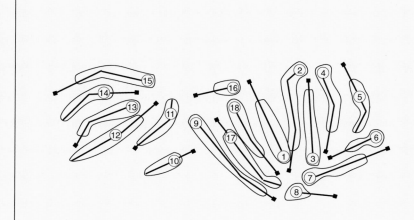

Hole	Metres	Par	Hole	Metres	Par
1	384	4	10	171	3
2	472	5	11	325	4
3	386	4	12	526	5
4	352	4	13	403	4
5	338	4	14	396	4
6	202	3	15	415	4
7	358	4	16	153	3
8	127	3	17	493	5
9	508	5	18	375	4
Out	**3,127**	**36**	**In**	**3,257**	**36**
			Out	**3,127**	**36**
			Totals	**6,384**	**72**

Rathsallagh House

Converted from Queen Anne stables the main house was burnt to the ground in 1798 this large, comfortable farmhouse is situated in 500 acres of peaceful parkland surrounded by some of the most beautiful countryside of Eastern Ireland.

The addition of full modern amenities has done nothing to spoil the traditional splendour of the house where welcoming log fires combine with full central heating to ensure your comfort, The delightful bedrooms are individually decorated with care and attention; all are large and luxurious and offer en suite bathrooms with enormous bath towels.

The atmosphere is happy and relaxed in this hotel with its huge variety of diversions. The 18 hole Championship Golf Course, set in 252 acres of mature parkland, was designed by Irish golfing legend Christy O'Connor Jnr and Peter McEvoy, former World Amateur Champion and English Captain. The course, which will open for play in May 1994, will not be restricted to residents and Members, although residents will enjoy a reduced green fee. Rathsallagh also has a hard tennis court, near the indoor heated swimming pool alongside the sauna which is upstairs from the full size billiard table. Croquet and

archery are practiced on the lawn, away from the noise of Clay Pigeon shooting with a CPSA Club Coach which it is also offered on the 530 acre estate. Alternatively, you could stroll around the award winning two acre walled garden, or relax with a whiskey in the fully licensed bar. For the racing enthusiast the hotel is ideally situated for the Irish National Stud, along with Curragh, Punchestown, and Goffs Sales Paddock.

For a change deer-stalking can be arranged, while your host, Joe O'Flynn, a former master of the local hunt can arrange fox-hunting in season. Besides the outstanding natural beauty of the surrounding areas there is also a variety of historic sites well worth a visit, not least of these being Glendalough and Russborough House.

At the end of such a day, the real log fire of the restaurant provides a pleasing welcome. The cooking is superb with the emphasis on fresh, local produce, while the too-tempting sweet trolley fairly groans with luscious offerings.

Naturally, Rathsallagh is fully able to cater for business meetings and offers, amongst other things, a fully equipped purpose-built Conference Room and Helipad.

Rathsallagh Country House and Restaurant
Dunlavin
Co Wicklow
Ireland
Tel: (010 353 45) 53112
Fax: (010 353 45) 53343

The 'K' Club (Straffan)

In timeless fashion, and without a care in the world the River Liffey meanders its way through the ancient Straffan Estate in Co. Kildare en route to Dublin and the Irish Sea. In 1988 the estate was acquired by Ireland's largest, and possibly most ambitious company, Jefferson Smurfit; undoubtedly the great attraction being the vast 19th century Straffan House, one of the most striking country houses in Ireland. Such a company, such an estate—a heady mix if ever there was one. For some time it had been the dream of company chairman Dr Michael Smurfit to develop a 'world class country club'. At Straffan he saw the potential for an extremely grand, even palatial 5 star hotel (the restored and extended Straffan House) and sufficient land to build a challenging championship length golf course, one good enough to host national and international tournaments. Thus the Kildare Country Club, or 'K' Club as everyone calls it, was born.

When it came to the design of the golf course the word 'challenging' was clearly given special emphasis, for though four leading golf architects submitted proposals for the 18 hole layout, it seems there was not much of a contest once Arnold Palmer and his team had presented their ideas. Palmer had already created one course in Ireland, the ultra-spectacular links at Tralee on the west coast, now was the opportunity to demonstrate his swashbuckling design theories on an inland site, just 25 miles south west of Dublin.

The new course, (which measures over 7,100 yards from its championship tees), was officially opened in 1991 and straightaway generated an enormous amount of interest. Initially, not all press coverage was favourable, although the criticisms were in no way directed at the quality or shape of the layout itself, rather they alluded to some teething problems with the course's drainage system. This however has now been fully rectified, and the 'K' Club can justifiably claim its place among the premier inland courses of Europe.

To suggest that Palmer has succeeded in creating a challenging course would be a gross understatement. With holes weaving their way through an extraordinary lunar-like landscape, the unsuspecting golfer is likely to be awestruck and amazed by some of the shots he is asked to take on... Straffan is no ordinary golf course.

First though, a couple of quick introductions. The Golf **Secretary** at the 'K' Club is the very personable **Ken Greene, tel: (01) 6273987,** and the **professional** is **Ernie Jones tel: (01) 6273111.** Visitors can make **tee reservations** by telephoning the hotel reception on **(01) 6273987.** All players must be golf club members and have a handicap; finally the green fee in 1994 was £77 on weekdays and £85 at weekends with reduced rates available for groups of 15 and over.

Time then for us to 'attack' Arnie's golf course. A long straight drive at the 1st, carrying the large fairway bunker should set up a relatively easy opening par five. The same, however, cannot be said of the 2nd where two very precise shots are essential. The drive must be perfectly positioned, for the approach is downhill to a smallish green guarded by trees on one side and water on the other. And so the gauntlet is laid down. There are two par threes in the first five holes, the 5th being the more demanding but for most people the round really comes alive at the par five 7th.

From tee to green this is one long, dramatic, 'S shaped' voyage of discovery as the hole double dog-legs its way over sand, rough and water and in between a plethora of colourful trees and shrubs. The green occupies its own pretty little island and is sandwiched between two arms of the River Liffey. A quaint old iron bridge transports us to and from the island. Our friend the River Liffey is an inseparable companion for the entire length of the 8th (a hooker's nightmare) and then comes the 9th, a truly intimidating stroke one hole.

There is absolutely no let up on the back nine, indeed the drama most definitely increases. The 12th is probably the best par three on the course; the tee shot here must be struck over a small lake to a superbly angled green—between the lake and green is a deep beach-like bunker where the sand literally runs into the water's edge. The downhill par five 13th rivals the 18th as the most exhilarating hole: like the 7th it is a double dog-leg with a highly illusive and heavily contoured green. From the 15th to the end of the round a series of heroic shots alongside or across water are called for. Two daring water carries in fact confront us at the 16th and a good drive at the last begs one final question: shall we risk a watery grave and go for the 18th green in two—a real grandstand finish in front of the magnificent clubhouse? Well, what would Arnie do?

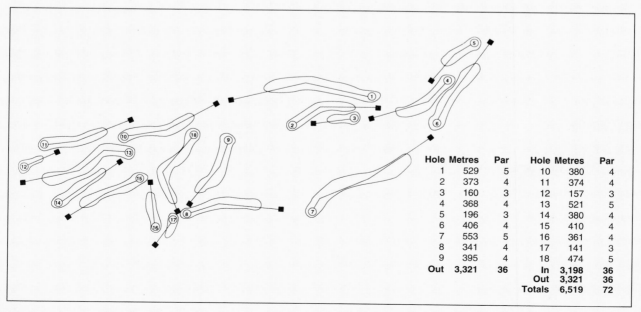

Hole	Metres	Par	Hole	Metres	Par
1	529	5	10	380	4
2	373	4	11	374	4
3	160	3	12	157	3
4	368	4	13	521	5
5	196	3	14	380	4
6	406	4	15	410	4
7	553	5	16	361	4
8	341	4	17	141	3
9	395	4	18	474	5
Out	**3,321**	**36**	**In**	**3,198**	**36**
			Out	**3,321**	**36**
			Totals	**6,519**	**72**

With its location just ten minutes from Dublin airport and only 20 minutes from the city centre, for any golfer visiting Dublin a round of golf at St Margaret's is a must. The course designers, Tom Craddock and Pat Ruddy, have created at St Margaret's Golf and Country Club a course which, within two years of opening, has been accoladed as one of Ireland's premier golfing venues.

The designers have turned a couple of hundred acres of flat farmland into a magnificent expanse of sculpted parkland. The modern design approach makes use of water hazards and each of the 18 holes is framed by manmade hills and huge undulating greens.

Challenging in terms of length the course has five par fives and four par threes - the rest being par fours. Flexible teeing allows the middle and high handicap golfer a fairer challenge on this course.

The par five 8th measures 525 yards and is set to become one of the most notorious holes in Europe. It features a lake to the left of the tee, a second lake to the right on the second shot and a third lake in front of the green. The 12th is perhaps the most picturesque of all the holes and features a generous rollercoaster fairway that dips between lakes and across a brook below the majestic elevated green.

The 18th hole is one of the finest in golf today and not for the faint hearted. The overall design of the course, the obvious attention to every small detail and the sheer beauty of the features all combine to inspire an excellent round of golf.

The clubhouse is designed with luxury in mind. It has a spacious bar ideal for relaxing after a challenging round of golf. The clubhouse also boasts a spike grill, luxury golf shop, an elegant restaurant and purpose-built conference suite. The overall effect is a welcoming building suitable for relaxing or conducting business. Corporate days and society outings are welcomed and expertly catered for under the guidance of Denis Kane and his experienced and friendly staff.

St Margaret's is designed as a place where golf is to be played recreationally and competitively. The club played host to the Women's Irish Holidays Open in July 1994 and over the last two years has played host to the Golf Writers Home Internationals, the Irish Seniors Open and the Cork Dry Gin Foursomes.

For intending visitors bookings are simple - phone Paul Henry, Director of Golf, to reserve a tee time (pre booking is recommended).

St Margaret's Golf & Country Club
St Margaret's
County Dublin
Ireland
Tel: (010 353 1) 8640 400
Fax: (010 353 1) 8640 289

I wonder what Old Tom Morris would have made of the recently opened St Margaret's Golf and Country Club. Not a lot probably. I'm not suggesting that he would necessarily disapprove of it but he probably wouldn't understand it. In fact, it would probably be as much a mystery to him as the jumbo jet aircraft at nearby Dublin Airport. Old Tom inhabited a very different world. It was Old Tom who designed the original golf links at Lahinch in Co. Clare and Lahinch is about as different from St Margaret's as it is possible for a golf course to be. In many ways (historically, geographically and technically for a start) Dublin's lavish new parkland layout is the antithesis of the famous west coast links, the so called 'St Andrews of Ireland'. One of the advantages of being a present day golfer, however, is that it is possible to play both courses and discover that such contrasting challenges can be equally enjoyable. Rather interestingly, in its 1993 ranking of 'Ireland's 30 Greatest Golf Courses' the Irish Golf Institute rated St Margaret's in 13th position, just one place behind Lahinch.

St Margaret's could be described as a 'state of the art' Championship golf course. The 13th place ranking referred to above emphasises, notwithstanding its great youth, just how highly regarded it is. The same panel voted St Margaret's the 'Best New Course of 1992' and the Tom Craddock and Pat Ruddy designed course is already being heralded as a future Irish Open venue. Precocious is not the word!

There is a favourite saying among purveyors of real estate that the two most important aspects of a property are its location.... and its location! Situated close to the international airport and not far from the centre of Dublin, no Club in Ireland is better placed to capture the attention of an ever increasing golf hungry public. Aesthetically speaking, the St Margaret's site was a fairly unremarkable piece of farmland before the bulldozers and the architects appeared on the scene. Now no one could ever describe St Margaret's as unremarkable - unrecognisable, yes. It is undoubtedly a very fine golf course and one without any obvious weaknesses; whether in time it will merit the accolade 'world class' remains to be seen. Perhaps the best thought is to pay it a visit for the St Margaret's Golf and Country Club is an extremely visitor friendly club.

Chiefly responsible for the welcoming atmosphere are the Club's **General Manager, Denis Kane** who can be contacted by telephone on **(01) 8640400** and the **Golf Director, Paul Henry**, tel: **(01) 8640416**. .There are no specific restrictions as to the time when visitors can play although advance booking is recommended. Finally, the green fees in 1994 were £30 per round during the week and £35 per round at weekends.

From its Championship tees, St Margaret's measures a shade under 7,000 yards, or in other words, when the elements are stirred it can be a brute! Most players of course will not have to confront the many challenges from the back markers but unlike on many courses, playing from the forward tees in no way diminishes the character of the holes. This is due largely to the fact that the real strength and flavour of St Margaret's lies in the great range of approach shots that the player is invited to take on. Perhaps the best example of this is provided by the 7th, where following a downhill drive the shot to the green invokes memories of the celebrated par three 12th at Augusta — with water (Ruddy's Creek?) and a bunker in front of the raised and narrow putting surface and twin bunkers posing menacingly behind the flag at the back of the green.

As one might expect on a modern Championship styled course, water not only features prominently, but shapes a number of fairways and greens at St Margaret's. The hole immediately following the 'slice of Augusta,' the dramatic par five 8th, illustrates the point perfectly. Here the golfer must avoid a lake to the left of the tee, another to the right of the fairway and a third which bisects the fairway immediately in front of the green — it all adds up to one of the most perilous journeys in Ireland!

On the back nine, the 12th hole is an absolute beauty but the 'piece de resistance' has to be the glorious finishing hole. The long, twisting par four 18th at St Margaret's features a dramatically positioned green which nervously overlooks a lake, which is in turn imperiously overlooked by the large clubhouse. It makes for a truly spectacular climax to the round although golfers might only feel comfortable playing this hole if wearing a blindfold. Blind shots at St Margaret's? Come back Old Tom.

Hole	Yards	Par	Hole	Yards	Par
1	365	4	10	395	4
2	160	3	11	365	4
3	510	5	12	480	5
4	455	4	13	200	3
5	175	3	14	400	4
6	465	4	15	180	3
7	370	4	16	535	5
8	525	5	17	510	5
9	395	4	18	450	4
Out	**3,420**	**36**	**In**	**3,515**	**36**
			Out	**3,420**	**72**
			Totals	**6,935**	**72**

Marlfield House is a fine house set in thirty-five acres of woodlands and gardens and was the principal residence of the Earl of Courtown. It has been converted by its present owners, Ray and Mary Bowe, whose aim is to meet the demands of the more discerning guest who insists on the best country house atmosphere.

Golfers will certainly not be disappointed by the quality of the courses close by, with Marlfield House ideally situated for the championship links of the European Club, one of Irelands most prestigious recent developments, and just two kilometres from the Courtown Course which has long been considered one of the finest on the east coast.

The award winning restaurant is a memorable experience and serves modern French cooking with a classical base. At the rear of the house is a spectacular conservatory. An inner, mirrored section reflects painted forest scenes and is snug in winter. An outer section opens to the gardens for summer dining. Vegetables, herbs and some fruits are grown in the kitchen garden and all local produce is made use of in the kitchen.

Accommodation is in nineteen superb rooms, including five luxurious junior suites and one magnificent master suite. These are lavishly decorated using period furniture and have huge marble en suite bathrooms, some with jacuzzis. Each of the junior suites has its own theme: Irish, Georgian, French etc.

Marlfield is only 80 kilometres from Dublin, in the heart of the countryside, situated on the Gorey to Courtown Road . This area is something of a sportsman's paradise with excellent fishing and shooting to be had in addition to the golf. It is also an area to be enjoyed for its glorious coastline and splendid sandy beaches and Marlfield House provides an ideal setting for touring the beauty spots of Wicklow and the south east of Ireland.

Marlfield House
Gorey
Co Wexford
Tel: (55) 21125
Fax: (55) 21572

> Rugged dunes, deep bunkers and sea breezes;
> fast running fairways, large undulating greens
> that invite the pitch-and-run approach
> and acres of tall waving marram grass.
> This is the very essence of golf - as it was
> at the beginning and was always meant to be'.
> *(Pat Ruddy)*

Legend has it that when W C Pickman peddled along the estuary from Baldoyle and saw the great stretch of linksland at Portmarnock he almost fell off his bicycle. Almost a century later, Robert Trent Jones was led deep into the sand hills at Ballybunion and has never been the same man since; it blew his mind. Imagine then how Pat Ruddy must have felt when he first saw the vast expanse of rugged dunes and waving marram grass just south of Brittas Bay in Co Wicklow. What effect on a man with golf in his soul?

Another legend is developing, for it is being claimed that Ruddy drove a JCB on to the same stretch of land in 1987 and didn't venture out the other side until 1993, and they believe it everywhere in Ireland, except at St Margaret's.

It is the proud boast of golfers at Mount Juliet that they play 'the course that Jack built' In Co Wicklow we can now experience the links that Pat built, and whatever else Pat Ruddy achieves in his life the European Club will stand as his monument to golf.

Let us straight away say that it has enormous potential. The word 'great' should be used very sparingly in relation to golf courses but the links at Brittas Bay is a great links. It has many great qualities. The sand hills are not of Ballybunion - like proportions: but they dwarf those at Portmarnock and Baltray. Better still, the golf course never leaves the dunes. There is balance and consistency and no feeling of mild disappointment as is sometimes expressed in relation to the final few holes at Lahinch and Newcastle — and indeed with regard to the first five at Ballybunion. The Irish Sea is the golfer's constant companion. You see it as you leave the 1st green, you hear it as you approach the 3rd and smell it as you stroll down the 7th... and you can almost touch it as you play along the 12th and 13th!.

There are at least five genuinely great holes. The beautifully flowing downhill 3rd, the 7th, with its fairway bordered by haunting marshland, the 8th, the 12th and the fabulous 17th which plunges through a secluded dune - lined valley - these could all be described as great holes, and one final treat - or is it shock? awaits at the 18th, but who are we to spoil the surprise?!

Ruddy's dream is that the European Club will one day be spoken of in the same breath as Ireland's 'Big Four' of Portmarnock, Portrush, Ballybunion and Newcastle. Most who have seen the course believe he has at least an evens chance of succeeding, and people who know Pat Ruddy will tell you that he eats such odds for breakfast.

We will probably have to wait a little while however before the European Club can be properly or fairly compared with the aforementioned 'Big Four' — it is still a trifle raw for one thing - but then the course was only fully opened for play in May 1993. What is certain is that you are made to feel very relaxed at Brittas Bay. A unique 'welcome to the family' atmosphere is developing. Ruddy says he wants to encourage a 'spirit of simplicity' and to recreate the mood of a time when golf was enjoyed in less hurried, less crowded and less pretentious circumstances. 'I've been to clubs where you see guys dressed like undertakers'. 'Golf is meant to be fun', he says.

The course and club facilities are open to visitors seven days a week. The only restriction as such is that the number of players is carefully controlled. Priority is naturally given to those who have made advance arrangements, so booking a tee time is recommended. The club's telephone number is **(0404) 47415**. The green fees in 1994 were set at £20 per round.

Brittas Bay is approximately 40 minutes south of Dublin and the European Club is slightly closer to the capital than Baltray (Co Louth) is to the north. It is often claimed that a golfer hasn't experienced the full flavour of Irish links golf until he or she has made a pilgrimage to Ballybunion. One day the same might be said about Brittas Bay. The golf course is genuinely amazing, and when a club is very personally run by a man whose motto in life is 'Grab some sticks and let's go golfing' how can you possibly resist?.

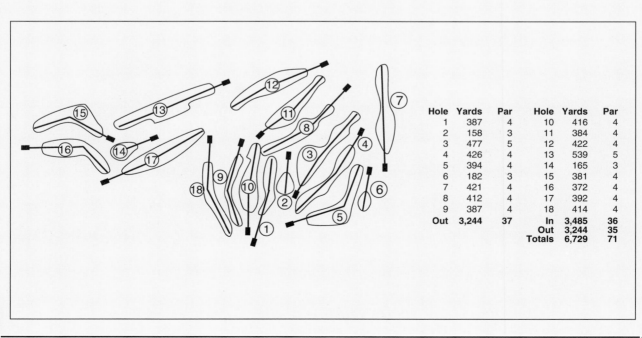

Hole	Yards	Par	Hole	Yards	Par
1	387	4	10	416	4
2	158	3	11	384	4
3	477	5	12	422	4
4	426	4	13	539	5
5	394	4	14	165	3
6	182	3	15	381	4
7	421	4	16	372	4
8	412	4	17	392	4
9	387	4	18	414	4
Out	3,244	37	In	3,485	36
			Out	3,244	35
			Totals	6,729	71

Continuing to wander down through the counties of Ireland, County Laois is the next we come across. There's only one 18 hole course, the **Heath** and no guesses as to the type of golf offered. The course is laid out on common land and rather like the Curragh, there's a fair chance that you'll spot more sheep than golfers. Stumbling into County Carlow we find probably the best inland course (aside from the new Mount Juliet) in south east Ireland. **Carlow** is a superb course: well bunkered and well wooded, it presents a considerable test of golf but a very fair one nonetheless. Carlow is highlighted later in this chapter. There are a number of convenient hotels in Carlow itself but for a real treat stay in Castledermot at **Kilkea Castle** (010 353) 503 45100, a splendidly converted 12th century castle. Kilkea has its own turf nursery and has recently laid out an 18 hole golf course in the grounds. A very popular restaurant is also found in Castledermot, the Doyles School House (010 353) 503 44282.

Kilkenny is one of those places that has to be visited. It's a town steeped in Irish history. In medieval times it housed the Irish Parliament, then there's the famous Kilkenny Castle, an impressive collection of churches and Kytelers Inn. The city's golf course is a bit of a youngster in comparison, but it's a fine parkland course, very typical of Ireland's better inland courses. The Newpark Hotel (010 353) 562 2122 is just one of several comfortable establishments in the town. Nearby, Thomastown is the setting for the magnificent new **Mount Juliet** complex (010 353) 562 4455, featuring 18 spectacular holes designed by Jack Nicklaus, and a luxurious country house hotel (see ahead). One mile from Thomastown and adjacent to Jerpoint Abbey is the Abbey House (010 353) 562 4192—a highly recommended guest house.

From Kilkenny it's a pleasant drive to **Borris** where there is an excellent 9 holer and it's certainly not a long way to Tipperary either. Visitors to the county with the famous name should slip a game in at **Clonmel**. This is a fairly isolated part of Ireland and you may just have the course to yourself on a quiet weekday. A good place to put the feet up after a game is the Hotel Minella (010 353) 522 2388, considered by many the best in this area, or alternatively, the Clonmel Arms Hotel (010 353) 522 1233. Not too far away in Cashel, (and be sure to visit the

magnificent Rock), the Cashel Palace Hotel (010 353) 626 1411 and its restaurant, the Four Seasons are quite outstanding. Before heading down to Waterford a quick recommendation for the 18 hole course at **Courtown**, close to the north Wexford coast which boasts some fabulous beaches—in fact the golden sands stretch practically all the way south to Wexford town. A charming place to stay when playing Courtown is Marlfield House (010 353) 552 1125 at Gorey, one of the finest country houses in Ireland.

The world famous Waterford crystal factory is reason enough for stopping a while in the Waterford area, but there are other sound reasons too. The first is **Waterford Castle**, the kind of place you dream about: an ivy-clad 12th century castle dominating a small island which can only be reached by ferry. Today, the castle is in fact one of Ireland's finest hotels (010 353) 517 8203, both sumptuous and intimate and also exceptionally welcoming. Moreover, the island isn't quite so small that the owners can't find space for a new 18 hole golf and country club! The course, designed by Ryder Cup golfer Des Smyth, opened in the summer of 1992. The other good reasons for visiting Waterford are **Tramore** Golf Club and **Waterford** Golf Club—both offer very good parkland golf. The former, just 15 minutes from Waterford, is a real test and is good enough to have staged the Irish Amateur Championship in 1987. The latter, however, is possibly more enjoyable having greater variety, especially on the back nine which features a magnificent downhill finishing hole. If ever there was a hole that tempted the golfer to open his shoulders and let rip, this is it—a good drive will run forever, a bad drive —well... Anyway, read on as the course is described in greater detail on a later page. Either side of Waterford there has been much golf course building activity and both **West Waterford** Golf Club at Dungarvon and **St Helen's Bay** are well worth inspecting from a base such as the Ferrycarrig Hotel (010 353) 53 22999.

But we end our journey at **Rosslare.** Having started our tour of south east Ireland on a heath, we end on a links. Rosslare may not have the glamour of a Portmarnock or a Royal Dublin but for lovers of the traditional game—rolling sand dunes and a hammering wind—it will do perfectly.

Artist: **Harry Elliot ON THE FAIRWAY** _Courtesy of_ **Burlington Gallery**

Hunter's Hotel, one of Ireland's oldest coaching inns, has been established for over 250 years from the days of post horses and carriages. Indeed some of the earliest written recommendations date back over 150 years and bear testimony to the hospitality of the Hunter family who have run the hotel for five generations. The owners today, The Gelletlie Family, are proud to carry on the traditions of their great great grandfather, John Hunter, who back in 1840 was considered to have the best inn in the county.

This area of Ireland is a sportsman's paradise and golfers especially can look forward to excellent accommodation, fine cuisine and friendly service with golf to match during their stay at Hunter's Hotel. Golf can be arranged, with transport at a number of fine courses in the area. Wicklow, Delgany and Woodenbridge are just three of eight courses within half an hour including the new European Club at Brittas Bay. This is a great golf links, the first to appear on Ireland's east coast this century and the 200 acres or so of natural dunesland that have been lovingly moulded into a links course present a great new challenge.

Hunter's Hotel is also an excellent base for, riding, hunting, tennis, swimming, hiking and on and on. The 'garden of Ireland' is at the guests doorstep with well known beauty spots such as Mount Usher Gardens, Powerscourt, Russborough House, Avondale House, Glendalough, the Devil's Glen and Roundwood all within easy reach. And for those keen to savour the atmosphere of another great Irish tradition, there is always the racing at Leopardstown, while the Curragh and Punchestown are about an hour or so away.

The character of this hotel lies in the charm and elegance retained from by gone days with antique furniture, open fires, fresh flowers, polished brass and wonderful gardens.

Hunter's Hotel
Newrath Bridge
Rathnew
Co Wicklow
Tel: 010353 404 40106
Fax: 010353 404 40338

Mount Juliet Estate—150 acres of unspoiled parkland in the south east of Ireland with a history that goes back to the 15th century. Today, it is Ireland's premier hotel and sporting estate, a beguiling combination of old and new which cannot fail to leave an indelible mark on even the most discerning international traveller.

The hotel offers several styles of deluxe accommodation. Guests can choose between the understated elegance of the gracious 18th century Mount Juliet House or the more sporting Hunters Yard where the Courtyard Rooms surround the ancient stable yard and the spacious Rose Garden Suites provide the ideal location for guests planning a longer stay.

Dining here is a delight. The Lady Helen Dining Room in Mount Juliet House is recognised as one of Ireland's most distinguished restaurants, while The Loft Restaurant in the Hunter's Yard offers relaxed dining in more informal surroundings. The cuisine in both restaurants is based on the best of the fine ingredients produced on the estate and in the surrounding area and is complemented by a fine selection of wines.

The striking decor of the private dining venues and conference rooms makes Mount Juliet the ideal out of town location for prestigious conferences and corporate entertainment, supported by all the necessary modern facilities plus superb hospitality and a wide range of sporting and recreational facilities.

The Jack Nicklaus designed golf course has earned a sterling reputation since opening in 1991. Described as the Augusta of Europe and home to the Irish Open in 1993 and 1994 it ranks as one of the top parkland courses in Europe. The unique David Leadbetter Golf Academy offers top class professional tuition on the three championship standard Academy holes (par 3, par 4 and par 5) and full indoor and video tuition facilities.

In addition to the estate's own stud farm, once the home of racing legends such as the Tetrach, the Tetratema and Mr. Jinks and now home to over 100 thoroughbreds, Mount Juliet also boasts one of the top equestrian centres in Ireland. Highly qualified instructors cater for all levels from beginners to serious cross country riders. The experienced angler can fish both the River Nore and King's River for salmon and trout while instruction for novices is also on hand. Coarse fishing and sea angling can be arranged locally. Clay target shooting and archery are also available on the estate as are tennis and croquet whilst for the less energetic, the superb leisure centre with heated pool, sauna, steam-room and gym is the ideal place to while away the hours when not exploring the estate's enormous woodlands an gardens on foot or by bicycle.

Whether it is for business or pleasure, there are few places to rival the unique ambience and lifestyle which one can experience at Mount Juliet.

Mount Juliet House
Thomastown
Co Killkenny
Tel: (010 353 56) 24455
Fax: (010 353 56) 24522

Joseph II of Austria (1741-1790) was an enlightened despot and a thoroughly miserable soul to boot. He wrote his own epitaph: 'Here lies a man who never succeeded in anything he attempted.' When, and let's hope it's a long, long way off, people begin to consider a fitting epitaph for Jack William Nicklaus someone should suggest, 'Here lies a man who succeeded in almost everything he attempted'.

Not content to go down in history as merely the greatest golfer who ever lived, the 'Golden Bear' is determined to establish himself as the finest golf course designer the world has known. Jack's original career goal was to better Bobby Jones' record of 13 Major Championship victories: by 1986 he had totalled 20. Many believe that he would have won even more Major titles had he not devoted so much of his energy to designing championship golf courses. But then again, had he not done so there would of course be no Muirfield Village, no St Mellion, no Glen Abbey... and no Mount Juliet.

Nicklaus once said, 'Building a golf course is my total expression. My golf game can only go on so long. But what I have learned can be put into a piece of ground to last beyond me'. Mount Juliet estate is a heavenly piece of ground, in fact 1500 acres of subliminally beautiful Irish countryside, through which the River Nore flows and on which Jack Nicklaus has built a masterly 18 hole golf course.

Situated approximately 75 miles south of Dublin (via the N7/N9) on the outskirts of Thomastown in Co. Kilkenny, Mount Juliet may just be the ultimate golfing oasis. The Mount Juliet Hotel, a splendidly refurbished 18th century mansion house, and the golf course have only recently opened yet the reputation of both is already immense. Some people are predicting that Mount Juliet will become the Turnberry or Gleneagles of Ireland, but there appears to be none of their overt 'flashiness' or commercial brashness. Everything about Mount Juliet seems very understated and the ambience is at once graceful and peaceful. In front of the great house, somewhere between the hotel reception and the 11th tee, is a veritable Garden of Eden. Amid the ancient oaks, beeches and lime trees a hundred colours dazzle the eye and Mount Juliet's famous parading pheasants can simply vanish into the floral background. It is the perfect place for an early morning 'get your mind together' stroll before going out and tackling Jack's formidable but spectacular parkland layout.

Unlike Gleneagles, golf at Mount Juliet is not restricted to residents and Golf Club members, although hotel guests do pay reduced green fees. Advance bookings can be made for any day of the week by telephoning the Club on **(056) 24725**. Both the **Golf Manager** and the **professionals, Todd Pyle and Nick Bradley** can be contacted on this number. Handicap certificates are required and the non-resident green fees for 18 holes in summer 1994 were £60 mid week and £65 at weekends. Special group rates are available and there are reductions for those teeing off after 5.30pm. Visitors may also wish to inspect Mount Juliet's impressive new David Leadbetter Golf Academy.

The course officially opened on 14th July 1991 and a vast crowd were present to watch Nicklaus play a friendly match against Christy O'Connor Snr. Even bigger crowds assembled in June 1993 to watch the Carrolls Irish Open, victory going to Nick Faldo—his third successive victory in the event—and twelve months later to see Bernhard Langer win the first Murphy's Irish Open.

Although it is certainly a mighty challenge from the back markers (all 7103 yards of it) each hole has four sets of tees so one needn't get too despondent! From the medal tees the course measures approximately 6650 yards and from the forward tees, 5500 yards, par 73.

When writing the piece on East Sussex National I fantasised about a 'dream nine holes' made up entirely from some of the finest holes on East Sussex National's West Course. To that nine I'm now going to add the 2nd, 3rd, 5th, 8th, 10th, 11th, 13th, 14th and 18th from the Mount Juliet course. This collection will provide three exceptional short holes: the 3rd (which has a serious water carry), the 11th (over a plunging valley occupied by a cascading stream and rockery) and the 14th (with its marvellous backdrop of trees); three par fours: the 2nd (a beautifully shaped dog-leg), the 13th (a hint of Augusta's back nine) and the 18th (reminiscent of the closing hole at St Mellion); as well as three outstanding par fives, namely the 5th, the huge 8th (a fabulous elevated tee here) and the 10th (where like the 5th a real sea of traps must be negotiated en route to a superbly angled green). A dream round for sure, but sweet dreams? Potential nightmares, I reckon!

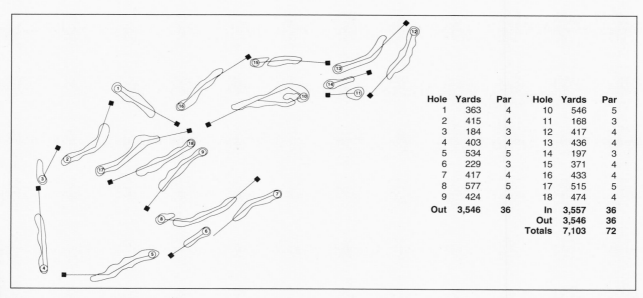

Hole	Yards	Par		Hole	Yards	Par
1	363	4		10	546	5
2	415	4		11	168	3
3	184	3		12	417	4
4	403	4		13	436	4
5	534	5		14	197	3
6	229	3		15	371	4
7	417	4		16	433	4
8	577	5		17	515	5
9	424	4		18	474	4
Out	**3,546**	**36**		**In**	**3,557**	**36**
				Out	**3,546**	**36**
				Totals	**7,103**	**72**

A beautiful, former Quaker mansion, Hotel Minella is an impressive stately home presiding over a stretch of the rippling River Suir. Tasteful modernisation blend into the background of the original 1863 building which commands nine acres of lovingly maintained grounds. All in all, a rare example of a hotel able to combine the comforts of the 20th century with the dignity and elegance of a bygone age which time, and three major wars seem to have tossed aside.

Clonmel itself - Cluain Meala - the Meadow of Honey, has aptly been described as the 'sportsman's paradise'. Long associated with many great names it is a renowned horse and greyhound breeding area. Few countries offer as much for the serious golfer, with courses ranging from parkland pleasures at Thurles to the justly famous and demanding hills of Clonmel, a mere two miles from the hotel. Both of these are 18 hole, par 71 courses. The hotel is happy to arrange an all inclusive golfing mini-holiday to ensure a more relaxed day.

For the racing enthusiast, this premier county is ideal. The Clonmel racecourse is just two miles from the Minella and less than an hour's drive away are the courses of Gowran, Tipperary, Wexford, Tramore, Mallow and Limerick.

For a diversion from these temptations why not try your hand at swimming, boating and canoeing on the Suir, mountain climbing in the Comeragh mountains and the beautiful Knockmealdown range. Tennis and badminton courts are nearby and croquet is available at the hotel. Take up the challenge of salmon and trout fishing on the rivers Nore, Tar, Anner and indeed the Suir or relax amidst the breathtaking scenery of the surrounding countryside. Pony trekking is easily arranged or simply take an entrancing walk.

The Minella offers a warm and friendly welcome at the end of a whirling day. Enjoy a quiet drink in the cocktail bar, overlooking the lawns and the banks of the Suir, and then move to the oak panelled dining room to sample some of the renowned Minella dishes, traditional Irish at its best, prime roast beef, grilled steaks and fresh fish, all complemented by a fine selection of wines.

All of the 45 bedrooms offer the perfect end to a perfect day. All have en suite bathrooms, colour television, direct dial telephone, hairdrier and alarm clock radio. Two executive suites have private jacuzzi and all offer a stunning morning view over the river or Comeragh Mountains.

Ideal for the business meeting, conference or private party, the hotel is able to accommodate anything from 10 to 600 people in a variety of function rooms. Facsimile and secretarial facilities are also readily available.

Hotel Minella
Clonmel
Co Tipperary
Ireland
Tel: (010 353 52) 22388/22417
Fax: (010 353 52) 24381

Many of the greatest prizes in golf come from Waterford. What a dazzling place! Home of the most famous crystal in the world, Waterford is a town that people have long been drawn to. In the early days they were not always welcome. First it was the Vikings: a race not exactly renowned for their good manners. A few centuries later if was Cromwell's Roundheads, a particularly wretched bunch who apparently named the spectacular hill that overlooks the town and its splendid bay, Mount Misery. Crystal came to Waterford in 1783 about 130 years after Cromwell's Roundheads, and then 130 years after the Penrose Brothers founded their glass manufacturing business, golf came to Mount Misery.

Waterford Golf Club was formed in March 1912, although the first nine holes was not officially opened until June 1913. The architect of this layout was Willie Park Jr of Musselburgh, a former British Open Champion and son of Willie Park Sr, the first ever winner of that event in 1860. Park's course was revised and extended to 18 holes in 1934 by another great Scottish golfer and celebrated architect, James Braid.

Whatever the Roundheads thought of Mount Misery, it makes a fine setting for a golf course. Although only a few miles from the sea, Waterford is regarded as one of the finest inland courses in Ireland. Ninety per cent of the course couldn't be described as anything other than classic parkland but on the highest parts of the course - on the top of Mount Misery if you like - there is just a hint of a moorland type of course, or even, if you really stretch your imagination, a Formby-like links.

Golfing visitors have always been welcome at Waterford. Subject to availability they may play on any day of the week. Naturally it is easier to arrange a game during the week but the only specific tee reservation at weekends is on Saturday when the 1st tee is often reserved for societies between 10:30am and 12:30pm. The Club's **Secretary, Joe Condon** can be contacted either in writing to: **Waterford Golf Club, Newrath, Waterford** or by telephone on **(051) 76748** (the code from the UK is (010 35351). The **professional, Eamonn Condon** can be reached on **(051) 54256** and the Club's fax number is (051) 53405.

The green fees at Waterford for 1994 were set at £15 during the week with £18 payable at weekends and on bank holidays. In terms of its location, Waterford the town is approximately two and a half hours drive from Dublin (via the N9/N7); about one hour south of Kilkenny (N9/N10) and 45 minutes west of Wexford (N25). There is an airport at Waterford, served daily from the UK. The Golf Club itself is to the North of Waterford, and from the town centre that means crossing the famous bridge and then taking the dual carriageway towards Kilkenny, exiting left after abut a mile and a half.

From the back tees, Waterford measures 5722 metres, or just under 6300 yards and has a fairly friendly par of 71. By no means is this Ireland's most difficult course but there is ample challenge nonetheless. The 1st demands an uphill drive to a blind target and is quite a testing opener. Immediately apparent on reaching the green is the quality of the putting surfaces at Waterford - undoubtedly among the best in Ireland. There are three short holes on the front nine and the 3rd and 7th both demand tricky downhill tee shots: the former requires little more than a deftly flighted pitching wedge but the green is surrounded by bunkers and can be very elusive. The 7th requires at least a medium iron and it is again very difficult to judge the distance accurately.

If the first nine holes are pleasant enough, the back nine at Waterford is quite something. The 11th, 12th and 13th make for a very attractive run of holes and the finish is quite spectacular with a superb par three (the 16th) being followed by an almost driveable par four and then a magnificent downhill 18th. The back tee for this classic closing hole couldn't have been better positioned. The 360 degree views over the surrounding countryside are quite awe-inspiring and the view down the narrow fairway is pretty invigorating too! In fact the fairway twists and turns downhill for almost the entire length of the hole. Ever hit a ball 350 yards? Here's your chance!

South east Ireland will never be as famous for its golf as the south west. Few, if any, areas of the world can compete with County Kerry and Ireland is always likely to be more famous for its links courses than for its inland tests, but there is still much to offer the golfer who journeys to this part of the world. Waterford is a fine course and not far away there is a good test at Tramore, while exciting things have been happening nearby at historic Waterford Castle and an hour and a half or so north of Waterford. Jack Nicklaus has built an outstanding Championship course at Mount Juliet. Waterford and its surrounds should force even the golfing misery to lick his lips with anticipation.

Hole	Metres	Par	Hole	Metres	Par
1	384	4	10	270	4
2	334	4	11	452	5
3	119	3	12	443	5
4	380	4	13	178	3
5	370	4	14	398	4
6	361	4	15	439	5
7	164	3	16	128	3
8	494	5	17	270	4
9	170	3	18	368	4
Out	**2,776**	**34**	**In**	**2,946**	**37**
			Out	**2,776**	**34**
			Totals	**5,722**	**71**

Like Scotland, Ireland is blessed with such a large number of outstanding links courses that overseas visitors tend to overlook its many inland treasures (each country having one great exception of course—Gleneagles in Scotland and Killarney in Ireland). In my view the links courses in Ireland represent the best collection in the world, but there is also much more to inland golf in the Emerald Isle than the twin gems of 'Heaven's Reflex'.

While it may be little known internationally, Carlow Golf Club has a proud reputation in Ireland. In 1978 it hosted the Irish Close Championship (normally the preserve of links courses) and in March 1992 a 24-strong panel of golfing experts ranked Carlow as the best inland course in Ireland after Killarney and the two new lavish developments at Mount Juliet and the Kildare Country Club. Strictly speaking, Carlow is a parkland type course and it certainly boasts a wealth of wonderfully mature trees, however, in places it has much more of a moorland, even heathland feel and the sub-soil is quite sandy. In fact Carlow has more than a hint of Yorkshire's Lindrick and Moortown about it—and it's just as good.

The course was designed by Tom Simpson, the architect who created the famous Old Course at Ballybunion and the magnificent links at Baltray, and opened in 1922; visitors have always been made very welcome. The current **Secretary** at Carlow is **Margaret Meaney** and she can be contacted by telephone on **(0503) 31695**. Advance bookings are recommended and although it is naturally much easier to arrange a game during the week, weekend golf is always a possibility. The 1994 green fees were set at £20 on weekdays and £25 at weekends. Weekly and fortnightly tickets can also be purchased and reduced rates are available for parties of 12 and over. Carlow's **professional** is **Andrew Gilbert** and he can be reached by telephone on **(0503) 41745**.

The county town of Carlow is located approximately 50 miles south of Dublin and the road linking each to the other is the N9. The same road joins Carlow with Thomastown (Mount Juliet), Kilkenny and Waterford to the south. The golf club is situated just to the north of the town, immediately off the Dublin Road.

From the championship tees Carlow is certainly no monster, measuring just under 6400 yards, (5844 metres) but it has a fairly tight par of 70 and is never 'torn apart'. The round commences with a pair of very contrasting par fours. The 1st is one of Carlow's toughest, a lengthy dog-leg left to a heavily guarded green: only a long straight drive up the right hand side of the fairway will suffice; at the 2nd, though, the sensible shot is to lay up with an iron off the tee, still leaving only a pitch to the green: a big smash with a driver might get you close to the green but it might also cause you to take a drop out of the water hazard. Probably the best two holes on the front nine are the stroke one 7th where the fairway meanders around to the left yet tries to throw your ball off to the right—a marvellously sited green here—and the spectacular downhill 8th where if you were prudent and held back on the 2nd tee no one could begrudge you now winding up and letting fly from this superbly elevated tee.

The real fun, however, is still to come. Carlow's back nine is exceptionally good and precision becomes the name of the game. A deft pitch is required over an attractive pond at the 10th and disaster can befall the shot that misses the green at the 12th: Carlow's rough is nothing if not punishing! A trio of par fours, the 14th, 15th and 16th guide you into deepest Co. Carlow; each is a really fine hole. The 16th, which is played through a tunnel-like valley, is perhaps the most demanding two-shotter of the entire round, and is followed immediately by the most celebrated par three hole. I mentioned 'precision' earlier, well, tackling the 17th at Carlow has been likened to threading a needle. How's your eyesight! The par five 18th offers the chance of a closing birdie and a grandstand finish as it tumbles downhill all the way back to the clubhouse. A good ending to a memorable round.

Carlow is less than 25 miles from Mount Juliet. It offers a very different type of challenge from the new Nicklaus designed course, but if you happen to be in this delightful part of 'Middle Ireland' why not play the pair? You won't regret it, that's for certain.

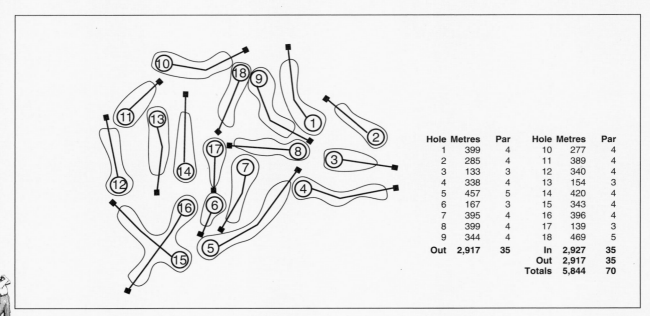

Hole	Metres	Par	Hole	Metres	Par
1	399	4	10	277	4
2	285	4	11	389	4
3	133	3	12	340	4
4	338	4	13	154	3
5	457	5	14	420	4
6	167	3	15	343	4
7	395	4	16	396	4
8	399	4	17	139	3
9	344	4	18	469	5
Out	**2,917**	**35**	**In**	**2,927**	**35**
			Out	**2,917**	**35**
			Totals	**5,844**	**70**

Ballyliffin GC
Rosapenna GC
Portsalon GC
ROSAPENNA
PORTSALON
BUNCRANA
N56
Letterkenny GC
LETTERKENNY
Narin & Portnoo GC
Ballybofey & Stranorlar GC
PORTNOO
Ballybofey
STRANORLAR
NARIN
BALLYBOFEY
DONEGAL
Donegal GC
BUNDORAN
Bundoran GC
N15
County Sligo GC
ROSSES POINT
SLIGO
Strandhill GC
Enniscrone GC
Belmullet GC
N59
BALLINA
Mulrany GC
Westport GC
Castlebar GC
WESTPORT
CASTLEBAR
KNOCK
Ballinrobe GC
ROSCOMMON
Roscommon GC
CLIFDEN
BALLINROBE
Athlone GC
CONG
ATHLONE
Connemara GC
N6
Galway GC
GALWAY
CLIFFS OF
MOHER
N67
N18
LAHINCH
Lahinch GC
Dromoland
Castle GC
CLARECASTLE
LIMERICK
Shannon GC
N7
Castletroy GC
TARBERT
Limerick GC
CASHEL
Ballybunion GC
TIPPERARY
N24
BALLYBUNION
N21
Tralee GC
N20
TRALEE
Dingle G.C.
Mallow GC
Dooks GC
Killarney
GLENBEIGH
KILLARNEY
Harbour Point GC
N70
CORK
Cork GC
Waterville G.C.
Muskerry GC
Douglas GC
WATERVILLE
KENMARE
Monkstown GC
BANTRY
N71
SKIBBEREEN

Resting in its 100 acre estate, is the historic mansion of Mount Falcon. Originally built in 1876 by John Fredrick Knox, it overlooks the Moy Valley towards the changing hues of the heathery slopes of the Ox mountains in the distance.

The owner, Constance Aldridge, plays the part of hostess to her visitors who quickly realise that in keeping with the tradition of the house, they will experience the friendliness and attention given to a personal guest rather than simply another booking. Here, you can relax beside a log fire in the tranquillity of gracious rooms filled with antique furniture and fresh flowers picked from the garden.

The superb menu is traditional country house cuisine. Frequently acclaimed in international good food guides, it includes local ingredients; fresh produce from the estate as well as well as fresh rod-caught salmon from the Mount Falcon Fishery on the River Moy. The delicious food is accompanied by a comprehensive selection of fine wines and after dinner, coffee and drinks are served in the drawing room.

There are ten bedrooms all enjoying views of the estate. All the bedrooms have private bathrooms as well as all the amenities you would expect of a good hotel.

Mount Falcon is the ideal base from which to explore the magnificent countryside of County Mayo. Beautiful beaches, rugged coastline, lakes and mountains are all on the doorstep as are fascinating sites of ancient Celtic history.

For the golfer, the first class 18 hole course of Enniscoe is only ten miles away and Ballina has a good 9 hole course. Horse riding is available in the area and the lively old fashioned town of Ballina is worth a visit.

For the serious fisherman, Mount Falcon has excellent facilities having catered for generations of country sportsmen. The River Moy is Ireland's most prolific salmon river and three miles away the large limestone loughs, Conn and Cullen, provide some of the finest fishing for brown trout in Europe.

In the winter months, the castle can arrange excellent rough shooting for woodcock and snipe.

Mount Falcon Castle
Ballina
Co Mayo
Ireland
Tel: (096) 70811
Fax: (096) 71517

Without any shadow of doubt some of the greatest golf courses in the world are to be found in the south west of Ireland. But as any Irishman worth his Guinness will tell you, great golf in the west of Ireland certainly isn't confined to the south western corner—it starts from County Donegal downwards. Apart from its magnificent golf, the south west is renowned for its beautiful scenery: majestic Killarney, the glorious Ring of Kerry and the Dingle Peninsula — stunning for sure but further north can be equally spectacular. This is what W M Thackeray had to say of the area around Westport: 'It forms an event in one's life to have seen the place, so beautiful is it, and so unlike all other beauties that I know of'. Clearly inspired, he continued: 'But the Bay—and the Reek which sweeps down to the sea—and a hundred islands in it, were dressed up in gold and purple and crimson, with the whole cloudy West in a flame'. Marvellous! And have you ever been to Connemara?

Donegal

And have you ever been to Donegal! I don't suppose many golfers are likely to begin a tour in the very far north and head all the way downwards but we shall have a go all the same. (It is possible I suppose if one were approaching from the Causeway Coast?) Let us start at **Ballyliffin** on the very northern tip of Donegal, not far from Malin Head. Now Ballyliffin is a course we overlooked in the early editions of Following The Fairways. This has now been rectified (see ahead). Suffice to say at this juncture, we believe it to be the most underrated course in Ireland and recommend that golfers stay overnight in the nearby Strand Hotel (010 353) 777 6107—it makes for a superb 19th hole base and, needless to say, the Proprietor is a club member!

Rosapenna is our next port of call. Like Ballyliffin it is somewhat isolated, but a fine 18 hole course nonetheless. It was laid out in 1893 by Old Tom Morris and is part links, part inland in nature, although I understand that nine new 'links holes' are presently being constructed. There are said to be more rabbits on this course than on any other—not a description of the members I might add! The place has a bleak beauty and the coast is very dramatic—note the spectacular nearby Atlantic Drive. The Rosapenna Golf Hotel (010 353) 745 5301 provides a comfortable and convenient base while those looking for really deluxe accommodation might consider Rathmullan House (010 353) 745 8188 in Rathmullan, a Georgian building with splendid gardens. Not far from Rosapenna there is a magnificently situated course at **Portsalon** and another delightfully old fashioned links at **Nairn and Portnoo**. Further inland, 18 holes can be played at **Letterkenny** and again at **Ballybofey & Stranorlar** where the Kee's Hotel (010 353) 743 1018 provides a perfect base for exploring the mountains and hills of Donegal.

Donegal town, famed for its tweeds and woollens, has one of the longest courses in Ireland measuring 7200 yards (try playing it in a fierce wind!) The course is actually outside of the county town at **Murvagh**. A truly great course this and again we explore it on a later page. There are a number of hotels in Donegal, but perhaps the best bet for golfers looking for a lively night is the Schooner Inn (010 353) 732 1671 on Upper Main Street. More sedate accommodation is to be found at Rossnowlagh, here the Sand House Hotel (010 353) 725 1777 enjoys superb views over Donegal Bay and there is a short 9 hole golf course within the hotel grounds. A little south of Rossnowlagh is **Bundoran**, another tough, though fairly open links. Right in the middle of the course is the Great Northern Hotel which has 150 rooms.

The West Coast Four- and more

Our next visit is a more established favourite. **County Sligo**, or **Rosses Point** as it is commonly known, is rated among the top ten courses in Ireland and is the home of the prestigious West of Ireland Amateur Championship. Laid out right alongside the Atlantic coast it is a true links and can be greatly affected by the elements. This great course is tackled ahead. County Sligo and surrounds is another charming area of Ireland. It is the country of W B Yeats and the landscape is dominated by the formidable Ben Bulben mountain. An outstanding seafood restaurant is located in Rosses Point—the Moorings (010 353) 982 5874. The Sligo Park Hotel (010 353) 716 0291, Ballincar House Hotel (010 353) 714 5361 and the Yeats Country Ryan Hotel (010 353) 717 7211 are all very convenient for the course. Just to the south of Sligo, Coopershill (010 353) 716 5108 is another fine hotel and at Colloney, Markree Castle (010 353) 716 7800 is quite superb. Rosses Point is marketed alongside Enniscrone, Westport and Connemara as one of the 'West Coast Four' but there are many other fine golfing challenges in this part of Ireland and a recommended neighbour of Rosses Point is the links at **Strandhill**, adjacent to County Sligo airport. Furthermore, at **Belmulett** in the far northwest of Co. Mayo, a magnificent links course is being constructed at Carn Beach amid Ballybunion-like sand dunes! A fun place to stay in Belmulett is the Drom Caoin (010 353) 978 1195 guest house.

Perhaps the most underrated of the West Coast Four is the delightful links at **Enniscrone**, laid out on the shores of Killala Bay; it is, to quote Peter Dobereiner, 'an undiscovered gem of a links.' The best places to stay nearby are the Downhill Hotel (010 353) 962 1033 in Ballina (the owner is a past Captain of the golf club!) and the Mount Falcon Castle (010 353) 967 0811. A short drive from Ballina and we reach **Westport**, Thackeray's paradise. The town nestles in the shadows of the massive Croagh Patrick mountain. It was on its peak that St Patrick is said to have fasted and prayed for 40 days. The golf course (from which there are many marvellous views of Croagh Patrick) is another on the grand scale—7000 yards when fully stretched. It's a relatively new course having been designed by Fred Hawtree in 1973. Although some holes run spectacularly along the shoreline (note particularly the superb par five 15th which curves around Clew Bay) Westport is most definitely a parkland type course and is a very friendly club. The Irish Amateur Championship has been played here twice in recent years. There is no shortage of good accommodation in Westport and many hotels offer golfing packages. One of the most comfortable hotels in town is the Hotel Westport (010 353) 982 5122 near Westport House, although the Castlecourt Hotel (010 353) 982 5444 is also popular with travel-weary golfers and in nearby Newport, Newport House (010 353) 984 1222 is first class and also highly commended for those seeking a more homely atmosphere in one of Ireland's top inns, Healy's Hotel (010 353) 945 6443. Approximately twenty miles away at Cong stands the redoubtable **Ashford Castle** (010 353) 924 6003 a place fit for a king and possibly the finest hotel in Ireland. Its setting on the edge of Lough Corrib is quite breathtaking; it also has a pleasant 9 hole golf course within the hotel grounds.

Connemara is located about 30 miles south of Westport amid very rugged country. It is a wild, remote and incredibly beautiful part of the world. The golf links at Ballyconneely must be one of the toughest courses that one is ever likely to meet — we visit it a few pages on. Despite the remoteness there are several first class establishments at hand. The best places for a night's stay are the Rock Glen Country House Hotel (010 353) 952 1035, the Ardagh Hotel and Restaurant (010 353) 952 1384. and the Abbeyglen Castle Hotel (010 353) 952 1201. All three are in Clifden. Another leading country houses is found close by in Cashel, the Cashel House Hotel (010 353) 953 1001.

On to Galway — a fascinating and lively city. Golfwise, there is the very established **Galway** Golf Club at Salthill, and the very new **Galway Bay** Golf and Country Club near Oranmore, the acclaimed creation of Christy O'Connor Jnr.

Galway has a number of centrally located hotels including The Great Southern Hotel (010 353) 916 4041 and Ardilaun House (010 353) 912 1433. In Spiddal, the Bridge House (010 353) 918 3118 is a cosy inn and at Oranmore, very convenient for Galway Bay, is the Oranmore Lodge Hotel (010 353) 919 4400.

Finally to a part of Ireland perhaps more renowned for its fishing than golf. The Roscommon-Athlone area doesn't have many courses but both **Athlone** Golf Club and **Roscommon** Golf Club are worth exploring and there is an exciting new course nearby, the **Glasson** Golf & Country Club. Among a number of pleasant places to stay we can recommend the Hodson Bay Hotel (010 353) 902 92444 surrounded by Athlone golf course itself.

Artist: **A Weaver PREPARING TO PUTT** *Courtesy of* **Burlington Gallery**

The Hodson Bay Hotel is located in Athlone at the very heart of Ireland on the edge of glorious Lough Ree, commanding breathtaking views of the islands and surrounding countryside. All bedrooms are en suite and equipped to the highest international standards.

L'Escale restaurant is intimate and well appointed, offering the discerning gourmet a menu specialising in fresh produce and local cuisine. The Waterfront bar is the meeting place for locals, golfers, businessmen and and holiday makers. An imaginative menu of food and beverages is offered in a warm and friendly environment

The hotel leisure centre provides facilities which include a heated indoor swimming pool, sauna, steamroom,solarium and fully equipped gymnasium. These facilities are complemented by various outdoor sporting activities on Lough Ree and the River Shannon which include fishing, boat trips, sailing, canoeing and wind surfing.

The Hodson Bay Hotel is a golfers paradise — its neighbour is the Athlone Golf Club, famous for its 18 hole championship course. Here, the golfer is assured a truly exciting and demanding game of golf. Directly across the lake is the new, Christy O'Connor (Jnr.) designed, Glasson Golf and Country Club. A challenging game awaits golfers on this course which already widely accepted as being potentially one of the finest championship courses in Ireland. The clubhouse, an elegant period residence, overlooks the 18th green and provides a spectacular view of Killinure Bay and the finishing six holes. For the beginner, Glasson has a golf academy consisting of three holes with a number of teeing-off points.

Five miles from the hotel is the Mount Temple Golf Course which is situated in one of Ireland's smallest villages — Mount Temple. This challenging course is built on a unique natural site with water hazards, rock, mature trees, natural undulations and wonderful views. Due to its natural terrain, the course is playable all year round. A short drive from the Hodson Bay Hotel will bring visitors to Ballinasloe's rolling parkland course with its magnificently refurbished clubhouse.

The hotel is the ideal venue for conferences. It has its own purpose built centre — the 'Clonmacnoise Suite' — which provides state of the art equipment and excellent conference support facilities. Delegates are offered the perfect ambiance for concentration on business and the perfect setting in which to relax.

Hodson Bay Hotel
Athlone
County Westmeath
Ireland
Tel: (010 353 902) 92444
Fax: (010 353 902) 92688

The Sand House Hotel is an oasis of comfort and tranquillity. It stands on the edge of the Atlantic Ocean overlooking Donegal Bay. Its unique rear garden is the vast ocean which laps onto miles of golden sands including the EC Blue Flag beach at Rossnowlagh. Over 40 years experience has fashioned the style with which you are greeted by the Britton family and their friendly staff at this delightful hotel.

The hotel's 40 en suite bedrooms are individually and tastefully decorated and furnished to a high standard of comfort. Each bedroom has coordinated fabrics and furnishings in classic country house style. Many overlook the sea and a limited number have four poster beds. In the elegant dining room guests can sample such house specialities as Donegal Bay salmon, sea trout, scallops, crab and lobster as well as prime beef, lamb, veal and game in season. Locally smoked salmon, fresh bay oysters and mussels are served throughout the day in the

cosy lounge bar. Guests can relax after dinner in the cocktail lounge or in one of the other two comfortable bars. Alternatively guests can appreciate the calm and beauty of the sea from the comfort of the delightful conservatory.

The Sand House Hotel is the ideal base in the northwest from which to explore Donegal's spectacular scenery and unique pleasures. Stracomer riding centre has excellent facilities, including trekking, and is just a 20 minute drive away. For the energetic the hotel has an all -weather tennis court, croquet and miniature golf. Swimming, board sailing, surfing, canoeing and water skiing can also be enjoyed right outside the hotel.

South Donegal is a golfer's paradise with a choice of three superb championship links within a 40 minute drive — Murvagh (15 minutes), Bundoran (20 minutes) and Rosses Point (40 minutes). Enniscrone and Strandhill are two other excellent links within easy reach.

The Sand House Hotel
Rossnowlagh
Donegal Bay
Ireland
Tel: (010 353 72) 51777
Fax: (010 353 72) 52100

The Irish have an inborn wanderlust that is perhaps rivalled only by Australians and New Zealanders. This partly explains how, wherever you go in the world, you bump into an Irishman, sooner rather than later. And why sooner rather than later, you'll hear the phrase 'to be sure' or 'tis grand'. It also partly explains why the names of numerous relatively small towns in Ireland are famous the world over: places like Limerick, Blarney and Tipperary for example. Another place that just about everybody has heard of is Donegal—not for its rhymes, kisses or songs of course but for its tweed. Yet like Limerick, Blarney and Tipperary not all that many people born outside Ireland have visited Donegal. Every golfer however, given the chance, should visit the country's most north westerly county: there are many wonderful courses here and they are all wonderfully uncrowded. And every brave golfer should visit Donegal, the county town itself, and play its majestic links at nearby Murvagh.

Why only every brave golfer? This is because to get the most out of Murvagh you must enjoy a mighty challenge- it is the longest golf course in Ireland. A local joke is that if you are a short hitter you can spend a full day at Murvagh and not complete 18 holes. Donegal really is a tiger of a links: from the Championship tees it measures just over 7300 yards (or 6633 metres as the card will tell you.) In reality, most of us are never going to tackle the links from the tiger tees and while it is still a very long course from the tees of the day, real challenge becomes entwined with real pleasure.

Murvagh enjoys considerable seclusion. It is not exactly off the beaten track—Donegal is only six miles away—but quite a bit of the course is bordered by some fairly thick woodland, and being situated on a peninsula, there is an added feeling of isolation. The other border of course is the great Atlantic Ocean.

Few golf clubs are as keen for visitors to come and experience the charms of their course as Donegal (the club is understandably proud of the fact that Nick Faldo visited the course in 1993). The green fees in 1994 were a modest £14 during the week with £18 payable at weekends and on bank holidays. The Club operates a timesheet system on Saturdays and Sundays and it is only at the weekend when restrictions are likely to apply. Donegal's **Secretary, John McBride** can be contacted by telephone on **(073) 34054** (or from the UK 010 353 73 34054) and by fax on (073) 34377. There is no professional at the Club but the Steward, **Eugene McLoughlin** is very helpful. Meals and snacks are available in the Clubhouse throughout the day although players are requested to place an order for meals before teeing off.

As already mentioned, Murvagh is approximately six miles from the centre of Donegal. The linking road is the N15 and the route off to the golf course is signposted. The town itself is about an hour's drive from the nearest airport which is at Sligo and again the route is the N15. Knock Airport is 80 miles away and Belfast 110 miles. Sligo Airport is obviously the most convenient and anyone playing golf at Donegal should try to include a game at County Sligo (or vice versa) ... Rosses Point and Murvagh—what a double for links enthusiasts!

Rather like at Rosses Point, the course opens with a fairly gentle hole. This time it is a par five and like every par five at Murvagh (there are four others) it is a dog-leg, but the approach to the green is not too demanding and the putting surface is fairly large. Things start to hot up at the 2nd. This is a very tough par four that plays every bit of its 416 yards. Thick, tangling rough lines the left hand side of the fairway on this hole and there is an out of bounds on the right; as for the green, it sits on a natural shelf.

Neither the 3rd or 4th is an easy hole and the 5th can be a horror. This is one of two really tremendous par threes at Donegal (the other is the 16th); here the tee shot must be struck perfectly to carry a ravine—mishit it slightly and you can be playing your second from sand 30 feet below the green. Beyond the green is the beach. A brilliant sequence of holes comes after the 5th. This is where the course runs close to Donegal Bay and the views (if you care to clamber up the sandhills) are tremendous.

Perhaps the most memorable holes on the back nine at Murvagh are the 10th, 11th and 15th, while the most demanding are the 12th and 16th. The former is once again a huge par five; from the back tees it would be a reasonable train journey and as on most three-shot holes the key is the second. If we are talking train distances then, as par threes go, the 16th must be the equivalent of the Trans-Siberian Express! One could sit behind this green all day and not see anyone reach the green with their tee shot. When the elements are stirred this is the kind of hole where, in days gone by, Jack Nicklaus would have peeled off his sweater and teed up with his driver. But then, Donegal is a place where another of those lovely Irish expressions 'good crack' takes on a new meaning.

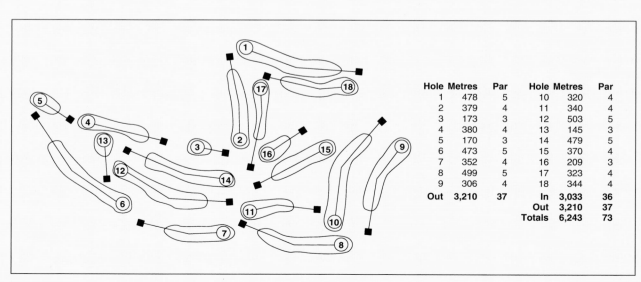

Hole	Metres	Par	Hole	Metres	Par
1	478	5	10	320	4
2	379	4	11	340	4
3	173	3	12	503	5
4	380	4	13	145	3
5	170	3	14	479	5
6	473	5	15	370	4
7	352	4	16	209	3
8	499	5	17	323	4
9	306	4	18	344	4
Out	**3,210**	**37**	**In**	**3,033**	**36**
			Out	**3,210**	**37**
			Totals	**6,243**	**73**

Slieve Russell

The unsuspecting traveller's first impression of the Slieve Russell Hotel is that it must be an incredible mirage. The knowledgeable golfer's lasting impression of Slieve Russell is that it is an extraordinary oasis.

Deep in the countryside of Co. Cavan a remarkable new hotel and Championship golf course has seemingly 'sprung from nowhere' and now demands to be discovered. Refreshingly, very little hype has coloured the emergence of Slieve Russell as one of Ireland's greatest golfing venues but then the quality of the product certainly hasn't needed the hard sell.

Ballyconnell is the place where it is all happening: a small town in a quiet, sleepy part of the world, one much more renowned as a fisherman's paradise than a golfer's — although this would appear set to change. The landscape of this part of Ireland is dominated by numerous lakes, hence all the fishing, and one other rather more unusual feature, drumlins. (Remember them from your geography studies of glacial drift?) These are curvaceous little hills or mounds and they are dotted all over the valleys of west Cavan. So a land of lakes and curvaceous mounds? Clearly Mother Nature intended...

Mother Nature aside, the founder and guiding force behind the development of Slieve Russell has been successful local entrepreneur, Sean Quinn. His original concept was for the 18 hole golf course to complement the extensive leisure facilities of a luxury 150 bedroomed hotel. The Slieve Russell Hotel in fact opened its doors in 1990 (to great acclaim it can be said) but sometime before the projected opening date for the golf course (summer 1992) it became apparent that this was to be no typical hotel resort type course. It would not have been hyperboles to suggest that the Slieve Russell construction team, lead by architect Paddy Merrigan, were busy creating a masterpiece. And now it is ready for all to inspect.

Hotel residents and non residents are equally welcome to play the course, although the latter not surprisingly pay higher green fees and should also possess official handicaps. There are no special tee time restrictions but bookings can be made by contacting the Club on **(049) 26444.** In 1994, the green fees for hotel residents were £14 between Sundays and Fridays and £20 on Saturdays per round, and for non residents £22 between Sundays and Fridays and £30 on Saturdays per round. **The Golf Manager at Slieve Russell, Andrew Mawhinny** and the **professional, Liam McCool** ensure that the requirements of all golfers are well attended to.

Paddy Merrigan's fingers must have tingled when he was first shown the proposed site for the 18 hole layout. These days it is becoming very rare for an architect to be introduced to such a naturally rolling, undulating piece of terrain. The installation of a good drainage system was the first very necessary requirement (the lakes didn't appear by chance). This was certainly achieved and is reflected, as the Slieve Russell course guide tells us, in a remarkably firm sod regardless of the prevailing weather conditions.

Slieve Russell is most definitely a parkland golf course although occasionally the extreme contouring — both natural and strategically introduced — produces an almost links type feel. Measuring in excess of 7,000 yards from the Championship tees it is also a big course in every sense of the word. Two large lakes, connected by a wandering stream are the dominant features of the design and are responsible for creating several outstanding and dramatic holes. Water in fact must be confronted as early as the 2nd, a truly marvellous swinging dog leg hole, where after trying to avoid the lake to the left of the fairway with the drive the approach must then be played over the stream to a raised and two tiered green. The severity of the undulations — including the putting surfaces! — will be understood by the time the roller coasting 3rd has been played. Both the 2nd and 3rd are superb par four holes but the quartet of par threes will probably create an even greater impression on the mind of the first time visitor, especially perhaps the 16th, which is an absolute gem of a short hole (and genuinely Augusta-like) and the amazing par five 13th, where for its entire length the fairway follows the curving edge of the second lake. You stand on the tee at the 13th and the green is straight ahead — the direct route to the flag however requires a water carry of some 400 yards!

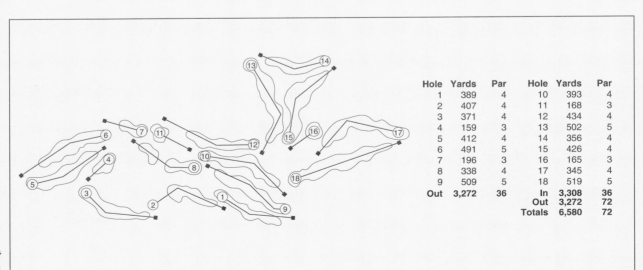

Hole	Yards	Par	Hole	Yards	Par
1	389	4	10	393	4
2	407	4	11	168	3
3	371	4	12	434	4
4	159	3	13	502	5
5	412	4	14	356	4
6	491	5	15	426	4
7	196	3	16	165	3
8	338	4	17	345	4
9	509	5	18	519	5
Out	**3,272**	**36**	**In**	**3,308**	**36**
			Out	**3,272**	**72**
			Totals	**6,580**	**72**

At first it was no more than a feint black spot on the horizon; then, as it passed by the side of the mountain it gained definition and the whirring sound of propeller blades could be made out: the helicopter was on schedule. Eventually, it landed and the great man got out; he said his hellos; joked with his friends and then played 18 holes. Nick Faldo was at Ballyliffin.

It happened in June 1993, exactly seven days before the Englishman was crowned Irish Open Champion for the third year in succession. His verdict on the Ballyliffin links? 'It is one of the most natural courses I have ever played.' He was also completely bowled over by the beauty of the setting and the extraordinary atmosphere of the place, indeed, so much so that he was heard to enquire as to the possibilities of obtaining employment as a window cleaner in the village! Nick Faldo had simply fallen under the spell—or put another way, he'd been 'Ballyliffined'.

Located in the far north of Donegal, close to Malin Head on the Inishowen Peninsula, Ballyliffin is Ireland's most northerly situated golf course. The position is as stunning as it is remote. Located between dark, dramatic hills on the one side and a sweeping bay on the other this is a veritable haven. But charms aside, what instantly hits everyone the moment they arrive at Ballyliffin is how natural a golf links this is. Golf has not been played here since the 16th century but you could easily imagine that it had. The sand dunes stretch as far as the eye can see. Amidst the dunes is the most perfect seaside grass and up, over, beside and around the dunes wend the fairways of Ballyliffin golf links. Stand on any tee of this course and the word to describe the fairway ahead is 'rippling'. The hole may dog-leg, it may climb or tumble downhill, but always it ripples. Add its geography to the equation and the unavoidable impression of Ballyliffin is that it is something of an Irish Royal Dornoch, and if that to the reader sounds like absurd flattery then I simply say, go and pay a visit!

For many people, it is a bit of a trek to put it mildly. Ballyliffin is about a two hour drive from Donegal, the route being via Letterkenny and Buncrana (travelling initially along the N15 and the N56). Buncrana is the starting point for the Inishowen 100 mile scenic drive which, if not as famous as the Ring of Kerry arguably offers comparable beauty and the road to Ballyliffin will guide you through some of this splendour. The nearest airport is just over the border at Derry, less than an hour away and not too far beyond Derry is the Causeway Coast and its much more famous golfing treasures.

Given the great distance that the traveller is probably coming from, it is always wise to contact the Club before setting off. The office telephone number is **(077) 76119** and the address for correspondence is; **Ballyliffin Golf Club, Ballyliffin, Cardonagh, Co. Donegal.** The green fees at Ballyliffin are extremely good value. In 1994 they were £10 per round midweek and £15 per round at the weekend. Individual visitors are welcome on any day of the week although there are some restrictions at weekends due to Club competitions.

There is a beautiful feeling of symmetry to a game of golf at Ballyliffin. The front nine and back nine each comprise two par threes, two par fives and five par fours (making up the total yardage of 6,524 yards, par 72). Parallels between the two nines continue in that the 1st and 10th holes are remarkably similar, both mildly dog-leg to the right and are immediately followed by longer dog-legs to the left. Both nines possess something that is becoming a rarity on newly designed courses, a good short par four hole. On the first half, it is the 3rd, with its ever narrowing fairway and where the tee shot must be targeted directly at the sea, and on the back nine it is the 14th, where the big hitter is teased into having a go for the green with his drive and of course is heavily punished if he fails to rise to the occasion. The 12th is a long and testing par three but the most memorable is the 5th, 'The Tank', where a long or medium iron must be struck perfectly to find an elevated plateau green surrounded by dunes.

If my theme of symmetry comes a little unstuck at the end of the two halves—the 9th measures a mere 110 yards and the 18th, 556 yards!—allow me to return to my rippling fairways and the 13th which runs very close to the shore. This is a real gem of a hole, it might even rival the 11th at Waterville as the best par five in Ireland — come to think of it though, how many better par threes are there than the 5th at Ballyliffin?

A visit to Ballyliffin is a truly unique experience. A warm welcome is guaranteed, and if you do go, mind you look closely at the local window cleaner... you never know!

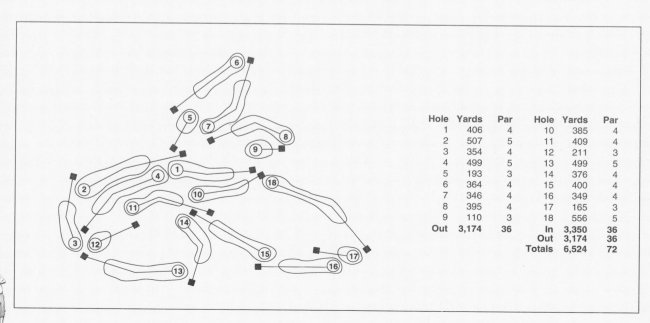

Hole	Yards	Par		Hole	Yards	Par
1	406	4		10	385	4
2	507	5		11	409	4
3	354	4		12	211	3
4	499	5		13	499	5
5	193	3		14	376	4
6	364	4		15	400	4
7	346	4		16	349	4
8	395	4		17	165	3
9	110	3		18	556	5
Out	3,174	36		In	3,350	36
				Out	3,174	36
				Totals	6,524	72

The Downhill Hotel is situated, not only very conveniently for the airports of Knock and Sligo (both 35 miles away) but also for some of the best golf on the west of Ireland. With the highly acclaimed links of Enniscrone almost on the doorstep, the grand course of Westport within a short drive and the true championship links of Rosses Point to the east, few golfers could ask for a more enjoyable challenge or a better place to stay.

This Grade A hotel offers excellent cuisine, personal and friendly service and fine facilities. Bedrooms are luxurious with television/video, satellite television, radio, telephone, tea and coffee making facilities and trouser press. The Downhill Hotel is situated in beautiful grounds and offers Frogs Pavilion Piano Bar, split level restaurant with extensive menu, swimming pool, sauna, gymnasium, squash, snooker room, sunbed and craft shop. If you are unable to escape from work, the Downhill offers excellent conference facilities and is equipped to meet the most exacting requirements.

Far away from polluted air and water, the Downhill Hotel lies next to the River Moy which is famous for its salmon fishing. Attached to Lough Conn and flowing into Killala Bay it provides an area rich in fresh and sea water fishing. Coarse angling is also available. The hotel staff are able to organise a boat for your day trip, be it on the lake, estuary or river (advance booking necessary). For that perfect game angling holiday come to the Moy and stay at the Downhill Hotel in the west of Ireland.

For those in search of a more peaceful break, a walk on one of the many beautiful sandy beaches or perhaps a scenic tour can always be recommended.

Downhill Hotel
Ballina
Co Mayo
Ireland
Tel: (010 353 96) 21033
Fax: (010 353 96) 21338

Which is the best golf course in Ireland? Is it the Old Course at Ballybunion? Or perhaps Portmarnock near Dublin? Or what about the two 'Royal' courses north of the border, Portrush and County Down? These are the four courses which invariably receive the most nominations in the age-old favourite 19th hole debate. They are, if you like, the four with the biggest reputations; but there is another golf course that many people believe deserves to be spoken of in the same breath and that is County Sligo, more commonly known as Rosses Point.

If we commit ourselves a little further, then of this magnificent five, Royal County Down at Newcastle has perhaps the strongest claim to possessing the finest front nine holes and Ballybunion the greatest back nine. But taking each of the eighteens as a balanced whole, Rosses Point must have a creditable claim; indeed Peter Alliss has been quoted as saying 'Rosses Point stands right at the very top of the list of Irish golf courses.' Another famous supporter of the west coast links which has hosted the West of Ireland Amateur Championship every year since 1923, is the great Tom Watson. If he were asked to name his three favourite links courses in Britain and Ireland (excluding those at which he won an Open Championship!) he would probably rattle off the names Ballybunion, Royal Dornoch and Rosses Point.

As well as having a glorious golf course, County Sligo Golf Club enjoys a glorious situation. The golf links (and the surrounding countryside) is dominated by the extraordinary mountain, Benbulben, which is a dead ringer for Cape Town's Table Mountain. Immediately adjacent to the links is a wonderfully sweeping bay with three beautiful beaches: little wonder that the scenery so intoxicated Ireland's greatest poet, W. B. Yeats.

Visiting golfers who wish to become similarly intoxicated by the golfing challenge are advised to contact the Club in advance. The **Secretary**, or **Golf Office** at Rosses Point can be contacted by telephone on **(071) 77134** (from the UK the code is 010 353 71) and by fax on (071) 77460. There is no firm requirement that visitors produce handicap certificates but they must, however, be players of a 'reasonable standard'. The Club's **professional, Leslie Robinson** can be reached by telephone on **(071) 77171**. Finally, the green fees for 1994 were £16 per round, £27 per day during the week and, subject to availability, £22 per round, £35 per day at weekends.

Rosses Point is often tagged 'remote', not as remote as Waterville but more so than most of Ireland's finest golfing attractions. Naturally, it depends where one is coming from but there is an airport (County Sligo) just 20 minutes drive away at Strandhill. The town of Sligo is no more than 10 minutes away from the links (via the R291 road); Donegal is about one hour's drive north (N15) and Westport approximately an hour and a half to the south west (N17/N5/N60).

The 1st at Rosses Point is a medium-length par four, fairly straight and gently uphill all the way to a well protected green. The 2nd, is much more severely uphill and the approach shot, although likely to be no more than a short iron can be very difficult to judge. On reaching the green at the 2nd, one can feel on top of the world, almost literally, for the panoramic view from here is as vast as it is sensational. Benbulben is genuinely awe-inspiring, a geological freak which, if located in a more widely known part of the world would be universally acclaimed. From such dizzy heights the Atlantic looks positively inviting—so does the downhill drive at the 3rd! This hole can be reached with two well struck shots but a series of fiendishly positioned bunkers await to punish the less accurate.

The 4th is a fine par three where the green sits on a natural plateau and this is followed by another vertigo-inducing tee shot at the 5th. The 6th is perhaps the weakest hole on the course and the 7th looks fairly straightforward for a stroke index one hole—that is until your second shot plummets into the brook in front of the green. The brook reappears on the 8th, which is a magnificent and much photographed dog-leg. The front nine concludes with the excellent par three 9th where the green is surrounded by bunkers.

The 10th and 11th offer the closest views of Benbulben and they are a very good pair of par fours. A fairly blind par five is followed by the difficult one-shot 13th, where the tee looks down over the sea and sands. Then comes Tom Watson's favourite. The 14th is a superb and extremely testing par four and when the wind is blowing can make even the 8th seem tame. If the wind is against on the 14th then it will be so again on the 15th, which is bad news because the drive needs to be carried far over some very wild dunes close to the shore. The 16th is the longest par three at Rosses Point and the 17th calls for a long uphill second to an amphitheatre green. Then at long last, comes a fairly gentle hole! It is the last and if you play it on a fine summer's evening you may be lucky enough to see the sun setting behind the 18th green: now, wouldn't that be the perfect end to a perfect round!

Hole	Metres	Par	Hole	Metres	Par
1	347	4	10	351	4
2	278	4	11	366	4
3	457	5	12	448	5
4	150	3	13	162	3
5	438	5	14	394	4
6	387	4	15	367	4
7	385	4	16	196	3
8	374	4	17	414	4
9	153	3	18	336	4
Out	**2,969**	**36**	**In**	**3,034**	**35**
			Out	**2,969**	**36**
			Totals	**6,003**	**71**

Adjoining the town of Newport and overlooking the tidal river and quay the impressive country mansion of Newport House stands guard over the centuries of history that form the backbone to its grounds and the surrounding countryside. Once the home of a branch of the O'Donel family, descended from the famous fighting Earls of Tir Connell and cousins to 'Red Hugh' of Irish history, it is now a superb example of a lovingly maintained Georgian Mansion House.

Encircled by mountains, lakes and streams, Newport is within easy reach of some of Ireland's most beautiful rivers. Renowned as an angling centre, it holds private salmon and sea-trout fishing rights to 8 miles of the Newport River; and the prolific waters of the stunning Lough Beltra West are close by. Less than twenty minutes drive from the hotel are Lakes Mask and Corrib, while the nearby Loughs Feeagh and Furnace are the site of the Salmon Research Trust of Ireland.

The discerning golfer has the pleasure of the 18-hole championship course at Westport as well as the more relaxed 9-hole course near Mulrany.

Outdoor activities are numerous amidst the breath-taking scenery of County Mayo. Riding is easily arranged or try swimming and diving on wide and often empty beaches, while hanggliding is a relatively new sport gaining popularity from the local Achill Cliffs. One of the best recreations though is simply walking across the ever changing panorama of mountain, forest and sea.

Warmth and friendliness fill this beautiful hotel in a country already famed for its hospitality. The house is furnished with a tasteful collection of fine antiques and paintings and the elegant bedrooms are individually decorated. Food is taken seriously, with much of the produce collected fresh from the fishery, gardens and farm. Home-smoked salmon and fresh sea-food are specialites, and all the dishes are complemented by a carefully chosen and extensive wine list.

Many of the staff have been long in the service of the estate, up to forty years in one case. Combine this with the solid background of the house and there is a rare feeling of continuity and maturity so rare in modern hotels today.

Newport House
Co. Mayo
Ireland
Tel: (010 353 98) 41222
Fax: (010 353 98) 41613

This old world hotel is situated in the heart of heart of Mayo's Lakeland District on the shores of Lough Cullen and Lough Conn. While retaining old world charm and character, it has a friendly atmosphere with professional standards. It was first opened in 1887 as a hotel by the Healy family and later became a Bianconni 'halting stop'. It still has features and remnants from the Bianconni era about the hotel. It is now a recognised country village inn.

In 1990, the McGeever family purchased the hotel and completely refurbished and restored it to its former character. The hotel has traditionally been a very popular establishment with the angling fraternity, with Ireland's premier salmon fishing river only five miles from the hotel, the River Moy and excellent trout and salmon fishing on Lough Conn and Lough Cullen.

Healys Hotel is an ideal location for golfers, being midway between Enniscrone Golf Course (20kms) and Westport Golf Course (25kms), both recognised international championship 18 hole courses. Castlebar is also just 15 kilometres away, another good 18 hole course, and two 9 hole courses, Ballina and Mullraney, are within 20 kilometres.

The hotel is just 20 miles from Knock Airport and transport can be arranged from the airport to the hotel. Car hire can also be arranged at very reasonable rates through the hotel.

The Lough Cullen Room restaurant overlooks Lough Cullen and is renowned for its game and fish dish specialities, using only the freshest of ingredients caught in the waters and woodlands of the locality.

Brendan and Julie McGeever and their staff endeavour to ensure that all their guests have a comfortable and memorable holiday in Ireland and you are certain to find the warmest of welcomes at Healys Hotel.

Healys Hotel
Pontoon
Foxford
Co Mayo
Ireland
Tel: (010 353 94) 56443
Fax: (010 353 94) 56572

The Ardagh Hotel & Restaurant

This quiet, family run hotel is located in the scenic heart of Connemara — which has long been regarded as the real emerald of Ireland. The Ardagh is situated on the edge of Ardbear Bay and is only three kilometres from Clifden, the county's capital.

The well-appointed bedrooms are en suite with central heating, direct dial telephone, colour television and tea/coffee making facilities. Large suites are also available overlooking the bay and the crystal clear waters of the Atlantic Ocean.

The owner-chef specialises in locally caught seafood and delicious home-grown vegetables — all complimented by an imaginative wine list. The restaurant has been awarded a rosette for excellent food from the A.A and also, a hospitality, comfort and restaurant award from the RAC. After dinner, guests may relax in one of the hotel's three lounges, one with an inviting fire, while reflecting on the constantly changing colours of Ardbear Bay.

The region of Connemara is famous for its outdoor pursuits: salmon and brown trout fishing, sea angling, horse riding and golf at the Connemara Golf Club can all be arranged by the hotel. Set against the spectacular backdrop of the Atlantic Ocean on one side and the distant Twelve Bens on the other, the Connemara Golf Club is the ideal venue for a challenging game of golf on the 18 hole championship links.

Places of interest which are near to the hotel include the sight and memorial of the first transatlantic flight, Kylemore Abbey and a tour of the Sky Road with its unsurpassed views of the Atlantic.

The Ardagh Hotel &
Restaurant
Clifden
Connemara
Ireland
Tel: (010 353 95) 21384
Fax: (010 353 95) 21314

Not many people reading this book will have visited the Moon and, unless N.A.S.A. is keeping an extraordinary secret under wraps, only one man has ever played golf there: our friend from La Moye and Fulford, Admiral Alan Sheppard. I suspect the closest most of us are ever likely to get to experiencing golf in a lunar-like landscape is if we visit Connemara on the west coast of Ireland.

While much of County Kerry basks in picture-postcard prettiness, the countryside of Connemara boasts a truly rugged kind of splendour. Some of Connemara appears almost pre-historic. Great grey rocks are strewn all over a hilly, green landscape. Connemara National Park is surely where Finn McCool and his giant buddies staged an all-night rock throwing party but forgot to clear up afterwards. The village of Ballyconneely is about as far west as you can go in Connemara without slipping into the Atlantic and Ballyconneely is where Connemara Golf Club is found.

Before 1973 it used to be reckoned that the only people who ventured this far west were lost. This of course was in the days before golf came to Ballyconneely. Connemara's Championship golf links is worth discovering: it may not be in quite the same league as Rosses Point to the north or Ballybunion to the south (but then which courses are?) But it is a wonderful golfing experience.

Ballyconneely is situated 9 miles south of Clifden, (where trans-Atlantic aviators Alcock and Brown fell to earth) a journey of perhaps 15 to 20 minutes along a fairly deserted road. Clifden is joined to Galway by the N59, a distance of approximately 50 miles, roughly an hour and a quarter by car, a journey though that no one should rush. According to Thackeray this is 'one of the most beautiful districts that is ever the fortune of the traveller to examine.' Thackeray was biased, but a thousand watercolours cannot lie. The N59 also links Clifden with Westport to the north east and the journey via Leenane, where 'The Field', which starred Richard Harris, was filmed is at least as dramatic.

Golfing visitors to Connemara are always made extremely welcome. Greatly responsible for the hospitable atmosphere at the Club is the **Secretary/ Manager John McLoughlin**. It is advisable to contact Mr McLoughlin in advance, tel **(095) 23502**, or fax (095) 23662 (from the UK the code is 010 353 95) to ensure that there aren't any tee reservations; moreover, during the summer months and at holiday weekends a starting sheet

system is operated. Subject to the above, and being able to provide proof of handicap there are no general restrictions on the times when visitors may play. Green fees for 1994 were set at £16 between May and September, £14 for the months of March, April and October and £10 during the winter months.

Few clubhouses enjoy a better vantage point than the one at Connemara. Perched on high ground there are not only some magnificent views over the ocean (particularly splendid when the western sun dips into the sea on a summer's evening) but also across much of the course. It is a wonderful place in which to relax. But first we must tackle the course.

The first seven holes at Connemara are frankly nothing special—not bad, but nothing special. To say that the course steps up a gear at the 8th would be a gross understatement. Some of the holes between the 8th and 18th are as good as any one is likely to play, 'so good they are nearly ridiculous' reckoned Irish golf writer Pat Ruddy. The first seven holes are by no means easy but apart from the excellent dog-legged 1st where from the tee the flag seems to be positioned somewhere in the middle of some particularly wild terrain, and the two short holes, the 3rd and the 6th, they are a bit of an up-and-down slog over what is easily the flattest part of the course.

The 8th however is a fine par four; it is the stroke index one hole and the approach is a very testing one to a broad but plateau green. As for the 9th, it is a real gem of a hole. Again a two-shotter, the player drives downhill from a magnificently placed high tee; over the player's shoulder as he drives is a mountainous backdrop, the famous Twelve Bens, and stretching out ahead is the sea, the great Atlantic Ocean—the next terra firma being Long Island.

If the 9th is a memorable hole, the par three 13th is out of this world. This is where landscape is replaced by moonscape. As at the 9th, an exhilarating downhill tee shot is called for. From the back tees a long-iron shot will be needed as the carry is all of 200 yards. The 14th, a par five, where you can really open the shoulders, and the 15th which is a little reminiscent of the 14th at Portmarnock with its uphill second to a shelf-like green, are two more marvellous holes. Water can play the devil at the 16th while the 17th and 18th are a pair of par fives that seem to stretch forever and a day.

If you've played Connemara from the back tees (well over 7000 yards) the chances are you'll be breathless by the finish. Breathless at Connemara—like being on the Moon.

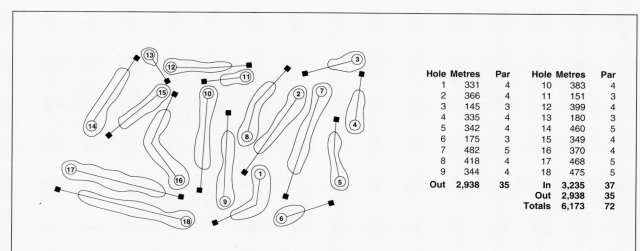

Hole	Metres	Par		Hole	Metres	Par
1	331	4		10	383	4
2	366	4		11	151	3
3	145	3		12	399	4
4	335	4		13	180	3
5	342	4		14	460	5
6	175	3		15	349	4
7	482	5		16	370	4
8	418	4		17	468	5
9	344	4		18	475	5
Out	**2,938**	**35**		**In**	**3,235**	**37**
				Out	**2,938**	**35**
				Totals	**6,173**	**72**

County Clare and County Limerick

We begin our brief tour of south west Ireland in County Clare where **Lahinch** is found. The famous links is featured ahead but ideas for staying in the area must include the excellent Aberdeen Arms Hotel (010 353) 658 1100—good food here also. In Ennis, Mungovans (010 353) 652 4608 offers first rate accommodation while slightly nearer Limerick in Newmarket-on-Fergus, Hunter's Lodge (010 353) 6136 8577 is inexpensive and **Dromoland Castle** (010 353) 6171 144 is for the true connoisseur. The person who stayed at Ashford Castle will probably be staying here. Again the hotel has a golf course although Dromoland's course has 18 holes and has recently been upgraded—it is detailed on a later page. Surrounded by the Dromoland Castle course, the Clare Inn Hotel (010 353) 6717 1161 is clearly very convenient for golfers who cannot afford to stay in the castle! Not far from Dromoland, **Shannon** Golf Club is also well worth a visit—friendly and a very good parkland golf course. Around Limerick, one of the more exciting developments in golfing terms is the new course at **Adare Manor** (010 353) 613 96566 in keeping with the grand style of the hotel. Another course with accommodation in the shape of twelve holiday cottages and well worth a visit is the Limerick Country Club (010 353) 613 51881, and golf is just one of a number of sporting pursuits to be enjoyed from the Clonlara Hotel (010 353) 613 54141.

Kerry's Gold

If we have crossed the Shannon via the Tarbert Ferry, **Ballybunion** is the first great club we come across in County Kerry. Like **Lahinch**, **Dromoland**, **Killarney**, **Waterville** and **Tralee** it's featured ahead. Killarney provides the most central base and as an enormously popular tourist destination has numerous hotels and guest houses. Undoubtedly one of the best places to base oneself is the Killarney Country Club (010 353) 644 4655, four miles from Killarney Golf Club at Faha: superb accommodation and a friendly welcome await. Among other fine establishments in Killarney are the Aghadoe Heights (010 353) 643 1768 (stunning views and an outstanding restaurant here), the Killarney Towers Hotel (010 353) 643 1038, the Muckross Park Hotel (010 353) 643 1938, the Great Southern (010 353) 643 1262, the very attractive Cahernane (010 353) 643 1895, the International (010 353) 643 1816 and the Castlerosse (010 353) 643 1144. Eating establishments are equally plentiful with Gabys (010 353) 643 2519, Foleys (010 353) 643 1217, and the aforementioned Aghadoe Heights Hotel restaurant unlikely to disappoint anybody. To the south of Killarney, the Park Hotel Kenmare (010 353) 644 1200 is where our friends from Dromoland Castle will now be heading. Also in Kenmare, Sheen Falls Lodge (010 353) 644 1600 is extremely welcoming and rapidly establishing itself as one of the finest hotels in the country. For an intimate and inexpensive stopover in Killarney, Kathleen's Country House Hotel is highly recommended (010 353) 643 2810 as is the friendly 19th Green guest house (010 353) 643 2868 which is almost adjacent to the famous golf club. **Tralee** is about 20 miles north west of Killarney. The links is actually some eight miles from the town itself; the journey takes a little longer than you expect but no golfer in the world would be disappointed when he reached this course. Perhaps the best hotel for golfers in Tralee itself is the Mount Brandon Hotel (010 353) 662 3333 but more adjacent in Barrow is the popular Barrow House (010 353) 663 6437 guest house. One hotel to match the quality of the golf at Ballybunion is undoubtedly the Glin Castle (010 353) 683 4173 while two hotels to note in Ballybunion are the Marine (068) 27522 — a good seafood restaurant here — and the Ballybunion Golf Hotel (068) 27111.

There are very reasonable 18 hole courses at **Dingle** (Ballyferiter) and **Dooks** but **Waterville** is the other great course in County Kerry. Waterville is one of the longest courses in Europe, when played from the back tees. It has its charm as well though and it has been described as 'the beautiful monster'. Suggestions for a 19th hole in Waterville include the elegant Waterville House (010 353) 667 4102, the Waterville Lake Hotel (010 353) 667 4133 and the Butler Arms Hotel (010 353) 667 4144. Two restaurants to savour here are the Huntsman and the Smugglers Inn. (A quick note here for Shamrock Cottages (010 353) 7497 6715, a group which boasts a fine selection of cottages in the most scenic locations.)

Cork and Tipperary

Coming down from rather dizzy heights, County Cork deserves a brief inspection. In the city itself, the **Cork** Golf Club at Little Island is decidedly worth a visit. Approximately five miles east of the town centre the course overlooks Cork Harbour and is one of the top ten inland courses in Ireland. It was at Little Island that one of Ireland's legendary golfers Jimmy Bruen learnt to play. Other golfing challenges near to Ireland's second city include **Muskerry**, **Monkstown**, **Harbour Point** and **Douglas**, plus two very fine new 18 hole courses, the much acclaimed **Fota Island**, which is not far from Cork Golf Club, and **Lee Valley**, which opened in 1993.

A delightful place to stay to explore and enjoy the golf, old and new, is Middleton Park (010 353) 216 31767 and other options include the Arbutus Lodge Hotel (010 353) 2150 1237 while less expensive, but equally welcoming, is the popular Rochestown Hotel (010 353) 2189 2233. Just outside Cork in Shanagarry is Ballymaloe House (010 353) 2165 2531, where the restaurant is particularly outstanding. Cork also boasts the Silver Springs Hotel (010 353) 2150 7533, which has numerous leisure facilities including its own 9 hole golf course. Not far away at **Mallow** the order of the day is an enjoyable round of golf followed by a relaxing stay at Longueville House (010 353) 224 7156... sheer bliss!

We complete this brief inspection of golf in the south west perhaps, but not a great distance from the delights of County Kerry. Between Tipperary and Cashel stands Dundrum House (062) 71116: a splendid hotel and an 18 hole golf course, **County Tipperary** Golf & Country Club, which we explore ahead.

RULE XIII
Worm casts *may* be removed · · · · without penalty · · ·

Charles Crombie RULE XIII Rosenstiel's

Adare Manor is a Gothic mansion set in 850 acres of parkland in the picturesque village of Adare in Ireland.

Home for the past two centuries to the Earls of Dunraven, Adare Manor has been lovingly transformed into a world class hotel with 64 luxury bedrooms. Located only 40 minutes from Shannon Airport and 20 minutes from Limerick, Adare offers the finest in Irish hospitality.

The restaurant which seats 64 people is famed for its wonderful European food with Irish influence. From its windows one can view the parterre gardens and the new Robert Trent Jones Snr. golf course located on the Manor grounds. The famous long gallery at Adare Manor, which is modelled on the Hall of Versailles, will seat over 200 for gala dinners.

Adare Manor has conference facilities for up to 200 delegates and offers full translation facilities and audio visual equipment. Leisure facilities include a gym, sauna, swimming pool and horse riding and claypigeon shooting are available within the grounds.

The new Robert Trent Jones Snr. golf course in Adare is a real stunner. The 18th hole is one of the finest par 5 finishing holes in the world, with the added attraction of a Gothic style mansion rising directly above the green.

When completed, the 16th will be one of the most scenic holes in the world with its backdrop of towering copper beech trees, spruces, cedars and oaks with views over a lake. The majesty of the course is intended to mirror the flavour and excellence of Augusta, perhaps the most celebrated golf course in the world. The course is due to be completed by the end of 1994.

Adare Manor
Adare
Co Limerick
Ireland
Tel: (010 353 61) 396566
Fax: (010 353 61) 396124

Some of the best golf in the world is to be found in south west Ireland and golfers looking for accommodation to match are cordially invited to sample the hospitality and service provided Glin Castle. Ideal for the celebrated links at Ballybunion and the great courses of Killarney, Tralee and Lahinch. Glin castle stands proudly in its wooden demesne on the banks of the River Shannon. Golfers taking advantage of the special tailor-made breaks of three days can expect nothing less than a warm welcome in the finest of Irish traditions as house guests in the home of the 29th Knight of Glin and Madam Fitzgerald.

The present Castle, which succeeds the medieval ruin in the village of Glin, was built in the late 18th century with entertaining in mind. Its toy fortress like quality is echoed by three sets of battlemented Gothic folly lodges, one of which is a restaurant — the Glin Castle Gate Shop. The entrance hall with its Corinthian pillars has a superb neo-classical ceiling. A series of reception rooms are filled with a unique collection of Irish 18th century furniture. Family portraits and Irish pictures line the walls and the library bookcase has a secret door leading to the hall and a very rare flying staircase.

The dining room windows catch the setting sun reflected in the river whilst inside, the room is filled with baronial oak furniture. Across the hall in the drawing room there is an Adam style ceiling and a matching inlaid Bossi chimney piece. Here frequently after-dinner coffee and conversation takes place.

After a stroll in the well kept grounds, the sitting room with its crackling fire makes a cosy gathering place for drinks. The cuisine is good country house cooking with fresh fruit, vegetables and fresh meat from the local butcher.

There are a variety of rooms available within Glin Castle, each with its own special appeal, including a four poster. The rooms are scattered with rugs and chaises longes and the walls are hung with interesting paintings and plates.

The Castle makes an ideal base for exploring the surrounding countryside and there is a hard tennis court in the walled garden.

Also close by is Foynes sailing club, whilst it is possible to hunt with the Limerick hounds at Adare. The countryside is breathtaking making it ideal for touring and there are important historical sights such as Lough Gur, Adare and many fascinating ruined castles and country houses. Credit Card Facilities: Visa, Access.

Glin Castle
Glin
Great Limerick
Ireland
Tel: (010 353 68) 34173 / 34112
Fax: (010 353 68) 34364

Ballybunion is a place of true pilgrimage. To golfers this is where gold has been struck, not once, but twice with two of the greatest golf courses in the world lying side by side. The Old Course at Ballybunion has long been regarded as the ultimate test in links golf. It lies in a remote corner of County Kerry close to the Shannon estuary amid the largest sandhills in the British Isles. It has a very wild beauty; no course could be closer to the sea and a number of the holes run right along the cliff edges. It's incredibly spectacular stuff and when the wind lashes in from the Atlantic, it is not a place for faint hearts.

The Old Course was begun in 1896 although a full eighteen holes were not completed until thirty years later. The renowned American writer Herbert Warren Wind said of the creation: 'It is the finest seaside course I have ever seen'. When Tom Watson first visited in 1981 (and he has returned many times since), he instantly supported Wind's contention and went on to tell the Members as much in a personal letter of thanks to the Club. What then of the New Course (now known as the Cashen Course) constructed in the mid 1980s? Architect Robert Trent Jones had this to say: 'When I first saw the piece of land chosen for the new course at Ballybunion, I was thrilled beyond words. I said it was the finest piece of links land I had ever seen. I feel totally confident that everyone who comes to play at Ballybunion will be as thrilled as I was by the unique majesty of this truly unforgettable course'.

Happily, Ballybunion isn't jealous of its treasures and visitors are always made to feel welcome. The **Golf Manager** at Ballybunion is **Jim Mckenna.** He can be contacted by telephone on **(068) 27146** or by fax on **(068) 27387.** The code from the UK is (010 353 68). The **professiona**l at Ballybunion, **Brian Callaghan,** can also be reached on the above number. A full day's green fee in 1994 was priced at £45 (or £50 in mid-summer). This entitles the visitor to a round over both the Old and the Cashen—not of course compulsory, but if the body can take it, and it's likely to receive a fair battering en route, it would be a tragedy not to play the pair. A single round over the Old Course was priced at £30 (£35) in 1994 with £20 (£25) payable for 18 holes on the Cashen.

Helped by the lavish praise of Messrs. Watson and Co. Ballybunion has become a lot busier in recent years and visitors should book some time in advance of intended play. Weekdays are naturally the easiest times for a visit

and Sundays should be avoided if a game on the Old Course is sought.

The nearest airports to Ballybunion are at Shannon, a distance of approximately sixty miles to the north east, and the new Kerry Airport at Farranfore, some thirty miles due south. Cork's airport is about eighty miles to the south east. From either Cork or Shannon the journey can take about an hour and a half but there cannot be a soul on earth who wouldn't enjoy a trek through the south west of Ireland. From Shannon, travel via Limerick and from Cork via Mallow and Listowel; from Ballybunion town the course is about a mile's drive along the coast.

There is certainly no shortage of land at Ballybunion and both courses can be stretched to 7000 yards—an alarming prospect! From the medal tees the two are of fairly similar length, the Old measuring 6503 yards, par 71, the Cashen 6477 yards, par 72. But don't be fooled by the scorecard, each is a monster when the mood takes it.

The truly great holes on the Old Course begin at the 6th which has a frighteningly narrow entrance to a plateau green. The 7th fairway runs its entire length along the shore—one of the most spectacular par fours one is likely to play. The 8th is a shortish downhill par three, but if you miss the green you can be in serious trouble. And so it continues with the 11th being perhaps the most famous hole on the course. The sight from the tee is intimidating to put it mildly; the Atlantic waves are beneath you to the right, with some enormous sand dunes to the left. The fairway drops in tiers until it finally culminates on a windswept plateau green overlooking the ocean. It is unquestionably one of the greatest two-shot holes anywhere in the world.

The Cashen Course is arguably more dramatic! The sand hills are even more massive, and some of the carries required from the tee are prodigious. Some people rate the course on a par with the Old. I wouldn't agree, although the back nine includes some truly magnificent holes.

The 19th at Ballybunion, which happens to be a brand new clubhouse opened by Tom Watson in 1993, is a grand place for recuperation. It is conveniently situated midway between nature's two masterpieces. Nowhere are stories swapped so enthusiastically and perhaps nowhere will you hear so often the phrase, 'Just wait until 'next time!' Gold diggers them all.

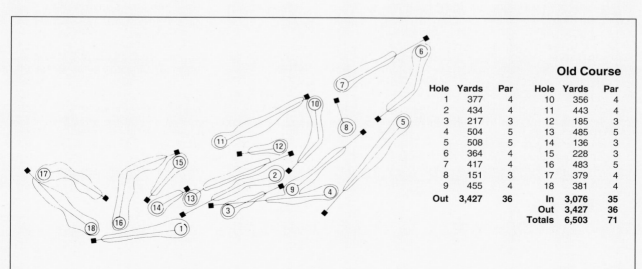

Set in eight and a half acres, the Aghadoe Heights Hotel, is renowned for its unique location, with breath-taking panoramic views of the lakes and mountains of Killarney, which provide a superb setting for one of South West Ireland's finest hotels. Sister hotel to Fredrick's in Maidenhead, the Aghadoe Heights enjoys a similar reputation for providing high standards of comfort, good food and personal service.

The elegance and style of the Aghadoe Heights is evident from the moment you step through the door into the warm and welcoming reception, with detailed personal touches displayed throughout in the rich tapestries and furnishings, crystal chandeliers, paintings and antiques.

Great care and attention to detail has gone into furnishing the hotel's 60 bedrooms and suites, to offer traditional comfort and modern facilities combined with simple touches of elegance. The bedrooms, fitted in mahogany, cherry wood or ash together with co-ordinated fabrics and furnishings, soft drapes and deep carpets give each room a distinct character. All rooms have direct dial telephone, radio, colour television with satellite network, trouser presses, hairdryers and mini-bars, together with spacious bathrooms offering full facilities, toiletries and bathrobes.

No stay at the Aghadoe is complete without sampling the culinary delights offered in 'Fredrick's at the Heights' the hotel's splendidly located roof-top restaurant. Fredrick's is receiving recognition from all the major guides and is now acknowledged as one of Ireland's finest restaurants. Cooking is Traditional French and the extensive menu features many fresh fish and seafood specialities for which County Kerry is so famous, all prepared under the direction of Executive Chef, Robin Suter. Guests may relax and enjoy a drink in the hotel's Cocktail and Heights Bars or sit and absorb the magnificent views from the terrace or the hotel's superbly appointed leisure area. This excellent facility includes a luxurious indoor swimming pool with special features such as a cascading waterfall, a pool bar and jacuzzi, together with a sauna, steambath, therapeutic plunge pool, solarium plus fitness and beauty treatment rooms.

With a superb location in the heart of Ireland's most spectacular scenery, the Aghadoe Heights is the ideal centre for a touring, sporting or simply relaxing holiday break. Five minutes away from, and overlooking Killarney's two 18 hole Championship Courses, the hotel is also within easy reach of Kerry's other premier golf courses such as Tralee, Ballybunion and Waterville. Guests may fish in season for salmon and trout on the hotel's own ten mile stretch of riverbank, or arrangements can be made for lake and deep sea fishing. A wide range of activities are available in the area from horse riding, pony trekking, tennis and shooting, to exploring the Ring of Kerry and the Dingle Peninsula. Every day offers so much that once having experienced the unrivalled hospitality of the Aghadoe Heights you will be counting the days until your return..

Aghadoe Heights Hotel
Killarney
Co.Kerry
Eire
Tel: (010 353 64) 31766
Fax: (010 353 64) 31345

Killarney is often described as 'paradise on earth', and not merely by we blasphemous golfers. This is Ireland's most famous beauty spot; somehow the lakes here seem a deeper and clearer blue and the mountains a more delicate shade of purple. It is a place where even the most miserable of wretches would be forced to smile.

The two golf courses of the Killarney Golf and Fishing Club take full advantage of the majestic surroundings. A Gleneagles afloat perhaps? Not really. The golf at Killarney is parkland rather than heathland, or moorland, but it can generate a similar degree of pleasure and, like Gleneagles, can be a welcome retreat from the tremendously testing links courses nearby. A place to soothe one's damaged pride.

Killarney has lived through a somewhat chequered history. Golf has been played here since the late 19th century. The first course was nothing grand, laid out in an old deer park owned by the Earl of Kenmare. However, in 1936 the Earl's very keen golfing heir, and a great character of his time, Lord Castlerosse, decided that Killarney deserved a course that would reflect the glorious setting. Eighteen holes were laid out by Sir Guy Campbell and the new course opened in 1939. Castlerosse, who had played a very active role in the design, was pleased with the creation but continued to suggest imaginative improvements, unfortunately, not all of which were carried through following his untimely death in 1943. In the 1970s a second eighteen holes were built and the two present courses, **Mahony's Point** and **Killeen** are each a combination of the old holes and the new. Basking beside the shores of Lough Leane and encircled by the splendour of the Macgillicuddy Reeks and the Carrauntoohill mountains, Killarney really is a golfer's dream.

The present **Secretary** at Killarney is the affable **Tom Prendergast**, who may be contacted by telephone on **(064) 31034** (from the U.K. (010 353 64) 31034). Any written correspondence should be addressed to The Secretary, **Killarney Golf and Fishing Club, O'Mahony's Point, Killarney, Co. Kerry, Ireland.** The Club's **professional, Tony Coveney** can be reached on **(064) 31615**. As seems to be the case with all of Ireland's great courses, visitors are warmly greeted—and they come from every foreseeable golfing country! There are no specific restrictions on playing during the week, although some do exist at the weekend, so it's always a good idea to telephone the Club before making any firm arrangements. The green fee at Killarney for 1994 was £26 per round, seven days per week. Handicap certificates are required for both courses.

Killarney is the most accessible of Kerry's golfing delights, the town being linked to both Limerick (70 miles) and Cork (60 miles) by major road. The nearest airport is at Farranfore (Kerry Airport). The Golf Club lies about three miles west of the town off Killorglin Road and is well signposted. Those staying in the area might note that Killarney is the starting point of the famous one hundred mile Ring of Kerry road, which takes in surely some of the most marvellous scenery to be enjoyed anywhere in the world.

In such a setting, inspired golf is clearly on the cards (or so one hopes!) Mahony's Point is still probably the better known of the two courses, largely on account of its spectacular finishing holes, although in 1991 and 1992 it was the much improved Killeen Course which hosted the Carrolls Irish Open, and on both occasions victory went to Nick Faldo. The Killeen is in fact the longer of the two courses, measuring 6426 metres, par 73, compared with Mahony's Point, which measures 6138 metres, par 72. Among the better holes on the Killeen Course are the dog-legged 1st, which follows the curve of Lough Leane's shore, the stunning par three 3rd, also alongside the water's edge and the exacting 13th—one of Castlerosse's favourites from the Campbell layout—a long par four which has a stream crossing the fairway to catch the mis-hit second.

On the Mahony's Point Course (which is scheduled to host the 1996 Curtis Cup) the celebrated finish begins at the par five 16th where the course returns toward Lough Leane. The 18th though is the hole that everyone remembers. It's a par three hole, which in itself is fairly unusual at the end of a round, and the tee shot is played directly across the edge of the lake, practically all carry. Rhododendron bushes and pine trees frame the green: very beautiful, yet potentially very treacherous. 'The best short hole in the world' enthused Henry Longhurst. He also suggested that it might be a fitting place to end one's days. I can think of many worse places than the 18th green on Mahony's Point, but to pass over the club's magnificent new 19th hole would be at best anti-social.

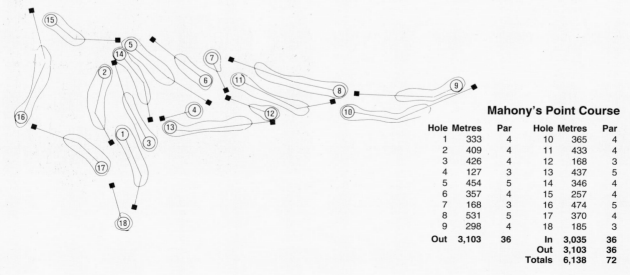

Mahony's Point Course

Hole	Metres	Par	Hole	Metres	Par
1	333	4	10	365	4
2	409	4	11	433	4
3	426	4	12	168	3
4	127	3	13	437	5
5	454	5	14	346	4
6	357	4	15	257	4
7	168	3	16	474	5
8	531	5	17	370	4
9	298	4	18	185	3
Out	**3,103**	**36**	**In**	**3,035**	**36**
			Out	**3,103**	**36**
			Totals	**6,138**	**72**

Artist: **Micheal Brown PREPARING TO PLAY** *Courtesy of:* **Burlington Gallery**

Kathleen's Country House

Kathleen's country house, winner of the 1993 RAC Small Hotel/Guesthouse of the Year, provides visitors with the opportunity to enjoy the best of both worlds — the standards to be expected from a first class hotel together with the comforts and warmth of an Irish home.

Set in peaceful scenic surroundings, with award-winning gardens, this is the ideal base for golf and for touring the Cork and Kerry region.

At Kathleen's, traditional hospitality and courteous personal attention are a way of life. The well-appointed bedrooms are en suite and have colour television, direct dial telephone and hairdriers. The accent is on comfort, with each room tastefully furnished and enjoying restful country views.

The elegant dining room is open for breakfast which is cooked to order from the award-winning menu. Home cooking, specialising in traditional wholesome dishes is a speciality.

Guests may enjoy a wide variety of activities during their stay at Kathleen's country house. There are heated indoor swimming pools nearby and many uncrowded beaches within 20 minutes drive. For the more energetic there are three 18 hole championship golf courses, and 9 hole courses, within five minutes drive. Enquiries/brochure available from owner/manager Kathleen O'Regan Sheppard.

Kathleen's Country House
Tralee Road
Killarney
County Kerry
Tel: (010 353 64) 32810
Fax: (010 353 64) 32340

Like the Beatles, there will never be another Arnold Palmer. In his prime he attacked golf courses the way Errol Flynn attacked pirates. He led golf away from its stuffy, gin and tonic, plus fours image and took a vast army of hero-worshipping fans with him. When he stopped winning golf tournaments around the world, Palmer became involved in golf course design. Now let's face it, a man whose middle name is 'Charge' is unlikely to construct 'humdrum' golf courses. Hardly. The courses Arnold Palmer designs are the sort that any golfer with high blood pressure really ought to steer well clear of. Tralee's golf course, perched on the edge of the incomparably dramatic coast of County Kerry, is one that should carry such a health warning.

Tralee (the golf course is actually eight miles west of the town at Barrow) understandably prides itself on being the first golf course that Arnold Palmer designed in Europe. Apparently, he had been looking to build across the water for some time but until the mid 1980s when he was approached by some remarkably astute Irish gentlemen he hadn't found a venue that suited. Doubtless the Irish chatted him up good and proper as only they can, but Palmer didn't need the Ancient Mariner's treatment. One look at the proposed site convinced him. 'I have never come across a piece of land so ideally suited for the building of a golf course', he declared.

For decades Tralee golfers had played on a rather ordinary 'town course.' When they discovered the tract of links land at Barrow they sensed they had discovered something very special—hence the bold approach to Palmer and the decision to 'quit town' and head for the coast.

The drive from Tralee to Barrow doesn't remotely hint at the pot of gold that awaits at the end of the long, winding road. The situation is sensational in the extreme and Palmer was the perfect choice to lay out a daring and heroic course alongside such a beautifully rugged coastal stretch: a seascape described by golf writer Peter Dobereiner as being 'in a different class even to California's Monterey Peninsula.'

The **Secretary** at Tralee is **Mr Peter Colleran**; he can be contacted by telephone on **(066) 36379** or by fax: (066) 36008. The code from the UK is (010 353 66). The Club's full address is, **Tralee Golf Club, West Barrow, Ardfert, County Kerry.** Visitors wishing to test their skills at Tralee must be in possession of a current handicap (the doctor's certificate is optional) and advance booking with the club is required. The best days to arrange a game at Tralee are Mondays, Tuesdays, Thursdays and Fridays when there are no general restrictions. On Wednesdays it is possible to tee off before 9.00 am or between 10.40 am and 12.30 pm. Weekend golf is possible between 11.00 am—12.30 pm. Finally, the green fees in 1994 were set at £25 per round midweek, £30 at the weekend.

Measuring 6252 metres (about 6900 yards) from the Championship tees, Tralee has the appearance of being two courses rather than one. The gentler outward half opens with an exacting par four where the second shot immediately guides you to the edge of the precipice—one of several greens overlooking the ocean and in this case, down over a vast, desolate beach that featured prominently in the film Ryan's Daughter. The 2nd is a banana-shaped par five that follows the cliff edges—invigorating stuff! Then comes the classic short 3rd across the rocks, a hole that often reminds American visitors of Pebble Beach. The view of the hole from the Championship tee is enough to make a brave man tremble. The 6th, 7th and 8th ('Palmer's Loop') offer more exhilarating golf and provide views of a ruined 12th century castle and an old smugglers' haunt, but it is the back nine holes that leave most first-timers gasping.

After passing in front of the Clubhouse and playing the 10th the golfer then disappears into another world, a world of extraordinarily wild and massive dunes. This is where Palmer (and Mother Nature) really went to town. In true Arnie fashion, desperately daring carries are the order of the day. The par four 12th is surely one of the most examining two-shot holes in golf. Although slightly downhill, it is invariably played into the teeth of the wind—and my how it can blow in these parts! The second must be fired over a huge ravine which continues around the left side of what is a painfully narrow table green. Barely do you have time to regain your breath when you must confront the par three 13th—there the tee shot must carry an even deeper chasm! As you play these holes, all around are magnificent vistas of the Atlantic Ocean, the Dingle Peninsula and the great sweep of Kerryhead. The drama doesn't let up and the downhill, par three 16th (reminiscent of the 15th at Ballybunion Old), and the dog-legged 17th (which is called 'Ryan's Daughter') are two more outstanding holes. On reaching the magnificently appointed clubhouse you will probably feel that you've tackled more than just an extraordinary golf course—you may even feel you have challenged Palmer head to head. But then that's Tralee—a unique golfing experience.

Hole	Metres	Par	Hole	Metres	Par
1	368	4	10	385	4
2	542	5	11	530	5
3	183	3	12	417	4
4	388	4	13	145	3
5	391	4	14	367	4
6	389	4	15	273	4
7	143	3	16	181	3
8	354	4	17	323	4
9	451	5	18	422	4
Out	**3,209**	**35**	**In**	**3,043**	**35**
			Out	**3,209**	**36**
			Totals	**6,252**	**71**

Geographically speaking, Waterville is something of an Irish Dornoch. No-one could pretend that it is anything but remote, but then who would really want it to be anything else? With remoteness comes the peace of a lost world; with remoteness comes charm.

Waterville sits at the far end of the Ring of Kerry; west of Waterville there is nothing for 2,000 miles, save the Atlantic Ocean, while completing the circle to the North, South and East are brooding mountains, majestic lakes, soft hills and babbling streams.

It may surprise some to learn that golf has been played at Waterville from at least as early as the 1870s; initially it was by those gallant and indominatable men who laid the trans-Atlantic cable, so bringing the New World close to the old. The land that these pioneering golfers played over was classic, sandy links terrain - greatly exposed to the elements, but neatly maintained by the local sheep.

Until the late 1960s Waterville was largely their own best-kept secret. About this time a second team of golfing pioneers led by the visionary Irish-American Jack Mulcahy determined that Waterville links should realise its full potential. 'Determined' is the word for in a few short years they, to adopt the words of leading Irish golf writer Pat Ruddy, 'transformed Waterville from a cosy localised scale to the pinnacles of world class'.

In the 20 years since 'modern' Waterville links opened for play it has been showered with praise; but there is also more to Waterville than spectacular golf. For one thing the 19th hole is one of the most comfortable clubhouses in Ireland and for lovers of golfing art and memorabilia it is a genuine treasure trove. And then there is Waterville House, the Irish residence of the owners of Waterville Links and a temporary home to guests who enjoy an intimate and timeless 'country house' ambience.

Built in the late 18th century and recently refurbished, Waterville House presides serenely on the shores of Ballinskelligs Bay. It has ten bedrooms all overlooking the pure waters of Butler's Pool (a favourite old fishing haunt of Charlie Chaplin) and the wider seascapes and landscapes of the Atlantic and the magnificent, untouched countryside. In addition to the warm hospitality and fine cuisine (note the hearty Irish breakfasts!) Waterville House offers its guests a heated pool, sauna, steam room, snooker and billiard room and golf practice facilities including a putting green.

Finally though, let us return to the nearby links and close with a few more choice words from Pat Ruddy, 'Waterville offers a person a splendid golfing challenge and a delicious taste of life as it must have been for primeval man - earth and clear sky, mountain and ocean and the ever present and teasing winds'.

Waterville House & Golf Links
Waterville
Co. Kerry
Ireland
Tel: (010 353 667) 4102
Fax: (010 353 667) 4482

How often have you read, or heard it said that 'Waterville is for the Big Man?' Given that Waterville is very much in the land of the Little People this sounds terribly exclusive. Wot, no Irishmen? Unlike Ballybunion, the name of the place sounds rather Anglo-French; the major influence however has undoubtedly been American. In fact, modern Waterville is very much the result of an American dream.

Oddly it was an American fisherman who first 'discovered' Waterville. Not your average fisherman, but one Charles Chaplin who regularly came here after the War to escape the clutches of stardom. In Waterville he found total peace (as well as some marvellous fishing).

The man we have to thank for creating the golfing majesty that is Waterville Links is an Irish-American, John A Mulcahy. Like all the others who had explored this part of the world he fell in love with the area, and like Castlerosse of Killarney fame he was both extremely wealthy and extremely crazy about golf. In the early seventies, Mulcahy talked to leading Irish course designer Eddie Hackett.......and the rest is history.

Immediately Mulcahy's Waterville opened for play, it was showered with the highest praise. Of course it helped that Mulcahy was able to bring his buddies over from America, and that they happened to include people like Sam Snead, Art Wall and Julius Boros, but their enthusiasm for Waterville and the beauty of its situation was genuine. In any event people like Henry Cotton, Tom Watson and Ray Floyd have since been and marvelled at the creation, the last named in particular who thought it, 'the finest links I have ever played'.

Today, more and more people are 'discovering' Waterville, although at most times the links is still relatively and wonderfully uncrowded. The reason for this is its remoteness. Waterville is 50 miles from Killarney and the nearest airport is at Farranfore, by car a journey time of approximately one and a half hours. The international airports at Cork and Shannon are 100 and 110 miles away respectively. But what a journey it is! The direct route from all points is via Killarney, and Killarney is the starting point for the Ring of Kerry, one of the most scenic roads in the world. Whether the approach to Waterville is 'along the top' via Killorglin and Cahiraveen (this is the quicker but less dramatic route) or 'along the bottom' via Kenmare and Parknasilla, much of the Ring of Kerry will be taken in. Nobody in their right minds could arrive at Waterville uninspired and surely nobody will leave on anything less than a high.

The 1994 green fee at Waterville was £35 per round, seven days per week. Second rounds are available on request. Tee times can be guaranteed by making an advance booking with the office, in this instance a 25 per cent deposit is payable one month in advance of the date of playing. The **Secretary/Manager** at Waterville is **Noel Cronin,** he can be contacted by telephone on either **(066) 74545 or (066) 74102** and by fax on (066) 74482. The Club's **professional, Liam Higgins** can be reached on **(066) 74102.**

The danger of encouraging the description of a golf course as being 'for the big man' is that it risks putting off anyone who cannot thump a ball 300 yards. Naturally it is an advantage (though not necessarily on every hole) to be able to hit the ball like the professional, Liam Higgins, who once holed in one at the 16th - all 350 yards of it!, but if you've got a twitchy short game, you are still going to be struggling, and besides, how often are you going to be asked to play Waterville from the Championship tees? From the forward and medal tees, Waterville is no more or less frightening than the other great links courses of Ireland and it is certainly as enjoyable.

Although there are some good holes on the front nine, notably the 3rd and 4th, it is the back nine at Waterville that everyone raves about. In golfing terms, this is life in the fast lane. The dunes are high and the fairways tumble; there are some spectacular carries and magnificent vantage points and three holes that are widely regarded as being world class; I refer to the 11th, 12th and 17th.

The 12th and 17th are both longish, short holes. On both the tee shots must be carried over a sea of dunes, and at the 12th, the 'Mass Hole', over a gaping gully as well. If the 12th tee is elevated then the 17th must be on a mini-mountain. In fact it is on 'Mulcahy's Peak', a purpose-built tower of a tee from which there is a superb view, not just down to the elusive green but across the entire links.

The 11th, 'Tranquillity' is rated by many to be the greatest par five in Ireland. The fairway winds its entire length beneath sand dunes that are reminiscent of Ballybunion or Birkdale. It is possible to reach the green in two, for much of the last eighty yards or so is downhill, but only if the drive has been perfectly positioned.

It's funny how the world not only turns but sometimes turns on its head. In the 19th century just about every self-respecting Irishman living in Co. Kerry wanted to explore America. Now every self-respecting American wants to explore Co. Kerry: to see the lovely Ring of Kerry and to play the glorious links of Kerry. But remember, Waterville isn't just for the Big Man, Waterville is for Everyman.

Hole	Yards	Par	Hole	Yards	Par
1	430	4	10	475	4
2	469	4	11	496	5
3	417	4	12	200	3
4	179	3	13	518	5
5	595	5	14	456	4
6	371	4	15	392	4
7	178	3	16	350	4
8	435	4	17	196	3
9	445	4	18	582	5
Out	**3,519**	**35**	**In**	**3,665**	**37**
			Out	**3,519**	**35**
			Totals	**7,184**	**72**

The Aberdeen Arms Hotel holds claim to being the oldest Golf Links Hotel in Ireland. Although completely refurbished in the last few years, it has been looking after guests since 1850 and the experience shows. With 55 luxury bedrooms, restaurants, bars, a health centre and conference centre, it is not only a haven for the discerning golfer but for the discerning traveller as well.

The bedrooms boast commanding views of both Lahinch's Golden Beach and the famous Golf Links. Each has private bathroom, direct dial telephone, in-house video channels and TV, hairdryer and hot drinks facilities.

Lahinch boasts two 18-hole courses. The Championship course is one of the world's classic golf links while the Castle Course is slightly more pleasant and less intimidating for the more leisurely golfer.

Take lunch in the Grill Room which is open all day and finish off the game in the Klondyke Bar - aptly named after the Lahinch's famous 5th hole. Relax in the evening over dinner in the restaurant, specialising in fresh seafood and the best of Irish local fayre, all complemented by an extensive wine list. Then wash away the strains of a day's golfing in the jacuzzi and sauna or, if you still have the energy try out the gym or floodlit tennis court.

For a diversion from golf, try the nearby facilities, such as horse riding, shore-angling and lake and river fishing. Shooting rights have also been obtained locally for the guests' convenience.

Aberdeen Arms Hotel
Lahinch
Co.Clare
Tel: (065)-81100
Fax: (065)-81228

On the rugged coast of County Clare, two miles from the spectacular Cliffs of Moher lies the 'St. Andrews of Ireland'.

In 1892, officers of the famous Black Watch Regiment stationed in Limerick discovered a vast wilderness of duneland. Being good Scotsmen, they knew at once that this was the perfect terrain for a golf links. On Good Friday 1893, Lahinch was duly founded. The obvious choice of person to design the course was 'Old' Tom Morris of St. Andrews. Tom accepted but then other than laying out the tees and greens, he felt there was little he could do. He said: 'I consider the links is as fine a natural course as it has ever been my good fortune to play over'. More praise was to follow. In 1928, Dr. Alister Mackenzie was invited to make a number of adjustments to the links. On completion he suggested that 'Lahinch will make the finest and most popular course that I, or I believe anyone else, ever constructed'. Not perhaps the most modest statement ever made but coming from a man who had just designed Cypress Point and who was soon to create the legendary Augusta, it can hardly be taken lightly.

Visitors wishing to play at Lahinch will find the Club extremely welcoming. The only restrictions are as follows: Monday to Friday between 9am and 10am and 12.00 to 1.30pm and at weekends between 8am and 11am and 12.30pm to 2pm. The present **Secretary** is **Mr. Alan Reardon**, who can be contacted by telephone on **(065) 81003** (from the UK (010 353 65) 81003. The **professional, Robert McCavery,** can be reached on **(065) 81408.**

Since Dr Mackenzie's alterations, there have been two 18 hole courses: the Championship Old Course and the shorter Castle Course, the latter having been extended from nine holes to eighteen in 1975. Green fees in 1994 to play on the Old Course were set at £30 per round, £40 per day between April and September with a reduced rate of £25 per round, £28 per day for midweek golf between January and March and in November and December.

Green Fees on the Castle Course were £18 per round, £28 per day (all year round). Certain discounts are available to those staying in local hotels (contact the club for details). Golfing Societies are equally welcome and bookings can be made for any day other than Sunday.

Travellers coming from Britain (or indeed Europe and America) should find Lahinch more accessible than any of the great links of Co. Kerry. International flights to Shannon are frequent and Lahinch is located approximately thirty miles to the north west of the airport. On leaving Shannon, Ennis is the town to head for, and thereafter, Ennistimon, just two miles from Lahinch. The road passes through some marvellous countryside, and incidentally, do try to visit the Cliffs of Moher—in places they rise to a sheer drop of over six hundred feet, the highest in Europe. Golfers on a west of Ireland pilgrimage approaching from Ballybunion should cross the Shannon via the Tarbert Ferry. It leaves every 30 minutes—on the hour and at half past.

The **Old Course** at Lahinch is not as tough as a Portmarnock or a Waterville; it doesn't have the length for a start, but then it's anything but straightforward. The golfer who enjoys the challenge of Ballybunion will fall in love with Lahinch. The seascapes are just as dramatic and the fairways twist and tumble in a similar fashion. A premium is placed on accurate tee shots and the slightest straying will put you amongst the dunes. Many greens sit on natural plateaux and can be tricky to hold. It isn't easy to select the best holes, for so many are memorable, but perhaps the finest sequence is found between the 7th and 10th—four really tremendous par fours. The most famous holes however are undoubtedly the 5th and 6th, both of which Mackenzie was forbidden to touch. Having won four Open Championships at Prestwick, 'Old Tom' clearly relished the blind shot and this is what is called for at both the 5th (Klondyke) and the 6th (Dell). Not too many quibble with the 5th—it is a par five, although the blind second shot is over a prodigious sand hill and the green is a further two hundred yards on. The 6th however, is a par three! The green nestles between two steep sand dunes and all the player sees from the tee is a white marker-stone placed on the fronting hill to indicate the current pin position—'hit and hope' perhaps, but charming all the same.

The par 70 **Castle Course** is literally over the road from the Old and occupies much more level ground. The fairways wind their way around the remains of O'Brien's Castle: it presents an attractive, if slightly less demanding challenge, and some £300,000 has recently been spent upgrading the course.

The Clubhouse at Lahinch is fairly small, but marvellously intimate and certainly an excellent place to adjourn to should the heavens open. And you'll have ample warning of the impending doom for legend has it that the goats that graze on the dunes will always make an early retreat towards the shelter of the 19th. A bit of Irish mist? Try telling that to the Members!

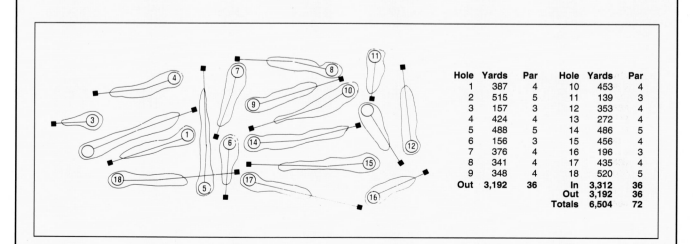

Hole	Yards	Par	Hole	Yards	Par
1	387	4	10	453	4
2	515	5	11	139	3
3	157	3	12	353	4
4	424	4	13	272	4
5	488	5	14	486	5
6	156	3	15	456	4
7	376	4	16	196	3
8	341	4	17	435	4
9	348	4	18	520	5
Out	**3,192**	**36**	**In**	**3,312**	**36**
			Out	**3,192**	**36**
			Totals	**6,504**	**72**

Limerick County Golf & Country Club

Limerick County Golf and Country Club is located just five miles south of Limerick City and 30 minutes from Shannon airport. The location of Limerick County is ideal for golfing visitors to Ireland's south-western region, packed as it is with facilities and services for the golfing tourist.

Designed by Des Smyth, the 6712 yard golf course meanders over an undulating pastoral setting, with the front nine offering rapid changes in elevation and the back nine, sited on flatter ground, throwing up subtle challenges designed into each hole by one of Europe's foremost golf architects.

Limerick County is more than a golf course — it is a golfing Mecca with a fully equipped golf school, a sumptuous clubhouse and twelve holiday villas. The golf school comprises an all-weather driving range, three practice holes and two practice putting greens. Tuition programmes are conducted by a first class team of golf professionals, under the direction of Philip Murphy — Director of Golf.

The clubhouse is a totally unique structure being circular in shape and enclosed in glass panels which provide panoramic views of the golf course and surrounding countryside. Its user facilities are state of the art including a steam room/jacuzzi in the changing areas and first class food and beverage service to accompany the stunning views from the upper floor of the building.

Twelve modern holiday villas nestle next to the first fairway and offer visitors the option of self catering or clubhouse dining during their stay. The Limerick County golf package is a complete one — accommodation, golf, tuition, informal practice, great hospitality and dedicated service, designed for the discerning traveller who appreciates first class amenities at realistic prices.

Limerick County is a natural gateway to the famous courses dotted around the south-western coastal area — Ballybunion, Lahinch, Killarney, Tralee are all within a 90 minute drive and this makes Limerick County the natural base of operations for the serious golf explorer. A golfing haven for your enjoyment.

Limerick County Golf and Country Club
Ballyneety
Limerick
Ireland
Tel: (010 353 61) 351881
Fax: (010 353 61) 351384

We all owe a great debt to televised pro-celebrity golf. Without it, how familiar would we be with 'Braid's Brawest' and the glorious colours of the King's Course at Gleneagles? And how familiar would we be with 'Tappie Toorie', Ailsa Craig and the lighthouse at Turnberry? Without it, how many of us would have even heard of Dromoland Castle?

When it comes to discussing magical locations Dromoland Castle has a head start over most—it is situated in the west of Ireland. Located in Co. Clare, overlooking the Shannon estuary, it is roughly equidistant from Connemara and Westport to the north and the Dingle Peninsula and the Ring of Kerry to the south; the Cliffs of Moher and the extraordinary prehistoric scenery of the Burren Country are even closer at hand. Golfwise it is within striking distance of Lahinch and Ballybunion, two of the greatest (and most famous) links courses in the world.

Yet for all the surrounding splendour, Dromoland Castle is a magical little kingdom of its own. Or that is what you can imagine the moment you drive through the castle gates and enter the beautifully wooded grounds of the estate. The castle itself (now of course a luxurious hotel) is quite majestic—as I suppose it should be, being the former ancestral home of the O'Briens, the direct descendants of Brian Boru, legendary 11th century High King of all Ireland. In front of the castle is a handsome lake, Dromoland Lough, and zig-zagging its way between the trees of the estate, occasionally glimpsing the lake and ocassionally glimpsing the castle are the emerald fairways of a challenging 18 hole golf course. All in all, Dromoland Castle isn't a bad place to while away a few days! But if you simply want to inspect the golf course then you don't have to be a resident or be accompanied by a club member: in fact visitors are not restricted in any way.

Golf Secretary, **John O'Halloran** and the **professional Philip Murphy** are the gentlemen most likely to welcome you. They may be contacted by telephone on **(061) 368444**. Tee times can be reserved and in 1994 the green fees were £20 on weekdays with £25 payable at weekends. The precise location of Dromoland Castle is immediately off the Limerick to Galway Road (the N7), 4 miles from Shannon (and its International Airport) at Newmarket on Fergus. Prior to 1985 there was only a 9 hole course at Dromoland and which, like the attractive 9 holer at Dromoland's sister castle, Ashford, was little more than a sporting, though enjoyable, 'holiday course'.

Anyone who played Dromoland before 1985 but hasn't done so since and is contemplating a visit is in for a pleasant surprise—and perhaps one or two shocks as well! Measuring 5719 metres (or just under 6300 yards), par 71 from the back tees it is a good test of golf and the quality and condition of the course is ever improving, as of course the two recent Pro-Celebrity Series bore witness to. All four professionals who played in the 1991 and 1992 events—Gary Player, Sandy Lyle, Hale Irwin and Sam Torrance—were complimentary of the layout and clearly relished playing amidst surroundings that were not only extremely picturesque but marvellously relaxing too.

Apart from a fairly open area between the 4th and 6th holes most of the fairways are bordered by rich woodland, which in fact is becoming richer by the week thanks to a novel 'Plant a Family Tree' scheme operated by a company called Forest Heritage Limited. Fancy putting down some roots in the 'Kingdom of Dromoland'? (Telephone (061) 71144 for details). Among the most beautiful trees are a number of mature copper beeches—wonderful—unless of course you happen to land behind (or in) one of them!

If one were to single out special holes at Dromoland then on the front nine the 2nd, 7th and 8th make for a splendid trio, comprising a spectacular dog-leg par five, a vertigo-inducing par three—a superb view of the castle and lake from this elevated tee—and a roller coaster of a par four where the fairway appears to tumble in every conceivable direction. On the back nine a new championship tee at the 10th has made the drive an all-or-nothing shot across the edge of the lake—perfect for the likes of Sandy Lyle! The 15th and 16th are an entertaining pair of par fours and the two short holes are attractive, but perhaps the best two holes on the back nine are the 11th and 18th. The former dog-legs sharply right and takes you alongside Lough Dromoland and through an avenue of resplendent trees; at the 18th you aim your tee shot at the lake, after which the fairway dog-legs sharply to the left and back towards the castle.

Just before you putt out on the final green take a deep breath and drink in the 360 degree views: magnificent towering trees, a peaceful lake, velvet fairways and, surveying all, Dromoland Castle. What more could you ask for?

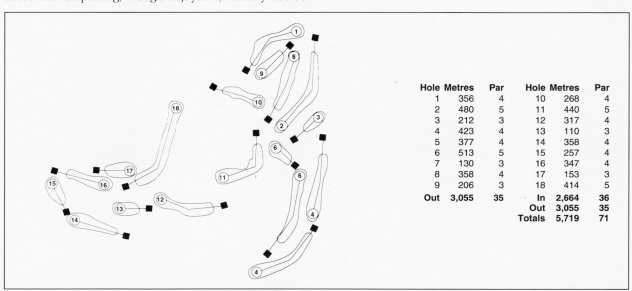

Hole	Metres	Par	Hole	Metres	Par
1	356	4	10	268	4
2	480	5	11	440	5
3	212	3	12	317	4
4	423	4	13	110	3
5	377	4	14	358	4
6	513	5	15	257	4
7	130	3	16	347	4
8	358	4	17	153	3
9	206	3	18	414	5
Out	**3,055**	**35**	**In**	**2,664**	**36**
			Out	**3,055**	**35**
			Totals	**5,719**	**71**

Midleton Park Hotel

On entering the warmth and elegance of Midleton Park Hotel, you will receive the luxury and personal service you deserve. The hotel is situated only ten miles from Cork Airport and Car Ferry Terminal and the business capital of the south, yet in a location very removed from city living and the interruptions of everyday life. Of all the counties in Ireland, Cork is the largest. In the path of the Mid Gulf Steam the climate is temperate, the scenery intoxicating and the choice of pursuits almost endless.

Golf is, of course, one of the specialities of the hotel and we have a selection of packages tailored to suit your requirements for that well deserved getaway.

For the golf fanatic, we are situated only four miles from the picturesque but challenging par 72 championship, Fota Island Golf Course which would satisfy the most discerning of golfers. For non golfers, we are just seven miles from the seaside village of Ballycotton with its unspoilt sandy beaches and relaxing mountain walks and at Fota Island Wildlife Park you can see the rarest species of wildlife from all five continents. No other county in Ireland offers such a fine tapestry of beauty,

historical riches and sporting and leisure possibilities.

To round off the perfect day, Midleton Park offers you the ideal place to relax with its luxurious guest rooms and award winning restaurant where you can sample our local cuisine and catches from the local waters. For a less formal atmosphere, there is the option of the comprehensive lounge menu which is available throughout the day. In the hotel bar you can indulge and sample the 'spirit of Ireland' in the local distilled and world famous Irish whiskeys. . . Jameson, Midleton Rare to name just two. You can also visit the 18th century distillery which has been restored.

The hotel also offers excellent business and conference facilities with three superior conference suites and four syndicate rooms catering from anything from2 to 400 delegates. . . Daily Delegate and 24 hour delegate rates are available on request.

The Midleton Park Hotel is a hotel where you can combine business and pleasure. Come and join us, you will discover a welcome as warm as the memories you will take back.

Midleton Park Hotel
Midleton
Co Cork
Ireland
Tel: (021) 631767
Fax: (021) 631605

Fota Island Golf Club, situated a few minutes drive east of Cork City, lies in the heart of a 780 acre estate which is listed in the **Inventory of Outstanding Landscapes of Ireland.** With Fota's internationally renowned Arboretum and Gardens nearby, the splendid woodlands are woven into a challenging par 72 championship course.

The terrain is gently undulating parkland, offering glimpses of Cork Harbour from various points around the course. While Fota is a new development, it eschews the modern trend towards "Americanised" courses. Fota is very much traditional in design and because of its location amid the mature woodlands, the impression is given of a course that has been there for generations.

Joint course architects were Irish Ryder Cup hero, Christy O'Connor, Jnr. and English amateur supremo, Peter McEvoy. Describing their design philosophy, Peter McEvoy wrote, "_Fota Island is not a piece of land, it is a place. It deserves the best. It is mature and should not have a shiny modern course imposed upon it, where earth moving has destroyed its feel and bunkers have been designed which look more at home in Florida_".

The American publication, **Golf Digest** couldn't agree more. "_For a breath of true golfing air, Fota Island, just outside Cork in Ireland, is the very place. Here the run up shot is given due regard. Almost every green invites more than one approach. Depending upon how you "see" the shot in your mind, you could be playing any one of three different clubs. In other words it makes you think. It's real golf._"

Golf Digest continues, "_Fota eschews Schwarzenegger-like brutality in favour of guile and subtlety_". This was achieved by the use of slopes and the positioning of hazards to dissuade the golfer from trying to overpower the course. Peter McEvoy explains,"_All too often nowadays golfers missing a green will end up in water or a bunker. At Fota, we have created many grassy hollows, dips and mounds to try to keep or even bring back pitching and chipping. A good course should test all these skills._". To accomplish this, Fota's bunkers are smaller than usual and generally placed in clusters. Little sand is seen from a distance, giving the impression of dark sinister hollows.

Fota's traditional approach means a ball can be played through the air and along the ground, The links-style "bump and run" is often called for. Holes like the 2nd, 4th, 10th, 11th, 15th and 18th use slopes and hazards to discourage golfers trying to overpower the course through the air. "_Not that it's easy_", say **Golf Digest,** "_You can still compile a sizeable score; it just happens more gradually_".

The signature hole at Fota is undoubtedly the 18th — a par 5, barely measures 500 yards. The tee shot must be threaded between a belt of woodland on the right and a copse of beech trees on the left. A long straight drive leaves the green exposed but not defenceless to a second shot — a cluster of pot bunkers in front and a lake behind provide ample food for thought. It is a hole where bold play can produce a 3 or a 7.

The 10th hole "Fuscia Hill" is another par 5 that winds it way down a hill to a green backed by water. It is a thinking man's hole. An iron off the tee and another off the fairway should normally produce regulation figures. Those wishing to challenge the hole can ruin a scorecard here.

The par threes are gentle holes from the regular tees but tigers from the backmarkers. The four pars are all strong holes — with the short picturesque 6th "Christy's Picnic" being the most memorable. A downhill tee shot into the "Deerpark" section of the course is followed by a short iron to a devilishly tricky elevated green.

Peter McEvoy best sums up Fota. "Most important of all was to use the beauty nature has given us, to highlight the trees and the water and — most importantly — give golfers the chance to notice".

Fota Island Golf Club
Fota Island
Carrigtwohill
County Cork
Ireland
Tel: (010 353 21) 883700
Fax: (010 353 21) 883713

Ancient Irish chieftains, the O'Dwyers of Kilnamanagh, once held the land whereon Lord Hawarden, The Earl of Montalt, built Dundrum House in 1730. Its elegant Georgian lines presided over a demesne of 2400 statute acres and consolidated Anglo Norman power in the area for nearly 200 years. The Hawardens sold the property to a religious order at the beginning of the century and the Crowe family bought the house and adjoining lands on the fish-rich Multeen River in 1978.

Austin and Mary Crowe have created a country manor house of style and warmth which again reflects the grace and elegance the house enjoyed in the 18th century. Open log fires greet guests on chilly spring and autumn evenings and the bar, with its beautiful stained glass windows is the perfect meeting place for guests, golfers and fishermen.

Each bedroom and suite enjoys the Georgian generosity of space and comfort as well as the modern additions of a direct dial telephone, television, central heating and en suite bathroom.

The old world atmosphere and hospitality is palpable in the dining room where fine linen laid tables receive the finest cuisine and wines. Whether your party is small or large, Dundrum House provides the perfect ambience for a perfect meal.

A wonderful golf course has been woven into the fabric of the mature Georgian estate, designed by top tour professional Philip Walton. Using the natural features of woodland and parkland, adorned by the Multeen River, Philip has created an exhilarating par 72 which provides a real test of golf.

Dundrum House Hotel
Dundrum
Cashel
Co Tipperary
Tel: (010 353 62) 71116
Fax: (010 353 62) 71366

Driving through the Irish countryside one is frequently distracted and occasionally dazzled. Ireland isn't known as the Emerald Isle for nothing. There is much truth in the legend that the landscape boasts some forty different shades of green (and none whatsoever in the complaint that the sky contains forty shades of grey). On the fertile plains of County Tipperary, in deepest rural Ireland another colour and a major distraction reveal themselves : it is the land of the Golden Vale and imperiously standing guard over this rich domain is the famous Rock of Cashel.

This striking natural phenomena, crowned by its ancient castle, cathedral and chapel, should cause any traveller pause and explore. The town of Cashel lies adjacent to the N8, the main highway linking Dublin to Cork and just six miles from Cashel along the R505 road is the village of Dundrum and a place every golfing traveller should pause and explore. The two principal reasons for stopping in Dundrum are the 18th century Dundrum House Hotel and the 18 hole golf course of the County Tipperary Golf and Country Club: the latter wraps around the former. Dundrum House is a distinguished Georgian mansion - now converted to a country house hotel but with no loss of character - and the golf course, a very recent addition to the scene, having opened for play in June 1993.

County Tipperary, or Dundrum, as people often call it, was designed by PGA European Tour Professional Philip Walton. It is a varied and impressive creation which can be stretched to 6709 yards (par 72) from the back tees.

Despite its youth the course is maturing very quickly - helped immeasurably by the fact that historic Irish country estates traditionally comprise a wealth of mature trees and Dundrum is no exception. In addition to a great spread of trees and wooded copses the River Multeen winds its way through the grounds affecting a number of holes (including, rather neatly, both the opening and closing holes) and, whilst not overdone,

small lakes have been fashioned to threaten wayward approach shots on a number of holes.

Residents and non residents are equally welcome to play at County Tipperary. The **Director of Golf, William Crowe** oversees all administrative matters. While booking in advance is not essential, reserving a tee time is always a good idea; this can be achieved by telephoning the Golf Shop on **(062) 71116**. Green fees for 1994 were set at £15 midweek and £20 at weekends.

The challenge commences then with the threat of the river. It meanders, very visibly, off to the right for the entire length of the long, dog-legged 1st - an intimidating start ! Trees also encroach on this hole, and they completely frame the fairway at the uphill par five 2nd, the beginning of an excellent trio of holes. Indeed the 2nd, 3rd and 4th provide the most attractive sequence on the front nine and it is where the golfer enjoys a feeling of splendid isolation. The 5th, 6th and 7th make up perhaps the weakest stretch - at least visually - of the round but the 8th offers a most exciting downhill drive and a tricky approach over water.

Holes 9 to 12 are played near to the front of Dundrum House and then, after a pleasant walk through the woods a second spectacular run of holes is confronted.

Thirty four ducks and a heron may greet you as you cross the pond at the swinging dog legged 13th (a hole that rivals the 4th as the best of the round) and, if so, you will more then likely meet them again as you leave the green at the short 15th. The closing holes tour the grounds at the back of the House and the 18th, with its stately trees and two tiered green positioned beyond the ubiquitous river makes for a very handsome finish.

Finding time to pause and explore the area around Cashel is therefore strongly recommended. In the heart of the county with the famous name, and situated within the shadow of the famous rock is Dundrum - a country house full of character and a golf course full of promise. Welcome to golf in the Golden Vale.

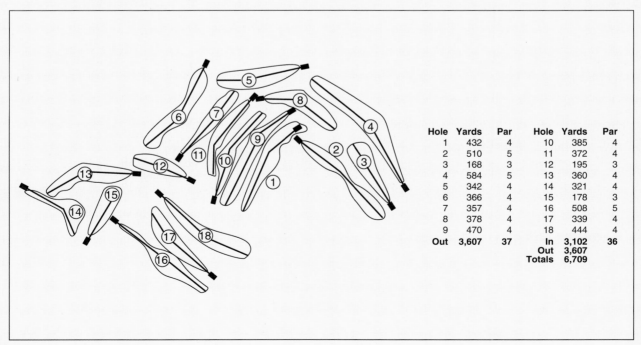

Hole	Yards	Par	Hole	Yards	Par
1	432	4	10	385	4
2	510	5	11	372	4
3	168	3	12	195	3
4	584	5	13	360	4
5	342	4	14	321	4
6	366	4	15	178	3
7	357	4	16	508	5
8	378	4	17	339	4
9	470	4	18	444	4
Out	**3,607**	**37**	**In**	**3,102**	**36**
			Out	**3,607**	
			Totals	**6,709**	

Clonlara Golf & Leisure is ideally situated in the heart of the west of Ireland, only a 20 minute drive from the centre of Limerick City and half an hours drive from Shannon airport. It is located in the grounds of Landscape House, which is now the home of Jill and Mike O'Connell, built in the 17th century, and stands on the banks of the majestic River Shannon.

The complex stands on 63 acres of mature parkland, which has been developed into a testing 9 hole, par 35, golf course. The centre offers a unique range of accommodation which includes nine self-catering apartments and two cottages, which are all fully furnished and individually designed. Each sleeps between four and six persons and all are fully equipped. There are a wealth of on site amenities to keep visitors occupied during their stay. The bar serves good food and there is entertainment once or twice weekly. In the games room visitors can choose to play either table tennis or pool and outside there are two tennis courts set within the walls of the old orchard. A babysitting service can be arranged if required and there is a children's play area and crazy golf to ensure an enjoyable time for the whole family. After a day on the course relax in the sauna or take a leisurely walk in the grounds.

Clonlara is a great centre for activity holidays with the Shannonside activity centre at Killaloe, 14 kilometres away, which provides virtually all types of watersports. Visitors can book coarse and game fishing as well as other activities. The centre is also ideally located for touring and sightseeing being close to Ireland's largest river, the Shannon, which leads into Lough Derg at Killaloe. To the west is County Clare with Aillwee Cave, the Cliffs of Moher, Bunratty Castle and Folk Park.

For further details contact:

Clonlara Golf & Leisure
Landscape House
Clonlara
County Clare
Tel: (010 353 61) 354141
Fax: (010 353 61) 354143

Key

*To avoid disappointment
it is advisable to telephone
in advance*

***Visitors welcome at most times
***Visitors usually allowed on
weekdays only*
**Visitors not normally permitted
(Mon, Wed) No visitors
on specified days*

Approximate Green Fees
A £30 plus
B £20 to £30
C £15 to £25
D £10 to £20
E under £10
F Greens fees on application

Restrictions
G Guests only
H Handicap certificate required
H (24) Handicap of 24 or less
L Letter of introduction required
*M Visitor must be a member of
another recognised club.*

WEST OF IRELAND

CO CLARE

Dromoland Castle G.C.
(061) 368144
Newmarket on Fergus
(18)6300 yards/***/B

Ennis G.C.
(065) 24074
Drumbiggle, Ennis
(18)5300 metres/**(Sun)/C

Kilkee G.C.
(065) 56048
East End, Kilkee
(9)6185 yards/***/F

Kilrush G.C.
(065) 51138
Parknamoney, Kilrush
(9)2739 yards/***/F

Lahinch G.C.
(065) 81003
Lahinch
(18)6702 yards/**/A
(18)5265 metres/**/D

Shannon G.C.
(061) 471849
Shannon Airport, Shannon
(18)6854 yards/**/B

Spanish Point G.C.
(065) 84198
Spanish Point, Miltown Malbay
(9)3820 yards/***/D

CO CORK

Bandon G.C.
(023) 4111
Castlebernard, Bandon
(18)5663 metres/***/D

Bantry Park G.C.
(027) 50579
Donemark, Bantry
(9)6436 yards/***/D

Berehaven G.C.
(027) 70039
Millcove, Castletownbere
(9)2400 yards/***/E

Charleville G.C.
(063) 81257
Ardmore, Charleville
(18)6380 yards/**/D

Cobh G.C.
(021) 812399

Ballywilliam, Cobh
(9)4338 metres/**(W/E am)/F

Cork G.C.
(021) 353451
Little Island, Cork
(18)6000 metres/**(Thurs)/B/H

Doneraile G.C.
(022) 24137
Doneraile, Cork
(9)5528 yards/**(W/E am)/F

Douglas G.C.
(021) 891086
Douglas, Cork
(18)5644 metres/**(Tues)/D

Dunmore G.C.
(023) 33352
Muckross, Clonakilty
(9)4464 metres/***(Sun)/E

East Cork G.C.
(021) 631687
Gortacrue, Midleton
(18)5207 metres/**/D

Fermoy G.C.
(025) 31472
Carrin Cross, Fermoy
(18)5550 metres/***(Mon/Wed pm)/F

Fota Island G.C.
(021) 883710
Carrigtwohill, Cork
(18)6886 yards/***/B/H

Frankfield G.C.
(021) 361199
Douglas, Cork
(9)5191 yards/***/E

Glengarriff G.C.
(027) 63150
Glengarriff
(9)4328 yards/***/D

Harbour Point G.C.
(021) 353094
Clash Road, Little Island, Cork
(18)6063 yards/***/B

Kanturk G.C.
(029) 50534
Fairy Hill, Kanturk
(9)5527 metres/***/E

Kinsale G.C.
(021) 772197
Ringenane, Belgooly
(9)5332 metres/**/D

Lee Valley G.& C.C.
(021) 331721
Clashanure, Ovens
(18)6800 yards/***/B/H

Macroom G.C.
(026) 41072
Lackaduve, Macroom
(9)5439 metres/***/D/H

Mallow G.C.
(022) 21145
Ballyellis, Mallow
(18)6559 yards/**(Tues)/D

Mahon G.C.
(021) 362480
Cloverhill, Blackrock
(18)4818 metres/***/E

Mitchelstown G.C.
(025) 24072
Mitchelstown
(15)5057 metres/***/D

Monkstown G.C.
(021) 841376
Parkgariffe, Monkstown
(18)6170 yards/***(Wed/Thurs)/B/H

Muskerry G.C.
(021) 385297
Carrigrohane, Blarney

(18)5786 metres/**(Wed/Thurs)/D

Raffeen Creek G.C.
(021) 378430
Ringaskiddy
(9)5800 yards/***/D

Skibbereen G.C.
(028) 21227
Licknavar, Skibbereen
(18)6000 yards/***/D

Youghal G.C.
(024) 92787
Knockaverry, Youghal
(18)6223 yards/***(Wed)/D

CO DONEGAL

Ballybofey & Stranorlar G.C.
(074) 31093
Stranorlar, Ballybofey
(18)5913 yards/**(Wed/Thurs/Fri)/D

Ballyliffin G.C.
(077) 76119
Ballyliffin, Cardonagh
(18)6524 yards/***/D

Buncrana G.C.
(077) 62279
Buncrana
(9)2020 yards/***/F

Bundoran G.C.
(072) 41302
Great Northern Hotel, Bundoran
(18)6960 yards/**/D

Cruit Island G.C.
(075) 43296
Kincasslagh, Dungloe
(9)5297 yards/***/E

Donegal G.C.
(073) 34054
Murvagh, Donegal
(18)7271 yards/***/D-C/H

Dunfanaghy G.C.
(074) 36335
Dunfanaghy, Letterkenny
(18)5066 yards/***/F

Greencastle G.C.
(077) 81013
Moville, Greencastle
(18)5386 yards/**/D

Gweedore G.C.
(075) 31140
Derrybeg, Gweedore
(18)6230 yards/***/E

Letterkenny G.C.
(074) 21150
Barnhill, Letterkenny
(18)6299 yards/***(Tues/Wed)/D

Nairn and Portnoo G.C.
(075) 45107
Nairn, Portnoo
(18)5950 yards/**(Sun)/F/H

North West G.C.
(077) 61027
Lisfannon, Fahon, Lifford
(18)6203 yards/***(Wed)/D

Otway G.C.
(074) 58319
Saltpans, Rathmullen
(9)4134 yards/***/E

Portsalon G.C.
(074) 59459
Portsalon, Letterkenny
(18)5844 yards/**/D

Redcastle G.C.
(077) 82073
Redcastle, Moville
(9)5528 yards/***/D

Rosapenna G.C.
(074) 55301
Downings, Rosapenna
(18)6254 yards/***/F

CO GALWAY

Athenry G.C.
(091) 94466
Palmerstown, Oranmore
(18)6000 yards/***(Sun)/D

Ballinasloe G.C.
(0905) 42126
Ballinasloe, Rossloss
(18)5800 metres/***/D

Connemara G.C.
(095) 23502
Ballyconnelly, Clifton
(18)6173 metres/***/C/H

Galway G.C.
(091) 22169
Blackrock, Salthill, Galway
(18)6376 yards/**(Tues)/C

Gort G.C.
(091) 31336
Laughtyshaughnessy, Gort
(9)4976 metres/***(Sun am)/F

Loughrea G.C.
(091) 41049
Bullaun Road, Loughrea
(18)5613 yards/***/D

Mountbellew G.C.
(0905) 79259
Shankhill, Mountbellew
(9)5564 yards/***/F

Oughterard G.C.
(091) 82131
Gortreevagh, Oughterard
(18)6150 yards/***/D

Portumna G.C.
(0509) 41059
Ennis Road,Portumna
(18)5776 yards/***/D

Tuam G.C.
(093) 28993
Barnacurragh, Tuam
(18)6321 yards/**/F

CO KERRY

Ballybunion G.C.
(068) 27146
Sandhill Road, Ballybunion
(18)6542 yards/***/A/H/L
(18)6477 yards/***/A/H/L

Castlegregory G.C.
(066) 39444
Stradbally, Castlegregory
(9)5488 yards/***/D

Ceann Sibeal G.C.
(066) 56255
Ballyferriter, Tralee
(18)6222 yards/***/D

Dooks G.C.
(066) 68205
Dooks, Killorglin
(18)6021 yards/**/C

Kenmare G.C.
(064) 41291
Kenmare, Killarney
(9)4400 yards/***/D

Killarney G.C.
(064) 31034
O'Mahony's Point, Killarney
(18)6378 metres/***/F/H
(18)6152 metres/***/F/H

Parknasilla G.C.
(0644) 5122
Parknasilla, Sneem
(9)4834 yards/***/D

Tralee G.C.
(066) 36379
West Barrow, Ardfert
(18)6900 yards/**(W/E am)/B/H

Waterville G.C.
(066) 74545

Ring of Kerry, Waterville
(18)7184 yards/***/A/H/L

CO LEITRIM

Ballinamore G.C.
(078) 44346
Crevy, Ballinamore
(9)5680 yards/***/F

Carrick on Shannon G.C.
(079) 67015
Woodbrook, Carrick on Shannon
(9)5584 metres/***/D

CO LIMERICK

Adare Manor G.C.
(061) 396204
Adare
(18)5700 yards/***/D

Castletroy G.C.
(061) 335261
Castletroy, Limerick
(18)6340 yards/**/B/H

Limerick G.C.
(061) 414083
Ballyclough, Limerick
(18)5767 metres/**(Tues)/B

Newcastle West G.C.
(069) 62015
Ardagh, Newcastle West
(18)5482 yards/***(Sun)/D

CO MAYO

Achill Island G.C.
(098) 43202
Keel, Achill
(9)2723 yards/***/F/H

Ballina G.C.
(096) 21050
Mossgrove, Shanaghy, Ballina
(9)5702 yards/***/D

Ballinrobe G.C.
(092) 41448
Castlebar Road, Ballinrobe
(9)5790 yards/***(Sun)/D

Ballyhaunis G.C.
(0907) 30014
Coolnaha, Ballyhaunis
(9)5393 yards/***/E

Belmullet G.C.
(097) 82292
Carn, Belmullet
(18)6016 metres/***/D

Castlebar G.C.
(094) 21649
Rocklands, Castlebar
(18)6109 yards/***(Sun)/D

Claremorris G.C.
(094) 71527
Rushbrook, Castlemaggaret,
Claremorris
(9)6454 yards/***/F

Mulrany G.C.
(098) 36262
Mulrany, Westport
(9)6380 yards/***/E

Swinford G.C.
(094) 51378
Brabazon Park, Swinford
(9)5230 yards/***/E

Westport G.C.
(098) 25113
Carrowholly, Westport
(18)6667 yards/***(Sun)/C

CO ROSCOMMON

Athlone G.C.
(0902) 92073
Hodson Bay, Athlone
(18)5928 metres/***/D

Boyle G.C.
(079) 62594
Roscommon Road, Boyle
(9)4957 metres/***/E

Castlerea G.C.

(0907) 20068
Clonalis, Castlerea
(9)5466 yards/***(Sun)/E

Roscommon G.C.
(0903) 26382
Moate Park, Roscommon
(11)5784 yards/**/D-E

CO SLIGO

Ballymote G.C.
(071) 83460
Carrigans, Ballymote
(9)5152 yards/***/E

County Sligo G.C.
(071) 77134
Rosses Point
(18)6603 yards/***(Tues)/C

Enniscrone G.C.
(096) 36297
Ballina Road, Enniscrone
(18)6720 yards/***/D

Strandhill G.C.
(071) 68188
Strandhill
(18)5937 yards/***/F

Tubbercurry G.C.
(071) 85849
Ballymote Road, Tubbercurry
(9)5478 metres/***/E

EAST OF IRELAND

CO CARLOW

Borris G.C.
(0503) 73143
Deerpark, Borris
(9)6026 yards/***/E

Carlow G.C.
(0503) 31695
Deer Park, Dublin Road, Carlow
(18)6347 yards/***/D

CO CAVAN

Belturbet G.C.
(049) 22287
Erne Hill, Belturbet
(9)5347 metres/***/E

Blacklion G.C.
(072) 53024
Toam, Blacklion
(9)6098 yards/***/E

Cabra Castle G.C.
(042) 67904
Kingscourt
(9)5839 yards/***/F

County Cavan G.C.
(049) 31283
Armore House, Drumellis, Cavan
(18)5519 metres/**(Wed/Fri)/D

Slieve Russell G.C.
(049) 26444
Slieve Russell Hotel, Ballyconnell
(18)7054 yards/***/B

Virginia G.C.
(049) 44103
Virginia
(9)4900 metres/***/E

CO DUBLIN

Balbriggan G.C.
(01) 8412173
Blackhall, Balbriggan
(18)6470 yards/***/D

Balcarrick G.C.
(01) 8436228
Corballis, Donabate
(18)5167 metres/**/D

Ballinascorney G.C.
(01) 512516
Ballinascorney
(18)5464 yards/***/F

Beaverstown G.C.
(01) 8436439
Beaverstown, Donabate
(18)6440 yards/***/D

Beech Park G.C.
(01) 580100
Johnstown, Rathcoole
(18)6303 yards/**/D

Castle G.C.
(01) 4904207
Woodside Drive, Rathfarnham
(18)6240 yards/**(Tues)/C

Carrickmines G.C.
(01) 2955972
Carrickmines, Dublin
(9)6103 yards/***/D/G

Clontarf G.C.
(01) 331892
Donnycarney House, Malahide
Road
(18)5447 yards/**(Mon)/C

Corballis G.C.
(01) 8436583
Donabate
(18)4971 metres/***/F

Deer Park Hotel G.C.
(01) 8322624
Howth Castle, Howth
(18)6647 yards/***/D
(9)3130 yards/***/E
(12)1810 yards/***/E

Donabate G.C.
(01) 8436346
Donabate
(18)6187 yards/**(Wed)/F

Dun Laoghaire G.C.
(01) 2803916
Eglinton Park, Dun Laoghaire
(18)5463 yards/***(Thurs/Sat)/C

Edmondstown G.C.
(01) 4932461
Edmondstown, Rathfarnham
(18)5663 metres/***/C

Elm Park G.C.
(01) 2693438
Nutley House, Donnybrook
(18)5485 metres/***/B

Finnstown Fairways G.C.
(01) 6280644
Newcastle Road, Lucan
(9)2695 yards/***/D

Forrest Little G.C.
(01) 8401183
Forrest Little, Cloghran
(18)6451 yards/**/F

Foxrock G.C.
(01) 2895668
Torquay Rd, Foxrock
(9)6234 yards/**/C

Grange G.C.
(01) 932832
Grange Road, Rathfarnham,
Dublin 16
(18)6068 yards/**(Tues/Wed
pm)/B

Hazel Grove G.C.
(01) 520911
Mount Seskin Road, Jobstown,
Tallaght
(9)5830 yards/**/D

Hermitage G.C.
(01) 6268491
Lucan
(18)6034 metres/**/B/L

Hollywood G.C.
(01) 8433406
Hollywood, Ballyboughal
(18)5834 yards/***/D/H

Howth G.C.
(01) 323055
Carriackbrack Road, Sutton
(18)6180 yards/**(Wed)/D

Island G.C.
(01) 8436104
Corballis, Donabate
(18)6658 yards/***/B

Killiney G.C.
(01) 2851983

Killiney
(9)6201 yards/***/D

Kilternan Hotel G.C.
(01) 2955559
Enniskerry Road, Kilternan
(18)5413 yards/***/D

Lucan G.C.
(01) 6282106
Celbridge Road, Lucan
(9)6554 yards/***/C

Luttrelstown Castle G.C.
(01) 8213237
Clonsilla, Dublin 15
(18)6384 metres/***/B-A

Malahide G.C.
(01) 8461611
Beechwood, The Grange, Malahide
(9)3176 yards/***/C-B
(9)3102 yards/***/C-B
(9)2895 yards/***/C-B

Milltown G.C.
(01) 976090
Lower Churchtown Road
(18)6202 yards/**/B

Newlands G.C.
(01) 4592903
Clondalkin
(18)6184 yards/**(Tues/Wed
pm)/F

Portmarnock G.C.
(01) 8462968
Portmarnock
(18)7182 yards/**/A/L
(9)3478 yards/**/A/L

Rathfarnham G.C.
(01) 4931201
Newtown, Rathfarnham, Dublin 16
(9)5787 yards/**(Tues)/C

Royal Dublin G.C.
(01) 8336346
Bull Island, Dollymount, Dublin 3
(18)6850 yards/**(Wed)/A/H

Rush G.C.
(01) 8437548
Rush
(9)6850 yards/**/D/H

St Annes G.C.
(01) 332797
Bull Island, Dollymount, Dublin 5
(18)6226 yards/**/D/L

St Margaret's G.& C.C.
(01) 8640400
St Margaret's, Dublin
(18)6900 yards/***/B-A

Skerries G.C.
(01) 8491567
Hackestown, Skerries
(18)5852 metres/*•*(Tues/Wed)/D-C

Slade Valley G.C.
(01) 582183
Lynch Park, Brittas
(18)5337 metres/**(Wed)/D

Stackstown G.C.
(01) 942338
Kellystown Road, Rathfarnham
(18)5952 metres/***/D-C

Sutton G.C.
(01) 8322965
Cush Point, Barrow Road, Sutton
(9)5522 yards/***(Tues/Sat)/D

Westmanstown G.C.
(01) 8205817
Clonsilla, Dublin
(18)6400 yards/***/D

CO KILDARE

Athy G.C.
(0507) 31729
Geraldine, Athy
(18)6308 yards/**/D

Bodenstown G.C.
(045) 97096
Bodenstown, Sallins
(18)6745 yards/**/E

Cill Dara G.C.
(045) 21433
Kildare Town
(9)6426 yards/***/D

Curragh G.C.
(045) 41714
Curragh
(18)6603 yards/***/D

Highfield G.C.
(0405) 31021
Highfield House, Carbury
(18)6278 yards/***/E

Kilcock G.C.
(01) 6284074
Kilcock
(9)/***/E

Kildare Country Club (`K' Club)
(01) 6273987
Straffan
(18)7200 yards/***/A/H

Killeen G.C.
(045) 66003
Killenbeg, Kill
(18)5212 yards/***/D

Knockanally G.& C.C.
(045) 69322
Donadea, N. Kildare
(18)6484 yards/***/D

Naas G.C.
(045) 97509
Kerdiffstown, Salins, Naas
(18)5660 metres/***/D

CO KILKENNY

Callan G.C.
(052) 25136
Geraldine, Callan
(9)5844 metres/***/E

Castlecomer G.C.
(056) 41139
Dromgoole, Castlecomer
(9)6515 yards/***/C

Kilkenny G.C.
(056) 22125
Glendine, Kilkenny
(18)6409 yards/***(Tues)/D

Mount Juliet G.C.
(056) 24725
Thomastown
(18)7143 yards/***/A

CO LAOIS

Abbey Leix G.C.
(0502) 31450
Abbey Leix, Portlaoise
(9)5680 yards/***/E

Heath G.C.
(0502) 26533
The Heath, Portlaoise
(18)6247 yards/***/D

Mountrath G.C.
(0502) 32558
Knockanina, Mountrath
(9)5300 yards/***/E

Portarlington G.C.
(0502) 23115
Garryhinch, Portarlington
(18)6324 yards/***/D/L

Rathdowney G.C.
(0505) 46170
Coulnaboul West, Rathdowney
(9)6086 yards/***/F

CO LONGFORD

County Longford G.C.
(043) 46310
Dublin Road, Longford
(18)6008 yards/***/E

CO LOUTH

Ardee G.C.
(041) 53227
Townparks, Ardee
(18)5833 yards/***(Wed)/D

County Louth G.C.
(041) 22329
Baltray, Drogheda
(18)6978 yards/***/F/H

Dundalk G.C.
(042) 21731
Blackrock, Dundalk
(18)6115 yards/***(not Tues/Sun)/D

Greenore G.C.
(042) 73212
Greenore, Dundalk
(18)6506 yards/***/D

Killinbeg G.C.
(042) 39303
Killin Park, Dundalk
(12)3322 yards/***/E

CO MEATH

Black Bush G.C.
(01) 8250021
Thomastown, Dunshaughlin
(18)6930 yards /***/D
(9)2800 yards/***/E

Gormanston College G.C.
(01) 8412203
Franciscan College, Gormanston
(9)2170 yards/*/F

Headfort G.C.
(046) 40857
Kells
(18)6543 yards/***(Tues)/D

Laytown and Bettystown G.C.
(041) 27170
Bettystown, Drogheda
(18)6254 yards/***/F

Royal Tara G.C.
(046) 25244
Bellinter, Navan
(18)5757 metres/**(Tues/Wed)/D
(9)3184 metres/***/D

Trim G.C.
(046) 31463
Newtownmoynagh, Trim
(18)6270 yards/***/D

CO MONAGHAN

Castleblayney G.C.
(042) 40197
Muckno Park, Castleblayney
(9)2678 yards/***/E

Clones G.C.
(049) 56017
Hilton Park, Scotshouse, Clones
(9)5790 yards/***/E

Nuremore G.C.
(042) 61438
Carrickmacross
(9)6246 yards/***/D

Rossmore G.C.
(047) 81316
Rossmore Park, Monaghan
(18)6082 yards/***/E-D

CO OFFALY

Birr G.C.
(0509) 20082
The Glenns, Birr
(18)6216 yards/***/D

Edenderry G.C.
(0405) 31072
Boherberry, Edenderry
(9)5791 yards/***/E

Tullamore G.C.
(0506) 21439
Brookfield, Tullamore
(18)6314 yards/***/D

CO TIPPERARY

Cahir Park G.C.
(052) 41474
Kilcommon, Cahir
(9)5690 yards/***/E

Carrick on Suir G.C.
(051) 40047

Garravoone, Carrick on Suir
(9)5948 yards/***(Sun)/E

Clonmel G.C.
(052) 21138
Lyreanearla, Mountain Road,
Clonmel
(18)6330 yards/**/D

County Tipperary G.& C.C.
(062) 71116
Dundrum House Hotel, Dundrum,
Cashel
(18)6682 yards/***/D

Nenagh G.C.
(067) 31476
Beechwood, Nenagh
(18)5483 metres/***/D

Rockwell College G.C.
(062) 61444
Rockwell College, Cashel
(9)4136 yards/*/F

Roscrea G.C.
(0505) 21130
Derryvale, Dublin Road, Roscrea
(18)5706 metres/***/D

Templemore G.C.
(0504) 31400
Manna South, Templemore
(9)5442 yards/***/E

Thurles G.C.
(0504) 21983
Turtulla, Thurles
(18)6494 yards/**(Tues)/F

Tipperary G.C.
(062) 51119
Rathanny, Tipperary
(18)6385 yards/***/D

CO WATERFORD

Dungarvan G.C.
(058) 41605
Knocknagranagh, Dungarvan
(18)6134 yards/***/D

Faithlegg G.C.
(051) 82241
Faithlegg House, Faithlegg
(18)6662 yards/***/C

Lismore G.C.
(058) 54026
Ballyin, Lismore
(9)5715 yards/***/E

Tramore G.C.
(051) 81247
Newtown Hill, Tramore
(18)6660 yards/***/D

Waterford G.C.
(051) 76748
Newrath, Waterford
(18)6237 yards/**/F

Waterford Castle G.C.
(051) 71633
The Island, Waterford
(18) 6500 yards/*/F/G

West Waterford G.C.
(058) 43216
Aglish Road, Coolcormack,
Dungarvan
(18)6771 yards/***/D

CO WESTMEATH

Delvin Castle G.C.
(044) 64315
Delvin
(18)6300 yards/***/D/H

Moate G.C.
(0902) 81271
Ballinagarby, Moate
(9)5348 yards/***/E

Mullingar G.C.
(044) 48366
Belvedere, Mullingar
(18)6370 yards/***/C

CO WEXFORD

Courtown G.C.

(055) 25166
Kiltennel, Gorey
(18)6435 yards/***(Wed)/D

Enniscorthy G.C.
(054) 33191
Knockmarshal, Enniscorthy
(18)6368 yards/***(Tues/Sun)/D

New Ross G.C.
(051) 21433
Tinneranny, New Ross
(9)6133 yards/***(Tues/Sun)/D

Rosslare G.C.
(053) 32203
Rosslare Strand, Rosslare
(18)6500 yards/***/C/H
(9)3153 yards/***/D/H

St Helens Bay G.& C.C.
(053) 33234
St Helens, Kilrane
(18)6163 yards/***/C

Wexford G.C.
(053) 42238
Mulgannon, Wexford
(18)6109 yards/***/D

CO WICKLOW

Arklow G.C.
(0402) 32492
Abbeylands, Arklow
(18)5770 yards/***/D

Baltinglass G.C.
(0508) 81350
Baltinglass
(9)5554 yards/***/E

Blainroe G.C.
(0404) 68168
Blainroe
(18)6681 yards/***/C

Bray G.C.
(01) 862484
Ravenswell Road, Bray
(9)5230 yards/**/C

Charlesland G.& C.C.
(01) 2876764
Greystones
(18)6739 yards/***/C-B
Coollattin G.C.
(055) 29125
Coollattin, Shillelagh
(9)6203 yards/***/D

Delgany G.C.
(01) 2874645
Delgany
(18)6000 yards/***/C

The European Club
(0404) 47415
Brittas Bay
(18)6729 yards/***/B

Greystones G.C.
(01) 2876624
Greystones
(18)5227 yards/***(Mon/Fri)/C-B

Old Conna G.C.
(01) 2826055
Ferndale Road, Bray
(18)6551 yards/**/B/H

Tulfarris Hotel & C.C.
(045) 64574
Blessington
(9)2806 yards/***/F

Wicklow G.C.
(0404) 67379
Dunbar Road, Wicklow
(9)5536 yards/***/D

Woodbrook G.C.
(01) 2824799
Dublin Road, Bray
(18)6541 yards/***(Tues/Wed)/F

Woodenbridge G.C.
(0402) 35202
Woodenbridge, Arklow
(9)6104 yards/***(Sat)/D

100 Greatest Golf Courses

As ranked by the 8th edition of Following The Fairways, August 1994

Top 50 Links Courses

1. **Royal Co. Down,** Newcastle, Co. Down, N. Ireland
2. **Ballybunion,** Co. Kerry, Ireland
3. **St Andrews,** Fife, Scotland
4. **Royal Birkdale,** Southport, Merseyside, England
5. **Muirfield,** Gullane, Lothian, Scotland
6. **Portmarnock,** Co. Dublin, Ireland
7. **Turnberry,** Ayrshire, Scotland
8. **Royal Portrush,** Co. Antrim, N. Ireland
9. **Hillside,** Southport, Merseyside, England
10. **Royal Dornoch,** Highland, Scotland
11. **Royal St George's,** Sandwich, Kent, England
12. **Carnoustie,** Tayside, Scotland
13. **Lahinch,** Co. Clare, Ireland
14. **Royal Porthcawl,** Mid Glamorgan, Wales
15. **Formby,** Merseyside, England
16. **Co. Sligo,** Rosses Point, Co. Sligo, Ireland
17. **Royal Liverpool,** Hoylake, Cheshire, England
18. **Co. Louth,** Baltray, Co. Louth, Ireland
19. **Saunton,** Devon, England
20. **Royal Troon,** Ayrshire, Scotland
21. **Waterville,** Co. Kerry, Ireland
22. **Portstewart,** Co. Londonderry, N. Ireland
23. **Rye,** E. Sussex, England
24. **Cruden Bay,** Grampian, Scotland
25. **Royal Lytham,** Lancashire, England
26. **Royal Aberdeen,** Grampian, Scotland
27. **European Club,** Brittas Bay, Co. Wicklow, Ireland.
28. **Machrihanish,** Campbeltown, Scotland
29. **Ballyliffin,** Co. Donegal, Ireland
30. **Royal St David's,** Harlech, Gwynedd, Wales
31. **Nairn,** Highland, Scotland
32. **Donegal,** Murvagh, Co. Donegal, Ireland
33. **Western Gailes,** Ayrshire, Scotland
34. **Prestwick,** Ayrshire, Scotland
35. **The Island,** Donabate, Co. Dublin, Ireland
36. **Burnham & Berrow,** Somerset, England
37. **Tralee,** Co. Kerry, Ireland
38. **Silloth on Solway,** Cumbria, England
39. **Hunstanton,** Norfolk, England
40. **Southerness,** Dumfries & Galloway, Scotland
41. **Prince's,** Sandwich, Kent, England
42. **Royal West Norfolk,** Brancaster, England
43. **Royal Cinque Ports,** Deal, Kent, England
44. **North Berwick,** Lothian, Scotland
45. **Murcar,** Aberdeen, Grampian, Scotland
46. **Connemara,** Co. Galway, Ireland
47. **La Moye,** Jersey, Channel Islands
48. **Royal Dublin,** Co. Dublin, Ireland
49. **Gullane, Lothian, Scotland**
50. **Royal North Devon,** Westward Ho! England

Top 50 Inland/Non Links Courses

1. **Woodhall Spa,** Lincolnshire, England
2. **Sunningdale,** Surrey/ Berkshire, England
3. **Mount Juliet,** Thomastown, Co. Kilkenny, Ireland
4. **East Sussex National,** Uckfield, E. Sussex, England
5. **Ganton,** North Yorkshire, England
6. **Wentworth,** Surrey, England
7. **Chart Hills,** Biddenden, Kent, England
8. **West Sussex,** Pulborough, W. Sussex, England
9. **Gleneagles,** Auchterarder, Perthshire, Scotland
10. **St Mellion,** Saltash, Cornwall, England
11. **Notts,** Hollinwell, Notts, England
12. **Walton Heath,** Surrey, England
13. **The 'K' Club,** Straffan, Co. Kildare, Ireland
14. **Blairgowrie,** Rosemount, Perthshire, Scotland
15. **The Berkshire,** Ascot, Berkshire, England
16. **St George's Hill,** Weybridge, Surrey, England
17. **The Wisley,** Woking, Surrey, England
18. **Killarney,** Co. Kerry, Ireland
19. **Woburn,** Buckinghamshire, England
20. **Lindrick,** South Yorkshire, England
21. **Swinley Forest,** Ascot, Berkshire, England
22. **Alwoodley,** West Yorkshire, England
23. **The London,** Ash, Nr. Sevenoaks, Kent, England
24. **Little Aston,** Sutton Coldfield, W. Midlands, England
25. **Royal Ashdown Forest,** E. Sussex, England
26. **Slaley Hall,** Northumberland, England
27. **Slieve Russell,** Ballyconnell, Co. Cavan, Ireland
28. **Frilford Heath,** Oxfordshire, England
29. **Moortown,** Leeds, W. Yorkshire, England
30. **Royal Worlington,** Suffolk, England
31. **Hanbury Manor,** Ware, Herts, England
32. **Carlow,** Co. Carlow, Ireland
33. **East Devon,** Budleigh Salterton, Devon, England
34. **Crowborough Beacon,** E. Sussex, England
35. **Isle of Purbeck,** Swanage, Dorset, England
36. **Portal,** Tarporley, Cheshire, England
37. **St Margaret's,** Co. Dublin, Ireland
38. **Bowood,** Calne, Wiltshire, England
39. **Malone,** Belfast, N. Ireland
40. **Ferndown,** Dorset, England
41. **Worplesdon,** Surrey, England
42. **The Oxfordshire,** Thame, Oxfordshire, England
43. **The Belfry,** Sutton Coldfield, W. Midlands, England
44. **Collingtree Park,** Northampton, England
45. **Nefyn & District,** Gwynedd, Wales
46. **Stoke Poges,** Buckinghamshire, England
47. **Letham Grange,** Tayside, Scotland
48. **Liphook,** Hampshire, England
49. **Woking,** Surrey, England
50. **Dalmahoy,** Edinburgh, Scotland

N. Arthur Lorraine **A MIXED FOURSOME** *Burlington Gallery*

Our Greatest Golf Courses

This is the third year that Following The Fairways has published a table ranking the top golf courses of Great Britain and Ireland. As stated in previous editions, there is nothing original in the concept of rating our greatest golf courses—both Golf World and Golf Monthly magazines produce their own tables—but there is a novelty in the way that Following The Fairways makes a distinction between links and non-links courses; in fact, we produce two separate lists. The rationale behind this being that, to quote from an earlier edition, 'to compare the Old Course at St Andrews with the Nicklaus Course at St Mellion is surely a bit like trying to contrast a Rembrandt with a Picasso?' Links golf is hardly a different game from inland golf, after all, the best golfers in the world tend to excel whatever the nature of the course, but the essential characteristics and challenges are surely both distinct and distinguishable.

Our criteria for passing judgement on the relative merits of the courses are as follows:

A The quality and character of the design (be it principally the work of Man or Mother Nature); specifically,

i) The variety of challenges offered;

ii) The degree of challenge (test);

iii) The quality of the hazards and the extent to which the course rewards the good shot and punishes the bad;

iv) The level of subtlety or drama (or both) incorporated in the design;

v) The memorability and individual character of the holes

B The quality of the terrain i.e. whether the land could be described as 'classic golfing country'; whether the best use has been made of the land and whether the course 'offends or blends' with the landscape.

C The natural beauty of the situation

D The feeling of 'occasion' experienced when playing—a mixture of history, tradition and reputation (which may be modern)

E The general and normal conditions of the course

The Top 50 Links Courses

The obvious potential criticism of the links ranking is the precedence given to Irish courses, particularly with Royal Co Down (Newcastle) and Ballybunion occupying the top two positions. No bias is intended (and there is no Irish blood in this editor!) It is simply felt that both Newcastle and Ballybunion are exceptional and extraordinary golf courses. Not only is a game at Ballybunion likely to set the golfer's pulse racing faster than at any other, as the fairways, fringed by massive sand dunes, rollercoast their way right alongside a dramatic shoreline, but the variety and subtlety required of the approach shots at Ballybunion may be unparalleled. As for Royal Co Down, is there a setting anywhere in the world to compare? And where is there a more demanding, challenging and interesting examination of classical links golf?

Most rankings that have been published over the years tend to accord slightly greater precedence to the Open Championship venues. This is understandable given that this event must provide the ultimate test for a great links course. However, it is interesting to note that according to many 'authorities' the top two rated courses in North America are Pine Valley and Cypress Point—neither of which has ever staged, nor probably will ever stage a Major Championship.

Opinions as to the relative merits of golf courses change, just as opinions on most subjects do, and golf courses can alter for better or worse, so inevitably there will be certain changes in our lists from year to year. Very few new links courses are being built these days, but the spectacular European Club in Co Wicklow has entered our listing and seems certain to climb higher in the next few years as it fully matures. The biggest move upwards in our ranking since their first publication has been achieved by Portstewart, although this has more to do with the settling down of the celebrated new holes that the club recently constructed than any revised opinion.

The Top 50 Inland/Non Links Courses

Our ranking of inland courses (or non-links courses i.e. it includes some cliff top courses, such as East Devon where the terrain is not that of a true links nature) is likely to change much more from year to year with the inclusion of a number of 'new' courses. It is interesting to note that 16 of the top 50 inland courses are less than 10 years old; this fact may cause some commentators to frown, but surely if a course is good enough then it is old enough. And anyone who has visited the likes of East Sussex National, particularly, we suggest, its less famous West Course and Mount Juliet will appreciate why they are so highly regarded. There are good new courses and there are bad new courses, just as there are good and bad old courses and just occasionally, a great new course comes along. Note the immediate inclusion in our Top 10 of Chart Hills, the outstanding Nick Faldo/Steve Smyers design in Kent which opened in 1993. Some courses mature more quickly than others but in next year's edition it is likely that a few more 'new' courses will make their way into the ratings. (Loch Lomond in Scotland, maybe, which was not officially open at the time these ranking were compiled).

Perhaps two other surprise inclusions among the top 10 on our second list are West Sussex (Pulborough) and St Mellion. Pulborough is an outstanding heathland course and has many of the qualities (and is as equally attractive) of Sunningdale; our view is that its reputation might be greater if it weren't so expert at hiding its light under a bushel. The Nicklaus Course at St Mellion is allegedly disliked by many professionals who find it too difficult: poor them! From the back tees it may well be the toughest inland course in the British Isles but that fact shouldn't preclude it from being one of the best—as Bernhard Langer once said, 'St Mellion sorts the men from the boys'. Besides, we've yet to meet an amateur golfer who wasn't captivated by the course.

A Personal View by the Editor, **Nick Edmund**

Gleneagles 28"x 21"

St Andrews 28"x 21"

Turnberry 28"x 21"

Royal Troon 28"x 21"

The Lady Golfer 10"x 12"

A Short Putt 10"x 12"

The Drive Off 10"x 12"

The Putting Green 10"x 12"

THE FIRST, KING'S COURSE
by Robert Wade   19″ × 27″

SEVEN IRON by Roy Perry   20″ × 30″

THE CADDIE
by Robert Wade   19″ × 27″

TO HALVE THE MATCH by Roy Perry 20″ × 30″

THE LUCKY DOG by Victor Venner   12″ × 16″

BALLESTEROS' HOLE, THE BELFRY
by Bill Waugh   10 ¾″ × 16″

ADRESSING THE BALL by Victor Venner   12″ × 16″

AUGUSTA NATIONAL,16th HOLE
by Bill Waugh   16 ¼″ × 24 ¼″

The Kensington West Collection

A range of fine sporting and leisure publications

Travelling The Turf

(tenth edition)
The complete guide to racecourses of Great Britain and Ireland. Travelling The Turf incorporates colour maps, extensive illustrations, many previously unpublished racing scenes with illuminating and witty analysis of every aspect of the racing scene. Comprehensive features on hotels, restaurants, pubs and bed and breakfasts are embellished with points and places of interest for the non-racegoer. A powerful resume of the worlds most stylish sport. Foreword by Peter O' Sullevan

Following The Fairways

(eighth edition)
The complete guide to the golf courses of Great Britain and Ireland. Following The Fairways contains a comprehensive directory of over 2,000 golf courses and in depth features on one hundred of the nation's most celebrated golfing challenges. An authoritative guide to the world's fastest growing leisure pursuit with a foreword by one of sports most celebrated personalities, Ian Botham.

Ping Women's Golf Year

The Ping Women's Golf Year - now in its second edition - offers an attractive and comprehensive annual review of the world of women's golf. Building on the great success of the pioneering 1st edition, the 2nd edition (Foreword by LPGA Hall of Fame member, Joanne Carner) is once again produced in full colour. The book includes approximately 150 photographs and captures all the excitement, style and drama of the women's game as the season unfolds in Europe, America and indeed in every corner of the globe. Both professional and amateur events are detailed and in addition to reflecting on the great moments of the past year, the book looks forward and previews the season ahead - and with Europe defending both the Solheim and Curtis Cups, what a season it promises to be!

Visions Of Sport

A celebration of the worlds leading photographic agency, Allsport. This unique collection of 160 sporting photographs covers a range of sports to delight the enthusiast as well as interest the amateur photographer. Articles by a select group of sporting celebrities include; David Gower, Rory Underwood, Daley Thompson and Alain Prost, coupled with a lively commentary, ensures a first class read. The book has been printed on the highest quality paper to ensure the outstanding photography appears in all its glory.

Visions of Golf

Visions of Golf is the definitive collection of golf photographs from Allsport, the worlds leading sports photographic agency. Well known golf personalities introduce sections on: - The Legends of Golf, The Major Championships (The U.S. Open, the Masters, the Open, U.S.P.G.A. Championship), Europe (both men and women's tours), America, the rest of the world (Asia, ANZ , Japan, Africa), Match Play golf (Ryder, Walker, Solheim, Curtis, Dunhill Cups) and to conclude, 30 pages on the world's golf courses. Supporting quotations and comments from the games greatest players accompany the photographs. Above all it is the quality of photography and the unique shots that make this an unrivalled publication

The Kensington Collection

As people continue to demand more for their money, so hoteliers have created all manner of short breaks to catch the imagination. The Kensington Collection has been produced to reflect this demand. It earmarks all manner of information from prices to what activities each hotel has to offer. Whether you enjoy a stroll in the country or a ride in a hot air balloon, you'll find something to enjoy, with an interesting foreword written by the Duke of Roxburghe.

Kensington West Productions publish a range of fine sporting and leisure publications, designed to suit the interest and pocket of one and all. We are renowned for producing books in full colour, superbly illustrated with art and photography of the highest quality, to grace the shelves of any library. Our sporting annuals also provide an infinite source of reading pleasure with their informed commentary and travel guidelines. From this wealth of experience comes our new pocket series, ideal reference works for both beginners and experts which make up in price what they lack in colour. No such problem with Visions of Sport, in our opinion quite simply the best value collection of sporting photographs ever assembled.

The Holiday Golf Guide

A colourful guide to popular golf resorts around the world, whose informed commentary makes easy reading and serves as a practical reference source. Destinations featured include all the traditional haunts of the itinerant British golfer and a sample of some of the more exotic locations to be found further afield. With summaries of major tour operators and the services they offer, The Holiday Golf Guide is an invaluable aid to anyone looking to book a golfing break.

Fishing Forays

Fishing Forays includes in-depth appraisals of famous beats, maps of lochs, lakes and rivers with helpful tips for beginners to the sport on where to fish. Contacts on particular waters make the book a first class investment and provide a short cut to finding how, when and where to fish the celebrated rivers of Britain and Ireland. An engaging summary of one of the world's most exclusive sports. Includes a foreword by Chris Poupard, Director of the Trout and Salmon Association.

Highland Spring

Produced by Highland Spring, world famous purveyor of Natural Mineral Water, The Watering Holes of Scotland is a comprehensive and picturesque guide to the heritage, hotels and restaurants of Scotland. Offering the best in Cuisine, leisure facilities and spectacular scenery, along with the world famous golf courses, this guide helps you to select your break at leisure. Enjoy too the humour and art found within the covers, together with a foreword from one of Scotland's most famous sons, Jackie Stewart.

Travelling the Turf, Following The Fairways and Fishing Forays are all available in black and white Pocket Guide Form.

Order Form

Title	Hardback	No.	Softback	No.
Travelling the Turf 1995	1 871349 42 7 £15.99		1 871349 47 8 £14.99	
Following the Fairways 1995	1 871349 52 4 £15.99		1 871349 57 5 £14.99	
Visions of Sport	1 871349 32 X £14.95			
Visions of Golf	1 871349 37 0 £14.99			
Ping Womens Golf	1 871349 273 £12.99			
The Kensington Collection			1 871349 966 £12.95	
The Holiday Golf Guide			1 871349 22 2 £7.99	
Fishing Forays 1994-1995	1 871349 869 £15.95		1 871349915 £14.95	
The Watering Holes of Scotland	1 871349 613 £20.00		1 871349567 £14.95	

No. of books _____

Total Value _____

Please send your order to Kensington West Productions Ltd, 5 Cattle Market, Hexham, Northumberland NE46 1NJ, Tel: 0434 609933 Fax: 0434 600066 Cheques (payable to Kensington West Productions Ltd) /Access/Visa/Amex/Diners

Card no _____ Address _____

Expiry Date _____

Hotel Index